AF701916

CONSTITUTION-BUILDING AFTER THE ARAB SPRING

How were post-Arab Spring constitutions drafted? What are the most significant elements of continuity and change within the new constitutional texts? What purposes are these texts designed to serve? To what extent have constitutional provisions been enforced? Have the principles of constitutionalism been strengthened compared to the past? These are some of the key questions Francesco Biagi addresses. *Constitution-Building After the Arab Spring: A Comparative Perspective* examines seven national experiences of constitution-building in the Arab world following the 2011 uprisings, namely those of Morocco, Algeria, Tunisia, Libya, Egypt, Syria, and Jordan. This interdisciplinary book, based largely on the author's own work and research in the region, compares these seven national experiences through four analytical frameworks: constitution-drafting and constitutional reform processes; separation of powers and forms of government; constitutional justice; and religion, women, and non-Muslims within the framework of citizenship.

Francesco Biagi is Associate Professor of Comparative Public Law in the Department of Legal Studies of the University of Bologna, Deputy Secretary General of the International Association of Constitutional Law (IACL-AIDC), Research Fellow at the Center for Constitutional Studies and Democratic Development, and Legal Consultant at the Max Planck Foundation for International Peace and the Rule of Law (Heidelberg). He is the author of *European Constitutional Courts and Transitions to Democracy* (Cambridge University Press 2020).

The best constitutional scholarship requires multiple skills. Francesco Biagi combines expert political analysis, legal acumen, and a regional focus to guide readers through the most tumultuous period in Arab politics.

Nathan J. Brown, Professor of Political Science and International Affairs, George Washington University

In this impressive and indispensable volume, Professor Biagi provides a comprehensive, richly theorized account of the myriad constitutional developments that took place in the Arab World from the start of the so-called "Arab Spring" in 2011 through the 2023 Tunisian parliamentary elections. Providing indispensable historical background to the events of this period and judiciously drawing upon theories of comparative law and comparative politics, Biagi insightfully identifies and explains connections between the experiences of different countries during this extraordinary decade of constitutional creation and implementation. He also explains cogently and convincingly why the process of constitution-building after the Arab Spring unfolded differently in different Arab countries and led to different results for their citizens. A *tour de force*.

Clark B. Lombardi, Dan Fenno Henderson Professor of Law and Director of Islamic Legal Studies, University of Washington School of Law

A must-read for anyone seeking to understand what went wrong after the "Arab Spring" and how constitutions are used by illiberal ruling regimes as an instrument of government. Seven constitution-building processes and political systems compared in 300 pages – a remarkable contribution to the study of comparative constitutional law and politics.

Nathalie Bernard-Maugiron, Senior Researcher, Université Paris Cité/IRD/Ceped

ASCL Studies in Comparative Law

ASCL Studies in Comparative Law publishes monographs and collections that broaden theoretical and practical knowledge of the world's many legal systems. Published under the direction of the American Society of Comparative Law, the *ASCL Studies* examine legal problems in a comparative light to advance legal science, develop technical insights, and promote greater cooperation across jurisdictional and cultural boundaries. This book series serves legal practitioners and those seeking to improve law and justice by publishing in-depth comparative studies of specific legal problems in every area of law.

The series has two general editors. David Gerber is Distinguished Professor of Law and Co-Director of the Program in International and Comparative Law at Chicago-Kent College of Law, Illinois Institute of Technology. He is past President of the American Society of Comparative Law. Mortimer Sellers is Regents Professor of the University System of Maryland and Director of the Baltimore Center for International and Comparative Law. He is past President of the Internationale Vereinigung für Rechts-und Sozialphilosophie.

Series Editors

David Gerber *Chicago-Kent College of Law*
Mortimer Sellers *University of Baltimore*

Editorial Board

Richard Albert *University of Texas*
David Clark *Willamette University*
Helge Dedek *McGill University*
James Feinerman *Georgetown University*
Richard Kay *University of Connecticut*
Maximo Langer *University of California Los Angeles*
Ralf Michaels *Max Planck Institute for Comparative and International Private Law*
Fernanda Nicola *American University*
Jacqueline Ross *University of Illinois*
Kim Lane Scheppele *Princeton University*
Franz Werro *Georgetown University*

External Advisory Board

Josef Drexl *University of Munich*
Diego Fernandez Arroyo *Institut d'etudes politiques de Paris*
Hongjun Gao *Tsinghua University*
Michele Graziadei *University of Turin*

Ko Hasegawa *University of Hokkaido*
Hisashi Harata *University of Tokyo*
Andreas Heinemann *University of Zurich*
Christophe Jamin *Institut d'etudes politiques de Paris*
Yong-Sun Kang *Yonsei University*
Claudia Lima Marques *Federal University of Rio Grande do Sul*
Bertil Emrah Oder *Koc University*
Amr Shalakany *American University of Cairo*

Constitution-Building After the Arab Spring

A COMPARATIVE PERSPECTIVE

FRANCESCO BIAGI
University of Bologna

CAMBRIDGE
UNIVERSITY PRESS

CAMBRIDGE
UNIVERSITY PRESS

Shaftesbury Road, Cambridge CB2 8EA, United Kingdom

One Liberty Plaza, 20th Floor, New York, NY 10006, USA

477 Williamstown Road, Port Melbourne, VIC 3207, Australia

314–321, 3rd Floor, Plot 3, Splendor Forum, Jasola District Centre, New Delhi – 110025, India

103 Penang Road, #05–06/07, Visioncrest Commercial, Singapore 238467

Cambridge University Press is part of Cambridge University Press & Assessment, a department of the University of Cambridge.

We share the University's mission to contribute to society through the pursuit of education, learning and research at the highest international levels of excellence.

www.cambridge.org
Information on this title: www.cambridge.org/9781009533645

DOI: 10.1017/9781009533669

© Francesco Biagi 2025

This publication is in copyright. Subject to statutory exception and to the provisions of relevant collective licensing agreements, no reproduction of any part may take place without the written permission of Cambridge University Press & Assessment.

When citing this work, please include a reference to the DOI 10.1017/9781009533669

First published 2025

A catalogue record for this publication is available from the British Library

Library of Congress Cataloging-in-Publication Data
NAMES: Biagi, Francesco, author.
TITLE: Constitution building after the Arab Spring : a comparative perspective / Francesco Biagi.
DESCRIPTION: Cambridge, United Kingdom ; New York, NY : Cambridge University Press, 2025. | Series: ASCL studies in comparative law | Includes bibliographical references and index.
IDENTIFIERS: LCCN 2024011582 (print) | LCCN 2024011583 (ebook) | ISBN 9781009533645 (hardback) | ISBN 9781009533669 (ebook)
SUBJECTS: LCSH: Constitutional law – Arab countries. | Constitutional history – Arab countries. | Constitutional amendments – Arab countries. | Separation of powers – Arab countries. | Legislative power – Arab countries. | Arab Spring, 2010– | Revolutions – Arab countries.
CLASSIFICATION: LCC KMC522 .B53 2025 (print) | LCC KMC522 (ebook) | DDC 342/.17492703–dc23/eng/20240317
LC record available at https://lccn.loc.gov/2024011582
LC ebook record available at https://lccn.loc.gov/2024011583

ISBN 978-1-009-53364-5 Hardback

Cambridge University Press & Assessment has no responsibility for the persistence or accuracy of URLs for external or third-party internet websites referred to in this publication and does not guarantee that any content on such websites is, or will remain, accurate or appropriate.

Ai miei genitori, Marina e Marco, e a mio fratello Lorenzo

A mia moglie Elena e alle mie figlie Arianna e Martina

Contents

Acknowledgments

There are many people I would like to thank. First and foremost, I wish to express my gratitude to my *maestri*, Giuseppe de Vergottini and Susanna Mancini, for their extraordinarily important teachings on comparative methodology and for their constant guidance and support in my research projects.

This book is the result of my activities in the Arab region over the past decade. In addition to conducting research and academic projects in a variety of Arab countries, I have provided training and consultancy (on various projects related to constitution-building and the rule of law) to governmental and judicial institutions in the Arab region (especially in Morocco, Jordan, and Palestine). Most of these activities have been organized by the Max Planck Foundation for International Peace and the Rule of Law (Heidelberg). I would like to thank Kathrin Maria Scherr and Johannes Krusemark-Camin, the directors of the Max Planck Foundation: These years at the Foundation, in which I served first as a senior research fellow and now as a legal consultant, have been of the utmost importance in allowing me to better understand, especially from a practical point of view, the main challenges of constitution-building processes in the Arab world and beyond.

I wish to thank Justin O. Frosini (the director of the Center for Constitutional Studies and Democratic Development [CCSDD], a research partnership between the University of Bologna and the Johns Hopkins University SAIS Europe) who has always supported my research projects at the CCSDD on constitutional transitions following the Arab Spring. Some of these projects have also been conducted within the framework of the activities of the Research Group on "Constitutionalism in Illiberal Democracies" of the International Association of Constitutional Law (IACL-AIDC). Moreover, it is thanks to the generous funding from the George Lawrence Abernethy Endowment for Research and Publications of the CCSDD that some of the editing costs of this book have been covered.

I am particularly grateful to Nathan J. Brown: I cannot thank him enough for all the support and help he gave me, especially in the latest stages of the drafting of this volume. Special thanks go also to Fadi Daou and Nayla Tabbara, with whom I share the passion for interfaith dialogue. Thanks to their precious advice, I was able to improve the chapter on citizenship, women, and non-Muslims.

Over the past few years, I have had the honor to regularly teach as a visiting professor at the University of Illinois College of Law, a place that I now consider my second home university. I am very grateful to Jason Mazzone for inviting me to Illinois, where I often have the chance to present to faculty members and students my work on the Arab world.

I wish to thank Siraj Khan and Islam Mohammed for their help: Our "Amman dialogues" are among the most intellectually stimulating conversations I have ever had. I will never stop learning from them. I would also like to thank Sana Alsarghali for her support: I have always benefited enormously from our meetings in Palestine and elsewhere.

I wish to thank my Italian colleagues, especially Tania Groppi, Luca Mezzetti, Andrea Pin, and Ciro Sbailò, with whom I have had the opportunity over the years to discuss the recent constitutional transformations in the Arab world. I would also like to thank Massimo Papa, my professor of Islamic law and my bachelor's thesis supervisor, for passing on to me his passion for Islamic legal studies.

I am also grateful to all other colleagues who, at various times and in various ways, gave me precious advice during the research and the drafting of this volume: Brahim Belguith, Nathalie Bernard-Maugiron, Philipp Bremer, Numan A. Elkhatib, Tamara El Khoury, Tom Ginsburg, Rainer Grote, Clark B. Lombardi, Karim Mezran, Laith K. Nasrawin, Tilmann J. Röder, Paul Saadeh, Anja Schoeller-Schletter, Adel Omar Sherif, and Arianna Vedaschi.

I must stress that I have been able to write this book because I have an amazing law school behind me, from which I graduated and where I now have the privilege to teach – the Department of Legal Studies of the University of Bologna. Thank you to the head of department, Michele Caianiello, and the deputy head of department, Federico Casolari. And thank you to Lidia Bonifati, Francesco Lucherini, Alessandro Martinuzzi and Leonardo Pierdominici.

I wish to extend my sincere thanks to David Gerber and Mortimer Sellers, the editors of the book series *ASCL Studies in Comparative Law*, for their support of this study. I would also like to thank Marianne Nield, Biju Singh, and the editorial staff at Cambridge University Press for their hard work.

Some sections of Chapters 1 and 3 were originally published, respectively, in "Constitution Drafting after the Arab Spring: A Comparative Overview" (2022) 29 *Indiana Journal of Global Legal Studies*, 1–57, and in "Constitutional Review after the Arab Spring: Reforms, Challenges and Perspectives" in Anja Schoeller-Schletter (ed.), *Constitutional Review in the Middle East and North Africa* (Nomos 2021), 161–187. Thanks to the editors and publishers for granting me the permission to incorporate these materials into the book.

Needless to say, any opinions expressed in this volume are solely my own. I am also solely responsible for any errors and omissions.

Introduction

Major constitutional reforms were adopted throughout the Arab world following the outbreak of the so-called "Arab Spring." During the protest movements, demonstrations and, in some cases, even revolutions that took place between the end of 2010 and the beginning of 2011 (but also in the following years), the Arab people not only called for profound political, social, and economic reforms but also demanded radical constitutional changes aimed at reinforcing safeguards for fundamental rights, strengthening the principle of separation of powers, and increasing the independence of the judiciary. A new wave of constitution-building thus began in the Arab world, one that – in the aspirations of the protesters – should have made a clean break with the previous autocratic or semi-autocratic regimes.

To what extent were the aspirations of demonstrators reflected in the post-2011 Arab constitutions and constitutional reforms? How were these documents drafted? What are the most significant elements of continuity and change within the new constitutional texts? What purposes are these texts designed to serve? To what extent have constitutional provisions been enforced? Have the principles of constitutionalism been strengthened compared to the past? These are some of the key questions this book addresses. Although the constitutional experiences of the Arab world were already objects of study in the past,[1] scholarly interest has developed significantly following the Arab Spring.[2] This can be partly explained by the

1 Among the comparative volumes on *pre*-Arab Spring constitutions, see, for example, Bernabé López García and Cecilia Fernández Suzor, *Introducción a los regímenes y constituciones árabes* (Centro de Estudios Constitucionales 1985); *Les constitutions des pays arabes: Colloque de Beyrouth, 1998* (Bruylant 1999); Nathan J. Brown, *Constitutions in a Nonconstitutional World: Arab Basic Laws and the Prospects for Accountable Government* (SUNY Press 2002); Maurizio Oliviero, *Il costituzionalismo dei paesi arabi. I. Le Costituzioni del Maghreb* (Giuffrè 2003); Chibli Mallat, *Introduction to Middle Eastern Law* (Oxford University Press 2007), 141ff.; Rainer Grote and Tilmann J. Röder (eds.), *Constitutionalism in Islamic Countries: Between Upheaval and Continuity* (Oxford University Press 2012).

2 Among the comparative volumes on *post*-Arab Spring constitutions, see, for example, Antoni Abat i Ninet and Mark Tushnet, *The Arab Spring: An Essay on Revolution and Constitutionalism* (Edward Elgar 2015); Justin O. Frosini and Francesco Biagi (eds.), *Political and Constitutional Transitions in North Africa: Actors and Factors* (Routledge 2015); Luca Mezzetti, *La libertà decapitata: Dalle*

fact that, especially at the beginning, these protest movements generated many expectations, so much so as to have even raised hopes regarding a *fourth* wave of democratization.[3] Furthermore, in some cases, important international actors were involved in the constitution-drafting processes: For example, the European Commission for Democracy through Law (known as the Venice Commission, the advisory body on constitutional issues of the Council of Europe) played a key role in the process that led to the adoption of the 2014 Tunisian Constitution, and the United Nations has been facilitating the current constituent processes in Syria and Libya. More generally, it was the magnitude of this new wave of constitution-building that attracted scholarly interest: In recent years, no regions in the world have witnessed the adoption of such a large number of new constitutions and constitutional reforms. These constitutional experiences often have many elements in common, although they are also characterized by significant differences. In some cases, these differences can be found even within the same country. One need only consider the differences in terms of the system of government, the place of Islam and *sharia*, gender equality, and the role of the constitutional court between the Egyptian Constitutions of 2012 and 2014, or between the Tunisian Constitutions of 2014 and 2022.

I.1 FOCUS OF THE BOOK

As indicated in the title, this volume focuses on the processes of *constitution-building* after the *Arab Spring* from a *comparative perspective*. What does each of these expressions specifically mean for the purposes of this book?

Constitution-building includes three main components, namely (1) the process of constitution-making or constitutional reform, (2) the substantive choices made by framers that are formalized in the new constitutional text, and (3) the process of constitutional enforcement. The analysis of these components represents the core of the book. The volume mainly focuses on seven national experiences of constitution-building, namely those of Morocco (constitution of 2011), Algeria (constitutional

Primavere arabe al Califfato (Editoriale Scientifica 2016); Rainer Grote and Tilmann J. Röder (eds.), *Constitutionalism, Human Rights, and Islam after the Arab Spring* (Oxford University Press 2016); Christophe Boutin, Jean-Yves De Cara, and Charles Nimer Saint-Prot, *Les constitutions arabes* (Karthala 2016); Nimer Sultany, *Law and Revolution: Legitimacy and Constitutionalism after the Arab Spring* (Oxford University Press 2017); Zaid Al-Ali, *Arab Constitutionalism: The Coming Revolution* (Cambridge University Press 2021); Ciro Sbailò, *Diritto pubblico dell'Islam mediterraneo. Linee evolutive degli ordinamenti nordafricani contemporanei: Marocco, Algeria, Tunisia, Libia, Egitto* (Wolters Kluwer – CEDAM 2022); Tofigh Maboudi, *The "Fall" of the Arab Spring: Democracy's Challenges and Efforts to Reconstitute the Middle East* (Cambridge University Press 2022); *Journal of Constitutional Law in the Middle East and North Africa*, special issue on "Arab Constitutional Responses to the Revolutions and Transformations in the Region" edited by Rim Turkmani and Tamara El Khoury (December 2023), www.jcl-mena.org

3. See Samuel Huntington, *The Third Wave: Democratization in the Late 20th Century* (University of Oklahoma Press 1991).

reforms of 2016 and 2020), Tunisia (constitutions of 2014 and 2022), Libya (draft constitution of 2017, and the on-going UN-facilitated constitution-making process), Egypt (constitutions of 2012 and 2014 – the latter being amended in 2019), Syria (constitution of 2012 and the ongoing UN-facilitated constituent process), and Jordan (constitutional reforms of 2011, 2014, 2016, and 2022). (In some cases, brief references will also be made to the constitutional experiences of other Arab countries.) The vast majority of these constitutional changes are directly related to the Arab Spring. However, even in those cases in which the link is less evident, there is still a connection with the 2011 uprisings. In Tunisia, for example, with the adoption of the 2022 constitution, President Kaïs Saïed aimed to mark a radical discontinuity with the 2014 constitution, which was one of the most important achievements of the 2011 Revolution. While some of the constitutional developments that have taken place in the region (e.g., in Yemen) have not been included in the book, the seven constitutional experiences covered in this work seem to be sufficiently representative in order to be able to identify the major features and trends characterizing this latest wave of constitution-building in the Arab world.

The *Arab Spring* is certainly not an accurate expression, especially from a scientific standpoint. When it was first used at the beginning of the 2011 uprisings, it was based on the presumption that the outcome of the transition processes in the region would be the establishment of a democratic regime, a fact that has clearly not occurred. The use of that expression shows that Guillermo O'Donnell's and Philippe C. Schmitter's teachings regarding the *uncertainty* of the outcome of transition processes had not been sufficiently considered. Indeed, in their seminal book *Transitions from Authoritarian Rule*, these two prominent scholars observed that

> the high degree of indeterminacy embedded in situations where unexpected events (*fortuna*), insufficient information, hurried and audacious choices, confusion about motives and interests, plasticity, and even indefinition of political identities, as well as the talents of specific individuals (*virtù*), are frequently decisive in determining the outcomes.[4]

In the past, the inaccuracy of the expression Arab Spring had prompted me not to use it altogether.[5] In this work, I have decided instead to rely on it nonetheless for two main reasons: First, after more than a decade, "Arab Spring" continues to be the most common and direct way to refer to the 2011 protest movements and revolutions throughout the region. Second, although it is imprecise and inaccurate, this

[4] Guillermo O'Donnell and Philippe C. Schmitter, "Tentative Conclusions about Uncertain Democracies" in Guillermo O'Donnell, Philippe C. Schmitter, and Laurence Whitehead (eds.), *Transitions from Authoritarian Rule* (The Johns Hopkins University Press 1986), 5.

[5] See Justin O. Frosini and Francesco Biagi, "Transitions from Authoritarian Rule Following the Arab Uprisings: A Matter of Variables" in Frosini and Biagi (eds.) 2015, *Political and Constitutional Transitions*, at pp. 161–162.

expression is also widely used in leading *scholarly* works. Thus, it seems that the effectiveness of the expression has prevailed over its form.

Although this volume focuses on the period from December 17, 2010 (when a young street vendor, Mohamed Bouazizi, set himself on fire in the town of Sidi Bouzid, Tunisia – an episode that is usually considered as the "official" starting point of the Arab Spring) to January 29, 2023 (when the second round of the December 2022–January 2023 parliamentary elections in Tunisia took place – elections that far from being an exercise in democracy will go down in history for record abstentionism), several references will also be made to the constitutional experiences in the region prior to the Arab Spring, thus showing both the *prius* and the *posterius*.

This book adopts a *comparative perspective*, which is essential in order to fully understand constitutional developments in the region. In particular, it compares and contrasts the seven national experiences referred to above through four analytical frameworks (rather than proceeding country by country). They are (1) constitution-drafting and constitutional reform processes; (2) separation of powers and forms of government; (3) constitutional justice; and (4) religion, women, and non-Muslims within the framework of citizenship. This approach *by topic* has appeared necessary in order to better examine the constitutional *trends* that followed the outbreak of the 2011 uprisings. A country-by-country analysis would have offered a wealth of details that a cross-cutting approach can hardly guarantee. However, it would most likely have hindered the identification and analysis of the trends prevailing throughout the region. Therefore, some details concerning the individual countries are missing, although the overall picture is probably clearer.

Ultimately, by providing a comprehensive comparative analysis of constitution-building processes after the 2011 uprisings, this volume aims to contribute to a more in-depth understanding of the social, political, and institutional dynamics in a region that has historically been very difficult to decipher.

I.2 METHODOLOGY

This volume adopts an interdisciplinary approach. Authoritative comparative legal scholars have repeatedly emphasized the crucial importance of such an approach in comparative studies. Pierre Legrand, for example, has stressed that the quality of comparison "not only depends on the brute knowledge" of foreign law but also "on the depth of a reflection which requires [the comparative scholar] to move to planets that are *a priori* unknown to him, such as anthropology, linguistics, sociology, history, cognitive psychology, and philosophy."[6] Without such an interdisciplinary approach, Legrand contends, the comparative scholar risks "regard[ing] social problems and their legal treatment as occurring in a cultural vacuum," perpetuating "the kind of dreary positivism which relegates comparative legal studies to a technical

[6] Pierre Legrand, *Le droit comparé* (Presses Universitaires de France 1999), 27.

exercise whose output is deeply flawed […].”[7] More recently, Ran Hirschl has argued that “the study of comparative constitutional law must open up to the social sciences,” toward “a more holistic approach to the study of constitutions across polities (comparative constitutional *studies*)” (emphasis in original).[8]

This book largely relies on the contributions of historians, political scientists, sociologists, and religious scholars. It could not have been otherwise, since in the Arab-Islamic world, all these subjects are intimately related to one another. Consider, for example, the role played by the king in the Moroccan legal system. The 2011 constitution vests him not only with temporal powers (as Head of State) but also with spiritual powers (as *Amir al-Mouminine*, i.e., Commander of the Faithful). His role as temporal leader and religious guide cannot be fully understood unless one considers that King Mohammed VI, as a member of the Alawi dynasty (which has ruled over the country since the mid-1600s), claims direct descent from Prophet Mohammed. Relying on different social sciences (particularly religious studies) is also necessary when examining the current challenges of citizenship in the Arab region. For example, certain categories of people – particularly women and non-Muslims – have thus far never been granted, *de jure* and *de facto*, the status of full citizens, also because of a certain interpretation of Islamic religious texts.

Thus, this volume seeks to present a comparison among “cultures,” as Peter Häberle puts it. Indeed, constitutional comparison only makes sense where it is immersed in the *culture* that forms the background to the different constitutional experiences.[9] In order to carry out this kind of comparison, my field experience of work and research in the region have been essential. The book would not have been the same without it.

I.3 PLAN OF THE BOOK

The book is comprised of four chapters.

Chapter 1 focuses on constitution-making and constitutional reform processes. After providing a brief historical overview of the four waves of constitution-drafting in the Arab world (which began in the mid-nineteenth century and spread into

7 Pierre Legrand, “The Same and the Different” in Pierre Legrand and Roderick Munday (eds.), *Comparative Legal Studies: Traditions and Transitions* (Cambridge University Press 2003), 276–277. In a similar vein, see also Giovanni Bognetti, *Introduzione al diritto costituzionale comparato* (Giappichelli 1994), 178–179. On the challenges in the use of history and, more in general, of an interdisciplinary approach in comparative law, see Giuseppe Franco Ferrari, “Comparazione e storia” (2021) 2 *Diritto pubblico comparato ed europeo*, 281ff.; Arianna Vedaschi, “Diritto comparato e interdisciplinarietà: tra innata vocazione e incompiuta realizzazione?” (2021) 2 *Diritto pubblico comparato ed europeo*, 301ff.

8 Ran Hirschl, *Comparative Matters: The Renaissance of Comparative Constitutional Law* (Cambridge University Press 2014), 191.

9 See Peter Häberle, *Verfassungslehre als Kulturwissenschaft* (Duncker & Humblot 1998), 28ff. In a similar vein, see also Paolo Ridola, *Esperienza Costituzioni Storia: Pagine di storia costituzionale* (Jovene 2019), 19ff.

the twenty-first century), this chapter examines closely the post-Arab Spring constitution-making and constitutional reform processes, focusing on the following elements: the body in charge of drafting the constitution and the role played by the ruling regime ("bottom-up" vs. "top-down" processes); the degree of openness and transparency of the process; the duration of the process; the role played by political parties; the role of civil society; the role played by external actors; the influence of previous domestic constitutions and their "reactivation"; and the influence of foreign constitutional models. The chapter shows that the vast majority of these processes were characterized by major flaws and shortcomings, a fact that not only contributed to weakening the democratic nature of the new constitutions but also had a negative impact on the legitimacy and sense of ownership of these texts and, ultimately, on the transition processes as a whole. Although it should not be idealized, the process that led to the adoption of the 2014 Tunisian Constitution was to a large extent a positive exception. Indeed, despite the extremely complicated political context and some serious episodes of violence, that process was characterized by a much stronger democratic spirit.

Chapter 2 discusses the systems of government and the distribution of powers under post-2011 Arab constitutions. It first examines the issue of the overconcentration of authority in the hands of the head of state (with the notable exception – again – of the 2014 Tunisian Constitution, which provided for a genuine semi-presidential system and a fairly robust system of checks and balances [at least on paper]). A special focus is placed on the emergency regimes: Despite some attempts to prevent abuses, the new constitutional provisions governing states of emergency continue to grant to the executive branch a significant degree of discretionary power. Furthermore, the chapter shows that not only horizontal but also vertical separation of powers has remained weak, and that this limited form of decentralization has favored the consolidation of authority at the central level. The last part of the chapter discusses the main reasons for the overconcentration of power, namely the constitutional tradition (characterized by two interrelated elements, i.e., the principle of unity of power and the historical dominance of the executive), the patriarchal family, the "top-down" constitution-making processes, and external influences. One of the major consequences of the overconcentration of authority was to undermine the principle of popular sovereignty. Indeed, far from belonging exclusively to the people, sovereignty in the Arab world continues to be *held* (and not only exercised) also by other subjects, namely political (and sometimes also military) leaders, around whom the entire system rotates.

Chapter 3, on constitutional justice, aims to establish whether the new Arab bodies for constitutional review have acquired the potential to subject the executive branch to adequate checks and thus contribute to the processes of democratization more effectively than in the past. In order to understand whether a new era for constitutional review in the Arab world has begun, the chapter first discusses the origins of constitutional review in the region, as well as the main reasons why, before the Arab Spring, constitutional courts and councils rarely acted as "counter-majoritarian" bodies. These reasons include their limited independence vis-à-vis the executive branch, deference toward the executive branch, the nature of constitutional review bodies, the "stranglehold" on access, and the political and social context in which these bodies carried out their action. The chapter then turns to an analysis of the major changes in the field of constitutional justice introduced by the post-2011 constitutions, including a limited strengthening of the independence of constitutional review bodies, the vesting of these institutions with judicial status, the broadening of access to these institutions, as well as a further expansion of their jurisdiction. The chapter also examines the role that constitutional courts and councils played in the transition processes that followed the outbreak of the Arab Spring, showing that in some countries these bodies exerted a strong influence on the direction of political and constitutional transitions, while in others the role of these bodies was much more limited. In general, constitutional courts and councils evinced a high degree of deference to the political authorities and thus made only limited contributions to securing the principles of constitutionalism. There are a few cases, however, in which these bodies delivered judgments unfavorable to the ruling regime and demonstrated a serious commitment to protecting fundamental rights and freedoms. Finally, the chapter discusses the most significant obstacles that constitutional courts and councils still need to overcome in order to emerge as effective guarantors of the principles of constitutionalism.

Chapter 4 examines issues of citizenship and religion, with a particular focus on the status of non-Muslims and women. The chapter shows how contrasting conceptions and practices of citizenship are the most appropriate prism for understanding how residents of Arab societies experience constitutional provisions. More specifically, after discussing the problematic notion of citizenship in the Arab world, the chapter analyzes the specific meaning and scope of citizenship in the post-2011 constitutional systems. Since non-Muslims and women are the two categories of people who in the past never enjoyed the status of full citizens in the Arab world, their treatment provides a litmus test for understanding whether constitutional framers have truly embraced *equal* citizenship. The chapter shows, on the one hand, that despite significant improvements with respect to the past, non-Muslims and women are still excluded from full citizenship, which remains a prerogative of male Muslims. On the other hand, however, over the past few decades – and in particular over the past few years – not only thinkers, scholars, feminists, and reformers but also prominent religious leaders and institutions have called for a more equality-based approach toward citizenship's rights for all people, irrespective of one's sex and religious belief. Given the profound influence that religion exerts on law and society in Arab countries, these calls might well lead to the adoption of legal reforms aimed at removing (or at least reducing) discrimination against women and non-Muslims, and might represent a first step toward replacing the differentiated citizenships that currently exist in Arab countries, with one single, full, and inclusive citizenship.

Ultimately, this chapter shows how different the interactions and relations between the state and individuals are, especially depending on one's sex and religious beliefs.

Thus, the sequence in the topics for analysis is the following: Chapter 1 examines *constitution-writing processes*; Chapters 2 and 3 focus on *state institutions and how they interact with each other*; and Chapter 4 looks at *how the state interacts with the society*.

The conclusions of the book bring things together with an analysis of the key lessons drawn from the discussion in the preceding chapters (1, 2, 3, and 4). Three main aspects have emerged. First, there exist numerous ambiguities, discrepancies, and contradictions concerning the role and functions of post-Arab Spring constitutional texts. These include (1) the idea of the constitution as a "charter of values" or as an "instrument of government"; (2) the integrative function of the constitution vis-à-vis societal fragmentation; and (3) the written and the unwritten constitution (*constitutional dichotomies*). Second, several constitutional provisions – especially those dealing with fundamental principles as well as rights and freedoms – have often remained little more than a dead letter, a fact that has generated major resentment, frustration, and anger among Arab people (*constitutional enforcement*). Third, although post-2011 constitutions are still being squeezed in a context marked by constrained constitutionalism, the Tunisian constitutional experience during the 2011–2021 period showed that the possibility of breaking with the tradition of previous autocratic regimes is not simply a mirage (*constitutional wishful thinking?*).

1

We the People or We the Rulers?

Constitution-Making and Constitutional Reform Processes

1.1 FOUR WAVES OF CONSTITUTION-DRAFTING IN THE ARAB WORLD

According to the periodization proposed by Nathan J. Brown, the Arab world has experienced four waves of constitution-making, which began in the mid-nineteenth century and spread into the twenty-first century.[1] The first wave – which involved not only the Arab world but also the broader Middle East – was mainly provoked by fiscal crisis, domestic turmoil, and foreign pressure. This led to the adoption of a constitution in Tunisia (1861 – considered the first constitution in the Arab world), the Ottoman Empire (1876), Egypt (1882), and Iran (1906).[2] All these constitutional texts were adopted under very similar circumstances: These countries were experiencing both near (or actual) bankruptcy and European pressure, and internal rebellion was rising. It comes as no surprise, then, that the main purpose of these documents was also similar – namely, to establish "more effective political mechanisms to address fiscal and security crises."[3] Indeed, most of the framers' concerns were related to the rationalization of administration of the country and the establishment of clear, accountable procedures for the use of public funds. The creation of a democratic government was certainly not the main issue, even though these constitutions did contain some traces of the principle of separation of powers as interpreted in the Western tradition (i.e., the separation of the three branches of government)[4] and provided for the recognition of a few fundamental rights and constitutional

[1] See Nathan J. Brown, "The Unsurprising but Distinctive Nature of Constitution Writing in the Arab World" in David Landau and Hanna Lerner (eds.), *Comparative Constitution Making* (Edward Elgar 2019), 448–453.

[2] On these constitutional experiences, see Nathan J. Brown, *Constitutions in a Nonconstitutional World: Arab Basic Laws and the Prospects for Accountable Government* (SUNY Press 2002), 15–34; Nathalie Bernard-Maugiron, *Droit contemporain des pays arabes* (Sirey 2023), 560–585.

[3] Brown, "Constitution Writing in the Arab World," at p. 449.

[4] See Tilmann J. Röder, "The Separation of Powers in Muslim Countries: Historical and Comparative Perspectives" in Rainer Grote and Tilmann J. Röder (eds.), *Constitutionalism in Islamic Countries: Between Upheaval and Continuity* (Oxford University Press 2012), 321. See also Chapter 2, Section 2.5.1.

guarantees.[5] Most of these constitutions were short-lived, mainly because of a hostile international environment and domestic divisions. The 1861 Tunisian Constitution (called "Law of the Tunisian State" – *qanun al-dawla al tunisiyya*) remained in force for only three years, as it was suspended in 1864. Similarly, the 1876 Ottoman Basic Law (*al-qanun al-asasi*), which had "a lasting impact on Arab constitutional history in that it provided a starting point for many subsequent [constitutions],"[6] was suspended in February 1878, after fewer than two years of operation, and then restored in 1908. In Egypt, the life of the 1882 Fundamental Ordinance (*al-la'iha al-asasiyya*) was even shorter, as it was repealed following the British occupation of the country in the same year. Only the 1906 Iranian Fundamental Law remained in force for quite some time – that is, until 1921.

The second wave of constitution-drafting in the Arab world began with the dissolution of the Ottoman Empire after World War I. One of the main reasons for issuing these constitutions was the desire to express national sovereignty.[7] Indeed, Arab drafters aimed to assert as much autonomy from European control as possible, even though they were often forced to acknowledge this control. This aim is particularly evident in the constitutions of Egypt (1923), Iraq (1925), Lebanon (1926), Transjordan (1928), and Syria (1930), all of which continued either to acknowledge the British or French mandate (Lebanon, Transjordan, and Syria) or at least to protect the interests of the mandated powers (Egypt and Iraq). The inclusion of these types of clauses was due to the fact that all these constitutions were drafted with massive foreign interference. In some cases, the mandated powers directly issued draft constitutions, which were then submitted to the local constituent assemblies, and specified the "redlines" (which corresponded to the interests they still had in the country) that could not be crossed.[8] In this second generation of Arab constitutions (which involved both monarchical and republican regimes), provisions on rights and freedoms were expanded compared to the previous generation, and the roles and functions of parliaments were partially strengthened. However, these constitutional guarantees were implemented only in rare circumstances.[9]

The end of World War II marked the beginning of the third wave of constitution-drafting in the Arab world. In some countries (e.g., in Jordan [1946], Libya [1951], Tunisia [1959], Kuwait [1962], and Algeria [1963]), the adoption of a constitution served the purpose, *inter alia*, of underscoring national sovereignty following decades of colonial dominance. Furthermore, unlike their predecessors, post–World War II

5 See, for example, Article 88 of the 1861 constitution of Tunisia (stipulating that all persons were equal before the law irrespective of the religion to which they belonged).

6 Nathan J. Brown, "Regimes Reinventing Themselves: Constitutional Development in the Arab World" (2003) 18 *International Sociology*, 36.

7 See Brown, "Constitution Writing in the Arab World," at pp. 451–452.

8 See Brown, *Constitutions in a Nonconstitutional World*, at pp. 35ff. and 67ff.

9 Ibid.

constitutions were very often ideological documents.[10] Socialist principles, for example, clearly influenced several constitutional experiences, including the constitutions of Algeria (1963 and 1976), Kuwait (1962), Egypt (1964 and 1971), and Syria (1973). This third generation of Arab constitutions was also characterized by a more prominent position granted to Islam, and sometimes also to *sharia*, with a view to ensuring a more effective enforcement of Islamic law.[11] Furthermore, another very important reason behind the promulgation of these constitutions was the rulers' desire to strengthen executive authority. This dominance by the executive, and in particular by the head of state, to the detriment of the other branches of government could be found in almost all Arab countries. Indeed, these constitutions, and their subsequent amendments,[12] enabled the rulers to enjoy near absolute powers, without any effective limitations.[13] It should also be noted that these texts contained bills of rights but usually left the concrete regulation of rights and freedoms to ordinary legislation, meaning that this legislation often resulted in the full-scale "hollowing out" of those very same rights.

The last Arab countries to adopt constitutions were the monarchies of the Arabian Peninsula, generally the most reluctant to issue constitutional documents – some of these do not even qualify themselves as constitutions, such as the 1992 Basic Law of Governance (*nizam asasi li'l-hukm*) of Saudi Arabia.[14] One of the main aims of these documents was to "address a critical concern of the peninsular monarchies: ensuring dynastic continuity and harmony of the ruling family."[15] Indeed, Gulf monarchies had often experienced royal depositions, coups, and irregular successions. Therefore,

10 See Brown, "Constitution Writing in the Arab World," at p. 452.

11 Suffice it to compare the Egyptian Constitution of 1923 (as an example of the second generation of Arab constitutions) with that of 1971 (as an expression of the third generation). Article 149 of the 1923 constitution contained, for the first time in Egypt's constitutional history, an explicit reference to Islam. Indeed, it stipulated that "Islam is the religion of the State and Arabic is its official language," a provision included in all of Egypt's subsequent constitutions. This article, however, never had any legal implication. Rather, it represented a way to emphasize Egypt's Islamic identity as opposed to British (and more generally Western) principles and values. See Yussef Auf, "Islam and Sharia Law: Historical, Constitutional, and Political Context in Egypt" *Atlantic Council* 4 (May 2016), www.atlanticcouncil.org/wp-content/uploads/2016/05/Islam_and_Sharia_Law.pdf. The 1971 constitution significantly amended this provision, by stipulating in Article 2 not only that Islam was the state religion and Arabic its official language but also that "principles of Islamic *Sharia* are a source of legislation." This provision was further strengthened in 1980, when the principles of *Sharia* became "the main" source of legislation. See Clark B. Lombardi, "Constitutional Provisions Making Sharia 'A' or 'The' Chief Source of Legislation: Where Did They Come From? What Do They Mean? Do They Matter?" (2013) 28 *American University International Law Review*, 754–758.

12 One need only consider the issue concerning the removal of the term limits for the presidents of the republic. In Egypt, for example, the 1980 amendment to the 1971 constitution included the removal of the two-term limit for the president of the republic, thus granting him the possibility to be re-elected indefinitely. In Tunisia, the 1959 constitution was amended in 2002 in order to remove the presidential three-term limit. In Algeria, the two-term limit for the president of the republic provided for by the 1996 constitution was removed following the 2008 constitutional reform.

13 See Chapter 2, Section 2.5.1.2.

14 The constitution of Kuwait, adopted back in 1962, is one of the few exceptions.

15 Brown, "Regimes Reinventing Themselves," at p. 42.

smooth transitions were very much needed, and this favored the adoption of constitutions containing clearer provisions addressing questions of successions.[16]

It should be noted that following World War II, there was a spate of constitution-making and constitutional reform processes. Algeria adopted four constitutions (1963, 1976, 1989, and 1996 – the latter being extensively amended in 2002, 2008, 2016, and 2020), Egypt adopted five (1956, 1964, 1971, 2012, and 2014), Syria adopted five (1950, 1953, 1962, 1973, and 2012), and Morocco adopted six (1962, 1970, 1972, 1992, 1996, and 2011). In Jordan, the constitution of 1952 was amended several times, including the major post-Arab Spring reform of 2011, followed by the amendments adopted in 2014, 2016, and 2022.

The fourth wave of constitution-writing in the Arab world started at the beginning of 2011 following the outbreak of the Arab Spring (even though the Iraqi Constitution of 2005 adopted after the fall of Saddam Hussein represented a sort of anticipation of this new generation of constitutions).[17] As is well-known, the event that is usually considered the beginning of the Arab Spring is December 17, 2010, when a young street vendor, Mohamed Bouazizi, set himself on fire in the town of Sidi Bouzid, Tunisia, as a sign of protest against the regime of President Ben Ali. This episode, and especially the death of Bouazizi on January 4, 2011, gave rise to mass protest demonstrations across the country, and, after a few days, Ben Ali, who had ruled over Tunisia for twenty-three years, was forced to flee the country. What happened in Tunisia acted as a catalyst for the rest of the Arab world, with protest movements, demonstrations, and, in some cases, even revolutions taking place across the entire region.[18] Arab people not only asked for radical political, social, and economic reforms but also called for major constitutional changes aimed at making a clean break from the previous autocratic or semi-autocratic regimes. New constitutions were thus promulgated in Morocco (2011), Syria (2012), Egypt (2012 and 2014 – the latter being amended in 2019), and Tunisia (2014 and 2022), and profound constitutional reforms were adopted in Jordan (2011, followed by amendments in 2014, 2016, and 2022) and Algeria (2016 and 2020). However, this new wave of constitution-drafting is not over. In Libya, for example, despite a hostile scenario of war and anarchy, a draft constitution was adopted in July 2017. This draft, however, still needs to be ratified in a referendum. In the light of the enormous difficulties in organizing the constitutional referendum (and the national elections), since March 2022 the United Nations have been facilitating a process aimed at finding a consensual constitutional basis for national elections. Furthermore, over the past few years, the United Nations have also been facilitating a process aimed at replacing

16 Ibid., pp. 42–44.

17 See Brown, "Constitution Writing in the Arab World," at pp. 452–453. Specifically on the 2005 Iraqi Constitution, see Zaid Al-Ali, *The Struggle for Iraq's Future: How Corruption, Incompetence and Sectarianism Have Undermined Democracy* (Yale University Press 2014).

18 On the factors explaining these protest movements, see Luca Mezzetti, *Diritto islamico: Storia, fonti, istituzioni, società* (Giappichelli 2022), 116ff.

the 2012 Syrian Constitution with a new constitutional text. As will be shown later, if this new wave of constitution-building has not produced the democratic change that the protestors expected (with the partial exception of Tunisia under the 2014 constitution), this is due in part to the serious deficits in the constitution-making and constitutional reform processes. The shortcomings that marked the previous waves of constitution-drafting have been addressed only to a limited extent.

1.2 CONSTITUTION-MAKING AFTER THE 2011 UPRISINGS

In the following sections, I look at the fourth and final wave of constitution-drafting in the Arab world. In particular, I focus on the constitution-making processes followed in Morocco, Syria, Tunisia, and Egypt, as well as on the constitutional reform processes that took place in Jordan and Algeria. I also examine the ongoing constituent process in Libya (both the process that led to the July 2017 draft constitution and the recent UN-led process) and the UN-facilitated process aimed at replacing the 2012 Syrian Constitution with a new constitutional document. In the comparative analysis of this fourth wave of constitution-drafting, I focus on the following elements: (1) the body in charge of drafting the constitution and the role played by the ruling regime ("bottom-up" vs. "top-down" processes), (2) the degree of openness and transparency of the process, (3) the duration of the process, (4) the role played by political parties, (5) the role of civil society, (6) the role played by external actors, (7) the influence of previous domestic constitutions and their "reactivation," and (8) the influence of foreign constitutional models.

1.2.1 *The Body in Charge of Drafting the Constitution and the Role Played by the Ruling Regime*

When examining constitution-making processes, first one must consider the body responsible for drafting the constitution and the procedure for selecting its members. A distinction that is often drawn in comparative studies on constitution-writing is between "top-down" processes, where the constitution is largely imposed by the governing regime, and "bottom-up" processes, characterized by an active participation of the civil society in the drafting process.[19] During previous waves of constitution-drafting in the Arab world, "top-down" processes were the norm, whereas genuine "bottom-up" processes were very rare. The first generation of Arab constitutions, for example,

> originated very much within the governing elite. They were not composed by constituent assemblies seeking to define the nature of the political community but by individuals or small groups of politicians who generally occupied very senior

[19] See, for example, Todd A. Eisenstadt, A. Carl LeVan and Tofigh Maboudi, *Constituents before Assembly: Participation, Deliberation, and Representation in the Crafting of New Constitutions* (Cambridge University Press 2017).

> positions. Often little public discussion surrounded their composition, even when they occasioned sharp private debate within the elite. And they were promulgated by rulers who made clear – though not always explicitly – that they could be taken away in the same manner that they were given. That is, the ruler or governing elite granted legitimacy to – rather than drew legitimacy from – the constitutional document.[20]

In a similar vein, during the second and third waves of constitution-making, the processes were very often driven and controlled directly by the ruling regimes, which appointed small committees with the task of drafting the new constitutional texts. In most cases, the members of these committees "were selected on the basis of their conservative predisposition and party loyalty and so any attempt to introduce progressive ideas to the process would have met with significant resistance."[21] This approach gave rise to some discontent. In Egypt, for example, the 1923 constitution was written by a committee appointed by the king, but some (including the political party *Wafd*) demanded that the constitution be drafted by a popularly elected Constituent Assembly.[22] Similarly, in Morocco, the requests coming from certain political and social forces to elect a Constituent Assembly (requests that began with the process leading to the adoption of the 1962 constitution) were always disregarded. The difficulties in electing a body of that type may be summarized by one commentator writing in 1963: "The Constituent Assembly is vested with supreme power and, in Morocco, *such supreme power lies with the King alone*"[23] (emphasis added).

Although they hardly qualify as genuine "bottom-up" processes, there are select few cases in which the adoption of a new constitution was not a mere imposition "from above." An interesting example is the process that led to the adoption of the 1926 constitution of Lebanon. A thirteen-member commission was vested with the task of consulting civil and religious leaders concerning the content of the future constitution. In particular, the commission prepared a questionnaire with twelve questions about the political regime (monarchy or republic), the quota system, Parliament (unicameralism or bicameralism), ministerial and presidential responsibilities, and the electoral system. The outcome of these consultations formed the basis for the work of the Representative Council, which was in charge of the drafting process.[24] One must

20 Brown, *Constitutions in a Nonconstitutional World*, at pp. 32–33.

21 Zaid Al-Ali, "The Arab Spring Constitutions: For Whose Benefit?" in Tom Ginsburg and Aziz Z. Huq (eds.), *Assessing Constitutional Performance* (Cambridge University Press 2016), 376.

22 See Brown, *Constitutions in a Nonconstitutional World*, at p. 37.

23 Ahmed Reda Guédira, "Une constituante ni nécessaire ni possible," 27 *Confluent* 67 (January 1963), cited in Mohamed Tozy, *Monarchie et Islam politique au Maroc* (Presses de Sciences Po 1999), 90–91. See also Francesco Biagi, "The 2011 Constitution-Making Process in Morocco: A Limited and Controlled Public Participation" in Tania Abbiate, Markus Böckenförde, and Veronica Federico (eds.), *Public Participation in African Constitutionalism* (Routledge 2018), 61.

24 See Edmond Rabbath, *La Constitution libanaise: Origines, textes et commentaires* (Publications de l'Université libanaise 1982), 15–19; Antoine Hokayem, *La genèse de la Constitution libanaise de 1926: Le contexte du mandat francais, les projets préliminaires, les auteurs, le texte final* (Les éditions universitaires du Liban 1996), 219.

also recall the 1950 Syrian Constitution and the 1959 Tunisian Constitution, which were both drafted by an elected Constituent Assembly. Remarkably, in Syria (but not in Tunisia),[25] even women were allowed to vote in the elections of the Constituent Assembly.[26] The constitution-making process that took place in Kuwait was also more democratic than the other processes in the region. Specifically, the task of drafting the 1962 constitution was granted to a Constituent Assembly composed of twenty elected members (which included representatives of Kuwait's merchant families, leaders of Bedouin groups, and an Arab nationalist leader), plus eleven ministers who had not won elections in their own right. This Assembly was assisted in its work by a group of foreign constitutional scholars, who prepared a first draft of the constitution.[27]

As will be discussed later, after the Arab Spring, most of the countries in the region continued to follow a "top-down" approach. This was the case for Syria, Morocco, Jordan, Algeria, Egypt (constitution of 2014), and Tunisia (constitution of 2022). On the contrary, the constitution-drafting processes of Tunisia (constitution of 2014), Egypt (constitution of 2012), and Libya followed a "bottom-up" approach. Post-2011 processes confirm the empirical findings of studies on comparative constitution-making processes, according to which, with some relevant exceptions, "top-down" processes are less likely to produce democratic texts,[28] whereas "bottom-up" processes tend to "tilt the odds in favor of democracy."[29] Indeed, "when constitutions are sovereign expressions of peoples' participation, constitutions better promote and protect democratic rights. In other words, citizens are better off when they live in a political world of their own making."[30] This was clearly the case of the 2014 Tunisian Constitution, which was the outcome of the only *genuine* "bottom-up" process in the region after the Arab uprisings.

1.2.1.1 "Bottom-Up" Processes

Between 2011 and 2014, Tunisia clearly followed a genuine democratic "bottom-up" process. The *pouvoir constituant* was entrusted to a Constituent Assembly directly elected by the population, on October 23, 2011, through a system of closed-list proportional representation. These were the first free and fair elections in the country after decades of authoritarian rule: More than 100 parties took part in this process, and twenty-seven party, independent, and coalition lists managed to win at least one

[25] See Bernabé López García and Cecilia Fernández Suzor, *Introducción a los regímenes y constituciones árabes* (Centro de Estudios Constitucionales 1985), 292.

[26] See Radwan Ziadeh, "The History of the Syrian Constitution" (2017) 22 *Syrian Studies Association Bulletin*, 11, https://static1.squarespace.com/static/613e6b4795ed212144c8ac79/t/655cf3f313960438da93da88/1700590584576/Vol+22+no+1+2017.pdf.

[27] See Nathan J. Brown, *The Rule of Law in the Arab World: Courts in Egypt and the Gulf* (Cambridge University Press 1997), 165–166; see also Section 1.2.6.

[28] Eisenstadt, LeVan, and Maboudi, *Constituents before Assembly*, at p. 84ff.

[29] Ibid., at p. 114ff.

[30] Ibid., at pp. 117–118.

seat in the Constituent Assembly (which also operated as an interim legislature).[31] The moderate Islamist party Ennahda won the elections with around 41 percent of the vote and obtained a relative majority of seats in the Constituent Assembly (89 out of 217). Owing to the adoption of the principle of "vertical equality," according to which electoral lists must be drawn up in such a way as to alternate between men and women,[32] women obtained 59 out of 217 seats in the Constituent Assembly (27 percent). This undoubtedly represented significant progress in women's representation compared to the past. The Independent High Authority for Elections, which replaced the Ministry of the Interior in the organization and oversight of the elections, contributed enormously to guaranteeing a democratic process.[33] This was demonstrated by the fact that the electoral results were not questioned and that the elections were considered free and fair by the international observers who monitored the process (including the Organization for Security and Cooperation in Europe, the European Union, and the Carter Center). In addition, the constitution, adopted in January 2014, was drafted with highly active participation by civil society, which had a strong impact on the final text of the document.[34]

In Egypt, the process that led to the adoption of the 2012 constitution marked a significant break from the past, because, for the first time in the country's history, the constitution was drafted by an *elected* body – namely, a Constituent Assembly elected by (an Islamist-dominated) Parliament. The process, however, did not have a quiet life and was marked by major democratic shortcomings. Specifically, the makeup of the Constituent Assembly – which included 66 Islamist members out of 100, who were mainly representatives of the Muslim Brotherhood's Freedom and Justice Party and the Salafi Al-Nour Party – was extremely contentious from the outset, and this led liberal and youth groups to file legal challenges claiming that this body did not sufficiently represent women, young people, and minorities. The Assembly was dissolved on April 10, 2012, by the Supreme Administrative Court on the grounds that it included members of Parliament. Indeed, relying on Article 60 of the March 30, 2011, Constitutional Declaration,[35] the Court stated that Parliament

[31] On pros and cons of having a constitution-making body working also as an interim legislature in non-democratic contexts, see Winluck Wahiu, *A Practical Guide to Constitution Building: An Introduction* (International IDEA 2011), 15–16; Kimana Zulueta-Fülscher and Sumit Bisarya, *(S)electing Constitution-Making Bodies in Fragile and Conflict-Affected Settings* (International IDEA 2018), 18–19.

[32] See Article 16 of the Decree-Law no. 35 of May 10, 2011. This provision was later confirmed in Article 24 of the Organic Law 2014–16.

[33] See Yadh Ben Achour, *Tunisie: Une révolution en pays d'Islam* (Cérès éditions 2017), 152.

[34] See Section 1.2.5.

[35] This Constitutional Declaration replaced the previous 1971 constitution and served as an interim constitution until the promulgation of the 2012 constitution. Article 60 stipulated that: "The members of the first People's Assembly and Shura Council (except the appointed members) will meet in a joint session following an invitation from the Supreme Council of the Armed Forces within 6 months of their election to elect a provisional assembly composed of 100 members which will prepare a new draft constitution for the country to be completed within 6 months of the formation of this assembly."

was vested with the power to elect the Constituent Assembly but could not elect its own members to such a body.[36]

After a series of complicated negotiations aimed at forming a more balanced body, a second Constituent Assembly was elected in June 2012. It was composed of 100 members: 39 seats were reserved for members of Parliament, 6 for judges, 13 for union representatives, 21 for public figures, 9 for legal experts, 5 for Al-Azhar, 4 for the Coptic Orthodox Church, 1 for the armed forces, 1 for the police, and 1 for the Ministry of Justice. However, the composition of this new Constituent Assembly was also contentious, as it still included members of Parliament and was dominated by the Islamists. Thus, its constitutionality was soon challenged in the courts, and a number of non-Islamist members (including representatives of liberal parties and the Church) decided to withdraw from it.[37] Uncertainty concerning the outcome of the constitution-making process was also due to the fact that, on June 14, 2012, the Supreme Constitutional Court struck down the law governing parliamentary elections and ordered the dissolution of the lower chamber of Parliament.[38] The Supreme Administrative Court repeatedly postponed its ruling on the legitimacy of the new Constituent Assembly and eventually referred to the Supreme Constitutional Court Law no. 79/2012, which, *inter alia*, granted the Assembly immunity from judicial dissolution.[39] The Islamists feared a new dissolution of the Constituent Assembly and, therefore, rushed to approve the new constitution on November 29, 2012, which was finally approved in a popular referendum on December 15 and December 22 of the same year.

The legitimacy of the constitution-making process continued to be controversial. Indeed, six months after the constitutional referendum, on June 2, 2013, the Supreme Constitutional Court struck down the electoral law for the upper house (*Shura* Council), as well as Law 79/2012, which had established the criteria for electing the members of the Constituent Assembly. Although the Court stated that the *Shura* Council could continue its functions until new parliamentary elections were

36 See Nimer Sultany, *Law and Revolution: Legitimacy and Constitutionalism after the Arab Spring* (Oxford University Press 2017), 309.

37 See Liliana Mihaila, "More Withdraw from Constituent Assembly," *Daily News Egypt* (November 18, 2012), https://dailynewsegypt.com/2012/11/18/more-withdraw-from-constituent-assembly/.

38 In this judgment, the Court also ruled Law no. 17 of 2012 (known as "Political Isolation Law") unconstitutional. This law prevented high officials during the Mubarak regime from holding important posts in the new state apparatus for a period of ten years. On this key decision, see Nathan J. Brown, "Egypt: A Constitutional Court in an Unconstitutional Setting" in Justin O. Frosini and Francesco Biagi (eds.), *Political and Constitutional Transitions in North Africa: Actors and Factors* (Routledge 2015), 44–46; Nathan J. Brown and Julian G. Waller, "Constitutional Courts and Political Uncertainty: Constitutional Ruptures and the Rule of Judges" (2016) 14 *International Journal of Constitutional Law*, 839ff.; Mohammad H. Fadel, "The Sounds of Silence: The Supreme Constitutional Court of Egypt, Constitutional Crisis, and Constitutional Silence" (2018) 16 *International Journal of Constitutional Law*, 945ff.

39 See Rainer Grote, "The Arab Republic of Egypt: Introductory Note" in *Oxford Constitutions of the World* (2014), 4–5.

held, and that the constitution remained valid, this judgment "contributed to the delegitimation of the 2012 Constitution."[40] Overall, it is fair to argue that the 2012 Egyptian Constitution was the outcome of a flawed "bottom-up" process.

Another "bottom-up" process marked by various shortcomings took place in Libya. Interestingly, some controversies that occurred in the process that led to the adoption of the 2017 draft constitution clearly recall the dynamics of the process that led to the adoption of the 1951 constitution. The composition of the drafting body and the procedure for selecting its members were certainly among the most controversial issues. In both cases, the Constituent Assembly was composed of sixty members – twenty members from each of the three historical regions of the country (namely, Tripolitania, Cyrenaica, and Fezzan). In 1950, the Committee of Twenty-One (responsible for making the key decisions concerning the creation of the National [Constituent] Assembly) ruled that the members of the Assembly would be directly appointed, without carrying out general elections. This raised some criticisms. Some members of the Committee of Twenty-One requested that the Assembly be formed through elections,[41] and the Political Committee of the Arab League, through its Secretary General Abdul Rahman Hassan Azzam, argued that an Assembly "composed of people who are selected and appointed, and not elected, did not have the right to make strategic decisions for the Libyan people."[42] Following the 2011 Revolution, the procedure for selecting the members of the Constitution Drafting Assembly was even more problematic. The original version of the Interim Constitutional Declaration of August 3, 2011, provided for direct appointment of the Assembly members. Subsequently, a 2012 amendment replaced direct appointment with general elections, but this amendment was ruled unconstitutional by the Supreme Court on procedural grounds. The "election vs. appointment" controversy was definitively settled by the amendment of April 2013, according to which the Constitution Drafting Assembly would be elected through universal direct suffrage.[43]

As to the composition of the Constituent Assembly, several issues emerged in both processes. In the light of the significant differences in terms of population, the criterion of equal representation of the three provinces was the first problematic point. In 1950, Fezzan had around 40,000 inhabitants, Cyrenaica had 300,000, and Tripolitania had 800,000.[44] In 2012 (two years before the elections of the Constitution Drafting Assembly), there were around 421,000 people in Fezzan, 1,361,000 in Cyrenaica, and 3,451,000 in Tripolitania.[45] The decision to allocate

40 Sultany, *Law and Revolution*, at p. 314.

41 See Ettore Rossi, "Il Regno unito della Libia" (October-December 1951) 10/12 *Oriente Moderno*, 161.

42 Ibid., at p. 168.

43 See The Carter Center, *The 2014 Constitutional Drafting Assembly Elections in Libya: Final Report* (2014), 12, www.cartercenter.org/resources/pdfs/news/peace_publications/election_reports/libya-06112014-final-.pdf

44 See Rossi, "Il Regno unito della Libia," at p. 165.

45 See Libya Data Portal, https://libya.opendataforafrica.org

twenty seats to each of the three regions regardless of population was founded on the idea that a lasting compromise would never be achieved if the regions were not equally represented.

The representation of minorities was another controversial issue. In 1950, the stance adopted by the Committee of Twenty-One did not seem very coherent. On the one hand, the Committee decided "against giving the Minorities the right of representation in the Assembly," but on the other hand, in its final resolution, it "pointed out that there was a genuine intention and a general feeling that all civil, religious, and social rights of minorities and foreigners should be safeguarded in the future constitution of Libya."[46] The issue concerning the representation of minorities was only partially addressed in the election law (Law no. 17 of 2013) for the 2014 elections of the Constitution Drafting Assembly. Indeed, only six seats (10 percent) were reserved for the ethnic minority groups: two for the Amazigh, two for the Tuareg, and two for the Tebu. The Amazigh, in particular, believed that this share failed to reflect their proportion of the population and, therefore, decided to boycott the elections and not participate in the constitution-making process. Despite initially participating, in June 2015, the representatives of the Tebu and the Tuareg, feeling that their requests were not seriously taken into consideration by the Arab majority of the Assembly, also decided to boycott the proceedings. This left the constituent body without any representatives from the minority groups.[47] Even women were not sufficiently represented in the Assembly, as they were only reserved six seats.

This very limited representation of ethnic minorities and women weakened the legitimacy of the Libyan Constitution Drafting Assembly, whose members were finally elected on February 20, 2014, through a majoritarian electoral system (first-past-the-post in individual constituencies). These elections, which saw a low turnout, were held amid a deteriorating security situation (some polling centers either did not open or were closed down) and a general disillusion of the population about the whole political process.[48] It should also be noted that over time, in addition to the representatives of the minority groups, other members withdrew from the Constitution Drafting Assembly, including some members from Western Libya, who denounced the "federalist inclinations" of the Assembly's working group and its attempt to divide the country with "regional quotas."[49] Eventually, the July 2017 draft constitution was approved by forty-three of the forty-four attending members

46 Ismail R. Khalidi, "Constitution of the United Kingdom of Libya: Background and Summary" (1952) 6 *Middle East Journal*, 222.

47 See Nedra Cherif, *Libya's Constitution: Between Conflict and Compromise* (European University Institute – Middle East Directions (MED) 2021/02) (March 2021), 4–6, https://cadmus.eui.eu/bitstream/handle/1814/70538/QM-09-21-057-EN-N.pdf?sequence=3&isAllowed=y

48 See Mohamed Eljarh, "Democracy Fatigue in Libya," *Foreign Policy* (February 26, 2014), https://foreignpolicy.com/2014/02/26/democracy-fatigue-in-libya/

49 Darin E. W. Johnson, "Conflict Constitution-Making in Libya and Yemen" (2017) 39 *University of Pennsylvania Journal of International Law*, 316.

of the Constitution Drafting Assembly,[50] but this document still needs to be ratified by the people in a referendum.[51] However, as discussed in greater detail later, in the light of the major difficulties in organizing the constitutional referendum (and the national elections), since March 2022, the United Nations has been facilitating a process aimed at reaching agreement between the representatives of the High Council of State (Western Libya) and the House of Representatives (Eastern Libya) on a consensual constitutional framework for national elections.[52]

1.2.1.2 "Top-Down" Processes

As noted earlier, after the Arab Spring, the majority of the countries in the region followed a "top-down" constitution-drafting process, that is, a process driven and controlled by the ruling regime. Syria is probably the clearest example of this approach. On October 15, 2011, a few months after the outbreak of civil war, President Bashar al-Assad issued Decree no. 33 appointing a twenty-nine-member committee (that only included three women) with the task of replacing the 1973 constitution with a new constitutional text in four months. In actual fact, only twenty-eight members participated to the work of the committee, as one of them, human rights lawyer Abdulhay Al-Sayed, decided to withdraw from it. Indeed, in his opinion the constitution should have been drafted by a popularly-elected Constituent Assembly.[53] The committee's chair handed the results of its work to President Assad on February 12, 2012, and a few days later, on February 26, the new constitution was ratified in a popular referendum.[54] The process, which was entirely orchestrated by Assad, was rightly depicted as a "sham."[55]

In Morocco and Jordan, the constitutional reforms represented to a large extent a mere "concession" by the king.[56] In Morocco, the new 2011 constitution, which was adopted in less than four months, was "granted" by the monarch and did not derive

[50] In this way, the Assembly achieved the required majority of 2/3+1 provided for by the Assembly's rules of procedure. See Nedra Cherif, "Libya's Constitutional Quagmire," *Konrad Adenauer Stiftung – Libya Brief no. 10* (June 2021), 4.

[51] On this referendum, see Section 1.2.5 in greater detail.

[52] See Section 1.2.6 in greater detail.

[53] See Ibrahim Daraji, "Syria: The Constitution of the 'Crisis' or the Crisis of the Constitution?", *Journal of Constitutional Law in the Middle East and North Africa*, special issue on "Arab Constitutional Responses to the Revolutions and Transformations in the Region" edited by Rim Turkmani and Tamara El Khoury (December 2023), 113–114, www.jcl-mena.org

[54] See Karim Atassi, *Syria, the Strength of an Idea: The Constitutional Architectures of Its Political Regimes* (Cambridge University Press 2018), 385ff.; Jacques el-Hakim and Taymour Harding, "Syria" (2010–2011) 16 *Yearbook of Islamic and Middle Eastern Law*, 180.

[55] Hugh Macleod and Annasofie Flamand, "Syria Referendum Called 'a Sham'," *GlobalPost* (February 27, 2012), www.pri.org/stories/2012-02-27/syria-referendum-called-sham

[56] See Francesco Biagi, "Will Surviving Constitutionalism in Morocco and Jordan Work in the Long Run? A Comparison with Three Past Authoritarian Regimes" (2014) 3 *Cambridge Journal of International and Comparative Law*, 1245ff.

from a democratically elected Constituent Assembly. Indeed, King Mohammed VI was the master of the entire constituent process: It was he who decided to replace the previous 1996 constitution; identify in his speech on March 9, 2011, the key elements on which the new constitution was to be based (a genuine "constituent speech")[57]; appoint the eighteen members of the Commission on Constitutional Reform, which had the task of drafting the new constitution (most of whom were university professors and activists from human rights associations); and, last, grant his approval to the draft presented to him by the President of the Commission, Abdeltif Menouni. In other words, Mohammed VI continued to pursue the tradition – which had begun with King Hassan II – of a "constituent King."[58] Thus, it is evident that the new constitutional text, which was ratified in a popular referendum on July 1, 2011, represents another *octroyée* constitution in Moroccan history.[59]

Like Mohammed VI of Morocco, King Abdullah II of Jordan steered the entire constitutional reform process. In April 2011, the monarch appointed a Royal Committee on Constitutional Amendments to propose reforms to the 1952 constitution. The composition of this body was harshly criticized:

1. Neither the prime minister nor any member of his cabinet had anything to do with the formation of the Commission. They were neither represented nor is it known if they were consulted.
2. Four out of the ten members were former prime ministers, while the other six members had formerly occupied ministerial positions.
3. Only three of the ten members were lawyers, but none of them was known to have written, published, or lectured on matters of constitutional law.
4. Up to the point when the Commission was formed, all the dignitaries who became members of this Commission were of the opinion that the constitution should not be amended in any reform effort and that no constitutional amendment should be permitted.[60]

The Committee held meetings for around four months, after which it submitted its proposals to the King. Abdullah II then directed the Government and Parliament to finalize the amendments within thirty days. The package of constitutional reforms was discussed and approved by the House of Representatives and the Senate, with minor changes, before being ratified by the king. The amendments were published in the Official Gazette on October 1, 2011.[61]

57 The speech of June 17 is available, along with all other official speeches of the Sovereign, online at www.maroc.ma/fr/discours-du-roi

58 Bernard Cubertafond, "La transition marocaine après le printemps arabe et la nouvelle Constitution" (2011) 5 *Les Études et Essais du Centre Jacques Berque*, 3.

59 See Biagi, "2011 Constitution-Making Process in Morocco," at p. 56ff.

60 Mohammad Hammouri, "Constitutional Reform and the Rise of Constitutional Adjudication in Jordan. Background, Issues, and Controversies" in Rainer Grote and Tilmann J. Röder (eds.), *Constitutionalism, Human Rights, and Islam after the Arab Spring* (Oxford University Press 2016), 725.

61 Ibid., at pp. 725–726.

This top-down approach also characterized the constitutional amendments adopted in 2014, 2016, and 2022.[62] The 2022 amendments, in particular, were part of a larger package of reforms.[63] In June 2021, King Abdullah II appointed a ninety-two-member "Royal Committee to Modernize the Political System," whose mission, to use the king's words, was

> to put forward new draft election and political parties laws; look into the necessary constitutional amendments connected to the two laws and the mechanisms of parliamentary work; and provide recommendations on developing legislation regulating local administration, expanding participation in decision-making, and creating a political and legislative environment conducive to the active engagement of youth and women in public life.[64]

In October 2021, the Royal Committee proposed a ten-year roadmap of political and constitutional reforms. The Government not only confirmed most of the Committee's proposals but also made its own suggestions that were aimed to further strengthen monarchical powers. In the first months of 2022, Parliament adopted both the constitutional and political reforms, which were then promulgated by the king.

In Algeria, the 2016 constitutional reform was approved a full five years after the April 15, 2011, speech in which President Abdelaziz Bouteflika announced his intention to amend the 1996 constitution. During that period, the regime acted as the absolute guiding force behind the reform, steering its progress, stipulating timescales, and, above all, deciding on its content without letting the people have any real say.[65] In fact, it is no coincidence that the reform has been defined as a "gift of the Emir."[66] The bill containing the constitutional amendment was subject to *ex ante* review by the Constitutional Council, which ruled that no aspect of the reform was unconstitutional.[67] The adoption of the reform by Parliament on February 7, 2016, was little more than a formality. Indeed, it was approved by an overwhelming majority, with 499 votes in favor, two against, and sixteen abstentions. As much as

62 See, for example, Sufian Obeidat, "Jordan's 2016 Constitutional Amendments: A Return to Absolute Monarchy?," *ConstitutionNet* (May 27, 2016), http://constitutionnet.org/news/jordans-2016-constitutional-amendments-return-absolute-monarchy; Sufian Obeidat, "Modernizing Jordan's Political System: The Unspoken Motivations," *ConstitutionNet* (July 29, 2021), https://constitutionnet.org/news/modernizing-jordans-political-system-unspoken-motivations

63 See Sean Yom and Wael Al-Khatib, "Democratic Reform in Jordan. Breaking the Impasse," *Project on Middle East Democracy – POMED* (February 2022), https://pomed.org/wp-content/uploads/2022/02/Yom_Khatib_Final-1.pdf

64 King Abdullah II, *Letter to Samir Rifai Entrusting Him With Chairing the Royal Committee to Modernise the Political System* (June 10, 2021), https://kingabdullah.jo/en/letters/letter-samir-rifai-entrusting-him-chairing-royal-committee-modernise-political-system

65 See Francesco Biagi, "The Algerian Constitutional Reform of 2016: A Critical Analysis" (2017) 17 *Global Jurist*, 2–4.

66 Bouhania Goui, "Algerian Angst: Can It Agree on Constitutional Change?," *Arab Reform Initiative – Policy Alternatives* (February 2015), 7, www.arab-reform.net/en/node/494

67 On this controversial judgment, see Biagi, "Algerian Constitutional Reform," at p. 3.

Bouteflika had stressed his desire to launch a process that would be as participatory as possible, in actual fact, it was not. Establishing commissions to reform the constitution (comprised of members – including university professors – appointed by Bouteflika himself) and conducting consultations with political parties and civil society served exclusively, according to a consolidated Algerian practice, to rubber stamp the wishes of the political leadership.[68]

Four years later, in 2020, the newly elected Algerian President Abdelmadjid Tebboune, who enjoyed the full support of the armed forces, decided to launch a new constitutional reform process in response to the massive protest demonstrations taking place in the country (the *Hirak* movement).[69] In his opinion, this reform was supposed to be "the cornerstone of the new Algeria."[70] However, most of the democratic shortcomings that had characterized the previous constitutional reform process were also present in this new one. Notwithstanding the calls for the election of a Constituent Assembly coming from civil society and some political parties,[71] Tebboune directly appointed a commission of experts (mainly university professors) and asked them to produce a new draft constitutional reform in three months.[72] Following the draft's release, the Government invited the population to submit their proposals on the draft reform. In actual fact, however, the regime's clampdown on opposition and dissent prevented any genuine open debate from taking place. After Parliament's approval, the draft was submitted to a referendum, which – in the regime's perspective – was supposed to strengthen the legitimacy of the reform. This popular consultation, however, was a major failure. While more than 66 percent of the voters backed the reform, the turnout was extremely low, with less than 24 percent of eligible voters participating.[73] One cannot fail to notice that this top-down process led by the political and military leadership was largely in contrast with Article 8 of the constitution, which stipulated (and still stipulates) that "[t]he constituent power shall belong to the people."

Although it cannot be considered an act of "largesse" by the head of state, the 2014 constitution of Egypt was mainly the outcome of a top-down process in which the President and the military were the two guiding forces. As is well known, the 2012 constitution proved to be short-lived. On July 8, 2013, following President Mohamed Morsi's removal from office, the army appointed Adli Mansour (former President of

68 See Ciro Sbailò, *Diritto pubblico dell'Islam mediterraneo. Linee evolutive degli ordinamenti nordafricani contemporanei: Marocco, Algeria, Tunisia, Libia, Egitto* (Wolters Kluwer – CEDAM 2022), 77.

69 On the *Hirak* movement, see volume 176 of the French journal *Pouvoirs* (2021).

70 "Le président Tebboune promulgue la révision de la Constitution," *L'Orient-Le Jour* (January 1, 2021), www.lorientlejour.com/article/1246710/le-president-tebboune-promulgue-la-revision-de-la-constitution.html

71 "Appel: Pour une Assemblée Constituante!," *El Watan* (March 3, 2019), www.elwatan.com/edition/actualite/appel-pour-une-assemblee-constituante-03-03-2019

72 See Zaid Al-Ali, "Algeria's Draft Constitution 2020," *IACL-AIDC Blog* (May 14, 2020), https://blog-iacl-aidc.org/2020-posts/2020/5/14/algerias-draft-constitution-2020

73 See Section 1.2.5 for more details.

the Supreme Constitutional Court) as interim President of Egypt. Mansour issued a Constitutional Declaration suspending the 2012 constitution and setting out a process for amending it. First, a ten-member committee of legal experts (which included judges from the ordinary courts, the Supreme Constitutional Court, the State Council, and law professors) was granted the power to propose amendments to the 2012 constitution.[74] The proposed changes were then submitted to a fifty-member Constituent Assembly, which, instead of simply discussing and approving the ten-member committee proposal,[75] decided to *rewrite* the constitution.[76] This Assembly represented the main stakeholders in Egyptian society, including political parties, workers, farmers, trade unions, federations, national councils, Al-Azhar, churches, armed forces, the police, and public figures. There was an additional requirement that provided that at least ten members of the Assembly be young people and women. It should be noted that only six seats were allocated to political parties: two for Islamist members, two for liberal members, one for a nationalist member, and one for a leftist member. Of the two Islamist representatives, one belonged to the Salafi Al-Nour Party, and the other was an independent Islamist personality who did not belong to any political party.[77] The decision to completely exclude the Muslim Brotherhood from the Constituent Assembly was part of the army's strategy of "Debrotherhoodization" of Egypt.[78] The last step in the constitution-making process consisted of the referendum held on January 15 and 16, 2014, when the people ratified the new document.

Unlike the previous 2012 constitution, where the Constituent Assembly was elected by Parliament, the 2014 constitution was drafted by commissions (both the ten-member committee and the fifty-member Constituent Assembly) whose members were appointed pursuant to a *presidential decree*.[79] This constitution-making process thus calls to mind the one followed to adopt the 1971 constitution. Specifically, this text was drafted by a committee directly appointed by President Sadat even though the regime ensured that the committee had representatives from across the ideological spectrum, including liberal members, Islamic scholars, and Coptic religious leaders.[80] The top-down approach followed in the process that led to the adoption of the 2014 constitution is also confirmed by the fact that public participation was overall rather limited and controlled from above. Even the 2019

74 As provided for by Article 28 of the 2013 Constitutional Declaration issued by Mansour.

75 As provided for by Article 29 of the 2013 Constitutional Declaration issued by Mansour.

76 See Sultany, *Law and Revolution*, at p. 250.

77 See Yussef Auf, "Egypt's Constitutional Committees," *Atlantic Council* (September 5, 2013), https://atlanticcouncil.org/blogs/menasource/egypt-s-constitutional-committees/

78 Sonia Farid, "Witch-hunt Politics in Egypt," *AlArabiya News* (July 9, 2013), https://english.alarabiya.net/en/views/news/middle-east/2013/07/10/Witch-hunt-politics-in-Egypt

79 As provided for by Articles 28 and 29 of the 2013 Constitutional Declaration issued by Mansour.

80 See Clark B. Lombardi, "The Constitution as Agreement to Agree: The Social and Political Foundations (and Effects) of the 1971 Egyptian Constitution" in Denis J. Galligan and Mila Versteeg (eds.), *Social and Political Foundations of Constitutions* (Cambridge University Press 2013), 409.

constitutional amendments to the 2014 constitution were the outcome of a hasty, secret process driven entirely by the ruling regime.[81]

In Tunisia, the process that led to the enactment of the 2022 constitution was diametrically opposed to the 2011–2014 constitution-making process. Indeed, the 2014 constitution was the result of a genuine "bottom-up" process, whereas the 2022 constitutional text can be qualified as the "Kaïs Saïed's Constitution," as the Tunisian President not only drove the process but also played a key role in the very drafting of the text.[82] His intention to "reform" the 2014 constitution (at that time there was no explicit reference to the adoption of a "new" constitution) was officially announced by Saïed for the first time in Presidential Decree no. 2021-117 of September 22, 2021,[83] two months after the proclamation of the state of exception in the country.[84] The first phase of the constitution-making process consisted of an online "public consultation" that was held between January 15 and March 20, 2022, whereas the second phase, the one related to the actual drafting of the constitutional text, began on May 19, 2022, with the adoption of Decree-Law No. 2022-30 by which the "National Consultative Commission for a New Republic" was created. This Commission – headed by Sadok Belaïd, university professor of public law, who was considered very close to Saïed – was composed of three sub-commissions: the Commission on Economic and Social Affairs (composed of representatives of some of the major civil society organizations and trade unions, including the Tunisian General Labor Union [UGTT]),[85] the Legal Commission (composed of the Deans of the country's Faculties of Law and Political Sciences), and the Commission for National Dialogue (composed of the members of the two previous commissions). The Commission on Economic and Social Affairs was required to make proposals in the light of the country's economic and social experience, while the Legal Commission was responsible for preparing a first draft of the new constitution. Finally, the Commission for National Dialogue, once it had received proposals from both commissions, was required to make a "synthesis" and submit

81 See in greater detail Sections 1.2.2 and 1.2.5.

82 On this constitution-making process, see International Commission of Jurists, *Fundamentally Flawed: Tunisia's 2022 Constitution-making Process* (June 2022), www.icj.org/wp-content/uploads/2022/07/Tunisia-draft-constitution-question-and-answer-briefing-2022-ENG.pdf; Aymen Bessalah, "Kaïs Saïed's National Monologue on a New Tunisian Constitution," *Project on Middle East Democracy – POMED* (June 2022), https://pomed.org/wp-content/uploads/2022/06/2022_06b_Bessalah_Snapshot.pdf; Francesco Biagi, "Tunisia: la Costituzione di Kaïs Saïed," *Diritti Comparati* (July 28, 2022), www.diritticomparati.it/tunisia-la-costituzione-di-kais-saied/

83 According to Article 22 of the Presidential Decree, the president was called upon to draw up "draft revisions related to political reforms with the assistance of a commission whose organization shall be established by presidential decree," and these draft revisions would be then submitted to a referendum by the president for final approval.

84 On the proclamation of the state of exception and on Presidential Decree no. 2021-117, see Chapter 2, Section 2.2.4.

85 However, some of these actors (including the UGTT) rejected the invitation to form part of the Commission. See Section 1.2.5 in greater detail.

the draft constitution to the President of the Republic by June 20. A new Decree-law, no. 2022-32 of May 25, then stipulated that the draft constitution to be submitted to referendum would be published by presidential decree by June 30, that is, ten days after the deadline for the submission of the draft by the Commission for National Dialogue.

While the Commission on Economic and Social Affairs met on at least three occasions, the Legal Commission never met[86] (or at most it met only once),[87] a fact that can be explained in the light of the Deans' refusal to participate in the constitution-making process in order to preserve the neutrality of their respective faculties. Saïed then tried to impose his will by issuing a new decree in which he explicitly indicated the names of the Deans appointed to serve on this Commission. To date, however, it is unclear who actually served on it. On June 18, two days before Sadok Belaïd handed over the draft constitution to Saïed, there appeared to have been a meeting between the Commission on Economic and Social Affairs and the Commission on Legal Affairs, a meeting that may also have been the only meeting of the Commission for National Dialogue provided for in Decree-Law No. 2022-30.[88]

On June 30, Saïed issued Presidential Decree no. 2022-578, which contained the text of the draft constitution to be submitted to a referendum. The text, however, was profoundly different from the draft submitted by Sadok Belaïd on June 20. Belaïd immediately distanced himself from the text issued by the President: In fact, on July 3, he handed over to the press the draft that he had submitted to Saïed (a draft that until then had not been made public), in order to show that it had nothing to do with the text published by the President. Belaïd also declared that the draft constitution was dangerous because, through certain provisions, it could "pave the way for a dictatorial regime."[89] Officially, nobody knows who actually drafted the final text of the constitution, but it is more than fair to assume that it was either Saïed himself (who was a university professor of constitutional law before he was elected President of Tunisia) or a small group of people under his direction. The flaws of the process, however, do not end there. On July 8, Saïed issued a new Presidential Decree, no. 2022-607, by which certain "errors" contained in the draft constitution published on June 30 were "corrected." This decree, however, far from merely correcting material errors, also provides for some substantive changes. For example, Article 5 of the constitution relating to the "objectives/aims" (*maqasid*) of Islam was amended by adding the expression "within the framework of a democratic system."[90]

86 See International Commission of Jurists, *Fundamentally Flawed*, at p. 3.

87 See Bessalah, "Kaïs Saïed's National Monologue," at pp. 7–8.

88 Ibid., at p. 8.

89 "Tunisie: l'auteur de la Constitution désavoue le projet amendé par Kaïs Saïed," *Jeune Afrique* (July 3, 2022), www.jeuneafrique.com/1358718/politique/tunisie-lauteur-de-la-constitution-desavoue-le-projet-amende-par-kais-saied/

90 On this issue, see Chapter 4, Section 4.2.1 in greater detail.

The constitution was then ratified in the referendum of July 25, 2022, which was held exactly one year after Saïed's proclamation of the state of exception. The vast majority of the voters backed the new constitution, but the turnout was extremely low.[91]

1.2.2 *Degree of Openness and Transparency of the Process*

Another element that must be considered when examining a constitution-making process is its degree of openness and transparency. In the first place, one must verify whether the meetings of the body in charge of drafting the constitution are open to the public. Regarding this aspect, two diametrically opposed processes of constitution-making were the 1787 Federal Convention in Philadelphia, which met in complete secrecy, and the 1789 French Constituent Assembly, which was fully public.[92] Jon Elster has stressed that secrecy is not an absolute evil, while, on the contrary,

> debates in front of an audience tend to generate rhetorical overbidding and heated passions that are incompatible with the kind of close and calm scrutiny that ought to be the rule when one is adopting provisions for the indefinite future. By denying the public admission to the proceedings and by keeping the debates secret until the final document has been adopted, one creates conditions for rational discussion that are less likely to prevail in the presence of an audience.[93]

However, Elster has argued that initial secrecy should be offset by subsequent publicity, for example, in the form of discussions in a plenary assembly: In fact, with total secrecy, "partisan interests and logrolling come to the forefront."[94] In this sense, the Spanish constituent process (1977–1978) was considered one that came closest to striking an "optimal balance"[95] between secrecy and publicity. Initially, in fact, the Constitutional Affairs and Public Freedoms Committee appointed a commission (*Ponencia*) (comprised of seven members from the main political parties) with the task of drawing up a draft constitution, and the decisions of this body were taken in secret. The draft constitution was only subsequently presented to Parliament (*Cortes*) and discussed publicly in both of its houses.[96]

91 See Section 1.2.5 in greater detail.

92 See Jon Elster, "Arguing and Bargaining in Two Constituent Assemblies" (2000) 2 *University of Pennsylvania Journal of Constitutional Law*, 345ff.

93 Jon Elster, "Legislatures as Constituent Assemblies" in Richard W. Bauman and Tsvi Kahana (eds.), *The Least Examined Branch: The Role of Legislatures in the Constitutional State* (Cambridge University Press 2006), 191.

94 Jon Elster, "Forces and Mechanisms in the Constitution-making Process" (1995) 45 *Duke Law Journal*, 395.

95 Ibid.

96 See Jorge de Esteban, "El proceso constituyente español, 1977–1978" in José Félix Tezanos Tortajada, Ramón Cotarelo García and Andrés de Blas Guerrero (eds.), *La transición democrática española* (Editorial Sistema 1989), 275ff.

In the Arab world, secrecy has generally been one of the trademarks of the work of constitution-drafting commissions.[97] Unfortunately, this lack of transparency and openness also characterized most of the post-2011 constitution-making and constitutional reform processes. In Morocco, Syria, and Jordan, for example, all meetings of the commissions responsible for drafting the constitutional reforms took place behind closed doors. No public sessions were envisaged. Only the 2021–2022 constitutional reform process in Jordan showed a higher degree of transparency and openness. For example, the website of the "Royal Committee to Modernize the Political System" contained all the Committee's proposals and internal documentation.[98]

In Algeria, the process that led to the 2016 constitutional reform was also largely "shrouded in mystery."[99] The first draft of the proposed amendments was only published in May 2014 – that is, more than three years after Bouteflika's speech in April 2011, when he announced his intention to reform the 1996 constitution. Moreover, consultations with the representatives of political parties and civil society showed a lack of transparency, and, in fact, their outcome was never made public.[100] The 2020 constitutional reform process addressed these shortcomings only in part. The meetings of the drafting commission appointed by Tebboune took place behind closed doors, but at least the draft reform was promptly released to the public at the beginning of May 2020 (there was a one-month delay due to the COVID-19 pandemic) when the government invited the people to submit their proposals.[101] However, the effects of this (partly) greater degree of transparency were watered down enormously by the lack of a genuine open debate.[102]

The process that led to the adoption of the 2014 Egyptian Constitution was also not particularly transparent. Live broadcast of the sessions of the Constituent Assembly was banned on several occasions,[103] not to mention the fact that the work of the ten-member committee of legal experts was surrounded by secrecy: "No details were officially published regarding the committee's work, or on its discussion or voting process."[104] Also the 2022 constitution-making process in Tunisia was characterized by the lack of transparency. First, the meetings of the "National Consultative Commission for a New Republic," which was responsible, *inter alia*, for submitting

97 See Al-Ali, "Arab Spring Constitutions," at p. 376.

98 The Committee's website is the following: https://tahdeeth.jo

99 Karim Mezran, "Constitutional Reforms in Algeria," *Atlantic Council* (January 12, 2016), www.atlanticcouncil.org/blogs/menasource/constitutionalreforms-in-algeria

100 See Biagi, "Algerian Constitutional Reform," at pp. 2–3.

101 See Madjid Zerrouky, "En Algérie, un projet de Constitution loin du rêve du Hirak," *Le Monde* (May 21, 2020), www.lemonde.fr/afrique/article/2020/05/20/en-algerie-un-projet-de-constitution-loin-du-reve-du-hirak_6040259_3212.html

102 See International Commission of Jurists, *Flawed and Inadequate: Algeria's Constitutional Amendment Process – A Briefing Paper* (October 2020), 5–8, www.icj.org/wp-content/uploads/2020/10/Algeria-NewConstitution-Advocacy-Analysis-Brief-2020-ENG.pdf

103 See Nathalie Bernard-Maugiron, "La constitution égyptienne de 2014: quelle réforme constitutionnelle pour l'Égypte?" (2015) 103 *Revue française de droit constitutionnel*, 516–517.

104 Auf, "Egypt's Constitutional Committees."

a draft constitution to President Saïed, took place behind closed doors. Second, the Commission never released a full official list of its members, and therefore "the public was only able to glean some of their identities from media coverage."[105] Third, Saïed did not publish the draft constitution submitted to him by Sadok Belaïd, the head of the Consultative Commission.[106] This draft was later made public by Belaïd himself in order to show that the text prepared by the Commission was different from the text submitted to the referendum by the President. Fourth, as recalled earlier,[107] officially nobody knows who drafted the final text of the constitution that was submitted to a referendum (even though it was probably either Saïed himself or a small group of people under his direction).

Bottom-up constitution-writing processes were characterized by a higher degree of openness and transparency. In Egypt, for example, the plenary sessions of the 2012 Constituent Assembly were widely publicized and broadcast live on television. Also in Tunisia, during the 2011–2014 constitution-making process, the sessions of the Constituent Assembly were broadcast live on television.[108] Furthermore, four drafts of the constitution (in August 2012, December 2012, April 2013, and June 2013) were made public, discussed, and revised before the final version was adopted. This increased enormously the chances for political parties, trade unions, associations, and civil society at large to have a concrete say on the final text of the constitution.[109] By way of comparison, in Morocco, the political and social organizations never really had the opportunity to make any comments or recommendations on the draft of the constitution because they only received a copy of it on the day before the king's speech to the nation (June 17, 2011) when the monarch announced that the constitutional referendum would take place on July 1.[110]

In the case of Libya, one must distinguish between the various elements. On the one hand, a certain degree of transparency was guaranteed by the fact that the Constitution Drafting Assembly, as the process moved forward, released a few drafts of the constitution. In addition to the preliminary draft of December 2014,

105 Bessalah, "Kaïs Saïed's National Monologue," at p. 3. In particular, it is not clear who really served on the sub-commission responsible for legal affairs (see Section 1.2.5).

106 Saïed was under no obligation to publish the draft, as Article 22 of the Decree-Law no. 2022-30 stated that "The results of the Commission's work are published by order of the President of the Republic."

107 See Section 1.2.1.2.

108 See Ben Achour, *Tunisie: Une révolution en pays d'Islam*, at p. 362.

109 See Section 1.2.5 for more details. However, it seems that also in Tunisia, some key decisions were made behind closed doors: "[…] specific language that could not be agreed upon by members of the constitutional committee were further discussed in the evening between the major political leaders. Oftentimes, the next morning, the rapporteur would bring a new sentence and the parties would agree automatically without further debates. Not all members of the committee knew about these secret meetings, which created some frustration among them. But is served to facilitate the process" (Tom Ginsburg and Sumit Bisarya, "Introduction: Constitution Makers on Constitution Making" in Tom Ginsburg and Sumit Bisarya (eds.), *Constitution Makers on Constitution Making: New Cases* (Cambridge University Press 2022), 16).

110 See Biagi, "2011 Constitution-Making Process in Morocco," at pp. 63–64.

the Assembly has thus far adopted a first draft in October 2015, a second draft in February 2016, a third draft in April 2016,[111] and a fourth, and potentially last, draft in July 2017.[112] On the other hand, the process took place predominantly behind closed doors. First, the Assembly's sessions were not broadcast. Second, the rules of procedure of the Assembly "require the documentation of all the debates of the assembly, [...] [b]ut the same rules indicate that this documentation work is meant to be transferred to the national archives upon completion of the [A]ssembly's work rather than being released for the purpose of public information during the drafting process."[113]

1.2.3 *Duration of the Process*

Although the duration of a constitution-drafting process can hardly provide definite answers – either in one way or another – on the democratic character of the process, the experiences of post-2011 Arab countries seem to confirm that very short or very long constitution-making periods are one of the distinguishing features of "non-democracies."[114] In most of these countries, the process was very short. In Morocco, it took less than four months to prepare the draft constitution, consult with the representatives of political parties and trade unions, and ratify the constitution in a popular referendum.[115] In Syria, the drafting committee prepared a draft constitution in four months, which was then submitted to a referendum for ratification. The whole process lasted four-and-a-half months.[116] In Jordan, it took around five months to adopt the 2011 amendments to the 1952 constitution. The timeframe imposed by the king was respected so scrupulously that the Senate (which, together with the Council of Ministers and House of Representatives, had been vested with the power to discuss the reform prepared by the drafting committee) decided to approve the

111 This draft was annulled by the Administrative Chamber of Al-Bayda's Court of Appeals in December 2016 due to a violation of the Assembly's rules of procedure. Indeed, since they could not achieve the required majority of 2/3+1 to adopt the draft, the members of the Constitution Drafting Assembly amended the Assembly's rules of procedure lowering the threshold to 2/3 of the Assembly's effective members (57) rather than of the official members (60). The Court ruled that this modification was in contrast with the Interim Constitutional Declaration. See Cherif, "Libya's Constitutional Quagmire," at p. 4, footnote 8.

112 This draft was annulled by the Administrative Court of Al-Bayda in August 2017 due to a violation of the Assembly's rules of procedure. According to the Court, there had been a violation of procedure as the vote took place during the weekend (Saturday) in violation of the Assembly's working rules. This ruling, however, was overturned by the Supreme Court in February 2018 with the argument that administrative courts had no jurisdiction over matters related to the Constitution Drafting Assembly. See Cherif, *Libya's Constitution*, at p. 10.

113 Omar Hammady, "The Role of Civil Society in the Libyan Constitution-making Process" in Abbiate, Böckenförde and Federico (eds.) 2018, *Public Participation*, at p. 165.

114 Justin Blount, Zachary Elkins and Tom Ginsburg, "Does the Process of Constitution-making Matter?" in Tom Ginsburg (ed.), *Comparative Constitutional Design* (Cambridge University Press 2012), 41.

115 See Biagi, "2011 Constitution-Making Process in Morocco," at p. 63.

116 See "Syrian Arab Republic: 2012 Constitution," *Refworld*, www.refworld.org/docid/5100f02a2.html

package of amendments without a single change just because it had been received only three days before the deadline.[117]

In Egypt, both the 2012 and the 2014 constitutions were drafted in around six months. In both cases, the need to meet the deadline was never seriously questioned and clearly prevailed over all other aspects of constitution-drafting, such as consensus-building, public participation, and the quality of the drafting. As noted earlier, in 2012, the Islamist-dominated Constituent Assembly, fearing another judicial dissolution, rushed to approve the new constitution, thus meeting the six-month deadline provided for by Article 60 of the 2011 Constitutional Declaration.[118] Very strict deadlines were also imposed during the process that led to the adoption of the 2014 constitution. The ten-member committee of legal experts was required to present the constitutional amendments within one month, and the fifty-member Constituent Assembly had a maximum of sixty days to finalize the text of the new constitution.[119]

The 2022 constitution-making process in Tunisia was also rushed. Officially, the process began on January 15, 2022 (which was the first day of the online "public consultation") and ended on July 25 the same year (when the constitutional referendum was held), that is, a little more than six months. The phase devoted to the actual drafting of the constitutional text was extremely short. It began on May 19, when the "National Consultative Commission for a New Republic" was created, but the first meeting of the Commission was held only on June 4.[120] This means that the Commission had just over two weeks before the June 20 deadline, when the head of the Commission was supposed to hand over the draft constitution to President Saïed.[121]

In all the above-mentioned cases, where the processes only lasted between four and six months, little room was allocated for debate, search for compromise, or involvement of civil society. This was due to a variety of reasons, including the top-down nature of the process, particularly in the cases of Morocco, Jordan, and Syria,[122] or the lack of willingness to adopt a consensual constitution, particularly in the case of the 2012 Egyptian constitution-making process,[123] or a combination of these reasons, as in the case of the 2022 Tunisian constituent process.[124]

The process that led to the 2016 constitutional reform in Algeria was also problematic, but for a diametrically opposed reason – namely, it took too long. As noted

117 See Hammouri, "Constitutional Reform," at p. 725.

118 Even though in the Constitutional Declaration of November 22, 2012, Morsi had extended the deadline by two months (Article 4).

119 It should be noted, however, that the Assembly granted itself the power to complete its work in 60 days *not counting official holidays* (Article 18 of the Constituent Assembly's Rules of Procedure, adopted on September 12, 2013).

120 It was when the sub-commission on economic and social affairs met for the first time.

121 See Bessalah, "Kaïs Saïed's National Monologue," at p. 3.

122 See Section 1.2.1.2 for more details.

123 See Section 1.2.4 in greater detail.

124 See Sections 1.2.1.2 and 1.2.4 for more details.

earlier, the amendments to the 1996 constitution were adopted a full five years after President Bouteflika had announced his intention to adopt a constitutional reform in April 2011. The timeframe of the process was entirely in the hands of Bouteflika, who froze it for years, then restarted it suddenly and, finally, kept postponing the presentation of the new text of the reform.[125] This extended process guided from above had at least two interrelated negative effects. First, the constitutional reform progressively lost momentum. Second, people lost interest in the reform.[126] In 2020, the constitutional reform process was much quicker. It lasted approximately ten months (i.e., from January 8, when Tebboune appointed the members of the Drafting Commission, to November 1, 2020, when the reform was ratified in the referendum). As happened in other countries in the region, however, the main concern of the regime was not to open democratic debate but, rather, to buy time to gain some legitimacy.[127]

Another constitution-drafting process that is lasting for too long is that taking place in Libya. Officially, the process began on February 20, 2014, when the Constitution Drafting Assembly was elected. Under the Interim Constitutional Declaration, as originally enacted in 2011, the Assembly had sixty days to draft the new constitution. This timeframe was subsequently extended to 120 days, which still proved to be completely unrealistic. The latest draft constitution was adopted on July 29, 2017, but this document has not yet been ratified in a popular referendum. As it was adopted seven years ago, the text is progressively losing its validity to the point that some commentators are wondering whether it should still be under consideration (maybe with some modifications) or whether it should be abandoned altogether.[128] The UN-led initiative that began in March 2022 has not thus far managed to reach agreement on a consensual constitutional basis for national elections.[129] In the light of the extremely problematic political and social situation in the country, it seems impossible to predict when the constituent process will be completed.

As far as the 2011–2014 Tunisian constitution-making process is concerned, the Constituent Assembly was elected on October 23, 2011, and the constitution was adopted on January 26, 2014, which means that the constitution-making period lasted for two years and three months. This seemed to be a reasonable duration, which

[125] See Biagi, "Algerian Constitutional Reform," at pp. 2–4.

[126] See Wissam Benyettou, "Will Algeria Start 2016 with a New Constitution? Long-awaited Constitutional Revision and the Road to Democratic Transition," *ConstitutionNet* (November 24, 2015), https://constitutionnet.org/news/will-algeria-start-2016-new-constitution-long-awaited-constitutional-revision-and-road

[127] See "La Constitution de 'l'Algérie nouvelle' ne fait pas consensus," *Le Monde Afrique* (May 12, 2020), www.lemonde.fr/afrique/article/2020/05/12/la-constitution-de-l-algerie-nouvelle-ne-fait-pas-consensus_6039444_3212.html

[128] See Zaid Al-Ali, *Libya's Final Draft Constitution: A Contextual Analysis (Version 2)*, International IDEA (December 2020), 2, https://constitutionnet.org/sites/default/files/2020-12/Libya%20analysis%20-%20Zaid%20Al-Ali%20%28December%202020%29%20%28English%29.pdf

[129] See Section 1.2.6 in greater detail.

allowed for negotiations among the political parties represented in the Assembly and guaranteed a very high degree of public participation. It should be noted, however, that the Assembly was supposed to finish its work in just one year.[130] A number of different reasons explain the delay in adopting the constitution, including the decision of the Assembly to start from a blank page[131]; the fact that the Assembly also acted as an interim legislature; the increasingly polarized political context, specifically following the assassinations of opposition leaders Chokri Belaïd on February 6, 2013, and Mohamed Brahmi on July 25, 2013; and the influence of the events that took place in Egypt following Morsi's removal from office.

The importance of the duration of the 2011–2014 Tunisian constituent process has been stressed by one of the members of the Constituent Assembly:

> The process succeeded, despite multiple counterrevolutionary attacks, political assassinations and sustained violence against Tunisians, which could have aborted the whole project. I believe this resiliency is due in part to the lengthy process, which was actually beneficial. Time was crucial. The very exercise of writing a founding text beyond our own individual lives, beyond the revolutionary moment, produced an effect among many drafters, which gradually refocused us on the long term.[132]

1.2.4 *The Role Played by Political Parties*

Generally speaking, political parties are often the protagonists of constitutional design (for better and for worse), especially when the constitution derives from a democratically elected Constituent Assembly. Following the Arab uprisings, the type of approach toward contentious issues by religious parties varied significantly from country to country. In Egypt, for example, the Muslim Brotherhood – which, together with the other Islamists, held almost 70 percent of the seats in the Constituent Assembly – assumed a winner-take-all attitude with regard to drafting the 2012 constitution. In particular, the Brotherhood made a number of concessions to the Salafists (including limiting the power of the Supreme Constitutional Court to interpret the principles of *sharia* and requiring Al-Azhar to be consulted in matters pertaining to *sharia*)[133] and considered the requests originating from non-Islamist parties only to a very limited extent. As noted earlier,[134] this resulted,

[130] As provided for by Decree no. 2011-1086 of August 3, 2011, "*portant convocation du corps électoral pour l'élection de l'Assemblée nationale constituante pour le 23 octobre 2011.*"

[131] See Section 1.2.7 for more details.

[132] Mabrouka M'Barek, "Makers of Our Own History: Upholding the Revolution and Unsettling Coloniality in the Drafting of Tunisia's 2014 Constitution" in Ginsburg and Bisarya (eds.) 2022, *Constitution Makers*, at pp. 151–152.

[133] See Nathan J. Brown and Clark B. Lombardi, "Contesting Islamic Constitutionalism After the Arab Spring. Islam in Egypt's Post-Mubarak Constitutions" in Grote and Röder (eds.) 2016, *Constitutionalism, Human Rights, and Islam*, at p. 255ff.

[134] See Section 1.2.1.1.

among other things, in the withdrawal of several non-Islamist members from the Constituent Assembly.

The approach by Ennahda in Tunisia during the 2011–2014 constituent process was diametrically opposed to this. In fact, Ennahda, which had a relative majority of seats in the Constituent Assembly, displayed its commitment to consensus and willingness to cooperate with the other secular parties represented in the Assembly from the outset of the constitution-drafting process. It thus formed a government coalition with the center-left Congress for the Republic and the social democratic party Ettakatol. Ennahda's approach, which featured "moderation and compromise,"[135] contributed enormously to the positive outcome of the process that led to the adoption of the 2014 constitution. Indeed, Ennahda took a step back and accepted the requests of secular parties in relation to some key aspects of constitutional design. For example, despite strong criticism from its base, Ennahda decided to withdraw its proposal to include a *sharia* clause in the constitution. Moreover, despite its preference for a parliamentary system, it eventually decided to accept the secular parties' calls for a semi-presidential form of government.[136] The reasons why Ennahda adopted such a moderate stance were partly practical in nature (e.g., Ennahda only had a *relative* majority in the Constituent Assembly), partly ideological (e.g., a parliamentary system was considered by Ennahda to be more consistent with the Islamic institute of *shura* [consultation]),[137] and partly influenced by the regional context (e.g., the civil war going on in Libya and the ousting of Morsi in Egypt pushed Ennahda to mitigate its positions).[138]

Notwithstanding this moderate approach, in the summer of 2013, the political climate in Tunisia was so complicated (for the reasons discussed earlier)[139] that the work of the Constituent Assembly was suspended. At that point, it was far from certain that the negotiating parties would be able to reach a final agreement. A crucial role in relaunching the transition process and, in particular, the work of the Constituent Assembly in the fall of 2013 was played by the National Dialogue Quartet, which was comprised of the Tunisian General Labor Union (UGTT), the Tunisian Confederation of Industry, Trade and Handicrafts (UTICA), the Tunisian Human Rights League (LTDH), and the Tunisian Order of Lawyers. The Quartet,

135 See Duncan Pickard, "Al-Nahda: Moderation and Compromise in Tunisia's Constitutional Bargain" in Frosini and Biagi (eds.) 2015, *Political and Constitutional Transitions*, at p. 19.

136 Ibid., at p. 19ff.

137 Ibid., at pp. 22–23. Indeed, according to Ennahda's founder and leader Rached Ghannouchi, "Islam, which enjoins the recourse to Shura (consultation) as a principle governing relations between political authority and the people, finds in democracy the appropriate instruments (elections, parliamentary system, separation of powers, etc.) to implement the Shura" (cited in John L. Esposito, "Islam and Civil Society" in John P. Esposito and Francois Burgat (eds.), *Modernizing Islam: Religion in the Public Sphere in the Middle East and Europe* (Rutgers University Press 2003), 79).

138 See Chawki Gaddes, "Il processo costituente (2011–14): fasi e protagonisti" in Tania Groppi and Irene Spigno (eds.), *Tunisia: La primavera della Costituzione* (Carocci 2015), 63.

139 See Section 1.2.3.

which was awarded the Nobel Peace Prize in 2015 "for its decisive contribution to the building of a pluralistic democracy in Tunisia in the wake of the Jasmine Revolution of 2011,"[140] favored dialogue and negotiations among the political parties represented in the Constituent Assembly, thus contributing to reaching a consensus on key aspects, including the timeline, of the constituent process.[141]

The consequences of this diametrically opposed approach in Tunisia and Egypt are evident and clearly show the difference between a *partisan* constitution and a *consensual* constitution. On the one hand, the short-lived 2012 Egyptian Constitution, which lacked a consensual approach, was perceived by many people as the constitution *of the Islamists* rather than the constitution of all Egyptians.[142] On the other hand, the 2014 Tunisian Constitution, which was a compromise among the main political forces represented within the Constituent Assembly, enjoyed, especially at the outset, a higher degree of legitimacy.

However, as also happened during previous waves of constitution-drafting, in many post-Arab Spring countries, the role played by political parties in constitution-making was quite limited overall, specifically due to the top-down nature of the processes. In Algeria, for example, during the process that led to the 2016 constitutional reform, representatives of political parties had more formal than substantive involvement, not to mention the fact that several political forces decided to boycott the consultations organized by the regime concerning that reform.[143] Political parties were also granted quite a limited role during the 2020 constitutional reform process. Not only did the regime exclude representatives of the political parties from the drafting commission but it also failed to even take into serious consideration most of the requests from the opposition forces, including the Islamist parties and the *Pacte pour l'alternative démocratique* (PAD), a platform of parties and associations linked to the *Hirak* movement.[144]

The process that led to the adoption of the 2014 constitution of Egypt also saw extremely limited involvement by political parties. As noted earlier, within the fifty-member Constituent Assembly, only six seats were allocated to political parties: two for Islamists, two for liberals, one for a nationalist, and one for a leftist. It should also be noted that the representation of Islamists was problematic for at least two reasons. First, the Muslim Brotherhood, which had won the previous elections, was completely excluded from the Constituent Assembly. In fact, out of the two Islamist representatives, one belonged to the Salafi Al-Nour Party, and one was an independent

140 *The Nobel Peace Prize for 2015* (October 10, 2015), www.nobelprize.org/prizes/peace/2015/press-release/

141 See Ben Achour, *Tunisie: Une révolution en pays d'Islam*, at p. 326.

142 On the differences between these two constitution-making processes, see also Justin O. Frosini and Francesco Biagi, "Transitions from Authoritarian Rule Following the Arab Uprisings: A Matter of Variables" in Frosini and Biagi (eds.) 2015, *Political and Constitutional Transitions*, at pp. 135–138.

143 See Biagi, "Algerian Constitutional Reform," at pp. 2–4.

144 "Algérie: l'avant-projet de réforme constitutionnelle laisse un goût d'inachevé," *Jeune Afrique* (May 12, 2020), www.jeuneafrique.com/943997/politique/algerie-lavant-projet-de-reforme-constitutionnelle-laisse-un-gout-dinacheve/

Islamist personality. Second, Islamists were underrepresented in the Assembly. At that time, the Islamist faction was "in no way less than fifty percent of Egyptian society [...]. Consequently, the allotment of the political parties' seats in the Committee of Fifty should have been split equally between the two main camps in Egypt, giving Islamists three seats and civil parties the other three."[145]

Even in Morocco, political parties played a rather marginal role in the drafting of the 2011 constitution despite the fact that their level of involvement was higher than in previous constituent processes.[146] On the one hand, there were no representatives of political parties in the commission responsible for drafting the 2011 constitution. On the other hand, parallel to the appointment of the commission, Mohammed VI ordered the establishment of a "Political Mechanism Accompanying the Constitutional Reform," a body comprised of representatives of political parties and trade unions and directed by his advisor Mohammed Moatassim, a university professor and constitutional law expert. This *mécanisme de suivi* was expected to facilitate dialogue and concerted action between the various political actors and was intended to operate as a channel for communication between the commission and the political and social organizations. While the establishment of such a body was an important innovation compared to the past, in actual fact, the body's role was severely limited. First, in the light of the strong tie between Moatassim and Mohammed VI, the function of this Political Mechanism was not only to facilitate dialogue between the Commission on Constitutional Reform and the political forces and trade unions but also to identify what was "politically acceptable to the palace and what was not."[147] Second, as noted earlier, the political and social organizations only received a copy of the draft constitution on the day before the king announced the constitutional referendum to the people. The delay in submitting a copy of the draft constitution represented a major obstacle to the political and social organizations' making comments and recommendations on the draft constitution.

Nevertheless, it must be emphasized that the proposals made by the political and social organizations were largely of the same tone as the constituent speech delivered by Mohammed VI on March 9, 2011. Indeed, most of the requests could already be found in the king's speech, and therefore they did not introduce any significant novelty into the debate. This passive position of the vast majority of the political parties is an excellent example of their "domestication"[148] by the Sovereign and confirms the "politics of consensus"[149] that has marked Morocco for a long

[145] Auf, "Egypt's Constitutional Committees."

[146] See Biagi, "2011 Constitution-Making Process in Morocco," at pp. 63–64.

[147] Michel Rousset, "L'interprétation des pouvoirs du roi dans la nouvelle Constitution" in Centre d'Études Internationales (ed.), *La Constitution marocaine de 2011: Analyses et commentaires* (L.G.D.J. 2012), 60.

[148] Driss Maghraoui, "Constitutional Reforms in Morocco: Between Consensus and Subaltern Politics" in George Joffé (ed.), *North Africa's Arab Spring* (Routledge 2013), 182.

[149] Ibid.

time. According to this notion, the role and absolute powers of the king are not questioned by the parties. Regardless of their ideological orientations, the parties "seem comfortable with not taking the initiative and leaving the palace full control of the political game and orientations of the country."[150] One of the very few cases in which a political party managed to influence the final text of the 2011 constitution was when the Islamist party *Parti de la justice et du développement* opposed the constitutional provisions which were considered to conflict with the country's Islamic identity.[151]

In the case of Jordan, the extremely limited role played by the political parties in constitutional design was related not only to the top-down nature of the process but also to the political system itself. Unlike Morocco, Tunisia, Egypt, and Algeria (which all have a – more or less, depending on the case – established party system), in Jordan, the politics of the regime and electoral law prevented for a long time the creation of real political parties. In the first place, it must be noted that political parties were banned from 1957 (when martial law was declared) to the early 1990s. Moreover, the electoral system in force in 2011 favored "tribal elites and local notables while discouraging the formation of political parties. This, together with the gerrymandering of districts, [...] produced structurally weak, unrepresentative parliaments."[152] Therefore, political forces were not structured or developed enough to be able to effectively contribute to the constituent debates. During the 2021–2022 constitutional reform process, the role played by political forces seemed to be higher compared to the past. Indeed, the "Royal Committee to Modernize the Political System" represented

> one of the largest royal committees ever formed and included dozens of oppositionists from most ideological currents. [...][U]nlike past royal reform commissions, this one included members of social and political movements that had loudly criticized the government in the past, such as the Muslim Brotherhood's Islamic Action Front (IAF) party as well as members of leftist and liberal movements.[153]

It should also be underlined that in April 2022, following the recommendations of the Royal Committee, Parliament adopted a new electoral law that is aimed at strengthening the parliamentary representation of political parties.[154]

In the case of Libya, in order to explain the weak role played by political parties in the constitution-making process, it is first necessary to stress that, following Gaddafi's rise to power, political parties were suspended and then suppressed. They

150 Ibid.

151 See Abdellah Tourabi, "Constitutional Reform in Morocco: Reform in Times of Revolution," *Arab Reform Initiative* (November 2011), 9–10, www.arab-reform.net/en/node/526

152 Marina Ottaway and Marwan Muasher, "Arab Monarchies. Chance for Reform, Yet Unmet," *The Carnegie Papers* (December 2011), 10, https://carnegieendowment.org/files/arab_monarchies1.pdf

153 Yom and Al-Khatib, "Democratic Reform in Jordan," at pp. 5–6.

154 See Chapter 2, Section 2.1.2 in greater detail.

were incompatible with the *Jamahiriyya*, the "republic of the masses," proclaimed by Gaddafi in 1977, in which people would directly exercise authority through congresses and committees.[155] In addition to this lack of both political experience and established political parties, it should also be considered that even if the election law did not formally prevent political parties from participating in the elections of the Constitution Drafting Assembly, "it was interpreted as barring candidates from being in any way affiliated with [political parties] and did not provide any avenue by which parties might nominate candidates."[156] The result was that "very few political figures made it to the [Assembly]. The assembly's members enjoyed only limited legitimacy as they were generally elected by a small number of voters reflecting rather their tribal or regional affiliations."[157] Only 45 percent of the 1.1 million Libyans who registered for the election turned up to cast their votes – less than 14 percent of the eligible voters in the country.[158]

It is not clear the extent to which the "Political and Administrative Isolation Law," adopted on May 5, 2013, affected the elections of the Constitution Drafting Assembly. This piece of legislation – which was very similar to the Egyptian "Political Isolation Law"[159] and recalled the "lustration laws" adopted in Central and Eastern Europe after the fall of the Communist regime[160] – prevented officials of the former Gaddafi regime from holding a position in legislative, executive, or constituent bodies (as well as positions of leadership in various other institutions, including the judiciary, universities, the military, and the media) for a ten-year period. While some scholars argued that this law affected "the set-up of the [Constitution Drafting Assembly],"[161] other analysts emphasized that "its implementation, in practice, did not have significant impacts on candidates."[162] Indeed, the High National Election Commission "submitted 700 candidate applications for review with the commission [responsible for applying the public office criteria], of which eight were isolated. Six of the eight isolated candidates appealed, and all successfully had their decisions overturned and were able to run in the elections."[163] This controversial law was officially repealed by

155 See Sami G. Hajjar, "The Jamahiriya Experiment in Libya: Qadhafi and Rousseau" (1980) 18 *The Journal of Modern African Studies*, 181ff.

156 The Carter Center, *2014 Constitutional Drafting Assembly Elections*, at p. 21.

157 Hammady, "Role of Civil Society," at p. 163.

158 See Eljarh, "Democracy Fatigue."

159 On the "Political Isolation Law," see earlier in footnote 38.

160 See Mark S. Ellis, "Purging the Past: The Current State of Lustration Laws in the Former Communist Bloc" (1996) 59 *Law and Contemporary Problems* 4, 181ff.; Wojciech Sadurski, *Rights before Courts: A Study of Constitutional Courts in Postcommunist States of Central and Eastern Europe* (Springer 2014), 343ff.; Angela Di Gregorio, *Epurazioni e protezione della democrazia: Esperienze e modelli di 'giustizia post-autoritaria'* (Franco Angeli 2012).

161 Felix-Anselm van Lier, "Constitution-Making as a Tool for State-Building? Insights from an Ethnographic Analysis of the Libyan Constitution-Making Process," *Max Planck Institute for Social Anthropology* (Working Paper no. 192) (2018), 9.

162 The Carter Center, *2014 Constitutional Drafting Assembly Elections*, at p. 23.

163 Ibid.

the House of Representatives (which is located in Tobruk, East Libya), but apparently this decision has not been accepted throughout the country.[164]

In all the above-mentioned cases, although they played a weak (or very weak) role, political parties did participate in the constitution-making processes. The case of Tunisia during the 2022 constituent process is different, as political parties were excluded altogether. Indeed, no party representative served on the "National Consultative Commission for a New Republic," not to mention the fact that some "independent national figures" (including some politicians) who had been invited to join the Commission's discussions refused to attend.[165] Kaïs Saïed's decision to sideline political parties comes as no surprise, especially if one considers that politicians and members of Parliament (especially Ennahda's members) were (and still are) among the main targets of the Tunisian President's attacks.

1.2.5 *The Role of Civil Society*

With very few exceptions,[166] during previous waves of constitution-making in the Arab world, public participation was generally very low, and the drafting bodies were not particularly representative of the different "souls" existing in Arab societies at that time. For example, during the second wave

> The variety of political, ideological, and religious orientations in the country were [...] rarely organized in political form to participate in the drafting process, nor did drafters see inclusive and democratic politics as a necessary part of constitution writing. Rulers continued to view their authority as prior to the constitutional text and sometimes moved outside its limits.[167]

In general terms, it is fair to say that, before the outbreak of the Arab Spring, people "played at best a passive role in shaping constitutional discourse."[168]

Over the past few decades, constitution-drafting processes have seen a much greater involvement of civil society compared to the past.[169] This is particularly

[164] See Katherine Ellena and Alexandra Brown, "Beyond Constitutional Reform to Elections. Libya Electoral Legal Framework Analysis," *International Foundation for Electoral Systems* (2019), 9, 28 and 46, www.ifes.org/sites/default/files/libya_electoral_legal_framework_analysis_november_2019.pdf

[165] See Bessalah, "Kaïs Saïed's National Monologue," at pp. 4–6.

[166] See Section 1.2.1.

[167] Brown, "Constitution Writing in the Arab World," at p. 451.

[168] Al-Ali, "Arab Spring Constitutions," at p. 376.

[169] See Abrak Saati, *The Participation Myth: Outcomes of Participatory Constitution Building Processes on Democracy* (Umeå University 2015); Umberto Allegretti, Cecilia Corsi and Giovanni Allegretti, "Constituent Process and Constituent Assembly: The Making of Constitutions Through the Larger Involvement of Citizens," *Forum costituzionale* (July 27, 2016), www.forumcostituzionale.it; Alexander Hudson, *The Veil of Participation: Citizens and Political Parties in Constitution-Making Processes* (Cambridge University Press 2021); Sujit Choudhry and Mark Tushnet, "Participatory Constitution-Making: Introduction" (2020) 18 *International Journal of Constitutional Law*, 173ff.

clear if one considers the cases of recent constitutions adopted in Africa,[170] Asia,[171] and Latin America.[172] Public participation also increased in post-Arab Spring constitution-making processes, even though in the majority of the cases people were not granted the power to effectively and substantially influence the drafting of the constitutional reforms.[173] Civil society was mainly involved from a *formal* – rather than a substantive – standpoint. In Algeria, for example, during the process that led to the adoption of the 2016 constitutional reform, political parties and some leading figures from civil society were officially invited by the political leadership to submit suggestions and proposals concerning the reform. Their involvement, however, was very limited and was mainly aimed at reinforcing the legitimacy and credibility of a process that was completely driven by the regime.[174] Something similar happened in 2020. President Tebboune repeatedly insisted that he wanted a consensual constitutional reform, but these words were not followed by deeds. Far from being a genuinely open and democratic consultation, it was a one-sided debate (especially during the period preceding the parliamentary approval of the reform), with very limited room for critical voices. Moreover, the whole process took place in quite a repressive environment, characterized by intimidations and arrests of activists and political militants.[175]

In Morocco, in addition to the "Political Mechanism Accompanying the Constitutional Reform" referred to above, political parties, trade unions, associations representing civil society, women, youth, and other organizations had the chance not only to submit "memoranda" (which in previous constituent processes represented the only instrument for submitting proposed constitutional amendments to the king) but also to meet with the members of the Commission responsible for drafting the constitution and to present their requests orally. This form of public

170 See Abbiate, Böckenförde and Federico (eds.) 2018, *Public Participation*; Yash Ghai, "Civil Society, Participation and the Making of Kenya's Constitution" in Landau and Lerner (eds.) 2019, *Comparative Constitution Making*, at p. 212ff.

171 See Melissa Crouch, "Constitution Making and Public Participation in Southeast Asia" in Landau and Lerner (eds.) 2019, *Comparative Constitution Making*, at p. 488ff.

172 See William Ortiz Jiménez, "Los Tres Nuevos Procesos Constituyentes en América Latina: Los Cambios Políticos y los Sujetos que los Impulsan" (2013) 38 *Diálogos de Saberes* 101ff.; David Landau, "Constituent Power and Constitution Making in Latin America" in Landau and Lerner (eds.) 2019, *Comparative Constitution Making*, at pp. 571–573.

173 See Tofigh Maboudi, *The "Fall" of the Arab Spring: Democracy's Challenges and Efforts to Reconstitute the Middle East* (Cambridge University Press 2022).

174 See Benyettou, "Will Algeria Start 2016 with a New Constitution?"; Xavier Philippe, "La Constitution Algérienne. Évaluation des Changements Après la Révision de Janvier 2016," *Democracy Reporting International* (June 2016), 2.

175 See Madjid Makedhi, "Le référendum sur la révision de la Constitution en quête de soutiens: Un projet qui peine à convaincre," *El Watan* (September 28, 2020), www.elwatan.com/edition/actualite/un-projet-qui-peine-a-convaincre-28-09-2020; Yasmina Allouche, "A Breakdown of Algeria's New Constitution," *Middle East Eye* (October 29, 2020), www.middleeasteye.net/news/algeria-new-constitution-breakdown; Zine Labidine Ghebouli, "Algeria: New Constitution, Old Balances," *Dustour Talk – JCL MENA* (March 23, 2021), http://jcl-mena.org/talk-entry.php?bid=9

participation, however, was strictly controlled by the monarchy, thus minimally affecting the content of the 2011 constitution.[176]

In Jordan, the 2011 constitutional reform process was characterized by very weak participation from civil society. Things got worse with the 2014 and 2016 reform processes (which lasted for less than three weeks), as citizens were not granted any role at all.[177] In the latest constitutional reform of 2022, the degree of involvement of civil society was a bit higher, especially if one considers that the "Royal Committee to Modernize the Political System" held several dialogues with civil society stakeholders, including the professional syndicates.[178]

In Egypt, both the 2012 and 2013 Constituent Assemblies were made up of five committees. One of them (named the "Drafting and Research Committee" during the 2012 constitution-making process and the "Communication and Community Dialogue Committee" during the 2013 process) was vested with the task of communicating with civil society and receiving people's comments and suggestions concerning the draft constitutions. Furthermore, the official website of both Constituent Assemblies allowed the people to submit their proposals and criticisms on the provisions of the constitutional drafts. With respect to the 2012 constitution-making process, a statistical analysis of the Constituent Assembly's sensitivity to public input shows that the Assembly was quite sensitive to citizens' proposals in the initial stages of the process. Afterward, however, especially following the boycott of the work of the Constituent Assembly by several non-Islamists, "constitution drafters appeared to become less responsive to public opinion and made very few changes to draft Articles based on suggestions from the online forum."[179]

The process that led to the adoption of the 2014 Egyptian Constitution was the object of harsher criticism. It was not clear, for example, how the proposals submitted to the Communication and Community Dialogue Committee "would be considered and viewed inside the [Constituent Assembly]. Moreover, the [Constituent Assembly]'s website, unlike the 2012 one, was not frequently updated and did not provide a proper electronic feedback mechanism from the [Constituent Assembly]'s members."[180] Thus, the impression was that public participation was "no more than a grant that [was] awarded subject to the discretion of the authorities."[181] Things got worse with the 2019 amendments, as the reform process took place in a very

[176] See Biagi, "2011 Constitution-Making Process in Morocco," at p. 63.

[177] See Osama Al Sharif, "Changes to Jordan's Constitution Raise Concerns," *Al-Monitor* (May 4, 2016), www.al-monitor.com/originals/2016/05/jordan-adopts-constitution-amendments-king-powers.html

[178] See Yom and Al-Khatib, "Democratic Reform in Jordan," at p. 6.

[179] Tofigh Maboudi and Ghazal P. Nadi, "Crowdsourcing the Egyptian Constitution: Social Media, Elites, and the Populace" (2016) 69 *Political Research Quarterly*, 717.

[180] Michael Meyer-Resende, "Egypt: In-depth Analysis of the Main Elements of the New Constitution," *Directorate-general for the External Policies of the European Union – Policy Department* (2014), 8, www.europarl.europa.eu/RegData/etudes/note/join/2014/433846/EXPO-AFET_NT(2014)433846_EN.pdf

[181] Mohamed Abdelaal, "The Flawed Public Participation in the Egyptian Constitutional Process" in Abbiate, Böckenförde and Federico (eds.) 2018, *Public Participation*, at p. 51.

repressive context, which made it almost impossible for Egyptians to express any criticism concerning the content of the amendments. Opposition members who tried to launch a campaign encouraging people to vote against the proposed constitutional amendments were arrested. A website hosting an online petition against the reform was blocked. Moreover, the voters were in some cases bribed and forced to vote in favor of the proposed amendments in the referendum.[182] Thus, compared with the 2012 and 2014 constitution-making processes, "the deterioration [was] dramatic."[183]

The Tunisian 2022 constitution-making process offers another example of a merely formal involvement of civil society. One need only consider the online "public consultation" (that took place through the "*e-istichara*" platform)[184] held at the outset of the constituent process, that is, between January 15 and March 20, 2022.[185] People were asked to answer a series of questions on various institutional, economic, and social issues. Although Kaïs Saïed called the consultation a "success," only 534,915 Tunisians participated in the vote, that is, about 7.5 percent of eligible voters. Not surprisingly, the results of the consultation coincided with Saïed's presidentialist ideas and vision. For example, 86 percent of those who participated in the vote would have liked to abandon the semi-presidential system and opt for a presidential form of government, and 92.2 percent were in favor of the possibility of withdrawing confidence from individual deputies before the end of their term. These suggested changes were then incorporated into the 2022 constitution.[186] Furthermore, some of the civil society organizations' and trade unions' representatives who had been invited to form the sub-commission on the economic and social affairs of the "National Consultative Commission for a New Republic" refused Saïed's invitation (including the Tunisian General Labor Union [UGTT], one of the most influential organizations in the country), as they considered the process a "charade."[187] It should also be recalled that the Deans of the country's Faculties of Law and Political Sciences refused to form part of the sub-commission on legal affairs as they wanted to preserve the neutrality of their faculties.[188]

The fact that in some countries, such as Morocco, Syria, Egypt, Algeria (2020 reform), and Tunisia (2022 constitution), the constitutional reform was ratified in a

182 See Timothy Kaldas, "Taking Dictatorship from De Facto to De Jure: Egypt's Constitutional Amendments," *ConstitutionNet* (May 1, 2019), http://constitutionnet.org/news/taking-dictatorship-de-facto-de-jure-egypts-constitutional-amendments

183 Gianluca Paolo Parolin, "Drifting Power Relations in the Egyptian Constitution: The 2019 Amendments" (2020) 3 *DPCE online*, 3177.

184 See https://e-istichara.tn

185 See Nidhal Mekki, "From 'Big Plans' to Improvisation: Where Is the New Tunisian Constituent Process Headed?," *ConstitutionNet* (April 29, 2022), https://constitutionnet.org/news/big-plans-improvisation-where-new-tunisian-constituent-process-headed

186 See Chapter 2, Section 2.2.5.

187 Bessalah, "Kaïs Saïed's National Monologue," at pp. 4 and 5–6.

188 See Section 1.2.1.2.

referendum is not enough to claim that these constitution-making processes were participatory.[189] Indeed, in all these countries, the regimes made every effort to promote the reforms as much as possible and strongly restricted those who promoted a boycott of the vote. In Morocco, where reports of fraud came from all over the country, even sermons by imams asked the population to vote "yes."[190] Thus, not surprisingly, the 2011 constitution was approved by 98 percent of voters, with a turnout of 73.5 percent. In Syria, where the referendum took place in the middle of the war, 57.4 percent of eligible voters cast ballots, and 89.4 percent of those voted in favor of the new constitution. The outcome of this consultation, however, was a foregone conclusion. Among the major shortcomings of the process was the fact that because of the flaws in the system, people managed to vote multiple times, and that no international observers had the chance to monitor the vote.[191] Also in Egypt, where the political atmosphere was particularly repressive, there was never going to be any doubt over the referendum results. Indeed, the 2014 constitution of Egypt was approved by 98.1 percent of the voters (with a turnout of 38.6 percent), and the 2019 amendments to the 2014 constitution were approved by 88.8 percent of the voters (with a turnout of 44.3 percent). In Tunisia, 94.6 percent of the voters backed the new constitution in the 2022 referendum, but only 30.5 percent of eligible voters went to the polls, a fact that demonstrates the strong disinterest in, or skepticism, or opposition to (depending on the cases) the President's project.[192] One cannot fail to notice that Article 142 of the 2022 Tunisian Constitution had expressly ruled out the possibility of the constitution being rejected in the referendum, as it states that "This Constitution enters into force *from the date of the proclamation of the final results of the referendum by the Independent High Authority for Elections*, and after the President promulgates it and orders its publication in a special issue of the Official Gazette of the Tunisian Republic" (emphasis added). It is clear, then, that all the above-mentioned popular consultations were much more similar to *authoritarian plebiscites* (which are motivated "by a desire to legitimize the autocrat's control of a polity") than to democratic referendums (which "allow the citizens to render a considered verdict on the constitution").[193] This is also what the Venice Commission had stated in its opinion no. 1085/2022 of May 27, 2022, when it had warned that there was a "risk" that the constitutional referendum in Tunisia "cannot be properly

[189] See Rüdiger Wolfrum, "Legitimacy of Constitution-making Processes. Reflections from the Perspective of International Law" in Grote and Röder (eds.) 2016, *Constitutionalism, Human Rights, and Islam*, at pp. 48–51. On the strengths and weaknesses of the use of referendums in constitution-making processes (with a specific focus on Africa), see Markus Böckenförde, "Letting the Constituent Power Decide? Merits and Challenges of Referenda in Constitution-making Processes in Africa" in Abbiate, Böckenförde and Federico (eds.) 2018, *Public Participation*, at p. 26ff.

[190] See Biagi, "2011 Constitution-Making Process in Morocco," at pp. 64–65.

[191] See Macleod and Flamand, "Syria Referendum Called 'a Sham'."

[192] See Biagi, "Tunisia: la Costituzione di Kaïs Saïed."

[193] Justin Blount, "Participation in Constitutional Design" in Tom Ginsburg and Rosalind Dixon (eds.), *Comparative Constitutional Law* (Edward Elgar 2011), 50.

prepared and becomes a de facto plebiscite on the person of the President of the Republic."[194]

It should be recalled that in the case of Morocco, the referendum also has an extremely important religious meaning, as the referendum is considered a "modern redefinition"[195] of two traditional institutes: the *bay'a* (pledge of allegiance to the king) and the *shura* (consultation). This instrument therefore aims to consolidate the spiritual link, the sacred covenant between the monarch – who is the *Amir al-Mouminine* (Commander of the Faithful)[196] – and the people. As a result, contesting "the project of the King would mean to commit a crime and to leave the community. It would mean to breach a divine duty and to commit a sacrilege."[197]

The referendum held to ratify the 2012 constitution of Egypt – where around 64 percent of the voters supported the new constitutional text – provided a more credible result[198] despite the turnout of 32.9 percent – extremely low, even by Egyptian standards.[199] The fear of a low turnout was precisely one of the main reasons why, in Algeria, President Abdelaziz Bouteflika decided that the 2016 constitutional reform should be adopted without any popular referendum.[200] Indeed, he did not follow the procedure that provides that proposed constitutional amendments must be approved by both Houses of Parliament and thereafter submitted to a referendum. Rather, he resorted to the procedure whereby if the Constitutional Council considers the constitutional reform in line with the constitution, the President of the Republic may promulgate the reform *directly*, provided that it has been approved by Parliament by a three-fourths majority. Bouteflika was aware that his popularity had fallen and that people had lost interest in the reform, and for this reason he decided not to resort to a popular consultation. Algerians' decidedly lukewarm reaction to the adoption of the 2016 constitutional reform suggests that these fears were well-founded.[201]

In 2020, Tebboune decided to change tactics, and after the Parliament's approval, the draft reform was submitted to a referendum. The purpose of this popular

194 Venice Commission, *Tunisia: Urgent Opinion on the Constitutional and Legislative Framework on the Referendum and Elections Announcements by the President of the Republic* (Opinion no. 1085/2022) (May 27, 2022), 14, www.venice.coe.int/webforms/documents/default.aspx?pdffile=CDL-PI(2022)026-e

195 El Houssain Abouchi, "La pratique référendaire dans le régime constitutionnel marocaine, 1962–2011: une analyse du contenu" in *Cinquante ans de vie constitutionnelle au Maroc: quel bilan?* (Publications de l'Association marocaine de Droit constitutionnel 2013), 56.

196 See Article 41 of the 2011 Moroccan Constitution.

197 Mohammed Madani, "La réforme constitutionnelle sous le règne de Mohammed VI: le processus et l'aboutissement" in Amina El Messaoudi and Manuel José Terol Becerra (eds.), *El poder constituyente en el mundo árabe* (Junta de Andalucía, Instituto Andaluz de Administración Pública 2012), 225.

198 Remarkably, the 2012 constitution was defeated in the referendum in three Governorates, including Cairo. See Parolin, "Drifting Power Relations," p. 3184.

199 As recalled earlier, the turnout for the 2014 referendum was 38.6 percent, and for the 2019 amendments was 44.3 percent.

200 See Biagi, "Algerian Constitutional Reform," at p. 3.

201 See Sarah Leduc, "Nouvelle Constitution en Algérie: entre 'avancée démocratique' et 'occasion ratée'," *France 24* (February 9, 2016), www.france24.com/fr/20160208-algerie-nouvelle-constitution-interview-hassan-moali-societe-civile-loi-corruption

consultation was to reinforce the legitimacy of the reform (and of Tebboune himself), but this move did not produce the effects he hoped for. Rather, the move turned out to be a serious blow for the regime. Indeed, while 66.8 percent of the voters backed the reform, the turnout was extremely low, with only 23.84 percent of eligible voters participating – Algeria's lowest ever for a major poll. This considerable boycott of the vote can be explained by the fact that the *Hirak* movement considered the new constitutional reform a mere perpetuation of the *status quo*, and large segments of the population were disenchanted by the many broken promises of the regime. Furthermore, the government's decision to hold the referendum on November 1 – the anniversary of the start of Algeria's 1954 War of Independence against France – was perceived by many as a form of instrumentalization by the regime.[202] Thus, the outcome of the referendum showed that the boycott had become "the largest political party"[203] in the country.

In Libya, civil society participated in the constituent process, especially during the first year after the election of the Constitution Drafting Assembly, when this body enjoyed quite widespread public support due to its lack of involvement in the political turmoil of the other state institutions. As the process moved forward, however, a number of factors contributed to hindering public participation. The major tensions between the country's West and East, which eventually led to a civil war, were the first and obvious reason: A "minimal level of stabilization and consensus is necessary to engage in constitution-drafting and for civil society's role to be effective."[204] Furthermore, due to the lack of a clear protocol and procedure for processing and analyzing the requests coming from citizens and civil society organizations, "[the requests'] content was neither discussed nor taken into consideration by thematic committees [of the Constitution Drafting Assembly] while drafting their respective chapters."[205] Another factor is related to the remoteness of the city of Al Bayda, in eastern Libya, where the Constitution Drafting Assembly held its meetings. In the first phase, this isolation helped the Assembly "to deliberate largely uninfluenced by political factions and armed militias," thus maintaining "its political independence" and, for a while, making the Assembly "the only largely uncontested and elected institution in the country."[206] The remoteness of the city and the deteriorating security situation, however, limited accessibility to the Assembly and made the meetings between the representatives of the civil society and the members of the Assembly much more difficult to organize. The result was that people lost faith in the constituent body, "as they felt that their concerns and

[202] See Allouche, "Breakdown."

[203] Amal Belalloufi, "Le régime en crise de légitimité après l'échec du referendum," *Le Devoir* (November 3, 2020), www.ledevoir.com/monde/afrique/588932/la-reforme-constitutionnelle-est-acceptee-en-algerie-avec-une-abstention-record

[204] Hammady, "Role of Civil Society," at p. 170.

[205] Ibid., at p. 166.

[206] van Lier, "Constitution-Making," at p. 12.

demands were not seriously taken into consideration in the constitution-making process."[207]

According to the Interim Constitutional Declaration (Article 30), the 2017 draft constitution needs to be ratified in a popular referendum in order to enter into force. In the first place, one should note that the outcome of this consultation (if it ever takes place) appears extremely uncertain. Indeed, many Libyans are disappointed in how this draft constitution regulated several key issues (e.g., identity, decentralization, and management of natural resources).[208] Even the constitutional provisions on minorities' rights and representation have often been deemed by ethnic minorities below their expectations, which pushed some of them to announce that they would boycott the referendum.[209] The Referendum Law, adopted in 2018, adds further uncertainty to the outcome of this consultation. Indeed, while the Interim Constitutional Declaration requested a two-thirds nationwide majority, this law divides Libya into three constituencies (Tripolitania, Cyrenaica, and Fezzan) and requires that the draft constitution be approved by a majority of the voters in each region. However, it is not clear not only whether these arrangements will be maintained or not but also (*rectius*: especially) whether the referendum will take place at all.[210] Indeed, the ratification of the draft constitution in a popular referendum has become more and more difficult, mainly due to security concerns and the persistent opposition to the draft among some communities.[211] This is one of the main reasons that pushed the United Nations in March 2022 to initiate a process aimed at finding a consensual constitutional framework for national elections.[212]

The constitution-making process featuring the highest degree of *de jure* and *de facto* popular participation was in Tunisia between 2011 and 2014.[213] In this case, people played a pivotal role, and it is not a coincidence that the 2014 constitution was often defined as "the Constitution of the people" or an example of a "participatory constitution."[214] People participated in the process in various ways, including through meetings between the members of the Constituent Assembly and the representatives of civil society (including students),[215] public demonstrations, and "e-participation." It should also be noted that four drafts of the constitution were

[207] Cherif, *Libya's Constitution*, at p. 7.
[208] Ibid., at p. 15.
[209] See van Lier, "Constitution-Making," at p. 17.
[210] See Cherif, *Libya's Constitution*, at pp. 11–12; Cherif, "Libya's Constitutional Quagmire," at p. 10ff.
[211] See Cherif, "Libya's Constitutional Quagmire," at p. 10.
[212] See Section 1.2.6 in greater detail.
[213] See Maboudi, "*Fall*," at p. 75ff.
[214] See Tania Abbiate, *La partecipazione popolare ai processi costituenti: L'esperienza tunisina* (Editoriale Scientifica 2016); Nedra Cherif, "Participation in the Tunisian Constitution-Making Process" in Abbiate, Böckenförde and Federico (eds.) 2018, *Public Participation*, at p. 69ff.
[215] These meetings took place not only in Tunisia but also in Italy and France, which are the two countries that host the largest communities of Tunisian emigrants. See Cherif, "Participation," at p. 76.

made public, and each of them was the object of intense debates and discussions among political and social actors, thus increasing the possibilities for civil society to have a concrete impact on the final text of the constitution.[216]

The serious consideration of public involvement is witnessed by the fact that in March 2013 a new provision was added to Article 104 of the Rules of Procedure of the Constituent Assembly, stating that "constituent commissions shall commit to considering the observations and proposals that emerged from the general debate and the national dialogue on the constitution, and this within 10 days of the date of reception of the report." This commitment did not remain a dead letter. In several cases, the points raised by citizens were directly translated into the text of the constitution.[217] Thus, for example, it was thanks to people's demands that the role of the opposition in Parliament was strengthened, the neutrality of the public administration and educational institutions was emphasized, and the youth's place and role in society were reinforced.[218] Moreover, the major protest demonstrations by women's associations were crucial for the (re)introduction of gender equality into the constitution.[219]

Although public involvement could have been even stronger,[220] the abovementioned examples clearly show that the Tunisian people, including women, actually had the chance to make their voices heard, thus *concretely* influencing the drafting of the constitution. To a large extent, this document reflected the pluralism characterizing Tunisian society and represented one of the pillars upon which the State was based. It must be stressed that popular constitution-making was fully achieved despite the fact that the constitution was not ratified in a popular referendum.[221] According to Article 3 of the December 2011 *Loi constituante* on the Provisional Organization of Public Authorities (better known as the "Little Constitution"), had the Constituent Assembly failed to adopt the constitution with a two-thirds majority, then a constitutional referendum would have taken place. However, there was no need for such a consultation as the final text was adopted by an overwhelming majority of 200 votes in favor, twelve against, and four abstentions.

216 See Rafaâ Ben Achour, "La Constitution tunisienne du 27 janvier 2014" (2014) 100 *Revue française de droit constitutionnel*, 784.

217 See Maboudi, "*Fall*," at p. 84ff.

218 See also Cherif, "Participation," at p. 79ff.

219 See Francesco Biagi, "Religion in Constitution-Making Processes: Comparative Perspectives" in Susanna Mancini (ed.), *Constitutions and Religion* (Edward Elgar 2020), 257–258.

220 See Badreddine Abdelkafi, "L'Assemblée Nationale Constituante et la société civile: quelle relation?" in *La Constitution de la Tunisie – Processus, principes et perspectives* (UNDP 2016), 148–149.

221 By way of comparison, even the 1996 South African Constitution – which was the outcome of a profoundly democratic process – was adopted without resorting to a popular referendum. See Hassen Ebrahim and Laurel E. Miller, "Creating the Birth Certificate of a New South Africa: Constitution Making after Apartheid" in Laurel E. Miller (ed.), *Framing the State in Times of Transition: Case Studies in Constitution Making* (United States Institute of Peace 2010), 120ff.

1.2.6 *The Role Played by External Actors*

Despite a global trend of growing involvement of the international community in constitutional design,[222] in many cases, the role played by external actors in post-Arab Spring constitution-drafting processes was quite limited. This limitation was often one of the consequences of the lack of transparency and openness that characterized these processes (e.g., in Morocco, Syria, Jordan, Algeria, and Tunisia [2022 constituent process]).[223] In some countries, there was also a desire to carry out a fully autochthonous process of constitutional design to mark a break from previous constitutions drafted with massive foreign intervention. As mentioned earlier, some of the second-generation Arab constitutions were directly crafted by the mandated powers and were then submitted to the local constituent assemblies.[224] In some cases, the constitutions adopted after World War II were also drafted mainly by the departing colonial powers.[225] This was very clear in the case of Morocco, where all five constitutions adopted in the last century (1962, 1970, 1972, 1992, and 1996) were written with the crucial contribution of prominent French scholars.[226] In his speech given on June 17, 2011, while presenting the project for the new constitution, King Mohammed VI proudly announced the end of this practice, as "for the first time in the history of our country, the Constitution [was] made *by the Moroccans for all the Moroccans*"[227] (emphasis added).

In the cases of Egypt, Algeria, Syria, and Tunisia (2022 process), the exclusion of external actors in drafting the constitutional reforms also had to do with the willingness to preserve the State's sovereignty, as well as the diffidence toward foreign (especially Western) intervention. This was implicitly made clear by Bouteflika in his speech given on April 15, 2011, while presenting the political, economic, and constitutional measures he intended to implement to respond to the protests. He declared that Algeria "rejects all foreign interferences and respects the decision of all people deriving from its national sovereignty."[228] Similarly, also in Egypt, constitution-drafting was

[222] See Cheryl Saunders, "International Involvement in Constitution Making" in Landau and Lerner (eds.) 2019, *Comparative Constitution Making*, at p. 69.

[223] See Section 1.2.2.

[224] See Section 1.1.

[225] See Charles M. Fombad, "The Evolution of Modern African Constitutions. A Retrospective Perspective" in Charles M. Fombad (ed.), *Separation of Powers in African Constitutionalism* (Oxford University Press 2016), 15.

[226] These scholars include Maurice Duverger, Jacques Robert, Georges Vedel, René-Jean Dupuy, and Michel Rousset. See Mohammed Madani, "Constitutionnalisme sans démocratie: la fabrication et la mise en œuvre de la Constitution marocaine de 2011" in Omar Bendourou, Rkia El Mossadeq and Mohammed Madani (eds.), *La nouvelle Constitution marocaine à l'épreuve de la pratique* (Éditions la Croisée des Chemins 2014), 44.

[227] The speech of June 17 is available, along with all other official speeches of the Sovereign, online at www.maroc.ma/fr/discours-du-roi

[228] The text of the speech is available online at www.afrique-asie.fr/1884-2/

considered an exclusively internal affair, and, in fact, the international community was only partially allowed to play a role during the referendum processes.[229] In the case of Syria, the exclusion of foreign actors from the constitution-making process can also be explained by the fact that the country was in the middle of a conflict. In the case of Tunisia during the 2022 constituent process, after the Venice Commission had issued Opinion no. 1085/2022 of May 27, 2022 – in which it had argued that in the light of the flaws characterizing the constituent process, "it [was] not realistic to plan to hold [the] constitutional referendum [...] in a credible and legitimate way"[230] – Saïed declared that this was a "blatant interference," that the Venice Commission was a "persona non grata in Tunisia," and he also threatened to suspend the country's membership of the Venice Commission and expel its representatives.[231]

The case of the 2011–2014 constitution-making process in Tunisia was the exact opposite. The high degree of participation of external actors was one of the distinguishing features of this constituent process and was a further manifestation of the transparency and openness of the process. Even if international involvement triggered suspicion among some members of the Constituent Assembly about foreign interference, most of the drafters were interested in the opinions and expertise of external actors on both the process of constitution-making and the content of the new constitution. The most active international organizations included the United Nations, the European Union, Democracy Reporting International, the International Institute for Democracy and Electoral Assistance (International IDEA), the Max Planck Institute for Comparative Public Law and International Law, the Carter Center, and the Venice Commission.[232] Notably, regional organizations such as the Arab League, the African Union, the Union of Arab Maghreb, and the Organization of Islamic Conference played only a marginal role in the process.[233]

Among the most significant interventions by these external actors is the Venice Commission's intervention. On June 3, 2013, the Speaker of the Constituent Assembly asked the Venice Commission to submit an opinion on the final draft constitution. In its observations, the Venice Commission recommended that the Constituent Assembly make certain changes to the provisions regarding fundamental principles and rights, as well as to the provisions of the chapters devoted to the legislature, the executive, and the judiciary, to ensure compliance with international standards and comparative

[229] See Abdelaal, "Flawed Public Participation," at pp. 48–49.

[230] Venice Commission, *Tunisia*, at p. 17.

[231] See "Saied Slams Venice Commission Over 'Interference' in Tunisia Affairs," *The Arab Weekly* (May 31, 2022), https://thearabweekly.com/saied-slams-venice-commission-over-interference-tunisia-affairs

[232] On the different roles played by these external actors, see Alicia Pastor y Camarasa, "Demystifying How Constitutions Are Made: External Actors' Modes of Actions in the 2014 Tunisian Constitution" (2022) 1 *Michigan Journal of Law & Society*, 51ff.

[233] See The Carter Center, *Constitution-making Process in Tunisia: Final Report, 2011–2014* (2015), 75–77, www.cartercenter.org/resources/pdfs/news/peace_publications/democracy/tunisia-constitution-making-process.pdf

best practices.[234] Interestingly, the Assembly did follow some recommendations of the Venice Commission, even some of those referring to extremely sensitive issues, such as the relationship between the State and Islam.[235] This major involvement of the Venice Commission might contribute to explaining why, almost ten years later, Saïed was so disturbed by the intervention of this body during the new constituent process.

Thus, even though the 2011–2014 Tunisian constitution-making process was a nationally driven and owned process, external actors provided important support to the Constituent Assembly. One may wonder why Tunisian drafters were particularly interested in foreign input. Tunisian drafters' interest can probably be explained by the desire to ground the new constitution in a dual legitimacy: internal and external. This dual legitimacy can be described as follows:

> The international community and (sometimes vague) comparative standards are being considered as a source of legitimacy in a way that becomes increasingly similar to the internal political process. Recent constitutions are thus also grounded on the acceptance by the international community, by showing that international standards and comparative best practices have been followed. In other words, the basic law […] has to persuade not only the country's citizens, but also other states and the international community as a whole. Thus, constitution-building […] is becoming bi-directional, being addressed to the inside (the national political community and society) as well as to the outside (international and comparative acceptance of the adopted text).[236]

It seems that, to a large extent, this objective was achieved in Tunisia. Indeed, the 2014 constitution has been considered profoundly innovative in the international field, thus representing a model in the Arab region and beyond.[237]

It must be emphasized that external technical intervention during constitution-drafting is not a novelty in the Arab world. One need only consider the process that led to the adoption of the 1962 Kuwaiti Constitution. Indeed, the Constituent Assembly was assisted in its work by a group of foreign constitutional scholars headed by 'Uthman Khalil Uthman (an Egyptian colleague of the prominent jurist 'Abd al-Razzaq al-Sanhuri), who prepared a first draft of the constitution. A constitutional committee revised this draft, made some changes, and then submitted it to the entire Assembly. The members of the Assembly raised a number of issues, but in most of the cases, they were convinced by the arguments made by 'Uthman in defense of the original draft. Thus, after some minor changes, the constitution was approved.[238]

234 See Venice Commission, *Opinion on the Final Draft Constitution of the Republic of Tunisia* (Opinion no. 733/2013) (October 17, 2013), www.venice.coe.int/webforms/documents/?pdf=CDL-AD(2013)032-e

235 See Biagi, "Religion in Constitution-Making Processes," at pp. 258–259. See also Chapter 4, Section 4.2.1.

236 Andrea Lollini and Francesco Palermo, "Comparative Law and the 'Proceduralization' of Constitution-Building Processes" in Julia Raue and Patrick Sutter (eds.), *Facets and Practices of State-Building* (Martinus Nijhoff 2009), 306.

237 See Rafaâ Ben Achour, "La Dyarchie dans la Constitution" in *La Constitution de la Tunisie – Processus, principes et perspectives* (2016), at p. 516.

238 The process is described in greater detail by Brown, *Rule of Law*, at pp. 165–166.

The ongoing constitution-making processes in Libya and Syria, which are both strictly linked to the peacemaking processes, are characterized by the massive involvement of the international community. In Libya, the United Nations Support Mission in Libya (UNSMIL) was established on September 16, 2011, with the mandate to "assist and support Libyan national efforts to [...] undertake inclusive political dialogue, promote national reconciliation, and embark upon the constitution-making and electoral process." Depending on who the special envoy for Libya was, the United Nations alternated phases featuring a low-profile approach with periods marked by much greater interventionism.[239] Although in some cases international actors managed to contribute positively to the various drafts of the Libyan Constitution, these organizations found a number of major obstacles while supporting the work of the Constitution Drafting Assembly. These obstacles included suspicion of foreign (especially Western) interference, the Constitution Drafting Assembly's lack of a clear protocol for cooperation with international actors, and security-related concerns. On this latter aspect, it should be stressed that by the time the Constitution Drafting Assembly started operating,

> [A]lmost all international organizations and embassies had relocated to Tunisia for security reasons. Accordingly, most events took place abroad in Tunisia, Egypt and Turkey, which made it impossible for a larger number of activists to be included and led to the emergence of a category of "permanent participants," limiting the rotation, and thus, the scope of beneficiaries.[240]

Furthermore, it has been argued that in some cases, the difficulties that the international actors faced were due to their lack of sufficient expertise and poor knowledge of the Libyan context.[241]

In the light of the major difficulties in organizing the referendum on the 2017 draft constitution (and the national elections), on March 3, 2022, the then Special Adviser to the Secretary-General on Libya, Ms. Stephanie Williams, launched an initiative to form a joint committee from the House of Representatives and the High Council of State "to agree on a firm constitutional basis for national elections."[242] The aim was to find an agreement between the competing governments currently existing in the country: the Government of National Unity (led by Abdul Hamid al-Dbeibah) and the High Council of State in Tripoli (Western Libya), on the one hand, and the Government of National Stability (led by Fathi Bashagha) and the House of Representatives in Eastern Libya, on the other hand.[243] Under the

[239] See Hammady, "Role of Civil Society," at pp. 168–170.

[240] Ibid., at p. 168.

[241] Ibid., at p. 170.

[242] *UNSMIL Statement on the UN-facilitated Joint HOR/HCS Committee Meeting* (March 21, 2022), https://unsmil.unmissions.org/unsmil-statement-un-facilitated-joint-horhcs-committee-meeting

[243] See International Peace Institute, Stimson Center and Security Council Report, *The Situation in Libya: Reflections on Challenges and Ways Forward* (June 2022), 2, www.stimson.org/wp-content/uploads/2022/07/Situation-in-Libya-Meeting-Note-Proofs26.pdf

auspices of the UN, the representatives of the High Council of State and the House of Representatives held three meetings in Cairo (in April, May, and June 2022) and one in Geneva (end of June 2022),[244] in which they reviewed the provisions of the 2017 draft constitution. According to the statement released by Special Adviser Ms. Williams after the Geneva meeting, the two bodies

> reached unprecedented consensus on a number of long-standing issues, including: the designation of the headquarters and distribution of seats for the two chambers of the legislative authority; division of responsibilities among the president, prime minister, cabinet and local government; the specific form of decentralisation, including the delineation of the number of governorates and their powers; a revenue allocation mechanism for the different levels of government; and increased representation for cultural components.[245]

However, the statement points out that "disagreement persists" on one specific issue, namely "the eligibility requirements for the candidates in the first presidential elections."[246] Therefore, "[w]hile the progress secured during three rounds of consultations in Cairo and this round in Geneva is significant, it remains insufficient as a basis to move forward towards comprehensive national elections."[247]

In the case of Syria, the international organizations – and in particular the United Nations – also have had a major involvement, as they have thus far "guided" the entire constitution-drafting process.[248] The movement toward constitutional reform started in June 2012 (just a few months after the adoption of the 2012 constitution in February of that year) with the Geneva Communiqué of the UN-backed Action Group for Syria, which made reference, *inter alia*, to the need to establish a "new constitutional order." This commitment was declared even more strongly in UN Security Council Resolution 2254 of December 2015. This resolution outlined the UN's support for a Syrian-led political process that "establishes credible, inclusive and nonsectarian governance and sets a schedule and process for drafting a new constitution" within six months. The resolution also recommended "free and fair elections, pursuant to the new constitution, to be held within 18 months" under

[244] This meeting in Geneva was only between the heads of the two bodies, namely the Speaker of the House of Representatives, Aguila Saleh Issa, and the President of the High Council of State, Khaled Mishri.

[245] *SASG Stephanie Williams' Statement on the High-level Meeting on Libya's Constitutional Track in Geneva* (June 30, 2022), https://unsmil.unmissions.org/sasg-stephanie-williams'-statement-high-level-meeting-libya's-constitutional-track-geneva

[246] Ibid. See also *United Nations Support Mission in Libya – Report of the Secretary-General (S/2022/632)* (August 19, 2022), 1–3, https://reliefweb.int/report/libya/united-nations-support-mission-libya-report-secretary-general-s2022632-enar. On this issue related to the eligibility requirements, see specifically Chapter 2, Section 2.1.6.

[247] *SASG Stephanie Williams' Statement on the High-level Meeting on Libya's Constitutional Track in Geneva* (2022).

[248] On constitution-making processes "guided" by international organizations see Giuseppe de Vergottini, *Diritto costituzionale comparato* (Wolters Kluwer – CEDAM 2022), 223ff.

UN supervision. Notwithstanding the numerous peace talks held in Geneva under the auspices of the UN (with strong support from the European Union), the Syrian Constitutional Committee (SCC) – the body responsible for adopting the new constitution – convened for the first time only in October 2019. The SCC is composed of 150 members: One-third are selected by Assad's government, one-third by the Syrian Opposition's Negotiations Committee, and one-third by the UN (this latter group includes members of Syrian civil society). The task of drafting the constitution has been granted to a smaller body composed of forty-five members – fifteen members from each "bloc."[249] The composition of the SCC, which was deeply influenced by external powers (particularly Russia and Turkey), has been harshly criticized, specifically due to the underrepresentation of Kurds (4 percent of the SCC – and there are no representatives of the Autonomous Administration of North and East Syria).[250] The negotiations, which are currently being held in Geneva and are especially facilitated by the UN special envoy for Syria, Geir Pedersen, have not produced any tangible results thus far, as neither side has shown a serious willingness to compromise. As of this writing, the Committee appears to have reached an impasse.[251]

The UN was not the only external actor involved in the Syrian constitution-writing process. Indeed, following the adoption of UN Security Council Resolution 2254 of December 2015, the Carter Center organized a series of workshops with a group of Syrian lawyers and academics to address what were presented as the shortcomings of the SC Resolution. These workshops considered the meaning of "inclusive transitional governing body with full executive powers" (provided for by the SC Resolution) and the constitutional and legislative changes necessary during the transition period to implement the Resolution. Three constitutional options were considered. First, the revision of the 2012 constitution; second, the adoption of a provisional constitution for the transitional period in the form of a constitutional declaration; third, the "re-activation" of the 1950 constitution for the interim period. The revision of the 2012 constitution was considered the preferred option. Specifically, it was suggested that executive powers be exercised jointly by the President of the Republic and the President of the Council of Ministers. The revision also suggested changing the composition of the Council of Minister (which would assume the functions of the Transitional Governing Body), the People's Assembly, and the Supreme Constitutional Court so as to include also opposition and independent representatives. As an alternative, the Carter Center suggested the adoption of a provisional Constitution, under which the President of the Republic and the Transitional Governing Body would jointly exercise executive powers. Neither the

[249] See Karam Shaar and Ayman Dasouki, "Syria's Constitutional Committee: The Devil in the Detail," *MEI@75* (January 6, 2021), www.mei.edu/publications/syrias-constitutional-committee-devil-detail

[250] Ibid.

[251] Security Council Report, *January 2023 Monthly Forecast*, www.securitycouncilreport.org/monthly-forecast/2023-01/syria-51.php

proposed revision of the 2012 constitution nor the proposed adoption of the interim constitution called into question President Assad's remaining in power during the eighteen months of the transitional period, even though both texts placed checks on his authority. The third option, namely the return to the 1950 constitution, was dismissed as "unrealistic." This work conducted by the Carter Center was published in the form of a working paper in June 2016.[252]

Even Russia tried to provide Syria with a new constitution. Indeed, on January 23–24, 2017, during the first round of the "Astana talks" (the Syria peace talks held in Astana, Kazakhstan, under the leadership of Russia, Iran, and Turkey), Moscow presented its draft proposal of a new Syrian Constitution,[253] which Konstantin Kosachev, the head of the Russian Senate's Foreign Relations Committee, referred to as Moscow's "contribution to catalyze the peace process."[254] On the one hand, this draft constitution introduced some positive elements (e.g., the recognition of the Kurdish autonomy and the use of minority languages),[255] but on the other hand, it was harshly criticized, especially due to the fact that it continued to provide for a strong concentration of authority in the hands of the President of the Republic.[256] This draft constitution, however, was never a serious option on the table, as it was soon rejected by both the Syrian government and the opposition.[257]

1.2.7 *The Influence of Previous Domestic Constitutions and Their "Reactivation"*

Following the Arab uprisings, one of the decisions that drafters had to make when crafting the new constitutions referred to the use of the previous constitutional texts. More specifically, the questions were: Should previous constitutions be used during the constitution-making processes? And if so, how and to what extent? In some cases (Jordan and Algeria), the constitutions were only amended – albeit extensively – and

[252] The Carter Center, *Syria's Transition Governance & Constitutional Options Under U.N. Security Council Resolution* 2254 (June 2016), www.cartercenter.org/resources/pdfs/peace/conflict_resolution/syria-conflict/principles-and-constitutional-provisions-may-8-2016.pdf. For a more detailed analysis of the three constitutional options considered by the Carter Center, see Atassi, *Syria*, at p. 446ff.

[253] The text of this draft constitution is available online at the following address: https://constituteproject.org/constitution/Syria_2017D?lang=en

[254] See Maxim A. Suchkov, "Russia Offers Outline for Syrian Constitution," *Al-Monitor* (January 27, 2017), www.al-monitor.com/originals/2017/01/russia-meeting-syria-opposition-moscow-constitution.html

[255] See, for example, Article 4 of the draft constitution, stipulating that Syrian citizens have the right to "educate their children in their native language," that "government agencies and institutions of Kurdish Cultural Autonomy shall use both Kurdish and Arabic equally," and that "each region shall have the right to use another majority language in addition to the official language as is regulated by the law, if such use was approved by a locally held referendum."

[256] See William Partlett, "Understanding the Origins of Russia's Constitutional Solution to the Syrian Conflict," *ConstitutionNet* (February 24, 2017), https://constitutionnet.org/news/understanding-origins-russias-constitutional-solution-syrian-conflict

[257] For a more detailed analysis of this draft constitution, see Atassi, *Syria*, at p. 451ff.

therefore their basic structure was largely preserved. On the contrary, all the other countries decided to adopt a brand-new constitutional document. In Morocco, Syria, and Egypt, the drafters relied quite extensively on previous constitutions. In Syria, for example, the 2012 constitution has been described as "a logical continuation and modernization of the 1973 constitution" rather than "a radical departure from it."[258] This comes as no surprise, also because the chair of the drafting committee, Mazhar al-Anbari, was the same person who also presided over the commission responsible for preparing the initial draft of the 1973 constitution.[259]

The case of Tunisia during the 2011–2014 process was different, as the members of the Constituent Assembly decided to start with a blank page. Starting from scratch has both pros and cons. If the drafters are seriously committed to making a clean break from the previous authoritarian regime, it seems wise not to use the previous illiberal constitution as the basis for deliberations. The risk, indeed, is to reincorporate the flaws of the previous text into the new constitutional document. In Egypt, for example, in 2012, the Constituent Assembly opted to use the 1971 constitution

> as a starting point for its deliberations. The effect is that while the [2012] constitution claims to be a product of the people's will, it is heavily influenced by the preceding decades of autocratic rule. So much so that many articles have simply been reproduced verbatim in the final text. Thus, although the new constitution solves some of the country's more important problems [...], its insistence on seeking inspiration from the 1971 constitution means that the same lapses recur, and the same arms-length relationship between the state and the people is maintained [...].[260]

In Tunisia, the decision to start with a blank page (*théorie de la feuille blanche*)[261] undoubtedly delayed the work of the Constituent Assembly. One might even claim that it contributed to increasing the difficulties of the constitution-making process itself. However, setting aside the previous 1959 constitution (which was repeatedly amended in the following decades) proved to be the right decision, as it helped the drafters to turn over a new leaf.

The case of Libya is peculiar, as the country was deprived of any formal constitution for a long time. Indeed, under his 41-year regime (1969–2011), Gaddafi ruled through the Constitutional Proclamation of December 11, 1969 (which was adopted following the *coup d'état* that removed King Idris from office) and various declarations. In particular, he set out his political philosophy, combining theories of nationalism, Islam, socialism, and populism in his *Green Book* (*al-kitab al-akhdar*). Gaddafi explicitly rejected the idea of having a constitution. In the Green Book, he

[258] Atassi, *Syria*, at p. 387.
[259] Ibid., at p. 308.
[260] Zaid Al-Ali, "The New Egyptian Constitution: An Initial Assessment of Its Merits and Flaws," *Open Democracy* (December 26, 2012), www.opendemocracy.net/en/new-egyptian-constitution-initial-assessment-of-its-merits-and-flaws/
[261] Ben Achour, *Tunisie: Une révolution en pays d'Islam*, at p. 312.

stated that "[t]he natural law of any society is either tradition (custom) or religion. Any other attempt to draft law for any society, outside these two sources, is invalid and illogical. Constitutions are not the law of the society."[262]

There is a Libyan constitutional text, however, that served (and might still serve) as an important reference during the constitutional debates – namely, the 1951 constitution, adopted under King Idris, which remained in force until the 1969 coup.[263] As the current constituent process got stuck and the current conditions in the country have thus far prevented the holding of national elections and the referendum aimed at ratifying the 2017 draft constitution, it has been proposed that the 1951 constitution – either in its original "federal" version of 1951 or in its amended "unitary" version of 1963[264] – be "reactivated" (with some modifications) as an interim constitutional framework. Then, as soon as the country stabilizes, Libyans would decide either to maintain this updated constitution or to draft a new constitutional text.[265] It has also been proposed to return to the 1951 constitution without any change of the form of government, a fact that would imply the reestablishment of the monarchy in the country.[266] What is certain is that, even without its reactivation, the 1951 constitution might still play a role in the constituent process, as certain provisions of this text could complement the acceptable parts of the 2017 draft constitution. Indeed, as both texts have strengths but also weaknesses, a careful "merging" of these two documents could eventually provide Libya with a more democratic constitution.[267]

As recalled earlier,[268] the possibility to reactivate a previous constitution was also discussed in Syria. Indeed, one of the constitutional options considered by the Carter Center to implement UN Security Council Resolution 2254 of December

[262] Muammar Gaddafi, *The Green Book* (Part I, The Law of Society) (1975).

[263] See Democracy Reporting International, *Assessment of the 1951 Libyan Constitution According to International Standards* (Briefing Paper 28) (July 2012), https://democracy-reporting.org/wp-content/uploads/2016/03/dri-ly-bp28-1951_libya_constitution.pdf

[264] The 1951 constitution provided for a federal system (comprising the three historical regions of Cyrenaica, Tripolitania, and Fezzan), whereas the 1963 constitutional reform abandoned it and created a unitary State.

[265] On this idea of the "reactivation" of the 1951 constitution, see Emadeddin Muntasser and Mohamed Fouad, "Libya Should Revive the 1963 Constitution," *MEI@75* (March 28, 2017), www.mei.edu/publications/libya-should-revive-1963-constitution; Edward P. Joseph, "Libya Needs Its Old Constitution If It Wants to Survive," *The National Interest* (July 4, 2018), https://nationalinterest.org/feature/libya-needs-its-old-constitution-if-it-wants-survive-24952; Karim Mezran and Wolfgang Pusztai, "Libya: Exploiting the Achievements of the Libyan Political Agreement," *ISPI* (January 9, 2019), www.ispionline.it/it/pubblicazione/libya-exploiting-achievements-libyan-political-agreement-21962

[266] See Mustafa El Sagezli, "A Return to a Constitutional Monarchy May Solve Libya's Problems," *Atlantic Council* (October 21, 2021), www.atlanticcouncil.org/blogs/menasource/a-return-to-a-constitutional-monarchy-may-solve-libyas-problems/

[267] A comparison between these two constitutional texts can be found in Duncan Pickard and Michael Meyer-Resende, "Libya: Comparison of Two Constitutional Texts According to International Standards of Democracy," *Democracy Reporting International* (November 24, 2020), https://democracyreporting.s3.eu-central-1.amazonaws.com/images/2015Constitutional-Comparison_Final_2020-11-17.pdf

[268] See Section 1.2.6.

2015 was to return to the 1950 constitution for the transitional period. This option, however, was ruled out as unrealistic.

In the future, the reactivation of the constitution might be an interesting option also in Tunisia. Indeed, in a future constituent process aimed at replacing the largely authoritarian constitution of 2022, Tunisians might consider reactivating – at least for an interim period – the democratic constitution of 2014 or some of its parts.

1.2.8 *The Influence of Foreign Constitutional Models*

Following the 2011 uprisings, all Arab drafters relied extensively on foreign constitutional models. Such a reliance occurred also during the previous waves of constitution-writing. During the second wave, for example, constitutional drafters relied extensively on the 1876 Ottoman Basic Law and some past European constitutions. The Egyptians looked specifically at the 1831 Belgian Constitution.[269] The Lebanese turned, in particular, to the 1875 French Constitution of the Third Republic, but some authors claim that some elements were also taken from the 1923 Egyptian Constitution and that the constitutions of Switzerland and the United States also served as a source of inspiration during the drafting process.[270] Also in the third generation of Arab constitutions, drafters borrowed heavily from European constitutions. In the Maghreb, they mainly turned to the 1958 French Constitution[271]; in Jordan, they looked specifically at the 1831 Belgian Constitution[272]; in Egypt, the drafters of the 1971 constitution referred to the constitutions of France and some Eastern European countries (such as Yugoslavia, Czechoslovakia, and the German Democratic Republic).[273] Arab drafters also considered constitutional experiences in the region. In addition to the 1876 Ottoman Basic Law, the 1971 Egyptian Constitution was the landmark text in the Arab world for a long time. For example, the 1973 constitution of Syria relied extensively on this Egyptian precedent. The case of Libya is particularly noteworthy, since the drafters of the 1951 constitution looked at a variety of countries:

> The Arab states of Egypt, Syria, Lebanon, and Iraq; the Asiatic states of Afghanistan, Iran, Indonesia, India, and Burma; the European states of Belgium, Switzerland, Greece, Norway, and Germany (Government of Bonn); some of the states of the Americas: the United States, Mexico, Canada, Venezuela, and Brazil; and the constitutions of the Union of South Africa and Australia.[274]

[269] See López García and Fernández Suzora, *Introducción*, at p. 35.

[270] See Cordelia Koch, "The Separation of Powers in a Fragmented State: The Case of Lebanon" in Grote and Röder (eds.) 2012, *Constitutionalism in Islamic Countries*, at p. 394.

[271] See Thierry Le Roy, "Constitutionalism in the Maghreb: Between French Heritage and Islamic Concepts" in Grote and Röder (eds.) 2012, *Constitutionalism in Islamic Countries*, at pp. 117–119.

[272] See Hammouri, "Constitutional Reform," at pp. 723–724.

[273] See Brown, *Constitutions in a Nonconstitutional World*, at pp. 80–81.

[274] Khalidi, "Constitution of the United Kingdom of Libya," at p. 225.

After the 2011 upheavals, Arab drafters not only took into consideration the recent constitutional reforms adopted in neighboring countries (thus giving rise, at least in part, to intraregional circulation) but were also often influenced by the standards typical of constitutional democracies and "global constitutionalism," which can be described as "the convergence among national constitutional systems in their structures and in their protections of fundamental human rights."[275] This influence explains the greater emphasis put on human dignity and the recognition and protection of fundamental rights and freedoms,[276] the strengthening of the binding force of international human rights treaties and conventions,[277] the reinforcement of "electoral justice" (with the establishment of electoral management bodies and the granting to the judiciary of the power to resolve electoral disputes),[278] and the inclusion of "limitation clauses" – that is, the clauses that are aimed at guaranteeing that the essence of fundamental rights is not affected by the implementing legislation.[279]

As was the case in the past,[280] French constitutional law continues to exert a strong influence in the Maghreb and beyond. In particular, Arab drafters drew inspiration from the constitutional reform adopted in France in 2008. This influence is very clear if one considers the decisions to give constitutional status to the parliamentary opposition in Morocco, Tunisia (constitution of 2014), and Algeria; to introduce concrete constitutional review (in the form of the "double-filter" system) in Jordan and Algeria[281]; or to vest the constitutional court with the power to review the presidential decision to uphold the state of exception in Tunisia (constitution of 2014).[282]

On the other hand, it must be stressed that all Arab constitutions continue to feature numerous references to national identity, such as Islam, the Arabic language, or membership of a specific geographical area (e.g., the Maghreb, the Great Maghreb, or the African continent). It should be noted that post-2011 constitutional texts have significantly "broadened their horizons," as they have often acknowledged the importance of external components and influences in forging national

275 Mark Tushnet, "The Inevitable Globalization of Constitutional Law" (2009) 49 *Virginia Journal of International Law*, 987.

276 See Andrea Pin, "Arab Constitutionalism and Human Dignity" (2017) 50 *The George Washington International Law Review*, 1ff.

277 See Said Mahmoudi, "International Human Rights Law as Framework for Emerging Constitutions in Arab Countries" in Grote and Röder (eds.) 2016, *Constitutionalism, Human Rights, and Islam*, at p. 535ff.

278 See Kaouthar Debbeche, "The Difficult Path toward Democracy: New Electoral Systems in Egypt, Libya and Tunisia" in Grote and Röder (eds.) 2016, *Constitutionalism, Human Rights, and Islam*, at p. 427ff.

279 See Francesco Biagi, "Women's Rights and Constitutional Implementation in the MENA Region: Challenges and Perspectives" in Claudia Padovani and Francesca Helm (eds.), *Rethinking the Transition Process in Syria: Constitution, Participation and Gender Equality* (Research-publishing.net 2018), 148.

280 See Le Roy, "Constitutionalism in the Maghreb," at pp. 117–119.

281 See Chapter 3, Section 3.3.3.

282 See Chapter 2, Section 2.3.

identity. From this point of view, the preamble to the 2011 constitution of Morocco is emblematic, as it declares, *inter alia*, that

> A sovereign Muslim State, attached to its national unity and territorial integrity, the Kingdom of Morocco intends to preserve, in its plenitude and diversity, its one and indivisible national identity. Its unity is forged by the convergence of its Arab-Islamist, Berber and Saharan-Hassanic components, nourished and enriched by its African, Andalusian, Hebraic and Mediterranean influences.

In a similar vein, the preamble to the Algerian Constitution declares: "Algeria, land of Islam, an integral part of the Great Maghreb, and an Arab and Amazigh, as well as Mediterranean and African country […]." Another state in which this confluence of international and domestic influences was particularly evident is Tunisia, where the 2011–2014 process of constitution-making has rightly been defined as "intermestic."[283]

1.3 A COMPARATIVE ASSESSMENT

The nature of a constitution is often strictly linked to the way it is drafted – hence the importance of analyzing constitution-making processes. Thus,

> [I]t would appear to be unimaginable, for example, for a despot to "impose" a liberal-democratic Constitution: in order for it to be genuinely liberal and democratic, it would need to be *decided* (not simply "accepted," and this is the reason for the weakness of all forms of plebiscite) by the people and/or their representatives.[284]

In most cases, post-Arab Spring constitution-making and constitutional reform processes addressed the flaws and shortcomings of the previous waves of constitution-drafting only to a limited extent. Indeed, many of these processes (which were often either too short or too long) followed a top-down approach, lacked transparency and openness, and were characterized by the limited involvement of political parties and civil society. In some cases, these new constitutional texts looked like mere "concessions" made by the head of state to the population. Furthermore, drafters often relied on the previous (largely autocratic) constitutions of their respective countries, a decision that favored the perpetuation of the *status quo*. In the light of past practices, which were often characterized by abuses by the former colonial powers, the decision of the drafters to reject foreign (especially Western) intervention in constitution-drafting is understandable. There were cases, however, in which these external actors contributed to a positive outcome of the process. In the case

[283] Sara Borrillo, "Women's Movements and the Recognition of Gender Equality in the Constitution-Making Process in Morocco and Tunisia (2011–2014)" in Ruth Rubio-Marín and Helen Irving (eds.), *Women as Constitution-Makers: Case Studies from the New Democratic Era* (Cambridge University Press 2019), 66.

[284] Antonino Spadaro, "La transizione costituzionale. Ambiguità e polivalenza di un'importante nozione di teoria generale" in Antonino Spadaro (ed.), *Le "trasformazioni" costituzionali nell'età della transizione* (Giappichelli 2000), 64.

of Tunisia (2014 constitution), for example, the recommendations of the Venice Commission helped strengthen the democratic nature of the constitutional text.[285] As to the influence of foreign constitutional models, the combination between elements typical of global constitutionalism and references to national identity is undoubtedly an interesting feature of post-Arab Spring constitutions. In some cases, however, this mix gave rise to ambiguous wording and contradictory provisions.[286]

The impression is that Arab drafters often adopted a short-term, partisan perspective, as if they were dealing with *ordinary* politics and not *constitutional* politics.[287] This is particularly evident if one considers the fact that adopting a new constitution or constitutional reform was rarely aimed at building a more democratic, just, and inclusive society. Less noble purposes were often at stake. In Egypt, for example, the constitution-making process was considered "a short-term political deal rather than a long-lasting social contract."[288] In 2012, the Muslim Brotherhood assumed a winner-takes-all attitude, while during the process that led to the adoption of the 2014 Egyptian Constitution, one of the main concerns of all the political and social forces represented in the Constituent Assembly was the "Debrotherhoodization" of the country.[289] Thus, both in 2012 and 2014, "a major faction of society was left out and the two Constitution-building processes were used by the most powerful groups to extend their advantage over their rivals and reinforce their own position in the state."[290] In the case of Morocco and Jordan, King Mohammed VI and King Abdullah II gave rise to what can be defined as "surviving constitutionalism"; in fact, both the 2011 Moroccan Constitution and the reform of the Jordanian Constitution mainly responded to the need to appease the people's discontent so as to ensure the regime's stability and continuity. The two kings allowed constitutional reforms to take place as long as their key powers and prerogatives were not questioned; their main purpose was not to democratize the country, but to guarantee their own survival.[291] Thus, the majority of post-2011

[285] See Venice Commission, *Opinion on the Final Draft Constitution*.

[286] See Chapter 4 para. 4.3.3.

[287] On the differences between ordinary politics and constitutional politics, see Bruce Ackerman, *We the People: Foundations* (Harvard University Press 1991), 6; Antonia Baraggia, "Constitutional Moment" in Rainer Grote, Frauke Lachenmann and Rüdiger Wolfrum (eds.), *Max Planck Encyclopedia of Comparative Constitutional Law* (Oxford University Press 2020), 1ff.; William Partlett and Zim Nwokora, "The Foundations of Democratic Dualism: Why Constitutional Politics and Ordinary Politics Are Different" (2019) 26 *Constellations*, 177ff.

[288] Yasmine Farouk, "Writing the Constitution of the Egyptian Revolution: Between Social Contract and Political Contracting (March 2011–July 2013)," *Arab Reform Initiative* (November 2013), 2, https://s3.eu-central-1.amazonaws.com/storage.arab-reform.net/ari/2013/11/02114149/Arab_Reform_Initiative_2013-11_Research_Paper_en_writing_the_constitution_of_the_egyptian_revolution_between_social_contract_and_political_contracting.pdf

[289] See Section 1.2.1.2.

[290] Nathalie Bernard-Maugiron, "State Powers and Constitution Drafting Processes in Post-Revolutionary Transitions in North Africa" in Senén Florensa (ed.), *The Arab Transitions in a Changing World: Building Democracies in Light of International Experiences* (IE Med 2016), 127.

[291] See Biagi, "Surviving Constitutionalism," at p. 1240ff.

constitution-writing processes can hardly be described as a genuine exercise of "higher lawmaking" – to use the well-known expression by Bruce Ackerman.[292]

All these deficits in constitution-making had at least two negative interrelated consequences, which both contributed to preventing a successful transition to democracy. First, these deficits produced constitutional texts addressing the protestors' demands only to a limited extent. For example, people had hoped to achieve a change in the form of government (e.g., from an "executive" monarchy to a "parliamentary" monarchy, or from a "hyper-presidential" system to a "semi-presidential" system), and more generally to reinforce the separation and balance of powers.[293] However, if the key prerogatives of the heads of state were largely left intact in the revised texts of most constitutions, thereby perpetuating the concentration of powers that has characterized these countries for a long time, this was also due to the top-down approach followed in the constitution-drafting processes. This approach clearly frustrated people's calls for major constraints on the prerogatives of kings and presidents.[294]

Second, the deficits in constitution-drafting extensively weakened the legitimacy of and sense of ownership over the new constitutions. Generally speaking, it is true that a bottom-up approach does not necessarily strengthen the democratic character of a constitution and does not automatically reinforce its legitimacy.[295] In the case of post-Arab Spring constitutions, however, one must observe that a higher degree of transparency and openness, as well as a greater involvement of civil society and political parties, probably would have contributed to developing documents closer to the people, thus reinforcing their sense of ownership over the new texts. Several factors demonstrate this weak public support for the new constitutional documents, including the very low turnout in the constitutional referendums,[296] the harsh criticisms coming from large parts of society toward both the constituent processes and the content of the new constitutional reforms,[297] and the recurrent protest demonstrations against, *inter alia*, the political, institutional, and constitutional arrangements.[298]

Although it should not by any means be idealized and romanticized,[299] in many ways, the 2011–2014 Tunisian constitution-making process was a positive exception.

[292] Ackerman, *We the People*, at p. 6.

[293] See Chapter 2.

[294] See Chapter 2, Section 2.5.3.

[295] See Claude Klein and András Sajó, "Constitution-Making: Process and Substance" in Michel Rosenfeld and András Sajó (eds.), *The Oxford Handbook of Comparative Constitutional Law* (Oxford University Press 2012), 424; Sultany, *Law and Revolution*, at pp. 236ff., 241ff., and 262; Eisenstadt, LeVan, and Maboudi, *Constituents before Assembly*, at pp. 114ff. and 131ff.

[296] See Section 1.2.5.

[297] See Section 1.2.5.

[298] The so-called "Arab Spring 2.0." See Marwan Muasher, "Is This the Arab Spring 2.0?," *Carnegie Endowment for International Peace* (October 30, 2019), https://carnegieendowment.org/2019/10/30/is-this-arab-spring-2.0-pub-80220

[299] The challenges in the drafting of the 2014 constitution are discussed by Mabrouka M'Barek, one of the members of the Constituent Assembly: M'Barek, "Makers of Our Own History," at p. 151ff.

Indeed, despite tremendous difficulties (including an extremely complicated political context marked by serious episodes of violence), the 2014 constitution represented the outcome of a democratic process in which the people were the real holders of the *pouvoir constituant*. The final text was a compromise among the main political forces represented within the Constituent Assembly and was drafted with the very active participation of civil society in a context featuring a high degree of transparency. The constant search for consensus, the resort to informal procedures, the decision not to rely on the previous 1959 constitution, and the critical openness to foreign actors (particularly the Venice Commission) and models also played crucial roles in ensuring the successful outcome of the process. Thus, it comes as no surprise that the 2014 constitution was one of the most democratic constitutional texts in the Arab world.[300] Furthermore, it enjoyed, especially at the outset, a higher degree of legitimacy and sense of ownership compared to the other post-Arab Spring constitutions. This can be explained by the fact that this document represented "the authentic reflection of the social expectations, fears, tensions and contradictions of the Tunisian society."[301] Indeed, unlike many other constitutional texts in the region, it was not an *octroyée* constitution. Rather, it was the product of the whole society. It has been rightly underlined that Tunisians "should be proud"[302] of the 2014 constitution, first and foremost because of the process that led to its adoption: "More important than the text of the constitution, the context in which it was drafted emerges as the hallmark of a society conscious of its rights, aware of its strength and capable to push the political class to act under its insightful control."[303] However, while Tunisian political forces managed overall to achieve a good result with the adoption of the 2014 constitution, they also displayed many limits and weaknesses during the process of constitutional enforcement.[304] In this phase, several important promises made to the people and incorporated into the constitution (e.g., in the field of socio-economic rights) were not maintained, a fact that created resentment and frustration among the population. Kaïs Saïed relied precisely on these sentiments when he started his illiberal-populist project in July 2021.

[300] See Tania Groppi, "La Constitution tunisienne de 2014: illustration de la globalisation du droit constitutionnel?" (2018) 114 *Revue française de droit constitutionnel*, 343ff.; Ben Achour, "La Constitution tunisienne du 27 janvier 2014," at p. 784.

[301] Ben Achour, *Tunisie: Une révolution en pays d'Islam*, at pp. 372–373.

[302] Ghazi Gherairi, "La Constitution de la IIe République: Clartés et ombres," *Leaders* (February 6, 2014), www.leaders.com.tn/article/13304-la-constitution-de-la-iie-republique-clartes-et-ombres

[303] Ibid. This seems to confirm the findings of recent studies on comparative constitution-making, according to which "the process that generates legal language is typically more important than the text itself" (Eisenstadt, LeVan, and Maboudi, *Constituents before Assembly*, at p. 143).

[304] See Democracy Reporting International, *La mise en œuvre de la Constitution tunisienne du 27 janvier 2014 au niveau du cadre juridique. Bilan* (September 2022), https://democracyreporting.s3.eu-central-1.amazonaws.com/images/63761f99ace6d.pdf. See also the Conclusions: Constitutional Dissonances, Sections C.2 and C.3.

2

Systems of Government and Distribution of Powers

More Concentration than Separation

2.1 THE CONCENTRATION OF AUTHORITY AT THE HORIZONTAL LEVEL

"Our problem in this country is an over-concentration of authority in the hands of the executive. We need a new constitution, with an effective parliament and an independent judiciary."[1] Thus spoke a demonstrator to an Al-Jazeera journalist in January 2011 in Tahrir Square, Cairo, during the revolution that led to the fall of Hosni Mubarak. What this Egyptian protestor said was certainly not an isolated case during the Arab Spring. Indeed, demonstrators in a number of Arab countries called for far-reaching political and institutional reforms, including both constraints on the prerogatives of heads of state (in both monarchies and republics) and the strengthening of the independence and powers of parliaments, judiciaries, and constitutional courts. In particular, protestors hoped to achieve a change in the system of government (e.g., from an "executive" monarchy to a "parliamentary" monarchy, or from a "hyper-presidential" regime to a "semi-presidential" system), and more generally to reinforce the separation and balance of powers and the system of checks and balances. However, despite these calls, Arab countries continue to be characterized by a very high – or rather excessive – concentration of authority in the hands of the head of state (and sometimes also of the military). Thus, the organization of state powers is one of the fields in which continuity with the past is more evident. In the words of Nathalie Bernard-Maugiron:

> The principle of separation of powers is devoid of substance and the head of state remains the keystone of the regime. He is the driving force and executor of the country's national and international policy, and no institution is able to constrain him or to challenge his way of managing power. Parliament shows great deference to the head of state and is often only a registration chamber for his decisions, while the government is an instrument for implementing his policy.[2]

1 Cited in Nathan J. Brown, "Constitutional Reform in the Arab Spring: A New Beginning or an Unhappy Ending?" in Noah Feldman and Nathan J. Brown (eds.), *Two Lectures on the Arab Spring* (Yale Law School – Occasional Papers 2013), 34.

2 Nathalie Bernard-Maugiron, *Droit contemporain des pays arabes* (Sirey 2023), 793–794.

In the following sections (Sections 2.1.1–2.1.6), I focus on the cases of Morocco, Jordan, Syria, Egypt, Algeria, and Libya. Tunisia is treated separately as it is a special case in the context of the Arab world, having alternated between a period (2014–2021) characterized by a democratic semi-presidential system and a period (2021–present) marked by an autocratic hyper-presidential regime.

2.1.1 *Morocco: The King Reigns and Governs*

In Morocco, during the demonstrations that took place in early 2011, protestors, including the members of the 20th February Movement, did not call into question King Mohammed VI. Several factors can explain the high degree of popularity and legitimacy enjoyed by the monarch.[3] First, the king, as a member of the Alaouite dynasty, claims direct descent from the Prophet Mohammed. Second, in contrast to other countries such as Tunisia, Egypt, or Libya, Morocco had embarked upon an important process of democratic reform in 1999, when Mohammed VI came to the throne. Third, the idea that, without the king and his "unifying role," the country would be ungovernable was very strongly rooted throughout the population.[4]

What the demonstrators in early 2011 wanted to achieve was a major change in the form of government. More specifically, they called for a shift from an *executive* monarchy (where the monarch "reigns and governs") to a *parliamentary* monarchy based, for example, on the Spanish or British model, where the king "reigns but does not govern."[5] During the constitution-making process, even some political parties expressed the desire that the prerogatives of the sovereign should be partially reduced. For example, the moderate Islamist force Justice and Development Party (PJD) called for the establishment of a High Council of State, to be charged with making key decisions regarding the country (including the power to declare war and a state of emergency, as well as to appoint senior officials in the state apparatus). The Socialist Union of Popular Forces asked that the Prime Minister be vested with the power to countersign the royal decrees (*zaha'ir*) concerning national defense,

3 According to a survey conducted in 2009 by the Moroccan newspapers *TelQuel* and *Nichane* and by the French newspaper *Le Monde*, 91 percent of Moroccans considered "positive" or "very positive" the first ten years of Mohammed VI's reign. See Ahmed Benchemsi, "Mohammed VI, despote malgré lui" (2013) 145 *Pouvoirs*, 25–26.

4 See Francesco Biagi, "The Pilot of *Limited* Change: Mohammed VI and the Transition in Morocco" in Justin O. Frosini and Francesco Biagi (eds.), *Political and Constitutional Transitions in North Africa: Actors and Factors* (Routledge 2015), 55.

5 Ibid., at pp. 63–67. According to Antonio Torres del Moral, *Estado de Derecho y democracia de partidos* (Editorial Universitas 2012), 341, a monarch who "reigns but does not govern" is he who exercises "a magistracy of authority and influence, a balancing, symbolic and integrating magistracy, a magistracy that enjoys the trust of the people. Hence its optimal position to encourage, warn, stimulate, suggest, advise, lubricate the functioning of the State machine and permeabilize all institutions, so that it can influence politics without taking an active part in it and always being above the parties in contention, whether they are political parties or state bodies."

internal security, and domestic affairs. Remarkably, the Authenticity and Modernity Party (PAM), considered by Moroccans as the party of the king, even proposed abolishing the "sacredness" of the person of the king – a proposal that was incorporated into the final text of the new constitution.[6] Furthermore, the vast majority of political forces called for the strengthening of the position and prerogatives of the Prime Minister. Thus, for example, according to several parties, including the PJD, the Socialist Union of Popular Forces, and the Independence Party (*Istiqlal*, the oldest political party in the country), the Prime Minister should be responsible for the appointment of senior officials within public institutions and companies, regional governments, and the public administration. The leftist Vanguard Party asked that the government no longer be accountable to the king and Parliament, but exclusively to Parliament.[7] Most political parties also agreed that the powers of Parliament should be reinforced, with respect to both the drafting of laws and the oversight of the executive branch. For example, the Authenticity and Modernity Party called for rules making it easier to table a motion of no confidence against the government. Among the most radical proposals, it is important to mention the Vanguard Party's call for the abolition of the upper chamber, namely the Chamber of Counsellors (*majlis al-mustasharin*), which had long been the object of harsh criticism due to its excessive powers.[8]

Most of these requests – which largely adopted the same tone as the constituent speech delivered by Mohammed VI on March 9, 2011, when the sovereign announced his intention to adopt a new constitution – were in fact accepted by the Commission on Constitutional Reform, which was responsible for drafting the new constitutional text. First, the new constitution considerably reinforced the prerogatives of the government. Indeed, while under the 1996 constitution the king was the effective holder of executive power (and the government often limited its action to the mere execution of the king's wishes), under the new constitution this power is shared between the sovereign and the government – more specifically, the Head of Government (*ra'is al-hukuma*) (which replaced the title of Prime Minister). Thus, the 2011 constitution created a sort of "executive dualism," even though (as discussed later) the king largely prevails over the Head of Government.

One of the major innovations refers to the appointment of the Head of Government. In fact, while under the previous Moroccan constitutions the Prime Minister was appointed at the discretion of the king, the 2011 constitution stipulates that the sovereign appoints the Head of Government from the party that received the most votes in the elections of the members of the House of Representatives (*majlis al-nuwwab*), "having regard to their results" (Article 47). This practice was introduced by King

[6] See Abdellah Tourabi, "Constitutional Reform in Morocco: Reform in Times of Revolution," *Arab Reform Initiative* (November 2011), 5–6, www.arab-reform.net/en/node/526

[7] Ibid., at pp. 6–7

[8] Ibid., at pp. 7–8.

Hassan II at the end of his reign and was followed on two occasions (following the 1997 and 2007 elections), although since it had no constitutional status it could be disregarded at any time, as occurred following the 2002 elections.[9] This new provision was immediately applied following the parliamentary elections in November 2011, when Mohammed VI appointed as Head of Government Abdelilah Benkirane, the leader of the PJD, the Islamist party that won the elections.

The 2011 constitution stipulates that members of the government are appointed by the sovereign, acting upon a proposal by the Head of Government; the latter may in turn request the king to remove one or more members of the government from office, either on his own initiative, or following their individual or collective resignation (Article 47). Moreover, the government is now no longer accountable to the king and Parliament, but exclusively to Parliament; in fact, Article 88 provides that the government takes up office after having obtained the confidence of the House of Representatives. Another significant novelty refers to the Council of Government (*majlis al-hukuma*). Indeed, while under the 1996 constitution this body, which was chaired by the Prime Minister, had no constitutional status and was limited to the function of preparing the decisions adopted by the Council of Ministers (*majlis al-uzara'*), the new constitution expressly recognizes its status and vests it with important functions. It is chaired by the Head of Government and now makes decisions in areas that previously fell under the exclusive competence of the Council of Ministers (Article 92). Furthermore, the Head of Government has been granted the power to dissolve the House of Representatives by a decree adopted in the Council of Ministers, after consultation with the sovereign, the President of the House of Representatives, and the President of the Constitutional Court (Article 104). Under the 1996 constitution, by contrast, this prerogative was vested exclusively in the king.[10]

Although the new constitution has significantly reinforced the Head of Government's powers, the king nonetheless remains the cornerstone of the system and continues to operate as the central figure in the country's most important decisions.[11] First and foremost, he still chairs the Council of Ministers, the body that resolves matters of decisive interest for the state. He also presides over the Higher Oulema Council (Article 41), and is the supreme Commander of the Royal Armed Forces (Article 53), the President of the Higher Council of the Judiciary, and also president of the new national security body, the Supreme Security Council (Article 54). Moreover, he has the power to dismiss one or more ministers after consultation with the Head of Government (Article 47), to appoint military positions (Article 53), as well as to dissolve the Houses of Parliament after consultation with the President

[9] See Francesco Biagi, "The Separation and Distribution of Powers under the New Moroccan Constitution" in Rainer Grote and Tilmann J. Röder (eds.), *Constitutionalism, Human Rights, and Islam after the Arab Spring* (Oxford University Press 2016), 502.

[10] Ibid., at pp. 502–503.

[11] See Juan José Ruiz Ruiz, "La Constitución marroquí de 2011 y el ensayo de parlamentarización de la monarquía" (2014) 164 *Revista de estudios políticos*, 33ff.

of the Constitutional Court and after informing the presidents of the two Houses of Parliament and the Head of Government (Article 96).[12]

Article 42 specifies that the king exercises his prerogatives through royal decrees (*zaha'ir*), which must be countersigned by the Head of Government. In this regard it should be pointed out that, while the *zaha'ir* that do not require countersignature by the Head of Government are now the exception, they do relate to matters of crucial importance: In addition to appointing the Head of Government (Article 47), they refer to the religious prerogatives inherent in the institution of the Commandership of the Faithful (Article 41), the appointment of the ten members of the Regency Council (Article 44), the dissolution of Parliament (Article 51), the approval of appointments of magistrates by the Higher Council of the Judiciary (Article 57), the proclamation of a state of exception (Article 59),[13] the appointment of half of the members of the Constitutional Court (Article 130), and the presentation of proposed constitutional amendments for referendum (Article 174).[14]

Following the 2011 constitutional reform, the Moroccan sovereign has undoubtedly lost much of his power in the legislative domain, but nevertheless still has some very significant prerogatives, which allow him to continue to play an influential role even in this area.[15] For example, he can request a second reading by Parliament (Article 95) and presides over the opening of the first session of Parliament, which provides him with the opportunity to provide inspiration for and guide legislative action (Article 65). Moreover (as will be discussed later), in his capacity as *Amir al-Mouminine* (Commander of the Faithful), he shares legislative power with Parliament as regards legislation pertaining to religious matters, family law, and the protection of rights and freedoms.

The king also continues to "interfere" in the fields of the judicial system and constitutional justice.[16] Indeed, judgments "are rendered and executed *in the name of the King* and by virtue of the law" (emphasis added) (Article 124), thus confirming the well-established principle according to which in Morocco (and in other Arab countries) justice is a delegated function.[17] He also approves by *zahir* the appointment of magistrates by the Higher Council of the Judiciary. This institution, which is still chaired by the sovereign, is composed of several members who are appointed by him. The king also appoints half of the members of the Constitutional Court, including the president (Article 130). Furthermore, the monarch has the right to grant pardons (Article 58).

Another extremely important innovation introduced by the 2011 constitution refers to the temporal and spiritual powers of the king, as Article 19 of the previous

12 See Biagi, "Separation and Distribution of Powers," at p. 503.
13 On the state of emergency, see Section 2.3.
14 See Biagi, "Separation and Distribution of Powers," at p. 503.
15 Ibid., at pp. 506–508.
16 Ibid., at pp. 508–510.
17 On the idea of justice as a delegated function, see Section 2.5.1.1 in greater detail.

constitutions has been "split" into two different provisions. This Article, defined within the literature as the "Supra-Constitution,"[18] for a long time represented the cornerstone of the Moroccan constitutional system and the most important source of the near-absolute powers of the sovereign, as it assigned the king both spiritual and temporal powers. It provided that:

> The King, Commander of the Faithful [*Amir al-Mouminine*], Supreme Representative of the Nation, the Symbol of the unity thereof, Guarantor of the perpetuation and continuity of the State, shall ensure respect for Islam and the Constitution. He shall be the Protector of the rights and freedoms of citizens, social groups and organizations. He shall guarantee the independence of the Nation and the territorial integrity of the Kingdom, within its authentic borders.

During the constitution-making process, only one party, the Vanguard Party, explicitly requested the elimination of this provision, claiming that "it was 'formulated vaguely' and gave unlimited powers to the King."[19] The 2011 constitution "split" this article into two provisions: Articles 41 and 42. The intention was to separate spiritual power from temporal power in order to remedy the "confusion" of powers. In particular, Article 41 sets forth the king's prerogatives in the religious sphere,[20] while Article 42 refers to the powers of the king in the secular domain.[21] From a symbolic point of view, the reform of the "old" Article 19 undoubtedly amounts to a true revolution. Indeed, for the first time in fifty years (that is, since the 1962 constitution was adopted), the most important provision of the Moroccan Constitution has been changed, thus losing its "sacredness." However, it is far from certain that this "split" will bring about any significant changes from a practical point of view. One need only consider the legislative power of the sovereign. Due to the splitting of Article 19 into two provisions, the king has lost his monopoly over legislation pertaining to religious matters, family law, and the protection of rights

[18] Anouar Boukhars, *Politics in Morocco: Executive Monarchy and Enlightened Authoritarianism* (Routledge 2011), 42.

[19] Tourabi, "Constitutional Reform," at p. 6.

[20] "The King, Amir al Mouminine [*Commander of the Faithful*], shall ensure respect for Islam. He shall be guarantor of freedom of worship. He shall preside over the Higher Oulema Council, which shall be entrusted with studying the issues submitted to it by the King. The Council shall be the only body empowered to issue officially approved religious opinions (fatwas) on the issues submitted to it, on the basis of tolerant principles, precepts and objectives of Islam […]. The King shall exercise, by royal decree, the religious prerogatives inherent in the institution of the Commandership of the Faithful; which are exclusively assigned to him under this article."

[21] "The King, Head of State, Supreme Representative, symbol of the unity of the nation, guarantor of the permanence and continuity of the State and supreme arbitrator between institutions, shall ensure compliance with the Constitution, proper functioning of constitutional institutions, protection of the nation's democratic options and of the rights and freedoms of citizens and communities, as well as compliance with the international commitments of the Kingdom. He shall be guarantor of the independence of the country and of the territorial integrity of the Kingdom, within its authentic borders […]."

and freedoms. Indeed – as is stressed by David Melloni[22] – in these areas, the monarch now shares legislative power with Parliament, which has been granted competence, *inter alia*, over family status and marital status, citizenship and the status of foreigners, as well as fundamental rights and freedoms (Article 71). However, in actual fact, Mohammed VI had consented to Parliament intervening in these fields *even in the past*: Indeed, both the new Code of Personal Status (from 2004) and the new Nationality Code (from 2006) were adopted by Parliament, despite relating to areas in which, in his capacity as *Amir al-Mouminine*, the king had always held sole competence.

Thus, while the 2011 constitution attributes significant new powers to the Head of Government and limits the sovereign's prerogatives in some areas, it does not by any measure establish a "parliamentary" monarchy (as stated in Article 1 of the constitution), in which the king's role is limited largely to the performance of ceremonial and representative functions.[23] In fact, Morocco remains an *executive* monarchy, albeit in some ways on a more limited scale compared to the past, as the monarch continues not only to reign but also to *rule*.[24] In particular, the constitution created a bicephalous executive, although the two heads are situated in very different positions. Indeed, the king is the real "ultimate leader" of the country, while the Head of Government is only a "second-in-command."[25] Furthermore, the sovereign continues to wear two hats, as he has remained both a temporal and a spiritual leader.

2.1.2 *Jordan: A "Presidential" Monarchy*

As in Morocco, in Jordan too, protestors' demands during the 2011 demonstrations "focused on changes *within the regime* rather than on regime change. All constituencies within the country strongly support[ed] the institution of the monarchy"[26] (emphasis added). Among the reasons explaining the popularity of King Abdullah II, one should recall the fact that the Hashemite House of Jordan (as the Alaouite Crown of Morocco) claims direct descent from the Prophet Mohammed, and that the monarchy serves as a "security blanket for all Jordanians regardless of their origins, providing protection for the country's various ethnic groups."[27]

22 David Melloni, "Le nouvel ordre constitutionnel marocain: de la 'monarchie gouvernante' à la 'monarchie parlementaire'?" in Centre d'Études Internationales (ed.), *La Constitution marocaine de 2011: Analyses et commentaires* (L.G.D.J. 2012), 40.

23 See Omar Bendourou, "La nouvelle Constitution marocaine du 29 juillet 2011" (2012) 91 *Revue française de droit constitutionnel*, 517ff. and 533ff.

24 The Moroccan regime was defined by Hassan II as a "*monarchie gouvernante*," and by Mohammed VI as a "*monarchie agissante*." See David Melloni, "La Constitution marocaine de 2011: une mutation des ordres politique et juridique marocains" (2013) 145 *Pouvoirs*, 6.

25 Biagi, "Separation and Distribution of Powers," at p. 505.

26 Marina Ottaway and Marwan Muasher, "Arab Monarchies. Chance for Reform, Yet Unmet," *The Carnegie Papers* (December 2011), 9, https://carnegieendowment.org/files/arab_monarchies1.pdf

27 Ibid.

The 2011 demonstrators demanded, *inter alia*, the removal of the Prime Minister, reform of the electoral system, the strengthening of representative institutions (e.g., the election of the Prime Minister by the House of Representatives (*majlis al-nuwwab*), and the popular election of the Senate [*majlis al-a'yan*]), with some of them (in particular the Islamists) calling for a transition to a parliamentary monarchy.[28] In the light of the weak and unrepresentative party system in the country, the contribution of political forces to the constitutional reform process was almost nonexistent.[29]

The 2011 reform of the 1952 constitution introduced a limited number of changes with respect to the system of government. These included a limitation on the government's power to issue temporary laws when Parliament has been dissolved, the establishment of a constitutional court for the first time in the country's history, the partial reinforcement of the independence of the judiciary, as well as various changes concerning the organization and oversight of electoral processes. As far as elections are concerned, the king lost the power to postpone elections indefinitely, an independent Electoral Commission replaced the Ministry of the Interior in organizing elections (Article 67(2)), and the judiciary replaced the House of Representatives in determining the validity of the elections of its members (Article 71).[30]

However, the 2011 reform did not affect the prerogatives of the king, who continues to hold near absolute powers and to be "immune from all liability and responsibility" (Article 30). The provisions of Chapter 3 of the constitution – on the general features of the branches of government – confirm this concentration of powers in the monarch's hands. Article 25 stipulates that "Legislative Power shall be vested in the Parliament *and the King* [...]"; Article 26 states that "Executive Power shall be vested *in the King*, and he shall exercise it through his Ministers in accordance with the provisions of this Constitution"; Article 27 declares that "The Judicial Power shall be independent and shall be exercised by courts of different types and levels. All judgments shall be issued in accordance with the law *in the name of the King*" (all emphasis has been added).[31]

[28] See Sean L. Yom, "Jordan in the Balance: Evaluating Regime Stability" (January 2013) 6 *CTC Sentinel*, https://ctc.westpoint.edu/jordan-in-the-balance-evaluating-regime-stability/; Francesco Biagi, "Will Surviving Constitutionalism in Morocco and Jordan Work in the Long Run? A Comparison with Three Past Authoritarian Regimes" (2014) 3 *Cambridge Journal of International and Comparative Law*, 1249. More generally, on the 2011 uprisings in Jordan, see Curtis R. Ryan, *Jordan and the Arab Uprisings: Regime Survival and Politics Beyond the State* (Columbia University Press 2018).

[29] See Chapter 1, Section 1.2.4.

[30] On these constitutional reforms, see Mohammad Hammouri, "Constitutional Reform and the Rise of Constitutional Adjudication in Jordan. Background, Issues, and Controversies" in Grote and Röder (eds.) 2016, *Constitutionalism, Human Rights, and Islam*, at p. 723ff.; Ibrahim Aljazy and Laith Nasrawi, "Positive Trends in Jordan: Constitutional Amendments of 2011" (2010–2011) 16 *Yearbook of Islamic and Middle Eastern Law*, 117ff.; Mohammed Torki Bani Salameh and Azzam Ali Ananzah, "Constitutional Reforms in Jordan: A Critical Analysis" (2015) 24 *Digest of Middle East Studies*, 139ff.

[31] On the idea of justice as a delegated function, see also Section 2.5.1.1.

Furthermore, it is emblematic that Chapter 4, Section I of the constitution – devoted to "The King and His Prerogatives" – was not altered by the 2011 constitutional reform. This means that the monarch retains the power to appoint and dismiss the Prime Minister and ministers at his absolute discretion (Article 35). One need only consider that King Abdullah II appointed seven different prime ministers between 2011 and 2020. Moreover, the sovereign ratifies and promulgates laws and orders the issue of any regulations necessary for their implementation (Article 31). The monarch appoints all members of the Senate (Article 36), and may dissolve both Houses of Parliament (Article 34). He is the Supreme Commander of the Armed Forces (Article 32), declares war, makes peace, and concludes treaties and agreements (Article 33(1)). He has the right to grant special pardons and to remit sentences (Article 38), as well as to confirm death sentences (Article 39). Furthermore, the king appoints and dismisses judges of the civil and *sharia* courts (Article 98), may declare a state of emergency or martial law (Articles 124 and 125),[32] and ratifies constitutional amendments (Article 126).

The 1952 constitution was also reformed in 2014, 2016, and 2022. All of these amendments further strengthened the king's prerogatives, including in particular his powers of appointment. The 2014 and 2016 amendments stated that (in contrast to the past) the appointments of the Crown Prince, the Vice-Regent, the Speaker and members of the Senate, the president of the Judicial Council, the president and members of the Constitutional Court, the Commander in Chief of the Army, the Director of Intelligence, and the Director of the Gendarmerie did not need to be countersigned by the Prime Minister or the minister or ministers concerned. The 2022 amendments not only confirmed these prerogatives but also granted constitutional status to other appointment powers that the king *de facto* already enjoyed. Indeed, the "new" Article 40 vests the king with authority to appoint and dismiss the Chief Justice, the head of the *Sharia* Judicial Council, the Grand Mufti, the Chief of the Royal Court, the Minister of the Royal Court, and the king's advisors without any requirement for countersignature.

The 2022 reform also provides for a National Security Council (*al-majlis al-amn al-qawmi*), which is composed of the Prime Minister, the ministers of Defense, Foreign Affairs, and the Interior, the Chief of Army, the Director of Intelligence, the Director of Public Security, and two members appointed by the king. The Council, which is responsible for security, defense, and foreign policy, convenes at the king's invitation, and its decisions are enforceable upon approval by the monarch (Article 122). This amendment provoked much criticism, as it was perceived as "a direct infraction on the executive and legislative branches."[33] These concerns were confirmed by the fact that the "council's regulations passed in April 2022 stipulate that

[32] On the declaration of the state of emergency and martial law, see Section 2.3.

[33] Tareq Al Naimat, "Constitutional Amendments in Jordan," *Carnegie Endowment for International Peace* (March 1, 2022), https://carnegieendowment.org/sada/86538

its meetings and deliberations are to be kept secret, while there is no mention of any role for the legislative branch in the council."[34]

Thus, one can hardly disagree with those commentators in the literature who argue that, especially following the latest reform packages, the Jordanian regime should be described as a "presidential" monarchy.[35] The only element, at least for the time being, that might move the country closer to a parliamentary monarchy is linked to the new electoral law adopted in April 2022. This law provides for some important innovations that are aimed at strengthening parliamentary representation not only of women and young persons but also of political parties. More specifically, the new law states, *inter alia*, that in the next elections, 41 out of 138 parliamentary seats will be allocated to political parties, and that the number of seats reserved to parties will gradually increase over the next few election cycles, eventually reaching 65 percent.[36] This change

> is expected to reduce the number of independent (that is, non-party affiliated) members of parliament, who currently dominate the lower house and often are conservatives, such as tribal notables and businesspersons who generally align with government positions. The idea is that, eventually, parliament should be filled with nothing but lawmakers from political parties – and in turn, those parties would gain the long-awaited power to form a government, to select a prime minister, and to undertake all the other desiderata of parliamentary democracy.[37]

Although this would undoubtedly be an important step, especially if one considers that the last (and only) time that the Jordanian Parliament selected the Prime Minister (Suleiman Nabulsi, who then formed his Cabinet) was in 1956, it is evident that the transition to a parliamentary monarchy would require much more than that.

2.1.3 *Syria: A Hyper-Presidential Regime*

Despite some relevant innovations – such as the replacement of the provision stating that the Ba'ath Party was "the leading party in the state and society" ("old" Article 8 of the 1973 constitution) with a new provision proclaiming the principle of "political pluralism" ("new" Article 8(1))[38] – the 2012 Syrian Constitution maintained the

34 Karim Merhej, "Latest Political Reforms in Jordan: Systemic Changes on the Horizon?," *The Tahrir Institute for Middle East Policy* (May 25, 2022), https://timep.org/commentary/analysis/latest-political-reforms-in-jordan-systemic-changes-on-the-horizon/

35 See Hammouri, "Constitutional Reform," at p. 735; Sufian Obeidat, "Jordan's 2016 Constitutional Amendments: A Return to Absolute Monarchy?," *ConstitutionNet* (May 27, 2016), www.constitutionnet.org/news/jordans-2016-constitutional-amendments-return-absolute-monarchy; Sufian Obeidat, "Modernizing Jordan's Political System: The Unspoken Motivations," *ConstitutionNet* (July 29, 2021), https://constitutionnet.org/news/modernizing-jordans-political-system-unspoken-motivations

36 See Merhej, "Latest Political Reforms."

37 Sean Yom and Wael Al-Khatib, "Democratic Reform in Jordan. Breaking the Impasse," *Project on Middle East Democracy – POMED* (February 2022), 7, https://pomed.org/wp-content/uploads/2022/02/Yom_Khatib_Final-1.pdf

38 The elimination of the "old" Article 8 was the main demand of opposition forces.

hyper-presidential regime provided for in the previous 1973 constitution. Indeed, the new constitutional text continues to vest the president with near absolute powers, to the point that it has been defined as "Assad's magic wand."[39]

The 2012 constitution states that the president is directly elected by the people (Article 86), whereas under the previous 1973 constitution the president was elected by means of a referendum on the sole candidate proposed by the People's Assembly upon the recommendation of the leadership of the Ba'ath Party ("old" Article 84). However, the potential of this (theoretically positive) innovation is significantly reduced by the fact that the requirements that must be met in order to be eligible for the presidency clearly favor the incumbent president, namely Bashar al-Assad. Indeed, the candidate must, *inter alia*, enjoy civil and political rights and must have not been convicted for a dishonorable felony. Furthermore, he must have been a resident in the country for no less than ten years continuously prior to nomination (Article 84). Not surprisingly, almost all former political prisoners fail to meet these conditions.[40] In addition, the candidate must have the support of at least thirty-five members of the People's Assembly (*majlis al-sha'b*) (Article 85(3)). However, in the light of the Ba'ath's political hegemony over Parliament, "it would not be possible for any candidate except Assad to collect the required 35 signatures from members of parliament, unless the president himself directs his followers to approve other candidacies."[41] All these rules explain why, out of twenty-four candidates who tried to register for the 2014 presidential elections, only three were allowed to do so by the Supreme Constitutional Court: Assad himself, and two unknown pro-government politicians.[42] Something similar happened also during the 2021 presidential election, when the Court permitted only Assad and two other candidates to stand for election.[43]

The president, who has been described as a "true republican monarch,"[44] is the master of the political and institutional system.[45] He is solely responsible for appointing the Prime Minister, his deputies, ministers, and their deputies, accepting their resignations, and dismissing them from office (Article 97). He lays down the general policy of the state and oversees its implementation (Article 98), and

[39] Qais Fares, "The Syrian Constitution: Assad's Magic Wand," *Malcolm H. Kerr Carnegie Middle East Center* (May 8, 2014), https://carnegie-mec.org/diwan/55541

[40] Ibid.

[41] Ibid.

[42] Ibid.

[43] Nigel Walker, "Syria: 2021 Presidential Election and Future Prospects," *House of Commons Library* (June 9, 2021), 4, https://researchbriefings.files.parliament.uk/documents/CBP-9250/CBP-9250.pdf

[44] Karim Atassi, *Syria, the Strength of an Idea: The Constitutional Architectures of Its Political Regimes* (Cambridge University Press 2018), 407.

[45] See Ibrahim Daraji, "Syria: The Constitution of the 'Crisis' or the Crisis of the Constitution?", *Journal of Constitutional Law in the Middle East and North Africa*, special issue on "Arab Constitutional Responses to the Revolutions and Transformations in the Region" edited by Rim Turkmani and Tamara El Khoury (December 2023), 121ff., www.jcl-mena.org

guarantees respect for the constitution, the regular functioning of public authorities, the protection of national unity, and the survival of the state (Article 96). He cannot be re-elected more than once, but his term of office is very long, that is, seven years (Article 88). Furthermore, the president assumes legislative powers "when the People's Assembly is not in session, or during sessions if absolute necessity requires this, or in the period during which the Assembly is dissolved" (Article 113(1)). The Assembly can revoke or amend this legislation only "by a majority of two thirds of the members registered for attending the session, provided that it constitutes no less than an absolute majority of all its members. Any such amendment or revocation shall not have retroactive effect." Should the People's Assembly fail to make such an amendment or revocation, the legislation in question "shall be considered approved" (Article 113(3)). The (extremely problematic) practice of presidential legislative decrees is well-consolidated in the history of Syria: "Under Hafez Assad almost 50 per cent of legislation was adopted by presidential legislative decrees and almost 50 per cent by acts passed by parliament. The percentage increased in favour of legislative decrees under Bashar Assad."[46]

Another provision that, due to its flexible language, gives the president significant scope for misusing his powers is Article 114, according to which "if a grave danger or a situation threatening national unity and the safety and integrity of the territories comprising the homeland should arise or prevent state institutions from fulfilling their constitutional responsibilities, the president of the Republic may take any urgent measures required by these circumstances in order to confront that danger." Moreover, the president is the Commander in Chief of the armed forces (Article 105), appoints civilian and military employees (Article 106), and "interferes" in the domains of the judicial system and constitutional justice. Thus, for example, he presides over the Supreme Judicial Council (Article 133) and appoints all justices of the Supreme Constitutional Court (Article 141).

2.1.4 *Egypt: The Supremacy of the President and the Armed Forces*

Following the January 25 Revolution, Egypt has adopted not just one but two constitutions: one in December 2012 and the other in January 2014. The 2012 constitution-drafting process was heavily influenced by the political and constitutional events that took place after the 2011 uprisings. In the first place, there was a general consensus among all political parties represented in the Constituent Assembly – both Islamists and liberals – concerning the need "to limit the presidency's powers in order to avoid the emergence of a new 'pharaoh.'"[47] It must also be recalled that the 2012

[46] Atassi, *Syria*, at p. 403.

[47] Zaid Al-Ali, "The New Egyptian Constitution: An Initial Assessment of Its Merits and Flaws," *Open Democracy* (December 26, 2012), www.opendemocracy.net/en/new-egyptian-constitution-initial-assessment-of-its-merits-and-flaws/

constitution relied heavily on the provisional constitution adopted by the Supreme Council of the Armed Forces (SCAF) on March 30, 2011 – a provisional constitution that in turn had absorbed the amendments made to the 1971 constitution that were approved in a referendum held on March 19, 2011.[48] The major innovations contained in the 2011 provisional constitution concerned the limitations imposed on some of the very broad prerogatives that the president had enjoyed under the previous 1971 constitution. Therefore, for the 2012 Islamist-dominated Constituent Assembly, it would have been hard to justify the exclusion of these democratic innovations, which were in fact incorporated into the new constitution. Thus, for example, a two-term limit for the president was introduced (Article 133), and the president's power to declare and extend a state of emergency was restricted (Article 148). Furthermore, the government was granted significant powers under Article 141, according to which the president exercised his "authority through the Prime Minister, his deputies and ministers," except for some areas, such as defense, national security, and foreign policy. The importance of this provision "only became apparent in March 2013 when the administrative court cancelled the president's signature of a decree, on the basis that the prime minister should have signed it."[49] Nevertheless, it must be recalled that the president continued to enjoy significant prerogatives. For example, he had the power to appoint one-tenth of the members of the *Shura* Council (the upper House of Parliament) (Article 128),[50] and was also responsible for appointing the heads of independent bodies and regulatory agencies (including the Anti-Corruption Commission, the Audit Commission, and the Central Bank) upon the approval of the *Shura* Council (Article 202). The Islamists in the Constituent Assembly also decided to expand the position and functions of Parliament, which they thought they would continue to dominate in future. This body was thus granted an important role in the formation of governments, could only be dissolved through a popular referendum, and was vested with considerable oversight powers.[51]

One institution that managed to preserve its privileged status under the 2012 constitution was the army, which has long been one of the main actors in the country's life. Indeed, "by laying low in the constitution-making process, the military got all it could reasonably have expected from a civilian-drafted document."[52] Remarkably, civilians

48 See Nathan J. Brown and Michele Dunne, "Egypt's Draft Constitutional Amendments Answer Some Questions and Raise Others," *Carnegie Endowment for International Peace* (March 1, 2011), https://carnegieendowment.org/2011/03/01/egypt-s-draft-constitutional-amendments-answer-some-questions-and-raise-others-pub-42817

49 Zaid Al-Ali, "Egypt's Third Constitution in Three Years: A Critical Analysis," *ConstitutionNet* (December 20, 2013), https://constitutionnet.org/news/egypts-third-constitution-three-years-critical-analysis

50 Traditionally, the presidential appointment of some members of the *Shura* Council was also a way to ensure the representation of the most vulnerable categories of people, including women and Christians.

51 See Al-Ali, "New Egyptian Constitution."

52 Tom Ginsburg, "The Real Winner in the Egyptian Constitution? The Military," *HuffPost* (December 7, 2012), www.huffpost.com/entry/egypt-draft-constitution-military_b_2259798

could still be tried by military courts for crimes that harmed the armed forces, in spite of the fact that both demonstrators during the Revolution and several members of the Constituent Assembly had identified the need to end military trials of civilians as a priority. However, the grip of the armed forces on the state intensified throughout 2011 and 2012, and this was then reflected in the final text of the constitution.[53]

The radically different political context following Mohammed Morsi's removal from power on July 3, 2013, had enormous consequences for the process that led to the adoption of the 2014 constitution. Now the key word uniting all the political and social forces represented in the Constituent Assembly was "Debrotherhoodization." The Muslim Brotherhood was in fact completely excluded from the drafting process, and the framers decided to weaken the role of Parliament (which turned into a unicameral body),[54] and to re-establish a hyper-presidential system, "under the assumption that the Brotherhood ha[d] little chance of winning the presidency any time soon."[55] The need to promote stability was the main argument made by the drafters to justify their decision to strengthen the prerogatives of the president,[56] an argument that is often heard in nondemocratic contexts.

The 2014 constitution "sw[ang] the pendulum back in favor of the president, although not to the 1971 constitution's extent."[57] In the first place, it should be stressed that the president appoints the Prime Minister at his discretion. It is only if the government does not obtain the confidence of a majority of the members of the House of Representatives (*majlis al-nuwwab*) that the president must appoint a Prime Minister on the basis of "the nomination of the party or the coalition that holds a plurality of seats in the House of Representatives" (Article 146(1)). The previous 2012 constitution stipulated that, if this government too did not secure the confidence of Parliament, then Parliament would elect a Prime Minister on its own, without any involvement by the president of the Republic (Article 139). By contrast, the 2014 constitution no longer contemplates this possibility. Indeed, if this government fails to obtain the confidence of Parliament within thirty days, it will be dissolved, and the president of the Republic will call for fresh elections (Article 146(1)). It has rightly been stressed that the risk of a dissolution of Parliament will push the latter to accept the candidate proposed by the president.[58]

Furthermore, in the event that the government is chosen from the party or coalition that holds a plurality of seats in the House of Representatives, the president

53 See Al-Ali, "New Egyptian Constitution."

54 As will be shown later, a bicameral Parliament was re-established with the 2019 constitutional reform.

55 Al-Ali, "Egypt's Third Constitution."

56 See Diana Serôdio, "Shaping Egypt's 2014 Constitution: Controversy and Negotiations" in Cornelis Hulsman (ed.), *The 2014 Egyptian Constitution: Perspectives from Egypt* (Tectum Verlag 2017), 66–67.

57 Al-Ali, "Egypt's Third Constitution." On the dominance of the president, see also Nathalie Bernard-Maugiron, "La constitution égyptienne de 2014: quelle réforme constitutionnelle pour l'Égypte?" (2015) 103 *Revue française de droit constitutionnel*, 529ff.

58 See Bernard-Maugiron, *Droit contemporain des pays arabes*, at p. 701.

has the power, in consultation with the Prime Minister, to choose the Ministers of Justice, the Interior, and Defense (Article 146(4)) – a prerogative that recalls the appointment of the so-called "ministers of sovereignty" (*wazarat siyadiah*).[59] Moreover, the president, who is the Head of State and head of the executive branch (Article 139), sets the general policy of the state (Article 150), may declare a state of emergency (Article 154),[60] represents the state in foreign relations, and concludes treaties and ratifies them after receiving approval from the House of Representatives (Article 151). He is the Supreme Commander of the Armed Forces (Article 152). The president also continues to exercise a strong influence in the legislative domain. In fact, if the House of Representatives has not yet been constituted, he may issue decrees that have the force of law (Article 156).[61] Moreover, he has the power to appoint 5 percent of the members of the House of Representatives (Article 102(4)). The president may also call referendums concerning issues relating to the supreme interests of the country (Article 157), thus "opening the possibility for a 'plebiscitary presidency' if ever the President encountered serious resistance from the House of Representatives."[62]

The president, however, was not the only beneficiary of the 2014 constitution. Indeed, at least two other institutions were granted a prominent role in the new constitutional text, namely the Supreme Constitutional Court and the army. The Court, in particular, was regranted full authority to interpret *sharia*, after the limitations to this role that had been introduced by the 2012 constitution.[63] The army continues to enjoy "extraordinary protections under the new constitution, cementing in law the powers and privileges that it already enjoys *de facto*, which are often described as a state in the state".[64] Indeed, the constitution, in its preamble, defines the army as a "pillar" of the modern Egyptian State and recalls how it had been decisive for the victory of the 2011 Revolution and had upheld the will of the people. Furthermore, it states that the National Defense Council "is responsible for attending to matters pertaining to the arrangements for ensuring the safety and security of the country" (Article 203(2)). This ambiguous expression may result in military interference in various areas of internal politics. This Council is also responsible for

59 On the "ministers of sovereignty," see in greater detail Section 2.5.1.2.

60 On the declaration of the state of emergency, see Section 2.3.

61 Article 156 specifies that when the new House of Representatives convenes, "if such decrees are not presented to the House and discussed, or if they are presented but not approved, their legality is revoked retroactively, without the need to issue a decision to that effect [...]."

62 Michael Meyer-Resende, "Egypt: In-depth Analysis of the Main Elements of the New Constitution," *Directorate-general for the External Policies of the European Union – Policy Department* (2014), 9, www.europarl.europa.eu/RegData/etudes/note/join/2014/433846/EXPO-AFET_NT(2014)433846_EN.pdf. On the use and abuse of referendums in Egyptian history, see Gianluca Paolo Parolin, "Il referendum in Egitto tra rivoluzione e riconfigurazione" (2014) 4 *Diritto pubblico comparato ed europeo*, 1801ff.

63 See Chapter 4, Section 4.2.2.

64 Meyer-Resende, "Egypt," at p. 10.

"discussing the budget of the Armed Forces, which is incorporated as a single figure into the state budget" (Article 203(2)). Moreover, the appointment of the Minister of Defense (who must be a military officer (Article 201)) must be approved by the Supreme Council of the Armed Forces for the first two presidential terms (Article 234).[65] Furthermore, despite strong opposition on the part of some members of the Constituent Assembly (in particular the younger ones), military courts continued to have broad jurisdiction over civilians.[66]

The 2019 amendments consolidated yet further the supremacy of the presidency and the armed forces in the country, to the detriment of the legislative and judicial branches. Despite the fact that Article 226(5) prohibits "under any circumstance" the amendment of those constitutional provisions that concern the re-election of the president of the Republic "unless the amendment brings more guarantees," the duration of the presidential term was extended from four to six years (Article 140), and a new provision was added (Article 241-bis), according to which this extension of the presidential term also applies to the *current* term, and that the *current* president has the right to be re-elected one more time. Specifically, this means that President Abdel Fattah Al-Sisi, who was re-elected for his second term in 2018, is allowed to remain in office until 2024, and will have the right to serve for an additional third term, which will end in 2030. Thus, Al-Sisi will be able to remain in power for "16 years in total or double the length of time he was constitutionally allowed when he took office in 2014."[67]

Furthermore, the 2019 amendments expanded the president's prerogatives with respect to the judicial and legislative branches of government. Indeed, the president is now vested with the power to appoint the head judges of the top judicial bodies, whereas in the past these positions were filled on seniority grounds, with judges managing their own affairs in terms of judicial appointments. The new Article 185 stipulates that the president appoints the head judges choosing from among the seven most senior judges in each judicial body, for a period of four years or until they reach the retirement age. It must be noted that presidential discretion in the appointment of senior judicial figures had already been provided for by Law no. 13 of 2017, the constitutionality of which was then challenged before the Supreme Constitutional Court. By granting constitutional status to this presidential discretion, the Court was prevented from ruling on its legitimacy.[68] The president was also granted a key role

65 As will be shown later, this temporal requirement was abandoned with the 2019 constitutional reform.

66 See Bassem Sabry, "Problems Ahead for Egypt Constitution Debate," *Al Monitor* (September 30, 2013), www.al-monitor.com/pulse/ar/originals/2013/09/egypt-constitution-highlights-new-draft.html; Serôdio, "Shaping Egypt's 2014 Constitution," at pp. 70–72.

67 Timothy Kaldas, "Taking Dictatorship from De Facto to De Jure: Egypt's Constitutional Amendments," *ConstitutionNet* (May 1, 2019), http://constitutionnet.org/news/taking-dictatorship-de-facto-de-jure-egypts-constitutional-amendments

68 See Gianluca Paolo Parolin, "Drifting Power Relations in the Egyptian Constitution: The 2019 Amendments" (2020) 3 *DPCE online*, 3181.

in the appointment of the General Public Prosecutor (Article 189) and the president of the Supreme Constitutional Court (Article 193), not to mention the fact that he chairs and appoints most of the members of a newly introduced Supreme Council of Judicial Bodies, which has jurisdiction over the conditions of appointment, promotions, and disciplinary action against members of the judiciary (Article 185). Furthermore, the prerogatives of the Council of State – historically, one of the most activist judicial bodies in the country – have been reduced (Article 190).

The establishment of the office of the Vice President might represent a threat to the president's rule. In actual fact, however, the reform partially waters down this innovation, as the president is not *required* to appoint a Vice President. Indeed, Article 150-bis only allows the president, should he decide to do so, "to appoint one or more Vice-Presidents, determine their competencies, delegate some of his duties to them, relieve them of their positions, and accept their resignation." An additional safeguard for the president's rule is offered by Article 160, which stipulates that, in the event of any temporary impediment, the president is replaced by the Vice President or the Prime Minister, but "the interim President or whoever temporarily assumes the presidency may not request any amendment to the constitution, dissolve the House of Representatives, dismiss the Government or stand as a candidate for President."[69]

The 2019 amendments also reintroduced the bicameral system. Indeed, in addition to the House of Representatives, the constitution provides for an upper house – the Senate (*majlis al-shuyukh*) – whose consultative prerogatives recall those exercised by the Consultative Council (*majlis al-Shura*) between 1980 (when it was provided for by the 1980 amendments to the 1971 constitution) and 2007 (when a new constitutional reform vested the Council with a more prescriptive role).[70] Two-thirds of the Senate's members are elected, whereas one-third are directly appointed by the president (Article 250). The first elections to this body were held in August–September 2020, with an extremely low turnout: approximately 14 percent in the first round and 10 percent in the second round. Not surprisingly, the vast majority of the seats went to the Nation's Future Party, which is closely connected to President Al-Sisi. Therefore, it is extremely likely that Parliament will continue to serve as a mere "rubberstamp"[71] for executive action.

The role of the army has been strengthened yet further, in both symbolic and practical terms. First, Article 200 stipulates that the armed forces are responsible for protecting "the Constitution, democracy, the fundamental constituents of the state, its civilian nature, as well as the people's achievements, rights and freedoms." Second, Article 204 further expands the jurisdiction of military courts over civilians so as to include those civilians who commit an "assault" against the military, rather

69 Ibid., at pp. 3183–3184.
70 Ibid., at pp. 3179–3181.
71 Kaldas, "Taking Dictatorship."

than only a "*direct* assault" as was the case under the original version of the 2014 constitution. Third, the temporal requirement originally provided for by the 2014 constitution, according to which the appointment of the Minister of Defense must be approved by the Supreme Council of the Armed Forces *for the first two presidential terms*, has been eliminated and has thus become a permanent arrangement (Article 234). It has been rightly pointed out that these amendments "are part of Al-Sisi's longstanding effort to consolidate and extend his rule over Egypt and reward the institution upon which he depends for power, the armed forces."[72] Indeed, it is well known that (with the exception of Mohammed Morsi) all Egyptian presidents have thus far hailed from the military. The situation in Egypt (and in some other Arab countries, including Algeria, as will be shown later) demonstrates that the president needs the support of the armed forces in order to be able to govern. Thus, the role played by the army was and still is so influential that Egypt can be described as the "triumph of the military over the civil state."[73]

2.1.5 *Algeria: The President and the Army Holding the Reins of the Country*

As was the case in Morocco and Jordan, in Algeria too, demonstrators did not call for regime change during the 2011 uprisings. Indeed, despite requests for major political and institutional reforms, the protests did not coalesce "into a nationwide opposition movement seeking the overthrow of the Bouteflika regime in the manner that happened in Tunisia, Egypt, and Libya."[74] This was due to a number of factors, including the memory of the 1990s civil war, the government's ability to buy social peace with oil and gas revenues, a strong security apparatus, as well as divisions in the opposition movement. Moreover, if the opposition found it so difficult to act against the regime, this was also due to the geography of the country as well as the characteristics of its population. Indeed, mobilizing a population with a low level of "homogeneity"[75] over an extremely vast territory (Algeria being the largest country in Africa) proved to be particularly complicated.[76] It was only during the 2019 mass protest demonstrations (the *Hirak* movement) that the Algerian people demanded an

72 Ibid.

73 Tilmann J. Röder, "State Control Over the Military or Military Control Over the State? A Comparison of Selected Arab Constitutions" in Grote and Röder (eds.) 2016, *Constitutionalism, Human Rights, and Islam*, at p. 290.

74 John P. Entelis, "Algeria: The Outlier State?" in Frosini and Biagi (eds.) 2015, *Political and Constitutional Transitions*, at p. 111.

75 Algeria's population is divided into various groups, some of which have specific linguistic and/or cultural identities (e.g., the Berbers in Kabylia, the Mozabites in Ghardaïa, and the Tuareg in the southern Sahara).

76 See Frédéric Volpi, "Algeria versus the Arab Spring" (2013) 24 *Journal of Democracy*, 104–105; Mohsin Khan and Karim Mezran, "No Arab Spring in Algeria," *Atlantic Council* (May 2014), 1, www.atlanticcouncil.org/wp-content/uploads/2014/05/No_Arab_Spring_for_Algeria.pdf; Entelis, "Algeria: The Outlier State?," at p. 107ff.

end to Abdelaziz Bouteflika's twenty-year rule and the dismantling of the "system" – known as "*le Pouvoir*," consisting in the military, the president of the Republic, and the National Liberation Front (the leading political party since Algeria's independence). As will be discussed later, Bouteflika eventually resigned on April 2, 2019.[77]

During the long process that led to the adoption of the 2016 constitutional reform, representatives of the civil society called for profound changes in the form of government, demanding in particular a limitation on the powers of the president of the Republic, as well as the establishment of the office of Vice President.[78] Although they were generally more moderate, requests made by political parties demanded the strengthening of the positions and powers of the Prime Minister and Parliament. More specifically, the National Liberation Front and other parties asked that the Prime Minister be selected from the list that wins the elections, as in the cases of Morocco and Tunisia. Certain proposals were aimed at reinforcing parliamentary mechanisms for oversight over the government. The right-wing Algerian National Front specifically asked for the establishment of a parliamentary regime.[79]

On the one hand, some of these requests were included in the 2016 reform. In the first place, the two-term limit for the president (which had been removed in the 2008 constitutional reform) was reintroduced. Furthermore, the reform introduced a requirement for the president to consult with the parliamentary majority when appointing the Prime Minister (Article 91). This provision was intended to ensure that the Prime Minister was an expression of the party that won the parliamentary elections. However, had the intention been to place a brake on the Head of State's discretion in the choice of the Prime Minister, the provision should not have been limited to establishing an obligation for the president to *consult* the parliamentary majority. For example, in Morocco and Tunisia (under the 2014 constitution), the constitutions introduced the rule that the head of state must appoint the head of government from the party that wins the most seats in the parliamentary elections.[80] This type of provision is decisively clearer and more stringent than that laid down in the 2016 reform of the Algerian Constitution. This constitutional reform also partially reinforced the independence of the judiciary and widened the grounds for access to the Constitutional Council.

77 See Emily Burchfield, "What's Next for Algeria's Popular Movement?," *Atlantic Council* (April 11, 2019), www.atlanticcouncil.org/blogs/menasource/what-s-next-for-algeria-s-popular-movement; Karim Mezran and Erin A. Neale, "Algerian Demonstrations: What They Mean for the Future of the Elite and the Country," *Atlantic Council* (February 27, 2019), www.atlanticcouncil.org/blogs/menasource/algerian-demonstrations-what-they-mean-for-the-future-of-the-elite-and-the-country

78 See Wissam Benyettou, "Will Algeria Start 2016 With a New Constitution? Long-awaited Constitutional Revision and the Road to Democratic Transition," *ConstitutionNet* (November 24, 2015), http://constitutionnet.org/news/will-algeria-start-2016-new-constitution-long-awaited-constitutional-revision-and-road

79 See Bouhania Goui, "Algerian Angst: Can it Agree on Constitutional Change?," *Arab Reform Initiative* (February 2015), 6–7, www.arab-reform.net/en/node/494

80 See respectively Sections 2.1.1 and 2.2.2.

On the other hand, however, the 2016 constitutional reform did not alter the excessive concentration of power in the hands of the president, with the consequence that the principle of the separation of powers – which was explicitly provided for in the constitution (Article 15) – remained more theoretical than substantive. Indeed, the president continued to be the dominant figure within the political and institutional system, occupying a position that was undoubtedly much more powerful than that of the Prime Minister and Parliament. More specifically, he was still the undisputed leader of the executive, maintained significant powers in relation to legislative issues, and could also exert a certain influence over the judiciary.[81] It should also be noted that one of the most pressing requests, namely the creation of the position of Vice President, was not accepted. This was in part due to the refusal by Bouteflika to allow himself to be assisted by a Vice President as this would have appeared to imply his inability to manage the affairs of the country, not to speak of the fact that the person holding that office could have appeared as a president in waiting. Another reason concerned the difficulties encountered by the various factions within the Algerian establishment in reaching agreement concerning a suitable person for such an appointment.[82]

In 2019–2020, the Algerian people – and in particular the *Hirak* movement – not only demanded an end to Bouteflika's regime but also called for *radical* political and institutional changes. This break with the past did not, however, take place as the 2020 constitutional reform continues to be characterized by a very high degree of continuity with the previous constitutional text.[83] This was the main reason why one of the members of the drafting commission decided to withdraw from it,[84] and was also the main criticism leveled by the *Pacte pour l'alternative démocratique* (PAD), a platform of parties and associations linked to the *Hirak* movement. The PAD, in particular, had called for the establishment of a transitional government and the adoption of a *new constitution*, and not simply the revision of the constitutional text inherited from the Bouteflika regime.[85]

81 See in greater detail Francesco Biagi, "The Algerian Constitutional Reform of 2016: A Critical Analysis" (2017) 17 *Global Jurist*, 7–10; Xavier Philippe, "Algérie: La Constitution algérienne – Evaluation des changements après la révision de janvier 2016," *Democracy Reporting International* (June 2016), 5ff., https://democracyreporting.s3.eu-central-1.amazonaws.com/images/3435DRI-Algerie-EU-BP84-2017-06.pdf

82 See Chérif Dris, "Quatrième mandat de Bouteflika: le parachèvement de la sanctuarisation du pouvoir présidentiel" (2014) 11 *L'Année du Maghreb* (online version).

83 See Zaid Al-Ali, "Algeria's Draft Constitution 2020," *IACL-AIDC Blog* (May 14, 2020), https://blog-iacl-aidc.org/2020-posts/2020/5/14/algerias-draft-constitution-2020

84 See "Révision de la Constitution: Un membre du comité d'experts démissionne," *Algerie Eco* (April 15, 2020), www.algerie-eco.com/2020/04/15/revision-de-la-constitution-un-membre-du-comite-dexperts-demissionne/; Yasmina Allouche, "A Breakdown of Algeria's New Constitution," *Middle East Eye* (October 29, 2020), www.middleeasteye.net/news/algeria-new-constitution-breakdown

85 See "Algérie: l'avant-projet de réforme constitutionnelle laisse un goût d'inachevé," *Jeune Afrique* (May 12, 2020), www.jeuneafrique.com/943997/politique/algerie-lavant-projet-de-reforme-constitutionnelle-laisse-un-gout-dinacheve/

As is the case in Egypt and Syria, Algeria has long been characterized by a system of government that is *formally* semi-presidential but *de facto* presidential (*rectius*: hyper-presidential), with the Head of State clearly dominating the political and institutional life of the country. While it is true that under the new constitutional reform the president of the Republic still remains the *dominus* of the entire system, it must be recognized that the 2020 reform has introduced some innovations that might place some checks on the president's authority. For example, no person may serve as president of the Republic for more than two "consecutive" or "discontinuous" terms (Article 88), the safeguards against potential abuses committed by the president during states of emergency have been partially strengthened (Articles 97ff.),[86] and the Constitutional Council has been replaced by a Constitutional Court (whose powers and prerogatives have been expanded) (Articles 185ff.). However, some proposals (including the [still] much-debated creation of the position of Vice President) were not confirmed in the final version of the reform.

One of the most interesting – and at the same time ambiguous – changes refers to the role of the Prime Minister/Head of Government and his relationship with the president of the Republic. Indeed, the constitution now stipulates that the government is headed by a Prime Minister (*al-wazir al-awwil*) when the legislative elections result in a "presidential majority," whereas the government is presided over by a Head of Government (*ra'is hukuma*) when the legislative elections result in a "parliamentary majority" (Article 103). The members of the government are appointed by the president of the Republic acting on a proposal of the Prime Minister or the Head of Government (as the case may be) (Article 104). The constitution goes on to provide that, in the event of a presidential majority, the president "charges the Prime Minister with the task of proposing a government and of developing an action plan for the implementation of the presidential program" (Article 105), whereas if the parliamentary elections result in "a majority other than the presidential majority," the president appoints a "Head of Government from the parliamentary majority and charges him with the task of forming his own government and of drawing up the program of the parliamentary majority" (Article 110) – this latter situation seeming to correspond (at least in part) to French-style *cohabitation*.[87] While in the event of a presidential majority (as occurred, e.g., following the 2021 parliamentary elections) one can reasonably expect the president to prevail clearly over the Prime Minister (as occurred in the past), in the event of a parliamentary majority the relationship between the president and the Head of Government is likely to be more complicated. However, the president retains certain prerogatives

[86] See Section 2.3 in greater detail.

[87] Indeed, as is well known, in case of cohabitation, the president belongs to one political party while the Prime Minister belongs to a different party. In France, this situation occurred three times, namely in the periods 1986–1988, 1993–1995, and 1997–2002. See the articles devoted to this issue in *Pouvoirs*, no. 91, 1999.

that allow him to politically influence the behavior of the Prime Minister/Head of Government. Indeed, the president has the power to dismiss the Prime Minister/ Head of Government at any time (Article 91(5)), and he can dissolve the People's National Assembly (*al-majlis al-sha'abi al-watani*) (the lower House of Parliament) and call for fresh elections (Article 151).

Alongside the president, the other key actor in the country is the army. Although until 2016 there were only a few references to its role in the constitution (in particular, Article 25),[88] in actual fact, the military has always exerted "a strong, indisputable grip on all the country's institutions."[89] Both the 2016 and 2020 reforms gave more "constitutional visibility" to the armed forces. In particular, the 2016 reform highlighted – within the preamble to the constitution – the fundamental role performed by it in the war of independence, along with its "exemplary commitment," "heroic readiness for sacrifice," and more generally, its "essential contribution" to the defense of the country and its citizens. The state was called upon to guarantee the "professionalization and modernization" of the Armed Forces and to ensure that they are provided with the equipment and resources in order to carry out their functions in the optimum manner. The 2020 reform took a further step by stating that the army can be deployed *outside* the national territory to support international peacekeeping missions, within the framework of the principles and objectives of the United Nations, the African Union, and the League of Arab States (Articles 31 and 91(2)). These provisions – marking the end of Algeria's doctrine of military noninterference – were harshly debated as they would allow the army to perform a more proactive role in the region (e.g., in the Sahel or in Libya).[90]

As in Egypt, in Algeria too, the support of the army is essential for the president in order to govern the country. It is no coincidence that in 2019, Bouteflika decided to resign after Ahmed Gaid Salah, Chief of Staff of the People's National Army, announced that he was siding with the Algerian people, and called for Bouteflika's removal from office.[91] More specifically, in the Communiqué of the National Defense Minister of March 30, 2019, Salah argued that Articles 7, 8, and 102 of the constitution should be applied. Article 7 stipulated that "The people shall be the

[88] This article stipulated the following: "The consolidation and development of the Nation's defensive potential shall be organized around the National People's Army. The National People's Army shall assume the permanent task of preserving national independence and defending national sovereignty. It shall also assume the task of protecting the unity and the integrity of the country, as well as defending its land, airspace and the various zones of its maritime domain." These provisions can currently be found in Article 30 of the constitutional text.

[89] Madjid Benchikh, "The Grip of the Army on Algeria's Political System" in Grote and Röder (eds.) 2016, *Constitutionalism, Human Rights, and Islam*, at p. 369.

[90] See Adlène Meddi, "Algérie: Tebboune dévoile son projet de réforme constitutionnelle," *Le Point Afrique* (May 8, 2020), www.lepoint.fr/afrique/algerie-tebboune-devoile-son-projet-de-reforme-constitutionnelle-08-05-2020-2374712_3826.php#

[91] See Sharan Grewal, "Why Algeria's Army Abandoned Bouteflika," *Brookings* (April 10, 2019), www.brookings.edu/blog/order-from-chaos/2019/04/10/why-algerias-army-abandoned-bouteflika/

source of all powers," Article 8 stated that "The constituent power shall belong to the people," and Article 102 made it possible to declare that the president was unfit to perform his duties in the event "of a serious and lasting illness." The communiqué indicated that the request to apply these provisions was founded on Article 25 of the constitution, which stipulates, *inter alia*, that the army is vested with "the permanent task of [...] defending national sovereignty." In this way, the People's National Army portrayed itself as the "custodian of the constitutional order."[92] Following Bouteflika's resignation, Salah acted as the "strongman," *de facto* leader of the country, and together with Interim President Abdelkader Bensalah played a key role in the organization of the December 12, 2019, presidential elections, which were won by Abdelmadjid Tebboune. The winner was dubbed as the "chosen one" on social media for being seen to be very close to Salah.[93] The army was thus the institution that made the key decisions in the 2019–2020 transition process.

2.1.6 *Libya: The Risk of Another "Strongman"*

The trend toward a very high concentration of power in the hands of the head of state is confirmed by the latest draft constitution of Libya, which was adopted by the Constituent Assembly in July 2017. Indeed, this text "places the president firmly at the top of the state's hierarchy of power,"[94] granting him very broad prerogatives. In the first place, the president, who is directly elected by the people for a five-year term (Articles 100–101), has full discretion in the appointment of the Prime Minister (Article 104(1)), is responsible for the formation of the government (Article 104(1)), and has exclusive authority to determine the general policies of the executive (Article 104(2)). Furthermore, when the two Houses of Parliament (namely the House of Representatives [*majlis al-nuwwab*] and the Senate [*majlis al-shuyukh*]) are not in session or if the House of Representatives has been dissolved, he may issue decrees with the force of law in the event of necessity or an urgent need for action (Article 108). He has the power of legislative initiative (Article 104(6)) and may call referendums (Article 106(3)). He is also the Supreme Commander of the Armed Forces (Article 106).

The conditions applicable to presidential candidates were (and still are) a matter of debate. These conditions are now less stringent compared to previous draft constitutions. There is one condition, however, that remains particularly problematic,

92 Mouloud Boumghar, "Le gant constitutionnel réversible: accessoire de l'uniforme militaire. Regard critique sur la crise constitutionnelle algérienne de 2019" (2019) 21 *L'Année du Maghreb* (online version).

93 "Algeria's Powerful Military Chief Ahmed Gaid Salah Dies," *BBC News* (December 23, 2019), www.bbc.com/news/world-africa-50891741. Salah died on December 23, 2019, a few days after the presidential elections

94 Zaid Al-Ali, *Libya's Final Draft Constitution: A Contextual Analysis (Version 2)*, International IDEA (December 2020), 9, https://constitutionnet.org/sites/default/files/2020-12/Libya%20analysis%20-%20Zaid%20Al-Ali%20%28December%202020%29%20%28English%29.pdf

that is, the one requiring dual nationals to renounce their second nationality one year prior to the date of the election (Article 99). This might represent a serious obstacle for General Khalifa Haftar, who holds Libyan and American citizenship and "who has made little secret of his presidential aspirations."[95] Thus, it comes as no surprise that disagreement between the House of Representatives (representing Eastern Libya) and the High Council of State (representing Western Libya) concerning the eligibility requirements for candidates in the first presidential elections was one of the main reasons that prevented the UN-led initiative launched in March 2022 from reaching agreement on a consensual constitutional framework for national elections.[96]

It should be noted, however, that the aim of the constitutional drafters "was not to restore a fully presidential system," as they were aware "of the risks that such a model could pave the way for a return of an authoritarian rule."[97] For this reason, a preliminary draft constitution of December 2014 had envisaged the *indirect* election of the president of the Republic, not to mention the fact that all draft constitutions that have thus far been adopted have always provided for some serious checks on executive authority. According to the 2017 draft constitution, the president can be re-elected only once (Article 101), and this provision cannot be amended (Article 195(2)). The Constitutional Court has been granted numerous prerogatives (Article 139), a number of independent constitutional bodies have been created (Articles 154ff.), and the independence of the judiciary is fully recognized, although many key aspects are left to implementing legislation, including the composition of the High Judicial Council (Article 126). Furthermore, the president has the power to declare a state of emergency and to request Parliament to declare martial law; however, the draft constitution provides for some temporal, procedural, and substantive safeguards (Articles 187ff.).[98]

Since the fall of Gaddafi, Libya has experienced war, disorder, violence, and anarchy. The system of government should be one of the essential components for guaranteeing order and stability in the country. The 2017 draft constitution envisages a strong presidency but provides for some important constraints on executive authority. It would be advisable to further strengthen the system of checks and balances before the constitution is finally ratified, otherwise there may be a risk of favoring the emergence of another "strongman" rather than a democratic leader.

95 Nedra Cherif, "Libya's Constitutional Quagmire," *Konrad Adenauer Stiftung – Libya Brief* no. 10 (June 2021), 8.

96 See SASG *Stephanie Williams' Statement on the High-level Meeting on Libya's Constitutional Track in Geneva* (June 30, 2022), https://unsmil.unmissions.org/sasg-stephanie-williams'-statement-high-level-meeting-libya's-constitutional-track-geneva; *United Nations Support Mission in Libya – Report of the Secretary-General (S/2022/632)* (August 19, 2022), 1–3, https://reliefweb.int/report/libya/united-nations-support-mission-libya-report-secretary-general-s2022632-enar. On the UN-led process, see Chapter 1, Section 1.2.6.

97 Cherif, "Libya's Constitutional Quagmire," at p. 8.

98 On the declaration of the state of emergency, see Section 2.3.

2.2 TUNISIA: FROM A SEMI-PRESIDENTIAL SYSTEM TO A HYPER-PRESIDENTIAL REGIME

Within any analysis of the separation of powers and systems of government following the 2011 uprisings, Tunisia must be treated separately. Indeed, unlike all the other countries in the region (as shown in Section 2.1), Tunisia was the only state that abandoned the previous system of one-man rule. In particular, the 2014 constitution provided for a semi-presidential system characterized by a bicephalous executive (president of the Republic and Head of Government) and a quite robust system of checks and balances (at least on paper). However, this system of government only lasted for seven years, when it was replaced with a hyper-presidential regime provided for by Presidential Decree no. 2021-117 of September 22, 2021. This choice was then confirmed in the 2022 constitution. The following sections (Sections 2.2.1–2.2.5) discuss the *evolution* and *involution* of the system of government in Tunisia, taking into account the social, political, and institutional context.

2.2.1 *Breaking with the Previous Authoritarian Presidentialism*

Following the outbreak of the 2011 Revolution, departing from the authoritarian presidentialism that characterized the regime of Zine El Abidine Ben Ali was undoubtedly one of the main priorities for both demonstrators and the political forces represented in the Constituent Assembly. "*Plus jamais la dictature*"[99] ("Never again a dictatorship") was indeed the watchword of all social and political forces in the aftermath of the Dignity Revolution.[100] However, the positions of political parties as to how this objective could be achieved differed significantly. On the one hand, Ennahda pushed for the introduction of a parliamentary system of government. Both ideological and tactical reasons accounted for this preference. In the first place, a parliamentary system was considered to be more in line with the Islamic institute of *shura* (consultation).[101] Indeed, as was explained by Ennahda's founder and leader Rached Ghannouchi, "Islam, which enjoins the recourse to Shura (consultation) as a principle governing relations between political authority and the people, finds in democracy the appropriate instruments (elections, parliamentary system, separation of powers, etc.) to implement the Shura."[102] Moreover, from a strategic standpoint, Ennahda's leaders felt confident that they would be able

[99] Yadh Ben Achour, *Tunisie: Une révolution en pays d'Islam* (Cérès éditions 2017), 331.

[100] See Rafaâ Ben Achour, "La Constitution tunisienne du 27 janvier 2014" (2014) 100 *Revue française de droit constitutionnel*, 792.

[101] See Duncan Pickard, "Al-Nahda: Moderation and Compromise in Tunisia's Constitutional Bargain" in Frosini and Biagi (eds.) 2015, *Political and Constitutional Transitions*, at pp. 22–23.

[102] Cited in John L. Esposito, "Islam and Civil Society" in John P. Esposito and François Burgat (eds.), *Modernizing Islam: Religion in the Public Sphere in the Middle East and Europe* (Rutgers University Press 2003), 79.

to win a majority of seats in Parliament in the following elections, thus putting them in a position to form a government.[103]

On the other hand, secular parties favored a presidential or semi-presidential system, "which they saw as the best way to check [Ennahda]'s power."[104] In general terms, they were convinced that if the president of the Republic were popularly elected, the people would consider a secular candidate to be more "reassuring" than an Islamist candidate. Moreover, in their view, a secular president would better be able to check the power of an Ennahda Prime Minister. Centrist parties were more inclined to embrace a US-style presidential system, whereas the center-left Congress for the Republic and the social democratic party Ettakatol (which formed the government coalition with Ennahda) supported a semi-presidential form of government.[105]

Eventually, Ennahda conceded and accepted a semi-presidential system. The 2014 constitution featured all three elements required by Maurice Duverger in order for a semi-presidential system to be considered as such: (1) The president is elected by universal suffrage; (2) he possesses considerable powers; and (3) he has opposite him a Prime Minister and ministers who enjoy executive power and can stay in office for as long as they enjoy the confidence of Parliament.[106] According to the 2014 constitution, executive power was exercised by the president and a government presided over by the Head of Government (Article 71). By splitting executive power between the president and the Head of Government, the framers aimed to establish "a system of checks and balances *within the executive branch*"[107] (emphasis added), so as to prevent the tyranny of one single man. Furthermore, the independence of the judiciary was significantly strengthened, and the Constitutional Court was vested with a number of key prerogatives, being conceived of as one of the pillars of the new constitutional order. Regrettably, however, the Court was never established and its absence has had major negative consequences on the operation of the political and institutional system.[108]

2.2.2 *The Semi-Presidential System under the 2014 Constitution*

According to Article 72 of the 2014 constitution, the president was the "Head of State and the symbol of its unity." He guaranteed "its independence and continuity" and ensured "respect for the Constitution." He was the Commander-in-Chief

103 See Rafaâ Ben Achour, "La Dyarchie dans la Constitution tunisienne" in *La Constitution de la Tunisie – Processus, principes et perspectives* (UNDP 2016), 517.

104 Pickard, "Al-Nahda," at p. 23.

105 Ibid., at pp. 22–24; Ben Achour, "La Dyarchie dans la Constitution tunisienne," at p. 517.

106 See Maurice Duverger, "A New Political System Model: Semi-presidential Government" (1980) 8 *European Journal of Political Research*, 166.

107 Marco Olivetti, "La forma di governo, tra parlamentarismo razionalizzato e semipresidenzialismo" in Tania Groppi and Irene Spigno (eds.), *Tunisia: La primavera della Costituzione* (Carocci 2015), 132.

108 See the following sections, as well as Democracy Reporting International, *Les effets de l'absence de la Cour constitutionnelle pendant la législature 2014–2019* (December 2019), https://democracyreporting.s3.eu-central-1.amazonaws.com/images/21732020-08-Tunisia-Effets-Abs-CC-Web-Fr.pdf

of the Armed Forces and had the power to determine the general policy of the state with regard to defense, foreign relations, and national security, to dissolve the Assembly of the Representatives of the People (*majlis nuwwab al-sha'b*) (i.e., the unicameral Parliament) in accordance with the provisions of the constitution, to chair the National Security Council, to declare war and make peace, to declare a state of exception,[109] and to ratify international treaties (Article 77). Moreover, he had the power of legislative initiative (Article 62), could return bills to Parliament (Article 81), and in exceptional circumstances could submit to a referendum draft laws adopted by Parliament concerning the ratification of treaties, freedoms and human rights, and personal status (Article 82). Furthermore, he appointed one-third of the judges of the Constitutional Court (Article 118(2)), the Mufti of the Tunisian Republic, and also individuals within the office of the presidency of the Republic, as well as in senior civil, military, and security-related positions (Article 78).

A rule that was clearly intended to avoid a drift toward authoritarianism was contained in Article 75, which stated that no person could be elected as president for more than two full terms, a limit that applied regardless of whether or not the two terms were consecutive or discontinuous (thus avoiding a Putin–Medvedev-style "job swap"). Moreover, this provision stipulated that the constitution could not be amended to increase the number or length of presidential terms (again in an attempt to avoid ploys used in other countries such as Venezuela or, again, Russia).[110] These provisions on presidential terms were also symbolically significant if it is considered that a constitutional reform adopted in 2002 under the Ben Ali regime had removed the three-term limit applicable to the president of the Republic.

Furthermore, while under the previous 1959 constitution the president could freely choose the Prime Minister, under the 2014 constitution he had to ask "the candidate of the party or the electoral coalition that won the largest number of seats in the Assembly of the Representatives of the People to form a government within a one month period, extendable once [...]" (Article 89(2)). If this period elapsed without any government being formed or if the confidence of the Assembly of the Representatives of the People was not obtained, the president had to "consult with the political parties, coalitions, and parliamentary groups, with the aim of asking the person judged most capable to form a government within a period of no more than one month to do so" (Article 89(3)).[111] Thus, unlike countries such as Jordan, Syria,

109 See in greater detail Section 2.3.

110 See Justin O. Frosini and Francesco Biagi, "Transitions from Authoritarian Rule following the Arab Uprisings: A Matter of Variables" in Frosini and Biagi (eds.) 2015, *Political and Constitutional Transitions*, at p. 160.

111 This is what happened following the 2019 parliamentary elections, in which Ennahda had obtained the highest number of seats. President Saïed asked Habib Jemli, Ennahda's candidate, to form a government, but Jemli did not obtain the confidence of Parliament. At that point, Saïed was entitled to select

or Egypt, where the head of state has full discretion as regards the appointment of the Prime Minister,[112] the case of Tunisia reflected that of Morocco and Algeria, where the results of the parliamentary elections bind the choice of the head of state when making this appointment. As regards the formation of the government, the constitution stipulated that the Head of Government should select ministers and the secretaries of state on his/her own initiative, except for the Ministers of Foreign Affairs and Defense, whose appointment had to occur in consultation with the president of the Republic (Article 89(1)).[113] Even the dismissal or acceptance of the resignation of these two ministers by the Head of Government could only occur in consultation with the president (Article 92).

Some constitutional provisions concerning the diarchal nature of the executive seemed to be problematic and could give rise to conflicts between the Head of State and the Head of Government. Article 91, for example, provided that the Head of Government "determines the state's general policy, taking into account the provisions of Article 77, and ensures its execution." On the one hand, this provision clearly affirmed the predominance of the Head of Government vis-à-vis the president of the Republic in the determination of the state's general policy. On the other hand, however, this had to occur "taking into account the provisions of Article 77," which stipulated, *inter alia*, that the president was responsible for determining the general policy of the state with regard to defense, foreign relations, and national security pertaining to the protection of the state and the national territory against all internal and external threats, after consultation with the Head of Government. Since the areas of defense, foreign policy, and national security are extremely broad and their scope can be interpreted in different ways, it was likely that divergent views could be expected between the president and the Head of Government in these matters.

Another controversial provision was the one governing the chairmanship of the Council of Ministers. Indeed, Article 93 first stated that "The Head of Government chairs the Council of Ministers," although it then went on to assert that

> it shall be mandatory for the president of the Republic to preside over the Council of Ministers in issues relating to defense, foreign policy and national security as concerns the protection of the state and the national territory from internal and

the person that in his opinion was "most capable" to form a government. Saïed asked Elyes Fakhfakh to form a government, and on February 27, 2020, Fakhfakh's technocratic government obtained the confidence of Parliament. See Bernard-Maugiron, *Droit contemporain des pays arabes*, at p. 699.

112 As recalled earlier (see Section 2.1.4), Article 146(1) of the 2014 Egyptian Constitution states that the president appoints the Prime Minister at his discretion. It is only if the government does not obtain the confidence of a majority of the members of the House of Representatives that the president must appoint a Prime Minister on the basis of "the nomination of the party or the coalition that holds a plurality of seats in the House of Representatives."

113 On the fact that this provision indirectly recalls the appointment of the "ministers of sovereignty," see footnote 278.

external threats. The president of the Republic may also attend other meetings of the Council of Ministers, in which case he shall chair the Council.

This provision was problematic not only in terms of interpretation of the scope of the fields of defense, foreign policy, and national security (as recalled earlier), but also because, if the president had decided to systematically attend the meetings of the Council of Ministers, he would have *de facto* become its permanent chair. This would have conflicted with the spirit of this article, which suggested that the chairmanship of the Council of Ministers by the president was not the norm but rather the exception.

The constitution vested the Head of Government with many other prerogatives. These included the power to initiate legislation (Article 62),[114] to create, amend, and dissolve public institutions, public enterprises, and administrative departments, as well as to appoint individuals in senior civil positions (Article 92). Furthermore, the Head of Government led the public administration (Article 92), exercised "general regulatory powers," and was responsible for issuing "individual" decrees that he signed following discussion in the Council of Ministers (Article 94).

As regards the relationship of confidence between the Government and Parliament, the Tunisian framers opted for the "constructive vote of no-confidence" according to the German and Spanish models, with the aim of reinforcing the stability of the executive. Indeed, Article 97(2) stipulated that "A vote of no-confidence in the government requires a vote by an absolute majority of the members of the Assembly of the Representatives of the People, *and the presentation of an alternative candidate to head the government* whose candidacy must be approved in the same vote [...]" (emphasis added). Alongside the "constructive vote of no-confidence," the constitution also provided for a question of confidence (*question de confiance*) to be tabled by either the president or the Head of Government. The latter could request Parliament to express its confidence (by an absolute majority of its members) in the continuation of the government in office. If this confidence was not granted, the government was considered to have resigned (Article 98(2)). The president of the Republic could also request Parliament to express its confidence (by an absolute majority of its members) in the continuation of the government in office. The president, however, could do so on a maximum of two occasions throughout the entire presidential term. If this confidence was not granted, the government was considered to have resigned (Article 99). From a comparative perspective, it should be noted that the power of the president to request a vote of confidence is clearly an exception. Indeed, such a vote was requested by an actor (the president) who was *external* to the

114 On the other hand, the government as a whole was responsible for ensuring the enforcement of laws (Article 92).

relationship of confidence between the Government and Parliament. One might wonder whether this was an instrument that the president could use "in order to get rid of a government that he does not like politically."[115]

2.2.3 *The First Parliamentary Term (2014–2019): A Conflictual Semi-Presidential System*

Being halfway between a presidential system and a parliamentary regime, the semi-presidential system is a hybrid form of government that can evolve in different ways, depending on a number of variables, including the prerogatives granted to the president in the text of the constitution, the political and party system, the charisma of the president and Prime Minister, and obviously the context in which it operates.[116] As has been noted in the literature, four main scenarios are possible.[117] First scenario: Although elected by universal suffrage and endowed with some personal powers, the president is only a "figurehead,"[118] who performs mainly ceremonial functions, in a manner reminiscent of the head of state in a parliamentary regime. This is the case, for example, of Iceland, Ireland, and Austria. Second scenario: The president is the real leader of the country and clearly prevails over the Prime Minister, who is a "second-in-command." With the exception of instances of *cohabitation*, this has been the case in the French Fifth Republic.[119] In many cases, however, this type of semi-presidentialism has degenerated into an authoritarian presidentialism/hyper-presidentialism, as has occurred in Russia and most Arab countries (including Tunisia under both the 1959 constitution[120] and – as will be shown later[121] – the 2022 constitution). Third scenario: The Prime Minister directs the general policy of the government, while the president acts as a counterweight and guarantor of the constitution. The president places some checks on executive action in order to avoid the tyranny of the majority. This more balanced form of semi-presidentialism can be found, for example, in Portugal and Finland.[122] Fourth scenario: The president acts not only as a counterweight to the Prime Minister, but also aims to direct the general policy of the government. As a consequence, tensions and conflicts often emerge between the president and the Prime Minister, thus giving rise to a conflictual semi-presidential system.[123]

115 Olivetti, "La forma di governo," at p. 144.
116 See Giovanni Sartori, *Comparative Constitutional Engineering: An Inquiry into Structures, Incentives and Outcomes* (Macmillan 1994), 121ff.
117 See Olivetti, "La forma di governo," at pp. 148–151.
118 Duverger, "A New Political System Model," at p. 167.
119 Ibid., at p. 170ff.
120 See Victor Silvera, "Le régime constitutionnel de la Tunisie: la Constitution du 1er juin 1959" (1960) 2 *Revue française de science politique*, 391ff.
121 See Section 2.2.5.
122 See Olivetti, "La forma di governo," at pp. 149–150.
123 Ibid., at p. 150.

Where did the Tunisian semi-presidentialism provided for by the 2014 constitution stand with respect to the four scenarios mentioned earlier? Since the text of the constitution envisaged a "*régime à géométrie variable*,"[124] the answer is not clear-cut. It is thus necessary to examine the political regime *in action*. It is apparent from an analysis of the first parliamentary term (2014–2019) that the country was characterized by a *conflictual* semi-presidential system. This is first of all due to the fact that the 2014 constitution vested both the president and the Head of Government with significant prerogatives and contained some problematic provisions that could give rise to conflicts between the two heads of the executive branch.[125] Moreover, it is also important to note that, far from adopting a "passive" stance, Beji Caid Essebsi, who served as president of Tunisia from December 31, 2014, until his death on July 25, 2019, was a charismatic leader who often imposed his will on the government's agenda. Finally, it is necessary to take into account the complex political context, involving a coalition government between, among others, Nidaa Tounes (a secular party founded by Essebsi in 2012) and Ennahda (Tunisia's main Islamist party), as well as an internal power struggle within Nidaa Tounes.

Political, institutional, and constitutional conflicts between the president and the Head of Government arose very soon. Only a year and a half after his appointment as Head of Government in February 2015, Parliament passed a motion of no-confidence in Habib Essid, who was then forced to resign. This came about as a result of a proposal made by President Essebsi a few weeks before to form a government of national unity – a move that clearly showed his dissatisfaction with Essid's actions. "*Guerre des chefs en Tunisie*" ("War of the Chiefs in Tunisia")[126]: This is how the French newspaper *Le Monde* described the political situation at that time – a description that would have also been appropriate in subsequent years. Indeed, Essebsi then appointed Youssef Chahed as Head of Government, "believing that he would be more docile toward his 'spiritual father.'"[127] In actual fact, however, Chahed asserted his constitutional authority and distanced himself from Essebsi (and from his ambitious son),[128] so much so that in 2018 he abandoned his party of origin (Nidaa Tounes) and created a new parliamentary group (Coalition nationale) and later a new party (Tahya Tounes).

One of the major constitutional clashes between Essebsi and Chahed concerned the procedure followed in the cabinet reshuffle carried out by Chahed in

[124] Salsabil Kelibi, "Séparation et équilibre des pouvoirs dans la Constitution tunisienne" in *La Constitution de la Tunisie – Processus, principes et perspectives* (2016), at p. 504.

[125] As shown in Section 2.2.2.

[126] Frédéric Bobin, "Guerre des chefs en Tunisie," *Le Monde* (July 25, 2016), www.lemonde.fr/international/article/2016/07/25/guerre-des-chefs-en-tunisie_4974259_3210.html

[127] Nidhal Mekki, "The Political Crisis in Tunisia: Is it a Consequence of the Semi-presidential Arrangement?," *ConstitutionNet* (December 7, 2018), https://constitutionnet.org/news/political-crisis-tunisia-it-consequence-semi-presidential-arrangement

[128] See Mokhtar Ben Henda, "Caid Essebsi père et fils: Virage ou mirage dynastique?," *Kapitalis* (September 4, 2018), http://kapitalis.com/tunisie/2018/09/04/caid-essebsi-pere-et-fils-virage-ou-mirage-dynastique/

November 2018. Essebsi complained that Chahed had not consulted him regarding the choice of new ministers. The constitution, however, stipulated that the Head of Government had full discretion over the selection of ministers, except for the Ministers of Foreign Affairs and Defense, whose appointment had to occur in consultation with the president of the Republic (Article 89(1)). Since the cabinet reshuffle did not affect these two ministries, Chahed was not under any constitutional obligation to consult Essebsi.[129] The situation was so tense that some commentators even stressed that, if Essebsi had not signed the decrees appointing the new ministers or if he had refused to swear them in, this behavior could have been interpreted as a serious breach of the constitution, thus potentially leading to the president's impeachment (Article 88).[130]

Even Chahed, however, did not comply fully with the constitution with respect to the change of the members of the government. Indeed, while Article 92 stated that the Head of Government was responsible for "creating, modifying and dissolving ministries [...] *after discussing the matter with the Council of Ministers*" (emphasis added), Chahed did not previously consult the Council of Ministers. Rather, he presented the cabinet reshuffle only at the *following* Council of Ministers. It has been stressed that the "initial procedural misstep" was not "a mere oversight" on the part of the Head of Government. Instead, "it could have been intended to avoid a possibility where the president could have sought to attend and preside meetings of the council of ministers, as anticipated in the constitution, which could possibly have derailed the reshuffle, considering the president's potential influence on some of the members of the council."[131]

The functioning of the political regime was seriously affected by the absence of the Constitutional Court. Indeed, the Court was responsible, *inter alia*, for resolving the conflicts between the president and the Head of Government concerning the allocation of powers (Article 101), for deciding on the impeachment of the president of the Republic (Article 88), as well as for declaring any temporary or permanent vacancy in the office of president of the Republic (Article 84). None of these functions was exercised during the period 2014–2019, as there was no body responsible for resolving the conflicts between the president and the Head of Government; there was no body that could have decided on any impeachment of Essebsi; and there was no body that could have declared a temporary vacancy in Essebsi's office (e.g., when he was hospitalized in June and July 2019) and that could have declared a permanent vacancy in his office when he died on July 25, 2019.[132]

[129] See Mekki, "Political Crisis in Tunisia."

[130] See Democracy Reporting International, *Les effets de l'absence de la Cour constitutionnelle pendant la législature 2014–2019*, at pp. 28–29, which also makes reference to another case in which it was raised the possibility to impeach President Essebsi.

[131] Mekki, "Political Crisis in Tunisia."

[132] See in greater detail Democracy Reporting International, *Les effets de l'absence de la Cour constitutionnelle pendant la législature 2014–2019*, at p. 25ff.

2.2.4 *Democratic Backsliding: Saïed's Declaration of the State of Exception and the Adoption of Presidential Decree no. 2021-117 on the "Exceptional Measures"*

The first two years of the second parliamentary term (2019–2021) were still marked by the persistence of conflicts and tensions. This time, however, these conflicts were not only between the president and the Head of Government but also between the president and Parliament – and more specifically, the Speaker of Parliament. Kaïs Saïed was elected president of Tunisia in September 2019, two months after Essebsi's death. Saïed was largely an outsider, as he was not associated either with a party or a parliamentary faction.[133] Following the resignation of Head of Government Elyes Fakhfakh on July 15, 2020, Saïed appointed Hichem Mechichi as the new Head of Government. Initially, Mechichi, who had a "technocratic profile," was perceived to be "close to Saied, but soon after the former's appointment, the situation changed."[134] Indeed, Mechichi distanced himself from the president and drew ever closer to the political parties supporting his government, including Ennahda and the secular parties Qalb Tounes and Tahya Tounes.[135] In January 2021, Saïed even rejected a cabinet reshuffle, preventing the newly-approved members of the government from swearing the oath of office.[136] The other institutional conflict was between President Saïed and Rached Ghannouchi, leader of Ennahda and Speaker of Parliament. Their views diverged significantly, especially as regards the notion of sovereignty and the exercise of power: Ghannouchi focused on the key role played by Parliament (as if Tunisia were a genuine parliamentary regime), whereas Saïed relied on a more "presidentialist" interpretation of the constitution.[137]

Against this backdrop of harsh political and institutional conflicts, on July 25, 2021, Kaïs Saïed invoked Article 80 of the constitution and declared a state of exception.[138] Four main measures were adopted by the president: (1) Head of Government Hichem Mechichi was dismissed; (2) Parliament's activities were frozen for thirty

[133] See Dario Cristiani, "Tunisia's Political Landscape a Decade after the Jasmine Revolution," *Atlantic Council* (December 17, 2020), www.atlanticcouncil.org/blogs/menasource/tunisias-political-landscape-a-decade-after-the-jasmine-revolution/

[134] Karim Mezran and Alissa Pavia, "Tunisia Was the Only Democracy to Blossom from the Arab Spring. Now It's a Mess," *Atlantic Council* (July 28, 2021), www.atlanticcouncil.org/blogs/menasource/tunisia-was-the-only-democracy-to-blossom-from-the-arab-spring-now-its-a-mess/?mkt_tok=NjU5LVdaWCowNzUAAAF-kuKsfoOsxCbduoSHJ1HS2lnFNBdPoSzAK_ns-4w7O7nOfOyhE5ZbjS_4joqyEpj1KaB52eeQPJAvPFbxMV85mkTMApB2BHgaBoyYGpMc

[135] Ibid.

[136] See "Constitutional Crisis Blocks New Tunisian Ministers from Oath of Office," *The Arab Weekly* (January 30, 2021), https://thearabweekly.com/constitutional-crisis-blocks-new-tunisian-ministers-oath-office

[137] See Frida Dahmani, "Tunisie: guerre froide entre Kaïs Saïed et Rached Ghannouchi," *Jeune Afrique* (July 2, 2020), www.jeuneafrique.com/mag/1007068/politique/tunisie-guerre-froide-entre-kais-saied-et-rached-ghannouchi/

[138] On the regulation of the state of exception in Tunisia, see Section 2.3.

days; (3) parliamentary immunity was suspended for all members of Parliament; and (4) President Saïed also announced that he would personally preside over the office of public prosecution. On August 23, the freezing of Parliament's activities and the suspension of parliamentary immunity were then extended "until further notice." These measures were clearly not compatible with the constitution.[139] For example, as far as the freezing of Parliament's activities is concerned, Article 80 of the constitution allowed the president to "take any measures necessitated by the exceptional circumstances," but also stipulated that "the Assembly of the Representatives of the People shall be deemed to be *in a state of continuous session throughout such a period*. In this situation, the president of the Republic cannot dissolve the Assembly of the Representatives of the People" (emphasis added).

Following the proclamation of a state of exception, President Saïed began to conduct a campaign of arrests involving activists, judges, journalists, and politicians, especially those affiliated with Islamist parties, which were the most critical voices of the measures taken by the president. In addition, a number of TV stations close to the Islamist front were shut down. The main targets of Saïed's attacks were Ennahda's members, who were depicted – relying on the Schmittean dichotomy *amicus-hostis* – as enemies of the state.

On September 22, 2021, Saïed took a further step and issued Presidential Decree no. 2021-117 on "exceptional measures," which granted him "full powers" (*pleins pouvoirs*, an expression that comes from the notion of *plenitudo potestatis*).[140] According to this Decree, parliamentary powers and immunity remained suspended (Articles 1 and 2); legislative power was exercised through law-decrees adopted by the Council of Ministers and promulgated by the president (Article 4); these decrees could not be annulled (by the courts) (Article 7); executive power was exercised by the president with the "assistance" of a government presided over by the Head of Government (Article 8); the president presided over the Council of Ministers (Article 10); he represented the State, decided on its general policy and took all fundamental decisions (Article 9); the government was accountable to the president (and not to Parliament) (Article 18), and only *implemented* the general policy of the state, according to the decisions made by the president (Article 17); the Provisional Authority Responsible for Verifying the Constitutionality of Bills was abolished (Article 21). In the preamble to this decree, President Saïed justified the adoption of these exceptional measures, arguing that the people had been prevented from exercising sovereignty, that the functioning of public powers had been hampered, that there was a real danger within Parliament, and that the principle according to which

[139] See International Commission of Jurists, *Tunisia: Judiciary Must Act as a Check on President's Power Grab* (August 3, 2021), www.icj.org/tunisia-judiciary-must-act-as-a-check-on-presidents-power-grab/; Eya Jrad, "Constitutional or Unconstitutional: Is That the Question?," *Arab Reform Initiative* (August 3, 2021), www.arab-reform.net/pdf/?pid=19421&plang=en

[140] See Giorgio Agamben, *State of Exception* (University of Chicago Press 2005), 5ff.

sovereignty belonged to the people prevailed over forms and procedures. According to a propagandistic move, on September 29, 2021, one week after the adoption of Presidential Decree no. 2021-117 on "exceptional measures," Saïed also designated a new Prime Minister – a woman – who was charged with the task of forming a new government. Nejla Bouden Romdhane thus became the first female Prime Minister in the Arab world.[141]

It should be noted that the duration of the state of exception was entirely dependent on President Saïed's discretion. Article 80 of the 2014 constitution – which is extremely similar to Article 16 of the 1958 French Constitution as amended in 2008 (as discussed later)[142] – stipulated that "Thirty days after the entry into force of [the exceptional] measures, and at any time thereafter, the Speaker of the Assembly of the Representatives of the People or thirty of the members thereof shall be entitled to apply to the Constitutional Court with a view to verifying whether or not the circumstances remain exceptional." However, since Parliament had been suspended and the Constitutional Court had not been established, the mechanism provided for by the constitution aimed at reviewing the upholding of the state of exception could not work. The failure to establish the Constitutional Court was also due to Saïed's decision in April 2021 to reject a bill that would have reduced the number of votes required for the election by Parliament of one-third of the Court's members from 145 to 131 (out of 217 members of Parliament). In his letter to Ghannouchi, Saïed justified his choice arguing that the Constitutional Court could not be established because the one-year deadline (provided for by Article 148(5) of the constitution)[143] for electing members of the Court had not been met.[144] Thus, Saïed regarded the deadline provided for under the constitution as a peremptory time limit rather than simply a recommended timeframe. This was undoubtedly very poor reasoning, also in view of the fact that, before being elected as president of Tunisia, Saïed had been a university professor of constitutional law.

Presidential Decree no. 2021-117 resulted in at least four extremely negative effects.[145] First, it introduced a *de facto* "super-Constitution" (i.e., the Decree itself), which partly replaced the 2014 constitution. This was confirmed by Article 20 of the Decree, which stipulated that "the preamble to the Constitution, Chapters 1 ['General Principles'] and 2 ['Rights and Freedoms'], as well as all the constitutional provisions that do not contrast with this Presidential Decree shall continue to be

[141] On this issue, see also Chapter 4, Section 4.3.1.

[142] See Section 2.3.

[143] This provision stated that the Constitutional Court should be established within a maximum of one year from the legislative elections. The legislative elections were held on October 26, 2014.

[144] See Yosra Ouanes, "Tunisie: le président Saïed refuse de promulguer la loi sur la Cour constitutionnelle," *Anadolu Ajansı* (April 4, 2021), www.aa.com.tr/fr/afrique/tunisie-le-président-saïed-refuse-de-promulguer-la-loi-sur-la-cour-constitutionnelle-/2197826

[145] See Francesco Biagi, "Tunisi: la primavera araba sfiorisce in stato d'eccezione" (2021) 4 *Quaderni costituzionali*, 962.

enforced." The hierarchy of sources of law was thus reversed: It was the constitutional provisions that had to be in line with the decree, and not the other way around. Second, the decree replaced the semi-presidential system provided for in the 2014 constitution with a hyper-presidential regime characterized by an overconcentration of powers in the hands of the president. Third, the decree struck a blow against representative democracy, in an attempt to establish a plebiscitary regime, based on the direct relationship between the president and the people. This came as no surprise, as Saïed had based his electoral campaign on criticism of elites and the political class, and the rhetoric of his speeches "has always revolved around the betrayal of the revolution by the institutions, which have been accused of abandoning the people and allowing corruption to run rampant: thus, from the outset the goal of Saïed has been to reverse hierarchies of power in order to return the management of the country to the 'betrayed' revolution and the people."[146] Fourth, the Decree laid the groundwork for a "top-down" constitutional reform process (i.e., a process driven and controlled directly by the president), which represented a major step back compared to the "bottom-up" process that led to the adoption of the 2014 constitution (i.e., a process characterized by the key role played by the population during the drafting of the constitution).[147]

On September 22, 2022, the African Court on Human and Peoples' Rights declared that Presidential Decree no. 2021-117 (and other presidential decrees relating to the state of exception) violated the African Charter on Human and Peoples' Rights.[148] The applicant was Mr. Ibrahim Ben Mohamed Ben Ibrahim Belguith, an advocate at the Court of Cassation of Tunisia. The African Court argued, in particular, that the following rights of the Charter had been violated: the right to have one's cause heard (Article 7(1)(a)), the right of the citizens to participate in the conduct of political affairs in their country (Article 13(1)), and the right to obtain guarantees for the protection of human rights and freedoms (Article 1). The Court ordered the Tunisian State to repeal Presidential Decree no. 2021-117 (and other presidential decrees relating to the state of exception), to take all measures necessary to ensure the operation of an independent Constitutional Court and remove all legal impediments thereto, and more generally to ensure a return to constitutional democracy within two years of the date on which the judgment was notified. Although it is highly unlikely that President Saïed will abide by this decision, this ruling is still of the utmost importance as it was issued by an independent regional court (the African Court), which unanimously certified that President Saïed's actions were not compatible with the principles of democracy, the rule of law, and human rights and freedoms.

146 Claudia Annovi, "La fine dell'eccezione tunisina?," *Centro Studi Internazionali* (July 29, 2021), www.cesi-italia.org/it/articoli/la-fine-delleccezione-tunisina

147 See Chapter 1, Sections 1.2.1.1 and 1.2.1.2.

148 Case *Ibrahim Ben Mohamed Ben Ibrahim Belguith* v. *Republic of Tunisia*. Application no. 017/2021 (September 22, 2022).

The process of democratic deterioration in Tunisia continued (*rectius*: further aggravated) in 2022. Saïed's attacks were initially directed against the Supreme Judicial Council. One of the few remaining state bodies still able to act independently, it was dissolved in February 2022 and replaced by a new "provisional" Supreme Judicial Council whose members were appointed directly by the president. Furthermore, at the end of March of the same year, President Saïed decided to dissolve Parliament. His decision came after more than half of its members had held an online session and voted to repeal the exceptional measures that he had used to seize power. Parliament's dissolution was another blatant violation of Article 80 of the 2014 constitution, which (as already recalled earlier) stipulated that, during a state of exception, "the President of the Republic cannot dissolve the Assembly of the Representatives of the People."

It should also be recalled that in order to further strengthen his control over the referendum on the new constitution, Saïed issued Decree-Law no. 2022-22 on the modification of the Independent High Authority for Elections (better known by its French acronym ISIE). This decree stipulated that it was the president (and no longer Parliament) who would appoint the members of the ISIE and reduced both the number of its members and its term of office. Furthermore, on September 13, 2022, Saïed issued Decree-Law no. 2022-54 (known as "Cybercrime Law"), which represents one of the latest measures adopted by the regime to silence the opposition. Indeed, this decree clearly violates the fundamental freedoms of expression and the press, as well as the right to privacy.

Moreover, on September 15, 2022, Saïed issued Decree-Law no. 2022-55 on the reform of the electoral law governing elections to the Assembly of the Representatives of the People, a measure that has rightly been defined as "another blow to Tunisia's democratic progress."[149] This decree, *inter alia*, replaces the previous system of proportional representation with a two-round majoritarian system, requires applications for candidacy to be submitted individually, removes quotas for women and candidates under 35, provides for overly burdensome requirements to be eligible to run for office, eliminates public financing of electoral campaigns, and gives the government the power to strip legislators from their offices and from candidacy for life if they are found guilty of receiving illicit donations.[150] The first parliamentary elections under the new electoral law were held in December 2022- January 2023. These elections, which were characterized by an extremely low turnout (about 11 percent in both rounds), led to an "atomized" Parliament[151] and a significant weakening of female representation.[152]

149 Sarah Yerkes and Mohammad Al-Mailam, "Tunisia's New Electoral Law Is Another Blow to Its Democratic Progress," *Carnegie Endowment for International Peace* (October 11, 2022), https://carnegieendowment.org/2022/10/11/tunisia-s-new-electoral-law-is-another-blow-to-its-democratic-progress-pub-88127

150 Ibid.

151 See Amira Souilem, "Tunisie: après les législatives, un Parlement sans coloration politique bien définie," *RFI* (February 1, 2023), www.rfi.fr/fr/afrique/20230201-tunisie-après-les-législatives-un-parlement-sans-coloration-politique-bien-définie

152 On female representation in Tunisia, see Chapter 4, Section 4.3.1.

All of these measures were depicted by Saïed as being not only perfectly compatible with democratic standards but also necessary to ensure the restoration of the democratic order in the country, thus following a typical illiberal-populist approach.

2.2.5 *Constitutionalizing the State of Exception: The Hyper-Presidential System in the 2022 Constitution*

The 2022 constitution, which was ratified in the referendum held on July 25, marks a radical departure from the 2014 constitutional text, replacing the semi-presidential form of government with a hyper-presidential regime.[153] The president is now the undisputed *dominus* of the institutional system: He is the leader of the executive branch, has wide and important legislative prerogatives, and can influence the work of the judiciary.[154] Thus, the 2022 constitution largely confirmed the system provided for under Presidential Decree no. 2021-117 on "exceptional measures," so much so that it can be argued that Kaïs Saïed – who not only drove the constitution-making process but also played a key role in the very drafting of the text[155] – *constitutionalized the state of exception*. Some constitutional provisions have even been taken over verbatim from the 2021 Presidential Decree. This is the case for Article 87 (the president exercises executive power "assisted" by a government headed by a Prime Minister), Article 100 (the president sets "the general policies of the State and defines its essential choices"), and Article 111 (the government may only ensure "the execution of the general policies of the State in accordance with the policy direction and choices of the President of the Republic"). The new constitution then stipulates that the president appoints the Prime Minister at his discretion and appoints ministers at the suggestion of the Prime Minister (Article 101). By contrast, the 2014 constitution severely limited the president's ability to choose, as he was required to appoint as Head of Government the leader of the party or coalition of parties that had won the largest number of seats in Parliament. Now the president can also dismiss the government and terminate the functions of any of its members, either by direction of the president himself or upon the recommendation of the Prime Minister (Article 102). The new constitution has also maintained the provision (that was also provided for in Presidential Decree no. 2021-117 on "exceptional measures") that states that the government is accountable only to the president (and not to

[153] See Zaid Al-Ali, "Tunisia's Draft Constitution Solidifies One-man Rule," *The Washington Post* (July 8, 2022), www.washingtonpost.com/politics/2022/07/08/tunisia-saied-coup-constitution-backsliding-democracy/; Ciro Sbailò, "La svolta inevitabile verso l'autoritarismo della Tunisia," *HuffPost* (July 26, 2022), www.huffingtonpost.it/blog/2022/07/26/news/referendum_in_tunisia_una_svolta_inevitabile-9945102/; Francesco Biagi, "Tunisia: la Costituzione di Kaïs Saïed," *Diritti comparati* (July 28, 2022), www.diritticomparati.it/tunisia-la-costituzione-di-kais-saied/

[154] See Nidhal Mekki, "The Project of the President's Constitution: Is It Time to Close the Democratic Parenthesis in Tunisia?," *ConstitutionNet* (July 25, 2022), https://constitutionnet.org/news/project-presidents-constitution-it-time-close-democratic-parenthesis-tunisia

[155] See Chapter 1, Section 1.2.1.2.

Parliament) (Article 112). The government must resign if Parliament passes a motion of no-confidence by a two-thirds majority (Article 115). Moreover, if a second motion of no-confidence is tabled during the same parliamentary term, the president may dissolve Parliament (Article 116).

The 2022 constitution also vests the president with the power to initiate legislation, and his bills "have priority" in the legislative process (Article 68). Budgetary bills and bills to ratify international treaties can only be presented by the president (Article 68), who also has the power to issue decrees under authority delegated by the Assembly of the Representatives of the People (i.e., the lower house) (Article 70), while the Assembly is in recess (Article 73), or after the Assembly has been dissolved (Article 80). Furthermore, the president may submit to referendum bills relating to the organization of public powers (Article 97). The president also has a veto power, which can only be overridden by Parliament by a two-thirds majority (Article 103). Parliament is no longer unicameral. Indeed, the new constitution retains the Assembly of the Representatives of the People, although supplements it with an upper chamber, the National Council (*al-majlis al-watani*) of Regions (*jihat*) and Districts (*aqalim*) (Articles 56–57 and 81ff.). The aim of the latter body, which is comprised of elected representatives from the regions and districts, is theoretically to strengthen territorial decentralization. However, as will be shown later,[156] the vertical separation of powers is not particularly enhanced in the 2022 constitution.

The president's prerogatives also include the power to appoint judges on the basis of a "recommendation" from the respective Supreme Council of the Judiciary (Article 120), to declare a state of exception (Article 96),[157] to initiate a constitutional reform process, and to submit to referendum a draft constitutional reform (Article 136). Moreover, although the constitution stipulates that the president may not serve for more than two terms (either consecutive or discontinuous) of five years each (Article 90) and that limits on re-election and the term in office may not be the object of a constitutional amendment (Article 136), Article 90 also stipulates that "In the event that elections cannot be held within the prescribed time due to war or *imminent danger*, the presidential term in office shall be extended by law until the causes that led to the delay of the elections come to an end" (emphasis added).[158] One cannot help but recall how in July 2021 Kaïs Saïed invoked precisely the existence of an "imminent danger" to justify the proclamation of a state of exception on the basis of Article 80 of the constitution. As further evidence of the almost total absence of mechanisms to control presidential action, one need only consider that the new constitution no longer contemplates any power for Parliament to impeach the president (who, under the 2014 constitution, would then be tried by the Constitutional Court [Article 88]). It is also significant that judges and members

[156] See Section 2.4.2.

[157] On the regulation of the state of exception, see more in detail Section 2.3.

[158] Admittedly, a similar provision could also be found in the 2014 constitution, that is, Article 75.

of the military and national security forces have been expressly deprived of the right to strike (Article 41).

Another clear sign of the weakening of the democratic system is the removal of the provisions, which were contained in the 2014 constitution, enshrining the full independence and neutrality of the army and the national security forces. Furthermore, several independent authorities are no longer contemplated in the new constitutional text, including the Audiovisual Communication Authority, the Human Rights Authority, the Authority for Sustainable Development and the Rights of Future Generations, and the Authority for Good Governance and Anti-Corruption.[159] It should also be noted that since he became president, although especially following the proclamation of the state of exception, Saïed has worked to prevent the establishment of independent constitutional bodies (such as the Constitutional Court), or has replaced them (as in the case of the Supreme Judicial Council) or modified them (as in the case of the Independent High Authority for Elections [ISIE]) with bodies placed under his direct control.

Thus, within the space of a year (July 2021 to July 2022), Kaïs Saïed succeeded in his intent to abolish the 2014 constitution, a document that he had always harshly criticized, especially because of the mechanisms limiting presidential authority. In other words, the system of checks and balances that represented the strength of the 2014 constitution was, in Saïed's eyes, simply an obstacle to his own actions.[160] Far from creating a "new Republic" (as the constitutional preamble emphatically proclaims), the 2022 constitution recalls in many respects the autocratic presidentialism that characterized the country under Ben Ali's regime. It is "one man's document,"[161] a type of text that Arab people are unfortunately very familiar with. Commenting on the results of Tunisia's 2019 presidential elections, Michel Camau pointed out that Kaïs Saied was not so much a "constitutionalist populist" ("*un constitutionnaliste populiste*") – a "reassuring definition that smells of academic propriety" – but rather a "populist constitutionalist" ("*un populiste constitutionnaliste*"), that is, a "populist determined to make his own idea of a constitution prevail, against winds and tides, as generally happens to populists once they come to power."[162] Recent events have shown that Camau was right: Since July 2021, Kaïs Saïed has imposed illiberal measures covered by a veneer of constitutionality and supported by a strong populist

[159] However, it should be noted that under the 2014 constitutional system, none of these institutions had been established, mainly because of the difficulties in the election of their members. See Democracy Reporting International, *La mise en œuvre de la Constitution tunisienne du 27 janvier 2014 au niveau du cadre juridique. Bilan* (September 2022), 84–91.

[160] See "Tunisia President Wants Debate on New Political System, Constitutional Amendment," *Reuters* (July 15, 2021), www.reuters.com/world/tunisia-president-wants-debate-new-political-system-constitutional-amendment-2021-06-15/

[161] Nathan J. Brown, "L'État C'est Qaïs," *Malcolm H. Kerr – Carnegie Middle East Center* (July 13, 2022), https://carnegie-mec.org/diwan/87496

[162] Michel Camau, "Un moment populiste tunisien? Temporalité électorale et temporalité révolutionnaire" (2020) 1 *Revue tunisienne de science politique*, 92.

rhetoric. The Tunisian President has thus joined the group of those democratically elected leaders who practice – in Kim Lane Scheppele's words – "autocratic legalism," dismantling *by law* (including constitutional law) the democratic system they inherited.[163]

2.3 EMERGENCY FRAMEWORKS: STILL A PARADIGM OF GOVERNMENT?

An analysis of the separation of powers and systems of government in the Arab world would not be complete without some specific consideration of the new constitutional provisions governing states of emergency. As is well known, in the past, Arab rulers – relying on the colonial emergency frameworks (in particular the French "*état d'urgence*" and the British "martial law") – often abused such mechanisms, under which the powers of the executive were even broader than normal.[164] Morocco experienced a state of exception under King Hassan II during the period 1965–1970, when the 1962 constitution was suspended. In Egypt, a state of emergency was declared in 1967, which lasted until 1980. Thereafter, following a break of eighteen months, it was re-imposed in 1981 and lasted until 2012. In Jordan, King Hussein imposed martial law in 1967 and lifted it in 1992. A state of emergency was in place in Algeria for nineteen years (from 1992 to 2011) and in Syria for forty-eight years (from 1963 to 2011). Therefore, in the Arab world, a provisional and exceptional measure was transformed – to use the words of Giorgio Agamben – into a "paradigm [or] technique of government."[165] Indeed, emergency rules were not so much aimed at countering threats to state security but rather to guarantee the survival and stability of the regime. This is also confirmed by the fact that emergency rules were often incorporated into *ordinary law* or sometimes even into *constitutional provisions*. This trend does not seem to be over yet, as is demonstrated by the 2022 Tunisian Constitution, which (as discussed earlier)[166] largely confirmed the system provided for in Presidential Decree no. 2021-117 on "exceptional measures."

Post-2011 Arab constitutions have addressed the problem of the "normalization of the exception" only in part.[167] In some cases, emergency provisions continue to be

[163] Kim Lane Scheppele, "Autocratic Legalism" (2018) 85 *The University of Chicago Law Review*, 545ff.

[164] For an analysis of the regulation of the state of emergency in pre-2011 Arab constitutions, see Arianna Vedaschi, *À la guerre comme à la guerre? La disciplina della guerra nel diritto costituzionale comparato* (Giappichelli 2007), 362ff., who also provides a classification of the different types of emergency regimes.

[165] Agamben, *State of Exception*, at p. 1ff.

[166] See Section 2.2.5.

[167] On the "normalization of the exception" from a comparative perspective, see Agamben, *State of Exception*, at p. 1ff.; Bruce Ackerman, "The Emergency Constitution" (2004) 113 *The Yale Law Journal*, 1029ff.; Günter Frankenberg, *Political Technology and the Erosion of the Rule of Law: Normalizing the State of Exception* (Edward Elgar 2014). On how Giorgio Agamben's ideas of the state of exception can help to understand the regulation and performance of political life in the Arab region, see Sanaa

characterized by loose wording and extremely limited restrictions. The 2012 constitution of Syria is emblematic. It states that the president of the Republic may declare a state of emergency (*halat al-tawari*) "and repeal it by a decree adopted within the Council of Ministers chaired by him approved by a majority of two thirds, provided that the decree is presented to the People's Assembly in its first session [...]" (Article 103). Furthermore, the constitution also stipulates that "if a grave danger or a situation threatening national unity and the safety and integrity of the territories comprising the homeland should arise or prevent state institutions from fulfilling their constitutional responsibilities, the president of the Republic may take any urgent measures required by these circumstances in order to confront that danger" (Article 114).

Virtually unlimited powers during a state of emergency are also granted to the executive in Jordan, where the provisions of the 1952 constitution governing emergency situations have not been changed following the 2011 reform. The constitution – which provides for two different types of states of exception, depending upon the seriousness of the emergency (Articles 124 and 125) – states that in the most dangerous cases, the king, on the basis of a decision made by the Council of Ministers, has the power to declare martial law and that during that time he may issue any instructions he deems necessary for the purpose of the defense of the kingdom, notwithstanding the provisions of any law in force (Article 125). When the situation does not require the proclamation of martial law, the king may declare a state of emergency on the basis of a decision made by the Council of Ministers. More specifically, "a law in the name of the Defense Law shall be enacted by virtue of which power shall be vested in the person specified by the law to take the necessary actions and measures, including the power to suspend ordinary laws of the State, in order to ensure the defense of the country" (Article 124). The state of emergency is currently regulated by Defense Law no. 13 of 1992, which is characterized by the fact that it remains "dormant" until it is "activated" by the monarch, as happened for instance on March 17, 2020, with the aim of curbing the spread of the COVID-19 pandemic.[168] The content of this Defense Law raises serious concerns, since it does not provide for any real safeguards (whether procedural, temporal, or substantive) against potential abuse on the part of the executive.[169]

In Morocco, the 2011 constitution lists the conditions that must be met in order for a state of exception (*halat al-istithna*) to be declared (i.e., a threat to the integrity of the national territory or events that hinder the proper functioning of the constitutional institutions). It also states that Parliament cannot be dissolved and that fundamental rights must be guaranteed during any period in which emergency powers are exercised (Article 59). Nevertheless, it is essential to stress that the king – after

Alsarghali, Simon Mabon and Adel Ruished (eds.), *States of Exception or Exceptional States: Law, Politics and Giorgio Agamben in the Middle East* (Bloomsbury Publishing 2022).

168 See Siraj Khan, "The State of Emergency and COVID-19: The Defence Law of Jordan 1992," unpublished manuscript.

169 Ibid.

having consulted with the Head of Government, the Presidents of the Houses of Parliament, and the President of the Constitutional Court – may declare a state of exception by royal decree (*zahir*) without any requirement for countersignature by the Head of Government (Article 42(4)), and without any requirement for approval by Parliament. Furthermore, the constitution does not provide for any temporal safeguards, as it only stipulates that the state of exception ends "as soon as the reasons which have justified it cease to apply" (Article 59(4)), and that the king is entitled to take all appropriate measures in order "to return, in the least time, to the normal functioning of the constitutional institutions" (Article 59(1)). Thus, the decision to assume exceptional powers, the nature and scope of such powers, and their duration are exclusively within the discretion of the monarch.[170]

Other post-2011 Arab constitutions have tightened up the provisions governing the state of emergency in order to make abuses of this sort more difficult. Nevertheless, in some cases, these provisions have proved not to be particularly effective. It is sufficient to consider the case of Egypt. Admittedly, the 2014 constitution offers more guarantees compared to the past (especially with respect to the 1971 constitution). In actual fact, however, this new regime has not prevented states of emergency from lasting indefinitely. First of all, the text of the 2014 Egyptian Constitution does not specify the exact circumstances under which a state of emergency (*halat al-tawari*) may be declared, thus leaving broad discretion to the president. Second, the constitution states that the president's declaration of a state of emergency must be approved by a majority of the members of the House of Representatives, but that it may only be extended by a two-thirds majority vote (Article 154(3)). It has rightly been argued that this mechanism recalls Bruce Ackerman's "supermajoritarian escalator,"[171] according to which a broader consensus is required for each prolongation of an emergency, thus incrementally increasing the power of the opposition to end the emergency if required.[172] However, since the vast majority of the members of the Egyptian House of Representatives are loyal to President Abdel Fattah Al-Sisi, Parliament *de facto* merely *ratifies* the president's decisions without exercising any effective oversight role. Third, the 2014 constitution stipulates that a presidential declaration of a state of emergency may last for a specified period not exceeding three months, which can only be extended for another similar period with Parliament's approval (Article 154(3)). However, President Al-Sisi has easily overcome this obstacle by *re-declaring* the state of emergency *the day after or a few days after* the expiration of the previous emergency period.[173] Having been initially

[170] See Melloni, "Le nouvel ordre constitutionnel marocain," at pp. 43–44.

[171] Ackerman, "Emergency Constitution," at p. 1047ff.

[172] See Islam Mohammed, "The Perpetual State of Emergency and the Reconstruction of National Security Threats in Egypt," unpublished manuscript. See also Elliot Bulmer, *Emergency Powers* (International IDEA 2018), 19, www.idea.int/sites/default/files/publications/emergency-powers-primer.pdf

[173] See Yussef Auf, "The State of Emergency in Egypt: An Exception or Rule?," *Atlantic Council* (February 2, 2018), www.atlanticcouncil.org/blogs/menasource/the-state-of-emergency-in-egypt-an-exception-or-rule/

declared in April 2017, the state of emergency in Egypt was continuously renewed until October 2021.

In Algeria, the 1996 constitution (as amended in 2020) dedicates an entire section to "Exceptional Situations" (Articles 97ff.), providing for the regulation of five different emergency regimes: the state of emergency, the state of siege, the state of exception, the general mobilization, and the state of war. Under all these exceptional circumstances, the president enjoys wide discretionary powers, even though the 2020 constitutional reform partially strengthened the safeguards against potential abuses. The state of emergency (*halat al-tawari'*) and the state of siege (*halat al-hisar*) are declared by the president "in case of compelling necessity," after having convened the High Council of Security and having consulted with the presidents of the two Houses of Parliament, the Prime Minister or the Head of Government (as the case may be),[174] and the President of the Constitutional Court, and may last for a maximum period of thirty days (Article 97(1)). The state of emergency and the state of siege can only be extended with the approval of Parliament meeting in joint session, although the constitution does not specify any maximum duration for such an extension (Article 97(2)). Moreover, in the light of the fact that the president is usually also the leader of the main political party in Parliament, and since no special majority is required (the constitution only requiring "Parliament's approval" (Article 97(2)), it is likely that it will not be difficult for the president to obtain such approval.

The state of exception (*halat al-istithna*) is declared by the president (after having consulted with the Presidents of the two Houses of Parliament and the President of the Constitutional Court, and also after having heard the High Council of Security and the Council of Ministers) "when the country is threatened by an imminent danger to its institutions, its independence or its territorial integrity" for a maximum period of sixty days, and during that period the president may "take any exceptional measures that are necessary in order to safeguard the independence of the Nation and the constitutional institutions of the Republic" (Article 98). The abovementioned weaknesses characterizing the state of emergency and the state of siege also characterize the state of exception. Indeed, the constitution does not specify a maximum duration for any extension of the state of exception and does not require Parliament (which must meet in joint session) to approve such an extension by a qualified majority (the constitution only requiring "the majority of the members of Parliament") (Article 98(5)). The president is also responsible for declaring a general mobilization (Article 99) and a state of war (Article 100) after having consulted with certain state institutions. Remarkably, during a state of war, the constitution is suspended and the president assumes all powers (Article 101).

The 2017 draft constitution of Libya provides for a state of emergency (*halat al-tawari'*) and martial law. The former may be declared in case of "calamity, siege or danger threatening the safety of the State" (Article 187), whereas the latter may

[174] See Section 2.1.5.

be declared "in case of war or a severe threat to national security" (Article 188). The state of emergency is declared by the president after having consulted with the Prime Minister and the Presidents of the two Houses of Parliament. The declaration needs to be approved (or rejected) by the *Shura* Council (i.e., Parliament), which must convene within three days of such declaration, and if it is in recess, it must convene within seven days (Article 187). The wording of this provision seems to suggest that the state of emergency comes into force immediately, even *before* it is approved by the *Shura* Council. Martial law is declared (and lifted) by the *Shura* Council upon a request by the president of the Republic. A declaration of martial law needs to be approved by an absolute majority of the members of the *Shura* Council within a three-day period (Article 188). The draft constitution provides for several safeguards. As regards the state of emergency, it contemplates, for example, a "supermajoritarian escalator" similar to the one existing in Egypt, whereby a presidential declaration of a state of emergency needs to be approved by a majority of the members of the *Shura* Council, but can only be renewed by a two-thirds majority of its members. Furthermore, the duration of the state of emergency must not exceed sixty days, and may be renewed for a period not exceeding sixty days (Article 187). As regards martial law, the draft constitution states that it cannot be imposed on the entire country, but only in specific regions (Article 188). Other safeguards that apply to both the state of emergency and martial law include limitations on restrictions on fundamental rights, judicial oversight over "all decisions and actions," and the prohibition on the dissolution of elected councils and amendment of the constitution (Article 189).

In Tunisia, the 2014 constitution provided for an interesting emergency regime that was deeply influenced by the constitutional reform adopted in France in 2008. Indeed, this reform introduced, *inter alia*, significant innovations to the constitutional provision governing the state of exception (Article 16), by vesting the *Conseil Constitutionnel* with the power to review the upholding of such a state. Article 80 of the 2014 Tunisian Constitution, which was extremely similar to (the new) Article 16 of the French Constitution, identified the conditions under which a state of exception (*halat al-istithna*) could be declared (i.e., "In the event of imminent danger threatening the nation's institutions or the security or independence of the country, and that hampers the normal functioning of the State") and stipulated that the president may declare such a state only after having consulted with the Head of Government and the Speaker of Parliament and after having informed the President of the Constitutional Court. Moreover, Parliament was deemed to be in a state of continuous session throughout such a period. In such situations, the president of the Republic could not dissolve Parliament and it was not possible to table motions of censure against the government. What made the Tunisian emergency framework different from the regimes existing in the other Arab countries (and in most countries around the world) was that the Speaker of Parliament or thirty of its members could apply to the Constitutional Court thirty days after the entry into force of the exceptional measures, and at any time thereafter, with a view to verifying whether or not the circumstances were still exceptional.[175] Unfortunately, these safeguards remained theoretical only. The state of exception was proclaimed for the first time in the country in March 2020 in order to combat the spread of the COVID-19 pandemic,[176] and was later proclaimed again on July 25, 2021, when Kaïs Saïed dismissed the Head of Government and suspended both Parliament's activity and parliamentary immunity. However, as already discussed earlier,[177] since the Constitutional Court had not been established, the mechanism provided for by the constitution for reviewing the upholding of a state of exception was unworkable, thus leaving to the president alone the decision as to whether to uphold such a state.

The 2022 constitution no longer involves the Constitutional Court in the process leading to the declaration and extension of a state of exception. Article 96 stipulates that the president of the Republic declares a state of exception after having consulted with the Prime Minister, the President of the Assembly of the Representatives of the People, and the President of the National Council of Regions and Districts, thus excluding altogether the President of the Constitutional Court. Furthermore, the Court is no longer vested with the power to review the upholding of a state of exception. The constitution now only stipulates that the exceptional measures "end as soon as the reasons which have justified them cease to apply" (Article 96), a provision that recalls Article 59(4) of the Moroccan Constitution. This means that the duration of a state of exception is entirely within the discretion of the president. Furthermore, one cannot fail to notice that the new emergency regime no longer requires Parliament to be in continuous session throughout a state of exception, as it only prevents the president from dissolving the two Houses of Parliament (Article 96).

It is apparent from the analysis of the post-2011 emergency frameworks described earlier that the head of state (whether this is a king or a president) has remained the undisputed leading actor in times of crisis, even though in some countries the role of Parliament has been reinforced, and new procedural, temporal, and substantive safeguards have been introduced. In many cases, however, these new democratic guarantees have not been sufficient to ensure respect for the principles of constitutionalism.

[175] The French framework is more "stringent" compared to the Tunisian one, since it also stipulates that sixty days after the exercise of the exceptional powers or at any moment thereafter, the Constitutional Council is entitled, *as of right*, to review the circumstances and make a decision (Article 16). This provision was absent in the 2014 Tunisian Constitution.

[176] Presidential Decree no. 2020-24 of March 18, 2020. See Avocats Sans Frontières, *The Tunisian Response to the Covid-19 Pandemic – When the State of Exception Overlaps With the State of Emergency* (July 1, 2020), https://asf.be/the-tunisian-response-to-the-covid-19-pandemic-when-the-state-of-exception-overlaps-with-the-state-of-emergency/. It should be noted that until March 2020, when facing security challenges, the executive resorted to a different emergency regime, namely the state of *emergency* (*état d'urgence*), which is regulated by Decree no. 78-50 of January 26, 1978 (adopted under Habib Bourguiba's rule). On the differences between the state of emergency and the state of exception, see Democracy Reporting International, *La mise en œuvre de la Constitution tunisienne du 27 janvier 2014 au niveau du cadre juridique. Bilan*, at pp. 73–76.

[177] See Section 2.2.4.

2.3.1 *The Role of Courts in Times of Crisis*

Under the post-2011 emergency regimes – as was the case in the past – the judiciary has not been granted any role in the process leading to the declaration or extension of a state of emergency. The only exception – as discussed earlier – was Tunisia under the 2014 constitution. This exclusion of the judiciary seems to be a major shortcoming, especially if one considers that in some countries – such as for example in Colombia[178] – courts' intervention has proved to be highly effective in preventing presidents from abusing the power to declare a state of emergency. However, it should be noted that, in the Arab world, the declaration of a state of emergency has long been considered by courts as an "act of sovereignty" (*a'mal al-siyada*), namely an act of the executive branch that falls outside the jurisdiction of the judiciary.[179] In Jordan, for example, the High Court of Justice ruled that "the King is the only person, who has the right to determine the existence or non-existence of the state of emergency, and this court cannot challenge such determination, otherwise the court would deprive the King of this power and give it to itself."[180] In a similar vein, the Supreme Court of Egypt argued that it could not review the declaration of a state of emergency since it was an "act of sovereignty,"[181] and this approach was subsequently followed by the Supreme Constitutional Court. Interestingly, in Egypt, this nonjusticiability doctrine was recently questioned by the State Council, which ruled that "the decision no. 587 of 2013 issued by the president of Republic to extend the declared state of emergency [...] for two months *is an administrative decision and is not considered an act of sovereignty* [...]"[182] (emphasis added). The State Council allowed for a limited review of the *formal* requirements for the proclamation of a state of emergency (namely, the duration of the emergency and its geographical scope). Although it continued to grant broad discretion to the executive, this decision is still an innovative one, as it partly departs from consolidated case law.

While they have not been granted any role in the process leading to the declaration and extension of a state of emergency (with the only notable exception of Tunisia under the 2014 constitution), in many cases, Arab courts have held that they

[178] See Katrin Merhof, "Building a Bridge between Reality and the Constitution: The Establishment and Development of the Colombian Constitutional Court" (2015) 13 *International Journal of Constitutional Law*, 718–719; Andrea Scoseria Katz, "Taming the Prince: Bringing Presidential Emergency Powers under Law in Colombia" (2020) 18 *International Journal of Constitutional Law*, 1201ff. From a comparative perspective, on the role of courts in the process leading to the declaration and extension of the state of emergency see Francesco Biagi, "Estados de emergencia y crisis pandémica: algunas reflexiones sobre el papel de los tribunales constitucionales" (2021) 1 *Asuntos constitucionales*, 62ff.

[179] On this doctrine, see Chapter 3, Section 3.2.2. in greater detail.

[180] High Court of Justice, February 24, 1952, *Journal of the Bar Association of Jordan* (1953), p. 54, cited in Sabah Mousa Al Momani, "Acts of Sovereignty as a Restriction on Judicial Control" (2020) 13 *Journal of Politics and Law*, 116.

[181] Judgment of April 3, 1976.

[182] Case no. 67/74029 (November 12, 2013), cited in Al Momani, "Acts of Sovereignty," at p. 119.

have jurisdiction to rule on the emergency measures adopted by state authorities in times of crisis. In the past, however, courts often displayed a very high degree of deference to political authorities in this field.[183] This approach has not changed significantly after the Arab Spring, although over the past few years, courts have issued some decisions offering greater protection for rights and freedoms. Thus, for instance, in 2013, the Supreme Constitutional Court of Egypt struck down Article 3 of the Emergency Law no. 162 of 1958, which granted the president of the Republic the power to arrest and search persons and places without judicial warrant.[184] In Tunisia, the administrative courts have annulled decisions imposing house arrests on the basis of Decree no. 78-50 regulating the state of emergency. For example, in a judgment issued on July 2, 2018, the Administrative Court of First Instance of Tunis argued that a decision to impose house arrest could not be issued on the basis of a decree but only on the basis of a *law*.[185] The reason was that according to Article 49 of the 2014 constitution, restrictions on constitutionally guaranteed rights and freedoms could only be imposed in the form of a law – and in particular in the form of an *organic law*, as stipulated by Article 65.[186]

2.3.2 *A Few Remarks on the COVID-19 Pandemic*

Following the outbreak of the COVID-19 pandemic, Arab rulers often relied on emergency provisions. In some cases – such as in Egypt and Algeria – they exploited this health crisis "to enact severe – albeit temporary – social control legislation" and "weaken potential opponents and critics in order to cement their hold on power."[187] While monarchs and presidents were the leading actors during this emergency, they rarely acted alone. Rather, a number of actors (including technical departments and ministries, civilian experts, the military, professional associations, as well as religious leaders and institutions) were often involved in decision-making processes concerning measures to be adopted in order to curb the spread of the virus.[188] Thus, during

[183] One need only consider the case of Egypt, where even during its more liberal and activist era (i.e., during the 1990s), the Supreme Constitutional Court declared the emergency state security courts in line with the constitution. See Tamir Moustafa, "The Political Role of the Supreme Constitutional Court: Between Principles and Practice" in Nathalie Bernard-Maugiron (ed.), *Judges and Political Reform in Egypt* (The American University in Cairo Press 2008), 95ff.

[184] Case no. 17, Judicial Year 15 (June 2, 2013). On this judgment, see also Chapter 3, Section 3.4.1.

[185] *Affaire* no. 150168 (July 2, 2018).

[186] A short summary of this decision can be found in Democracy Reporting International, *La mise en œuvre de la Constitution tunisienne au niveau du cadre juridique. 30 septembre 2019 – 9eme édition* (2019), 47.

[187] Frederick Kempe and Giampiero Massolo, "Preface" in Karim Mezran and Annalisa Perteghella (eds.), *The Politics of Pandemics: Evolving Regime-Opposition Dynamics in the MENA Region* (ISPI-Atlantic Council 2020), 10, www.ispionline.it/en/publication/politics-pandemics-evolving-regime-opposition-dynamics-mena-region-28410

[188] See Alessia Melcangi, "Regime Responses in Egypt and Algeria" in Karim Mezran et al. (eds.), *The Impact of COVID-19 on Either Shore of the Mediterranean* (Atlantic Council 2020), 9ff., www.atlanticcouncil.org/wp-content/uploads/2020/09/Covid-on-Both-Shores-Report_Final.pdf

this health crisis, there appeared to be a higher degree of collegiality compared to past security-related emergencies – although this collegiality did not always prevent abuses. In the light of their major influence, it is worth stressing the role played by religious institutions and leaders (including Al-Azhar), who were often requested to issue opinions (*fatawa*) concerning the compatibility with *sharia* of the measures adopted by state authorities in order to contain the spread of the virus. In most cases, the religious authorities confirmed the legitimacy of these measures and called on the faithful to respect them.[189]

2.4 GREATER BUT STILL VERY WEAK: THE VERTICAL SEPARATION OF POWERS

Historically, Arab states were characterized by highly centralized and unitary systems of government, in most cases leaving little or no room for decentralization, regionalism, or federalism. Put differently, not only the horizontal but also the *vertical* separation of powers was extremely weak. The very few Arab countries that could be classified (at least from a formal point of view) as "federal" include Libya and the United Arab Emirates. Libya adopted a federal system (comprising the three historical regions of Cyrenaica, Tripolitania, and Fezzan) in 1951, although the 1963 reform of the 1951 constitution abandoned it and created a unitary state. The United Arab Emirates has been a federal state since 1971. The seven Emirates forming the country (namely, Abu Dhabi, Dubai, Sharjah, Ras Al-Khaimah, Ajman, Umm Al-Quwain, and Fujairah [Article 1 of the constitution]) exercise sovereignty over their own territories in all matters that do not fall within the jurisdiction of the Union (Article 3).

Currently, aside from the constitution of the UAE, the 2005 Iraqi Constitution is the only constitutional text in the Arab world to classify the country as "federal" (Article 1). More specifically, Article 116 stipulates that "The federal system in the Republic of Iraq is made up of a decentralized capital, regions, and governorates, as well as local administrations." Currently, Iraqi federalism is asymmetric. Indeed, until now the only region to have been created is Kurdistan, with the Kurdistan Regional Government (KRG) as its official ruling body. However, apart from Kurdistan, the Baghdad central government has managed to preserve its broad authority over the rest of country.[190] Indeed, "[a]lthough the 2005 constitution

[189] See Maria Chiara Locchi, "La risposta all'emergenza sanitaria Covid-19 nei paesi a maggioranza musulmana: alcune considerazioni comparative" (2020) 2 *DPCE online*, 2186–2187; Chiara Pellegrino, "Le autorità religiose islamiche al tempo del Coronavirus," *Fondazione Oasis* (April 30, 2020), www.oasiscenter.eu/it/le-autorita-religiose-islamiche-al-tempo-del-coronavirus

[190] On Iraq's territorial organization, see Ali Al-Mawlawi, "Salvaging State Legitimacy in Iraq through Decentralization" in Aslı Ü. Bâli and Omar M. Dajani (eds.), *Federalism and Decentralization in the Contemporary Middle East and North Africa* (Cambridge University Press 2023), 120ff.; Zaid Al-Ali, "Constitutional Legitimacy in Iraq. What Role Local Context?" in Rainer Grote and Tilmann J. Röder

backed a devolution of powers to regions and provinces along the lines that Kurdish leaders envisaged, flaws in the document and the need for supporting legislation have allowed successive governments in Baghdad to resist limits on the power of the federal government."[191] On September 25, 2017, the KRG organized a nonbinding independence referendum, where approximately 92 percent of voters expressed their desire to start a process of secession from Iraq. However, the refusal by the central government and several foreign states to recognize this consultation or its outcome clearly shows the difficulties associated with the independence option, at least for the time being. In February 2022, the Iraqi Supreme Court issued two extremely controversial judgments, which clearly show that the relations between Baghdad and the KRG remain problematic[192]: In one of these decisions, the Court barred a Kurdish politician from running for the presidency after a complaint was filed against him over corruption charges,[193] while in the other judgment, the Court ruled the 2007 Oil and Gas Law of the Kurdistan Region unconstitutional, obliging Kurdistan to hand over all oil produced by oil fields in the Kurdistan Region.[194]

Since the 2011 uprisings, some Arab countries (Jordan, Egypt, Algeria, and Syria) have remained heavily centralized, whereas others (Morocco, Tunisia [under the 2014 constitution], and Libya) have provided for a limited decentralization of an administrative (rather than political) nature. The following sections (Sections 2.4.1–2.4.3) examine these two groups in greater detail.

2.4.1 *Major Centralization: Jordan, Egypt, Algeria, and Syria*

In Jordan, neither the 2011 reform nor the subsequent amendments adopted in 2014, 2016, and 2022 affected the very few constitutional provisions on local government (Articles 120 and 121), thus keeping the heavily centralized system of government

(eds.), *Constitutionalism in Islamic Countries: Between Upheaval and Continuity* (Oxford University Press 2012), 652ff. Specifically on the Kurdish question, see Peter Bartu and Aidan MacEachern, "The Devil Is in the Details. Iraqi Kurdistan's Evolving Autonomy" in Bâli and Dajani (eds.) 2023, in this note, at p. 183ff.; Bawar Bammarny, "The Legal Status of the Kurds in Iraq and Syria" in Grote and Röder (eds.) 2016, *Constitutionalism, Human Rights, and Islam*, at p. 480ff.

191 Raad Alkadiri, "Federalism and Iraq's Constitutional Stalemate," *Chatham House* (November 2020), p. 2, www.chathamhouse.org/sites/default/files/2020-11/2020-11-27-iraq-federalism-alkadiri.pdf.pdf

192 These decisions are extremely controversial also because the Federal Supreme Court has not yet been formed in accordance with the 2005 Constitution. The existing Court is a Court that was established in 2004 by a provision in the 2004 Law of Administration for the State of Iraq for the Transitional Period.

193 See "Iraqi Court Bars Veteran Zebari from Running for Presidency," *Al Jazeera* (February 13, 2022), www.aljazeera.com/news/2022/2/13/iraqi-court-bars-zebari-from-running-for-presidency-state-media

194 See Majida S. Ismael, "The Federal Supreme Court of Iraq From Interpreting to Amending the Constitution: KRG's Oil Judgement as an Example," *Kurdistan 24* (April 3, 2022), www.kurdistan24.net/en/opinion/27484-The-Federal-Supreme-Court-of-Iraq-from-interpreting-to-amending-the-constitution:–KRG's-oil-judgement-as-an-example; "Iraq's Invalid Supreme Court is Used Against Kurds Again," *Washington Kurdish Institute* (February 26, 2022), https://dckurd.org/2022/02/26/iraqs-invalid-supreme-court/

in place. The new Decentralization Law and the revised Municipalities Law (both passed in 2015) are characterized by several flaws and made very little progress in the decentralization process.[195] In Egypt, the 2014 constitution stipulates that the state "ensures support for administrative, financial, and economic decentralization" (Article 176), and that the local administrative units include governorates, cities, and villages (Article 175). The regulation of most issues relating to local government (including the powers and competences of the administrative units) is left to implementing legislation. The result of this territorial arrangement is that Egypt has remained "one of the most centralized countries in the world."[196]

In a similar vein, in Algeria, the 2020 constitutional reform introduced minor changes to the local government. The constitution stipulates that the "local communities of the State shall be the municipality and the wilaya," and that in order to ensure "an economic and social balance, as well as better management of the needs of less developed populations and municipalities, the law may provide for specific provisions for some of them" (Article 17). Furthermore, the "relationships between the State and the local communities shall be based on the principles of decentralization and deconcentration" (Article 18). This very limited degree of decentralization stands in sharp contrast with the size of the country and the composition of its population. Indeed, Algeria is the largest country on the African continent, with a population divided into various groups, some of which have specific linguistic and/or cultural identities (e.g., the Berbers in Kabylia, the Mozabites in Ghardaïa, and the Tuareg in the southern Sahara). As noted by John P. Entelis

> a failure to appreciate this reality of political geography has been and continues to be a distinctive factor in explaining why the Algerian state has never been able to fully enforce its political will and why those seeking the state's overthrow confront the same challenge. In short, geography neutralizes incumbents and insurgents alike in their quest to alter the political status quo.[197]

In Syria, the decentralization system is quite complex, as one must distinguish between the territory controlled by the Assad government (around 63 percent), the territory governed by opposition forces (around 11 percent), and the territory under the control of Kurdish forces (around 25 percent).[198] In government-controlled

[195] See Wael Al Khatib, *Decentralization in Jordan* (Konrad Adenauer Stiftung 2020), www.kas.de/documents/279984/280033/Publikation+Dezentralisierung.pdf/8823fcf8-1ea9-0f43-d91d-6321311904f3?version=1.0&t=1587493676422

[196] Rana Khazbak, "In Egypt, There Is No Local Government," *Mada Masr* (March 28, 2016), www.madamasr.com/en/2016/03/28/opinion/u/in-egypt-there-is-no-local-government/

[197] Entelis, "Algeria: The Outlier State?," at p. 112. On the fact that the geography of the country played a role also during the demonstrations held against the regime between January and February 2011, see Section 2.1.5.

[198] "Map of Military Control Across Syria at the End of 2022 and the Beginning of 2023," *Jusoor Center for Studies* (January 2, 2023),. https://jusoor.co/en/details/map-of-military-control-across-syria-at-the-end-of-2022-and-the-beginning-of-2023

regions, the system of government is very centralized. The 2012 constitution continues to provide for a unitary state, thus perpetuating the centralization that has characterized the country since the Ba'ath Party's seizure of power in 1963. The constitutional text only dedicates two provisions to local government: Article 130, which states that "[t]he Syrian Arab Republic consists of administrative units [...]," and Article 131, which stipulates that "[t]he organization of local administration units is based on the principle of decentralization of authorities and responsibilities [...]." The regulation of almost all local governance issues is left to ordinary legislation, which still consists of the "Local Administration Law" no. 107 of October 2011. This piece of legislation, however, which "was intended to signal democratic reforms under the guise of devolution of powers to municipalities, [...] failed to go far enough in undoing the government's authoritarianism, retaining key elements of control on which the Ba'ath Party had come to depend."[199] Furthermore, several important provisions of Law no. 107 have not been implemented.[200]

In the territory under their control, the opposition forces implemented a system of decentralization that drew inspiration from Law no. 107. However, unlike in government-controlled regions, "where decentralization was little more than a facade to maintain political control," in these areas "decentralization was thrust on local bodies of the Opposition as a matter of practical necessity, and invested them with real power and authority."[201] But "without a center around which these bodies could cohere, and in the face of a constant onslaught from both the government and more hardline Islamist rebels, the long-term viability of this system was constantly imperiled."[202] Since December 2016, the vast majority of opposition-control areas have been retaken by government forces. Indeed, as recalled earlier, currently less than 11 percent of the territory is under the control of the opposition.

The remaining Syrian territory is governed by the Kurdish forces. As is well known, like in Iraq, also in Syria, the Kurdish question remains extremely problematic. In the 2012 constitution, the existence of Kurds is completely ignored, despite the fact that they form the largest ethnic minority in the country, constituting an estimated 10 percent of the population.[203] The constitution only guarantees, in very general terms, "the protection of cultural diversity of the Syrian society with all its components and the multiplicity of its tributaries" (Article 9). In 2012, in the midst of the conflict, Kurdish militias forced the Syrian army to withdraw from Kurdish-inhabited areas in the north of the country, specifically the Rojava region. Afterward, in 2014, the Rojava authorities proclaimed the (*de facto*) autonomy of the

[199] Samer Araabi and Leila Hilal, "Decentralization in State Disintegration. An Examination of Governance Experiments in Syria" in Bâli and Dajani (eds.) 2023, *Federalism and Decentralization*, at p. 349.

[200] Ibid., at p. 350.

[201] Ibid., at p. 357.

[202] Ibid.

[203] See Bammarny, "Legal Status of the Kurds," at pp. 490–492.

region from the Syrian government and adopted a constitutional document, whose official name was the "Social Contract of Rojava Cantons in Syria."[204] This text, which has been described as "extraordinarily progressive,"[205] incorporated the ideas and principles of the polity system known as "democratic confederalism," as theorized by the Kurdistan Workers Party (PKK) leader Abdullah Öcalan. This system, which is based on the principles of autonomy, direct democracy, environmentalism, feminism, and self-governance, aims to foster coexistence in multicultural societies by transcending the notion of the nation state.[206] A new constitutional text was then adopted in 2016, namely the "Social Contract of the Democratic Federation of Northern Syria,"[207] which continues to be grounded on the principles of "democratic confederalism."[208] According to this document, the region is administered by decentralized self-governing units (Articles 47ff.) and is based on the "co-presidency system," with the aim of guaranteeing "equal representation of both genders" in all "political, social, administrative and other fields" (Article 12). It should be stressed that, unlike Kurdish leaders in Iraq, the Rojava authorities did not claim independence. Indeed, the 2014 Social Contract stated that the regions of Rojava formed "an integral part of Syria" and that this represented "a model for a future decentralized system of federal governance in Syria" (Article 12). In a similar vein, the preamble to the 2016 Social Contract stipulated that the region was "part of the united Syrian democratic federalism," thus expressing the willingness of the Rojava authorities to create a federal Syria.[209] However, the region lost part of its autonomy following the Turkish invasion in October 2019, also in the light of the fact that the leaders of Rojava (whose official name is now the "Autonomous Administration of North and East Syria" [AANES]) were forced to invite Syrian and Russian forces into their territory for protection.[210]

Although the draft constitution for Syria prepared by the Russian government in 2017 was rejected by all political forces, it still contains some interesting features in relation to territorial arrangements, which are worth considering. The draft states that the Syrian Republic (it is significant that the expression "Syrian *Arab* Republic" has been abandoned) consists of "constituent parts," and that the

[204] The text is available online here: https://civiroglu.net/the-constitution-of-the-rojava-cantons/

[205] Bammarny, "Legal Status of the Kurds," at p. 492.

[206] See Stefano Marinelli, "The 2016 Rojava Social Contract: A Democratic Experiment of Civil and Social Rights in Northern Syria," *International Law Blog* (October 24, 2016), https://internationallaw.blog/2016/10/24/the-2016-rojava-social-contract-a-democratic-experiment-of-civil-and-social-rights-in-northern-syria/

[207] The text is available online here: https://internationalistcommune.com/social-contract/

[208] See Marinelli, "2016 Rojava Social Contract."

[209] See also Lorenzo Cremonesi, "Sconfitta Isis, noi curdi vogliamo ora una Siria federale e democratica," *Il Corriere della Sera* (March 29, 2019), www.corriere.it/esteri/19_marzo_29/sconfitta-isis-noi-curdi-vogliamo-ora-siria-federale-democratica-4b1ef910-5236-11e9-95de-b93fcff37bd3.shtml

[210] See Mazloum Abdi, "If We Have to Choose Between Compromise and Genocide, We Will Choose Our People," *Foreign Policy* (October 13, 2019), https://foreignpolicy.com/2019/10/13/kurds-assad-syria-russia-putin-turkey-genocide/

organization of the local authorities is based on the principle of decentralization (Article 15). Furthermore, the draft contains some provisions specifically dealing with the Kurdish question. Compared to the currently applicable 2012 constitution, this represents *per se* a step forward. Article 4 stipulates that Syrian citizens have the right to "educate their children in their native language," that "government agencies and institutions of Kurdish Cultural Autonomy shall use both Kurdish and Arabic equally," and that "each region shall have the right to use another majority language in addition to the official language as regulated by the law, provided that such usage has been approved by a locally held referendum." The preamble to the draft constitution also proclaims a commitment to respect the Declaration on the Rights of Persons Belonging to National or Ethnic, Religious and Linguistic Minorities. On the other hand, however, the draft contains some questionable points. In particular, it stipulates that the relationship between the central government and the local authorities, their mandate, financial revenues, control over their work, the appointment or election of their representatives, as well as the status of the Kurdish Cultural Autonomy are regulated by *law* (Article 15), thus leaving the possibility for the central government to significantly limit the scope of Kurdish autonomy.

Within the current constitution-making process, which is being carried out under the supervision of the United Nations,[211] Kurds only comprise 4 percent of the Syrian Constitutional Committee (SCC), the body responsible for replacing the 2012 constitution with a new constitutional text. Worse still, the Democratic Union Party (PYD), which exerts the greatest influence in the Rojava region, has been completely excluded from the SCC due to its strong ties with the PKK, which is regarded as a terrorist organization by Turkey, the European Union, and the United States. The lack of representatives from the "Autonomous Administration of North and East Syria" in the constitution-drafting process is a major flaw, which should be addressed.[212] Their representation seems to be essential, *inter alia*, in order to reach agreement on the territorial organization of the country.

2.4.2 *Limited Decentralization: Morocco, Tunisia, and Libya*

In Morocco, the 2011 constitution stipulates that "the territorial organization of the Kingdom is decentralized" and is "founded on an advanced regionalization" (Article 1). More specifically, the territorial entities of which the country is comprised are the regions, the prefectures, the provinces, and the municipalities (Article 135).[213] The process of advanced regionalization started to be implemented with the adoption

[211] See in greater detail Chapter 1, Section 1.2.6.

[212] See Karam Shaar and Ayman Dasouki, "Syria's Constitutional Committee: The Devil in the Detail," *MEI@75* (January 6, 2021), www.mei.edu/publications/syrias-constitutional-committee-devil-detail

[213] See the special issue of the *Revue marocaine d'administration locale et de développement* (REMALD), no. 93 (2015) on "La régionalisation avancée: fondements et principes constitutionnels."

of three Organic Laws, namely Organic Law no. 111-14 on the regions, Organic Law no. 112-14 on prefectures and provinces, and Organic Law no. 113-14 on municipalities.[214] Although the degree of regionalization is certainly higher than it was in the past, the territorial organization of Morocco is much more similar to the French *administrative* decentralization than to the Italian or Spanish regionalism, where sub-state entities (respectively, the *regioni* and the *Comunidades Autonomas*) are granted full *political* autonomy.[215] This is also confirmed by the fact that regions in Morocco are only granted *regulatory* (and not legislative) powers (*pouvoir réglementaire*) (Article 140(2)).

Far from being resolved, the long-standing question of Western Sahara remains one of the most sensitive issues in Morocco. It is significant that Article 42(2) of the constitution stipulates that the king is the "Guarantor [...] of the territorial integrity of the Kingdom *within its authentic frontiers*" (emphasis added). The Autonomy Plan for Sahara proposed by the Moroccan authorities in 2007 envisages a "Sahara autonomous region," which would clearly represent an exception to the type of regionalism provided for under the 2011 constitution.[216] For example, the Sahara region would be granted *political* autonomy and its Parliament would be vested with *legislative* power. Therefore, if incorporated into the Moroccan Constitution, this new arrangement would lead to a form of *asymmetric* regionalism.[217] However, as the Polisario Front claims full sovereignty over this territory, an autonomous Sahara region within Morocco does not seem to be a viable option, at least for the time being.

In Tunisia, whereas the 1959 constitution merely contained a single provision on "Local Communities" (Article 71), the 2014 constitution dedicated an entire section to "Local Government" (Title VII). Local authorities, which included municipalities, regions, and districts, were vested with more competence and enjoyed a much higher degree of autonomy than they had in the past (Articles 131–142).[218] As in Morocco, however, this autonomy was only of an administrative (rather than political) nature. Indeed, Article 132 stipulated that "Local authorities shall enjoy legal personality as well as financial and administrative autonomy. They shall manage local affairs in accordance with the principle of free administration." Moreover, Article 134(3) only vested local authorities with regulatory (and not legislative)

[214] Respectively, *Zaha'ir* no. 1-15-83, no. 1-15-84, and no. 1-15-85, of July 7, 2015.

[215] See Abdelhamid Adnane, "Tratamiento jurídico-constitucional de los entes territoriales en Marruecos y los indicadores de la autonomía mermada del poder regional" (June 24, 2020) *Federalismi.it*, 36ff., www.federalismi.it

[216] See François-Paul Blanc, "La régionalisation et la Constitution de 2011: genèse et prospective" in Centre d'Études Internationales (ed.) 2012, *La Constitution marocaine de 2011*, at p. 326ff.

[217] For a deeper analysis of Morocco's advanced regionalization and the question of Western Sahara, see Omar Yousef Shehabi, "'Dans ses Frontières Authentiques'? Morocco's Advanced Regionalization and the Question of Western Sahara" in Bâli and Dajani (eds.) 2023, *Federalism and Decentralization*, at p. 268ff.

[218] See Lofti Tarchouna, "Il decentramento territoriale: novità e sfide" in Groppi and Spigno (eds.) 2015, *Tunisia*, at p. 152ff.

powers. In 2018, the Tunisian Parliament adopted the Code of Local Authorities,[219] which was one of the most important pieces of legislation implementing Title VII of the constitution. It was a "*méga Code*" comprising 400 articles. Its enforcement, however, was severely hindered by the fact that the majority of its implementing decrees were not adopted.[220] During the same year (2018), the first free and fair local elections in the history of the country were held. Although this undoubtedly represented a very important step toward the consolidation of a democratic system, the process of decentralization did not produce the desired results in terms of the distribution of competences between the central government and local authorities, cooperation and coordination among local authorities, as well as the strengthening of social and public services.[221]

Following his election as president of the Republic in 2019, on several occasions, Kaïs Saïed expressed his intention to proceed with a decentralization of power. His idea was to "reverse the pyramid of power," building up democracy "from the grass roots."[222] More specifically, according to the Tunisian president, the system needed to be re-established around "local popular assemblies created at delegation level (second-order administrative districts), regional assemblies, and last, a national assembly whose members are indirectly elected or drawn by lot from local assemblies."[223] This scheme, however, can hardly be found in the 2022 constitution. The very few traces of the "democracy from the bottom-up" include the brief reference to "local assemblies" (Article 75), the revocability of elected representatives' mandates by voters (Article 61),[224] as well as the creation of an upper House, the National Council of Regions and Districts, which is comprised of elected representatives from the regions and districts (Article 81). The vertical separation of power seems to be very weak, at least in formal terms. One need only consider that the 2014 constitution devoted an entire chapter, Chapter 7, to "Local Power," which

[219] Law no. 2018-29 of May 9, 2018.

[220] On the difficulties in the enforcement of this code, see Democracy Reporting International, *La mise en œuvre de la Constitution tunisienne du 27 janvier 2014 au niveau du cadre juridique. Bilan*, at pp. 94–101.

[221] On the challenges of decentralization in Tunisia, see International Crisis Group, *Décentralisation en Tunisie: consolider la démocratie sans affaiblir l'État* (Rapport Moyen-Orient et Afrique du Nord, no. 198) (March 26, 2019), www.crisisgroup.org/fr/middle-east-north-africa/north-africa/tunisia/198-decentralisation-en-tunisie-consolider-la-democratie-sans-affaiblir-letat; Abdessalam Jaldi, "Tunisie: la démocratie à l'épreuve de la crise de la IIème République," *Policy Center for the New South* (February 2022), 8–9, www.policycenter.ma/sites/default/files/2022-02/PP_03-22_Jaldi%20%281%29.pdf; Intissar Kherigi, "Decentralization Reforms in Post-Revolution Tunisia. The Struggle Between Political and Bureaucratic Elites" in Bâli and Dajani (eds.) 2023, *Federalism and Decentralization*, at p. 140ff.

[222] Jaldi, "Tunisie," at p. 17ff.

[223] Eric Gobe, "Saïed's Constitution, an Authoritarian Project Behind a Bottom-up Curtain," *ISPI* (July 21, 2022), www.ispionline.it/it/pubblicazione/saieds-constitution-authoritarian-project-behind-bottom-curtain-35847

[224] This issue is regulated by Decree no. 2022-55 on the reform of the electoral law governing the elections to the Assembly of the Representatives of the People.

contained twelve articles, whereas Chapter 7 of the 2022 constitution, on "Local and Regional Bodies," only contains one article (Article 133) (as was the case under the 1959 constitution). Article 133 of the 2022 constitution – which has been taken over almost verbatim from Article 71 of the 1959 constitution – merely stipulates that municipal, regional, and district councils will look after local and regional interests in accordance with the law, without clarifying the type of autonomy (administrative or political) granted to these sub-state entities.

In Libya, the system of decentralization introduced by Law no. 59 of 2012 on the "Local Administration System" has contributed, at least partially, to addressing some of the country's governance challenges. Indeed, it has been argued that "amid national political paralysis, [...] Libya has witnessed some progress at the local level."[225] Having said that, Law no. 59 is characterized by a series of shortcomings and the system of decentralization remains largely incomplete.[226] It is clear, then, that "a future constitution [...] must substantively address the decentralization issue."[227] Not surprisingly, the territorial organization of the state was an extremely sensitive issue during the constitution-making process.[228] Chapter 6 of the 2017 draft constitution concerns local government. More specifically, Article 143 refers to the "principle of expanded decentralization [...] within the unity of the State," and Article 144 states that the country will be divided into governorates, municipalities, and other administrative levels. The decentralized entities are only granted administrative (rather than political) autonomy. Indeed, Article 145 (the wording of which is identical to Article 132 of the 2014 Tunisian Constitution [recalled earlier]) stipulates that "Local authorities shall enjoy legal personality as well as financial and administrative autonomy. They shall manage local affairs in accordance with the principle of free administration." The composition of Parliament's upper chamber is a clear concession to those who called for the establishment of a federal country. Indeed, despite the fact that the tri-regional federal option (as originally provided for under the 1951 constitution) has been abandoned, the Senate is supposed to guarantee representation for these three historical regions: thirty-two seats are granted to the Western region (Tripolitania), twenty-six to the Eastern region (Cyrenaica), and twenty to the Southern region (Fezzan) (Article 75). Moreover, the Senate has been vested with

[225] Karim Mezran and Elissa Miller, "The Promise – And Limits – Of Stabilization through Local Governance in Libya" in Bâli and Dajani (eds.) 2023, *Federalism and Decentralization*, at p. 318.

[226] Ibid., at p. 323ff.

[227] Ibid., at p. 329.

[228] See Democracy Reporting International, *Decentralisation in Libya* (August 2013), https://democracy-reporting.org/en/office/libya/publications/report-decentralisation-in-libya; Karim Mezran and Mohamed Eljarh, "The Case for a New Federalism in Libya," *Atlantic Council* (December 23, 2014), www.atlanticcouncil.org/publications/issue-briefs/the-case-for-a-new-federalism-in-libya; Nedra Cherif, "Libya's Constitution: Between Conflict and Compromise," *European University Institute – Middle East Directions (MED)* 2021/02 (March 2021), 20–21, https://cadmus.eui.eu/bitstream/handle/1814/70538/QM-09-21-057-EN-N.pdf?sequence=3&isAllowed=y; Al-Ali, "Libya's Final Draft Constitution," at pp. 13–15.

the power to approve laws related to local governance (Article 79(2)).[229] One compromise struck between "centralists" and "federalists" has been to maintain Tripoli as the sole capital (Article 3),[230] while distributing some key institutions among other cities, namely Benghazi in the East (the seat of both Houses of Parliament) (Article 90) and Sabha in the South (the seat of the Constitutional Court) (Article 135). As regards the management of natural resources (particularly oil and gas) and the distribution of revenues generated by them, the framers opted to leave the regulation of most of these issues to implementing legislation. In the past, the centralized and state-controlled economic system failed to ensure a fair distribution of revenues from natural resources, particularly to the producing regions (east and south), which remained marginalized under the Gaddafi regime.[231] Therefore, addressing this issue will certainly be one of the priorities for any future government in Libya.

2.4.3 *Decentralization: A Plant that Still Has to Take Root*

The vertical separation of powers in the Arab world is certainly greater than it was in the past. However, it is still too weak, thus favoring the consolidation of authority in the hands of the executive branch at the central level. Sub-state entities should be granted a greater role not only because they are better placed in order to understand and address people's needs but also because they can impose important checks on the government's action. When sub-state entities do not exist or are granted extremely limited prerogatives, this bulwark is absent. In any case, territorial organization is likely to remain a sensitive topic in the region. For instance, in Morocco, the issue of Western Sahara continues to be extremely controversial; in Syria, the Rojava authorities aim to create a federal country; in Libya, many "federalists" in Cyrenaica are not satisfied with the territorial arrangement provided for under the 2017 draft constitution, as they would had preferred the tri-regions federal option;[232] and in Tunisia, it remains to be seen whether and to what extent Kaïs Saïed will try to implement his ideal of "democracy from the bottom-up."

2.5 REASONS FOR THE CONCENTRATION OF POWERS

The previous sections (Sections 2.1–2.4) established that the concentration of power, both at the horizontal and at the vertical level, continues to be a distinguishing feature of most Arab countries. The following sections (Sections 2.5.1–2.5.4) examine the reasons for this overconcentration of authority, which include the constitutional

[229] See Cherif, "Libya's Constitution," at p. 21.

[230] The 1951 constitution, on the contrary, provided for two capitals: Tripoli and Benghazi (Article 188).

[231] See Cherif, "Libya's Constitution," at p. 21.

[232] See Felix-Anselm van Lier, "Constitution-Making as a Tool for State-Building? Insights From an Ethnographic Analysis of the Libyan Constitution-Making Process," *Max Planck Institute for Social Anthropology* (Working Paper no. 192) (2018), 16. It should be noted that this resistance from the

tradition (characterized by two interrelated elements, namely the principle of unity of power and the historical dominance of the executive), the patriarchal family, the "top-down" constitution-making processes, and external influences.

2.5.1 *The Constitutional Tradition*

The principle of the separation of powers is not alien to the Islamic world. Some forms of separation of powers can be traced back to the earliest phases of Islamic statehood, even though this concept differs from the one that emerged in the West. Indeed,

> unlike the relationship between executive, judicial, and legislative powers in modern democracies, the classical Muslim balance of powers was not between government entities but rather between the government as a whole and the non-governmental forces of scholarly academia. Neither had absolute power over the law, and each institution recognized the other's presence and role in the system.[233]

Thus, a distinction was drawn between ruler-made law (*siyasah*, literally "administration" or "management"), on the one hand, and scholar-crafted law (*fiqh*, literally, "understanding"), on the other hand.[234] *Siyasah* and *fiqh* were two different types of law: While the former was generated according to the will of the rulers (namely, kings, sultans, and caliphs), who were responsible for adopting and enforcing laws aimed at maintaining safety, security, and justice, the latter was (and still is) the outcome of the hermeneutic effort (*ijtihad*) of religious scholars to interpret *sharia*.[235] Traditionally, *fiqh* scholars were extremely deferential to rulers, and in a similar vein, rulers generally respected the authority of *fiqh* scholars.[236] This gave rise to an "effective separation of powers in which neither realm – rulers or scholars – had full control over societal norms."[237]

Traces of the principle of the separation of powers as interpreted within the Western tradition (i.e., the separation between the three branches of government) can be found in the first constitutions adopted in the Islamic world, namely the 1861 constitution of Tunisia, the 1876 Ottoman Basic Law, the 1882 Egyptian

"federalists" in Cyrenaica might influence the outcome of the referendum on the draft constitution. Indeed, while the Interim Constitutional Declaration requested a two-thirds nationwide majority, the 2018 Referendum Law divides Libya into three constituencies (Tripolitania, Cyrenaica, and Fezzan) and requires that the draft constitution be approved by a majority of the voters in each region. As of this writing, however, it is not clear whether these arrangements will be maintained or not and also whether the referendum will take place at all. See Chapter 1, Section 1.2.5.

233 Asifa Quraishi, "The Separation of Powers in the Tradition of Muslim Governments" in Grote and Röder (eds.) 2012, *Constitutionalism in Islamic Countries*, at p. 63.

234 Ibid., at pp. 64–47.

235 Ibid., at pp. 64–66.

236 As also stressed by Noah Feldman, *The Fall and Rise of the Islamic State* (Princeton University Press 2012), 6, who argues that *fiqh* scholars were a "powerful and effective check on the ruler(s)."

237 Quraishi, "Separation of Powers," at p. 67.

Fundamental Ordinance, as well as the 1906 Iranian Fundamental Law.[238] The 1861 constitution of Tunisia partially constrained the absolute power of the Head of State (the *Bey*) by establishing a regime under which he shared some of his prerogatives with the ministers and the Supreme Council. This body was responsible, *inter alia*, for protecting the constitution as well as the laws and the rights of inhabitants (Article 60), and also had the power of legislative initiative (Article 62). Moreover, the judiciary enjoyed a certain degree of independence, as judges could not be removed from office except in a limited number of cases (Articles 28 and 60). The 1876 Ottoman Basic Law provided for executive bodies (especially the Council of Ministers) and a Parliament (General Assembly) comprised of a Chamber of Deputies and a Chamber of Notables. In actual fact, however, the Sultan continued to wield almost unchecked executive and legislative powers. The only branch of government that seemed to enjoy greater independence was the judiciary, as the Basic Law explicitly guaranteed the irremovability of judges (Article 81). In Egypt, the 1882 Fundamental Ordinance was a short constitutional text primarily aimed at regulating the prerogatives of the Consultative Assembly of Representatives. This elected body was granted the power to enact legislation and oversee the public finances. Moreover, the cabinet was accountable to the Assembly. This document – which reduced the *Khedive*'s discretion only in part – was repealed during the same year in which it was adopted (1882) following the British occupation of the country.

The 1906 Iranian Fundamental Law was probably the constitutional text of that period that came closest to the idea of the separation of powers as interpreted within the Western tradition. This Fundamental Law was drafted by a National Consultative Assembly, which relied heavily on Western models, including in particular the 1831 Belgian Constitution.[239] The National Consultative Assembly was granted a key role with respect to legislative and financial matters, business concessions, and infrastructure projects. One year after the Fundamental Law was adopted, a Supplement to it was introduced, which *explicitly* provided for the principle of the separation of powers. Indeed, Article 27 of this Supplement stipulated that

> The powers of the Realm are divided into three branches. First, the legislative branch, the task of which is the enactment or amelioration of laws, is composed of His Imperial Majesty, the National Consultative Assembly, and the Senate [...] Second, the judicial branch, by which is meant the determining of rights, pertains exclusively to the ecclesiastical tribunals in matters relating to the ecclesiastical law, and to the civil courts in matters relating to ordinary law. Third, the executive branch, which appertains to the King, that is to say, the laws and ordinances are

[238] See Tilmann J. Röder, "The Separation of Powers in Muslim Countries. Historical and Comparative Perspectives" in Grote and Röder (eds.) 2012, *Constitutionalism in Islamic Countries*, at p. 321ff.; Bernard-Maugiron, *Droit contemporain des pays arabes*, at p. 560ff. See also Chapter 1, Section 1.1.

[239] See Röder, "Separation of Powers," at p. 332.

carried out by the Ministers and State officials in the august name of His Imperial Majesty in such manner as the Law defines.

Furthermore, Article 28 of the Supplement stated that "The three abovementioned branches shall in all cases remain distinct and separate from one another." However, this constitutional text has never been particularly influential in the Arab world.[240]

It should be noted however that, notwithstanding the abovementioned historical models, and notwithstanding the strong influence of Western constitutionalism, the principle of the separation of powers has rarely taken root in the constitutional traditions of Arab countries, which have by contrast often been characterized by two interrelated elements, namely the principle of *unity of power* and the *historical dominance of the executive.*

2.5.1.1 The Principle of Unity of Power

In some Arab countries, the principle of unity of power has undoubtedly been one of the most important elements of the constitutional architecture. In Algeria, for example, the first two postcolonial constitutions – adopted, respectively, in 1963 and 1976 – were clearly inspired by socialist principles and were modeled around this idea of unity of power. The regime, indeed, was founded on a single party, the National Liberation Front. The preamble to the 1963 constitution, in particular, explicitly rejected both presidential and parliamentary systems of government and stated that only a single-party regime could guarantee stable institutions. Subsequently, the 1976 constitution defined the socialist model as an "irreversible option" (Article 10) and confirmed the single-party system (Articles 94–95). Under this model, "the single-party is responsible for deciding the policies of the state, and the state bodies are responsible for their implementation. At the top level, the structures of the state and of the party blend into the figure of the president of the Republic, the Secretary General of the single-party, whose prerogatives span the entire constitutional field."[241] According to this notion of unity of power, "the President is everything [*le President est tout*]: in the party, in the state, in political decision making, in the law, in the implementation of the law, in the surveillance of the whole society, he is everything."[242]

[240] See Nathan J. Brown, *Constitutions in a Nonconstitutional World: Arab Basic Laws and the Prospects for Accountable Government* (SUNY Press 2002), 29.

[241] Mohammed Abdelwahab Bekhechi, "Remarques sur l'évolution du droit constitutionnel algérien de l'indépendance à la révision constitutionnelle de 1996" in *Les Constitutions des Pays arabes: Colloque de Beyrouth*, 1998 (Bruylant 1999), p. 38, footnote 26. On the one-party system in Algeria and other Arab countries, see also Maurizio Oliviero, *Il costituzionalismo dei paesi arabi. I. Le Costituzioni del Maghreb* (Giuffrè 2003), 36–38.

[242] Yadh Ben Achour, "Conclusions générales" in *Les Constitutions des Pays arabes: Colloque de Beyrouth*, 1998 (1999), at p. 321.

Although under the 1989 and 1996 constitutions the single-party system was abandoned in favor of a multi-party system, all references to the socialist model were eliminated and the separation of powers was formally proclaimed, it appears that this idea of unity of power has continued to exert a strong influence on the Algerian constitutional framework. This has also had negative implications with respect to the independence of the judiciary. For example, the 2016 reform introduced a provision according to which the president of the Republic acted as the "guarantor of the independence of the judiciary" (Article 156). While provisions of this type are not unknown in the Arab world (having been adopted for example in Morocco [Article 107(2) of the Moroccan Constitution] and Syria [Article 132 of the Syrian Constitution]), it is difficult to understand – given the context within which they operate – how they can genuinely promote the independence of the judiciary. By contrast, there is a risk that they may further reduce the already weak separation of powers that is typical of many countries in the region. In the case of Algeria, this risk seems to be particularly evident, also in view of the fact that the president of the Republic is often defined as "the first magistrate of the country" – in Arabic, "*el qadi al awal fi el bilad*," in French, "*le premier magistrat du pays*."[243] While in French "*magistrat*" has more than one meaning (in a broad sense, it refers to any holder of an element of public authority), in Arabic "*qadi*" refers specifically to a *judge*. Thus, to construe the president of the Republic as "*el qadi al awal fi el bilad*" might even imply that the president is the supreme judicial authority in the country, and is even entitled (if necessary) to overturn decisions made by the highest courts. It has been rightly pointed out that this ambiguous expression recalls an idea of justice based on the unity of power – a concept that characterized (as mentioned earlier) the Algerian system, especially under the 1963 and 1976 constitutions.[244] Within this constitutional framework, there was no independence of the judiciary: Indeed, justice was "a specialized function of a single revolutionary power, the unity [of which] being produced by the Head of State."[245] It must be noted that, following the 2020 reform, the constitution no longer provides that the president is the guarantor of the independence of the judiciary. This role has now been vested in the Supreme Judicial Council (Article 180).

The case of Syria largely recalls that of Algeria. The Ba'athist provisional constitutions of 1964, 1969, and 1971, as well as the permanent constitution of 1973, clearly disregarded the principle of separation of powers for ideological reasons. Indeed, these constitutional texts "were all part of a 'popular democracy' political philosophy borrowed from communist regimes in which the separation of powers

[243] See Chérif Bennadji, "De l'ambigüité des rapports entre le président de la République et le pouvoir judiciaire en Algérie: de l'usage de la formule 'le président de la République, Premier magistrat du pays'" (2007) III *L'Année du Maghreb* (online issue).

[244] Ibid.

[245] Ibid.

was merely a separation of *functions*" (emphasis added).[246] The political and institutional system revolved around the Ba'ath Party, which was defined as "the leading party in the state and society" (Article 8 of the 1973 constitution). Despite the fact that in the new 2012 constitution all references of socialism have been abandoned, and that the "new" Article 8 has replaced the mention to the Ba'ath party with the principle of "political pluralism," the new constitutional text has maintained the overconcentration of authority in the hands of the president of the Republic, thus confirming the prevalence of the principle of unity of power over the principle of separation of powers.

Another country where the principle of unity of power has always held a prominent position is Morocco. Although all three kings who have reigned over the country since its independence (i.e., Mohammed V, Hassan II, and Mohammed VI) have stressed the importance of the principle of the separation of powers in their official speeches, it has never been implemented in the way it is implemented in Western consolidated democracies.[247] Indeed, the Moroccan constitutional order used to place above it the principle of unity of power, as embodied in the monarchy. As has been pointed out by prominent Moroccan scholar Abdeltif Menouni, this power is "one of the fundamental realities, keystones and cement of the [...] constitutional system" and is "unique, originary and oriented."[248] It is *unique* because the king is the only authority to enjoy simultaneous religious, historical, and legal-rational legitimacy. He stands above the political parties and electoral competition.[249] It is an *originary* power because the constitution is not the source of legitimacy for royal power, but rather only acknowledges the existence of the monarchical institution and identifies the consequences of the king's supremacy. It is the sovereign who holds the constituent power and who decides concerning the time and extent of any constitutional reforms.[250] It is an *oriented* (*finalisé*) power because the power held by the king is not unlimited. For instance, according to Article 19 of the previous constitutions, the sovereign was responsible for guaranteeing the continuity of the state, respect for Islam and the constitution, the protection of the rights of citizens, the independence of the nation, and the territorial integrity of the realm. This is the "permanent mission" that the constitution ascribed (and still ascribes) to the king.[251]

The Moroccan constitutional order was then characterized by two opposing principles: the principle of the separation of powers, on the one hand, and the principle

[246] Atassi, *Syria*, at p. 402.

[247] See Abderrahim El Maslouhi, "Séparation des pouvoirs et régime parlementaire dans la nouvelle Constitution marocaine" in Centre d'Études Internationales (ed.) 2012, *La Constitution marocaine de 2011*, at p. 86.

[248] Abdeltif Menouni, "Constitution et séparation des pouvoirs" in Driss Basri, Michel Rousset and Georges Vedel (eds.), *Trente années de vie constitutionnelle au Maroc* (L.G.D.J. 1993), 180.

[249] Ibid., at pp. 180–182.

[250] Ibid., at pp. 182–185.

[251] Ibid., at pp. 185–187.

of unity of power, on the other hand.[252] The leading literature, the case law of the Constitutional Chamber of the Supreme Court and official royal speeches acknowledged the existence of both principles within the Moroccan constitutional order but repeatedly pointed out that *the monarchical institution was not involved in the separation of powers*, despite the king being the leader of the executive branch and exerting his influence over the legislature and the judiciary. Indeed, *the king was considered to be above such a separation of power*. Thus, according to Abdeltif Menouni:

> [...] the Constitution, and especially the practice of the institutions, intersect with two movements whose nature is different, but which mutually complete and clarify each other. The first affirms the *unity of political power* and defines the channels through which it will spread; the second, which is more restricted and is *present especially at the level of constitutional sub-system, allows for a separation of the bodies and collaboration among the political functions*, but only [...] subject to significant limits.[253] (emphasis added)

On October 27, 1970, Ahmed Bahnini, President of the Constitutional Chamber of the Supreme Court, declared:

> To assert that the Constitution has transferred sovereignty from the King to the Nation is not correct [...] What clearly emerges from the Constitution is that the Nation has wanted to ascribe to the King a supremacy with respect to the heavy responsibilities that the Constitution, the function of Imam and the Islamic traditions [...] have assigned to him. *In the light of this supremacy, the King, among his prerogatives, holds the power to control all levers of state*, without any exception.[254] (emphasis added)

In his speeches, Hassan II most clearly expressed the idea that the king was not involved in the separation of powers. For example, on May 22, 1977, he stated: "*If there is a separation of powers, this would not be at our level, but at a lower level*, because the king was asked to supervise and decide on the politics of his country, with the assistance of the executive branch represented by his government, and of the legislative branch: Parliament"[255] (emphasis added). Similarly, on October 9, 1987, he declared: "I have said and I repeat that *for Me*, humble servant of God and first servant of Morocco, *there is not a real separation of powers*. I am the father of everyone, of the legislator and of the executor, of the young and of the old man, of the strong and of the weak [...]"[256] (emphasis added).

If under the new 2011 constitution (as mentioned earlier[257]), the king still has spiritual and temporal powers, remains the head of the executive branch, maintains significant

[252] See El Maslouhi, "Séparation des pouvoirs," at p. 86ff.
[253] Menouni, "Constitution et séparation des pouvoirs," at pp. 179–180.
[254] Cited in El Maslouhi, "Séparation des pouvoirs," at p. 87.
[255] Ibid.
[256] Cited in Menouni, "Constitution et séparation des pouvoirs," at p. 193.
[257] See Section 2.1.1.

prerogatives in the legislative domain, and continues to "interfere" in the judicial system, thus transcending the separation of the three branches of government, this is also due to the fact that the principle of unity of power is still in place and continues to prevail over the principle of the separation of powers. This has negative implications also for the independence of the judiciary. As recalled earlier, courts' judgments "are rendered and executed *in the name of the King* and by virtue of the law" (emphasis added) (Article 124 of the constitution), thus confirming the well-rooted principle according to which in Morocco justice is a *delegated* function. Historically, the judge (*qadi*) was the authority delegated by the Sultan to exercise the judicial power.[258] In modern Morocco, this idea of justice as a delegated function has been confirmed both by the courts and the king. For example, in the *arrêt* "Société agricole Abdelaziz" of March 20, 1970, the Administrative Chamber of the Supreme Court ruled that:

> Considering that His Majesty the King exercises his constitutional competences in his capacity as Imam of the Faithful in accordance with Article 19 of the Constitution and that in this regard he cannot be considered as a mere administrative authority pursuant to Article 1 of *Zahir* of 2 Rabia 1 – 1377 (27/9/1957) [...]; considering that the *judicial function is one of those tasks responsibility for which falls in the first place to the Commander of the Faithful*; that the *judge performs this function by mere delegation*; that the *judgments are rendered and executed in the name of His Majesty* in accordance with Article 83 of the Constitution [...].[259] (emphasis added)

More recently, King Mohammed VI underscored this close link between justice and Commandership of the Faithful. Indeed, he argued that justice "is intrinsically part of the tasks of the supreme 'imamate,'"[260] and that "justice is the responsibility of the Commandership of the Faithful, and the King is the Guarantor of the independence of the judicial power."[261]

Another clear example of a country where, historically, the principle of the separation of powers has not been taken very seriously is Egypt. Gamal Abdel Nasser himself even admitted that any notion of the separation of powers was merely a mirage. In 1963, for example, he stated:

> I'm against the principle of the separation of powers, and I consider the carrying out of this separation an enormous illusion. Why? Because in reality there is no such

[258] See Menouni, "Constitution et séparation des pouvoirs," at p. 190; Nadia Bernoussi and Abderrahim El Maslouhi, "Les chantiers de la 'bonne justice'. Contraintes et renouveau de la politique judiciaire au Maroc" (2012) 91 *Revue française de droit constitutionnel*, 482–484.

[259] Administrative Chamber of the Supreme Court, *arrêt Société propriété agricole Abdelaziz contre Président du Conseil et Ministre de l'Agricolture* (March 20, 1970), cited in Menouni, "Constitution et séparation des pouvoirs," at p. 190.

[260] Message of the king to the participants in the international seminar on "L'avenir de la justice au 21e siècle," organized in Rabat by the Supreme Court on November 21, 2007, cited in Bernoussi and El Maslouhi, "Les chantiers de la 'bonne justice'," at p. 483.

[261] Royal speech of August 20, 2009.

> thing as the separation of powers; because whoever has the majority in parliament takes over the executive and legislative powers. Thus the political leadership that has the majority also has two things: executive power and legislative power, and, consequently, judicial power. For, no matter what they say about its independence, the judicial power is subordinate to the legislative power.[262]

The current 2014 constitution (as amended in 2019), which is characterized by the strong dominance of the president of the Republic and the army,[263] shows that the notion of the separation of powers (despite being formally recognized [Article 5]), is still particularly weak.

2.5.1.2 The Historical Dominance of the Executive

Executive dominance has long been a distinguishing feature of Arab countries. As has been pointed out by Noah Feldman, "[i]f there is a single characteristic feature of the states that arose in the wake of the collapse of the Ottoman Empire over the course of the twentieth century, it is undoubtedly an unchecked executive dominating the rest of the government and, through it, society itself."[264] Colonialism prevented any institutional model of divided or balanced government from emerging, although even afterward, once they became independent, Arab States promulgated constitutions as a way "to organize or augment state authority. Unchecked executive authority, poorly developed rights provisions, succession mechanisms that fail to make the leadership in any sense accountable, and escape hatches to allow rulers to violate their own rules [were] the hallmark [of] almost all Arab Constitutions."[265]

Examples abound of this historical dominance of the executive (and specifically of the head of state) in the Arab world. In Jordan, for example, the 1952 constitution granted the king near absolute powers. In fact, the government, Parliament, and (at least in part) also the courts (in particular the special courts) were *de facto* under the control of the monarchy. Things did not improve over time: Between 1954 and 1984, "28 amendments were made to the constitution, effectively increasing the power of the executive branch at the expense of other branches."[266] Martial law – imposed by King Hussein in 1967 and lifted in 1992 – and the ban on political parties between 1956 and 1992 further contributed to turning Jordan into a "police state."[267]

In Morocco, before the promulgation of the 2011 constitution, five different constitutions had been adopted (in 1962, 1970, 1972, 1992, and 1996), all of which entered into force under the reign of Hassan II. Under these constitutions, the prerogatives

[262] Cited in John Waterbury, *The Egypt of Nasser and Sadat: The Political Economy of Two Regimes* (Princeton University Press 1983), 343.
[263] See Section 2.1.4.
[264] Feldman, *Fall and Rise*, at p. 88.
[265] Brown, *Constitutions in a Nonconstitutional World*, at p. 92.
[266] Hammouri, "Constitutional Reform," at p. 724.
[267] Ibid.

of the monarch were practically unchecked. The key provision on which the sovereign's power was based was Article 19, which gave him (as mentioned earlier)[268] both secular and spiritual powers: He was the Head of State, the Supreme Representative of the Nation, and the *Amir al-Mouminine* – that is, the Commander of the Faithful. The democratic changes introduced under the 1992 and 1996 constitutions (such as the establishment of the Constitutional Council and the Economic and Social Council, as well as stronger protection for fundamental rights) did not significantly change the illiberal nature of the state.[269]

Egypt is another relevant example, as the country was characterized for a long time by authoritarian presidentialism. The 1971 constitution has often been considered within the literature as an effective instrument of the illiberal regimes of Presidents Sadat and Mubarak: In fact, it granted the president broad executive and legislative powers (both in ordinary and exceptional circumstances), as well as significant prerogatives in the judicial field. The constitutional amendments adopted in 2005 and 2007 did not introduce an effective system of checks and balances; on the contrary, in some cases, these reforms further strengthened the presidential nature of the regime. Consequently, the "overpowering authority of the president, in practice, was almost unlimited."[270]

The 1973 constitution of Syria, which drew heavily on the 1971 Egyptian Constitution, granted the president sweeping powers, with very weak checks on his authority. Indeed, the country was characterized by an "outright presidentialization of the regime with a ubiquitous head of state within all the wheels of power (executive and legislative)."[271] The president had the power, *inter alia*, to appoint and chair the cabinet, to dissolve Parliament, to assume legislative authority in exceptional circumstances, to hold public referenda concerning important issues affecting the country's highest interests, to declare a state of emergency, and to appoint all the members of the Supreme Constitutional Court.[272] The 1973 constitution represented a very important tool in the hands of Hafez al-Assad and (afterward) Bashar al-Assad in exercising their authoritarian rule over the country for decades.

It should be stressed that the Heads of State maintained control over the executive branch even during the (rare) periods in which the prime ministers belonged to one of the opposition parties. This is very evident if one considers the case of Morocco. In 1998, the policy of "alternance" (according to which members of the

[268] See Section 2.1.1.

[269] See Biagi, "Pilot of *Limited* Change," at pp. 51–52.

[270] Nathalie Bernard-Maugiron, "Strong Presidentialism. The Model of Mubarak's Egypt" in Grote and Röder (eds.) 2012, *Constitutionalism in Islamic Countries*, at p. 384. See also Kristen Stilt, "Constitutions in Authoritarian Regimes. The Egyptian Constitution of 1971" in Tom Ginsburg and Alberto Simpser (eds.), *Constitutions in Authoritarian Regimes* (Cambridge University Press 2014), 111ff.

[271] Atassi, *Syria*, at p. 318.

[272] See Peter B. Heller, "The Permanent Syrian Constitution of March 13, 1973" (1974) 28 *The Middle East Journal*, 53ff.

opposition parties could be appointed to government office – the so-called "*gouvernement d'alternance*") was implemented for the first time in the country. Thus, King Hassan II appointed as Prime Minister Abderrahmane Youssoufi, the Secretary of the Socialist Party *Union Socialiste des Forces Populaires*. However, this did not significantly limit the prerogatives of the king, especially because the so-called "ministers of sovereignty" (*wazarat siyadiah*) (including the ministers for the Interior, Defense, Foreign Affairs, Justice, and Habous and Islamic Affairs) continued to be directly appointed by the sovereign.[273] In a 2001 interview, the monarch "found it necessary to deny that there were two governments, one inside the palace and one outside, all the while asserting that the king had 'special responsibilities' for foreign affairs, defense, the interior, religious affairs, and justice. Moroccan kings have long held the defense portfolio personally."[274] Far from being abandoned, this practice is still apparent, as shown by the formation of the government led by Abdelilah Benkirane following the 2011 elections. Indeed, whereas Benkirane had declared that the era of the ministries of sovereignty was over, in actual fact he was forced to leave the appointment of some ministries (including the ministers for Defense, Habous and Islamic Affairs, and Agriculture) to the discretion of Mohammed VI.[275]

In a similar manner to previous Moroccan constitutions, the 2011 constitution does not distinguish between ministries of sovereignty and other ministries. It falls to the king to recommend "one particular individual rather than another" for a ministry of sovereignty, "depending upon the political situation and his personal relations with the Head of Government."[276] While in Morocco, the appointment of the ministers of sovereignty has remained a constitutional *convention*, in Egypt, this practice has been recognized *in the text of the constitution itself*. Indeed (as recalled earlier),[277] in the event that the government is chosen from the party or coalition that holds a plurality of seats in the House of Representatives, the president of the Republic has the power, albeit in consultation with the Prime Minister, to select the Ministers of Justice, the Interior, and Defense (Article 146(4)). By granting full constitutional status to this practice, the Egyptian framers ensured the predominance of the president over the government, even in those cases in which the Prime Minister is not chosen at the president's full discretion (Article 146(1)). On the one hand, the inclusion of an explicit constitutional provision concerning the selection of the ministers

[273] Ali Lmrabet, "Maroc: la véritable histoire d'Abderrahman Youssoufi," *Middle East Eye* (August 15, 2020), www.middleeasteye.net/fr/opinion-fr/maroc-abderrahman-youssoufi-nationaliste-socialiste-premier-ministre-histoire

[274] Michael Herb, "Princes and Parliaments in the Arab World" (2004) 58 *The Middle East Journal*, 381–382.

[275] See Omar Bendourou, "La consécration de la monarchie gouvernante" (2012) VIII *L'Année du Maghreb* (online issue).

[276] Didier Maus, "L'exécutif dans la Constitution marocaine de 2011" in Centre d'Études Internationales (ed.) 2012, *La Constitution marocaine de 2011*, at p. 73.

[277] See Section 2.1.4.

of sovereignty makes this practice more "binding."[278] On the other hand, however, the specific identification of these ministries (Justice, the Interior, and Defense) might (albeit not necessarily) hinder the president's selection of *other* ministries of sovereignty. In Morocco, on the contrary, where this practice remains informal and uncodified, the king seems to be freer to decide – depending on the political circumstances – which ministries have to be considered as *wazarat siyadiah*.

If the executive (and specifically the head of state) was able to maintain its predominance in the political and institutional systems, this is also because parliaments and courts (including constitutional courts) – which in theory should be "centres of potential resistance"[279] to the executive branch – only rarely placed adequate checks on the head of state. Parliaments were traditionally very weak actors in the Arab world. In most of the cases, the head of state had *de facto* full control over these institutions (thanks both to an extremely limited political pluralism, as well as to his power to appoint part [or sometimes even all][280] of their members), with the consequence that the main task of parliaments was merely to ratify decisions taken by the president or the king. These bodies played a more active role in only a few cases. Indeed, as has been recalled by Nathan J. Brown,

> Jordan's parliament deposed a king, Kuwait's parliament has brought down ministers, and the Palestinian parliament in the making has already engaged in sharp confrontations with the government over corruption and other issue, even if it has retreated at the last minute. Some Arab parliaments have been so bothersome to the political authorities that they have been suspended: in Egypt, Jordan, Algeria, Kuwait, Morocco, and Bahrain independent governments have shut down obstreperous parliaments for extended (and unconstitutional) periods.[281]

Similarly, before the Arab uprisings, courts (and in particular constitutional courts) acted as real "counter-majoritarian" bodies only in a few instances.[282] The paradox is

278 Another constitutional text containing a provision partially recalling the concept of ministries of sovereignty was the 2014 Tunisian Constitution. Article 89(1) stated that the ministers were selected by the Head of Government, but the Ministers of Foreign Affairs and Defense were selected "in consultation with the President of the Republic." The difference with Egypt, however, is evident: While in Egypt the *president* is the one who holds the power (in consultation with the Prime Minister) to appoint the Ministers of Justice, the Interior, and Defense, in Tunisia it was up to the *Head of Government* (in consultation with the president) to select the Ministers of Foreign Affairs and Defense.

279 Giovanni Bognetti, *Dividing Powers: A Theory of the Separation of Powers*, English edition by Antonia Baraggia and Luca Pietro Vanoni (Wolters Kluwer – CEDAM 2017), 62.

280 As for example in Saudi Arabia.

281 Brown, *Constitutions in a Nonconstitutional World*, at p. 112; see also Bernard-Maugiron, *Droit contemporain des pays arabes*, at pp. 799–800. More specifically, on the role played by parliaments in Gulf monarchies, see Gianluca Paolo Parolin, "Winter Is Coming. Authoritarian Constitutionalism Under Strain in the Gulf" in Grote and Röder (eds.) 2016, *Constitutionalism, Human Rights, and Islam*, at p. 149ff.

282 Among the very few Arab constitutional courts that placed effective checks on the executive branch (at least on occasion), one can mention the Supreme Constitutional Court of Egypt and the Constitutional Council of Lebanon. See Chapter 3, Section 3.2.5.

that, in some cases, they even contributed to *strengthening* (rather than constraining) the prerogatives of the head of state. In Morocco, for example, the Constitutional Council was originally created with the primary purpose of upholding the dominant position of the monarchy.[283] In a similar vein, the Supreme Court too was always firmly in favor of upholding the king's constitutional powers and competences.[284] In Tunisia, the Constitutional Council was conceived more as an ally of the executive branch than as a counter-majoritarian body. Indeed, for the first eleven years of its existence (1987–1998), the Council was only able to issue advisory opinions, which were confidential and communicated exclusively to the president of the Republic, who was the only authority entitled to refer bills to the Council. Although following a series of reforms, it ceased to be a purely advisory body, the Council never fully acquired full decision-making or judicial powers.[285] It should also be stressed that, in several countries (including Egypt, Kuwait, and Jordan), courts often relied on the doctrine of the "acts of sovereignty" in order to allow the executive branch to exercise broad discretionary powers.[286]

Finally, as recalled earlier,[287] it must be considered that this "historical" dominance of the executive was also the consequence of a long tradition of highly centralized and unitary systems of government. Indeed, administrative centralization reflected the centrality and supremacy of the executive branch (and specifically of the head of state) within the political and institutional system.

2.5.2 *The Patriarchal Family*

Although at first sight the model of family might not seem to exert an influence over the political regime of a country, in actual fact there is a quite evident correlation between the two. In the context of the Arab world, the patriarchal family has largely contributed to the establishment of nondemocratic systems of government characterized by an overconcentration of authority in the hands of the head of state. As has been stressed by Yadh Ben Achour:

> It is in fact in domesticity, in the family that the true Constitution of a people resides. Before going to the collective, the true Constitution of a people is established in the family, and it is in the family that all the political values and representations are formed. The authoritarian family, in which there is only male and sovereign authority, is the best breeding ground for the formation of dictators. The liberal family, in which there is a balance between the weight of the man, the masculine, and the weight of the feminine, the weight of the father and that of the mother, prepares the

283 See Rainer Grote, "Constitutional Review in Arab Countries. Down of a New Era?" in Grote and Röder (eds.) 2016, *Constitutionalism, Human Rights, and Islam*, at p. 687. See also Chapter 3, Section 3.2.3.

284 One need only consider the *arrêt Société propriété agricole Abdelaziz* recalled earlier. See Section 2.5.1.1.

285 See Chapter 3, Section 3.2.3. in greater detail.

286 On the doctrine of "acts of sovereignty," see Chapter 3, Section 3.2.2 in greater detail.

287 See Section 2.4.

> democratic spirit. The principle of virility and the principle of sovereignty, which unfortunately still characterize some large sections of Arab societies, are not made to promote democratization.[288]

In the light of the above, Ben Achour has rightly pointed out that, before taking into consideration the "political Constitution of a country," it is necessary to examine the "basic Constitution of the society, namely *family law*"[289] (emphasis added). It is well known that personal status laws, which represent the "stronghold"[290] of *sharia*, have proved to be profoundly resistant to change, despite recurring calls by liberals and feminists to make changes. It has only been over the past few decades that some Arab countries have reformed their Family Codes or Nationality Codes with the aim of strengthening women's rights and gender equality. From this point of view, Tunisia has been at the forefront of the Arab world since the adoption of the Personal Status Code in 1956.[291] Even Morocco (thanks to the reform of the Personal Status Code (*Moudawana*) in 2004)[292] and (although to a more limited extent) Algeria (thanks to the reform of the Family Code in 2005)[293] represent positive examples.[294] As far as the Nationality Codes are concerned, it should be recalled that Tunisia, Egypt, Algeria, and Morocco have introduced maternal *ius sanguinis* as a way of attributing nationality to children (in addition to paternal *ius sanguinis*).[295]

Despite these positive changes, one can hardly disagree with Leila Ahmed when she argues that family law in Islamic countries – which mainly reflects a *patriarchal interpretation of religious texts* (particularly the Quran and the Sunna) – is the cornerstone of the system of "male privilege and male control over women."[296] Thus, for example, according to the personal status laws of several Arab countries, the husband is the head of the family,[297] wives must obey their husbands, and the husbands are, in some cases

[288] Ben Achour, "Conclusions générales," at p. 315. In a similar vein, see also Massimo Papa, "L'evoluzione storica del costituzionalismo nei Paesi arabi tra Islam e modernità" in Eberhard Kienle et al., *Islam, democrazia e diritti* (Clueb 2007), 16.

[289] Ben Achour, "Conclusions générales," at p. 315.

[290] Massimo Papa and Lorenzo Ascanio, *Shari'a* (il Mulino 2014), 109.

[291] See Sana Ben Achour, "Le Code tunisien du statut personnel, 50 ans après: les dimensions de l'ambivalence" (2007) II *L'Année du Maghreb*, 55ff.

[292] See Katie Zoglin, "Morocco's Family Code: Improving Equality for Women" (2009) 31 *Human Rights Quarterly*, 964ff.

[293] See Nahas M. Mahieddin, "L'évolution du droit de la famille en Algérie: nouveautés et modifications apportées par la loi du 4 mai 2005 au Code algérien de la famille du 9 juin 1984" (2007) II *L'Année du Maghreb*, 97ff.

[294] It should be noted, however, that after independence, only Tunisia adopted a progressive family code. The 1957–58 Code of Personal Status adopted in Morocco remained faithful to the prevailing Islamic legislation. In Algeria, family law became caught in a paralyzing gridlock between reformist and conservative tendencies for more than two decades after independence in 1962. Finally, a conservative family code was adopted in 1984. See Mounira Charrad, *States and Women's Rights: The Making of Postcolonial Tunisia, Algeria, and Morocco* (University of California Press 2001).

[295] On this issue, see Chapter 4, Section 4.1.

[296] Leila Ahmed, *Women and Gender in Islam* (Yale University Press 1992), 242.

[297] Including in Tunisia (see Article 23(4) of the Code of Personal Status).

and under certain conditions, allowed to chastise their wives.[298] Furthermore, the rules on inheritance – most of which are taken directly from the Quran – do not always provide for equal treatment for men and women (it is well known, e.g., that the Quran stipulates that the son's share of inheritance must be twice that of the daughter's).[299]

It seems extremely unlikely that Arab countries will completely abandon the system of one-man rule if the model of the patriarchal family remains in place. Again, in the words of Yadh Ben Achour: "The democratic family influences the democratic state."[300]

2.5.3 *"Top-down" Constitution-making Processes*

Another very important reason that accounts for the concentration of powers in the Arab world is related to the constitution-making processes. Indeed, as has been analyzed in much greater detail in Chapter 1,[301] after the Arab uprisings, several countries followed a "top-down" process, in which the ruling regime acted as the absolute guiding force. In Egypt (2014 constitution) and Algeria, the processes of constitutional reform were led by the political and military leadership. In Syria, Morocco, and Jordan, the "top-down" nature of the process was also very evident, as the head of state had the first and the final say on the content of the new or amended constitutions, thus giving the impression that these new documents were simply a "concession" by the respective head of state, and not so much the result of the popular will. In Tunisia, the process that led to the adoption of the 2022 constitution was entirely driven by President Kaïs Saïed. In all instances, political parties, trade unions, social organizations, and civil society were not granted the power to effectively and concretely influence the drafting of constitutional reforms. Thus, not surprisingly, the result of this "top-down" approach was that kings and presidents (and sometimes also the army) were able to hold on to most of their key prerogatives, thereby perpetuating the concentration of powers that has characterized these countries for a long time.

2.5.4 *External Influences*

Aside from the role played by constitutional tradition, the patriarchal family, and the "top-down" constitution-making processes, another reason that accounts for the concentration of powers in the Arab world concerns external influences. First and

[298] See Sura 4:34.

[299] See Sura 4:11. For a comparative overview of family law in Arab countries, see Jamal J. Ahmad Nasir, *The Islamic Law of Personal Status. Third Revised and Updated Edition* (Brill 2009); Bernard-Maugiron, *Droit contemporain des pays arabes*, at p. 863ff. For a comparative overview of the legal status of women in Arab countries, see Jamal J. Ahmad Nasir, *The Status of Women Under Islamic Law and Modern Islamic Legislation. Third Edition of the Revised and Updated Work* (Brill 2009).

[300] Ben Achour, "Conclusions générales," at p. 316.

[301] See Chapter 1, Section 1.2.1.2.

foremost, it is necessary to consider the *Zeitgeist*, that is, the spirit of the times.[302] According to Juan J. Linz and Alfred Stepan, "when a country is part of an international ideological community where democracy is only one of many strongly contested ideologies, the chances of transiting to and consolidating democracy are substantially less than if the spirit of times is one where democratic ideologies have no powerful contenders."[303] According to Linz and Stepan, the effect of a *Zeitgeist* that is favorable or unfavorable to democracy can be easily understood if one compares the Europe between the two world wars (when democracy was only one of several contested ideologies, such as communism, fascism, authoritarian constitutional monarchy, and Catholicism) with the Europe of the late 1970s and the 1980s (when the democratic ideal had no major contenders).[304]

The current Arab world, where the *Zeitgeist* is certainly not entirely favorable to democracy, seems much more similar to the Europe between the two world wars than to the Europe of the late 1970s and the 1980s. Indeed, while the democratic ideal is increasingly consolidating itself among the people (the 2011 uprisings are a clear demonstration of this tendency),[305] nevertheless the region is still very much influenced by nondemocratic ideologies, such as authoritarian monarchy, authoritarian presidentialism and authoritarian military, as well as Islamist fundamentalism. All these ideologies, although for different reasons, support the concentration of power in the hands of a single person or institution, whether the king (e.g., in the Gulf monarchies[306] or – albeit to a lesser extent – in Morocco and Jordan),[307] the president (e.g., in Syria, Egypt, Algeria, and Tunisia [after 2021], or even Palestine),[308] the military (e.g., in Libya,[309] Egypt,[310] or Algeria[311]), or the caliph (in the so-called

[302] See Juan J. Linz and Alfred Stepan, *Problems of Democratic Transition and Consolidation: Southern Europe, South America, and Post-Communist Europe* (The Johns Hopkins University Press 1996), 74.

[303] Ibid., at p. 74.

[304] Ibid., at pp. 74–75.

[305] In its 2021–2022 public opinion survey across the Middle East and North Africa, the Arab Barometer has shown that Arab citizens are worried that democracy can't deliver either good politics or stable and healthy economies. At the same time, however, most people believe that democracy remains the best system of government. See Michael Robbins, "Arab Citizens Know Democracy's Not Perfect. They Want It Anyway," *The Washington Post* (July 21, 2022), www.washingtonpost.com/politics/2022/07/21/arab-citizens-know-democracys-not-perfect-they-want-it-anyway/

[306] See Ottaway and Muasher, "Arab Monarchies," at p. 14ff.

[307] See respectively Sections 2.1.1 and 2.1.2.

[308] On the case of Syria, Egypt, Algeria, and Tunisia (after 2021), see respectively Sections 2.1.3–2.1.5 and 2.2.4; on the case of Palestine, see Sanaa Alsarghali, "An (Un)constitutional Hangover? An Analysis of the Current Palestinian Basic Law in Light of Palestine's Constitutional Heritage" (2017) 2017 *University of Illinois Law Review*, 497ff.

[309] The reference is to General Khalifa Haftar, commander of the Libyan National Army. See Jon Lee Anderson, "The Unravelling. In a Failing State, an Anti-Islamist General Mounts a Divisive Campaign," *The New Yorker* (February 23 and March 2, 2015), www.newyorker.com/magazine/2015/02/23/unravelling

[310] See Section 2.1.4.

[311] See Section 2.1.5.

"Islamic State" [IS], also known as ISIS, ISIL, or Daesh).[312] This model has been reflected in the new constitutional frameworks and continues to represent the paradigm of government for most Arab countries.

Geopolitics is another external factor that should not be underestimated. The major involvement of Russia in the Syrian conflict offers an excellent example. On January 23–24, 2017, during the first round of the so-called "Astana talks" (namely, the Syria peace talks held in Astana, Kazakhstan, under the leadership of Russia, Iran, and Turkey), Moscow presented its draft proposal for a new Syrian Constitution.[313] On the one hand, it must be recognized that this draft constitution introduced some positive elements that represent a step forward compared to the current 2012 constitution. For example, as recalled earlier,[314] the draft contains some provisions dealing with the Kurdish question, regulating the use of minority languages, and proclaiming a commitment to respect the Declaration on the Rights of Persons Belonging to National or Ethnic, Religious and Linguistic Minorities. On the other hand, however, this draft constitution caused some perplexity, having being described as "an important example of a nonliberal constitutional model put forward as a solution to one of the world's most intractable conflicts."[315] These concerns refer specifically to the system of government. Indeed, by relying heavily on the constitutional model of the Eurasian countries (including for example Kazakhstan),[316] the draft constitution continues to provide for a strong concentration of authority in the hands of the president of the Republic. According to the draft constitution, the president, *inter alia*, appoints the Prime Minister and the ministers (Article 64), issues decrees, edicts, and instructions (Article 57), concludes international treaties (Article 58), may call referendums on important issues that affect the higher interests of the country (Article 59), and is the Commander in Chief of the Armed Forces (Article 60). Moreover, while the draft constitution states that the same person cannot hold the office of president for more than two consecutive terms, it still provides for a very long term in office, specifically seven years (Article 49). Furthermore, there are

312 Indeed, the "Islamic State" was characterized by a "pyramidal and personalistic structure, whose leader is the caliph […], who is the supreme religious and political authority, since he enjoys an absolute (executive) power, which is exercised on behalf of Allah" (Arianna Vedaschi, "Da al-Qaida all'IS: il terrorismo internazionale si è fatto Stato?" (2016) 1 *Rivista trimestrale di diritto pubblico*, 68). From 2014 until his death in 2019, the Caliph of the "Islamic State" was Abu Bakr al-Baghdadi. On the profoundly unclear and ambiguous nature of the "Islamic State," see Wael B. Hallaq, *The Impossible State: Islam, Politics, and Modernity's Moral Predicament* (Columbia University Press 2013); Massimo Campanini, "Il concetto ambiguo di 'Stato islamico'" (2014) 3 *Storia del pensiero politico*, 369ff.; Vedaschi 2016, in this note, at p. 42ff.

313 See Chapter 1, Section 1.2.6.

314 See Section 2.4.1.

315 William Partlett, "Understanding the Origins of Russia's Constitutional Solution to the Syrian Conflict," *ConstitutionNet* (February 24, 2017), https://constitutionnet.org/news/understanding-origins-russias-constitutional-solution-syrian-conflict

316 Ibid.

certain constitutional provisions that – by following a "Eurasian-style Syrian presidency"[317] – grant the president the power "to supervise and unify all branches of power in the state."[318] Indeed, the president is the "guarantor of the independence, unity, and territorial integrity of the country" (Article 55(1)), ensures the "continuous operation of public authorities" (Article 55(2)), and acts as an "intermediary for the State authorities, and between the State and the society [...]" (Article 55(3)).

The 2017 draft constitution for Syria proposed by Russia was rejected by both the Syrian government and the opposition. Still, it clearly shows the potential risks of external influences: "the Russian drafters s[aw] the solution to Syria's civil war as one that concentrates state power in one strong central government, rather than dispersing it."[319]

2.6 A POPULAR *AND GOVERNMENTAL* SOVEREIGNTY

Based on a superficial analysis of post-2011 Arab constitutions, one might have the impression that the new constitutional systems are rooted in the principle of the separation of powers, and that sovereignty (*al-siyada*) – interpreted as "supreme and absolute power"[320] – belongs exclusively to the people. Admittedly, this is what the new constitutional texts often formally proclaim. The 2014 Egyptian Constitution, for example, stipulates that "the political system is based on [...] the separation and balance of powers" (Article 5), and that "sovereignty belongs to the people alone [...]. They are the source of power" (Article 4). In a similar vein, the 1996 Algerian Constitution (as amended in 2020) provides that "the State is founded on the [principle] of [...] separation of powers" (Article 15), and that "the people are the source of all powers. National sovereignty belongs exclusively to the people" (Article 7). The 2012 Syrian Constitution is even more vocal when it comes to popular sovereignty: "Sovereignty is an attribute of the people and no individual or group may claim sovereignty. Sovereignty is based on the principle of the rule of the people, by the people and for the people. The people exercise their sovereignty within the aspects and limits prescribed in the Constitution" (Article 2).

A closer look, however, suggests a different reading. As has been shown in this chapter, the system of checks and balances – which aims to ensure that the branches of government oversee one another in order to prevent tyranny and despotism – continues to be weak. Post-2011 Arab constitutions still provide for (albeit to a lesser extent than in the past) an extremely high concentration of authority in the hands of the head of state (and in some cases also of the military), thus favoring the continuation in office of illiberal or hybrid regimes. This weak separation of powers – both in

317 Ibid.
318 Ibid.
319 Ibid.
320 See Michel Troper, "Sovereignty" in Michel Rosenfeld and András Sajó (eds.), *The Oxford Handbook of Comparative Constitutional Law* (Oxford University Press 2012), 350.

horizontal and vertical terms – is due to different reasons, including constitutional tradition, the patriarchal family, top-down constitution-making processes, and external influences. In 1999, Yadh Ben Achour argued that "rule or die" was the "principle and the fundamental vice of Arab political regimes."[321] Twenty-five years later, most Arab countries have not yet completely abandoned this formula. Tunisia was the only post-Arab Spring country to have made a clear departure from the previous system of one-man rule, although since 2021 President Saïed has re-established a hyper-presidential regime.

This overconcentration of powers has seriously undermined the principle of popular sovereignty. Far from belonging exclusively to the people, sovereignty in the Arab world continues to be *held* (and not only exercised) also by other subjects, namely political (and sometimes also military) leaders, who are the fulcrum around which the entire system rotates. Thus, it is a popular *and governmental* sovereignty. In some cases, this seems to be explicitly acknowledged within the text of the constitution itself. In Morocco and Jordan, for example, sovereignty does not belong to the people. Rather, it belongs to the *ummah* (i.e., the community of believers).[322] This suggests the idea of *national* sovereignty, rather than popular sovereignty.[323] As is well known, people and nation should not be treated as synonyms: "the people is viewed as a reality, a group of citizens living in a country, whereas the nation is an abstract entity made up not only of citizens but also of the *long-term general interests that may transcend the interests of citizens*"[324] (emphasis added). In the case of Morocco and Jordan, the main interpreter of these "long-term general interests" is obviously the respective king, who is the "engine" behind all constitutional reforms, leads the executive branch, participates in the legislative function, and has key prerogatives in the judicial domain. This means that the "general will" is expressed not only by the people but also (often *mainly*) by the head of state.

Constitution-making processes, constitutional provisions, constitutional conventions, and judicial interpretation confirm that a large (often *the largest*) share of sovereignty continues to be held by presidents, kings, and military leaders. Examples abound. Since the Arab uprisings these subjects have often acted as if they – and not so much the people – were the holders of the *pouvoir constituant* ("We the rulers")[325]; most constitutions still do not place effective limitations on political (and military) authorities and do not provide for an effective system of checks and

[321] Ben Achour, "Conclusions générales," at p. 321.

[322] The Moroccan Constitution stipulates that "Sovereignty belongs to the Nation [*ummah*], which exercises it directly, by way of referendum, and indirectly, by the intermediary of its representatives" (Article 2), and the Jordanian Constitution states that "The Nation [*ummah*] is the source of powers. The Nation shall exercise its powers in the manner prescribed in this Constitution" (Article 24).

[323] See Bernard-Maugiron, *Droit contemporain des pays arabes*, at pp. 661–662.

[324] Troper, "Sovereignty," at p. 366.

[325] See Chapter 1.

balances during both ordinary political circumstances and in times of emergency[326]; the practice of appointment by the head of state of the "ministers of sovereignty" often continues to be applied; the doctrine of the "acts of sovereignty" is still (ab) used by courts; in some countries (such as Morocco and Jordan) judicial decisions are not given in the name of the people, but "in the name of the King."[327] And the list might go on.

A well-known saying concerning the French Constitution of 1799 goes as follows: "*Qu'y a-t-il dans la Constitution? Il y a Bonaparte.*"[328] It would be misleading to affirm that in post-2011 Arab constitutions, there is only the head of state (and sometimes also the military). However, it seems fair to argue that the excessive prominence granted to these actors has seriously eroded the principles of separation of powers and popular sovereignty. Bonaparte, in other words, is still too present in most new Arab constitutional systems.

[326] See Carl Schmitt, *Political Theology: Four Chapters on the Concept of Sovereignty* (original volume of 1922) (translated by George Schwab) (University of Chicago Press 2005), 47: "Sovereign is he who decides on the exception."

[327] See Article 27 of the Jordanian Constitution and Article 124 of the Moroccan Constitution.

[328] "Qu'y a-t-il dans la Constitution? Il y a Bonaparte" Le mot circule dans Paris en 1800," *L'Histoire en citations*, www.histoire-en-citations.fr/citations/qu-y-a-t-il-dans-la-constitution#cit-1696

3

Counter-majoritarian Institutions?

The Role of Constitutional Courts and Councils

3.1 THE ORIGINS OF CONSTITUTIONAL REVIEW OF LEGISLATION IN THE ARAB WORLD

Contrary to what one might expect, the first attempts to introduce constitutional review of legislation in the Arab world date back to the mid-nineteenth century, specifically to the 1861 Tunisian Constitution, which was the very first constitution in the region. Indeed, Article 60 stated that the Supreme Council, "guardian of the Fundamental Pact and the laws, and protector of the rights of the inhabitants," was responsible for opposing the promulgation of legislative acts contrary "to the principles of the law, the equality of inhabitants before the law and the principle of irremovability of judges [...]." Another proto-constitutional review experience in the region is that of Morocco, with its 1908 draft constitution. Indeed, this text, which never came into force, stipulated that the Advisory Council and the Council of Notables had the power to verify the compatibility of administrative acts and legislative provisions with the constitution (Articles 34 and 54). In Iraq, the 1925 constitution vested the High Court with the task of ascertaining the constitutionality of laws and regulations (Articles 83 and 86).

The case of Egypt is quite peculiar, as constitutional review of legislation was introduced *de facto* in the country through a judgment delivered by the State Council (*majlis al-dawla*) on February 10, 1948.[1] In this decision, the State Council declared, in the first place, that judicial review of the constitutionality of laws did not infringe the principle of separation of powers:

> There is nothing in Egyptian legislation to prevent Egyptian courts from examining the constitutionality of laws, let alone decree-laws, either as to form or merits. The assertion that discussing the constitutionality of law would represent a disregard for the principle of separation of powers through the interference of the Judicial Authority in the work of the Legislative Authority [...] is refutable. On the contrary, discussing the constitutionality of laws is actually an application of this principle

[1] Case no. 65/1 (February 10, 1948).

> and contributes directly to carrying it out [...] If one of the three powers violates the principle of the Constitution, it goes outside the domain defined for the exercise of its jurisdiction. If it could successfully invoke the principle of separation of powers to free itself from all constitutional rules, the situation would result in anarchy.[2]

The State Council then proclaimed the principle of hierarchy of laws (*lex superior derogat legi inferiori*) and established a duty for the judiciary to refrain from applying any law at odds with constitutional provisions (the so-called "doctrine of abstention control"), even though the 1923 constitution did not vest courts with such a power:

> It follows therefore that if there is a contradiction between an ordinary law and the Constitution in any case presented to the courts, they are obliged, in the performance of their judicial functions, and for the reasons above indicated, to resolve this problem. There is no doubt that they must subordinate the ordinary law and give preponderance to the constitutional law as a law of superior authority. In so doing the courts do not infringe the domain of the legislative power so long as they do not themselves create a law, or order the annulment of the law, or the stopping of its implementation. They merely resolve a judicial question in indicating the law which must be applied between two contradictory laws. If the ordinary law is not applied in a given case it is because the Constitution has superiority over all other laws. The judge and the legislator alike must respect this superiority.[3]

According to the prominent Egyptian scholar Abd al-Razzaq al-Sanhuri, the introduction of constitutional review of legislation (in the form of abstention control) was "the most important decision that the Egyptian judiciary has issued in the modern era [and] a point of real transformation in the position of the Egyptian courts in this matter."[4] al-Sanhuri confirmed the State Council's arguments by noting as follow:

> The applicable constitutional principle is that powers should be exercised in accordance with the Constitution. The parliament contradicts this principle if it issues legislation that opposes the Constitution. Rather than apply unconstitutional laws, the judges record this violation. Thus it is permitted that judges look at the constitutionality of laws – indeed it is their duty to do so – in order to prevent application of legislation which, in their estimation, infringes the Constitution.[5]

The doctrine of abstention control recalled the decentralized model of constitutional review.[6] Indeed, it could be exercised by all courts, irrespective of their jurisdiction

[2] Cited in Enid Hill, "Establishing the Doctrine of Judicial Review in Egypt and the United States" in Eugene Cotran and Adel Omar Sherif (eds.), *The Role of the Judiciary in the Protection of Human Rights* (Kluwer Law International 1997), 324–325.

[3] Ibid., at pp. 325–326.

[4] Ibid., at p. 328.

[5] Ibid., at p. 329.

[6] See Islam Mohammed, "Supreme Constitutional Court of Egypt (Al-Mahkamah al-Dustūrīyah al-'Ulȳ)" in Rainer Grote, Frauke Lachenmann and Rüdiger Wolfrum (eds.), *Max Planck Encyclopedia of Comparative Constitutional Law* (Oxford University Press 2022), 3.

or level.[7] Furthermore, as clarified by the State Council in a following judgment,[8] the declaration of unconstitutionality produced *inter partes* effects, as the legislative provision was declared nonoperative only with respect to the specific case under review, and only affected the parties involved. The consequence was that the same legislative provision could be viewed differently by the same court in another case, as well as by other courts in different cases.[9] Since the unconstitutional provision could never be declared void, and its operative force remained intact with respect to other cases, the risk was that contradictory judgments concerning the same constitutional issue could be produced.[10] Nonetheless, Egyptian courts continued to exercise their power of abstention control until the adoption of Decree-Law no. 81 of 1969, which vested the Supreme Court with the exclusive power of constitutional review.

The doctrine of abstention control of Egyptian origins proved influential, as it was also adopted in other Arab countries, including Jordan, for example. On the one hand, the 1952 Jordanian Constitution vested a High Court with the power to interpret the provisions of the constitution following a request to this effect by the Council of Ministers and the Houses of Parliament (Article 122). On the other hand, according to settled case law, ordinary courts were required to refrain from applying any laws or regulations that violated the constitution. The approach of the Jordanian judiciary evolved over time.[11] At the outset, courts were quite reluctant to carry out constitutional review of legislation, as demonstrated by the judgment delivered by the Court of Appeal of Jerusalem in 1953.[12] In this decision – which was issued during the period (1950–1967) in which Jordan controlled the West Bank and East Jerusalem, including the Old City – the Court of Appeal held that it did not have jurisdiction to review the constitutionality of legislation: "The Court is not entitled to scrutinize the constitutionality of these laws […] as long as they are adopted by Parliament and ratified by His Majesty the King."[13] In the following years, however, Jordanian courts (including the Court of Cassation) adopted the doctrine of abstention control as a way of guaranteeing the supremacy of the constitution.[14]

7 For example, on February 7, 1952 (case no. 386/20), the Criminal Chamber of the Court of Cassation refrained from applying a provision of a law that was in contrast with the constitutional principle of nonretroactivity of criminal laws. See Nathalie Bernard-Maugiron, *Le politique à l'épreuve du judiciaire: la justice constitutionnelle en Égypte* (Bruylant 2003), 39.

8 State Council, case no. 568/3 (June 30, 1952).

9 See Awad Mohammad El-Morr, Abd El-Rahman Nossier and Adel Omar Sherif, "The Supreme Constitutional Court and Its Role in the Egyptian Judicial System" in Kevin Boyle and Adel Omar Sherif (eds.), *Human Rights and Democracy: The Role of the Supreme Constitutional Court of Egypt* (Kluwer Law International 1996), 38.

10 Ibid. See also Bernard-Maugiron, *Le politique à l'épreuve du judiciaire*, at p. 40.

11 See Mohammed S. M. Ghazwi, *The Development of Monitoring the Constitutionality of Laws and Regulations in Light of the Jordanian Constitution of 1952* (Amman 2015), 10.

12 Case no. 312/1953.

13 I am grateful to Professor Numan A. Elkhatib, former Justice of the Constitutional Court of Jordan, for bringing this judgment to my attention.

14 See Numan A. Elkhatib and Nesreen M. Domour, "The Constitutional Court of Jordan and Its Relation to Ordinary Courts" (2021) 11 *The Lawyer Quarterly*, 695; Ghazwi, *Monitoring the Constitutionality*, at pp. 9–10.

In other countries, however, the doctrine of abstention control was explicitly rejected. In Kuwait, for example, in the eleven years between the adoption of the constitution and the establishment of the Constitutional Court (1962–1973), scholars debated over whether ordinary courts could review the constitutionality of laws. Some scholars argued that courts were not entitled to do so since the constitution had vested a "competent judicial body" (Article 173) with the constitutional review function, thus excluding ordinary courts.[15] Other scholars, on the contrary, stated that judges were required to refrain from applying legislative acts that were at odds with the constitution (the doctrine of abstention control), as the latter was the supreme norm and therefore ordinary laws were required to comply with it. Kuwaiti courts chose the former path. In 1970, for example, the Court of Appeals stated that it could not rule on the constitutionality of a legislative act since the constitution granted this power to a "competent judicial body," which the legislator had not yet established.[16]

The power of courts to review the constitutionality of legislation was a sensitive issue also in Tunisia, where the original version of the 1959 constitution had not explicitly vested any authority with the power to review the constitutionality of legislation. In an interesting judicial saga that occurred prior to the Constitutional Council being granted constitutional status,[17] the point of contention was whether ordinary courts were entitled to ascertain the constitutionality of laws.[18] The first phase of the saga occurred on December 24, 1987, when the Court of First Instance of Kairouan declared its competence to review the constitutionality of legislation, based on the principle of hierarchy of laws. According to the Court, this competence "confirm[ed] the principle of separation of powers by ensuring that the legislative power would be prevented from imposing on the judicial power a law that contravened the Constitution [...], as this would hinder the independence of the judicial authority and would limit its function of enforcement of legal norms upon which the Constitution ultimately rests."

In the second phase of the saga, the Court of Appeals of Sousse, on April 11, 1988, upheld the decision of the Court of Kairouan, stating that even if the constitution had not expressly granted such a power to any authority, it still had not prevented courts from ascertaining the constitutionality of laws. Thus, constitutional review of legislation was justified precisely by the silence of the constitution on this matter. Unlike the Court of Kairouan, which had found the law to be in line with the

[15] Article 173 stipulates that "The Law shall determine the competent judicial body to deal with the settlement of disputes in respect to the constitutionality of laws and regulations and shall determine this body's jurisdiction and the procedure it shall follow. [...]."

[16] See Yousri Elassar, "Le contrôle de la constitutionnalité des lois au Koweït" in *Les Constitutions des Pays arabes: Colloque de Beyrouth, 1998* (Bruylant 1999), 248–250; Nathan J. Brown, *The Rule of Law in the Arab World: Courts in Egypt and the Gulf* (Cambridge University Press 1997), 172–173.

[17] On how the Tunisian Constitutional Council's status evolved over time, see Section 3.2.3.

[18] The judicial saga is analyzed in detail by Rafaâ Ben Achour, "Vicissitudes du contrôle de constitutionnalité des lois" (1988) 4 *Annuaire international de justice constitutionnelle*, 541ff.

constitution, the Court of Appeals of Sousse ruled that the Law of November 7, 1959, on associations was at odds with Article 8 of the constitution, which recognized freedom of association.

The third and final phase of the saga occurred on June 1st, 1988, when the Court of Cassation overturned the decision of the Court of Appeals of Sousse, stating that ordinary courts were not entitled to rule on the constitutionality of laws. The Court of Cassation reasoned that the Tunisian Constitution did not contemplate the constitutional review of legislation, and that the risk of vesting ordinary courts with such a power would be to "establish a *government of judges*, whose will [...] could contravene the will of the nation" (emphasis added). This latter argument was clearly influenced by French legal thought. One need only consider the work of Eduard Lambert, *Le gouvernement des juges et la lutte contre la législation sociale aux États-Unis*,[19] in which the French scholar argued that in the United States, the decentralized system of judicial review, along with other factors, had given rise to judicial supremacy where the legislature and the executive branches of government were subordinate to the judicial branch, thus producing a serious imbalance in institutional power. Interestingly, the decision of the Court of Cassation also echoed the judgment of the Egyptian State Council of February 10, 1948 (recalled earlier). Indeed, according to the Court of Cassation, constitutional review could have provoked "anarchy and disorder," and the law could have lost its credibility.

As will be discussed in greater detail later,[20] the issue concerning the courts' power to review the constitutionality of legislation was to resurface in Tunisia after the 2011 Revolution. Indeed, administrative courts declared their competence to carry out constitutional review not only in the period 2011–2014 but also after the adoption of the 2014 constitution, notwithstanding a constitutional provision that explicitly prevented courts from ascertaining the constitutionality of legislation (Article 148(7)).

3.2 CONSTITUTIONAL REVIEW BODIES PRIOR TO THE ARAB SPRING

After obtaining their independence or over the following decades, a number of Arab countries, following a trend taking place all across the globe,[21] established a system for reviewing the constitutionality of legislative acts. Before the outbreak of the Arab uprisings, the majority of countries had opted for a "centralized" model, in which

[19] Edouard Lambert, *Le gouvernement des juges et la lutte contre la législation sociale aux Etats-Unis* (Marcel Giard & Cie 1921).

[20] See Section 3.4.2.

[21] See, for example, Tom Ginsburg, *Judicial Review in New Democracies: Constitutional Courts in Asian Cases* (Cambridge University Press 2003); Wojciech Sadurski (ed.), *Constitutional Justice, East and West: Democratic Legitimacy and Constitutional Courts in Post-Communist Europe in a Comparative Perspective* (Kluwer Law International 2002); Francesco Biagi, *European Constitutional Courts and Transitions to Democracy* (Cambridge University Press 2020).

constitutional review was carried out by a specialized, *ad hoc* constitutional court or council. In Morocco, Mauritania, Algeria, Tunisia, and Lebanon, the drafters, drawing inspiration from the French *Conseil Constitutionnel*, provided for constitutional councils. Kelsenian-style (or *quasi* Kelsenian-style) constitutional courts were established in Egypt, Syria, Kuwait, and Bahrain. Other countries, by contrast, granted the Supreme Court the power to review the constitutionality of legislation: This was the case, for example, in Iraq, Yemen, the United Arab Emirates, and Libya.[22] In Jordan, a hybrid system of constitutional review was in place. As recalled earlier,[23] a High Court was granted the power to interpret the provisions of the constitution, whereas according to settled case law, ordinary courts refrained from applying legislative acts that were considered in conflict with the constitution.

Despite being provided for in most Arab constitutions, constitutional review bodies rarely guaranteed respect for constitutional principles or protection for fundamental rights and freedoms[24] – the Egyptian Supreme Constitutional Court and the Lebanese Constitutional Council being (at least on occasion) among the very few exceptions. As discussed later, a number of different reasons explain the inability of these institutions to act as effective defenders of constitutionalism: (1) limited independence vis-à-vis the executive branch; (2) deference toward the executive branch; (3) the nature of constitutional review bodies; (4) the "stranglehold" on access; (5) the political and social context (with the Egyptian and Lebanese [partial] exceptions).

3.2.1 A *Limited Independence vis-à-vis the Executive Branch*

It has rightly been pointed out that "the prestige and the capacity of the constitutional court to fulfil its role as guardian of the constitution crucially depend on its ability to distance itself from the political branches of government."[25] This was not the case for most constitutional courts and councils prior to the Arab Spring, as these bodies typically enjoyed very limited independence vis-à-vis the executive branch.

First and foremost, in several Arab countries, the Head of State dominated the system of appointment of the members of constitutional review bodies. In Syria, for example, all the justices of the Supreme Constitutional Court were appointed by the president of the Republic. In Morocco, half of the members of the Constitutional

22 In Libya, the constitutional chamber of the Supreme Court, responsible for verifying the constitutionality of laws, was suspended for long periods of time both under the Gaddafi regime, and under the post-2011 constitutional framework. See Nathalie Bernard-Maugiron, *Droit contemporain des pays arabes* (Sirey 2023), 546.

23 See Section 3.1.

24 See Nathan J. Brown, "Judicial Review and the Arab World" (1998) 9 *Journal of Democracy*, 89.

25 Rainer Grote, "Models of Institutional Control: The Experience of Islamic Countries" in Rainer Grote and Tilmann J. Röder (eds.), *Constitutionalism in Islamic Countries: Between Upheaval and Continuity* (Oxford University Press 2012), 225.

Council were appointed by the king (including the President of the Court), while the other six were selected by the Speakers of both Houses of Parliament. In Tunisia, the president of the Republic had the power to appoint all the members of the Constitutional Council until 2002. Afterward, the appointment system was changed in order to reduce the Head of State's involvement in the selection process. Out of nine members comprising the Council, four were appointed by the president of the Republic and two by the President of the Chamber of Deputies; moreover, the First President of the Court of Cassation, the First President of the Administrative Court, and the First President of the Court of Auditors were *ex officio* members of the Council. However, this appointment system *de facto* continued to give the president of the Republic control over the Council. Indeed, "as the President of the Republic [was] also the chief of the dominant party in Parliament, it [was] improbable that the President of the Chamber of Deputies [would] appoint members of the constitutional council who [did] not enjoy the trust of the President of the Republic."[26]

In Algeria, all three branches of government were involved in the appointment system. Indeed, out of nine members comprising the Council, three were appointed by the president of the Republic, four by Parliament, one by the Supreme Court, and one by the Council of State. However, as was the case in Tunisia, the Head of State's dominance over the legislature gave him control over the selection process. One of the clearest demonstrations of the very close link between the executive branch and the Constitutional Council occurred in 2012, when President Abdelaziz Bouteflika appointed the then Minister of Justice, Tayeb Belaiz, as President of the Council. Belaiz did not resign his position as Minister of Justice and retained both positions for a few months, thus clearly violating the principle of the separation of powers as well as the most basic rules on incompatibility of office.[27]

Also in Egypt, the executive exercised strong control over appointments to the Supreme Constitutional Court (SCC). In fact, according to the Law no. 48 of 1979 on the SCC, the Chief Justice was appointed by the president of the Republic, and even associate justices were appointed by presidential decree. However, when appointing them, the president had to choose between two nominees, one chosen by the Chief Justice and one by the General Assembly of the Court (which consisted of all members of the Court). It should be noted, however, that for the first two decades of its existence (i.e., during the 1980s and 1990s), the Court followed

> an *informal* procedure whereby the President promoted the most senior serving justice on the SCC to be Chief Justice. For the other justices on the SCC, the Chief Justice and the General Assembly of the Court [...] each nominated one

[26] Imen Gallala-Arndt, "Constitutional Jurisdiction and its Limits in the Maghreb" in Grote and Röder (eds.) 2012, *Constitutionalism in Islamic Countries*, at p. 239.

[27] See Francesco Biagi, "Constitutional Review in Algeria Following the 2016 Reform: With Particular Reference to the 'Exception of Unconstitutionality'" in Anja Schoeller-Schletter (ed.), *Constitutional Review in the Middle East and North Africa* (Nomos 2021), 98.

> candidate, and the President appointed one of these two candidates (SCC Law Article 5). In practice, the Chief Justice and the General Assembly of the Court always nominated the same person, whom the President would then appoint. In effect, the SCC became a self-perpetuating body, relatively free from executive control.[28] (emphasis added)

This informal mechanism came to an end in the early 2000s, when President Mubarak reasserted his formal authority over the selection process. Indeed, he appointed a Chief Justice who was loyal to his government and also packed the Court with friendly judges, taking advantage of the fact that neither the 1971 constitution nor the Law no. 48 of 1979 specified the number of Court members. As a consequence of this "silence," an indeterminate number of judges was possible. Therefore, "if a Chief Justice and President both dislike[d] the decisions of majority on the Court, they [could] collude to pack the court with justices sympathetic to their views."[29] This is precisely what happened in the early 2000s, when Mubarak appointed additional loyal members in order to shift the balance in his favor.

The eligibility for reappointment of the members of constitutional review bodies represented another serious threat to the independence of these institutions. In Syria, for example, the four-year term could be renewed, while in Tunisia, the three-year term was renewable twice. There are clear dangers to the renewability of judicial tenure. Since the court members "rely on continued executive support for their tenure [they] have little incentive to exercise any measure of judicial independence."[30]

3.2.2 *Deference toward the Executive Branch*

The weakness of constitutional review bodies was also closely linked to their deference toward the political authorities, and in particular toward the executive branch. A clear demonstration of this deference is apparent in the doctrine whereby "acts of sovereignty" (*a'mal al-siyada*) fall outside the jurisdiction of the judiciary. This doctrine, of French origins (*actes de gouvernement*), recalls the "political question doctrine" typical of the United States. The notion of acts of sovereignty is rather vague. In general terms, an act of sovereignty is something which states – and in particular the holder of executive authority – do by virtue of their status as sovereign actors, encompassing measures taken both at the domestic and international level. Thus, these acts often relate to matters of internal security, public order, and foreign

28 Center for Constitutional Transitions – International IDEA, *Constitutional Courts After the Arab Spring: Appointment Mechanisms and Relative Judicial Independence* (2014), 58, www.idea.int/sites/default/files/publications/constitutional-courts-after-the-arab-spring.pdf

29 Clark B. Lombardi, "Egypt's Supreme Constitutional Court: Managing Constitutional Conflict in an Authoritarian, Aspirationally 'Islamic' State" (2008) 3 *Journal of Comparative Law*, 242.

30 Center for Constitutional Transitions – International IDEA, *Constitutional Courts*, at p. 30.

policy. Clearly, the aim of acts of sovereignty is to allow the executive branch to exercise broad discretionary power.[31]

The doctrine was prevalent in Egypt. It was applied for the first time during the colonial era by the mixed courts, and afterward it was followed by ordinary courts, administrative courts, the Supreme Court, and also by the Supreme Constitutional Court.[32] ʿAbd al-Rahman Nusayr, a former Vice President of the Egyptian Supreme Constitutional Court, pointed out that

> The general guidance given by the [Supreme Constitutional Court] in this concern is that such political questions (or acts of sovereignty) are closely interrelated with the sovereignty of the State internally and externally, and encompass, by their nature, profound political considerations which justify giving the legislative or executive branches full discretionary power in order to realize the security and well-being of the country. As a result, this category of political questions (or acts of sovereignty) may not be subjected to judicial control, neither on its constitutionality nor its legality. [...] [N]either in its earlier or in its recent decisions has the court given precise criteria for both acts of sovereignty and/or political questions, preferring to give itself, case-by-case, the power to determine whether or not the challenged law is considered an act of sovereignty or a political question.[33]

Not surprisingly, in many cases, constitutional courts abused the doctrine of acts of sovereignty in order to avoid striking down laws that were clearly unconstitutional. In Kuwait, for example, the Constitutional Court "has been faced with cases in which the doctrine has been cited in its most extreme forms to justify actions that were incontrovertibly unconstitutional. The court has not endorsed the argument that the executive's violation of the constitution is an act of sovereignty, but it has not repudiated it either."[34] In Egypt, the judiciary considered declarations of a state of emergency to fall outside the scope of judicial review, as they were considered to result from an act of sovereignty.[35]

It should be pointed out that, far from having disappeared, this doctrine continues to be applied by constitutional review bodies in the region, especially in the most politically sensitive cases. In 2018, for example, the Egyptian Supreme Constitutional Court relied on this doctrine in order to legitimize the executive's controversial decision to cede sovereignty over the Tiran and Sanạfir islands to Saudi Arabia.[36]

[31] See Mohamed Maher Abouelenen, "Judges and Acts of Sovereignty" in Nathalie Bernard-Maugiron (ed.), *Judges and Political Reform in Egypt* (The American University in Cairo Press 2008), 181ff.

[32] Ibid., at p. 182ff.

[33] Cited in Brown, *Rule of Law*, at p. 121.

[34] Nathan J. Brown, *Constitutions in a Nonconstitutional World: Arab Basic Laws and the Prospects for Accountable Government* (SUNY Press 2002), 157.

[35] See in greater detail Chapter 2, Section 2.3.1.

[36] Case no. 37 and 49, Judicial Year 38 (March 3, 2018). See Karim Adel Kebaish, "Tiran and Sanafir: A Historical and Constitutional Argument Opposing the Territorial Cession of the Tiran and Sanafir

3.2.3 *The Nature of Constitutional Review Bodies*

While the role of constitutional courts and councils should be to place checks on the government majority and to protect rights and freedoms, in some Arab countries, constitutional review bodies were mainly conceived as institutions aimed at *protecting* or *advising* the executive branch. In Morocco, for example, the Constitutional Council "was originally created with the primary purpose of upholding the dominant position of the monarchy enshrined in the constitution. It was allowed to venture into other fields, and in particular into the field of fundamental rights, as long as this was not seen as incompatible with its primary role."[37] Thus, the Council was considered as the "*chien de garde de l'exécutif*"[38] and "the protector of royal prerogatives."[39]

Another emblematic case is that of Tunisia. For a long time (i.e., until 1987), the country did not have any constitutional review mechanism in the form of a constitutional court or council, as the president of the Republic was the institution responsible for guaranteeing respect for the 1959 constitution. A Constitutional Council was established in 1987 by presidential decree,[40] and was subsequently granted constitutional status in 1995. The Tunisian framers relied on the French model of constitutional review. Indeed, the Council was mainly a political body, and was in fact responsible for reviewing the constitutionality of legislation only prior to enactment (*ex ante* review). Unlike its French counterpart, however, the only institution entitled to refer bills to the Council was the president of the Republic. Moreover, for the first eleven years of its existence, the Council was only able to issue *advisory opinions*, which were *confidential* and *communicated exclusively to the president of the Republic*.[41] Therefore, the main task of the Constitutional Council was to advise the president of the Republic in his role of "guarantor […] of respect for the Constitution" (Article 41 of the 1959 constitution).[42]

Islands to Saudi Arabia" (2019) 97 *Texas Law Review*, 835ff. For other decisions where the Supreme Constitutional Court relied on this doctrine, see Mohammed, "Supreme Constitutional Court of Egypt," at pp. 8–9.

37 Rainer Grote, "Constitutional Review in Arab Countries. Down of a New Era?" in Rainer Grote and Tilmann J. Röder (eds.), *Constitutionalism, Human Rights, and Islam after the Arab Spring* (Oxford University Press 2016), 687.

38 Omar Bendourou, "Le Conseil constitutionnel et les droit fondamentaux" (2004) 56 *Revue marocaine d'administration locale et de développement*, 37. As is well known, this expression was originally used by Michel Debré to describe the French *Conseil Constitutionnel*.

39 Youssef Fassi Fihri, "Le Conseil constitutionnel marocain et le contrôle du législateur organique" in Omar Bendourou, Rkia El Mossadeq and Mohammed Madani (eds.), *La nouvelle Constitution marocaine à l'épreuve de la pratique* (Friedrich Ebert Stiftung 2014), 154.

40 Decree no. 87-1414 (December 16, 1987).

41 See Gallala-Arndt, "Constitutional Jurisdiction," at p. 252.

42 See Rafâa Ben Achour, "Le contrôle consultatif de la constitutionnalité des lois par le Conseil constitutionnel tunisien" in *Constitutions et pouvoirs: Mélanges en l'honneur de Jean Gicquel* (Montchrestien – L'extenso éditions 2008), 18; Rafâa Ben Achour and Abdessalem Lachaal, "Le contrôle de la constitutionalité des lois (état de la question)" (1991) 7 *Annuaire international de justice constitutionnelle*, 647–648.

The Council ceased to be a mere advisory body in 1998, when a constitutional amendment introduced the rule that the Council's opinions should be respected by all public authorities (unless they concerned the issues set out in Article 72(3) of the constitution, i.e., the issues subject to facultative jurisdiction) (Article 75(1) Const.). Furthermore, in 2004, Organic Law no. 52/2004 introduced the obligation to publish the Council's decisions in the Official Gazette (with the exception of the issues subject to facultative jurisdiction) (Article 28), thus officially putting an end to the abovementioned confidentiality and enabling public authorities to take note of the opinions of the Council.[43] Following these innovations, the Council "[was] no longer an advisory body strictly speaking, but [was] not yet a decision-making body and [was] certainly not a jurisdictional body."[44]

The peculiar nature of the Tunisian Constitutional Council was also reflected in the type of constitutional review that this body was entitled to exercise. Indeed, according to Article 72 of the 1959 constitution, the Council was responsible for verifying the "conformity" (*conformité*) or the "compatibility" (*compatibilité*) of bills with the constitution. Examining the "conformity" of a legislative act with the constitution is the standard function exercised by constitutional courts and councils. It involves comparing two legal texts, so as to ensure that the bill (or the statute law) complies with the constitution. The notion of "compatibility" is different. As explained by Rafaâ Ben Achour, the notion of compatibility "admits the existence of a certain divergence or even certain derogations" from the constitution, to the point that a legislative act is considered compatible with the constitution so long as there is not a "manifest contradiction" between these two texts.[45] The notion of compatibility granted a wide "margin of appreciation" to the Tunisian Constitutional Council, which relied on it in order to "save" certain controversial and disputable bills.[46]

3.2.4 *The "Stranglehold" on Access*

The procedural gateways to constitutional courts and councils represented another major weak point of these institutions. Indeed, in a number of countries, constitutional standing to refer cases to constitutional review bodies was significantly limited, with the obvious consequence of drastically reducing the overall number of legislative acts on which these institutions could rule. This "stranglehold" on access was very evident in the Maghreb countries. In the first place, only (usually very few) *political* authorities had standing to refer a case to the constitutional council. In Tunisia, for instance, as already mentioned earlier,[47] the president of the Republic

[43] See Gallala-Arndt, "Constitutional Jurisdiction," at p. 252.

[44] Ben Achour, "Le contrôle consultatif de la constitutionnalité des lois par le Conseil constitutionnel tunisien," at p. 23.

[45] Ibid., at p. 22.

[46] Ibid., at pp. 22–23.

[47] See Section 3.2.3.

was the only authority entitled to refer bills to the Constitutional Council. Another example is Algeria, where only the president of the Republic and the Speakers of the two Houses of Parliament could apply to the Constitutional Council.

Even when the procedural gateways were broader, still very few cases were referred to the constitutional councils. One need only consider the case of Morocco, where the 1996 constitution granted the power to appeal to the Constitutional Council not only to the king, the Prime Minister, and the Speakers of the two Houses of Parliament but also to the parliamentary opposition (i.e., one-quarter of the members of either House of Parliament). However, over the period 1994–2013, the opposition only applied to the Constitutional Council *four* times,[48] despite considerable doubts as to the constitutionality of a whole series of laws. This can be explained on both legal and political grounds. As to the former, it was not always easy for opposition parties to achieve a quorum of one-quarter of the members of either House.[49] As to the political grounds, the opposition often displayed a passive stance, due mainly to a more general attitude prevalent among Moroccan political parties. Indeed, in some cases, constitutionally controversial bills were not referred to the Council, having attracted a "consensus" among the different parties represented in Parliament.[50] This confirms the "politics of consensus," which has characterized Morocco for many decades. According to this notion, the role and absolute powers of the sovereign are not a matter for discussion or difference of opinion among the political parties. The latter, regardless of their ideological orientations, are happy to leave the palace full control over the key decisions for the country.[51] In addition, if the opposition applied to the Constitutional Council only in highly rare circumstances, this was also due to "its perceived bias in favor of the government," as the Council was always "firm in the defence of government prerogatives."[52]

Another aspect worth stressing is that since they were largely modeled on the French *Conseil Constitutionnel*, constitutional councils in the Maghreb were only empowered to review the constitutionality of legislation before its promulgation (*ex ante* review). Algeria was the only country in the Maghreb in which constitutional review was possible, not only *ex ante* but also *ex post*. In fact, Article 165 of the 1996 constitution stipulated that the Constitutional Council was required to rule by an

48 See Mohammed Amine Benabdallah, "Préface" in Mohammed Benyahya (ed.), *Les grandes décisions de la jurisprudence du Conseil Constitutionnel [1994–2013]* (Publications de REMALD 2013, no. 31), 20.

49 See Nadia Bernoussi and Abderrahim El Maslouhi, "Les chantiers de la 'bonne justice'. Contraintes et renouveau de la politique judiciaire au Maroc" (2012) 91 *Revue française de droit constitutionnel*, 499.

50 This occurred, for example, in relation to the Law of May 28, 2003, on combating terrorism, and to the Law of November 11, 2003, on the entry and residence of foreign nationals in the Kingdom of Morocco, emigration, and illegal immigration. See Bendourou, "Le Conseil constitutionnel et les droit fondamentaux," at p. 37.

51 See Driss Maghraoui, "Constitutional Reforms in Morocco: Between Consensus and Subaltern Politics" in George Joffé (ed.), *North Africa's Arab Spring* (Routledge 2013), 182.

52 Gallala-Arndt, "Constitutional Jurisdiction," at p. 254.

avis in relation to laws, treaties, and regulations that were not yet executed, and otherwise to rule by a *décision*.

It should be noted, however, that even when *ex post* review was admitted, only *political* authorities could apply to the constitutional council (*abstract* review). Indeed, in Algeria, the institutions that were granted constitutional standing both in *ex ante* and *ex post* review were the president of the Republic and the Speakers of the two Houses of Parliament. Ordinary courts, on the contrary, were not given the power to challenge the constitutionality of laws before the Council. This undoubtedly reduced the chances for the constitutional councils to rule on legislative acts that violated constitutional rights and freedoms. Egypt and Kuwait were the only Arab countries characterized by *concrete* review, as the ordinary courts were entitled to refer questions of constitutionality to the constitutional court.

3.2.5 *The Political and Social Context (with the Egyptian and Lebanese [Partial] Exceptions)*

Finally, it is essential to take into account the political and social context within which constitutional review bodies exercised their powers. As has been pointed out by Mauro Cappelletti, "no dictatorial or oppressive regime has ever accepted an effective, and not merely nominal, system of constitutional justice."[53] The very few constitutional courts that have managed to carry out their functions effectively despite the fact that they were operating under authoritarian regimes may be seen as exceptions that confirm the rule.[54] One of these exceptions is given by the Supreme Constitutional Court of Egypt. During the first phase of its existence (1980–1985), the Court focused on the safeguarding of economic and property rights, thus fulfilling the expectations of Presidents Sadat (initially) and Mubarak (subsequently). However, by mid-Eighties the Court also started to protect civil and political rights. As a result, the Court clashed directly with the executive, which was opposed to political liberalization. Moreover, from the early Nineties, under the presidency of Chief Justice Awad Mohammed El-Morr, the Court – adopting an expansive reading of the 1971 constitution – began to rely on international human rights treaties and conventions in order to guarantee even more effective protection for fundamental rights and freedoms.[55] Interestingly, the Court often also promoted a liberal and modernist interpretation of the principles of *sharia*, always with the aim

53 Mauro Cappelletti, *Dimensioni della giustizia nelle società contemporanee: Studi di diritto giudiziario comparato* (il Mulino 1994), 69.

54 On the role of judicial bodies in autocratic regimes, see Tom Ginsburg and Tamir Moustafa (eds.), *Rule by Law: The Politics of Courts in Authoritarian Regimes* (Cambridge University Press 2008).

55 For an analysis of this case law, see Boyle and Sherif (eds.) 1996, *Human Rights and Democracy*; Cotran and Sherif (eds.) 1997, *Role of the Judiciary*, at pp. 1–76; Nathalie Bernard-Maugiron, "La Haute Cour constitutionnelle égyptienne, gardienne des libertés publiques" (1999) 2 *Égypte/Monde arabe*, 17ff.; Bernard-Maugiron, *Le politique à l'épreuve du judiciaire*, at p. 161ff.

of safeguarding human rights, including women's rights.[56] As a result, from 1985 until the late Nineties (a period known as "the golden age" of the Constitutional Court), despite the limits discussed earlier (such as a strong executive control over the appointment of the Court's members, or the (ab)use by the Court of the doctrine of acts of sovereignty), the Supreme Constitutional Court, which had initially been conceived as an ally of the Government, managed to achieve and maintain autonomy from the executive branch and turned into a body that (at least on occasion) constrained the regime.[57]

Nonetheless, "there were important limits to [the Court's] activism. At odds with its strong record of rights activism, the [Court] ruled Egypt's emergency state security courts constitutional. It also delayed issuing a ruling on the constitutionality of civilian transfers to military courts."[58] As recalled earlier, during the early 2000s, President Mubarak put an end to the Court's boldness by packing it with regime-friendly judges. Emblematic of this was his appointment of Fathi Nagib as the new Chief Justice, the person "who had drafted the vast majority of the government's illiberal legislation over the previous decade."[59] In this way, the regime managed to transform the Court back into a less activist and less liberal institution.[60]

Another example of a constitutional review body that managed to act (at least on occasion) as a defender of constitutionalism is the Lebanese Constitutional Council. Unlike many other countries in the region, Lebanon has never experienced a fully autocratic regime, even though the social, political, institutional, and religious context has long been highly complicated. Despite such a context and certain flaws in its design, the Council contributed to strengthening the democratic character of the Lebanese constitutional system.[61] First of all, its presence and its ability to strike down laws as unconstitutional represented a "dissuasive element,"[62] forcing the government and Parliament to pay more attention to the elaboration of legislative acts in order to ensure their compliance with the constitutional text. Furthermore, the Council made some important decisions in the field of electoral disputes[63] and in the field of the

56 See also Chapter 4, Sections 4.2.2 and 4.3.2.

57 On how the Court managed to do so, see Nathan J. Brown et al., *Authoritarianism from the Inside: How and When State Institutions Realize Autonomy Under Authoritarian Regimes* (forthcoming).

58 Tamir Moustafa, "The Political Role of the Supreme Constitutional Court: Between Principles and Practice" in Bernard-Maugiron (ed.) 2008, *Judges and Political Reform*, at p. 95.

59 Ibid., at p. 103.

60 See Tamir Moustafa, *The Struggle for Constitutional Power: Law, Politics, and Economic Development in Egypt* (Cambridge University Press 2007), 178–219; Lombardi, "Egypt's Supreme Constitutional Court," at p. 242ff.

61 See Nada Youssef, "Le Liban: la transition inachevée vers l'État de droit" (2013) 95 *Revue française de droit constitutionnel*, 751–752; Francesco Biagi, "La Costituzione del Libano" in Luca Mezzetti (ed.), *Codice delle Costituzioni. Paesi islamici. Vol. VI.3* (Wolters Kluwer – CEDAM 2023), 327ff.

62 Pierre Gannagé, "Le Conseil constitutionnel libanais" in *Les Constitutions des Pays arabes: Colloque de Beyrouth, 1998* (1999), at pp. 270–271.

63 See Conseil Constitutionnel, *Recueil des décisions du Conseil constitutionnel 1994–2016 – Volume 2: Décisions relatives au contentieux électoral* (Beirut 2017).

protection of fundamental rights.[64] Thus, for example, the Council guaranteed the protection of the right to vote,[65] the principle of equality,[66] the autonomy of confessional groups in the management of their religious affairs,[67] the right of defense and recourse to justice,[68] as well as the right of property.[69] Also noteworthy is a judgment delivered in 2017,[70] in which the Council gave emphasis to the principle of transparency in legislation, and the principles relative to the annual and universal nature of the state budget and the consequent impossibility of levying taxes in the absence of one. The relevance of this decision can be explained in the light of the state's failure to adopt a new budget for thirteen consecutive years. Following this judgment, which was "an unprecedented attempt at restoring constitutional rule against years of recurrent violations that had gone unchallenged," annual budgets "made their comeback, restoring a certain sense of constitutional normalcy."[71] In some of its rulings, the Council even relied on international human rights treaties and conventions.

Interestingly, the Council, according to settled case law, argued that the fundamental principles proclaimed in the preamble to the 1926 constitution constituted an integral part of the constitutional text and therefore should be included within the parameter for constitutional review. Suffice it to consider the decisions concerning the principle of the separation of powers,[72] the democratic nature of the legal system,[73] and popular sovereignty.[74] Thus, the Lebanese Constitutional Council followed the example of the French *Conseil Constitutionnel* that, in the landmark judgment *Libertè d'association* of July 16, 1971, held that the preamble to the 1958 constitution (that made reference, *inter alia*, to the 1789 Declaration of the Rights of Man and of the Citizen and to the preamble to the 1946 constitution) was part of the parameter for constitutional review (*bloc de constitutionnalité*).[75]

That said, it must be stressed that the Lebanese Constitutional Council's role of guardian of the constitution was significantly hindered by the composition itself of

64 See Conseil Constitutionnel, *Recueil des décisions du Conseil constitutionnel 1994–2016 – Volume 1: Décisions relatives à la constitutionnalité des lois* (Beirut 2017).
65 *Décision* no. 2/1997.
66 *Décision* no. 1/2000.
67 *Décision* no. 2/2000.
68 *Décision* no. 5/2000.
69 *Décision* no. 4/2000. On all these decisions, see Youssef, "Le Liban," at pp. 751–752.
70 *Décision* no. 5/2017.
71 Tamara El Khoury, "Back to Basics: When Stating the Obvious is Groundbreaking," *IACL-AIDC Blog* (June 22, 2021), https://blog-iacl-aidc.org/menaregion/22-6-21-back-to-basics-when-stating-the-obvious-is-groundbreaking
72 *Décisions* no. 2/1999, no. 2/2002, and no. 1/2005.
73 *Décision* no. 1/2013.
74 *Décision* no. 7/2014.
75 On this ruling of the *Conseil Constitutionnel* and the value of the preamble to the 1958 Constitution, see Justin O. Frosini, *Constitutional Preambles: At a Crossroads Between Politics and Law* (Maggioli 2012), 64ff.; Wim Voermans, Maarten Stremler and Paul Cliteur, *Constitutional Preambles: A Comparative Analysis* (Edward Elgar 2017), 105ff.

the Council (which was strongly influenced by the quota-sharing principle)[76] and by the fact that the Council received only a very limited number of constitutional challenges (a fact that can be explained, *inter alia*, by limited access to the Council).[77] Furthermore, in some politically sensitive cases, the Council preferred to dismiss the challenges even if the constitutionality of the laws was particularly doubtful.[78]

3.3 CONSTITUTIONAL REVIEW IN POST-2011 CONSTITUTIONS

The new constitutions or constitutional reforms adopted following the Arab uprisings introduced a number of major innovations in the field of constitutional review.[79] Some countries established a constitutional court for the first time in their history (Jordan in 2012 and Palestine in 2016);[80] meanwhile in Libya, although the constitution-making process is still ongoing, the last draft constitution from July 2017 provides for a constitutional court. Other countries (e.g., Morocco, Tunisia, Algeria, and Kuwait) have reinforced the position and the prerogatives of their constitutional review bodies, and in Egypt, the Supreme Constitutional Court remains a highly powerful and influential institution.[81]

There are various different reasons why these new constitutional review bodies have become – at least from a *formal* perspective – such a fundamental element of the new constitutional frameworks. On the one hand, the establishment or reinforcement of these institutions represented a way of addressing demands made by protesters during the 2011 demonstrations – protesters who were calling, *inter alia*, for the creation of a state based on the rule of law and a more effective protection for rights and freedoms. On the other hand, the willingness to adopt constitutions that are more closely aligned with international standards (even if only at a formal level) became strongly apparent, and constitutional review – as is well known – is now considered as an essential element of a democratic country. In other cases, the establishment of a constitutional court appeared to be linked to political dynamics,

[76] See Nizar Saghieh, "Lebanon's Constitutional Council: Access Blocked to Protect the Consensus System?" in Schoeller-Schletter (ed.) 2021, *Constitutional Review*, at pp. 124–127.

[77] Ibid., at pp. 129–130. On limited access to the Council, see Section 3.5.

[78] Ibid., at p. 130ff.

[79] See Justin O. Frosini and Francesco Biagi, "Transitions from Authoritarian Rule following the Arab Uprisings: A Matter of Variables" in Justin O. Frosini and Francesco Biagi (eds.), *Political and Constitutional Transitions in North Africa: Actors and Factors* (Routledge 2015), 139ff.; Grote, "Constitutional Review," at p. 677ff.; Schoeller-Schletter (ed.) 2021, *Constitutional Review*.

[80] It should be clarified that in Palestine, the Constitutional Court had already been provided for under the Basic Law of 2003, and that the Law on the Constitutional Court had been adopted in 2006 (Law no. 3 of 2006, which was subsequently amended in 2017 [Law no. 19 of 2017]). On the Constitutional Court of Palestine, see Osayd Awawda, *The Palestinian Constitutional Court: An Assessment of Its Independence Under the Emergency Regime* (Cambridge Scholars Publishing 2022).

[81] On the influence and impact of the Egyptian model of constitutional review and of the Supreme Constitutional Court's case law in the Arab region, see Mohammed, "Supreme Constitutional Court of Egypt," at pp. 14–15.

including in particular the need to provide a "constitutional veneer" for decisions made by the regime.

In the following sections (Sections 3.3.1–3.3.4), I examine some of the most significant innovations introduced by the recent constitutional reforms, including (1) a limited strengthening of the independence of constitutional review bodies, (2) the vesting of these institutions with judicial status, (3) the broadening of access to these institutions, and (4) a further expansion of their jurisdiction.

3.3.1 A *Limited Strengthening of the Independence of Constitutional Review Bodies*

In the wake of the Arab Spring, some countries reinforced the independence of constitutional courts and councils, for example, by limiting the excessive influence of the executive branch in the appointment process. This was undoubtedly the case of Tunisia, where the 2014 constitution involved all three branches of government on an equal footing in the selection of the members of the Constitutional Court: four were appointed by the president of the Republic, four by the Assembly of the Representatives of the People, and four by the Supreme Judicial Council. However, the 2022 constitution (as will be discussed later) completely abandoned this appointment system.

The 2017 draft constitution of Libya also involves all three branches of government in the selection of the twelve members of the Constitutional Court. Indeed, six are appointed by the High Judicial Council, three by the president of the Republic, and three by the legislative branch. However, since the composition of the High Judicial Council is not indicated in the draft constitution, but has to be determined by the implementing legislation, it is difficult to fully assess the real "weight" that each of these three institutions will have in the appointment process.

Generally speaking, the involvement of a wide range of actors in the appointment process is extremely important not only because it reduces, at least in part, the excessive interference of a single institution or party[82] but also because it "fosters a broad sense of political investment in the court," as "all actors have an incentive to continue supporting the court even when they are on the losing side of its decisions."[83] Furthermore, this appointment procedure contributes to ensuring that the Constitutional Court is in tune with the society in which it operates. In fact, a court "whose decisions do not in any way reflect society's values and concerns is unlikely to retain the public's support, and will either come to be disregarded as an unjust body or dismantled by the elected branches."[84]

82 See Giacomo Delledonne, "Appointing and Electing Constitutional Judges. An Evolving Comparative Landscape" in Martin Belov (ed.), *The Role of Courts in Contemporary Legal Orders* (Eleven International Publishing 2019), 162.

83 Center for Constitutional Transitions – International IDEA, *Constitutional Courts*, at p. 9.

84 Ibid., at p. 28.

Other changes have also contributed to protecting the new Arab constitutional review bodies from political influence. First of all, the countries that still do not provide for a fixed term in office are now clearly in a minority. This is the case, for example, of Syria where the 2012 constitution continues to provide that the four-year term of the members of the Supreme Constitutional Court can be renewed. Thus, in 2022, several constitutional justices (including the President of the Court, Mohammad Jihad al-Laham), after serving a first term, were reappointed to the bench.[85] Furthermore, a number of countries have enhanced the qualifications that members of constitutional review bodies must hold, such as the level of education and professional expertise that they must have obtained, the minimum or maximum age at the time of appointment, or the list of professions or offices that are incompatible with appointment to constitutional review bodies (usually political positions).[86]

In most Arab countries, however, the head of state continues to dominate the appointment system of the members of constitutional courts. In Syria, for example, the 2012 constitution still grants the president of the Republic the power to select all justices of the Supreme Constitutional Court. Similarly, the 1952 Jordanian Constitution (as amended in 2011) states that all the members of the Constitutional Court are appointed by the monarch. In Morocco, the 2011 constitution continues to vest the king with the power to select half of the members of the Constitutional Court, including the President (while the other half is selected by Parliament). It should be noted that both in Morocco and Jordan (in the latter case following the 2016 constitutional reform), the king's appointment of the members of their respective constitutional courts does not need to be countersigned by the government, thus leaving full discretion to the monarch.

In Egypt, the original version of the 2014 constitution had granted a key role to the General Assembly of the Court (which is composed of all the Court's members) in the selection process. Indeed, the Assembly was responsible for selecting the Court's Chief Justice from among the most senior Deputy Chief Justices (i.e., the associate justices) of the Court. Moreover, the Assembly had the power to choose the Deputy Chief Justices, who were then appointed by presidential decree. The 2019 reform to the 2014 constitution, however, radically changed the selection process, as the president of the Republic now has full control over this process. Indeed, the Chief Justice is directly appointed by the president of the Republic, choosing from among the five most senior Deputy Chief Justices of the Court. The Chief Justice's role is of the utmost importance, since he "controls the [Court]'s docket and oversees the process of writing the Court's decisions."[87] The president of the Republic also appoints the

[85] See Syrians for Truth and Justice, *The Supreme Constitutional Court in Syria: A Formal Independent Tool in the Hands of the President* (August 2022), 3, https://stj-sy.org/wp-content/uploads/2022/08/The-Supreme-Constitutional-Court-in-Syria-.pdf

[86] See Center for Constitutional Transitions – International IDEA, *Constitutional Courts*, at p. 89ff.

[87] Ibid., at p. 59.

Deputy Chief Justices of the Court, choosing between two nominees: one nominated by the General Assembly of the Court, and one nominated by the Chief Justice.

The 2012 constitution had introduced an important new provision, according to which the Supreme Constitutional Court was to be composed of the President and ten justices, thus remedying the failure by the previous constitution of 1971 to specify the number of the Court's members. However, this change proved to be short-lived, as the 2014 constitution no longer specifies the number of justices on the Court: It only states that the Court must be composed of a president and a "sufficient number" (*'adad kaf*) of justices (Article 193). In a similar vein, even the 2012 Syrian Constitution stipulates that the Supreme Constitutional Court "consists of *at least* seven members" (Article 141) (emphasis added). On May 16, 2022, President Assad issued Decree no. 127, which increased the number of constitutional justices to eleven. Currently, the Syrian Supreme Constitutional Court includes six judges, three lawyers (including the President of the Court), and two university professors.[88] In order to avoid the risks inherent in the court-packing schemes mentioned earlier, a fixed number of justices would have been preferable.

In the case of Algeria, one should distinguish between the 2016 reform of the 1996 constitution and the 2020 reform. The 2016 reform increased the number of the members of the Constitutional Council from nine to twelve, and involved all three branches of government in the appointment process. Indeed, the president of the Republic appointed one third (four) of the members of the Council, including the President and the Vice President of the Council; a further third were elected by Parliament (two judges by the People's National Assembly and two by the Council of the Nation), while the remaining third were appointed by the judiciary (two members by the Supreme Court and two by the Council of State).

The 2020 reform, however, introduced profound modifications. In the first place, the Constitutional Council was replaced by a Constitutional *Court*. As to the selection process, four members (including the President) are appointed by the president of the Republic, one by the Supreme Court (among its members), one by the Council of State (among its members), and "six are elected by suffrage from among the professors of constitutional law" (Article 186). As to these latter members (who form half of the members of the Court), the constitution specifies that the president of the Republic is responsible for deciding "conditions and modalities for [their] elections" (Article 186). On August 4, 2021, President Tebboune issued Presidential Decree no. 21-304, which regulated these elections. According to this decree, the right to vote is granted to every active university teacher of public law (Article 8). As to the eligibility requirements, any candidate must, *inter alia*, be at least fifty years old, have the rank of professor, have been a teacher of constitutional law for at least five years, have made scientific contributions in the field, have at least twenty years' experience in law in an institution of higher education, enjoy civic and political rights, not have been handed down any

88 See Syrians for Truth and Justice, *Supreme Constitutional Court*, at p. 3.

definitive conviction depriving him or her of liberty, and not have been affiliated with a political party for at least three years preceding the election (Article 9). The elections of the six professors of constitutional law as members of the Constitutional Court were held on October 14, 2021: According to the National Electoral Commission in charge of supervising these elections, 2,253 teachers of public law participated in the vote, with a 75.25 percent turnout.[89] This type of election of the constitutional court members is singular from a comparative perspective. Indeed, it also differs from those few cases (such as Bolivia[90]) in which the members of the constitutional court are elected by universal suffrage. In the case of Algeria, half of the constitutional justices are elected by a highly specific category of people, namely by university teachers of public law. It should also be noted that the conditions and modalities for the election of these members of the Court can easily change, as they are not regulated by the constitution and the implementing legislation, but are left to the sole discretion of the president of the Republic. This power, combined with the direct selection of one-third of the members (including the President), gives the president of the Republic significant control over appointments to the Constitutional Court.[91]

In Tunisia, the 2022 constitution states that the nine members of the Constitutional Court are appointed "by decree" (presumably by *presidential* decree) (Article 125). More specifically, "[a] third of these members are the most senior chamber presidents of the Court of Cassation, a third are the most senior presidents of the cassation chambers or the consultative chambers of the Administrative Court, and a last third are the most senior members of the Court of Accounts" (Article 125). Thus, the selection process of the constitutional justices has been completely changed with respect to the 2014 constitution, which involved all three branches of government on an equal footing (as recalled earlier).[92]

89 See "Proclamation de la liste des professeurs de droit constitutionnel élus," *Algérie Press Service* (October 18, 2021), www.aps.dz/algerie/129061-cour-constitutionnelle-proclamation-de-la-liste-des-professeurs-de-droit-constitutionnel-elus

90 See Article 198 of the Constitution. Article 19 of Law no. 027 of July 6, 2010 (Law on the Plurinational Constitutional Tribunal) specifies that nominations are made before the Plurinational Legislative Assembly, which, by a two-thirds vote of its members, will define a preselection of candidates, whose list will then be sent to the Plurinational Electoral Body. On this system, see Millán Terán and Óscar Antonio, "El sistema electoral para la elección de los magistrados del Tribunal Constitucional Plurinacional" (2015) 35 *Ciencia y Cultura*, 107–132.

91 See International Commission of Jurists, *Flawed and Inadequate: Algeria's Constitutional Amendment Process – A Briefing Paper* (October 2020), 15–16, www.icj.org/wp-content/uploads/2020/10/Algeria-NewConstitution-Advocacy-Analysis-Brief-2020-ENG.pdf

92 On the new selection process of the members of the Constitutional Court, see Nidhal Mekki, "The Project of the President's Constitution: Is It Time to Close the Democratic Parenthesis in Tunisia?," *ConstitutionNet* (July 25, 2022), https://constitutionnet.org/news/project-presidents-constitution-it-time-close-democratic-parenthesis-tunisia; Siraj Khan, "A Comparative Analysis of the Draft Constitutions of Tunisia 2022: Zero-Sum Games," *Konrad Adenauer Stiftung – Rule of Law Programme Middle East and North Africa* (July 2022), 11, www.kas.de/documents/265308/22468903/A+Comparative+Analysis+of+the+Draft+Constitutions+of+Tunisia+2022+Zero-Sum+Games.pdf/4a68ee42-6ca4-31b2-78f2-4aeccca3e3b4?version=1.0&t=1674460240919

3.3.2 *The Shift toward a "Judicialization" of Constitutional Review Bodies*

Before the Arab Spring, the strong influence of the French model of constitutional review was largely responsible for the mainly *political* character of constitutional review bodies in the Maghreb countries (and indeed beyond, such as in Lebanon). This political nature was apparent in a series of features: (1) the name itself: "constitutional council" (*majlis dusturi*) instead of "constitutional court" (*mahkama dusturiyya*) clearly indicated the nonjudicial status of these bodies; (2) the appointment and composition: Members of constitutional councils were mainly appointed by political actors (and in particular by the head of state), and were not usually required to have any legal background in order to be selected; (3) the type of constitutional review: With the sole exception of Algeria (which also provided for *ex post* review), the Maghreb countries only provided for *ex ante* review, as constitutional scrutiny was only allowed during (and not after) the legislative process, that is, prior to the enactment of the law; (4) constitutional standing: Only political authorities (such as the head of state, the prime minister, the speakers of the houses of parliament, and in some cases also the parliamentary opposition) were entitled to apply to constitutional councils (abstract review); ordinary courts, on the other hand, were not granted the power to challenge the constitutionality of legislative acts (concrete review).[93]

Many post-2011 constitutions in the Maghreb have completely overturned this political model, moving toward the "judicialization" of constitutional review, in the form of Kelsenian-style (or *quasi*-Kelsenian-style) constitutional courts. First, constitutional councils have changed their name and are now called constitutional "courts" (as in Morocco, Tunisia, and following the 2020 reform also in Algeria). Second, in some countries (such as Tunisia [under the 2014 constitution] and Algeria), different branches of government – including the judiciary – were/are involved in the process of appointing the members of constitutional courts. Thus, political actors are no longer the only institutions empowered to select their members.[94] Third, in most cases, a legal background has become an essential requirement for appointment to the bench (as in Morocco,[95] Tunisia,[96]

93 On all these features, see in greater detail Gallala-Arndt, "Constitutional Jurisdiction," at p. 239ff.

94 In Morocco, by contrast, half of the members of the Constitutional Court are appointed by the king, and half by Parliament, without any involvement of the judiciary (Article 130).

95 The 2011 Constitution stipulates that the members of the Constitutional Court are chosen from among those persons with an advanced qualification in law and with judicial, doctrinal or administrative expertise who have exercised their profession for more than fifteen years, and are recognized for their impartiality and probity (Article 130(5)).

96 The 2014 Constitution provided that three-quarters of the members of the Constitutional Court were "legal experts with at least 20 years of experience" (Article 118(1)), and that the president and the vice-president were "specialists in law" (Article 118(4)). The 2022 Constitution states that the Court must be composed exclusively of career judges (from the Court of Cassation, the Administrative Court, and the Court of Accounts) (Article 125).

and Algeria[97]). Fourth, in addition to *ex ante* review (which continues to be a distinguishing feature of these systems), constitutional courts in the Maghreb have now been vested with the task of reviewing the constitutionality of legislation also *after* its promulgation (*ex post* review). In particular (as will be discussed in Section 3.3.3), authority to challenge the constitutionality of legislative acts has also been vested in ordinary courts (concrete review), as is the case for example in Morocco, Tunisia, and Algeria. Fifth, the reinforcement of the judicial character of constitutional courts is also evident if one considers that the binding status of the decisions of these bodies has been further consolidated. In Tunisia, for example, while (as discussed earlier) under the 1959 constitution the Constitutional Council never fully lost its mainly advisory function, the 2014 constitution specified that the Constitutional Court was "an independent judicial body" (Article 118), and that its decisions were "binding on all authorities and published in the Official Gazette" (Article 121). These latter provisions were maintained in the 2022 constitution (Articles 125 and 129).

It is important to stress that the "judicialization" of constitutional review bodies has not been characteristic only of Maghreb countries, but has been a common feature throughout most post-2011 Arab countries. In Egypt and Syria, for example, the new constitutions have maintained the judicial status of the Supreme Constitutional Court. In addition, recently established constitutional review bodies, namely the constitutional courts of Jordan and Palestine, are clearly judicial bodies. Also, the 2017 draft constitution of Libya has granted the constitutional court judicial status. This trend represents a significant innovation, which should contribute to a more effective protection of rights and freedoms.

3.3.3 *The Broadening of Access*

Calls within the literature[98] and in some cases by the members of constitutional review bodies themselves (such as in Algeria[99] and Jordan[100]) to broaden access to constitutional courts and councils have been accepted by constitutional framers in

[97] The 2020 constitutional reform has not only provided that the members of the Court must have at least twenty years of legal experience and must have followed a training in constitutional law (Article 187) but has also required that half of the members of the Court be professors of constitutional law (Article 186(3)).

[98] See Chibli Mallat, *Introduction to Middle Eastern Law* (Oxford University Press 2007), 208–210; Bendourou, "Le Conseil constitutionnel et les droit fondamentaux," at p. 37; Gallala-Arndt, "Constitutional Jurisdiction," at p. 258.

[99] See Tayeb Belaiz, "Allocution de M. Tayeb Belaiz, Président du Conseil Constitutionnel, à l'ouverture de la journée d'étude organisée à Alger, le 22 avril 2013, sur le thème 'L'extension de la saisine du Conseil Constitutionnel'" (2013) 2 *Revue du Conseil Constitutionnel*, 52.

[100] See Max Planck Foundation for International Peace and the Rule of Law, *The Constitutional Court System in the Hashemite Kingdom of Jordan: High-Level Roundtable with the Constitutional Court and the Court of Cassation of Jordan (October 10–13, 2016)* (Heidelberg 2016–2017), 19.

most Arab countries. In the first place, they have decided to increase the number of governmental bodies with standing to apply to constitutional courts and councils (abstract review). In Algeria, for example, only the president of the Republic and the speakers of the two Houses of Parliament had standing to apply to the Constitutional Council, while the 2020 constitutional reform vested this power also in the Prime Minister/Head of Government[101] and the parliamentary opposition (i.e., forty members of the People's National Assembly and twenty-five members of the Council of the Nation). In Tunisia, the broadening of access to the Constitutional Court has been even more evident. In fact, while under the 1959 constitution, the president of the Republic was the only political authority entitled to apply to the Council, the 2014 constitution granted constitutional standing also to the Head of Government and thirty members of the Assembly of the Representatives of the People, and the 2022 constitution states that the constitutionality of laws can also be challenged by thirty members of the Assembly of the Representatives of the People or by half of the members of the National Council of Regions and Districts.

However, a system of constitutional review can hardly be successful if only political actors – albeit increased in number – are entitled to apply to constitutional courts and councils. Therefore, the decision by most Arab framers to include (alongside abstract constitutional review) also *concrete* constitutional review has undoubtedly represented a major step forward. Under this system, when an ordinary judge concludes (either following a request by one of the parties or *ex officio*, depending on the country) that the law to be applied to the specific case violates the constitution, he/she must stay the proceedings and refer a question of constitutionality to the constitutional court, either directly or through the highest courts (as will be discussed later). The system of concrete review is likely to increase the chances of these bodies ruling on the constitutionality of legislative acts that violate fundamental rights and freedoms.

In the past, this procedural gateway was extremely rare in the Arab world and was to be found in very few countries, including Kuwait and (in particular) Egypt, where it has been very successful: "citizens have been able to bring an enormous number of constitutional claims, both minor and momentous, to the attention of the [Egyptian Supreme Constitutional Court]. As a practical matter, then, courts have [...] permitted citizens ample access to the [Supreme Constitutional Court]."[102]

A distinction must however be drawn between countries that adopted a "single-filter" system and countries that adopted a "double-filter" system. Indeed, some states – including Egypt, Kuwait, Palestine, Tunisia (under the 2014 constitution),[103] and now also Jordan – followed the system that can be found, for example, in Italy, Germany,

[101] On the difference between the Prime Minister and the Head of Government in Algeria, see Chapter 2, Section 2.1.5.

[102] Lombardi, "Egypt's Supreme Constitutional Court," at p. 240.

[103] In Tunisia, this system was very peculiar, as will be shown later.

and Spain, where all courts – including lower courts – can *directly* refer questions of constitutionality to the constitutional court (single-filter system). In Tunisia, a textual analysis of the 2022 constitution (Article 127) seems to suggest that the single-filter system has been maintained, but the concrete functioning of this mechanism needs to be clarified by the implementing legislation. Other countries – including Algeria and from 2012 to 2022 also Jordan – on the contrary, followed the French model (introduced by the 2008 constitutional reform (*Question Prioritaire de Constitutionnalité*) [QPC])[104] whereby lower courts must refer the question of constitutionality to the apex courts (e.g., the Court of Cassation and the Council of State), which then decide whether or not to refer the question to the constitutional court (double-filter system).

Comparative examples show that the double-filter system can be rather problematic, especially at the outset, as it can foster tensions between the highest courts and the constitutional court, and can hinder access to constitutional justice. For example, between 1951 and 1956, Germany adopted an access route that had strong similarities with the double-filter system. Specifically, courts could only refer a question of constitutionality to the *Bundesverfassungsgericht* via the supreme courts. These courts did not have the power to block the referral, but had the right to submit to the Constitutional Court their own opinion concerning the question referred by the lower courts. However, within the practice of the *Bundesgerichtshof* (the supreme court in civil and criminal matters),

> such opinions began to take the form of all but complete judgments on constitutionality and were published in the official collection of the *Bundesgerichtshof*'s decisions, sometimes before the Constitutional Court had rendered its decision. In 1955, the Constitutional Court declared that the supreme courts were not allowed to submit their opinions. In response, all five supreme court presidents addressed a note of protest to the President of the Constitutional Court. Finally, in July 1956, the Federal Constitutional Court Act was amended and the participation of supreme courts in the procedure of judicial referrals was abolished.[105]

Also in France, the introduction of the double-filter system was not without its difficulties. Indeed, during the first years of operation of the *Question Prioritaire de Constitutionnalité*, the Court of Cassation (although not the Council of State)[106] displayed a certain level of resistance when referring cases to the Constitutional Council – as was also recalled by the President of the French Constitutional Council Laurent Fabius during a visit to the Algerian Constitutional Council in

[104] See Federico Fabbrini, "Kelsen in Paris: France's Constitutional Reform and the Introduction of a Posteriori Constitutional Review of Legislation" (2008) 9 *German Law Journal*, 1297ff.; *Pouvoirs* (2011), no. 137 (specifically devoted to the *Question Prioritaire de Constitutionnalité*).

[105] Lech Garlicki, "Constitutional Courts versus Supreme Courts" (2007) 5 *International Journal of Constitutional Law*, 51.

[106] See Marthe Stefanini, *Le filtrage opéré par le Conseil d'État* (Rapport de recherche – Aix-Marseille Université 2013), 1ff., www.researchgate.net/publication/281356900_Le_filtrage_opere_par_le_Conseil_d'Etat

February 2017.[107] The reasons for this initial reluctance on the part of the Court of Cassation include its disinclination to perform this new role, and its hesitancy in altering the judicial equilibrium.[108]

Similar problems have also arisen (or may arise) in the Arab countries that adopted this model. In Jordan, for example, during the first decade of the Constitutional Court's activity (2012–2022), the very low number of judgments issued by this body appeared to be related – among other things – specifically to some reluctance on the part of the Court of Cassation to refer questions of constitutionality to the Constitutional Court.[109] For this reason, some constitutional justices recommended switching to a single-filter system.[110] This suggestion was eventually followed in 2022, when the constitutional reform and the amendments to the Law on the Constitutional Court replaced the double-filter system with a single-filter mechanism – an innovation that might promote access to the Constitutional Court, thus strengthening the role, the legitimacy, and the credibility of that body.

In Algeria, the double-filter system was introduced by the 2016 constitutional reform (and then confirmed in the 2020 reform),[111] and is regulated by Organic Law no. 18-16 on the "exception of unconstitutionality" (*exception d'inconstitutionnalité*), which entered into force on March 7, 2019.[112] Before the entry into force of the 2020 constitutional reform, the Constitutional Council had delivered four judgments concerning an exception of unconstitutionality. In all cases, the "exceptions" were raised by the Supreme Court and the contested legislative provisions referred to certain articles of the Code of Criminal Procedure.[113]

The risks of adoption of a double-filter system had previously been emphasized by the Venice Commission. Indeed, in a document published in 2011 concerning the procedural gateways to constitutional review bodies, the Commission had stressed that "from the viewpoint of human rights protection it is more expedient and efficient to give *courts of all levels* access to the Constitutional Court" (emphasis added).[114]

[107] See Laurent Fabius, "La question prioritaire de constitutionnalité en France 2010–2017: les principaux enseignements" (2017) 8 *Revue du Conseil Constitutionnel*, 118–119.

[108] See Nicolas Molfessis, "La résistance immédiate de la Cour de Cassation à la QPC" (2011) 137 *Pouvoirs*, 89ff.; Pierre de Montalivet, "QPC et 'dialogue des juges'" (2018) 116 *Revue française de droit constitutionnel*, 927.

[109] According to the official website of the Constitutional Court, the Court delivered 18 judgments in 2013, 7 in 2014, 4 in 2015, 3 in 2016, 4 in 2017, and 7 in 2018. See www.cco.gov.jo/en-us/Documents/The-Court-in-Numbers

[110] See Max Planck Foundation for International Peace and the Rule of Law, *Constitutional Court System*, at p. 19; Elkhatib and Domour, "Constitutional Court of Jordan," at p. 696.

[111] The 2020 constitutional reform introduced the rule according to which not only a legislative provision but also a provision of a *regulation* may be the object of an exception of unconstitutionality (Article 195).

[112] For an in-depth analysis of the double-filter system in Algeria, see Biagi, "Constitutional Review in Algeria," at p. 95ff.

[113] For a discussion of the first two decisions (namely Decision no. 01/D.CC/EI/19 and Decision no. 02/D.CC/EI/19 of November 20, 2019), see Biagi, "Constitutional Review in Algeria," at p. 106ff.

[114] Venice Commission, *Study on Individual Access to Constitutional Justice* (Study no. 538/2009) (January 27, 2011), 18, www.venice.coe.int/WebForms/documents/default.aspx?pdffile=CDL-AD(2010)039rev-e

In Morocco, the adoption of a single-filter system had been recommended by the National Human Rights Council, which had pointed out that the double-filter system "is cumbersome and may create intermediate steps between individuals and constitutional justice." Also, the length of time of the procedure "may impact pending cases and make it difficult for individuals to access constitutional justice."[115] Parliament, nevertheless, did not follow this recommendation and in February 2018 adopted Organic Law 86-15 on the "exception of unconstitutionality," introducing a double-filter mechanism.[116] However, this Organic Law did not enter into force, as it was ruled partially unconstitutional by the Constitutional Court in the decision 70-18 of March 6, 2018.[117]

The system of concrete constitutional review that can be found in Syria is extremely peculiar, as it seems to be halfway between the single-filter system and the double-filter system. Indeed, according to the 2012 constitution (Article 147(2)(a)) and Law no. 7 of 2014 on the Supreme Constitutional Court (Articles 11 and 38), the constitutionality of legislation cannot be challenged during a process before a lower court. It can only be challenged during an appeal process. Thus, only appellate courts – namely the Courts of Appeal, the Court of Cassation, and the High Administrative Court – are entitled to refer questions of constitutionality to the Supreme Constitutional Court. In order to refer a question of constitutionality, the challenged law must be necessary to resolve the case and the claim needs to be serious. It should be noted that, up until now, most constitutional challenges have been rejected by the Supreme Constitutional Court on procedural grounds.[118]

When assessing the effectiveness of concrete constitutional review, it is also particularly important to consider whether ordinary judges can refer a question of constitutionality only following a request by one of the parties to the case, or also *ex officio*. While some countries have vested judges with the power to refer a question *ex officio* (e.g., Egypt, Kuwait, and Palestine), other countries (e.g., Algeria, Jordan, Syria, and Tunisia) have preferred not to grant such a prerogative to the courts, which are only permitted to refer a question if either party to the case should so request. In relation specifically to Tunisia under the 2014 constitutional framework,

[115] National Human Rights Council, *The Organic Law Relating to the Exception of Unconstitutionality – Memorandum* (Rabat 2013), 5, www.ceja.ch/images/CEJA/DOCS/Bibliotheque/Doctrine/Maroc/CNDH/ENGLISH/Memorandum/The%20exception%20of%20unconstitutionality-%20memorandum.pdf

[116] See Juan José Ruiz Ruiz, "Las constituciones de las primaveras árabes y su implementación: el caso de Marruecos" (2018) 179 *Revista de estudios políticos*, 119–120.

[117] See Abdelhaif Chentouf, "Exception d'inconstitutionnalité des lois: le gouvernement contraint de revoir sa copie," *Challenge* (June 24, 2019), www.challenge.ma/exception-dinconstitutionnalite-des-lois-le-gouvernement-contraint-de-revoir-sa-copie-111234/

[118] See Ibrahim Daraji, "Syria: The Constitution of the 'Crisis' or the Crisis of the Constitution?", *Journal of Constitutional Law in the Middle East and North Africa*, special issue on "Arab Constitutional Responses to the Revolutions and Transformations in the Region" edited by Rim Turkmani and Tamara El Khoury (December 2023), 133-134, www.jcl-mena.org

it should be noted that this exclusion had been maintained despite the fact that the Venice Commission, in its opinion on the draft Organic Law on the Constitutional Court, recommended that the ordinary courts be granted the power to refer questions of constitutionality *ex officio*.[119] Furthermore, Article 56 of the Organic Law on the Constitutional Court (no. 2015-50 of December 3, 2015) appeared to suggest that ordinary judges were not permitted to assess the merits of a party's request to refer a question of constitutionality to the Constitutional Court.[120] In other words, it appeared that the referral was automatic, and that the ordinary courts were not permitted to ascertain the seriousness of the issue.[121] Since the Constitutional Court was never established under the 2014 constitutional framework, this uncertainty was never clarified. Following the adoption of the 2022 constitution (Article 127), it remains to be seen how this issue will be regulated by the implementing legislation.

Kuwait and Palestine should also be considered in regard to access to constitutional justice, as they have recently taken a further step. In these two countries, individuals have been granted the right to petition the constitutional court *directly*, in a way that recalls the individual constitutional complaints that can be found, for example, in Spain (*recurso de amparo constitucional*) and Germany (*Verfassungsbeschwerde*). In Palestine, the Law on the Constitutional Court no. 3 of 2006 (as amended by Law no. 19 of 2017) provides that the Constitutional Court must review the constitutionality of a legislative act on the basis of an "original direct lawsuit [...] raised by the aggrieved person" (Article 27(1)). In Kuwait, the Law no. 109 of 2014 has granted any natural or legal person the power to petition the Constitutional Court directly. In order to file an individual complaint against a legislative act, the complainant must have serious reasons to suspect that a provision of the constitution may have been violated, as well as a direct personal interest. The law also stipulates that, when submitting the petition, the person must deposit 5,000 Kuwaiti dinars (around 16,300 USD) as a guarantee.[122] This large amount of money risks excessively impeding access to the Constitutional Court – especially for women, who are usually financially dependent on their husbands.

119 See Venice Commission, *Opinion on the Draft Institutional Law on the Constitutional Court of Tunisia* (Opinion no. 817/2015) (October 26, 2015), 8, www.venice.coe.int/webforms/documents/?pdf=CDL-AD(2015)024-e By contrast, in other cases the framers decided to follow the recommendations of the Venice Commission, as for example when increasing the number of the authorities entitled to apply to the Constitutional Court for *ex ante* review. See Venice Commission, *Opinion on the Final Draft Constitution of the Republic of Tunisia* (Opinion no. 733/2013) (October 17, 2013), 30, www.venice.coe.int/webforms/documents/?pdf=CDL-AD(2013)032-e

120 Article 56 stipulates that "when an exception of unconstitutionality is raised before the courts, the latter must immediately transmit the issue to the Constitutional Court (*doivent renvoyer immédiatement l'affaire à la Cour constitutionnelle*)."

121 See Democracy Reporting International, *La Cour Constitutionnelle tunisienne: Analyse de la physionomie de l'institution après l'adoption de la Loi organique du 3 décembre 2015* (2016), 14.

122 See Fawaz Aljidie, *The Kuwaiti Constitutional System* (Kuwait City 2018), 186ff.

It should be noted that one of the major differences between the individual constitutional complaint mechanisms introduced in Palestine and Kuwait and those existing in Spain and Germany is the scope of the constitutional courts' review. Indeed, in Palestine and Kuwait, individuals are only entitled to file an individual complaint against a legislative act. In Spain and Germany (and in other European countries), however, individual complaints usually refer to "fundamental rights infringements by the regular judiciary or by the administration [...]. It is less common for complainants to (be able to) assert that the legislature has violated their fundamental rights by passing a particular piece of legislation."[123]

3.3.4 *A Further Expansion of Jurisdiction*

It is well known that the core function of constitutional courts and councils is to review the constitutionality of legislation. Over the last few decades, however, these bodies have also been granted a number of functions over and above the constitutional review of legislation *stricto sensu*, namely the so-called "ancillary functions."[124] This has also occurred in the Arab world, where constitutional review bodies – even before the 2011 uprisings – were vested with the task, for example, of reviewing the validity of elections (e.g., in Morocco, Algeria, Syria, Lebanon, and Kuwait), ascertaining the incapacity of the president of the Republic (e.g., in Algeria) or the vacancy of that office (e.g., in Algeria and Tunisia [under the 2014 constitution]), deciding on the impeachment of the president of the Republic (e.g., in Syria and Tunisia [under the 2014 constitution]), resolving conflicts between state authorities (e.g., in Egypt), adjudicating on disputes between the central government and sub-state entities (e.g., in the United Arab Emirates and Iraq), or reviewing the constitutionality of international treaties (e.g., in Algeria and Tunisia).

It is noteworthy that in certain cases, these ancillary functions *prevailed* over the constitutional review of legislation. In Algeria, for example, in the light of the "stranglehold" on access recalled earlier, the bulk of the Constitutional Council's decisions did not involve constitutional review, but consisted rather in ruling on the regularity of legislative elections, presidential elections, and referendums, as well as proclaiming the results of these electoral processes. In other words, the role of the Algerian Council was mainly that of an "arbiter of electoral life"[125] of the country. In a similar vein, the Moroccan Constitutional Council has been compared to the

123 Maartje de Visser, *Constitutional Review in Europe: A Comparative Analysis* (Hart 2015), 143.

124 See Tom Ginsburg and Zachary Elkins, "Ancillary Powers of Constitutional Courts" (2008) 87 *Texas Law Review*, 1431ff. For a focus on European constitutional courts, see de Visser, *Constitutional Review*, at p. 155ff.

125 Romain Graëffly, "Le Conseil constitutionnel algérien. De la greffe institutionnelle à l'avènement d'un contentieux constitutionnel?" (2005) 5 *Revue de droit publique*, 1403.

"sleeping beauty castle"[126] in the field of constitutional review. Indeed, in the period 1994–2013, the vast majority of its decisions (724 out of 913) related to the regularity of elections of the members of Parliament and of referendum procedures.[127] Thus, the impression was that the Algerian and Moroccan Councils were more similar to Latin American electoral courts rather than constitutional review bodies strictly speaking.[128]

The constitutional reforms adopted in the wake of the Arab Spring have, in numerous cases, further expanded the jurisdiction of constitutional courts. The case of the Tunisian Constitutional Court under the 2014 constitution is emblematic of this trend. In the first place, as also discussed in Chapter 2,[129] the Court was granted a key role in the functioning of the political regime. Indeed, it was responsible for resolving the conflicts between the president of the Republic and the Head of Government concerning the allocation of powers (Article 101), for deciding on the impeachment of the president of the Republic (Article 88), for declaring the temporary and permanent vacancy of the office of the president of the Republic (Article 84), as well as for reviewing the upholding of a state of exception (Article 80). In addition to that, the Court was vested with the power to review the constitutionality of constitutional amendments not only on procedural grounds but also on substantive grounds (Articles 120(2) and 144).[130] Another important function included the power to review the constitutionality of international treaties before the draft law approving them was signed (Article 120(3)). All these ancillary functions – that were never concretely exercised as the Court was never set up – confirm once again that this body would have been a fundamental component of the political and constitutional order.[131]

The 2022 Tunisian Constitution eliminated many of the abovementioned ancillary powers, including that of resolving conflicts between the president of the Republic and the Head of Government concerning the allocation of powers, that of deciding on the impeachment of the president of the Republic, and that of reviewing

[126] This was the metaphor used by Robert Badinter, cited in Nadia Bernoussi, "La Constitution de 2011 et le juge constitutionnel" in Centre d'Études Internationales (ed.), *La Constitution marocaine de 2011: Analyses et commentaires* (L.G.D.J. 2012), 211.

[127] See Benabdallah, "Préface," at p. 19. On the role of the Moroccan Constitutional Council in the electoral processes, see Adil Moussebbih, "L'office du Conseil constitutionnel marocain, juge électoral" (2017) 110 *Revue française de droit constitutionnel*, 437ff.

[128] On electoral justice in Latin America, see José de Jesús Orozco Henríquez, *Justicia electoral comparada de América Latina* (Universidad Nacional Autónoma de México 2019).

[129] See Chapter 2, Sections 2.2.3 and 2.2.4.

[130] On this power of courts in a comparative perspective, see Yaniv Roznai, *Unconstitutional Constitutional Amendments: The Limits of Amendment Powers* (Oxford University Press 2017); Richard Albert, *Constitutional Amendments: Making, Breaking, and Changing Constitutions* (Oxford University Press 2019), 217ff.

[131] On the effects of the absence of the Constitutional Court in the Tunisian legal system, see Democracy Reporting International, *Les effets de l'absence de la Cour constitutionnelle pendant la législature 2014–2019* (December 2019), https://democracyreporting.s3.eu-central-1.amazonaws.com/images/21732020-08-Tunisia-Effets-Abs-CC-Web-Fr.pdf

the upholding of a state of exception. The elimination of these ancillary functions can easily be explained by the illiberal turn that has occurred in the country since the proclamation of the state of exception in July 2021. Indeed, the semi-presidential form of government (characterized by a dual executive, that is, the president and the Head of Government) was replaced by a hyper-presidential regime; the president cannot be impeached any longer; and the possibility to extend the duration of the state of exception indefinitely is an essential component of Kaïs Saïed's strategy – as demonstrated in the period 2021–2022.

Algeria is another country where the Constitutional Council has traditionally been vested with a number of ancillary functions.[132] The 2016 and 2020 reforms have further expanded the jurisdiction of the Council (now Court). One of the most interesting innovations introduced by the 2020 reform has consisted in vesting a series of institutional actors (i.e., president of the Republic, Speakers of the two Houses of Parliament, Prime Minister/Head of Government,[133] as well as forty deputies or twenty-five members of the Council of Nation) with the power to apply to the Constitutional Court in case of disputes among "constitutional powers" (Article 192(1)). The same actors are also entitled to apply to the Court to request an interpretation of one or more constitutional provisions (Article 192(2)).

As will be shown in greater detail later, some ancillary functions of the Algerian Constitutional Court have been crucial in the regulation of constitutional reform processes as well as transition processes.[134] As to the former, the 2020 reform has maintained the provision enabling the constitution to be amended without a popular referendum. In fact, if the proposed constitutional amendment is upheld as constitutional by the Constitutional Court, the president of the Republic may promulgate the amendment law directly, provided that it has been approved by Parliament by a majority of three-fourths of the members of both Houses (Article 221). This latter procedure was followed in relation to the constitutional reforms taking place in 2002, 2008, and 2016. Furthermore, certain ancillary functions (in particular, the Court's power to decide on the regularity of electoral processes [Article 191], and to rule that the office of the president of the Republic is permanently vacant [Article 94]), were very important in regulating the transition process following the decision by Abdelaziz Bouteflika not to run for a fifth term in office and to resign on April 2, 2019.

Other relevant ancillary functions of the Algerian Constitutional Court include the power to verify the constitutionality of international treaties prior to their ratification (Article 190) and to extend the timeframes for holding new presidential elections up to a maximum period of sixty days in the event that any of the second-round candidates should die or be subject to a lawful impediment (Article 95). Moreover,

[132] See Biagi, "Constitutional Review in Algeria," at pp. 96–100.

[133] On the difference between Prime Minister and Head of Government in Algeria, see Chapter 2, Section 2.1.5.

[134] See Section 3.4.3.

the President of the Court must be consulted by the president of the Republic concerning any declaration of a state of emergency or a state of siege (Article 97), state of exception (Article 98), war (Article 100), or in the event of the dissolution of the People's National Assembly (Article 151), while the Court as a whole must be consulted in case of extension of the parliamentary term (Article 122). Furthermore, under certain extreme circumstances (e.g., if the office of President of the Council of the Nation is vacant at the time of the resignation or death of the president of the Republic), the President of the Constitutional Court assumes the duties of Head of State (Article 94).

Also the Egyptian Supreme Constitutional Court is vested with some important ancillary functions, including for instance that of providing statutory interpretation, resolving conflicts of jurisdiction between different judicial bodies, and resolving conflicts concerning the execution of two contradictory final judgments. In 2021, the Law on the Court was amended in order to grant the Court the power to "review the constitutionality of the decisions of international organizations and institutions, and also the judgments of foreign courts that are required to be implemented against the Egyptian state."[135] Interestingly, the Report of the Committee on Constitutional and Legislative Affairs concerning the draft bill on amending the Law on the Court stated that the rationale behind this amendment was "protecting Egyptian national security" from international decisions that "may not rest on any legal legitimacy." However, this report did not clarify what could constitute an illegitimate international decision that would threaten the Egyptian national security.[136] The impression is that with these amendments to the Law on the Court, Egypt "is unilaterally creating a judicial review step and in essence giving the [Court] the power to stop enforcement. Though these amendments will not change whether or not a judgment or decision is binding on Egypt, they do provide cover for Egyptian authorities to use domestic law to avoid international obligations."[137]

Assigning ancillary functions to constitutional courts and councils comes with its advantages and drawbacks. On the one hand, one of the major advantages – as pointed out by Tom Ginsburg and Zachary Elkins – is that these bodies represent

> political insurance in the face of uncertainty. Constitutional designers know there will be political conflict down the road, but they cannot anticipate who will be on what side of the issues and may anticipate that they are not in the majority. This will, *ceteris paribus*, lead them to empower a downstream actor who can fill gaps in the constitution and resolve disputes so as to maintain the system.[138]

135 Article 27 bis, Law no. 48 of 1979 (as amended in 2021).

136 See Mohammed, "Supreme Constitutional Court of Egypt," at p. 6.

137 Mai El-Sadany and Yasmin Omar, "Egypt's Constitutional Court Amendments: The International System On Its Own Terms," *Carnegie Endowment for International Peace* (July 12, 2021), https://carnegieendowment.org/sada/84941

138 Ginsburg and Elkins, "Ancillary Powers," at p. 1454.

On the other hand, ancillary functions also entail disadvantages. First of all, vesting a high number of powers in constitutional courts risks overloading these institutions, thus hindering the effectiveness of their activity. Moreover, granting them the power to resolve issues of high political sensitivity risks undermining their image as technical, neutral, and independent bodies. This could also undermine the courts' legitimacy.[139]

The ancillary functions examined earlier can be found in various countries worldwide, and not only in the Arab region. A peculiar function that may be vested specifically in courts in Islamic countries is the power to interpret *sharia*, as is the case for example in Egypt. As analyzed in greater detail in Chapter 4,[140] during the process that led to the adoption of the 2012 constitution, the Islamists (and in particular the Salafists) changed certain constitutional provisions with the aim of forcing the Supreme Constitutional Court to depart from its previous liberal interpretation of *sharia* principles and adopt a more traditional interpretation of Islam. Afterward, the 2014 constitution regranted to the Constitutional Court full authority in interpreting *sharia*. Suffice it to consider the preamble to the constitution, which states that in defining the principles of *sharia*, "the point of reference for the interpretation thereof is the relevant texts in the collected rulings of the Supreme Constitutional Court."

Another Constitutional Court that has long played a key role in the interpretation of *sharia* is that of Kuwait. In some cases, this body favored a moderate, relatively progressive interpretation of *sharia*, in a way that echoed (at least in part) its Egyptian counterpart.[141] On November 28, 1992, for example, the Court held that the provisions of the Kuwaiti Commercial Code allowing for the charging of interest were in line with the constitution, since Article 2 of the constitution makes *sharia* "a main source" and not "the only source" of legislation.[142] In other cases, the Court specifically protected women's rights. In a judgment delivered on October 20, 2009, for instance, the Court stated that a provision of the Personal Status Law requiring a woman's husband or male guardian to grant her permission to obtain a passport was in conflict with Articles 29 (principle of equality), 30 (personal liberty), and 31 (freedom of movement) of the constitution. One week later, on October 28, 2009, the Constitutional Court also ruled that female lawmakers were free not to wear the *hijab* while in Parliament.[143]

[139] Ibid., at p. 1457ff.

[140] See Chapter 4, Section 4.2.2.

[141] See Ran Hirschl, *Constitutional Theocracy* (Harvard University Press 2010), 115.

[142] See William Ballantyne, "Commercial Law: The Conflict in Shar'ia and Secular Law Public Policy" in Sohrab Behdad and Farhad Nomani (eds.), *Islam and the Everyday World: Public Policy Dilemmas* (Routledge 2006), 152–153.

[143] On these judgments concerning women's rights, see Hirschl, *Constitutional Theocracy*, at pp. 115–117; Fawaz Almutairi, "The Kuwaiti Constitutional Court and Its Role in Protecting the Fundamental Liberties" in Schoeller-Schletter (ed.) 2021, *Constitutional Review*, at p. 148ff.

A Constitutional Court that, once established, is likely to interpret *sharia* is that of Libya. Although (as in Egypt and Kuwait) the 2017 draft constitution does not expressly grant this power to the Court, Article 6 stipulates that *sharia* is "a source of legislation," and Article 136 states that the members of the Constitutional Court appointed by the president and the legislative branch must have an advanced degree in the areas of law, political science, and *sharia*. Furthermore, this competence would be in line with the country's constitutional history. Indeed, under the Gaddafi regime, Libya largely lacked a functioning judicial system, but the Supreme Court (that had been established by the 1951 constitution) was preserved, with some modifications. In particular, it was divided into five chambers, one of which was precisely devoted to *sharia* cases.[144]

3.4 THE ROLE OF CONSTITUTIONAL COURTS AND COUNCILS IN THE TRANSITION PROCESSES

The role of constitutional courts and councils in the transition processes following the Arab Spring varied significantly from country to country. In Egypt, for example, the Supreme Constitutional Court proved to be an "interventionist constitutional court,"[145] exerting a strong influence on the direction of the transition. In Tunisia, on the one hand, the Constitutional Council decided on two extremely sensitive political and constitutional issues at the very beginning of the transition process. On the other hand, however, the Constitutional Court provided for by the 2014 constitution, which was designed as a key institution within the state architecture, was never set up. In Algeria, the Constitutional Council was heavily involved in the process leading to the adoption of the 2016 constitutional reform, and in the transition following the resignation of Abdelaziz Bouteflika in April 2019, but in both situations, the Council displayed a high degree of deference to the political and military authorities. In other cases (as for example in Jordan and Morocco, and even more so in Syria), the role of the constitutional review bodies in the transition processes was much more limited.

In general terms, unlike constitutional courts in other regions (e.g., in Europe),[146] most Arab constitutional review bodies had neither the willingness nor the authority to deliver judgments aimed at achieving a clean break with the previous authoritarian past. Having said that, it would be misleading to affirm that constitutional courts and councils have only rubber-stamped the decisions of the executive branch. Indeed, as will be shown later, after 2011, the case law of these bodies has not always

[144] See Center for Constitutional Transitions – International IDEA, *Constitutional Courts*, at pp. 16–17.

[145] Nathan J. Brown and Julian G. Waller, "Constitutional Courts and Political Uncertainty: Constitutional Ruptures and the Rule of Judges" (2016) 14 *International Journal of Constitutional Law*, 839; see also Ciro Sbailò, "Elezioni presidenziali in Egitto: quando le Corti vogliono guidare le transizioni" (2012) 3 *Quaderni costituzionali*, 646–649.

[146] See Biagi, *European Constitutional Courts*.

been characterized by self-restraint. In a few cases, constitutional justices have delivered judgments unfavorable to the ruling regime, and on occasion have shown a serious commitment to the protection of rights and freedoms.

3.4.1 *Egypt*

The Egyptian Supreme Constitutional Court (*al-mahkamah al-dusturiyah al-'ulya*) has remained the strongest and boldest constitutional court in the Arab world, as demonstrated by the crucial (and often controversial) role played in the transition process from Mubarak regime. As put it by Nathan J. Brown, "[r]evolutions are not friendly times for courts, constitutions, and the rule of law. [...] But it is still remarkable how much a judicial actor [i.e. the Supreme Constitutional Court] was able to play a pivotal role in such an unfriendly environment."[147]

From the outset, the Court clashed with the Muslim Brotherhood, which had won the first free and fair elections after the fall of Mubarak, while showing its support for the military. On June 14, 2012, for example, the Court struck down parts of the law governing parliamentary elections and ordered the dissolution of the (Islamists-dominated) lower chamber of Parliament.[148] The parliamentary election law provided for a mixed system, that is, two-thirds of the deputies elected by a system of proportional representation, and one-third by a uninominal system. The law forced individual candidates to compete only in the uninominal system while allowing political party members to compete on either ballot. According to the Court, this system violated the principle of equality and popular sovereignty. The timing of the ruling is one of the various reasons that led to the accusation that the Court issued a political decision aimed at weakening the Brotherhood. The Court had struck down electoral laws on similar grounds even in the past, but it had always taken several years for its judgments to be handed down. On this occasion, by contrast, the Court "issued its ruling hours after hearing the arguments."[149]

On June 14, 2012, the Supreme Constitutional Court also declared Law no. 17 of 2012 (known as the "Political Isolation Law") to be unconstitutional.[150] This law prevented high officials during the Mubarak regime from holding important posts in the new state apparatus for a period of ten years. The consequence of the Court's decision was to allow Ahmed Shafiq – the last Prime Minister to serve under Mubarak administration before the outbreak of the 2011 Revolution – to run for the 2012 presidential elections. Shafiq narrowly lost out in the second round of the

[147] Nathan J. Brown, "Egypt: A Constitutional Court in an Unconstitutional Setting" in Frosini and Biagi (eds.) 2015, *Political and Constitutional Transitions*, at p. 33.

[148] Case no. 20, Judicial Year 34 (June 14, 2012).

[149] Brown, "Constitutional Court in an Unconstitutional Setting," at p. 37.

[150] Case no. 57, Judicial Year 34 (June 14, 2012). See Mohammad H. Fadel, "The Sounds of Silence: The Supreme Constitutional Court of Egypt, Constitutional Crisis, and Constitutional Silence" (2018) 16 *International Journal of Constitutional Law*, 948–949.

elections to Mohammed Morsi, gaining 48.27 percent of the vote, compared to Morsi's 51.73 percent.

On June 2, 2013 (i.e., six months after the adoption of the 2012 constitution), the Supreme Constitutional Court delivered two judgments on the constitutionality of the electoral law for the upper House (*Shura* Council),[151] and of the law establishing the criteria for electing the members of the Constituent Assembly, the body that drafted the 2012 constitution.[152] The Court argued that the electoral law for the *Shura* Council was partially at odds with the constitution but that this House of Parliament could continue to function until new elections for the lower House were held. The Court also struck down the law establishing the criteria for electing the members of the Constituent Assembly, but stated that the 2012 constitution remained valid as it had been approved by the people in a referendum.[153] The Court demonstrated a certain caution in these highly ambivalent judgments, but at the same time managed to cast a shadow on the legitimacy of the 2012 constitution.[154]

On June 2, 2013, the Supreme Constitutional Court also struck down Article 3 of the Emergency Law no. 162/1958, which granted the president of the Republic the power to arrest and search persons and places without judicial warrant.[155] According to the Court, this provision was in conflict with the "fundamental freedoms of the citizens" and represented "an assault on the sanctity of their homes and private places." This ruling was very important as it put an end to "the legal base upon which the governing regimes, for decades, arrested thousands of citizens."[156] Also in this case, the timing of the decision had an evident political flavor. Indeed, the Court decided to hand down its decision in this case only in June 2013, while the Brotherhood was in power, despite the fact that the constitutionality of Article 3 of the Emergency Law had been challenged twenty years previously, in April 1993.[157] However, this is an area the Court "had not dared to tread in the Mubarak years."[158] To do so "would have been institutional suicide."[159] But in 2013, the emergency law "became fair game for the [Court]."[160]

President Morsi was removed from office on July 3, 2013, following a coup d'état supported by the military. The latter decided to appoint as Interim president of the

151 Case no. 112, Judicial Year 34 (June 2, 2013).

152 Case no. 166, Judicial Year 34 (June 2, 2013).

153 On these decisions, see Yussef Auf, "What Does the Supreme Constitutional Court's Decision Mean?," *Atlantic Council* (June 5, 2013), www.atlanticcouncil.org/blogs/menasource/what-does-the-supreme-constitutional-court-s-decision-mean/

154 See Nimer Sultany, *Law and Revolution: Legitimacy and Constitutionalism after the Arab Spring* (Oxford University Press 2017), 314.

155 Case no. 17, Judicial Year 15 (June 2, 2013).

156 Yussef Auf, "The State of Emergency in Egypt: An Exception or Rule?," *Atlantic Council* (February 2, 2018), www.atlanticcouncil.org/blogs/menasource/the-state-of-emergency-in-egypt-an-exception-or-rule

157 Ibid.

158 Brown, "Constitutional Court in an Unconstitutional Setting," at p. 46.

159 Moustafa, Political Role of the Supreme Constitutional Court," at p. 108.

160 Brown, "Constitutional Court in an Unconstitutional Setting," at p. 46.

Republic Adli Mansour, the Chief Justice of the Supreme Constitutional Court, whose decision to accept this position "seemed to signal approval of the coup."[161] A few days later, on July 8, Mansour issued a constitutional declaration providing a roadmap for amending the 2012 constitution. As a further demonstration of the influence exerted by the Supreme Constitutional Court (and more generally of the judiciary) on the constitution-making process, it should be recalled that the ten-member Committee, responsible for proposing amendments to the 2012 constitution, included – in addition to two judges from the ordinary courts, two from the State Council, and four professors of constitutional law – two justices of the Supreme Constitutional Court. The constituent process ended in January 2014 with the entry into force of the new constitution. Not surprisingly, this new constitutional text restored the Supreme Constitutional Court's status and competences, which had been narrowed under the 2012 constitution.[162]

It should be emphasized that the Court radically changed its attitude after Morsi's fall. Indeed, it "stepped back from considering fundamental political questions,"[163] thus abandoning its bold and interventionist approach, and returning to a lower institutional profile. The Court was not particularly active in the field of protection of fundamental rights and freedoms either. However, there are a few decisions that are worth recalling. In 2016, for example, the Court declared the Protest Law no. 107/2013 partially unconstitutional. In particular, the constitutional justices struck down Article 10 of the Protest Law, which granted the Ministry of the Interior immediate authority to cancel, postpone, or modify the route of a protest demonstration without judicial review.[164] Such a court authorization was then introduced in 2017 following an amendment to the Protest Law.[165] Another interesting judgment was delivered in 2017, when the Court granted Coptic civil servants the right to paid leave for one month to enable them to make a pilgrimage to the holy city of Al-Quds (Jerusalem), in the same way as Muslim civil servants are entitled to paid leave of thirty days for the pilgrimage to Mecca (*hajj*).[166] In 2019, the Court made reference to several human rights instruments in a case involving the right to freedom of association before declaring the unconstitutionality of Article 42 of Law no. 84 of 2002, which vested the Minister of Social Affairs with the power to dissolve community associations.[167]

161 Clark B. Lombardi, "Constitutions of Arab Countries in Transition: Constitutional Review and Separation of Powers" in *IEMed Mediterranean Yearbook* (2014), 128, www.iemed.org/wp-content/uploads/2021/02/Constitutions-of-Arab-Countries-in-Transition-Constitutional-Review-and.pdf

162 For example, the framers had limited the Court's power to interpret *sharia*. See in greater detail Chapter 4, Section 4.2.2.

163 Brown and Waller, "Constitutional Courts," at p. 849.

164 See David Risley, "What Egypt's Court Ruling on Protest Law Means," *MEI@75* (December 14, 2016), www.mei.edu/publications/what-egypts-court-ruling-protest-law-means

165 See "TIMEP Brief: Protest Law," *The Tahrir Institute for Middle East Policy* (November 9, 2018), https://timep.org/reports-briefings/timep-brief-protest-law/

166 Case no. 153, Judicial Year 32 (February 4, 2017). On this ruling, see also Chapter 4, Section 4.2.2.

167 Case no. 84, Judicial Year 39 (February 2, 2019).

Over the past few decades, the Egyptian Supreme Constitutional Court has stood out compared to its counterparts in the region, as it has proved to be a body capable of achieving and consolidating its autonomy from the ruling regime. Its activism during the Morsi regime is one of the latest examples. Various reasons explain this autonomy, including the high degree of linkages and institutionalization enjoyed by the Court.[168] Indeed, the Court has over time developed strong linkages with the broader judicial establishment and state apparatus, as well as with legal advocacy groups and human rights NGOs. Following the 2011 Revolution, for example, the Court formed an alliance with the military, challenging the Morsi government. Furthermore, the Court is highly institutionalized, in the sense that its members have articulated a sense of mission, have developed a corporate identity that guides the Court in setting its own agenda, and more generally the Court is an institution that is deeply rooted in the Egyptian political landscape.[169]

As discussed earlier, after the fall of Morsi and the subsequent seizure of power by Al-Sisi, the Court has opted for a much more cautious approach. It would be a mistake, however, to declare that body defeated. Indeed, the Court "has accumulated half a century of experience as an adaptable rope-a-dope fighter, one that picks its exchanges carefully and has demonstrated a unique skill in weathering punches and allowing adversaries to tire themselves out as the court becomes more sure of its own footing."[170]

3.4.2 *Tunisia*

Interestingly, in Tunisia, the Constitutional Council – which had hardly ever been at the center of the political-institutional game in the past – soon became one of the protagonists of the transition process, deciding two extremely important political and constitutional issues. In the first place, the Council was asked to decide on who should assume the presidency of the Republic following Zine El-Abidine Ben Ali's fall in January 2011. This highly sensitive issue involved two provisions of the 1959 constitution, that is, Articles 56 and 57. According to Article 56, in case of *temporary* impediment, the president of the Republic could delegate his powers to the Prime Minister, while Article 57 provided that in case of *permanent* impediment, the presidency *ad interim* would pass to the Speaker of the Chamber of Deputies, who would be responsible for organizing the next presidential elections. Mohamed Gannouchi, Ben Ali's Prime Minister, had invoked Article 56 upon Ben Ali's departure on January 14, thus becoming the interim president of the Republic. However, the following day, on January 15, the Constitutional Council

[168] See Brown et al., *Authoritarianism from the Inside*.
[169] Ibid.
[170] Ibid.

ruled that since Ben Ali had left the country without delegating his prerogatives to the Prime Minister, and in the light of the "current circumstances" existing in the country, Ben Ali's departure met the requirements of Article 57 and therefore the Speaker of the Chamber of Deputies (Fouad Mebazaa) had to immediately assume the interim presidency of the Republic. Mohamed Gannouchi remained as Prime Minister.[171]

After the resolution of the problem concerning the vacancy of the presidency, the other key issue to be addressed concerned the exercise of legislative power, since the Chamber of Deputies and the Chamber of Councillors were "completely discredited" and, therefore, "were not any longer politically capable of exercising legislative power."[172] On February 3, 2011, the Constitutional Council was requested by the interim president to rule on the constitutionality of the bill authorizing the president to rule by decree-laws until the end of the interim period (sixty days). This bill, which *de facto* delegated legislative power to the interim president, relied on Article 28(5) of the 1959 constitution, according to which the Chamber of Deputies and the Chamber of Councillors could vest the president of the Republic with the power to adopt decree-laws for a "limited period" and for a "specific objective." Once this period expired, the decree-laws were required to be submitted to Parliament for approval. The Constitutional Council ruled that as the period of the delegation was limited, the objective of such delegation (despite its broad nature) was sufficiently determined, and that the country was experiencing a transitional phase, the bill was "perfectly in line" with the constitution.[173] This decision was described as "the homage that the Constitutional Council, instrument of the deposed ancient regime, paid to the Revolution during this farewell session."[174] Indeed, one month later, the Council was officially dissolved by Decree-Law no. 2011-14 of March 23, 2011 on the "Provisional Regulation of Public Powers."

According to the 2014 constitution, the Constitutional Court should have been established within at most one year from the date of the first legislative elections (Article 148(5)). However, as reiterated, this body was never set up. First of all, this was due to a lack of agreement among the political forces, which prevented the two-third majority required for the parliamentary appointment of one-third of the members of the Court from being achieved. Several members of Parliament feared that one ideological trend could prevail over another within the Court, a fact that was perceived as problematic since a number of extremely sensitive constitutional provisions (e.g., on religion and gender equality) could be interpreted in very

[171] See Rafaâ Ben Achour and Sana Ben Achour, "La transition démocratique en Tunisie: entre légalité constitutionnelle et légitimité révolutionnaire" (2012) 92 *Revue française de droit constitutionnel*, 718–719.

[172] Yadh Ben Achour, *Tunisie: Une révolution en pays d'Islam* (Cérès éditions 2017), 280.

[173] See Yadh Ben Achour, "La révolution tunisienne dans ses manifestations constitutionnelles. La première phase de transition (14 Janvier 2011–16 Décembre 2011)" in *La Constitution de la Tunisie – Processus, principes et perspectives* (UNDP 2016), 45–47.

[174] Ben Achour, *Tunisie: Une révolution en pays d'Islam*, at p. 280.

different ways.[175] The failure to establish the Court is also attributable to the actions of President Saïed. Indeed, in April 2021, he rejected the draft law aimed at lowering the quorum for the parliamentary appointment of one-third of the constitutional judges, a measure that would have made it easier to achieve the majority needed for such an appointment. The reasons put forward by Saïed to justify his rejection are rather far-fetched, even considering that, prior to his election as President of Tunisia, he was a university professor of constitutional law. In his view, the Court could not be established since the constitution's one-year deadline for the creation of such a body had not been met. For Saïed, therefore, this deadline was to be considered a peremptory time limit rather than merely a recommended timeframe.[176]

The 2014 constitution stipulated that before the establishment of the Constitutional Court, constitutional review would be carried out by a "Provisional Authority in charge of ascertaining the constitutionality of bills," composed of the first President of the Court of Cassation (as a President of the Authority), the first President of the Administrative Court, the first President of the Audit Court, as well as three members, legal experts, each appointed on an equal basis by the President of the National Constituent Assembly, the president of the Republic, and the Head of Government (Article 148(7)). This Provisional Authority was responsible for reviewing the constitutionality of legislation before its promulgation (*ex ante* review) upon request of the president of the Republic, the Head of Government, or at least thirty members of Parliament.[177]

The Provisional Authority was established by Law no. 2014-14 of April 18, 2014, and exercised its functions until September 22, 2021, when it was abolished by Kaïs Saïed through Presidential Decree no. 2021-117 on "Exceptional Measures" (Article 21). This body, which issued fifty-three judgments (seven judgments per year on average),[178] proved to be quite ineffective. In part, this was due to its "inherent weakness."[179] Indeed, the prerogatives of the Provisional Authority were much narrower compared to those of the Constitutional Court: The former was only entitled to verify the constitutionality of bills, whereas the latter was also responsible for ascertaining the constitutionality of constitutional amendments, international treaties, and the rules of procedure of the Assembly of the Representatives of the People (always on an *ex ante* basis), as well as legislation (on an *ex post* basis, through the "exception of unconstitutionality"). In addition to that, unlike the Constitutional Court,[180] the

[175] See Democracy Reporting International, *La mise en œuvre de la Constitution tunisienne du 27 janvier 2014 au niveau du cadre juridique. Bilan* (September 2022), 72, https://democracyreporting.s3.eu-central-1.amazonaws.com/images/63761f99ace6d.pdf

[176] Ibid., at pp. 65–67.

[177] Article 3 of the Organic Law on the Provisional Authority no. 2014–14 of April 18, 2014.

[178] See Democracy Reporting International, *Mise en œuvre de la Constitution tunisienne du 27 janvier 2014 au niveau du cadre juridique. Bilan*, at p. 68.

[179] Democracy Reporting International, *Les effets*, at p. 14.

[180] See Section 3.3.4 and Chapter 2, Sections 2.2.3 and 2.2.4.

Provisional Authority did not have the power to make key decisions concerning the functioning of the political regime (e.g., resolving conflicts between the president and the Head of Government concerning the allocation of powers, deciding on the impeachment of the president of the Republic, or reviewing the upholding of a state of exception).

Another reason for the weakness of the Provisional Authority was related to certain shortcomings of the Organic Law on the functioning of this body. Indeed, in certain cases, some provisions of this Organic Law *de facto* prevented the Provisional Authority from making a decision. This was mainly due to a combination of three rules. First, the need for an absolute majority of the Authority's members in order to make a decision (Article 21); second, the parity composition of the Authority (six members) (Article 4); third, the nonpreponderance of the President's vote in the event of a tie vote. The failure to reach an absolute majority within the Authority led to a "*blocage*" (blocking)[181] of this body, which was then forced to return the bills to the president of the Republic. Such a "*blocage*" was considered as a form of "denial of constitutional justice."[182]

In the light of the abovementioned weaknesses, it comes as no surprise that the role played by the Authority was not effective in protecting the constitution and that its decisions were frequently the object of harsh criticism.[183] This was mainly due to the fact that its case law was characterized by poor reasoning and that the Authority often avoided taking a clear stance on highly politicized issues.[184] Furthermore, the Authority considered certain bills of dubious constitutionality to be in line with the constitution.[185]

It should be emphasized that the Constitutional Court and the Provisional Authority in charge of ascertaining the constitutionality of bills were not the only actors in the field of constitutional review. Indeed, after the 2011 Dignity Revolution, the administrative courts declared that, in the absence of a constitutional review body, they were entitled to check the constitutionality of legislation. For example, on November 7, 2013, the Administrative Court of Tunis stated that administrative judges were duty-bound to verify the compliance of laws with the constitution

181 Democracy Reporting International, *Les effets*, at p. 17.

182 Leïla Chikhaoui, "Le renvoi des recours au Président de la République: 'Déni de justice' ou silence dynamique?" in *Mouvances du droit. Études en l'honneur du professeur Rafâa Ben Achour. Tome 1* (Konrad Adenauer Stiftung 2015), 263ff., cited in Democracy Reporting International, *Les effets*, at p. 17.

183 For an analysis of the case law of this body, see, for example, Democracy Reporting International, *Les effets*, at pp. 15–17; Democracy Reporting International, *La mise en œuvre de la Constitution tunisienne au niveau du cadre juridique. 30 septembre 2019 – 9eme édition* (2019), 43–45; Juan José Ruiz Ruiz, "Justicia constitucional transicional y jurisdicción constitucional en la Constitución tunecina de 2014" (2016) 19 *Revista general de derecho público comparado*, 31ff.; Hana Ben Abda, "The Provisional Instance of Tunisia: An Insufficient Substitute for a Constitutional Court," *IACL-AIDC Blog* (July 15, 2021), https://blog-iacl-aidc.org/menaregion/the-provisional-instance-of-tunisia-an-insufficient-substitute-for-a-constitutional-court-ddjlw

184 See Ben Abda, "Provisional Instance of Tunisia."

185 See Democracy Reporting International, *Les effets*, at p. 15ff.

and with international conventions ratified by Tunisia.[186] After the adoption of the 2014 constitution and the establishment of the Provisional Authority, administrative courts continued to engage in the constitutional review of legislation despite a constitutional provision explicitly preventing courts (all courts, including administrative courts) from ascertaining the constitutionality of legislation (Article 148(7)). The administrative judges relied on two main arguments. First, they stated that each judge had the duty to safeguard rights and freedoms and to guarantee the supremacy of the constitution, as provided for by Articles 49 and 102 of the constitution. Second, they argued that the prohibition for courts to verify the constitutionality of legislation only applied if the constitutional review body had already verified the constitutionality of the contested law.[187] This bold interpretation was very problematic as it made the administrative court a *de facto* "complementary" constitutional court. It is extremely likely that the Constitutional Court would have not tolerated sharing its exclusive competence in this field with other courts, as Article 120 of the constitution explicitly stated that the Constitutional Court was the "sole body" competent to oversee the constitutionality of legislation.[188]

Tunisia is a particularly interesting laboratory in the field of constitutional review and democracy also if one considers that the proposal to establish an International Constitutional Court came precisely from the former Tunisian President of the Republic, Mohamed Moncef Marzouki. The latter first proposed this idea in an article in the French newspaper *Libération* published in 1999 (when he was a political opponent of the Ben Ali regime), and then relaunched the idea after the 2011 Revolution, when he became president of the Republic.[189] He also presented it to the General Assembly of the United Nations. The ambitious aim of this Court would be to contribute to "better eradicate tyranny and to establish and institutionalize democracy in the world."[190] Preventing dictatorship and despotism by means of a judicial mechanism is, on the face of it, a fascinating and intriguing idea. However, many questions (and perplexities) arise when passing from words to deeds. Who would appoint the members of the Court? What would form the parameter of review? Who would have standing to lodge a claim before the Court? How wide would the jurisdiction of the Court be? How would the decisions of the Court be enforced? Moreover, the proposal touches a sensitive contemporary

[186] See *Arrêt* of the Administrative Court (*Assemblée plénière*) no. 134855. See Ruiz Ruiz, "Justicia constitucional transicional," at pp. 25–27.

[187] See Administrative Court, judgments no. 126863 (March 18, 2014), no. 125265 (December 3, 2014), and no. 150168 (July 2, 2018). See Democracy Reporting International, *Les effets*, at p. 24.

[188] See Democracy Reporting International, *Les effets*, at p. 24.

[189] See Yadh Ben Achour, "An International Constitutional Court. Bulwark Against the Erosion of Constitutional Democracy" in Grote and Röder (eds.) 2016, *Constitutionalism, Human Rights, and Islam*, at pp. 756–757.

[190] "General Presentation of the Project for the Establishment of an International Constitutional Court" in Asma Ghachem and Henri Pallard (eds.), *Une Cour Constitutionnelle Internationale au service du droit démocratique et du droit constitutionnel: Actes du colloque* (Konrad Adenauer Stiftung 2015), 287.

debate in international law, that is, whether or not there is an international right to democracy. The "Project for the Establishment of an International Constitutional Court," prepared by an *ad hoc* international commission, responds to some of the abovementioned questions. Still, it will not be easy to overcome all the theoretical and practical difficulties that the establishment and functioning of an International Constitutional Court would involve.[191]

3.4.3 *Algeria*

In Algeria, the Constitutional Council was heavily involved both in the process leading to the adoption of the 2016 constitutional reform, and in the transition following the resignation of Abdelaziz Bouteflika in April 2019. As to the former, the Council was asked to ascertain the constitutionality of the bill containing the 2016 constitutional reform, which affected the preamble and all four titles comprising the constitution. In its ruling issued on January 28, 2016, the Council declared that no aspect of this reform was unconstitutional.[192] This decision was harshly criticized, since some provisions of the reform did not seem to comply with the constitution and contradicted what the Council had stated in some of its previous rulings.[193] A clear example refers to the articles concerning the eligibility requirements for certain public offices and political functions. Article 63 of the 1996 constitution (as amended in 2016) introduced the requirement of "exclusive Algerian nationality" as a prerequisite for eligibility for "high public office" and "political functions," which need to be identified in the implementing legislation. Moreover, Article 87 stipulated that any candidate for president of the Republic must hold – *inter alia* – an "immaculate" Algerian nationality, in the sense that the candidate must never have acquired another nationality, must have been resident within the country for at least ten years prior to standing, the candidate's father and mother must be Algerian by birth, and the candidate's spouse must hold Algerian nationality only and be Algerian by birth.

It is significant that these criteria – in particular those relating to the spouse – are diametrically opposed to what the Constitutional Council had stated in some of its past decisions. For example, in a decision issued in 1989,[194] the Council struck down the provisions of the electoral law requiring that candidates for parliamentary

[191] On this (potential) Court, see in much greater detail Ben Achour, "International Constitutional Court," at p. 741ff.; Ghachem and Pallard (eds.) 2015, *Une Cour Constitutionnelle Internationale*; Laith K. Nasrawin, "Towards the Establishment of an International Constitutional Court" (2017) 10 *Vienna Journal on International Constitutional Law*, 386ff.; Richard Albert, "Does the World Need an International Constitutional Court?" (2023) 3 *Rutgers International Law and Human Rights Journal*, 1 ff.

[192] *Avis* no. 01/16 A.RC/CC (January 28, 2016).

[193] See Francesco Biagi, "The Algerian Constitutional Reform of 2016: A Critical Analysis" (2017) 17 *Global Jurist*, 5ff.

[194] Decision no. 1 – D.L.CC-89 (August 20, 1989).

elections and the spouse of the presidential candidate must be Algerian by birth, as these criteria violated the principle of nondiscrimination and various international treaties (in particular the 1966 International Covenant on Civil and Political Rights and the 1981 African Charter on Human and Peoples' Rights). This ruling was confirmed a few years later, in 1995,[195] when an ordinance required once again a certificate of Algerian nationality from the president's spouse. Furthermore, in a judgment delivered in 2004,[196] the Constitutional Council declared unconstitutional the requirement that candidates for judicial school must have held Algerian nationality "for at least ten years."

However, in the judgment upholding the constitutionality of the 2016 reform, the Constitutional Council did not take into account any of these decisions. Indeed, the Council ruled that Article 63 of the constitution (which – as mentioned earlier – required "exclusive Algerian nationality" as a prerequisite for eligibility for "high public office" and "political functions") "does not violate human or citizens' rights" and that Article 87 of the constitution (on the eligibility criteria for the president) does nothing other than "consolidate the high constitutional tasks vested in the president of the Republic."

It should also be noted that the Constitutional Council provided no justification for delivering almost identical decisions – over a span of only a few years – on the issue concerning the term limits for the president of the Republic, notwithstanding the fact that constitutional amendments had diametrically opposite effects. Indeed, in 2008, the Council, upholding as constitutional the removal of the two-term limit, ruled that this constitutional amendment had strengthened the democratic system as it would enable the people to choose, on a fully sovereign basis, whether or not to place their trust in the president once again.[197] Eight years later, when assessing the reintroduction of that limit, the Council (in the judgment upholding the constitutionality of the 2016 reform) expressed itself in essentially the same terms, pointing out that the principle of democratic alternation reinforces the democratic system and enables the people to choose freely their own representatives through regular, free, and fair elections.

The Constitutional Council also issued some key rulings regulating the transition process after President Bouteflika's decision not to run for a fifth term in office and to resign on April 2, 2019. As is well known, Bouteflika's decision was made in the wake of several weeks of mass protests throughout the country (the *Hirak* Movement). In actual fact, the Constitutional Council had already made a questionable decision on March 13,[198] when it simply took note of the fact that the presidential elections had been revoked by a (presumably unconstitutional) presidential decree adopted

[195] Decision no. 1 – D.O.CC-95 (August 6, 1995).
[196] *Avis* no. 02/A.LO/CC/04 (August 22, 2004).
[197] *Avis* no. 01/08 A.RC/CC (November 7, 2008).
[198] Decision no. 07/D.CC/19 (March 13, 2019).

by Bouteflika on March 11.[199] Following Bouteflika's resignation, the Constitutional Council ruled that the office of president of the Republic was definitively vacant, and gave notice of this fact to Parliament (Article 102(4) and (5) of the 1996 constitution, as amended in 2016).[200] The duties of Head of State were then assumed by the President of the Council of the Nation, Abdelkader Bensalah, who was entitled to remain in office for a maximum of ninety days, during which presidential elections were to be organized (Article 102(6)). These were scheduled for July 4, 2019, although due to a lack of eligible candidates, they had to be postponed. Indeed, the Constitutional Council – which continued to be vested with the task of deciding on the regularity of electoral processes (Article 182(2) and (3)) – rejected applications by both candidates due to the lack of a sufficient number of signatures endorsing them as candidates and irregularities when collecting them,[201] with the consequence that the election could not be held on July 4, 2019 and had to be postponed.[202] With the aim of guaranteeing the continuity of state institutions, the Constitutional Council clarified in a Communiqué that it was for the provisional Head of State – whose ninety-day term expired on July 9, 2019 – to call a new election and to complete the process of electing a new president of the Republic.[203] These rulings attracted harsh criticism, and the Constitutional Council was accused of giving a "constitutional veneer" to decisions made by the political and military leadership.[204]

The presidential elections were eventually held on December 12, 2019, and saw the victory in the first round of the former Prime Minister and Minister of Housing, Abdelmadjid Tebboune. In the meantime, in September 2019, an electoral commission (*Autorité nationale indépendante des élections*) had been set up and the Organic Law no. 16-10 of August 25, 2016, on the electoral system had been amended. Despite the fact that their constitutionality was questionable on various grounds,[205] the Constitutional Council upheld both the Organic Law establishing the electoral commission and the Organic Law reforming the electoral system. Only minor aspects of these laws were struck down as unconstitutional.[206] Furthermore, on November 9, 2019, the Council validated the list of candidates for the presidential elections (after rejecting nine appeals by candidates who had been excluded by the Electoral Commission),[207] and on December 16 proclaimed the final results of the elections.[208]

[199] See Mouloud Boumghar, "Le gant constitutionnel réversible: accessoire de l'uniforme militaire. Regard critique sur la crise constitutionnelle algérienne de 2019" (2019) 21 *L'Année du Maghreb* (online version).
[200] Declaration of April 3, 2019.
[201] Decisions no. 18/D.CC/19 and no. 19/D.CC/19 (June 1, 2019).
[202] Decision no. 20/D.CC (June 1, 2019).
[203] Communiqué of June 2, 2019.
[204] Boumghar, "Le gant constitutionnel réversible."
[205] See Souhila Hammadi, "Lois organiques encadrant les élections: Bâclage des procédures et violation de la Constitution," *Algeria-Watch* (September 16, 2019), https://algeria-watch.org/?p=72559
[206] *Avis* no. 01/A.L.O/19 and *Avis* no. 02/A.L.O/19 (September 14, 2019).
[207] Decision no. 36 /D.CC/19 (November 9, 2019).
[208] Proclamation no. 03/P.CC/19 (December 16, 2019).

The judgments delivered during both the 2016 and 2019 transition processes once again threw into considerable doubt the Constitutional Council's effective independence from the political and military authorities. However, this comes as no surprise, since the Algerian Council had also displayed a high degree of deference toward the ruling regime in the past.[209]

3.4.4 *Jordan, Morocco, and Syria*

In Jordan and Morocco, the role of the constitutional review bodies in the transition processes was much more limited compared to that of the constitutional courts and councils in Egypt, Tunisia, and Algeria. In Jordan, the 2011 constitutional reform provided for a Constitutional Court, which in itself is a major innovation, as the country, despite recurrent calls for the establishment of such a body,[210] did not have a constitutional court.[211] The Court was established in 2012 and has thus far encountered great difficulties in fully displaying its potential. The reasons for the Court's weakness include the appointment system (which seriously threatens the independence of the Court, as all members are directly selected by the king),[212] the "stronghold" on access (due to the "double-filter" system that characterized the Court's system until the 2022 constitutional reform),[213] and more generally the deference of the Court toward the ruling regime. Notwithstanding this complicated picture, the Court issued some interesting decisions. In Judgment no. 4 of 2013, for example, it relied on Article 128 of the constitution (which provides for a "limitation clause"), stressing that Parliament must "regulate the exercise of rights [...] in a manner that is not detrimental to the fundamentals of these rights or adversely affects them." Furthermore, in its Interpreting Decision no. 6 of 2013, the Court proclaimed the right of public employees to form trade unions, relying – *inter alia* – on the 1948 Universal Declaration of Human Rights, the 1966 International Covenant on Civil and Political Rights, as well as the 1966 International Covenant on Economic, Social and Cultural Rights. More recently, the Court protected the principle of the

209 See Biagi, "Constitutional Review in Algeria," at p. 96ff.; Graëffly, "Le Conseil constitutionnel algérien," at p. 1398ff.

210 The intention to establish a Constitutional Court had already been announced by the government in 1989. See "Jordan Plans to Lift Martial Law," *The New York Times* (December 20, 1989), www.nytimes.com/1989/12/20/world/jordan-plans-to-lift-martial-law.html). On the call for the establishment of a Constitutional Court, see Michelle L. Burgis, "Judicial Reform and the Possibility of Democratic Rule in Jordan: A Policy Perspective on Judicial Independence" (2007) 21 *Arab Law Quarterly*, 162–163; Muddather Abu-Karaki, Raed S. A Faqir and Majed Ahmad K. Marashdah, "Democracy & Judicial Controlling in Jordan: A Constitutional Study" (2011) 4 *Journal of Politics and Law*, 180ff.

211 See Laith K. Nasrawin, "Protecting Human Rights Through Constitutional Adjudication – Jordan as a Case Study" (2016) 25 *Digest of Middle East Studies*, 264ff.

212 See Sufian Obeidat, "The Independence of Constitutional Judges: The Case of Jordan" in Schoeller-Schletter (ed.) 2021, *Constitutional Review*, at p. 47ff.

213 See Section 3.3.3.

independence of the judiciary (Judgment no. 2 of 2018), and declared the supremacy of international treaties ratified by Parliament over domestic law (Interpreting Decision no. 1 of 2020).[214]

In Morocco, the Constitutional Council was involved in particular in the process of enforcement of the 2011 constitution, as it reviewed a number of organic laws implementing this constitutional text (indeed, in Morocco, organic laws are subject to *mandatory* constitutional review). This was a significant task as these organic laws refer to key issues (including language, political parties, rights, Parliament, the government, the judiciary, the Constitutional Court, the "advanced" regionalization system, and many others), thus representing *de facto* an "extension" of the 2011 constitution.[215] In several cases, however, the decisions of the Constitutional Council were the object of criticism, either because they upheld provisions whose constitutionality was doubtful,[216] or because of their "unpredictability," "lack of coherence," and "poor reasoning."[217] More generally, the Council never established itself as a body capable of protecting fundamental rights and freedoms, and continued to be seen as "a tool by which the King retained a veto over legislation."[218] The process leading to the establishment of the Constitutional Court,[219] which replaces the Constitutional Council, was long and problematic. The Organic Law no. 66-13 on the Constitutional Court was promulgated on August 13, 2014, but the Court was set up only three years later, in April 2017, with the appointment of its President and members. What is still missing is another crucial piece of legislation, namely the Organic Law on the "exception of unconstitutionality," which (as already indicated earlier)[220] was declared partially unconstitutional by the Constitutional Court in the decision 70–18 of March 6, 2018.

The Supreme Constitutional Court of Syria is the typical example of a constitutional court aimed at protecting and strengthening the position of the president of the Republic, rather than placing checks on his actions. Indeed, as recalled earlier, all the members of the Court are selected by the president, the four-year term of constitutional justices is renewable, and the number of the Court's members is not fixed, as the constitution provides that the Court must consist "of at least seven members" (Article 141). In addition to that, it is also emblematic that the Court is prevented from ascertaining the constitutionality of laws that have been submitted to referendum by

[214] On these (and other important) judgments delivered by the Constitutional Court, see Zaid Eyadat and Laith Nasrawin, *The Constitutional Court of Jordan: Evaluating 10 Years of Service & Future Expectations* (Konrad Adenauer Stiftung – Rule of Law Program Middle East & North Africa 2021), 8ff.

[215] See Fassi Fihri, "Le Conseil constitutionnel marocain et le contrôle du législateur organique," at p. 153.

[216] See Ruiz Ruiz, "Las constituciones de las primaveras árabes y su implementación: el caso de Marruecos," at p. 121.

[217] Fassi Fihri, "Le Conseil constitutionnel marocain et le contrôle du législateur organique," at pp. 154 and 157.

[218] Lombardi, "Constitutions of Arab Countries in Transition," at p. 126.

[219] On this body, see Bernoussi, "La Constitution de 2011 et le juge constitutionnel," at p. 207ff.

[220] See Section 3.3.3.

the president and that have obtained the approval of the people (Article 148). Among the few decisions issued by the Court following the adoption of the 2012 constitution, one can recall those related to verifying the eligibility requirements for presidential elections, requirements that clearly favor the incumbent president, namely Bashar al-Assad.[221] Thus, in the 2014 and 2021 elections, the Court only permitted Assad and two other candidates to stand for elections.[222] Overall, the Supreme Constitutional Court of Syria is clearly an instrument in the hands of Assad, at least for the time being.

3.5 CHALLENGES AND PERSPECTIVES

As Clark B. Lombardi has pointed out, in the Arab region there is currently "more constitutional review than ever before [...], and the institutions empowered to perform it have, at least on paper, new independence and power."[223] In fact, compared to the past, Arab constitutional review bodies have significantly strengthened their position within the new constitutional frameworks, not to mention the fact that public opinion now seems to be more aware of the crucial significance of these institutions. However, constitutional courts and councils have thus far exploited their potential only in rare circumstances. There are numerous significant obstacles that these bodies must still overcome in order to contribute more effectively to the processes of democratization.

In the first place, it should be noted that in several countries, the legitimacy of these institutions is often questioned. Indeed, in many cases, due to the "counter-majoritarian difficulty," constitutional courts and councils are not readily accepted by other constitutional bodies and political actors. In Kuwait, for example, some members of Parliament called for the abolition of the Constitutional Court, arguing – *inter alia* – that Parliament was the only institution that reflected the popular will.[224] In Lebanon, most of the political class is unwilling to strengthen the status and powers of the Constitutional Council, since "they don't want to be controlled by any institution."[225] Thus, the "mighty problem"[226] of constitutional review of legislation is still very much present in today's Arab world.

The limited independence of constitutional review bodies vis-à-vis the executive branch remains a serious problem, especially if one considers that in most countries,

[221] Indeed, according to the Constitution, the Court is responsible for verifying the eligibility requirements in presidential elections (Article 85).

[222] See Chapter 2, Section 2.1.3.

[223] Lombardi, "Constitutions of Arab Countries in Transition," at p. 132.

[224] See Habib Toumi, "Kuwaiti MPs Call for Abolishing Constitutional Court," *Gulf News* (January 7, 2019), https://gulfnews.com/world/gulf/kuwait/kuwaiti-mps-call-for-abolishing-constitutional-court-1.61290332

[225] Issam Sleiman and Robert Poll, "Towards a Reform in Lebanon? Interview with the President of the Constitutional Council Issam Sleiman," *VerfassungsBlog* (June 20, 2018), https://verfassungsblog.de/towards-a-reform-in-lebanon-interview-with-the-president-of-the-constitutional-council-issam-sleiman/

[226] Mauro Cappelletti, "The 'Mighty Problem' of Judicial Review and the Contribution of Comparative Analysis" (1980) 53 *Southern California Law Review*, 409ff.

the Head of State continues to exert excessive influence over the appointment system. Such a limited independence contributes to explaining the fact that constitutional courts and councils, rather than placing checks on the political branches, often uphold or even strengthen the dominant position of the governing authorities. This is particularly evident when these bodies rely on the doctrine of the "acts of sovereignty" so as to allow the executive branch to exercise even broader discretionary power.

Moreover, access to constitutional courts and councils (although significantly expanded) is still quite problematic. Suffice it to consider the adoption of the "double-filter" system (rather than the "single-filter" system) or the decision to prevent the ordinary courts from referring questions of constitutionality *ex officio*. In Lebanon, despite recurrent calls for widening access to constitutional justice,[227] the constitutionality of laws can only be challenged within fifteen days of their publication in the Official Gazette,[228] not to mention the fact that only political[229] and religious authorities[230] are entitled to apply to the Constitutional Council, whereas the ordinary courts are not granted this power (Article 19 constitution).

Poor legislative drafting is another element that must be taken into account. Indeed, ambiguities and gaps in the laws regulating the organization and functioning of constitutional courts hinder the functioning and actions of these bodies, thus weakening the system of constitutional review overall. In addition, in some cases these laws have not been updated, thus giving rise to legal uncertainties. In Jordan, for example, the Law on the Constitutional Court[231] continued to refer to the High Court of Justice[232] even when this body was replaced in 2014 by the Administrative Court (court of first instance) and the High Administrative Court (court of second instance).[233] Since the Law on the Constitutional Court was not updated, it was not clear whether the High Administrative Court could refer a question of constitutionality to the Constitutional Court directly, or whether it had to refer the question of constitutionality to the Court of Cassation.[234] The law was amended only in 2022, when the "double-filter" system was replaced by a "single-filter" mechanism.

[227] See, for example, Conseil constitutionnel and Fondation Konrad Adenauer (eds.), *Extension des attributions du Conseil constitutionnel au Liban. Actes du séminaire organisé par le Conseil constitutionnel et Fondation Konrad Adenauer le 6/5/2016. Débat autour du Projet élaboré par le Président du Conseil constitutionnel Issam Sleiman* (Beirut 2017).

[228] Article 19 of Law no. 250/1993.

[229] Namely, the president of the Republic, the Speaker of Parliament, the Prime Minister, and at least ten members of Parliament (Article 19 of Law no. 250/1993).

[230] The heads of the legally recognized religious confessions are entitled to apply to the Constitutional Council only in matters concerning personal status, freedom of belief, and religious exercise, as well as freedom of religious education (Article 19 of Law no. 250/1993).

[231] Law no. 15 of 2012.

[232] Article 11(3)(D) of Law no 15 of 2012.

[233] Law no. 27 of 2014.

[234] See Max Planck Foundation for International Peace and the Rule of Law, *Constitutional Court System*, at p. 17.

Delays in implementing the new constitutional provisions on constitutional review represent another *punctum dolens*. In Morocco, for example, the constitution was adopted in 2011, although the Constitutional Court was only established in 2017, and the Organic Law regulating the "exception of unconstitutionality" has not yet been promulgated. In Tunisia, where the constitution entered into force in 2014, the Organic Law on the Constitutional Court was adopted in 2015, but the Constitutional Court was never set up. Comparative experiences, however, show that postponing the establishment of constitutional review bodies and the enactment of the relevant laws risks weakening the "innovative force" that these institutions have when they are set up in a timely manner.[235]

The social and political context (as already noted many times) represents another obstacle that clearly hinders the action of constitutional courts, especially if one considers that these bodies can contribute to "the transition to liberal constitutional democracy if, but only if, a nation has already made a good start in that direction. An independent and vigorous constitutional court is the child of liberal democracy, and without that kind of polity, a constitutional court cannot function effectively."[236] Unfortunately, with the (partial) exception of Tunisia until July 2021, this precondition has largely been absent in the Arab world. Because of this difficult context, constitutional courts and councils have thus far delivered founding, landmark judgments only in very rare circumstances.[237] Despite the autocratic setting, the constitutional review body in the Arab region that much more than others has managed to achieve and maintain a significant degree of autonomy vis-à-vis the ruling regime, at least during certain periods of time, is the Supreme Constitutional Court of Egypt. But even the justices of this Court are aware that there are certain "red lines" imposed by the governing authorities that cannot be crossed, otherwise this would have fatal repercussions for the Court.[238]

It would be naïve to expect the obstacles mentioned earlier to be overcome in the short term, as the problems related to constitutional review in the region are not only technical but also of political and cultural nature. However, it would be equally naïve to think that Arab constitutional courts are marginal bodies that will inevitably remain as such. Thus, the future of these bodies is much more uncertain and complex than one would expect.

[235] See Biagi, *European Constitutional Courts*, at pp. 192–193.

[236] Herman Schwartz, *The Struggle for Constitutional Justice in Post-Communist Europe* (University of Chicago Press 2000), 226.

[237] On this issue, with a special focus on the Moroccan Constitutional Council, see Bernoussi and El Maslouhi, "Les chantiers de la 'bonne justice'," at pp. 506–507.

[238] Nathan J. Brown, for example, recalls the fact that in a personal interview he conducted in Cairo in December 1996, a leading justice of the Egyptian Supreme Constitutional Court remarked about the Court's "dragging its heels on a constitutional challenge to the authority of military courts to try civilians in a private conversation 'I would love to eliminate military trials. But if we did that, it would be the last judgment the court issued'." See Brown and Waller, "Constitutional Courts," at p. 843, footnote 62.

4

Religion, Non-Muslims, and Women

The Challenges of Citizenship(s)

4.1 THE PROBLEMATIC NOTION OF CITIZENSHIP IN THE ARAB WORLD

For a long time, the only form of membership accepted within traditional Islamic culture was a *confessional* membership based on *religious affiliation*. Indeed, the Islamic community embraced all those who shared the same faith in Islam.[1] This form of religious citizenship (*ius religionis*) also characterized the Ottoman Empire, under which the *millet* (i.e., the religious community) system operated. According to this system, non-Muslims (specifically Christians and Jews) were granted some (limited) powers to regulate their own affairs (including religious affairs), under the overall supremacy of the Ottoman administration.[2] However, non-Muslims never enjoyed full citizenship rights: For example, they had to pay a special tax (*jizya*) (see later), and were excluded from the army, the state administration, and also politics.[3] The notion of equal citizenship, which transcends one's religion, was (partially) introduced for the first time in the Islamicate world during the "reorganization" (*Tanzimat*) of the Ottoman Empire in the nineteenth century. Indeed, the Edict of Gülhane (1839) and the Reform Edict (1856) abandoned the previous *millet* system and provided for (at least formal) legal equality between Muslims and non-Muslims.[4] This process continued in 1869, when the Sublime Porte adopted the first Law on Citizenship, which confirmed the abandonment of religious citizenship. The law provided for the principle of paternal *ius sanguinis* (Article 1), and stated

1 See Gianluca Paolo Parolin, *Citizenship in the Arab World: Kin, Religion and Nation-State* (Amsterdam University Press 2009), 41.

2 See Efrat Aviv, "Millet System in the Ottoman Empire" in *Islamic Studies* (Oxford University Press) (November 28, 2016), www.oxfordbibliographies.com/view/document/obo-9780195390155/obo-9780195390155-0231.xml

3 See Giorgio Del Zanna, "Società civile, pluralismo e minoranze in Turchia" in Barbara Airò and Massimo Zaccaria (eds.), *I confini della cittadinanza nel nuovo Medio Oriente* (Viella 2015), 33.

4 See Maurits H. van den Boogert, "Millets: Past and Present" in Anh Nga Longva and Anne Sofie Roald (eds.), *Religious Minorities in the Middle East: Domination, Self-Empowerment, Accommodation* (Brill 2012), 33ff.

that any individual born on Ottoman soil to foreign parents could apply for Ottoman nationality three years after coming of age (Article 2). Acquisition by naturalization required continued residence of at least five years (Article 3). Citizenship could also be obtained due to individual merit (Article 4). A departure from past practice was clearly apparent in the fact that "[a]mong the modes of acquisition of Ottoman citizenship, conversion to Islam was not listed."[5] Admittedly, Ottoman institutions continued to consider conversion to Islam as a valid reason for granting citizenship under Article 4; however, in contrast to the past, "citizenship by conversion could be demanded, but not imposed."[6]

The *Tanzimat* and the first Ottoman Law on Citizenship represented the first steps in a long process. Subsequently, Arab nationalism (which rose to prominence with the weakening and defeat of the Ottoman Empire in the early twentieth century) and the process of self-determination from European colonialism "emphasised the need to unify citizens of different religions to increase the possibility of success against foreign oppression."[7] Thus, the concept of citizenship was more related to a "specific geographical area than to a religious faith."[8] Over time, Western models exerted a significant influence also on the nationality codes adopted in various countries in the region. While for a long time paternal *ius sanguinis* was the norm (and maternal *ius sanguinis* the exception), in Egypt, Algeria, and Morocco, maternal *ius sanguinis* was introduced as a way of attributing nationality to children (in addition to paternal *ius sanguinis*) in 2004, 2005, and 2007, respectively. In Tunisia, since 1963 the Nationality Code has granted Tunisian nationality to any child born in Tunisia to a Tunisian mother; moreover, since 1993, Tunisian nationality has also been granted to any child born to a Tunisian mother outside Tunisia.[9]

Notwithstanding these developments, the concept of citizenship has long struggled to gain acceptance in the Arab world. One of the explanations lies in the fact that the notion of citizenship seems to be very difficult to reconcile with that of the Islamic *ummah*, namely the community of believers.[10] According to the Quran (Sura 3:110), the Islamic *ummah* is the best community: "You are the best 'Ummah ever raised for mankind. You bid the Fair and forbid the Unfair, and you believe

5 Parolin, *Citizenship in the Arab World*, at p. 74.

6 Ibid.

7 Marco Demichelis, "Citizenship and Equity. An Excursus Within the Nahda, Islamic Pluralism and Religious Exclusivism" in Airò and Zaccaria (eds.) 2015, *I confini della cittadinanza nel nuovo Medio Oriente*, at p. 24.

8 Ibid.

9 See Parolin, *Citizenship in the Arab World*, at p. 79ff. Most Arab countries, however, still do not recognize equality between men and women when it comes to attributing nationality to children. See Nathalie Bernard-Maugiron, *Droit contemporain des pays arabes* (Sirey 2023), 830.

10 See Walid Larbi, "Le statut du citoyen dans les structures traditionnelles d'appartenance et d'organisation politique islamique" in Rafâa Ben Achour (ed.), *Constitution, citoyenneté et justice constitutionnelle: Entre exigence démocratique et recompositions territoriales* (Centre de publication universitaire 2014), 260ff.

in Allah [...]." The modern notion of citizenship in the Western world refers to a bundle of rights enjoyed on equal terms by all members of a certain nation. It is founded on the participation of all people in the *res publica*, without any form of discrimination (including religious discrimination). The *ummah*, on the contrary, is not so much based on the notion of equality. Rather, it has a clear religious foundation: people belong to this community *because of their Islamic faith*. The *ummah* is a community founded on a religious bond and centered on the Quran. As the term itself indicates (*ummah*), it is a community of believers. This explains why, unlike citizenship (which has a strong territorial dimension [the state]), the *ummah* has a "universalist, cross-territorial character."[11] Religion is not just a matter of personal belief but also (*rectius*: mainly) consists in membership of a community.[12] This helps to explain why the abandonment of the Islamic religion (apostasy, *ridda*) is perceived as a *betrayal* of such a community.[13]

Albeit with some exceptions, two categories of people who historically suffered particular discrimination in the territories of Islam (*dar al-islam*) and who were not granted the status of full citizens, both *de jure* and *de facto*, were non-Muslims and women.[14] When examining the legal and social status of non-Muslims, one must differentiate – on the basis of the distinction made by the Quran – between the "People of the Book" (*Ahl al-Kitab*, mainly Christians and Jews),[15] on the one hand, and all the other non-Muslims (particularly polytheists [belonging to "associationism"]), on the other hand.[16] While the latter were not tolerated, the former, who were considered as *dhimmis* (which is the non-Quranic title for the People of the Book), were tolerated, and were granted the right to practice their religion. However, the condition of *dhimmitude* came with its own price. Indeed, in exchange for the protection afforded to them by the authorities, Christians and Jews were required to pay a special tax, known as the *jizya*, which had to be paid by demonstrating humility.[17]

11 Ibid., at p. 266.

12 Ibid., at p. 270.

13 On this issue, see Section 4.2.3 in greater detail.

14 On this issue, see in particular the following works by Abdullahi Ahmed An-Na'im: "Religious Minorities under Islamic Law and the Limits of Cultural Relativism" (1987) 9 *Human Rights Quarterly*, 1ff.; "Mahmud Muhammad Taha and the Crisis in Islamic Law Reform: Implications for Interreligious Relations" (1988) 25 *Journal of Ecumenical Studies*, 1ff.; "Beyond *dhimmihood*: Citizenship and Human Rights" in Robert W. Hefner (ed.), *The New Cambridge History of Islam. Volume 6. Muslims and Modernity: Culture and Society Since 1800* (Cambridge University Press 2010), 314ff.; "Islam, Sharia and Democratic Transformation in the Arab World" (2012) 87 *Die Friedens-Warte*, 27ff.

15 Although Christians and Jews are the "People of the Book" *par excellence*, other religions (such as Zoroastrians and Sabians) "have been allotted, or deprived of, or considered close to the title *Ahl al Kitab* according to circumstance" (Nayla Tabbara, "Islam and Other Religions" in Fadi Daou and Nayla Tabbara, *Divine Hospitality: A Christian-Muslim Conversation* (World Council of Churches Publications 2017), 73).

16 See Tabbara, "Islam and Other Religions," at pp. 71–73.

17 On the *jizya* and the other tax imposed to non-Muslims (i.e., the *kharag*), see Nicola Melis, "Lo statuto giuridico degli ebrei dell'Impero ottomano" in Martino Contu, Nicola Melis and

This was in line with the requirement stipulated by the Quran (Sura 9:29) in the well-known "verse of the *jizya*": "Fight those who believe not in God nor the Last Day, nor hold that forbidden which hath been forbidden by God and His Apostle, nor acknowledge the Religion of Truth [even if they are] of the People of the Book; [fight them] until they pay the *jizya* with willing submission, and feel themselves subdued." This verse (*ayah*) – along with other verses dealing with non-Muslims such as Sura 2:191: "Kill them wherever you come upon them and drive them out of the places from which they have driven you out". – was often followed literally, without any kind of historical contextualization, a practice that led to violence and abuses.[18]

The relationship between Muslims and the People of the Book was influenced for centuries by the "Pact of Umar," a treaty that, according to tradition, was signed by the second Caliph Umar ibn al-Khattab with the Christians of Syro-Palestine, after they had been conquered by the Islamic army. This treaty "set out the conditions upon which the Christians were to be granted the right to live and be protected from assault."[19] These conditions included, *inter alia*, restrictions on freedom of worship, prohibitions on public displays of their religion, the duty to be discrete in their religious practices, as well as the requirement that the appearance of non-Muslims be different from those of Muslims.[20] Christians and Jews living in the *dar al-islam* were required to respect similar obligations for a long time, up until the *Tanzimat* of the Ottoman Empire in the nineteenth century. Indeed, as well as having to pay the *jizya*, at some points in time they were forced to wear specific clothing or signs, were only allowed to ride donkeys (and not horses), and were required to comply with various restrictions when building or renovating their places of worship (churches and synagogues). In Moroccan cities, the Jewish community was constrained into specific districts (known as *mellah*). More generally, the People of the Book had to live in a condition of subservience.[21] It should be noted that the condition of all the other non-Muslims was even worse. African polytheists, for example, were not granted any form of tolerance: "In the event of capture or conquest, they were offered the choice between conversion and slavery, and sometimes both at the same

Giovannino Pinna (eds.), *Ebraismo e rapporti con le culture del Mediterraneo nei secoli XVIII–XX* (Giuntina 2003), 144ff.

18 On the lack of historical contextualizations, see Massimo Papa, "L'Islam e la violenza: un excursus giuridico" in Francesca Maria Corrao and Luciano Violante (eds.), *L'Islam non è terrorismo* (il Mulino 2018), 57–58.

19 Mariz Tadros, "Christianity in North Africa and West Asia" in Kenneth R. Ross, Mariz Tadros and Todd M. Johnson (eds.), *Christianity in North Africa and West Asia* (Edinburgh University Press 2018), 21.

20 Ibid., at pp. 21–22.

21 For a history of Christians and Jews in the Middle East and North Africa, see, respectively, Philip Jenkins, *The Lost History of Christianity: The Thousand-Year Golden Age of the Church in the Middle East, Africa and Asia – And How It Died* (HarperOne 2008), and Georges Bensoussan, *Les Juifs du monde arabe: La question interdite* (Odile Jacob 2017).

time."[22] Notwithstanding these discriminations, as will be shown later,[23] there were periods during which Muslims and non-Muslims coexisted peacefully, there were instances of interfaith dialogue, and there were attempts to place greater emphasis on the verses of the Quran that call for openness and respect toward other religions.

The legal and social status of women was equally problematic, although for different reasons. Obviously, women were (and still are) part of the *ummah*. However, mainly due to a patriarchal interpretation of the religious texts they suffered major injustices and discrimination (as is often the case with all other major religions, including Christianity).[24] In the words of Leila Ahmed:

> establishment Islam (institutional and legal Islam) [...] [is] intolerant of all understandings of the religion except its own, which is authoritarian, implacably androcentric, and hostile to women [...]. There is no ambiguity within establishment Islam and its laws on the treatment of men and women, or on their different, and women's distinctly inferior, rights before the law. [...] The controls on women, the limitations on their participation in the economy, their exclusion from many fields of activity in their society, including politics, their subjection to a code of law with fundamental inequalities and, worse, systematic cruelty – all were features of many previous Muslim societies [...]. Women [...] can be oppressed and deprived of rights not just for being dissidents but merely for being women.[25]

The Quran does contain some controversial verses that – if not properly contextualized – can easily lead to a patriarchal interpretation, a fact that had extremely negative consequences on the social and legal status of women. One example of this is provided in Sura 4:34:

> Men are in charge [*qawwamun*] of women by [right of] what Allah has given one over the other and what they spend [for maintenance] from their wealth. So righteous women are devoutly obedient [*qanitat*], guarding in [the husband's] absence what Allah would have them guard. But those [wives] from whom you fear arrogance – [first] advise them; [then if they persist], forsake them in bed; and [finally], strike them [*adribu-hunna*]. But if they obey you [once more], seek no means against them. Indeed, Allah is ever Exalted and Grand.

This verse refers, in the first place, to men's *qawama*, which encompasses not only protection and maintenance but also guardianship over women. In turn, women have to be loyal and obedient toward men. Furthermore, men can discipline women who are disloyal and disobedient, and even dispense beatings if necessary. According to Abdullahi Ahmed An-Na'im, these principles, and the related *Sunna* of Prophet Mohammed, "have been taken as the basis for a wide variety of rules

[22] Bernard Lewis, "L'islam et les non-musulmans" (1980) 3–4 *Annales*, 789.

[23] See Section 4.4.2.

[24] On women's discrimination because of a patriarchal interpretation of Christian religious texts, see Section 4.4.2.8 in greater detail.

[25] Leila Ahmed, *Women and Gender in Islam* (Yale University Press 1992), 225, 230, and 231.

signifying women's inferior status [...]. Other verses requiring women to be veiled and confined to the home are also used to support restrictions and limitations on women."[26] However, as will be shown later,[27] the Quran also contains other verses that suggest an egalitarian approach between men and women. Unfortunately, this different (and more progressive) reading of religious texts has thus far never prevailed in Arab countries – with the (partial) exception of Tunisia since the mid-twentieth century.

It is therefore evident that in the *dar al-islam* citizenship *optimo jure* was for a long time only granted to Muslims – and in particular only to *male* Muslims. Women (particularly Muslim women), Christians, and Jews were considered, *de jure* and *de facto*, "second-class" citizens. Non-Muslim women and the followers of religions other than Christianity and Judaism (in particular polytheistic religions) were granted an even lower status, and in many cases could hardly qualify as citizens of any sort.

Thanks to the strong influence of Western constitutional models, the term "citizen" already appeared in many Arab constitutions during the twentieth century, especially after these countries gained independence from European powers. However, it has been in particular in the post-2011 constitutions that the term "citizenship" (*al-muwatana*) has clearly entered into several Arab constitutional texts. It is fair to say that this concept has been very much emphasized in some of these new documents. In Morocco, for example, the 2011 constitution states that the constitutional regime of the kingdom is founded, *inter alia*, on "participatory, citizen democracy" (*al-dimuqratiyya al-muwatina al-tasharukiyya*; *démocratie citoyenne et participative*) (Article 1(2)). The 2012 Syrian Constitution stipulates that citizenship is "a fundamental principle which involves rights and duties enjoyed by every citizen and exercised according to law" (Article 33(2)), and that citizens have equal rights and duties (Article 33(3)). In Tunisia, the 2014 constitution stated that "Tunisia is a civil state based on citizenship, the will of the people, and the supremacy of law" (Article 2), but this provision was eliminated in the 2022 constitution. In Egypt, citizenship had already been incorporated into the 1971 constitution by the 2007 reform. Indeed, while the original version of Article 1 of the 1971 constitution stated that Egypt was characterized by "a socialist, democratic system based on the alliance of the working forces of the people," following the 2007 reform, this provision stipulated that Egypt was "a democratic state based on citizenship." The 2012 constitution not only maintained the reference to citizenship but also explained what citizenship consisted of. Indeed, Article 6 stated that the political system was based, *inter alia*, on the principle of "citizenship, under which all citizens are equal in public rights and duties." This explanatory clause was eliminated in the 2014 constitution, which only states that Egypt is "a republican, democratic system based on citizenship and

[26] An-Na'im, "Religious Minorities," at p. 13.

[27] See Section 4.4.1.

the rule of law" (Article 1). In Jordan, the 2022 constitutional amendments added a new paragraph to Article 6, stipulating that "The state guarantees the promotion of the values of citizenship, tolerance and the rule of law […]" (Article 6(7)).

In all the abovementioned countries, the notion of citizenship seems to convey the idea of *equality* (*al-musawa*) in terms of rights and duties. This largely recalls the (modern) concept of citizenship in the Western world. Indeed, in the words of Michel Rosenfeld, "[m]odern citizenship is equal citizenship and premised on the universal axiom that all human beings are inherently equal."[28] In Syria, this concept is mentioned in quite explicit terms within the text of the constitution itself (citizenship is "a fundamental principle which involves rights and duties enjoyed by every citizen" (Article 33(2)). In Tunisia, the translation of the 2014 constitution into vernacular Tunisian prepared by the Tunisian Association of Constitutional Law states: "which means that all the people in it are equal (*kif kif*)."[29] In Egypt, the fact that the 2014 constitution no longer includes the explanatory clause contained in the 2012 constitution ("citizenship, under which all citizens are equal in public rights and duties" [Article 6]) does not seem to provide a sufficient basis to argue that the Egyptian framers rejected this notion of equal citizenship. Indeed, this notion is indirectly recalled in other provisions of the constitution, such as for example in the preamble ("We are drafting a Constitution that achieves equality between us in rights and duties with no discrimination. We are the citizens. We are the Egyptian people, sovereigns in a sovereign homeland. This is our will and this is the Constitution of our revolution"), or in Article 19 ("Every citizen has the right to education with the aim of […] establishing civilizational and spiritual values and the concepts of citizenship, tolerance and non-discrimination"). In Jordan, it is significant that the new reference to citizenship has been included under the umbrella of the provision proclaiming the principle of equality and nondiscrimination (Article 6). In Morocco, the constitution suggests that the concept of citizenship is not only related to the idea of equality but also to that of political participation ("participatory, citizen democracy" (Article 1(2)).[30]

The special place granted to citizenship in many post-2011 constitutions, as well as the fact that the concept of citizenship seems to be associated with equality, are *per se* significant innovations. What needs to be clarified, however, is whether and to what extent this idea of equal citizenship is reflected in other constitutional provisions, specifically those on non-Muslims' and women's rights. Indeed, since non-Muslims and women are the two categories of people *par excellence* who in the past never enjoyed the status of full citizens in the Arab world, their treatment provides

28 Michel Rosenfeld, *The Identity of the Constitutional Subject: Selfhood, Citizenship, Culture and Community* (Routledge 2009), 213.

29 Cited in Gianluca Paolo Parolin, "The Buzz and Fuzz of 'Citizenship' in North African Constitutions" in Airò and Zaccaria (eds.) 2015, *I confini della cittadinanza nel nuovo Medio Oriente*, at p. 98.

30 See Parolin, "Buzz and Fuzz of 'Citizenship'," at p. 98.

a litmus test for understanding the real intentions of Arab framers. Did they really embrace the notion of *equal* citizenship? Or did they still rely (at least in part) on the notion of *religious* citizenship? To what extent were constitutional provisions in these fields implemented? I try to answer these questions in the following sections (Sections 4.2 and 4.3).

4.2 NON-MUSLIMS' RIGHTS UNDER POST-2011 CONSTITUTIONAL SYSTEMS

Post-Arab Spring constitution-making processes confirm that religion is often an extremely contentious issue in constitutional design.[31] In general, the presence of religion in contemporary constitutions is very common.[32] What makes Arab constitutions different from most other constitutional documents is the "unusual degree of attention on the relationship between religion *and law*"[33] (emphasis added). Indeed, "State and religion are too foreign to love each other and too close to be separate. These are two categories that will never get along because they have different objectives, but that can never be separate because they are intertwined by the nature of things."[34]

A comparative analysis of post-2011 constitutions shows that they differ significantly from country to country when it comes to religious freedom and the rights of non-Muslims, although it is possible to identify some common trends. In the first place, it should be noted that most constitutions prohibit discrimination on the grounds of religion. This requirement was first stipulated in the 1861 constitution of Tunisia, which is considered to be the first constitution in the Arab world. Indeed, it provided that "All subjects of the kingdom, irrespective of the religion they belong to, are equal before the law [...]" (Article 88), and repeated at several points that the various rights listed in the constitution were granted to all subjects of the kingdom "irrespective of the religion they belong to" (Articles 86ff.).

That said, it should be noted that the notion of religious freedom in most Arab countries is much narrower in scope than it is under Article 18 of the 1948 Universal

[31] See Asli Ü. Bâli and Hanna Lerner (eds.), *Constitution Writing, Religion and Democracy* (Cambridge University Press 2017); Francesco Biagi, "Religion in Constitution-making Processes: Comparative Perspectives" in Susanna Mancini (ed.), *Constitutions and Religion* (Edward Elgar 2020), 253ff.

[32] Statistics also confirm this "ubiquity of religion in constitutions" (Francois Venter, *Constitutionalism and Religion* (Edward Elgar 2015), 87): Out of 194 constitutions in existence today, 186 contain the world "religion"; 183 include some forms of protection of religious freedom; and 114 mention the words "God," "the divine," or other deities. See Asli Ü. Bâli and Hanna Lerner, "Introduction" in Bâli and Lerner (eds.) 2017, *Constitution Writing*, at p. 6; Iván C. Ibán, "God in Constitutions and Godless Constitutions" in W. Cole Durham, Jr. et al. (eds.), *Law, Religion, Constitution: Freedom of Religion, Equal Treatment, and the Law* (Routledge 2013), 37ff.

[33] Nathan J. Brown, "The Unsurprising but Distinctive Nature of Constitution Writing in the Arab World" in David Landau and Hanna Lerner (eds.), *Comparative Constitution Making* (Edward Elgar 2019), 448.

[34] Yadh Ben Achour, "Conclusions générales" in *Les Constitutions des Pays arabes: Colloque de Beyrouth*, 1998 (Bruylant 1999), 312.

Declaration of Human Rights, which proclaims that "Everyone has the right to freedom of thought, conscience and religion; this right includes freedom to change his religion or belief, and freedom, either alone or in community with others and in public or private, to manifest his religion or belief in teaching, practice, worship and observance." Indeed, in the Arab region, freedom of *conscience* – which includes the right "to choose a religion, to change religion, or not to have a religion"[35] – is guaranteed only very rarely (as for example in the Lebanese and Tunisian Constitutions), a fact that obviously makes conversion from Islam to another religion particularly difficult. The exclusion of freedom of conscience from most Arab constitutions is far from surprising since, under *sharia*, apostasy is not allowed.[36] Some constitutional texts (including, for example, the constitutions of Egypt and Syria) guarantee freedom of *belief*, whereas other constitutions (including, for example, the constitutions of Morocco, Jordan, and Algeria) only recognize freedom of *worship*, which guarantees the exercise of religious practices. Tunisian Constitutions (both from 2014 and 2022) expressly recognize freedom of conscience, belief, and worship.[37] It is clear that the differences in wording that can be found in the provisions of Arab constitutions on religious freedom appear subtle, but in actual fact have major substantial implications.[38] In all countries, religious freedom is often subject to various limitations and restrictions.[39]

Another aspect that is common to virtually all Arab countries is that Christians and Jews – being part of the People of the Book (*Ahl al-Kitab*) – are granted much preferential treatment compared to other non-Muslims (especially the followers of polytheistic religions), a fact that (as explained earlier) is rooted in the predominant interpretation of the Quran and in *fiqh*.[40] For example, while the 2014 Egyptian Constitution recognizes that freedom of belief is absolute, it grants the freedom to practice religious rituals and to establish places of worship only to the "divinely revealed religions," that is, Islam, Christianity, and Judaism (Article 64). This shows that the influence exerted by Islam and *sharia* on the interpretation of religious freedom and non-Muslims' rights is still strong.

Another trend that is worth emphasizing is that a significant number of constitutional texts guarantee full political rights – and particularly the right to be elected

35 Yadh Ben Achour, *Tunisie: Une révolution en pays d'Islam* (Cérès éditions 2017), 355; see also Rafâa Ben Achour, "La Constitution tunisienne du 27 janvier 2014" (2014) 100 *Revue française de droit constitutionnel*, 787.

36 See Rudolph Peters and Gert J. J. De Vries, "Apostasy in Islam" (1976–1977) 17 *Die Welt des Islams*, 1ff.

37 See Article 6 of the 2014 constitution, and Articles 27 and 28 of the 2022 constitution. See Section 4.2.1 in greater detail.

38 See Nathan J. Brown, "Citizenship, Religious Rights, and State Identity in Arab Constitutions: Who is Free and What Are They Free to Do?" in Nehal Bhuta (ed.), *Freedom of Religion, Secularism, and Human Rights* (Oxford University Press 2019), 54.

39 On new approaches to the protection of religious freedom and religious minorities in the region, see Andrea Pin, *Religious Freedom Without the Rule of Law: Getting the Middle East Right* (Brill, forthcoming).

40 See Section 4.1.

as head of state – only to Muslims. This comes as no surprise if one considers that political rights are probably citizenship rights *par excellence*, and their full enjoyment has historically been granted only to Muslims. Thus, the concept of *religious* citizenship continues to be present in today's Arab world.

All of these aspects are particularly worrying also in the light of the large-scale emigration of non-Muslims from Arab countries that began during the twentieth century and continued into the twenty-first century. This exodus has involved particularly Jews and Christians, who had previously constituted stable and historic communities in the region, dating back to centuries before the time of Prophet Mohammed. While in 1945 there were about 900,000 Jews living in the Arab world,[41] today Jews have almost completely disappeared from the region: Morocco has one of the largest remaining Jewish communities with approximately 3,000 members, while there are around 1,500 Jews in Tunisia. However, in most Arab countries, Jews amount to a few hundred people, and in some cases even fewer.[42] Jews mainly left Arab countries after the establishment of the State of Israel in 1948 (known among Arabs as "*al-nakba*," i.e., "the catastrophe") and in the aftermath of the Arab-Israeli Six-Day War in 1967. Most of them emigrated to Israel, Europe, the United States, or other Western countries.

The number of Christians has also drastically fallen. They accounted for 13.6 percent of the region's population in 1910, but only 4.2 percent in 2010.[43] Following the 2011 Arab uprisings, the exodus of Christians has increased further, with many deciding to emigrate due to wars, conflicts, atrocities perpetrated by ISIS, and various forms of discrimination and persecution.[44] It is generally believed that the fall of the old dictatorships contributed significantly to the weakening of the protection of religious minorities, including Christian minorities.[45] According to the

41 See Carole Basri, "The Jewish Refugees from Arab Countries: An Examination of Legal Rights – A Case Study of the Human Rights Violations of Iraqi Jews" (2003) 26 *Fordham International Law Journal*, 659.

42 See Joshua Castellino and Kathleen A. Cavanaugh, *Minority Rights in the Middle East* (Oxford University Press 2013), 85ff.

43 See Todd M. Johnson and Gina A. Zurlo, "Ongoing Exodus: Tracking the Emigration of Christians from the Middle East" (2013–2014) 3 *Harvard Journal of Middle Eastern Politics and Policy*, 40. On the exodus of Christians, see also Giovanni Sale, *Isis, Islam e cristiani d'oriente* (Jaca Book 2016), 145ff.; Andrea Riccardi, "La sconfitta del Califfato sarà il ritorno dei cristiani," *Il Corriere della Sera* (November 5, 2017), 24; Andrea Riccardi, "La nuova 'resurrezione' cristiana in Medio oriente," *Il Corriere della Sera* (April 21, 2019), 26.

44 See Gina A. Zurlo, "A Demographic Profile of Christianity in North Africa and West Asia" and Ewelina Ochab, "Religious Freedom" in Ross, Tadros and Johnson (eds.) 2018, *Christianity*, respectively, at pp. 10ff. and 371ff.; Andrea Pin, "Religious Persecution and Constitution Building in the Middle East: The Rule-of-Law Conundrum" (2022) 97 *Notre Dame Law Review Reflection*, 245ff.

45 See Huma Haider, *The Persecution of Christians in the Middle East*, Institute of Development Studies (February 16, 2017), 4, https://opendocs.ids.ac.uk/opendocs/bitstream/handle/20.500.12413/13055/K4D_HDR_Persecution%20of%20Christians%20in%20the%20Middle%20East.pdf;jsessionid=A2BBDB58992018CD5B3E2F28511CB7ED?sequence=142

2022 World Watch List published by Open Doors, the persecution of Christians is "extreme" in Libya, Yemen, and Saudi Arabia, and "very high" in Sudan, Iraq, Syria, Qatar, Egypt, Algeria, Mauritania, Morocco, Tunisia, Oman, Jordan, and Kuwait.[46] Arab Christians are currently facing an existential threat.[47] Iraq is one of the most emblematic cases. Since the fall of Saddam Hussein in 2003, the Christian community has dwindled by 83 percent, from around 1.5 million to just 250,000.[48] According to other sources, the number has fallen even lower, that is, to approximately 146,000.[49] The proclamation by ISIS of the "Caliphate" in Iraq and Syria in 2014 contributed enormously to the plight of Christians in these countries. When ISIS invaded Mosul (Iraq) in June 2014, Christians were issued with an ultimatum: convert to Islam, pay the *jizya*, or face death. Christian homes were marked with the Arabic letter *nun* (i.e., "n"), for *Nasarah* (i.e., Nazarene), a term Muslims used throughout the centuries but that nowadays Christians reject. In the "Annual Report on Human Rights and Democracy in the World" issued on December 14, 2016, the European Parliament argued that "some of the oldest Christian communities are in danger of disappearing, especially in North Africa and the Middle East."[50]

The only Arab states that have seen an increase in their Christian population are some Gulf countries, due to the influx of significant numbers of Christian migrant workers from Asia (particularly from India and the Philippines) and in part also from Africa. Thus, for example, Christians currently comprise approximately 5 percent of the population of Saudi Arabia (a percentage that roughly corresponds to the proportion of Muslims living in the European continent),[51] 7 percent of the population of the United Arab Emirates, and 10 percent of the population of Bahrain and Kuwait.[52] It should be noted, however, that these people are foreigners who temporarily live and work in these countries, and therefore cannot by any means be considered as citizens.

46 Open Doors, *World Watch List 2022* (2022), https://cms.evangelicalfocus.com/upload/2022-01-19-11:49_MapaWWL2022.pdf

47 See Janine di Giovanni, *The Vanishing: The Twilight of Christianity in the Middle East* (Bloomsbury 2021).

48 See Frank Gardner, "Iraq's Christians 'close to extinction'," *BBC News* (May 23, 2019), www.bbc.com/news/world-middle-east-48333923

49 See Gian Guido Vecchi, "Il viaggio di un francescano tra i cristiani decimati in Iraq," *Il Corriere della Sera* (December 19, 2019), 25.

50 European Parliament, *Annual Report on Human Rights and Democracy in the World and the European Union's Policy on the Matter 2015* (December 14, 2016), point no. 146, www.europarl.europa.eu/doceo/document/TA-8-2016-0502_EN.pdf?redirect

51 See Pew Research Center, *Europe's Growing Muslim Population* (November 29, 2017), www.pewresearch.org/religion/2017/11/29/europes-growing-muslim-population/

52 See Philip Jenkins, "Premessa dell'autore all'edizione italiana" in Philip Jenkins, *La storia perduta del Cristianesimo: Il millennio d'oro della Chiesa in Medio Oriente, Africa e Asia (V–XV secolo). Come è finita una civiltà* (EMI 2016), 17–19. The experience of being a Christian in the Gulf has been described by Bishop Paul Hinder in his book *Als Bischof in Arabien: Erfahrungen mit dem Islam* (Herder 2016).

Although in much smaller numbers compared to the Gulf countries, over the past twenty years even Morocco, and in part also Tunisia, have become a destination for migrants, including Christian migrants (mainly from sub-Saharan Africa), who are permanently settling in these countries in increasing numbers.[53] This phenomenon, which has contributed to the "revival" of some Christian churches, can be largely explained in the light of the enormous difficulties that sub-Saharan migrants face in reaching Europe.[54] Interestingly, in 2012, a theological institute – the Al-Mowafaqa Ecumenical Institute of Theology – was established in Rabat, Morocco, on the initiative of the Catholic and Protestant Churches, with the aim of promoting ecumenism, as well as intercultural and interreligious dialogue.[55]

4.2.1 *Tunisia*

In Tunisia, during the 2011–2014 constitution-drafting process, the first matter of contention regarded the decision over whether (or not) to establish Islam as the state religion. Article 1 of the 2014 constitution retained the same wording as Article 1 of the previous 1959 constitution: "Tunisia [*Tounes*] is a free, independent, sovereign state [*dawla*]; *its religion is Islam* [*al-islam dinha*], its language is Arabic, and its system is republican" (emphasis added).[56] In Arabic, "*al-islam dinha*" can refer both to the "state" and "Tunisia."[57] Thus, this provision is characterized by evident ambiguity as it can be interpreted in two different ways, that is, either as establishing Islam as the state religion or as declaring that Islam is the religion of the majority of the population. Under the former interpretation, Islam is the religion of state institutions, whereas the latter interpretation underscores a sociological and identitarian aspect, resulting from the fact that 99 percent of the Tunisian population is Muslim. Since the adoption of the 1959 constitution, the latter interpretation has prevailed, and it has indeed been stressed that, thanks to this interpretation, *Islam has reigned* in Tunisia, but the *state has governed*.[58]

The fourth (and final) draft constitution published on June 1, 2013 maintained the wording of Article 1 of the 1959 constitution, although also introduced an "eternity clause" (Article 141) listing a series of constitutional principles that could not be amended, including "Islam as the State religion." The report on this draft

53 See Sophie Bava and Katia Boissevain, "Migrations africaines et variations religieuses: les églises chrétiennes du Maroc et de Tunisie" (2020) 32 *Migration Société*, 115ff.

54 See the podcast "Chrétiens au Maroc: une renaissance portée par les migrants subsahariens," *RFI* (December 24, 2021), www.rfi.fr/fr/podcasts/orient-hebdo/20211224-chrétiens-au-maroc-une-renaissance-portée-par-les-migrants-subsahariens

55 See its website: www.almowafaqa.com

56 As it will be shown later, unlike the 1959 constitution, Article 1 of the 2014 constitution also contained a provision stipulating that "This article might not be amended."

57 See Jean-Philippe Bras, "Un État 'civil' peut-il être religieux? Débats tunisien" (2016) 156 *Pouvoirs*, 60.

58 See Pietro Longo, "L'Islam nella nuova Costituzione: dallo Stato neutrale allo Stato 'protettore'" in Tania Groppi and Irene Spigno (eds.), *Tunisia: La Primavera della Costituzione* (Carocci 2015), 111.

constitution prepared by a committee of experts appointed by the president of the Republic[59] highlighted a contradiction between the civil character of the state (provided for in Article 2) on the one hand, and the proclamation of Islam as the religion of the state (declared in Article 141) on the other hand. The report recommended that Article 141 be amended as follows: "No constitutional amendment may cause prejudice to Article 1 or Article 2 of the Constitution."[60] A similar observation was also made by the Venice Commission, which had been requested to submit an opinion on this draft constitution by the Speaker of the Constituent Assembly on June 3, 2013. The Venice Commission pointed out that "the reference to Islam as the state religion as a non-amendable principle contained in Article 141 goes far beyond the wording of Article 1, which states that Islam is the religion of Tunisia (= of the majority of Tunisians)."[61] According to the Venice Commission, Article 141 was inconsistent, in particular, with Article 2 of the constitution, which stipulated that Tunisia was a "civil state" (*dawla madaniyya*).[62]

In the light of the observations made by the committee of experts and by the Venice Commission, the Constituent Assembly decided to remove Article 141 and maintain the wording of Article 1 (Islam as the religion of Tunisia) and Article 2 (Tunisia as a civil state). A paragraph was also added to both provisions, stating that "This Article may not be amended." The Constituent Assembly thus clearly promoted an interpretation of Article 1 according to which Islam was not the state religion, but rather the *religion of the majority of the population* (as it had been interpreted in the past). Therefore, Tunisia continued to be one of the very few Arab countries (together with Syria and Lebanon, for example) not to proclaim Islam as the religion of the state. It should also be stressed that the recommendations of the Venice Commission in relation to Article 1 were not perceived as undermining the state's sovereignty and were in fact incorporated into the new constitution, thus showing a willingness on the part of the Tunisian framers to comply with international standards and comparative best practices.

The inclusion of a *sharia* clause in the 2014 constitution was also vigorously debated. On the one hand, Ennahda pushed for the incorporation of this clause into the constitution. Some of its members called for a provision stating that "*sharia* is the main source of legislation." An internal Ennahda draft constitution presented in February 2012 included a lighter version according to which *sharia* would only be "a" source of legislation. This draft also provided for the establishment of a High *Sharia* Council responsible for verifying the conformity of legislative acts with *sharia*. It should also be recalled that, on January 23, 2012, Sadok Chourou, former President

59 This commission was composed of nine members and presided over by the prominent Tunisian jurist Yadh Ben Achour.

60 See Ben Achour, *Tunisie: Une révolution en pays d'Islam*, at pp. 353–354.

61 Venice Commission, *Opinion on the Final Draft Constitution of the Republic of Tunisia* (Opinion no. 733/2013) (October 17, 2013), 8, www.venice.coe.int/webforms/documents/?pdf=CDL-AD(2013)032-e

62 Ibid., at pp. 7–8.

of Ennahda, even called for the introduction of *hudud* punishments, which range from public lashing to public stoning to death, the amputation of hands, and the death penalty. On the other hand, secular parties strongly opposed a constitutional recognition of *sharia*, and accused Ennahda of trying to establish a religious state.[63]

The clashes among political forces within the Constituent Assembly reflected the differing views in civil society. Indeed, in mid-March 2012, both supporters and opponents of the introduction of a *sharia* clause into the constitution gathered in demonstrations in order to express their views. On March 25 of the same year, Ennahda's leadership took a step back, announcing its decision to withdraw its proposal to introduce a *sharia* clause into the constitution. This decision can be explained not only in the light of the hostility displayed by a large share of the population to such a proposal[64] but also in the light of Ennahda's political strategy characterized by moderation and compromise.[65]

The place and role of religion proved to be a very sensitive issue also during the 2022 constitution-making process. Prior to submitting the text of the draft constitution to President Kaïs Saïed, Sadok Belaïd, the head of the "National Consultative Commission for a New Republic," declared in an interview that "80 percent of Tunisians are against extremism and the use of religion for political ends" and that his intention was to "erase Article 1 [of the 2014 Constitution] in its current form."[66] The draft constitution presented to Saïed on June 20, 2022, did in fact remove the provision stating that Islam was the religion of Tunisia, and only maintained the reference in the preamble to the teachings of Islam and its objectives/aims (*maqasid*). Shortly after receiving the draft constitution, Saïed declared in an interview that the new constitution would not enshrine Islam as the religion of Tunisia. More specifically, he stated that "The next Constitution of Tunisia won't mention a State with Islam as its religion, but of belonging to an *ummah* which has Islam as its religion. The *ummah* and the State are two different things."[67]

The 2022 constitution, which was drafted with the direct involvement of Saïed himself,[68] no longer refers to Islam as the religion of Tunisia, but rather contains

63 See Ben Achour, *Tunisie: Une révolution en pays d'Islam*, at p. 350.

64 See Tania Abbiate, "The Cross-cutting Issue of Religion in the Tunisian Participatory Constitution-making Process" in Tania Abbiate, Markus Böckenförde and Veronica Federico (eds.), *Public Participation in African Constitutionalism* (Routledge 2018), 285.

65 See Duncan Pickard, "Al-Nahda: Moderation and Compromise in Tunisia's Constitutional Bargain" in Justin O. Frosini and Francesco Biagi (eds.), *Political and Constitutional Transitions in North Africa: Actors and Factors* (Routledge 2015), 21.

66 See "Tunisia Expert Drafting New Constitution Says No Reference to Islam," *France 24* (June 6, 2022), www.france24.com/en/live-news/20220606-tunisia-expert-drafting-new-constitution-says-no-reference-to-islam

67 See "No State Religion Says Tunisia President After Receiving Draft Constitution," *The Arab Weekly* (June 21, 2022), https://thearabweekly.com/no-state-religion-says-tunisia-president-after-receiving-draft-constitution

68 See Chapter 1, Section 1.2.1.2.

a highly ambiguous and controversial provision, namely Article 5. This provision stipulates that "Tunisia is part of the Islamic *ummah*, and the State alone, within the framework of a democratic system, must endeavor to achieve the objectives (*maqasid*) of Islam in the preservation of life, honor, property, faith, and freedom." In the first place, it should be stressed that the reference to the aims/objectives of Islam was removed from the preamble and incorporated into Article 5, a fact that facilitates the implementation of this provision.[69] Second, this article as it appeared in the draft constitution published on June 30, 2022, was amended only a few days later, on July 8, by Presidential Decree no. 2022-607, which "corrected" certain "errors" contained in the draft constitution.[70] However, far from correcting a material error, this provision was substantially amended by the addition of the expression "within the framework of a democratic system." Third, the "objectives" mentioned in the constitution in part diverge from what are traditionally considered to be the *maqasid al-sharia*, namely the preservation of faith, life, intellect, property, and lineage.[71] Fourth, it is also unclear what effects this provision will have on the Tunisian legal system. While according to some commentators this article could open the door for the creation of a theocratic state (also in the light of the fact that the 2022 constitution no longer defines Tunisia as a "civil" state, as the 2014 constitution did in Article 2),[72] others believe that this provision would not place the state in a subordinate position with respect to religion, but would rather make it the true interpreter of the divine will, allowing it to identify the goals of Islam.[73]

Tunisia represents a special case in the Arab region also because it is one of the very few countries in which freedom of conscience is expressly recognized in the constitution. Freedom of conscience was first proclaimed in the 1959 constitution (Article 5), was subsequently maintained in the 2014 constitution (Article 6), and can now be found in the 2022 constitution (Article 27). Its recognition, however, proved to be extremely problematic during the process that led to the adoption of the 2014 constitution. Indeed, the first three draft constitutions only guaranteed freedom of belief and the practice of religious rituals. The absence

[69] See Siraj Khan, "A Comparative Analysis of the Draft Constitutions of Tunisia 2022: Zero-Sum Games," *Konrad Adenauer Stiftung – Rule of Law Programme Middle East and North Africa* (July 2022), 13, www.kas.de/documents/265308/22468903/A+Comparative+Analysis+of+the+Draft+Constitutions+of+Tunisia+2022+Zero-Sum+Games.pdf/4a68ee42-6ca4-31b2-78f2-4aeccca3e3b4?version=1.0&t=1674460240919

[70] See in greater detail Chapter 1, Section 1.2.1.2.

[71] See Khan, "Comparative Analysis," at pp. 12–15.

[72] See Nidhal Mekki, "The Project of the President's Constitution: Is It Time to Close the Democratic Parenthesis in Tunisia?," *ConstitutionNet* (July 25, 2022), https://constitutionnet.org/news/project-presidents-constitution-it-time-close-democratic-parenthesis-tunisia

[73] On this debate, see Nathan J. Brown, "L'État C'est Qaïs," *Malcolm H. Kerr – Carnegie Middle East Center* (July 13, 2022), https://carnegie-mec.org/diwan/87496; Sharan Grewal, Salah-Dean Satouri and Ian DeHaven, "Tunisia's New Constitution Will Only Worsen Its Political Crisis," *The Brookings Institution* (July 6, 2022), www.brookings.edu/blog/order-from-chaos/2022/07/06/tunisias-new-constitution-will-only-worsen-its-political-crisis/

of freedom of conscience was heavily criticized by secularists, both outside and within the Constituent Assembly.[74] Following debates among the political parties represented in the Assembly, freedom of conscience was introduced into the fourth draft constitution of June 1, 2013, and was subsequently retained in the final 2014 constitution.

During the 2011–2014 constituent process, the religious cleavage between Islamists and secularists also concerned the proposal made by Ennahda to introduce the crime of blasphemy into the Criminal Code and the Constitution, with the aim of safeguarding the Islamic identity of Tunisia. However, following strong opposition from the secular parties and large segments of the population, this proposal was eventually abandoned.[75] Another extremely controversial point that emerged at the very end of the drafting process concerned the interdiction on *takfir*, which refers to the "pronouncement that someone is an unbeliever (*kafir*) and no longer Muslim."[76] One of the socialist members of the Constituent Assembly, Monji Rahoui, had proposed that Article 1 of the constitution be amended so as to expressly proclaim Islam as the religion of the people, rather than the religion of the state. In response to this proposal, Habib El-Louz, one of the most prominent Ennahda members, stated that Rahoui was an unbeliever and an enemy of Islam. Ennahda immediately released a statement distancing itself from the statement made by El-Louz, stressing that this was not the official position of the party. This episode provoked anger among many secular members of the Constituent Assembly, who requested (and obtained) the introduction of a provision prohibiting *takfir*.[77]

It proved to be extremely complicated to arrive at a compromise between the religious and secular components of the Tunisian Constituent Assembly. The most evident example of these difficulties is represented by the final version of Article 6 of the 2014 constitution, which has been defined as a "constitutional *pot-pourri*, proclaiming one thing and also its opposite."[78] This Article provided as follows:

> The state is the guardian [*ra'iya*] of religion. It guarantees freedom of belief [*mu'taqad*] and conscience [*damir*], the free exercise of religious practices [*mumarasat al-sha'a'ir al-diniyya*] and ensures the neutrality of mosques and places of worship from all partisan instrumentalization. The state undertakes to disseminate the values of moderation and tolerance and the protection of the sacred [*muqaddasat*], and the prohibition of all violations thereof. It undertakes likewise to prohibit and combat calls for *takfir* and the incitement of violence and hatred.

74 See, for example, Abdelwahab Meddeb, "Une constitution inacceptable," *Leaders* (April 27, 2013), www.leaders.com.tn/article/11300-abdelwahab-meddeb-une-constitution-inacceptable

75 See Abbiate, "Cross-cutting Issue," at pp. 286–287.

76 John L. Esposito, "Takfir" in *The Oxford Dictionary of Islam* (Oxford University Press 2003), www.oxfordreference.com/display/10.1093/acref/9780195125580.001.0001/acref-9780195125580-e-2319

77 See Longo, "L'Islam nella nuova Costituzione," at pp. 114–115; Pickard, "Al-Nahda," at p. 22.

78 Ben Achour, *Tunisie: Une révolution en pays d'Islam*, at p. 357.

This provision raised a number of sensitive questions. For example, does the expression "The state is the guardian of religion" mean that all religions are protected by the state, or only Islam? What does the "sacred" (*muqaddasat*, literally "the sacred things," with plural form) consist in? How can the prohibition on *takfir* be balanced with freedom of expression (recognized by Article 31)? As was easily predictable, no definite answers were offered to these questions during the period 2014–2022, when the 2014 constitution was in force.

The 2022 constitution still guarantees freedom of belief, conscience, and worship (Articles 27 and 28) and has removed the most controversial provisions contained in the previous Article 6. Thus, for example, it no longer refers to the role of the state as the "guardian of the religion" and to the state's responsibility to protect the "sacred" and to fight "against calls for *takfir*." However, the new constitutional text still contains some contradictory provisions. One need only consider the contradiction (which could already be found in the 2014 constitution) between, on the one hand, the provision stipulating that the president of the Republic must be a Muslim (Article 88) and, on the other hand, the provisions guaranteeing freedom of conscience (Article 27) and the equality of all citizens before the law without any discrimination (Article 23).[79]

Over the past few years, the Tunisian courts have issued some interesting judgments in the field of religious freedom, displaying a remarkable degree of openness. In 2017, for example, the Court of First Instance of El Kef stated that the best interest of the child does not necessarily entail the child being brought up in the Islamic faith. Other factors – related to his/her physical and psychological well-being – are more important. Furthermore, the Court invoked the child's freedom of conscience (guaranteed in the constitution), rejecting the principle according to which a child whose father is Muslim must necessarily embrace the Islamic religion. For these reasons, the Court decided to award custody of the children to a mother whose second husband was a non-Muslim.[80]

In 2018, the Court of First Instance of Tunis became the second court in the Arab world (after the Court of Appeals in Beirut, Lebanon)[81] to recognize gender reassignment by allowing the applicant, who had undergone surgery abroad, to change

[79] A provision stipulating that the president of the Republic must be Muslim can also be found in the constitutions of Syria (Article 3) and Algeria (Article 87).

[80] Court of First Instance of El Kef, case no. 44801 (December 12, 2017). For a comment on this judgment, see Imen Gallala-Arndt, "Tracing Tunisian Case Law on Freedom of Religion, Equality and Islamic Law" in Anja Schoeller-Schletter and Robert Poll (eds.), *Balancing Individual Rights, Religious Law and Equality: Landmark Decisions From Egypt, Kuwait and Tunisia* (Konrad Adenauer Stiftung – Rule of Law Programme Middle East and North Africa) (April 2021), 39ff., www.kas.de/documents/265308/265357/Balancing+Inidividual+Rights%2C+Religious+Law+and+Equality.pdf/5e4cd2b6-372f-f15e-f462-23cdeb1e9a3a?version=1.0&t=1617987215625

[81] See Anealla Şafdar, "Transgender Ruling in Lebanon An 'Empowering' Moment," *Al Jazeera* (February 6, 2016), www.aljazeera.com/features/2016/2/6/transgender-ruling-in-lebanon-an-empowering-moment

sex and name in the civil registry. The Court relied on international law, foreign law, and foreign case law, as well as on *fiqh*. Indeed, although gender reassignment is usually prohibited, Islamic scholars agree that "exigency suspends prohibitions." The Court ruled that the change of gender was not capricious, but had been dictated specifically by a real exigency.[82]

Currently, very few non-Muslims live in Tunisia. The Jewish community, for example, was approximately 30,000 in 1962, whereas now there are only between 1,500 and 1,600 Jews remaining in the country, most of whom live in and around Tunis, as well as on the island of Djerba and in the neighboring town of Zarzis.[83] The few synagogues that are still open bear witness to the particular importance of the Jewish-Tunisian heritage, as "the history of Jews of Tunisia is inseparable from national history."[84] As regards the Christian community, the Ministry of Religious Affairs estimates that there are approximately 30,000 Christians, most of whom are foreigners[85] (mainly Europeans and [as discussed earlier] migrants from Sub-Saharan Africa).[86] Jews and Christians are generally allowed to worship freely and the government provides security for their religious services, even though services and processions outside places of worship are generally not allowed (with a few exceptions).[87] The construction of new churches and the ringing of church bells are prohibited.[88] Proselytism is not prohibited, although the law criminalizes forced conversions. Over the past few years, the number of Muslim converts to Christianity has risen, but because of the violence and ostracism that these individuals have to face from their families and society at large, they often keep their conversions secret.[89]

It should be noted that in Tunisia – and in many other Arab countries – the persistence of the conversion as a social taboo is also related to colonialism. For a long time, Christianity was considered an internal affair of the French/European

82 Court of First Instance of Tunis, Judgment no. 12304 (July 9, 2018). For a comment on this decision, see Gallala-Arndt, "Tracing Tunisian Case Law," at p. 42ff.

83 See Castellino and Cavanaugh, *Minority Rights*, at p. 99.

84 Abdelkrim Allagui, *Juifs et musulmans en Tunisie* (Tallandier 2016), 137.

85 See US Department of State – Office of International Religious Freedom, *2021 Report on International Religious Freedom: Tunisia* (June 2, 2022), www.state.gov/reports/2021-report-on-international-religious-freedom/tunisia/

86 On Christian migrants who decide to settle in Tunisia (and Morocco), see above Section 4.2.

87 For example, the tradition of the procession of the Virgin of Trapani used to take place in the streets of the town of La Goulette (near Tunis) on August 15 of every year until the end of the Fifties. This celebration was resumed on August 15, 2017, but in a less visible way, in the interior courtyard of the church. See Antonino Cusumano, "Una Madonna di frontiera, tra la Sicilia e la Tunisia" (2020) 44 *Dialoghi mediterranei*, www.istitutoeuroarabo.it/DM/una-madonna-di-frontiera-tra-la-sicilia-e-la-tunisia/

88 See US Department of State – Office of International Religious Freedom, *2021 Report on International Religious Freedom: Tunisia*.

89 Ibid. See also Open Doors International – World Watch Research, *Tunisia: Full Country Dossier* (January 2022), https://opendoorsanalytical.org/wp-content/uploads/2022/01/Tunisia-Full-Country-Dossier-January-2022-revised.pdf; Katia Boissevain, "Algeria and Tunisia" in Ross, Tadros and Johnson (eds.) 2018, *Christianity*, at p. 45ff.

community. This contributed to the creation of a "causal link between Christianity and colonialism"[90] which is still present in the collective memory of Tunisian people. The idea is that "every Christian can only be a foreigner and every Tunisian is 'naturally' Muslim."[91] Thus, these conversions are seen as operating a "gap in the perfect correspondence between Islam and *tunisianité* [creating a] disjunction between religion and nationality."[92]

4.2.2 *Egypt*

During the post-2011 constituent processes in the Arab region, what usually generated debate and controversy was *what* the constitution should say about Islam and *sharia* – for example, the recognition or nonrecognition of Islam as the state religion (as occurred in Tunisia) or, more frequently, the inclusion or noninclusion of a *sharia* clause (as occurred, again, in Tunisia), or the type of *sharia* clause that should be included (as occurred in Libya). It was only in a few cases that debate revolved around *who* had the authority to speak for Islam and to interpret *sharia*. This was, for example, the case of Egypt. Indeed, in this country, the proclamation of Islam as the state religion (Article 2) was taken for granted, and even the presence of a *sharia* clause was not seriously debated (the original wording of Article 2 of the 1971 constitution was "principles of *sharia* are *a* main source of legislation" [emphasis added], whereas following the 1980 constitutional reform, principles of *sharia* became "the" main source of legislation, and this wording was confirmed both in the 2012 and 2014 constitutions).[93] Rather, it was the role played by the *institution responsible for interpreting sharia*, namely the Supreme Constitutional Court, that generated major divisions. It should be recalled that between 1980 (when the Court was set up) and 2012 (when the new constitution came into force), the Court took

90 Donia Saadi, "From Mosque to Church: What Challenges Face Tunisian Converts to Christianity," paper presented at the Roundtable on "The Effect of Religious Laws on Rights, Equality and non-Discrimination: Citizenship and Subsidiary Rights Affected by Religious Laws in the MENA Region," organized by the MENA Legal Network and the Konrad Adenauer Stiftung, Lebanon (July 26–27, 2023).

91 Ibid.

92 Katia Boissevain, "Le baptême adulte de chrétiens tunisiens: rituel public d'un engagement privé" (2014) *Cahiers d'études du religieux. Recherches interdisciplinaires* (online), special issue, https://journals.openedition.org/cerri/1408

93 During the process that led to the adoption of the 2012 constitution, one can recall the proposal made by the Salafists to replace the wording of Article 2 of the constitution from "principles of *sharia*" to "*sharia*" (see Bernard-Maugiron, *Droit contemporain des pays arabes*, at p. 672). One can also recall the proposal made by one member of the 2013 Constituent Assembly to change the wording "principles of *sharia* are *the* main source of legislation" to "principles of sharia are *a* source of legislation" (see Diana Serôdio, "Shaping Egypt's 2014 Constitution: Controversy and Negotiations" in Cornelis Hulsman (ed.), *The 2014 Egyptian Constitution: Perspectives from Egypt* (Tectum Verlag 2017), 59). The *sharia* clause, however, never became a serious issue of contention during the constitution-making processes.

the view, in the light of Article 2 (which stipulated, as mentioned earlier, that "principles of *sharia* are the main source of legislation"), that Parliament was required to abide by *sharia* principles when drafting laws, and that any legislation at odds with these principles would have to be declared unconstitutional.[94] The Court also clarified that legislation could only be ruled unconstitutional on the basis of "absolute" principles of *sharia* (i.e., principles that are absolutely certain with respect to their authenticity and meaning), but not also due to "relative" principles (i.e., principles the authenticity and meaning of which are not certain). Moreover, legislation had to be consistent with the "aims/objectives" of *sharia* (*maqasid al-sharia*).[95] It is indicative that up until now only two provisions have been declared unconstitutional by the Court because of their contrast with Article 2.[96] It is also crucial to point out that, when interpreting *sharia* principles, the Court often "reflected liberal modernist sensibilities,"[97] thus promoting liberal values and the protection of human rights, including women's rights.[98] This approach can also be explained by the fact that the Court "refused to recognize supra-constitutional value to the principles of *sharia*," considering the constitution as an "organic unity" and "a coherent set of homogeneous and non-contradictory principles," and interpreting Article 2 "in the light of the other constitutional provisions."[99]

The Salafists, who were strongly opposed to this liberal understanding of Islam, imposed their view during the process that led to the adoption of the 2012 constitution, confirming the power of the Supreme Constitutional Court to review the compatibility of laws with *sharia* principles, while however limiting the possibility to interpret

94 See in particular case no. 20, Judicial Year 1 (May 4, 1985). In this ruling, the Court clarified that only laws adopted *after* the 1980 amendment of Article 2 of the constitution had to be consistent with the principles of *sharia*. Following this amendment, the principles of *sharia* ceased to be "a" main source of legislation and became "the" main source of legislation.

95 See case no. 7, Judicial Year 8 (May 15, 1993). See also case no. 8 of Judicial Year 17 (May 18, 1996), available in English in Nathan J. Brown and Clark B. Lombardi, "The Supreme Constitutional Court of Egypt on Islamic Law, Veiling and Civil Rights: An Annotated Translation of Supreme Constitutional Court of Egypt Case No. 8 of Judicial Year 17 (May 18, 1996)" (1996) 21 *American University International Law Review*, 437ff.

96 See Judgment no. 28/15 (December 5, 1998), and Judgment no. 113/26 (January 15, 2006). See Bernard-Maugiron, *Droit contemporain des pays arabes*, at p. 680.

97 Nathan J. Brown and Clark B. Lombardi, "Contesting Islamic Constitutionalism After the Arab Spring. Islam in Egypt's Post-Mubarak Constitutions" in Rainer Grote and Tilmann J. Röder (eds.), *Constitutionalism, Human Rights, and Islam after the Arab Spring* (Oxford University Press 2016), 254.

98 See "Constitutional Jurisprudence on Fundamental Rights: Digest of Selected Cases" in Kevin Boyle and Adel Omar Sherif (eds.), *Human Rights and Democracy: The Role of the Supreme Constitutional Court of Egypt* (Kluwer Law International 1996), 229ff.; Clark B. Lombardi, "Egypt's Supreme Constitutional Court: Managing Constitutional Conflict in an Authoritarian, Aspirationally 'Islamic' State" (2008) 3 *Journal of Comparative Law*, 246–249; Tamir Moustafa, *The Struggle for Constitutional Power: Law, Politics, and Economic Development in Egypt* (Cambridge University Press 2007), 178ff.; Ran Hirschl, *Constitutional Theocracy* (Harvard University Press 2010), 105ff.; Ciro Sbailò, *Principi sciaraitici e organizzazione dello spazio pubblico nel mondo islamico: Il caso egiziano* (CEDAM 2012), 214ff.

99 Bernard-Maugiron, *Droit contemporain des pays arabes*, at p. 680.

these principles in a modernist fashion. Indeed, the 2012 constitution maintained the same wording as Article 2, while also including a new provision laying down a specific definition of *sharia* principles, namely Article 219, which stipulated that "The principles of Islamic *sharia* include comprehensive evidences [*al-adilla al-kulliyya*], methodological rules [*al-qawa'id usuliyya*], jurisprudential rules [*al-qawa'id fiqhiyya*], as well as the reliable sources according to the Sunni schools of jurisprudence [*madhahib*]." The aim of this article was to force the Court to depart from its previous jurisprudence and adopt a more traditional interpretation of Islam. Furthermore, again in an attempt to constrain the interpretative authority of the Court, the constitution introduced a new provision (Article 4), stipulating a requirement to consult Al-Azhar in matters relating to *sharia*.[100] The Constitutional Court issued only one judgment concerning the implementation of Article 2 under the 2012 constitution. The decision was issued on June 2, 2013, just one month before the constitution was suspended. Interestingly, the Court applied Article 2 on the basis of its previous jurisprudence, without making any reference to Article 219 and without seeking Al-Azhar's advice.[101]

The 2012 constitution was short-lived, as it was suspended in July 2013 following the fall of President Morsi, and it was replaced by a new constitution in January 2014. Only two Islamists were represented in the fifty-member Constituent Assembly, with the consequence that liberals were able to re-establish the authority of the Supreme Constitutional Court to interpret *sharia*. Indeed, the framers maintained the wording of Article 2, but eliminated Article 219, did not confirm the consultative role of Al-Azhar, and included within the preamble a provision stating that in defining the principles of *sharia*, "the point of reference for the interpretation thereof is the relevant texts in the collected rulings of the Supreme Constitutional Court."[102]

The status and rights of non-Muslims were also heavily debated during constitution-making processes. This was due especially to the fact that Egypt hosts the largest Christian community in the Arab world. The vast majority of its members belong to the Coptic Orthodox Church, which is currently led by Pope Tawadros II. Due to a lack of definite and reliable demographic data, estimates of the number of Egyptian Christians vary significantly. Official governmental statistics refer to Copts as composing 6 percent of the population, whereas church leaders refer to much higher numbers. Ten percent is the most commonly used figure in news coverage of Egypt.[103] The 2012 constitution introduced a provision stipulating that "[t]he principles of the laws of Egyptian Christians and Jews are the main source of legislation regulating their personal status, religious affairs, and selection of spiritual

[100] See Brown and Lombardi, "Contesting Islamic Constitutionalism," at pp. 255–258.

[101] Judgment of June 2, 2013, no. 41. See Nathalie Bernard-Maugiron, "La place du religieux dans le processus constitutionnel en Égypte après 2011" (2018) 181 *Archives de sciences sociales des religions*, 53–54.

[102] See Brown and Lombardi, "Contesting Islamic Constitutionalism," at pp. 255–258.

[103] See Michael Wahid Hanna, "Excluded and Unequal. Copts on the Margins of the Egyptian Security State," *The Century Foundation* (May 9, 2019), https://tcf.org/content/report/christian-exclusion-from-egypts-security-state/#easy-footnote-bottom-2

leaders" (Article 3). The introduction of this provision, which represented a concession made by Islamists in order to make up for the numerous references to Islam and *sharia*,[104] attracted harsh criticism on the grounds that it would complicate the legal status of other religious denominations, including for example the Baha'is.[105] Upon request by the leaders of the various churches, this provision was retained in the 2014 constitution (Article 3), although some members of the Constituent Assembly proposed that its scope be expanded to cover all non-Muslims.[106] Interestingly, some Coptic associations objected to the inclusion of this article, stating that it would grant too much authority to churches over their followers, and that a reference to general Egyptian law – which is more flexible than Christian laws in relation to the dissolution of marriage – would be preferable.[107]

The preferential treatment (compared to other non-Muslims) for the People of the Book was also confirmed in other constitutional provisions. On the one hand, both the 2012 constitution (Article 43) and the 2014 constitution (Article 64) recognize freedom of belief (*hurriyyat al-i'tiqad*): This freedom is considered "inviolable" in the 2012 constitution and "absolute" in the 2014 constitution. On the other hand, however, both constitutional texts grant the freedom to practice religious rituals and to establish places of worship only to the followers of the "heavenly religions" or "divinely revealed religions" (*al-adyan al-samawiyya*; *religions célestes*), namely Islam, Christianity, and Judaism (the Abrahamic religions) (Article 43 of the 2012 constitution and Article 64 of the 2014 constitution). Therefore, these followers are the only ones who are allowed to practice their religious rituals in public.[108] The constituent debates show that, despite some critical voices (especially within the fifty-member Constituent Assembly that drafted the 2014 constitution), most framers wished to exclude other religious denominations, particularly the Baha'is.[109] The conditions for the followers of this religion are still particularly difficult, as they continue to be discriminated against on various grounds.[110] A serious problem concerns cemeteries. A few years ago, the members of the Baha'i community had requested

[104] See Nathalie Bernard-Maugiron, "La constitution égyptienne de 2014: quelle réforme constitutionnelle pour l'Égypte?" (2015) 103 *Revue française de droit constitutionnel*, 528.

[105] See Bassem Sabry, "Problems Ahead For Egypt Constitution Debate," *Al Monitor* (September 30, 2013), www.al-monitor.com/pulse/ar/originals/2013/09/egypt-constitution-highlights-new-draft.html

[106] See Bernard-Maugiron, "La constitution égyptienne de 2014," at p. 528.

[107] Ibid., at pp. 528–529.

[108] See Diana Serôdio, "A Comparison of the 2012 and 2014 Constitutions" in Hulsman (ed.) 2017, *2014 Egyptian Constitution*, at p. 77.

[109] See Mohamed Gamal Ali, "Exclusively for Adherents of 'Divinely Revealed' Religions?! How Did the Preparatory Work for the Egyptian Constitutions Discuss Issues of Freedom of Religion and Belief?," *Religioni, diritti ed economie nello spazio mediterraneo* (REDESM) (September 26, 2022), www.redesm.org/2022/09/26/exclusively-for-adherents-of-divinely-revealed-religions-how-did-the-preparatory-work-for-the-egyptian-constitutions-discuss-issues-of-freedom-of-religion-and-belief/

[110] See Amr Ezzat, "The Fundamental Rights of Baha'is: An Excellent Opportunity to Expand Religious Freedom in Egypt," *Egyptian Initiative for Personal Rights* (January 4, 2022), https://eipr.org/en/blog/amr-ezzat/2022/01/fundamental-rights-baha'-excellent-opportunity-expand-religious-freedom-egypt

that the Alexandria Governorate allocate a piece of land to be used as a burial site for its members because, currently, only a single cemetery space in Cairo is available to the followers of this religious denomination. This has resulted in the depletion of the cemetery's capacity and forced families of deceased Baha'is to transport their loved ones' remains to Cairo from all across the country. However, the Alexandria authorities rejected the request, arguing that they did not have authority to allocate cemetery space. On December 21, 2021, the Administrative Court of Alexandria ruled that the Governorate was not forced to allocate a piece of land to be used by the Baha'is as a burial site, stating that the Egyptian state recognizes only Islam, Judaism, and Christianity as religions and that the Baha'is are not recognized as a religious denomination. The judgment delivered by the Administrative Court of Alexandria was then upheld, on December 20, 2022, by the Appeals Examination Circuit of the Supreme Administrative Court.[111]

This strict interpretation of religious freedom – which is the norm in the Arab world – has been very much influenced by a landmark judgment issued by the Egyptian Supreme Court in 1975:

> The preparatory works for Articles 12 and 13 of the 1923 Constitution, which were drawn on by previous constitutions, show that the constitutional protection for freedom of worship enshrined in these articles only applies to the three religions of the book, and this upon condition that the practice of worship does not cause any disruption to public order, which is largely comprised of Islamic law. The practice of Bahaism does not thus fall within the scope of this constitutional protection, because on the one hand Bahaism cannot be considered as one of these three religions and on the other hand the practice of Bahaism can cause problems for public order within a Muslim country.[112]

It should be noted that the framers of the 2014 constitution provided additional protection for Christian minorities. In particular, they introduced a transitional provision (Article 235), which stipulates that, during its first legislative term after the entry into force of the constitution, the House of Representatives must issue a law concerning the construction and renovation of churches in order to guarantee Christians the freedom to practice their religious rituals. This law, which was passed by Parliament on August 30, 2016, has been criticized because it still imposes various restrictions that are likely to continue to discriminate against Christians.[113] These

[111] See George Sadek, *Egypt: Supreme Administrative Court Rejects Petition to Obligate Local Administrative Authorities to Allocate Burial Site for Baha'i Religious Minority*, Library of Congress (January 25, 2023), www.loc.gov/item/global-legal-monitor/2023-01-24/egypt-supreme-administrative-court-rejects-petition-to-obligate-local-administrative-authorities-to-allocate-burial-site-for-bahai-religious-minority/

[112] Supreme Court of Egypt, case no. 7, Judicial Year no. 2 (March 1, 1975), cited in Ayman Mohamed-Afify, "La Constitution égyptienne de 2014: entre traditions et tendances révolutionnaires" (2015) 101 *Revue française de droit constitutionnel*, 136.

[113] See "Egypt: New Church Law Discriminates Against Christians," *Human Rights Watch* (September 15, 2016), www.hrw.org/news/2016/09/15/egypt-new-church-law-discriminates-against-christians

restrictions concerning the construction and renovation of churches have thus far been the norm in Egypt, despite some court rulings upholding the right to build places of worship for Christians. For example, in a well-known judgment issued in 1952, the Supreme Administrative Court, presided over by 'Abd al-Raziq al-Sanhuri, ruled that the stipulations for granting permission for the establishment of places of worship

> should not be used as a pretext to pose unjustified obstacles that hinder the establishment of such places, since such a practice would violate the freedom of performing religious rites. The permission mandated by the [firman] was not intended to be used to hinder the performance of religious rites, but to ensure that the places of worship are established in a respectable environment that fits the dignity and purity of the religious practices and does not cause any friction with other religious communities. Within these reasonable parameters, the permission should be granted. Furthermore, legislation should be promulgated to stipulate and simplify the requirements for establishing a place of worship. Once the requirements are met, the permission should be granted within a timeframe to be specified by the legislator. Since the permission was not granted within the specified timeframe, the applicant was free to establish the place of worship applied for.[114]

However, the principles enunciated in this ruling have only been respected in a few cases. The practice has been to *hinder*, rather than facilitate, the construction or renovation of places of worship for Christians.

The 2019 amendments to the 2014 constitution strengthened the representation of Christians in Parliament. Indeed, Article 244, as originally worded, stated that Christians (together with other categories of people, including, for example, young persons and people with disabilities) must be granted "appropriate representation" in the first House of Representatives to be elected after the adoption of the constitution. The 2019 amendments eliminated this temporary requirement, making "appropriate representation" (which is specifically regulated by Law no. 46 of 2014) a permanent fixture of the lower house. As far as the representation of Christians in public institutions is concerned, it should also be noted that, for the first time in the history of this institution, a Christian – Bolis Fahmy Eskandar – was appointed as President of the Supreme Constitutional Court in February 2022.[115]

Over the last few years, the Egyptian courts have issued some judgments that have been particularly favorable to Christians. In 2017, for example, the Supreme

[114] Supreme Administrative Court, case no. 6510, Judicial Year no. 5 (December 16, 1952), cited in Nabil Abdel Fattah, "The Political Role of the Egyptian Judiciary" in Nathalie Bernard-Maugiron (ed.), *Judges and Political Reform in Egypt* (The American University in Cairo Press 2008), 80.

[115] See "Egypt Appoints First Christian President of Supreme Constitutional Court," *Daily News Egypt* (February 9, 2022), https://dailynewsegypt.com/2022/02/09/egypt-appoints-first-christian-president-of-supreme-constitutional-court/

Constitutional Court granted Coptic civil servants the right to paid leave of one month in order to make a pilgrimage to the holy city of Al-Quds (Jerusalem), in the same way as Muslim civil servants have the right to paid leave of thirty days for the pilgrimage to Mecca (*hajj*).[116] In this decision, the Court relied extensively on constitutional history, emphasizing that since the 1923 constitution, all Egyptian constitutional texts have consistently recognized both the principle of equality before the law and freedom of belief. According to the Court, the law cannot discriminate without justification among the followers of different religions. On the other hand, however, the Court pointed out that, although the 2014 constitution no longer refers to the need to respect public order and morals while practicing religious rituals, this requirement still needs to be respected: "It is obvious and self-evident in the Constitution and shall be enforced even if the text lacks it." In Egypt and in many other Arab countries, the notions of public order and morals are often invoked by state authorities to justify restrictions to fundamental rights and freedoms (including religious freedom).[117]

Egyptian courts also recently ruled that Christian law must be applied in matters of inheritance involving Christians. A very innovative decision was issued on November 24, 2019, by the seventh circuit of the Helwan Family Court of Personal Matters – Guardianship.[118] The point of contention regarded the fact that an inheritance had been distributed in accordance with *sharia*, according to which the son's share of the inheritance must be twice that of the daughter's. However, the deceased and his heirs were Copts, and the defendants did not object to the application of Christian law, which gives the same inheritance rights to both men and women. The applicant also referred to Article 3 of the 2014 constitution, which gives Christians the right to apply principles of the Christian law in their personal matters. The Court ruled in favor of the applicant, applying the relevant articles of the Coptic Orthodox regulation and of the constitution.[119] A similar decision had been made three years earlier, in 2016, when the Cairo Court of Appeal applied the Coptic Orthodox regulation concerning matters of inheritance.[120] These rulings are extremely important because they represent a clean break with the past, when Egyptian courts – relying on the case law of the Court of Cassation – applied the *sharia* law concerning matters of inheritance to both Muslims and non-Muslims on public order grounds.[121]

116 Case no. 153, Judicial Year 32 (February 4, 2017). For a comment of this decision, see Yussef Auf, "Equality in the Jurisprudence of the Supreme Constitutional Court of Egypt" in Schoeller-Schletter and Poll (eds.) 2021, *Balancing Individual Rights*, at pp. 6–8.

117 On the (ab)use of the notion of public order by Egyptian courts in order to limit religious freedom, see Bernard-Maugiron, *Droit contemporain des pays arabes*, at pp. 856–859.

118 Case no. 3743 (November 24, 2019).

119 See Eman Muhammad Rashwan and Ahmad Ali Lotief, "Egypt" in Richard Albert et al. (eds.), *2019 Global Review of Constitutional Law* (ICONnect – Clough Center 2020), 109.

120 Ibid., at pp. 109–110.

121 Ibid., at p. 109.

Despite the developments mentioned earlier, the condition of Christians remains particularly difficult, as they continue to be victims of harsh discrimination. This discrimination manifests itself in many ways, such as

> in the near-complete exclusion of Copts from positions of authority in the government, with Coptic representation in the military and police forces capped at an unofficial 1% and completely denied in the intelligence service. This is also true in other sectors of the state bureaucracy, including the complete exclusion of Copts from university leadership positions such as presidents and deans. State discriminatory policies are also evident in the near-complete exclusion of Coptic history from the educational system and the absence of Copts and their interests from the state-controlled media.[122]

Furthermore, over the past few years, there have been numerous terrorist attacks against Christians, and their places of worship have also been frequently attacked, especially on Christian holy days. In some cases, girls have been kidnapped by Islamist extremists with the aim of forcing them to marry Muslims.[123] More generally, "the lack of serious law enforcement and the unwillingness of local authorities to protect Christians leave them vulnerable to all kinds of attacks, especially in Upper Egypt."[124]

4.2.3 *Morocco*

While in Egypt, all three Religions of the Book have been expressly recognized and granted special status, in Morocco, the 2011 constitution recognizes only Islam and Judaism as components of the national religious identity, leaving out Christianity. Indeed, the preamble stipulates that Morocco, a "sovereign Muslim State," is "forged by the convergence of its Arab-Islamist, Berber and Saharan-Hassanic components, nourished and enriched by its African, Andalusian, *Hebraic* and Mediterranean influences" (emphasis added). Remarkably, one of the closest advisors to King Mohammed VI is a Jew, André Azoulay, who also served as an advisor to King Hassan II.[125] This special status granted to Jews – which can be explained

122 Samuel Tadros, "Egypt" in Ross, Tadros and Johnson (eds.) 2018, *Christianity*, at p. 76.

123 See Harriet Sherwood, "Christians in Egypt Face Unprecedented Persecution, Report Says," *The Guardian* (January 18, 2018), www.theguardian.com/world/2018/jan/10/christians-egypt-unprecedented-persecution-report; US Department of State – Office of International Religious Freedom, *2021 Report on International Religious Freedom: Egypt* (June 2, 2022), www.state.gov/reports/2021-report-on-international-religious-freedom/egypt/; "Dossier Copti" (June 2017) *Missioni Consolata*, 35ff.

124 Open Doors International – World Watch Research, *Egypt: Full Country Dossier* (January 2022), 6, https://opendoorsanalytical.org/wp-content/uploads/2022/01/Egypt-Full-Country-Dossier-Revised-24-January-2022.pdf

125 In an interview given in 2007, Mr. Azoulay said that "I am part of a very snobbish club, I am its only member. From Mauritania to Central Asia, in no other Muslim country you will find a person of Jewish faith with such a responsibility. I am very proud of my King and my people." See Cecilia Zecchinelli, "L'ebreo del Marocco che cerca i Giusti fra gli islamici," *Il Corriere della Sera* (November 4, 2007), 14.

by their historical presence in the country[126] – had already been provided for in the Code on Personal Status, namely the *Moudawana* (as reformed in 2004). Indeed, Article 2 states that "Moroccans of Jewish faith shall be governed by the provisions of the Hebraic Moroccan Family Law." These rules are enforced by Hebrew personal status chambers within the ordinary courts, formed by rabbis. However,

> there are now only two courts, in Casablanca with five judges and in Tangier with one judge, which decide an average of one hundred to two hundred cases per year, mainly inheritance cases. The judges are civil servants of the Ministry of Justice, but must be trained in Israel, and they render their decisions in Arabic, in the name of the King.[127]

Article 3 of the Royal Decree promulgating the Moroccan Nationality Code provides that the *Moudawana* applies to all Moroccans (with the exception of Moroccan Jews, who are subject to their own rules on personal status), and that the following rules only apply to Moroccans who are neither Muslims nor Jews: (1) polygamy is prohibited; (2) the rules governing breastfeeding do not apply; and (3) a decree of divorce may only be issued by a judicial authority following an attempt at conciliation between the parties and an inquiry into the grounds for the petition for divorce. This means, for example, that Moroccan Christians and Baha'is are not allowed to marry according to their own religious rites. Rather, they must follow the provisions of the *Moudawana*, which is largely inspired by *sharia*.[128] Obviously, this situation has raised discontent among Christians and Baha'is, who feel severely discriminated against.

One of the most sensitive debates throughout the process that led to the adoption of the 2011 Moroccan Constitution – which still proclaims that Islam is the state religion (Article 3) and lacks a *sharia* clause – concerned the formulation of the provision on religious freedom. Initially, the Commission on Constitutional Reform had proposed introducing a clause guaranteeing freedom of conscience. However, the Islamist Justice and Development Party strongly opposed the introduction of this

[126] Morocco has hosted one of the most important Jewish communities in the Arab world, especially before the birth of the State of Israel in 1948. Part of the literature has stressed that Muslims and Jews peacefully coexisted in Morocco (see, e.g., Taha Tayebi, "Religious Minorities in the Sherifian Kingdom of Morocco: Change and Lack of Change" in Hamza Tayebi and Jochen Lobah (eds.), *Dynamics of Inclusion and Exclusion in the MENA Region: Minorities, Subalternity, and Resistance* (Hanns Seidel Foundation 2019), 133), whereas other authors have emphasized that Jews were severely discriminated and persecuted (see, e.g., Bensoussan, *Les Juifs du monde arabe*). Currently, according to Jewish community leaders, there are an estimated 2,000 to 3,500 Jews in the country. See US Department of State – Office of International Religious Freedom, 2021 *Report on International Religious Freedom: Morocco* (June 2, 2022), www.state.gov/reports/2021-report-on-international-religious-freedom/morocco/

[127] Bernard-Maugiron, *Droit contemporain des pays arabes*, at p. 518.

[128] See "Au Maroc, des chrétiens se battent pour que leur mariage soit reconnu par les autorités," *Info Chrétienne* (June 12, 2018), www.infochretienne.com/maroc-chretiens-se-battent-mariage-soit-reconnu-autorites/

article, threatening to vote against the new constitution in the popular referendum. Indeed, in the eyes of the Islamists, this would have represented an attack on Morocco's Islamic identity. In the light of this virulent opposition, the provision on freedom of conscience was abandoned and the old formula, which only grants freedom of worship (*hurriyya mumarasa al-shaai'r al-diniyya*; *libre exercice des cultes*) to all people (Article 3), was retained.[129]

In the years following the adoption of the 2011 constitution, the issue of apostasy was addressed in two important pronouncements of the Higher Oulema Council, which according to the constitution is the only body empowered to issue officially approved religious opinions (Article 41). In 2012, the Council issued a *fatwa* in which it argued, relying on classic arguments of the Islamic tradition, that a Muslim who changes his or her religion should be punished by death. Five years later, in 2017, the Council issued a diametrically opposed opinion, arguing that apostasy no longer merited the death penalty. The Council explained that the Prophet's *hadith* that "whoever changes his religion, kill him" had to be understood in the context of seventh-century Arabia, which was characterized by conflicts between Muslims and non-Muslim groups. Thus, apostasy entailed the *betrayal* of one's community. In the words of the Council: "the killing of the apostate is meant for the traitor of the group, the one disclosing secrets, [...] the equivalent of *treason in international law*" (emphasis added).[130] This interpretation of apostasy seems to be more in line with the spirit of the 2011 constitution, as well as the vision of King Mohammed VI. The constitution places great emphasis on the notion of a "moderate" Islam (preamble and Article 1(3)), and the Monarch, who is the Commander of the Faithful (*Amir al-Mouminine*) and "guarantor of freedom of worship" (Article 41), has repeatedly expressed his willingness to protect religious freedom and religious minorities.[131] For example, in a speech given in 2016 during the conference held in Marrakesh on the "Marrakesh Declaration on the Rights of Religious Minorities in Muslim-Majority Lands,"[132] the king stressed that he is the Commander of *all* the Faithful: "As *Amir al-Mouminine* [...], we are responsible for preserving the rights of Muslims and non-Muslims without distinction between them."

However, the situation in the country remains very problematic for non-Muslims, including Christians. For example, the authorities continue to deny Moroccan citizens the right to Christian or civil marriage and funeral services, as well as the right to establish churches. Furthermore, even though apostasy is not a crime, proselytism is punishable by law, as the Criminal Code criminalizes "anyone who employs

[129] See Abdellah Tourabi, "Constitutional Reform in Morocco: Reform in Times of Revolution," *Arab Reform Initiative* (November 2011), 9ff., www.arab-reform.net/en/node/526

[130] See Anne-Bénédicte Hoffner, "Au Maroc, les apostats ne sont plus passibles de la peine de mort," *La Croix* (February 8, 2017), www.la-croix.com/Religion/Islam/Au-Maroc-apostats-sont-plus-passibles-peine-mort-2017-02-08-1200823368

[131] See Tayebi, "Religious Minorities," at p. 134ff.

[132] In this chapter, see Section 4.4.2.4.

incitements to shake the faith of a Muslim or to convert him to another religion [...]" (Article 220).[133] As recalled earlier, over the past two decades, an increasing number of Christian migrants from Sub-Saharan Africa have settled in Morocco.[134]

4.2.4 *Jordan*

In Jordan, the 2011, 2014, 2016, and 2022 reforms did not affect any constitutional provisions on religion. Thus, the constitution still proclaims Islam as the state religion (Article 2), lacks a *sharia* clause, includes religion as one of the grounds on which discrimination is prohibited (Article 6(1)), and guarantees freedom of worship ("free exercise of all forms of worship and religious rites [*hurriyyat al-qiyam bi-sha'a'ir al-adyan*] in accordance with the customs observed in the kingdom, as long as these are consistent with public order or morality" [Article 14]). Furthermore, the constitution provides for civil courts, religious courts, and special courts, with religious courts divided into *sharia* courts and tribunals of the other religious communities that have been recognized by the government (Articles 104 and 108). Both *sharia* courts and the tribunals of the other religious communities have jurisdiction over personal status issues and apply the religious law of the respective religious community (Articles 105ff.).

Christians – who comprise around 2–3 percent of the population – make up the most numerous non-Muslim religious community in the country. Antoine Fleyfel argued that Jordan can be described, at least in part, as "the Kingdom of the happy Christians,"[135] stressing that Jordanian Christians live under better conditions compared to Christians living in most Arab countries.[136] On the one hand, it is true that Christians "enjoy a calm and stable existence"[137] and are granted special status in the political and institutional system. For example, according to the electoral law adopted in April 2022, they are allocated nine of the 138 parliamentary seats, not to mention the fact that they often hold positions in the government and in other public institutions (including for example the Constitutional Court). This can be explained by the fact that King Abdullah II has always promoted freedom of religion, the protection of religious minorities, and interfaith dialogue.[138] It is

[133] See US Department of State – Office of International Religious Freedom, *2021 Report on International Religious Freedom: Morocco*; Open Doors International – World Watch Research, *Morocco: Full Country Dossier* (January 2022), https://opendoorsanalytical.org/wp-content/uploads/2022/01/Morocco-Full-Country-Dossier-January-2022.pdf; Jack Wald, "Morocco and Western Sahara" in Ross, Tadros and Johnson (eds.) 2018, *Christianity*, at p. 41ff.

[134] See Section 4.2.

[135] Antoine Fleyfel, *Géopolitique des Chrétiens d'Orient: Défis et avenir des chrétiens arabes* (L'Harmattan 2014), 75.

[136] Ibid., at p. 94. On the conditions of Jordanian Christians, see also "Dossier Giordania" (November-December 2022) 6 *Terra Santa*, 27ff.

[137] Paulo Maggiolini and Iyad Twal, "Jordan" in Ross, Tadros and Johnson (eds.) 2018, *Christianity*, at p. 152.

[138] See, for example, the "Amman Message," the "Common Word Between Us and You" Letter, and the discussion paper on the "Rule of Law and Civil State" (see Section 4.4.2.1). Furthermore, on

emblematic that, in exercising the Custodianship over Holy Sites in Jerusalem, the Hashemite Monarch has not only safeguarded Islamic holy sites but also Christian holy sites. In 2016, for example, he donated funds to restore Christ's Tomb in the Church of the Holy Sepulcher in Jerusalem.[139]

On the other hand, however, Christians continue to experience various forms of discrimination, especially in employment.[140] Converts from Islam are those who face the most difficult conditions. Although apostasy is not punished by law,

> Some converts to Christianity from Islam continued to report ostracism as well as physical and verbal abuse from their families and communities, and some worshipped in secret due to the social stigma they faced. Some converts reported persistent threats of violence from family members concerned with protecting traditional honor. Religious leaders reported continued online hate speech directed towards religious minorities and moderates, frequently through social media.[141]

Furthermore, Jordanian Christians often have a *dhimma* mentality, which causes "excessive conformism and self-censorship," limits their presence in the public sphere, and favors "a passive acceptance of the positions of whoever intends to impose the logic of majority rule."[142]

Education is another very sensitive field. In 2016, for example, when authorities limited textbooks' Islamic content (e.g., including pictures of women without head coverings or significantly reducing the references to Quranic verses), major protests occurred in the country, as these changes were regarded as an attempt to alienate students from their Islamic values. Textbooks were even burnt as a sign of protest.[143]

It should also be noted that the government continues to deny official recognition to some religious groups, including Baha'is and Jehovah's Witnesses.[144]

March 29, 2019, at the Basilica of St. Francis, in Assisi, Italy, King Abdullah II of Jordan was awarded the "Lamp of Peace" for his efforts in human rights, peacebuilding, and inter-religious dialogue. See "Lamp of Peace Awarded in Assisi to King of Jordan," *Ansa.it* (March 29, 2019), www.ansa.it/ansamed/en/news/nations/italy/2019/03/29/lamp-of-peace-awarded-in-assisi-to-king-of-jordan_b132904f-8bd1-4fa2-b585-302ec9754cc8.html

139 See "Custodianship over Holy Sites," *King Abdullah II Official Webpage*, https://kingabdullah.jo/en/page/the-hashemites/custodianship-over-holy-sites

140 See Open Doors International – World Watch Research, *Jordan: Full Country Dossier* (December 2021), https://opendoorsanalytical.org/wp-content/uploads/2022/01/Jordan-Full-Country-Dossier-December-2021.pdf

141 US Department of State – Office of International Religious Freedom, *2021 Report on International Religious Freedom: Jordan* (June 2, 2022), www.state.gov/reports/2021-report-on-international-religious-freedom/jordan/

142 Maggiolini and Twal, "Jordan," at pp. 161–162.

143 See Diaa Hadid, "Jordan Tones Down Textbooks' Islamic Content, and Tempers Rise," *The New York Times* (October 14, 2016), www.nytimes.com/2016/10/15/world/middleeast/jordan-tones-down-textbooks-islamic-content-and-tempers-rise.html

144 See US Department of State – Office of International Religious Freedom, *2021 Report on International Religious Freedom: Jordan*.

4.2.5 *Algeria*

The constitution of Algeria proclaims Islam as the state religion (Article 2) and lacks a *sharia* clause. As in Morocco,[145] implicit references to the Islamic religion can be found in the constitutional provisions referring to "national constants." Thus, for example, Article 34(2) (as amended following the 2020 constitutional reform) provides that no restriction of rights and freedoms may be imposed except "for reasons related to [...] the protection of national constants [*al-thawabit al-wataniyya*]." It must also be stressed that the original version of this constitutional text, adopted in 1996, guaranteed freedom of *conscience*, and this freedom was also maintained in the constitutional reforms of 2008 and 2016. However, following the latest reform of 2020, freedom of conscience is no longer proclaimed in the Algerian Constitution. The new Article 51 only guarantees freedom of *worship*: "Freedom of opinion shall be inviolable. Freedom of worship [*hurriyya mumarasat al-'ibada*; *liberté d'exercice des cultes*] shall be guaranteed and exercised in compliance with the law. The State shall guarantee protection for places of worship from any political or ideological influence." This change clearly represents a step backward compared to the previous text, and could even lead to greater discrimination against religious minorities. The 2020 constitutional reform also confirmed the provision prohibiting non-Muslims from running for the presidency (Article 87).

Even linguistic rights became controversial on religious grounds during the latest constitutional reform process. Indeed, one of the main reasons explaining the opposition of Islamist parties to the 2020 constitutional reform regarded the status granted by the constitution to *Tamazight*, the language spoken by the Berbers. Indeed, not only did the 2020 reform confirm *Tamazight* as a "national" and "official" language (Article 4) but it also included this language – alongside Arabic – under the fundamental principles that cannot be subject to constitutional amendment (Article 223). Islamist parties – including the *Front de la Justice et du Développement* and the *Mouvement pour la société et la paix* – strongly opposed any recognition of full equality between *Tamazight* and Arabic, arguing that this would entail a serious threat to national identity, the role of Islam, and the language of the Quran.[146]

In Algeria, the law does not prohibit conversion from Islam, although the proselytizing of Muslims by non-Muslims is a criminal offense. Algeria used to host a significant number of Jews. However, between the Sixties and the Eighties, most of them left the country.[147] In today's Algeria, the Jewish community has *de facto*

[145] See Section 4.3.3.

[146] See "Révision de la Constitution: Tamazight cible des islamistes," *Algerie ECO* (October 6, 2020), www.algerie-eco.com/2020/10/06/revision-de-la-constitution-tamazight-cible-des-islamistes/; Arezki Saïd, "Algérie: pourquoi les islamistes continuent de s'opposer à l'amazigh," *Jeune Afrique* (October 12, 2020), www.jeuneafrique.com/1057038/politique/algerie-pourquoi-les-islamistes-continuent-de-sopposer-a-lamazigh/

[147] See Castellino and Cavanaugh, *Minority Rights*, at p. 92.

disappeared. Indeed, some religious leaders estimate there are fewer than 200 Jews in the country. As regards the Christian community, estimates of their number range from 20,000 to 200,000, although this number might be even higher.[148] Since the early 1990s, there has been a "discreet conversion movement"[149] from Islam to Christianity (mainly the Evangelical Church), particularly in Kabylia, the Berber region in the north of the country. This can be explained by the fact that in Kabylia, "the religious choice is also a political one, set in the debate about Berber specificity, distinct from the Arab identity and therefore from the Muslim one. Their claim to a specific Algerian identity is consequently strengthened."[150]

Although some Christian communities are well integrated into society, Christians are often victims of discrimination. For example, in several cases, they have been fined (or even arrested) on proselytism charges. In general, Christian converts tend to keep a low profile due to concerns for their personal safety and the potential for legal, family, career, and social problems. Furthermore, some Christian groups are forced to use homes or businesses as "house churches" due to government delays in issuing the necessary legal authorizations to build or renovate their places of worship.[151] Moreover, since 2019, some churches have been closed down by Algerian authorities.[152]

4.2.6 *Syria*

In Syria, the 2012 constitution does not differ significantly from the previous 1973 constitution as far as religion is concerned. In the first place, in contrast to most other Arab constitutions, Islam is not proclaimed as the state religion. Article 3 of the 2012 constitution only stipulates that the religion of the president of the Republic must be Islam, as was also provided for under the previous Syrian constitutional texts. Moreover, as far as the *sharia* clause is concerned, the framers of the 2012 constitution chose to maintain the term *fiqh* instead of *sharia*: "*fiqh* is a main source of legislation" (Article 3). This is another difference compared to the vast majority of Arab constitutions, which usually use the term *sharia*.[153] As is well known, *fiqh* is

148 See US Department of State – Office of International Religious Freedom, *2021 Report on International Religious Freedom: Algeria* (June 2, 2022), www.state.gov/reports/2021-report-on-international-religious-freedom/algeria/

149 Boissevain, "Algeria and Tunisia," at p. 45.

150 Ibid., at p. 50.

151 See US Department of State – Office of International Religious Freedom, *2021 Report on International Religious Freedom: Algeria*; see also Open Doors International – World Watch Research, *Algeria: Full Country Dossier* (December 2021), https://opendoorsanalytical.org/wp-content/uploads/2022/01/Algeria-Full-Country-Dossier-December-2021.pdf

152 See "Témoignage d'un pasteur algérien: 'La foi chrétienne en Algérie est difficile mais Dieu nous donne beaucoup de joie et de courage'," *Info Chrétienne* (February 25, 2022), www.infochretienne.com/temoignage-dun-pasteur-algerien-la-foi-chretienne-en-algerie-est-difficile-mais-dieu-nous-donne-beaucoup-de-joie-et-de-courage/

153 See Razi A. Diab Esq, "Religion and the Law in Syria," *Arab Center for International Humanitarian Law and Human Rights Education (ACIHL)*, https://acihl.org/articles.htm?article_id=26

the Islamic jurisprudence, which covers the activity carried out by jurists in order to understand *sharia* and to elaborate and systematize principles and rules taken from *sharia*.[154] As also occurred in previous constitution-making processes,[155] the decision by the Syrian framers not to make Islam the religion of the state, but at the same time to introduce a *sharia* clause, reflected a willingness to strike a balance between the aspirations of the religious minorities, on the one hand, and those of the Islamists, on the other hand. At the same time, the retention of the term *fiqh* instead of *sharia* can also be interpreted in terms of the desire of the Ba'ath regime to maintain a more "secular" spirit.[156] A significant degree of continuity can also be found with respect to religious freedom. Article 3 of the constitution stipulates that "the State shall respect all religions [*jami' al-adyan*], and shall ensure the freedom to perform all rituals [*hurriyyat al-qiyam bi-jami' sha'a'iriha*] that do not prejudice public order," while Article 42 states that "freedom of belief [*al-i'tiqad*] shall be protected in accordance with the law." Furthermore, no discrimination is permitted on religious grounds (Article 33(3)). Article 3 also specifies that "the personal status of religious communities shall be protected and respected."

Prior to the outbreak of the Syrian Revolution in 2011, the condition of Christians (who comprised approximately 10 percent of the population) was satisfactory overall, especially when compared to that of Christians living in other Arab countries. In addition to the right to practice their religion, they held important positions in the public administration and sometimes also in the representative institutions (Parliament and Government) and in the army, had their own religious courts, could build new churches, and had the right to Sunday rest. In addition, major Christian holidays such as Christmas and Easter were officially celebrated.[157] This high degree of protection for Syrian Christians was granted in exchange for their loyalty and full political support for the Ba'ath regime,[158] in a way that recalls (at least in part) the dynamics between religious minorities and autocratic regimes in many other Arab countries. It should be recalled that both Hafez al-Assad and his son Bashar belong to the Alawite community, which accounts for around 10 percent of the population. Many have argued that the regime's concern for Christians can be explained in the light of the minority status of the president's religious denomination, within the framework of an *alliance between minorities*.[159]

154 See Massimo Papa and Lorenzo Ascanio, *Shari'a* (il Mulino 2014), 24.

155 See Clark B. Lombardi, "Constitutional Provisions Making Sharia 'a' or 'the' Chief Source of Legislation: Where Did They Come From? What Do They Mean? Do They Matter?" (2013) 28 *American University International Law Review*, 743ff.

156 See Massimo Papa, "L'evoluzione storica del costituzionalismo nei Paesi arabi tra Islam e modernità" in Eberhard Kienle et al., *Islam, democrazia e diritti* (Clueb 2007), p. 18, footnote 27, who refers to the 1973 constitution, but his observation seems relevant even for the 2012 constitutional text.

157 See Fleyfel, *Géopolitique des Chrétiens d'Orient*, at pp. 190–195.

158 Ibid., at p. 190.

159 See, for example, Salma Mousa, "To Protest or not to Protest? The Christian Predicament in the Syrian Uprising" (2012) 17 *Syrian Studies Association Bulletin*, 4; Fleyfel, *Géopolitique des Chrétiens*

The Syrian conflict, which broke out in March 2011, and the subsequent atrocities perpetrated by ISIS (particularly in the city of Aleppo, which was home to some 150,000 Christians before the war; there are around 30,000 remaining today)[160] have worsened the condition of Christians tremendously and have forced most of them to abandon their country.[161] Indeed, out of the 1.5 million Christians who lived in Syria before the war (around 10 percent of the population), it is estimated that only 300,000 have remained (less than 2 percent of the population).[162] Those who still live in Syria have to face discrimination and violence at the hands of violent extremist groups.[163] It has been rightly pointed out that, since the outbreak of the war, Christians have been experiencing a real "tragedy" in their country.[164] The long list of Christians killed or missing includes the Bishops of Aleppo, Greek Orthodox Boulos Yazigi, and Syriac Orthodox Yohanna Ibrahim, who were kidnapped in 2013, as well as Father Paolo Dall'Oglio, a Jesuit priest who served for three decades at the Deir Mar Musa promoting interfaith dialogue (also kidnapped in 2013). As regards the other religious minorities, before the civil war, there was a small Jewish community in Aleppo and Damascus, but it is likely to have disappeared.[165] Jehovah's Witnesses are banned, as this community is considered by the government to be a "politically-motivated Zionist organization."[166] As a result, the US Commission on International Religious Freedom (USCIRF) has categorized Syria as a "country of particular concern" for particularly severe violations of religious freedom.[167]

In order to strengthen its hold on the religious field, in November 2021, President Assad abrogated the position of Mufti and redistributed his powers to a jurisprudential

d'Orient, at p. 190. According to Castellino and Cavanaugh, *Minority Rights*, at p. 110, "The vested interest of the current Asad regime in maintaining a Christian alliance has, in large part, contributed to a symbiotic relationship."

[160] See "War and Economic Crisis in Aleppo Cause Christians to Flee," *Vatican News* (December 13, 2021), www.vaticannews.va/en/church/news/2021-12/syria-war-christian-tobji-joseph.html

[161] On the condition of Christians before and after 2011 see Razek Siriani, "Syria" in Ross, Tadros and Johnson (eds.) 2018, *Christianity*, at p. 105ff.

[162] See "Report: Number of Christians in Syria Dropped from 1.5 Million to 300,000," *The Syrian Observer* (November 18, 2022), https://syrianobserver.com/news/80226/report-number-of-christians-in-syria-dropped-from-1-5-million-to-300000.html

[163] See US Department of State – Office of International Religious Freedom, *2021 Report on International Religious Freedom: Syria* (June 2, 2022), www.state.gov/reports/2021-report-on-international-religious-freedom/syria/

[164] Gian Micalessin, *Fratelli traditi. La tragedia dei cristiani in Siria. Cronaca di una persecuzione ignorata* (Cairo 2018). On the persecutions and discriminations against Christians, see also Open Doors International – World Watch Research, *Syria: Full Country Dossier* (December 2021), https://opendoorsanalytical.org/wp-content/uploads/2022/01/Syria-Full-Country-Dossier-December-2021.pdf

[165] See US Department of State – Office of International Religious Freedom, *2021 Report on International Religious Freedom: Syria.*

[166] Ibid.

[167] See Elizabeth Hagedorn, "US Government Watchdog Calls Out Syria for Religious Freedom Abuses," *Al-Monitor* (April 21, 2021), www.al-monitor.com/originals/2021/04/us-government-watchdog-calls-out-syria-religious-freedom-abuses

council, the *majlis al-ilmi al-fikhi*, chaired by the Minister of Religious Endowments. The position of Mufti had already been hollowed out in 2018, when Law no. 31 reduced life tenure to three years.[168]

4.2.7 *Libya*

In Libya, it was not the place of Islam that generated major debate during the constitution-making process (its recognition as the official religion of the state was indeed taken for granted), but rather the place of *sharia*.[169] Unlike Tunisia, however, where the debate revolved around the issue as to whether or not a *sharia* clause should be introduced in the constitution, in Libya the point of contention had to do with the role that *sharia* "should play and what level of detail needed to be included in the draft constitution."[170] In general terms, the population and the members of the Constituent Assembly overwhelmingly favored the introduction of a *sharia* clause, although opinions differed as to its formulation. Some people preferred a light version (such as *sharia* as "a" or "a main" source of legislation), while others pushed for a stronger formula (such as *sharia* as "the main" or "the sole" source of legislation).[171] Finding a compromise proved to be extremely complicated. According to the July 2017 draft constitution, *sharia* is "a source of legislation," which is certainly a much lighter and less controversial version compared to the *sharia* clauses contained in the previous draft constitutions. The April 2016 draft, for example, stated that "[…] *sharia* shall be the source of legislation in accordance with the recognized doctrines and interpretations without being bound to a particular jurisprudential opinion on discretionary matters […]" (Article 8).

The special recognition granted to Islam and *sharia* can be found in many other provisions of the 2017 draft constitution of Libya. Article 27, for example, states that "The family that is established on *sharia*-based marriage between a man and a woman shall be the foundation of society. It shall be founded on religion, ethics, complementary roles between its members, as well as on affection and mercy […]." Article 52 stipulates that "educational curricula" are based, among other things, on "the teachings and values of the Islamic religion." Nor is the National Council for Human Rights immune from this approach, as its task is to reinforce and promote the culture of human rights and public liberties "provided for in Islamic *sharia* and

168 See Michael Young, "An Excommunication in Damascus," *Malcolm H. Kerr – Carnegie Middle East Center* (November 19, 2021), https://carnegie-mec.org/diwan/85816

169 See Ragab Saad, "A Constitution That Doesn't Protect Rights and Freedoms: Libya Writes Its Constitution," *Atlantic Council* (August 3, 2017), www.atlanticcouncil.org/blogs/menasource/a-constitution-that-doesn-t-protect-rights-and-freedoms-libya-writes-its-constitution/

170 Nedra Cherif, *Libya's Constitution: Between Conflict and Compromise* (European University Institute – Middle East Directions (MED) 2021/02) (March 2021), 14, https://cadmus.eui.eu/bitstream/handle/1814/70538/QM-09-21-057-EN-N.pdf?sequence=3&isAllowed=y

171 Ibid., at pp. 14–15.

international conventions" (Article 159). The draft constitution also provides for a *Sharia* Research Council, responsible for expressing opinions on matters referred to it by state authorities, addressing religious issues, and issuing opinions (*fatawa*) (Article 161). Some of these provisions are clearly not in line with international standards and comparative best practices, as they contradict, for example, the principles of equality and freedom of religion and belief.

In the Arab world, there is a general consensus among constitutional framers that religious freedom can be limited – even severely – but cannot be excluded outright from a constitution. The exceptions to this rule are very rare. These include, for example, the 1991 constitution of Mauritania (which stipulates that Islam is the religion of the people and the state [Article 5], but does not mention freedom of belief and worship, and does not list religion as one of the grounds on which discrimination is prohibited), as well as the July 2017 draft constitution of Libya. Indeed, this text does not contain any specific provision guaranteeing the free exercise of religious practices and does not include religion among the grounds on which discrimination is prohibited. In addition, the draft constitution stipulates that the president of the Republic, the Prime Minister, the Ministers, and the members of the House of Representatives and the Senate must be Muslims (see Articles 99, 113, 69, and 76). The president of the Republic must also be born to Muslim parents (Article 99). Admittedly, some Arab constitutions (e.g., Syria, Algeria, Tunisia, and Mauritania) grant the right to be elected only to Muslims, although this requirement only applies to the presidency of the republic. In a similar vein, in Morocco, Jordan, and other Arab monarchies, the king must be Muslim. In the latest draft constitution of Libya, however, Islamic faith is a prerequisite for election to *all* of the highest representative institutions (i.e., presidency of the republic, government, and Parliament). As discussed earlier, this approach clearly recalls the idea of *religious* citizenship, which was a distinctive feature of Muslim-majority countries for a long time.[172]

The constitutional provisions mentioned earlier raise serious concerns for religious and ethnic minorities and stand in sharp contrast not only with international standards and most Arab constitutions but also with the previous 1951 Libyan Constitution, as well the current interim constitution, namely the 2011 Constitutional Declaration. The 1951 constitution did include religion as one of the grounds on which discrimination was prohibited (Article 11), and stated that "[f]reedom of belief [*al-i'tiqad*] shall be absolute. The state shall respect all religions and faiths and shall ensure to Libyans and to foreigners residing in its territory freedom of belief and the liberty to practice religious rites so long as this does not prejudice public order and morality" (Article 21). The current interim constitution stipulates that "The State shall guarantee for non-Muslims the freedom to practice their religious rites" (Article 1) and that "Libyans shall be

[172] See Section 4.1.

equal [...] without distinction on the grounds of religion, belief, language, wealth, gender, kinship, political opinions, social status, or tribal, regional or familial status" (Article 6). Thus, in order to address the extremely serious shortcomings in the field of religious freedom, Libyans could rely on the 1951 constitution and the 2011 Constitutional Declaration.[173]

The condition of non-Muslims is extremely difficult in today's Libya, especially for converts from Islam, who face threats of violence, dismissal from employment, and hostility from their families and communities.[174] The lack of a single central government that can impose order and stability in the country has made the situation even more precarious for non-Muslims, including Christians.[175] It should be recalled that Libya was the scene of one of the most infamous attacks on Christians in recent years. Indeed, on February 15, 2015, twenty-one Egyptian Copts kidnapped from the city of Sirte were beheaded by Isis after refusing to convert to Islam.[176]

4.3 WOMEN'S RIGHTS AND GENDER EQUALITY AFTER 2011

During the post-2011 constitution-making processes, discussions concerning women's rights and nondiscrimination clauses in some cases generated major divisions between Islamists and secularists. These divisions were also reflected within the women's movements. On the one hand, it must be recognized that the new Arab constitutions significantly reinforced the provisions on women's rights and gender equality, thus marking a positive discontinuity with previous constitutional texts. On the other hand, however, the path toward creating real equality between men and women in the Arab region is still very long and difficult. Indeed, women continue to be discriminated against (more or less explicitly) on various grounds. The social, cultural, and religious context is the factor that, more than others, caused the strongest resistance to the adoption of more gender-sensitive constitutional documents – the case of Tunisia being a partial exception. The constituent debates clearly demonstrated that the patriarchal mentality that considers women as "second-class" citizens is still extremely strong, and will not be uprooted easily.

[173] On the role that the 1951 constitution can play, see also Chapter 1, Section 1.2.7.

[174] See US Department of State – Office of International Religious Freedom, *2021 Report on International Religious Freedom: Libya* (June 2, 2022), www.state.gov/reports/2021-report-on-international-religious-freedom/libya/

[175] See Open Doors International – World Watch Research, *Libya: Full Country Dossier* (January 2022), 6, https://opendoorsanalytical.org/wp-content/uploads/2022/01/Libya-Full-Country-Dossier-Revised-January-2022.pdf; see also Akram Habib, "Libya" in Ross, Tadros and Johnson (eds.) 2018, *Christianity*, at p. 52ff.

[176] On this event, see Martin Mosebach, *The 21: A Journey into the Land of Coptic Martyrs* (Plough Publishing House 2019).

4.3.1 *Tunisia*

Tunisia has long been at the forefront of the Arab word when it comes to women's rights and gender equality. One need only consider that the 1956 Code of Personal Status still represents the most progressive family code in the Arab world,[177] and that in 1973 Tunisia became the first (and up until now the only) Arab state to allow women to obtain an abortion on demand during the first trimester.[178] However, strongly conflicting views were aired in the country during the 2011–2014 constitution-making process as far as women's rights and gender equality were concerned. Difficulties started to emerge as soon as the first draft constitution of August 2012 was released. Indeed, this text contained an extremely controversial provision (Article 28), which stipulated that "The State shall guarantee the protection of the rights of women and shall support the gains thereof as true partners to men in the building of the nation and as having a role *complementary* thereto within the family" (emphasis added). The point of contention was obviously the term "complementary." Although the Arabic term "*yetekaamul*" can be translated either as "complementary" (which is the most common translation – in French "*complémentaires*") or as "integrate with one another" (indicating a sense of fulfillment and unity between men and women), it is certain that the term "equality" (*al-musawa*; *égalité*) was missing from this article.[179] The risk of incorporating such an equivocal provision into the constitution was evident. As pointed out by Imen Gallala-Arndt,

> Considering women to be complements to men jeopardizes gender equality and opens the door to discriminatory interpretation of the law or even to the undoing of the advancements made by women in the Code of Personal Status. Women would not then be considered full citizens. They could not enjoy their rights as human beings or citizens, but only in the function of their role within the family as a mother or a wife. Such a provision could be used as a justification for the

[177] This Code, *inter alia*, prohibits polygamy and repudiation (*talaq*) and mandates the consent of both spouses prior to marriage. On this Code, see Sana Ben Achour, "Le Code tunisien du statut personnel, 50 ans après: les dimensions de l'ambivalence" (2007) II *L'Année du Maghreb*, 55ff.

[178] In 1965, Tunisia legalized abortion in the first three months of pregnancy for women with five children or more. Eight years later, in 1973, this right was extended to all women, regardless of their number of children, during the first trimester. See Bénédicte Gastineau, "Légalisation de l'avortement et planification familiale: l'expérience tunisienne," *Séminaire International "Santé de la Reproduction en Afrique"* (Abidjan, November 9–12, 1999), https://horizon.documentation.ird.fr/exl-doc/pleins_textes/2022-03/010029691.pdf It should be noted that countries in the MENA region usually permit abortion only if the mother's life is in danger. Some countries also permit abortion in cases of a risk to the mother's physical or mental health, fetal impairment, or rape. Currently, in the MENA region, only Tunisia and Turkey allow *elective* abortions.

[179] See Mounira M. Charrad and Amina Zarrugh, "Equal or Complementary? Women in the New Tunisian Constitution after the Arab Spring" in Andrea Khalil (ed.), *Gender, Women and the Arab Spring* (Routledge 2015), 104–105.

legalization of traditional gender roles with women confined to stay at home or justify polygamy if a first wife is barren.[180]

This wording aroused considerable criticism among secularists and a number of women's associations, who organized major protest demonstrations (in particular on August 13, 2012, on Tunisian Women's Day, which commemorates the adoption of the 1956 Code of Personal Status), calling for the removal of the term "complementarity" from the constitution. Given the vehement reaction against this provision, Ennahda declared that Article 28 had been misunderstood, and accepted to remove the term "complementarity." The principle of gender equality was clearly proclaimed already in the second draft constitution from December 2012, as well as in later drafts and in the final constitution of 2014. Indeed, Article 21 stipulated that "All citizens, male and female, have equal rights and duties, and are equal before the law without any discrimination. The state guarantees freedoms and individual and collective rights to all citizens, and provides all citizens the conditions for a dignified life."

It must be stressed that the complementarity/equality debate was one of the main reasons for the division between Islamist women and secular feminists. Indeed, "the women of Nahda agreed with gender equality in the public sphere, which they were already living up to by the simple fact of being in Parliament, while the main problem was about the recognition of equality in the family, in the private sphere, where the women of Nahda conceptualised the correctness of the gender division of labour."[181] Secular feminist associations, on the contrary, called for full gender equality both in the public and in the private sphere, largely relying on the liberal Western narrative of "Women's rights are human rights," which is reflected in some international documents such as the Convention on the Elimination of All Forms of Discrimination against Women (CEDAW), the International Covenant on Civil and Political Rights (ICCPR), and the International Covenant for Economic Social and Cultural Rights (ICESCR).[182]

As far as the CEDAW is concerned, Tunisia was the first Arab country to withdraw all of its reservations to this Convention in April 2014. These reservations referred to Articles 9 (gender equality in relation to the passing on of nationality to children), 15 (the right of a woman to choose her own domicile), and 16 (gender equality in the field of marriage and family law). Although this withdrawal undoubtedly marked a historical turning point not only in Tunisia but also in the Arab world at large, the Tunisian government decided to retain the general declaration that Tunisia "shall

[180] Imen Gallala-Arndt, "Tunisia After the Arab Spring. Women's Rights at Risk?" in Grote and Röder (eds.) 2016, *Constitutionalism, Human Rights, and Islam*, at p. 611.

[181] Sara Borrillo, "Women's Movements and the Recognition of Gender Equality in the Constitution-Making Process in Morocco and Tunisia (2011–2014)" in Ruth Rubio-Marín and Helen Irving (eds.), *Women as Constitution-Makers: Case Studies from the New Democratic Era* (Cambridge University Press 2019), 63.

[182] Ibid., at pp. 64–66.

not take any organizational or legislative decision in conformity with the requirements of this Convention where such a decision would conflict with the provisions of Chapter 1 of the Tunisian Constitution." Chapter 1 stipulated, *inter alia*, that the religion of Tunisia was Islam, an expression that (as shown earlier)[183] gives rise to very different interpretations.

The 2014 Tunisian Constitution was by far the most advanced Arab Constitution with regard to women's rights and gender equality. In addition to Article 21 mentioned earlier, one should recall, for example, the preamble (which referred to the "equality of rights and duties between all citizens, male and female"), Article 34 ("The state seeks to guarantee women's representation in elected assemblies"), Article 40 ("Work is a right for every citizen, male and female. […] All citizens, male and female, shall have the right to decent working conditions and to a fair wage"), as well as Article 46 ("The state commits to protect women's accrued rights and work to strengthen and develop those rights. The state guarantees the equality of opportunities between women and men to have access to all levels of responsibility in all domains. The state works to attain parity between women and men in elected assemblies. The state takes all necessary measures in order to eradicate violence against women").

Thanks to the principle of "vertical equality," according to which electoral lists must be drawn up in such a way as to alternate between men and women, women obtained 59 out of 217 seats in the Constituent Assembly (i.e., 27 percent),[184] and Ennahda held a majority of the seats that were occupied by women (42 out of 59). This undoubtedly represented progress in women's representation compared to the past. By guaranteeing alternation between men and women in the electoral lists, the principle of vertical equality represented a significant improvement, although it was not immune to criticism, as was demonstrated by the elections for the Constituent Assembly (2011) and the subsequent parliamentary elections (2014 and 2019). Indeed, since the electoral law did not specify the position that women must have in the electoral lists, political parties tended to place men (rather than women) in the highest positions. In this way, small parties that only won one seat did not have any female representation in Parliament. The principle of "horizontal equality" tries to remedy this shortcoming by providing that "political parties will be obliged to respect the equality of sexes, not only in the same list but also between the lists that they present in different constituencies in such a way that if in Constituency A the lead candidate of a list is a man, the lead candidate in Constituency B must be a woman."[185] In a

[183] See Section 4.2.1.

[184] Article 16 of Decree-Law no. 35 of May 10, 2011. This provision was later confirmed in Article 24 of the Organic Law 2014–16.

[185] Nidhal Mekki, "The Law on Local and Regional Elections: A Step Towards Local Democracy in Tunisia," *ConstitutionNet* (March 27, 2017), https://constitutionnet.org/news/law-local-and-regional-elections-step-towards-local-democracy-tunisia

judgment delivered in 2014,[186] the "Provisional Authority in charge of verifying the constitutionality of bills"[187] ruled that, by contemplating only the principle of vertical equality and not also that of horizontal equality, the proposed Organic Law 2014–16 did not violate the constitution since the principle of "vertical equality" already complied with the constitutional provisions on women's representation in elected assemblies (Article 34(2) Const.) and on parity between men and women in elected assemblies (Article 46(3) Const.).

Three years later, in February 2017, the electoral law for *municipal* and *regional* elections not only provided for the principle of vertical equality but also for that of horizontal equality.[188] The different effects of the principles of vertical *and* horizontal equality compared to the principle of vertical equality alone can be easily seen if one compares the outcome of the May 2018 municipal elections with that of the October 2019 parliamentary elections. In the latter elections, women obtained 26 percent of parliamentary seats, whereas in the former elections, women obtained 47 percent of the municipal council seats, and a woman from the Ennahda party, Souad Abderrahim, was elected as mayor of Tunis, as the first woman elected to that role.

However, Tunisia can no longer be considered a model in the region in terms of women's representation in Parliament. Indeed, in September 2022, President Saïed issued Decree no. 2022-55 on the reform of the electoral law governing elections to the Assembly of the Representatives of the People. (Provisions on the newly created secondary legislative chamber, the National Congress of Regions and Districts, are due to be issued at a later date.)[189] This decree, *inter alia*, eliminated the principle of vertical equality. As a consequence, following the December 2022–January 2023 parliamentary elections, only twenty-five women obtained seats, as against 129 men (i.e., 16.2 percent, which represents a significant step backward compared to the past).[190]

The adoption of Organic Law no. 2017-58 of August 11, 2017, on the elimination of violence against women was another important measure aimed at promoting gender equality in the country, as well as being a key step in the process of implementing the 2014 constitution. Among the most relevant innovations, the law imposes harsh sanctions for sexual harassment in public spaces and makes it

186 Judgment no. 2-2014 (May 18, 2014).
187 On this body, see Chapter 3, Section 3.4.2.
188 Article 49 nonies para. 3 of Organic Law no. 2017-7 (February 14, 2017).
189 See Sarah Yerkes and Mohammad Al-Mailam, "Tunisia's New Electoral Law Is Another Blow to Its Democratic Progress," *Carnegie Endowment for International Peace* (October 11, 2022), https://carnegieendowment.org/2022/10/11/tunisia-s-new-electoral-law-is-another-blow-to-its-democratic-progress-pub-88127
190 Seven seats reserved for the diaspora remained vacant in the absence of candidates in the constituencies. See "Tunisie/législatives: 154 députés dont 25 femmes au nouveau parlement et 7 sièges encore vacants," *XinhuaNet* (January 31, 2023), https://french.news.cn/20230131/f77f6d59d6414f26a0bb776fb1b8430d/c.html

easier to prosecute domestic violence (Articles 15 and 16). Moreover, it calls for the Ministries of Education, Religious Affairs, Health, Social Affairs, Justice, and the Interior to organize training on how to prevent and handle cases of violence against women (Articles 7ff.) and stipulates that the younger generations should be educated concerning human rights and gender equality (Article 7). In 2017, Tunisia also joined a movement across the Arab world to abolish so-called "marry your rapist laws," which allow rapists to escape prosecution if they marry their victims. Thus, Article 227bis(4) of the Tunisian Criminal Code, which contemplated this "escape route" for rapists, was repealed.[191] Despite the fact that similar provisions are still in force in a number of Arab countries, the past few years have seen a trend toward their abolition. Indeed, Egypt and Morocco repealed their laws in 1999 and 2014, respectively, and in 2017, Jordan and (in part) Lebanon[192] also joined Tunisia in this group of countries.[193]

In August 2017, former President Beji Caid Essebsi established a "Commission for Individual Freedoms and Equality," which was instructed to prepare a report on reforms in the field of human rights and gender equality. This report, which was published in June 2018, contained a series of proposals aimed at ensuring compliance by Tunisian legislation with the 2014 constitution and international treaties and conventions. The most controversial proposal was undoubtedly the plan to introduce full equality between men and women in relation to inheritance – a proposal that had originally been made by Essebsi himself.[194] Due to the mainstream interpretation of the rules on inheritance contained in the Quran, gender equality in this field has always been regarded as a taboo in the Arab world. Essebsi's project, however, was not implemented, as his successor, Kaïs Saïed, from the outset voiced clear opposition to equality between the sexes in relation to inheritance.[195]

It is also worth recalling that, following a proposal by former President Essebsi, the circular issued on November 5, 1973, by the Minister of Justice prohibiting the celebration of marriages between a Muslim woman and a non-Muslim man was repealed in September 2017. In actual fact, however, it is far from certain that this

[191] See Article 15 of Organic Law no. 2017-58.

[192] In Lebanon, the "marry your rapist law" has been maintained in two situations in which the sexual relation is practiced with a girl between 15 and 18 (Articles 505 and 518 of the Criminal Code). See "L'article 522 abrogé, mais ses effets maintenus dans deux situations," *L'Orient Le Jour* (February 16, 2017), www.lorientlejour.com/article/1035419/larticle-522-abroge-mais-ses-effets-maintenus-dans-deux-situations.html

[193] See Elspeth Dehnert, "As Lebanon, Jordan, Tunisia End 'Marry-Your-Rapist' Laws, Where Next?," *The New Humanitarian* (August 22, 2017), www.newsdeeply.com/womenandgirls/articles/2017/08/22/as-lebanon-jordan-tunisia-end-marry-your-rapist-laws-where-next

[194] See Democracy Reporting International, *La mise en œuvre de la Constitution tunisienne au niveau du cadre juridique. 30 septembre 2019 – 9eme édition* (2019), 30–31; Sari Hanafi and Azzam Tomeh, "Gender Equality in the Inheritance Debate in Tunisia and the Formation of Non-Authoritarian Reasoning" (2019) 3 *Journal of Islamic Ethics*, 207ff.

[195] See "Tunisian President Rejects Gender Equality in Inheritance," *The Arab Weekly* (August 14, 2020), https://thearabweekly.com/tunisian-president-rejects-gender-equality-inheritance

repeal has actually permitted this type of interfaith marriages in the country. Indeed, Article 5 of the Personal Status Code, which stipulates that "the two spouses must not be affected by any instance of *religious impediment*" (emphasis added), was *not* repealed, and therefore some mayors refused to celebrate marriages between Muslim women and non-Muslim men, relying on this provision of the Family Code.[196] Article 5 was indeed interpreted by these mayors in the light of mainstream *fiqh*, according to which Muslim women are *not* allowed to marry non-Muslim men (even if they are Christian or Jewish).

The 2022 constitution has maintained, with the same wording, most of the key provisions on women's rights and gender equality contained in the 2014 constitution. Thus, Article 23 stipulates that "All citizens, male and female, have equal rights and duties, and are equal before the law without any discrimination," Article 46 states that "Work is a right for every citizen, male and female. [...] All citizens, male and female, shall have the right to decent working conditions and to a fair wage," and Article 51 declares that

> The State commits to protect women's accrued rights and work to strengthen and develop those rights. The State guarantees the equality of opportunities between women and men to have access to all levels of responsibility in all domains. The State works to attain parity between women and men in elected assemblies. The State takes all necessary measures in order to eradicate violence against women.

Some of these constitutional provisions, however, are no longer reflected in the implementing legislation. For example, as discussed earlier, Decree no. 2022-55 on the reform of the electoral law governing the elections to the Assembly of the Representatives of the People has abolished the principle of vertical equality, a measure that has significantly reduced female representation in Parliament.

In terms of women's representation in politics, it should also be recalled that, on September 29, 2021, one week after the adoption of Presidential Decree no. 2021-117 on the "exceptional measures," President Kaïs Saïed appointed a woman, Nejla Bouden Romdhane, as the new Head of Government. In this way, Romdhane became the first female Prime Minister in the Arab world, a fact that is, in itself, welcome news. However, it is difficult not to perceive in this choice by Saïed a *captatio beneloventiae* in a propagandistic light.

4.3.2 *Egypt*

In Egypt, the diametrically opposed composition of the 2012 and 2013 constitution-making bodies, as well as the political climate in which these institutions were operating, had a profound impact on the recognition of women's rights and gender

[196] On this issue, see Democracy Reporting International, *La mise en œuvre de la Constitution tunisienne au niveau du cadre juridique. 30 septembre 2019 – 9eme édition*, at pp. 27–28.

equality. In 2012, the mobilization of feminist associations could do little to prevent the Islamist-dominated Constituent Assembly from adopting a constitution that reflected a very conservative vision of society. However, at least one important objective was achieved. Specifically, Article 68 of the draft constitution – which corresponded to Article 11 of the previous 1971 constitution – stipulated that "The state shall guarantee the harmonization between the duties of woman toward the family and her work in society, ensuring her equality of status with man in fields of political, social, cultural and economic life *insofar as this does not violate the rules of Islamic jurisprudence*" (emphasis added). Feminists feared that, in the light of the new political climate, this provision would be used to further reduce women's rights. Eventually this article was removed from the 2012 constitution, but other problematic provisions were retained, such as Article 10, which stipulated, *inter alia*, that "The State [...] shall ensure the reconciliation between the duties of a woman towards her family and her work." This provision not only recalled the principle of complementarity (instead of equality) but also seemed to contrast with the principle of nondiscrimination, since it imposed on women the obligation to work and to take care of their families, without imposing any equivalent duty on men. Furthermore, the Islamist members of the Constituent Assembly refused to accept requests made by feminist associations, which were calling for the introduction of constitutional provisions on the protection of women against gender-based violence, on the establishment of the minimum marriage age at eighteen, as well as on the country's commitments to international treaties and conventions of which it was a signatory, such as the CEDAW.[197]

The political climate in which the 2013 constitution-making process took place was certainly more favorable to the promotion of women's rights. First of all, only two Islamists were represented in the fifty-member Constituent Assembly. Moreover, unlike the vast majority of the women represented in the 2012 Constituent Assembly, the five women represented in the 2013 Assembly "presented a bloc that pushed almost consistently for an expansion of rights," and most of them "had a strong track record of championing women's rights."[198] These five women, supported by feminist associations, managed to forge alliances with liberal members in the Assembly, and as a result, a more gender-sensitive constitution was adopted. Article 11, for example, reads as follows:

> The State commits to achieving equality between women and men in all civil, political, economic, social, and cultural rights in accordance with the provisions of this Constitution. The State commits to taking the necessary measures to ensure appropriate representation of women in the houses of Parliament, in the manner specified by law. It grants women the right to hold public posts and high

[197] See Mariz Tadros, "Negotiating Women in Egypt's Post-Mubarak Constitutions (2012–2014)" (2020) 16 *Politics & Gender*, 16.

[198] Ibid., at p. 18.

> management posts in the State, and to appointment in judicial bodies and entities without discrimination. The State commits to the protection of women against all forms of violence, and ensures women empowerment to reconcile the duties of a woman toward her family and her work requirements. The State ensures care and protection and care for motherhood and childhood, and for breadwinning, and elderly women, and women most in need.

Even though this provision incorporated several requests made by feminist associations (such as protection for women against all forms of violence), some of the shortcomings characterizing the previous 2012 constitution were not addressed. For example, Article 11 still provides that the state must ensure the reconciliation "of the duties of a woman towards her family and her work requirements," thus maintaining the gender stereotype discussed earlier. Even the clause guaranteeing "appropriate representation [*tamthil munasib*] of women in the houses of Parliament" was rigorously debated. A previous formulation granted women "just and balanced" (instead of "appropriate") representation, although this wording encountered the unexpected hostility of some members of the Constituent Assembly belonging to the liberal New Wafd Party, as well as to the trade unions of journalists, lawyers, and medical doctors. It was feared that the expression "just and balanced" would end up granting women excessive representation in elected institutions. Alternative terms were then discussed (including "just," "suitable," "balanced," and "appropriate"), and the Assembly eventually agreed on the term "appropriate."[199] The 2019 amendments to the 2014 constitution strengthened the representation of women in the House of Representatives, stating that "at least one quarter of the seats shall be allocated to women" (Article 102(1)).

Another important achievement of the 2014 constitution was the introduction of Article 93, which proclaims the state's commitment to the international conventions of human rights ratified by Egypt, including the CEDAW. Even the introduction of Article 80 – which sets the age of majority at eighteen – represents a significant step forward. Indeed, during the 2012 constitution-making process, Salafists opposed to the inclusion of a similar provision, taking the view that the silence of the constitution on this point would have favored the continuation of the practice of child marriages[200] – a practice that is still common in some rural areas of Egypt (especially in Upper Egypt) despite the fact that the 2008 Child Law sets the minimum age of marriage at eighteen years.[201]

One of the various reasons accounting for the extremely difficult condition of Egyptian women is the problem of sexual harassment. During the demonstrations held in Tahrir Square that led to the fall of President Mubarak in 2011 and President

[199] See Serôdio, "Shaping Egypt's 2014 Constitution," at pp. 61–62.
[200] Ibid., at pp. 63–64.
[201] See UNICEF, *Child Marriage in the Middle East and North Africa – Egypt Country Brief* (2017), www.unicef.org/mena/media/1796/file/MENA-CMReport-EgyptBrief.pdf.pdf

Morsi in 2013, a number of women protesters were sexually assaulted and even forced to take virginity tests.[202] This is not particularly surprising if one considers that, according to a report prepared by the United Nations (UN) in April 2013, 99.3 percent of women declared that they had been subjected to some form of sexual harassment.[203] The discriminatory approach toward women can also be exemplified by the proposal made by a member of Parliament in October 2016 to conduct mandatory virginity tests for women seeking university admission. The aim of these tests was to prevent informal marriages (known as *gawaz orfy*) between young people who choose to have sex before marriage.[204]

In some cases, courts have issued judgments that have contributed to (partially) strengthening women's rights. This is particularly evident if one considers the case law of the Supreme Constitutional Court during its "golden age" (1990–2000). Thus, for example, the Court ruled that the right of a married woman to seek a divorce in the event of her husband's new marriage was consistent with the constitution, and that this right was guaranteed even if the man had not been obliged under his original marriage contract not to marry another woman.[205] In another case, the Court ruled that the prohibition on the members of the State Council from marrying foreign women was unconstitutional.[206] More recently, in a judgment delivered in 2017, the Court ruled that women who take extended unpaid maternity leave should still receive full annual pay increases. The Court argued that the annual increases granted to women employees represent a right that strengthens their purchasing powers in the face of inflation, and that this right should not be denied to employees on unpaid maternity leave.[207]

4.3.3 *Morocco*

In Morocco, women were particularly active during the 2011 constitution-making process. As in Tunisia, however, the differences between Islamist women and progressive feminist associations were quite evident. It is emblematic, for example, that during the 2011 demonstrations, two different slogans were heard: "for progressive groups, 'Women and men are equal in rights' (*al-nisāʾ wa-l-rijāl fi-l huqūq bhal*

[202] See Xan Rice, "Egyptians Protest Over 'Virginity Tests' on Tahrir Square Women," *The Guardian* (May 31, 2011), www.theguardian.com/world/2011/may/31/egypt-online-protest-virginity-tests

[203] See United Nations Women, *Study on Ways and Methods to Eliminate Sexual Harassment in Egypt* (April 2013), 6, https://s3-eu-west-1.amazonaws.com/harassmap/media/uploaded-files/287_Summaryreport_eng_low-1.pdf

[204] See "Egyptian Lawmaker's Call for Virginity Tests Draws Fire," *VOA News* (October 2, 2016), www.voanews.com/a/egyptian-lawmaker-call-for-virginity-tests-draws-fire/3533612.html

[205] Case no. 35, Judicial Year 9 (August 15, 1994).

[206] Case no. 23, Judicial Year 16 (March 18, 1995).

[207] See "Women Workers Must Receive Annual Pay Increases During Unpaid Maternity Leave: Egypt's Constitutional Court," *Ahram Online* (May 6, 2017), https://english.ahram.org.eg/NewsContent/1/64/268220/Egypt/Politics-/-Women-workers-must-receive-annual-pay-increases-d.aspx

bhal); for Islamist groups, 'Women and men are equal in the struggle' (*al-nisā' wa-l-rijāl finnidāl bhal bhal*)."[208] The feminist associations submitted to the Commission responsible for drafting the new constitution at least three memoranda, in which they called for the recognition of gender equality and full citizenship for women, the criminalization of violence against women, the promotion of real equality between women and men in access to decision-making positions, and respect of international conventions on human rights, including in particular the CEDAW.[209] Within the Commission, the issue of gender equality was much less problematic compared to other questions, and in fact, most requests were accepted and incorporated into the 2011 constitution. For this reason, feminist movements decided to support a "Yes" vote in the constitutional referendum. This led to a sharp division with the 20th February Movement (namely, the movement leading the protest demonstrations), which, by contrast, promoted a boycott of the vote due to the top-down nature of the constitution-drafting process.[210]

The new Moroccan Constitution represents a major step forward in terms of women's rights and gender equality compared to the past. Indeed, Article 8 of the previous 1996 constitution only granted "political" rights to women, whereas Article 19 of the 2011 constitution declares that

> The man and the woman enjoy, in equality, the rights and freedoms of civil, political, economic, social, cultural and environmental character, enounced in this Title and in the other provisions of the Constitution, as well as in the international conventions and pacts duly ratified by Morocco and this, with respect for the provisions of the Constitution, of the constants of the Kingdom [*thawabit al-mamlaka; constantes du Royaume*] and of its laws. The State works for the realization of parity between men and women. An Authority for parity and the struggle against all forms of discrimination is created, to this effect.

This provision, however, is quite ambiguous. Indeed, equality between women and men must respect the "provisions of the Constitution," "the constants of the Kingdom," and "its laws." First of all: What do the "constants of the Kingdom" consist in? These "constants" seem to include the Islamic religion, as underlined by King Mohammed VI in his constituent speech on March 9, 2011, in which he announced to the people his decision to adopt a new constitution ("The sacredness of our constants which are the subject of national unanimity, namely Islam as the state religion [...]"), and as stipulated in Article 1 of the constitution itself ("The Nation [*ummah*] relies in its collective life on certain *federative constants* [*thawabit jami'a; constantes fédératrices*]," which include, *inter alia*, the "moderate Islamic religion").[211] Second, it seems extremely hard to reconcile respect for the

[208] Borrillo, "Women's Movements," at p. 47.
[209] Ibid., at pp. 49–51.
[210] Ibid., at pp. 52–54.
[211] See Bernard-Maugiron, *Droit contemporain des pays arabes*, at p. 828.

"international conventions and pacts duly ratified by Morocco" (which include, for example, the CEDAW) with the "laws" of the Kingdom, which are often at odds with these international obligations, especially in the field of personal status. Thus, it has been rightly stressed that Article 19 allows for two diametrically opposed interpretations in relation to the principle of gender equality: one "in favor of universalism" and the other "toward conservatism."[212]

A similar ambiguity also refers to the status of international human rights treaties and conventions. On the one hand, the constitution implicitly proclaims its supremacy over international norms, as stated in Article 55(4) ("If the Constitutional Court [...] declares that an international commitment contains a provision contrary to the constitution, its ratification may only intervene after the revision of the Constitution"). On the other hand, however, the preamble, which is "an integral part of this Constitution," stipulates that Morocco "grant[s] to international conventions duly ratified by it – within the framework of the provisions of the Constitution, the laws of the Kingdom, respect for its immutable national identity [*huwayatiha al-wataniyya al-rasikha*], and upon publication of these conventions – supremacy over domestic law [*al-tashri'at al-wataniyya; législation nationale*] of the country," and also requires Morocco "to harmonize the relevant provisions of its national legislation accordingly." One cannot help but wonder how the primacy of international conventions can be guaranteed if at the same time respect for the "immutable national identity" (which seems to include also the Islamic religion) must be ensured. One need only consider the tensions between the CEDAW and some provisions of the Code on Personal Status (*Moudawana*).[213]

The use of ambiguous wording and contradictory provisions is not unusual in constitution-drafting. Rather, it forms part of the "incrementalist" strategies, on which framers often rely when they are unable to reach a clear agreement.[214] In the case of Morocco, the abovementioned ambiguities concerning women's rights and the status of international treaties represented a compromise between the position of the Islamist parties (which argued that international norms had to be consistent with Islamic principles and rules – and for this reason in the past always opposed any withdrawal of reservations in matters concerning equality between men and women) and the position of progressive parties (which advocated for the supremacy of international treaties and conventions, especially those on human rights).[215] Striking a balance between the need to respect international norms on the one

[212] Nadia Bernoussi, "Morocco's Constitutional Court After the 2011 Reforms" in Grote and Röder (eds.) 2016, *Constitutionalism, Human Rights, and Islam*, at p. 705.

[213] See Bernard-Maugiron, *Droit contemporain des pays arabes*, at pp. 844–845.

[214] These "incrementalist" strategies also include the deferral of certain matters to ordinary legislation, or the inclusion within the constitution of nonjusticiable clauses. See Asli Ü. Bâli and Hanna Lerner, "Designing Constitutions in Religiously Divided Societies" in Bâli and Lerner (eds.) 2017, *Constitution Writing*, at p. 378ff.

[215] See Tourabi, "Constitutional Reform," at pp. 8–9.

hand, and the preservation of national identity on the other, seems to be, now more than ever, one of the major challenges confronting Arab countries.[216]

Domestic violence is undoubtedly one of the major problems that Moroccan (and more in general Arab) women have to face. On November 23, 2016 (i.e., two days before the International Day for the Elimination of Violence against Women), a program on Moroccan state television showed women how to use makeup to cover up evidence of domestic violence, thus helping them to "carry on with [their] daily life," as the host said at the end of the segment.[217] The message conveyed by the program was particularly worrying, especially in the light of the fact that, according to a government survey conducted in 2009/10, two-thirds of women had experienced physical, psychological, sexual, or economic violence.[218] Furthermore, some provisions of the Criminal Code on violence against women are hardly compatible with the 2011 constitution.[219]

Strong resistance toward the recognition of equality between men and women can also be found among judges. A study has shown that Moroccan courts tend to interpret several key provisions of the (rather progressive) *Moudawana* (as reformed in 2004) in quite conservative terms. For example, the Code raised the minimum marriage age for women from fifteen to eighteen years, thus aligning it with the required age for men (Article 19). Marriages between minors should thus be the exception (Article 20). In practice, however, things are very different. Indeed, in 2020, out of 19,266 requests, courts authorized more than 13,000 marriages between minors (especially in rural areas).[220] This conservative approach taken by Moroccan courts can be explained by the fact that "the judge [...] tends to be moralistic in his application of the Code, taking into account social conventions more than the spirit of the law."[221] One should also recall the decision issued by the Constitutional

[216] See Francesco Biagi, "Women's Rights and Constitutional Implementation in the MENA Region: Challenges and Perspectives" in Claudia Padovani and Francesca Helm (eds.), *Rethinking the Transition Process in Syria: Constitution, Participation, and Gender Equality* (Research-publishing .net 2018), 149–150.

[217] See Youssef Ait Akdim, "Au Maroc, œil au beurre noir cherche poudre libre pour maquillage de violences," *Le Monde* (December 7, 2016), www.lemonde.fr/afrique/article/2016/12/07/au-maroc-il-au-beurre-noir-cherche-poudre-libre-pour-maquillage-de-violences_5045016_3212.html

[218] See Royaume du Maroc – Haut-Commissariat au Plan, *Enquête nationale sur la prévalence de la violence à l'égard des femmes au Maroc 2009* (2012), www.abhatoo.net.ma/maalama-textuelle/developpement-economique-et-social/developpement-social/societe/femmes/enquete-nationale-sur-la-prevalence-de-la-violence-a-l-egard-des-femmes-au-maroc-2009

[219] See Hanae Chaieri, "La armonización del código penal de Marruecos con la constitución de 2011: la tutela del orden público nacional frente a la protección penal de las libertades" in Gerardo José Ruiz-Rico Ruiz et al. (eds.), *Derecho penal y garantías constitucionales: Una perspectiva iberoamericana* (Tirant lo Blanch 2020), 377–379.

[220] See "Mariage des mineures au Maroc: Un phénomène 'dur à cuire,'" *La Quotidienne* (August 3, 2022), https://laquotidienne.ma/article/infos-societe/mariage-des-mineures-au-maroc-un-phenomene-dur-a-cuire

[221] Mohamed Mouaqit, "Disposition culturelle/axiologique du juge et interprétation du nouveau code de la famille" in *Le code de la famille: Perceptions et pratique judiciaire* (Fondation Friedrich-Ebert 2007), 187.

Council on July 25, 2014, which struck down the provision of Organic Law no. 66-13 on the (new) Constitutional Court requiring "a representation of women" within the Court.[222] According to the Council, this form of positive discrimination contrasted with the principles of equality and nondiscrimination, and the legislature was not entitled to predetermine the presence of women in this public institution. This ruling – which partially echoed the judgment issued in 2014 by the Tunisian "Provisional Authority in charge of verifying the constitutionality of bills" on the representation of women in Parliament[223] – can hardly be considered to be consistent with the spirit of the 2011 constitution.

In the Throne Speech delivered on July 30, 2022, King Mohammed VI hinted at the need for a new reform of the *Moudawana*, in order to further strengthen women's rights. Indeed, he argued that "At first, the Family Code represented a real leap forward; now it is no longer sufficient as such. The experience in fact revealed some obstacles that prevented the reform initiated from being completed and the expected objectives from being achieved."[224]

4.3.4 *Jordan*

In Jordan, the reforms of 2011, 2014, and 2016 did not change any of the constitutional provisions concerning women. In 2011, the Royal Committee responsible for amending the constitution considered the possibility of including sex among the grounds on which discrimination is prohibited but eventually "opted to keep [it] off of the list for religious and political reasons."[225] Therefore, Article 6(1) of the 1952 constitution continued to stipulate that "Jordanians shall be equal before the law. There shall be no discrimination between them as regards to their rights and duties on grounds of race, language or religion," without mentioning sex. In this way, the Jordanian Constitution held the sad record of being among the very few constitutions in the world not to include sex among the grounds on which discrimination is prohibited.

Although Article 6(1) has retained its previous wording, it seems fair to argue that the 2022 constitutional reform has largely addressed this shortcoming. In the first place, the constitution now addresses Jordanian citizens in both the masculine *and the feminine* tense. More specifically, the feminine tense has been introduced into the title of the Second Chapter of the Constitution (which contains Article 6). Before the 2022 amendment, the title was "Rights and Duties of *Jordanians*" (emphasis added): When translated into Arabic, "Jordanians" referred to both men

[222] Judgment no. 943–2014 (July 25, 2014).

[223] See Section 4.3.1.

[224] See Mohamed Badrane, "Moudawana 2023, année de la grande réforme?," *Aujourd'hui le Maroc* (December 28, 2022), https://aujourdhui.ma/actualite/moudawana-2023-annee-de-la-grande-reforme

[225] Marwan Muasher, "Jordan's Proposed Constitutional Amendments–A First Step in the Right Direction," *Carnegie Endowment for International Peace* (August 17, 2011), https://carnegieendowment.org/2011/08/17/jordan-s-proposed-constitutional-amendments-first-step-in-right-direction

and women, but it was a masculine term, which corresponded "to the standards of written Arabic back in the 1950s, when groups of people were referred to using masculine terms."[226] Now, the amended version of the title reads: "Rights and Duties of *Jordanian Men and Women*" (emphasis added). This change provoked a heated discussion in Parliament, especially because some conservative lawmakers regarded it as a threat to morality. A video shows some members of Parliament throwing punches and hurling threats and insults at one another[227] – a fact that demonstrates how sensitive this topic still is in the country. In addition to the use of gender sensitive language, the 2022 reform also amended Article 6 with the aim of strengthening the rights of women, people with disabilities, and young persons. As far as women are concerned, Article 6(6) stipulates that "The State guarantees women's empowerment and support to have an active role in building society in a way that ensures equal opportunities based on justice and equity and protects them from all forms of violence and discrimination."

The 2022 constitutional reform is in line with the "Comprehensive National Plan for Human Rights for the Years 2016–2025" launched by King Abdullah II in 2016. In general terms, this initiative aims to review legislation in order to make it more compatible with the constitution and the international human rights treaties and conventions ratified by Jordan. A specific section is devoted to the protection of women's rights: Its objective is to put an end to discriminatory practices, guaranteeing equal opportunities, and providing a safe environment for women in the family, at work, and in society.[228]

4.3.5 *Algeria*

In Algeria, the 2016 constitutional reform strengthened women's rights and the principle of gender equality by introducing, for example, a new provision stipulating that the state must promote "parity between men and women in the labor market" and encourage "the advancement of women in positions of responsibility in public institutions and administrations, as well as at a company level" ("old" Article 36, current Article 68). The 2020 constitutional reform took a further step forward by introducing a provision stipulating the state's duty to protect women against all forms of violence "in public space, in the professional sphere and in the private sphere" (Article 40). The reinforcement of women's rights and the principle of gender equality was, however, a sensitive issue. Indeed, this was regarded by some Islamist parties as a

[226] Lena Aloul, "Today, History Was Made," *The Jordan Times* (January 2, 2022), www.jordantimes.com/opinion/lena-aloul/today-history-was-made

[227] See Celine Alkhaldi, "Jordanian Lawmakers Trade Punches in Parliament Amid Heated Discussion on Women's Rights," *CNN* (December 29, 2021), https://edition.cnn.com/2021/12/29/middleeast/jordan-parliament-fight-intl/index.html

[228] Specifically on the issue of domestic violence, see Laith K. Nasrawin, "Protection Against Domestic Violence in Jordanian Law and International Conventions" (2017) 31 *Arab Law Quarterly*, 363ff.

threat to the identity of Algerian society, to the stability of the country, and also to *sharia*. For this reason, for example, during the process that led to the 2016 reform, the Islamist party *Mouvement pour la société et la paix* decided to boycott the consultations organized by the commission to reform the constitution.[229]

Following the 2011 uprisings, Organic Law no. 12-03 of January 12, 2012, strengthened the representation of women in Parliament by providing for a gender quota. More specifically, the law imposed quotas for women candidates for Parliament, which varied between 20 and 50 percent depending on the number of seats in each electoral district (Article 2). This led to a significant increase in female representation: Following the 2012 and 2017 elections, respectively, 31.6 percent and 25.8 percent of the seats of the lower house were held by women. However, the quota system was abolished almost ten years later by Ordinance no. 21-01 of March 10, 2021, on the electoral system. This Ordinance no longer refers to gender quotas. Rather, it stipulates that lists must, *inter alia*, ensure "parity between women and men" (Article 191(3)), thus forcing political parties to include in a list the same number of men and women. However, this system *de facto* facilitates the exclusion of women: The election of a certain percentage of women is no longer guaranteed, as voters can choose the candidates they want, regardless of gender. Not surprisingly, in the 2021 elections, women obtained only 8 percent of the seats in the lower house. The case of Algeria confirms the importance of gender quotas in the Arab world. Following the 2011 uprisings, alongside Tunisia and Egypt (recalled earlier), gender quotas have also been adopted in Morocco, Jordan, and Libya.[230]

Among the numerous examples of the patriarchal and conservative mentality that still prevails throughout the country,[231] it is worth recalling that, in the 2017 and 2021 parliamentary elections – according to a practice also followed in other Arab countries – numerous female candidates were presented on campaign posters without

[229] See Bouhania Goui, "Algerian Angst: Can it Agree on Constitutional Change?," *Arab Reform Initiative – Policy Alternatives* (February 2015), 7, www.arab-reform.net/en/node/494

[230] Specific details on each individual country can be found in the Gender Quota database provided for by International IDEA (www.idea.int/data-tools/data/gender-quotas). It should be noted that a greater representation of women in some Arab countries' parliaments has also been favored by the adoption of systems of proportional representation, which replaced the previous majoritarian systems. See Kaouthar Debbeche, "The Difficult Path Toward Democracy. New Electoral Systems in Egypt, Libya, and Tunisia" in Grote and Röder (eds.) 2016, *Constitutionalism, Human Rights, and Islam*, at p. 436ff. Indeed, proportional systems tend to favor the election of women and make the quota system work better. See Drude Dahlerup and Lenita Freidenvall, "Gender Quotas in Politics. A Constitutional Challenge" in Susan H. Williams (ed.), *Constituting Equality: Gender Equality and Comparative Constitutional Law* (Cambridge University Press 2009), 29ff.

[231] The Code of Personal Status was reformed in 2005. This reform partially reinforced women's rights, but to a more limited extent compared, for example, to the reform of the Code of Personal Status (*Moudawana*) adopted in Morocco in 2004. See Nahas M. Mahieddin, "L'évolution du droit de la famille en Algérie: nouveautés et modifications apportées par la loi du 4 mai 2005 au Code algérien de la famille du 9 juin 1984" (2007) II *L'Année du Maghreb*, 97ff.

their faces, thus giving rise to the phenomenon of "ghost candidates." Moreover, in many cases, not only were women's faces erased but they were also replaced by the same generic drawing of a woman in *hijab*.[232]

4.3.6 *Syria*

In Syria, the 2012 constitution prohibits discrimination, *inter alia*, on grounds of sex (Article 33(3)) and stipulates that "[t]he State guarantees women all opportunities enabling them to effectively and fully participate in political, economic, social and cultural life. The State shall endeavor to remove restrictions that prevent their development and participation in building society" (Article 23). However, despite this provision (which was also contained in the previous 1973 constitution), decision-making positions in Syria are largely held by men, a fact that has pushed women activists to call for institutionalized mechanisms for the political inclusion of women. The lack of equal participation is evident also if one considers the role played by women during the 2011 Revolution. At the outset of the Revolution, women "actively participated in peaceful protests," but once "the revolution became complicated by the regime's brutal indiscriminate violence against civilians, the revolution was co-opted by men and effectively became a man's domain."[233] Despite this extremely difficult context, "women found ways to continue their work," for example, by "organizing nonviolent protests, documenting human rights violations, and [contributing to] the foundation of civil society."[234]

With respect to the current UN-facilitated political and constitutional processes, some important efforts have been made in order to strengthen women's representation. More specifically, the UN Special Envoy and the Syrian Opposition established a "Women's Advisory Board" and a "Women's Consultative Committee," respectively, with the aim of addressing the problem of the lack of inclusion of women at the decision-making level.[235] As regards the Syrian Constitutional Committee (which is the body responsible for adopting the new constitution), 27 percent of its members are women. This percentage is higher than it has been for many other Arab constitution-making bodies, but is below the 30 percent percentage that is usually regarded as a "critical mass"[236] needed in order for women to be able to make a significant contribution to representative institutions.

[232] See "Ces candidates qui se voilent la face," *El Watan* (April 14, 2017), www.elwatan.com/actualite/ces-candidates-qui-se-voilent-la-face-14-04-2017-343261_109.php; "En Algérie, l'inclusion des femmes en politique reste sélective," *VOA* (June 9, 2021), www.voaafrique.com/a/en-algérie-l-inclusion-des-femmes-en-politique-reste-sélective-/5922165.html

[233] Mariam Jalabi, "Rethinking Transition in Syria, Gender Equality, and Constitution" in Padovani and Helm (eds.) 2018, *Rethinking the Transition Process in Syria*, at p. 102.

[234] Ibid., at pp. 102–103.

[235] Ibid., at p. 103.

[236] Stina Laserud and Rita Taphorn, *Designing for Equality. Best-fit, Medium-fit and Non-favourable Combinations of Electoral Systems and Gender Quotas* (International IDEA 2007), 4, www.idea.int/sites/default/files/publications/designing-for-equality.pdf

4.3.7 *Libya*

A country where women have encountered enormous difficulties in making their voices heard during the constitution-making process is Libya. In the first place, it must be recalled that only six seats were reserved for women in the Constitution Drafting Assembly (i.e., 10 percent). Furthermore, the fact that, due to security reasons, the majority of the meetings with international organizations took place abroad (mainly in Tunisia, Egypt, and Turkey) had a negative impact on women's participation. Indeed, "the practice in Libya is that women would not travel alone. Therefore, most female participants had to ensure that a male member of the family would be available to accompany them and that the hosting organization would also cover the expenses."[237] This practice preventing women from traveling abroad alone was confirmed in February 2017, when military officials controlling the eastern part of the country (which is under the command of General Khalifa Haftar) prohibited women under the age of sixty from traveling abroad on their own.[238]

This weakness of female participation in the constitution-drafting process helps to explain why the provisions on women contained in the latest draft constitution from 2017 have merits, but also flaws. On the one hand, the draft stipulates that men and women are equal before the law (Article 7), grants equal opportunities to all citizens (Article 16), and requires the state to pass laws guaranteeing protection for women, raising their position in society, eliminating the negative culture and social customs that detract from their dignity, prohibiting discrimination against them, ensuring their rights in elections, and giving them opportunities in all areas (Article 49). Moreover, the National Council for Human Rights has been vested, *inter alia*, with the task of supporting women in enforcing their rights and ensuring that they are not discriminated against (Article 159).

On the other hand, however, the draft constitution stipulates that marriage is not founded on equality between the spouses, but rather on the "complementary roles between its members" (Article 27). Furthermore, the draft no longer acknowledges the right of women to pass Libyan nationality on to their children – a fact that represents a major step back compared to the previous April 2016 draft constitution, which stated that "anyone born from a Libyan mother is Libyan" (Article 12). This issue is particularly sensitive in Libya, where according to Law no. 24 of 2010 on Libyan Nationality, women "can theoretically transfer their nationality to their children even if married to a non-Libyan. In practice, however, the implementing regulations include complex procedures and restrictions that render the legal provision ineffective."[239]

[237] Omar Hammady, "The Role of Civil Society in the Libyan Constitution-making Process" in Tania Abbiate, Markus Böckenförde and Veronica Federico (eds.), *Public Participation in African Constitutionalism* (Routledge 2018), 168.

[238] See "Libya's Eastern Authority Bans Women Travelling Solo," *BBC News* (February 20, 2017), www.bbc.com/news/world-africa-39027619

[239] Cherif, *Libya's Constitution*, at p. 16 footnote 70.

4.4 CALLING FOR FULL AND INCLUSIVE CITIZENSHIP FOR NON-MUSLIMS AND WOMEN

The previous sections (Sections 4.2 and 4.3) have demonstrated that the idea of equal citizenship, which seems to be suggested in some articles of post-2011 Arab constitutions,[240] is only reflected to a limited extent in the provisions concerning non-Muslims and women. Indeed, despite significant improvements with respect to the past, these categories of people are still largely excluded from full citizenship, which remains a prerogative of *male Muslims*. This confirms that citizenship is an "*exclusionary* concept," "the key mechanism for inclusion and exclusion, distinguishing insiders from outsiders," and that states act as "gatekeepers"[241] (emphasis added).

The questions that now arise are the following: Is full and equal citizenship for all possible in the Arab world? If so, how can it be achieved? Although providing a comprehensive response would go well beyond the scope of this chapter, one can at least argue that such full and equal citizenship can hardly be achieved without considering two spheres of influence that are closely interrelated, namely the *political* sphere and the *religious* sphere. At the *political* level, the previous sections (Sections 4.2 and 4.3) have shown that in the highest and noblest moments of politics, namely the drafting of a constitutional text and its enforcement, Arab framers have often preserved the *status quo*, largely excluding non-Muslims and women from full citizenship. At the *religious* level, despite a general conservative approach, there have recently been some extremely important developments, which may have a profound influence on the idea of citizenship in the region. Indeed, as will be discussed in the following sections (Sections 4.4.1 and 4.4.2), over the past few decades – and in particular over the past few years – not only thinkers, scholars, feminists, and reformers, but also prominent religious leaders and institutions have called for a more equality-based approach toward citizenship's rights for all people, irrespective of one's sex and religious belief. This approach – which is often based on a different (i.e., more egalitarian) interpretation of Islamic religious texts, and specifically the Quran – appears to be extremely promising and may even lead more readily to the adoption of constitutional and legislative reforms aimed at removing (or at least reducing) discrimination against women and non-Muslims, thereby moving toward full and inclusive citizenship.

However difficult this may be, one should recall that radical changes in the interpretation of *sharia* have already occurred. The abolition of slavery is a good example. For a very long time slavery in Muslim-majority countries was taken for granted. Over time, however, this approach radically changed, as modern interpretations started to consider slavery to be in contrast with *sharia*. Tunisia was the

[240] See Section 4.1.

[241] Norman Dorsen et al., *Comparative Constitutionalism: Cases and Materials* (Third Edition) (West Academic Publishing 2016), 565.

first country in the Islamicate world to abolish this practice between 1841 and 1846, and at present, no Muslim state legally accepts slavery.[242]

4.4.1 *Thinkers, Scholars, Feminists, and Reformers*

The first examples of Arab thinkers and reformers who placed the abolition of discrimination against women at the core of their analysis can be found at the end of the nineteenth century and during the initial years of the twentieth century. For example, in a series of newspaper articles published during the 1880s and 1890s, the Egyptian thinker Muhammad 'Abdu proclaimed equality between men and women, stressing the need to reform laws affecting women, such as those concerning polygamy and divorce. In his opinion, the original intent of the Quran had been ignored, and it was necessary to pursue reforms, including legal reforms, to correct the harmful practices that had developed.[243]

In his books *Tahrir al-mar'a* (*The Liberation of Women*) and *Al-Mar'a al-gadida* (*The New Woman*), published respectively in 1899 and 1900, the Egyptian thinker Qasim Amin argued that *sharia* provides for equality between men and women, and that women's education is an important tool for combating discrimination. It should be noted, however, that according to Amin, a woman only needed to complete primary-school education, as this type of education was sufficient in order to perform her role as a wife and mother.[244]

The Tunisian scholar Tahar Haddad adopted a much more progressive approach compared to that of Amin, as he called for *full* gender equality. Indeed, in his book *'Imra' tuna fi 'l-sari'ah wa 'lmugtami'ah* (*Our woman, the Islamic Legislation and the Society*) published in 1930, he argued that polygamy should be abolished, the regulations concerning divorce should be profoundly reformed, and women should be treated equally also in the field of inheritance. Haddad denounced discrimination and prejudices against women, arguing that they resulted from an incorrect interpretation of Islam.[245]

The need for a different (i.e., more egalitarian) interpretation of religious texts, and specifically the Quran, has also been emphasized by various scholars over

[242] See William Gervase Clarence-Smith, *Islam and the Abolition of Slavery* (Oxford University Press 2006); see also the conversation between Talal Asad and Abdullahi Ahmed An-Na'im, *Religion, Law, and the Politics of Human Rights: Talal Asad and Abdullahi An-Na'im in Conversation* (September 29, 2009), 2–3, https://mkotifssrcorgohy6thb.kinstacdn.com/wp-content/uploads/2009/11/Talal-Asad-and-Abdullahi-An-Naim-in-conversation.pdf

[243] As recalled by Ahmed, *Women and Gender*, at p. 140.

[244] See Qasim Amin, *"Tahrir al-mar'a." The Liberation of Women: A Document in the History of Egyptian Feminism* (The American University in Cairo Press 1993) (originally published in 1899), and Qasim Amin, *"Al-Mar'a al-gadida." The New Woman: A Document in the Early Debate on Egyptian Feminism* (The American University in Cairo Press 1995) (originally published in 1900).

[245] See Tahar Haddad, *Notre femme, la législation islamique et la société* (Editions ANEP 2012) (originally published in 1930).

the past few decades. One need only consider, for example, the works of Asma Lamrabet,[246] Ziba Mir-Hosseini,[247] Amina Wadud,[248] and Nayla Tabbara.[249] Their works represent some of the most important interpretive readings of the Quran written by women, after fourteen centuries of Islamic thought that had produced a legacy of interpretive readings of this Holy Book written almost entirely by men.[250] Lamrabet, Mir-Hosseini, Wadud, and Tabbara place special emphasis on those verses of the Quran that proclaim moral and spiritual equality between men and women. These verses include Sura 2:187 ("[…] [Women] are clothing for you and you are clothing for them"), Sura 2:229 ("Wives have rights corresponding to those which husbands have, in equitable reciprocity"), Sura 9:71 ("The believers, both men and women, are guardians of one another"), and Sura 33:35, which states that

> Indeed, the Muslim men and Muslim women, the believing men and believing women, the obedient men and obedient women, the truthful men and truthful women, the patient men and patient women, the humble men and humble women, the charitable men and charitable women, the fasting men and fasting women, the men who guard their private parts and the women who do so, and the men who remember Allah often and the women who do so – for them Allah has prepared forgiveness and a great reward.

The abovementioned scholars also examine the most controversial verses that have been used, up until now, to limit women's public and private roles, and even to justify violence toward women (such as Sura 4:34, recalled earlier),[251] revealing that their original meaning and context defy such interpretations. Interestingly, these scholars not only argue for an alternative reading of religious texts regarding women and gender, but in many cases also offer a more egalitarian interpretation of the verses of the Quran concerning the relationship between Muslims and non-Muslims, thus confirming the strict relationship between the condition of women and that of non-Muslims.[252]

[246] See, for example, Asma Lamrabet, *Women in the Qur'an: An Emancipatory Reading* (Kube Publishing 2016).

[247] See, for example, Ziba Mir-Hosseini, *Journeys Toward Gender Equality in Islam* (Oneworld Academic 2022).

[248] See, for example, Amina Wadud, *Qur'an and Woman: Rereading the Sacred Text from a Woman's Perspective* (Oxford University Press 1999).

[249] See, for example, Nayla Tabbara, *L'Islam pensé par une femme* (Bayard 2018).

[250] The first Muslim woman to emerge in the field of Quranic studies was the Egyptian Aisha 'Abd al-Rahman (1913–1998), better known by her pen name Bint al-Shati, "the daughter of the shore." Her most famous theological text is *The Rhetorical Explanation of the Holy Quran* (*Tafsir al-bayani li-l-Quran al-karim*, 1962–1968). See Margherita Picchi, "A Woman Amongst the Sheikhs: The Qur'anic exegesis of Bint al-Shāṭi," *Fondazione Oasis* (January 13, 2021), www.oasiscenter.eu/en/woman-amongst-sheikhs-quranic-exegesis-bint-al-shati

[251] See Section 4.1.

[252] See, for example, Tabbara, *L'Islam pensé par une femme*, and Tabbara, "Islam and Other Religions," at p. 71ff.

As far as feminist movements are concerned (which emerged in the Arab world at the end of the nineteenth century and during the initial years of the twentieth century), one can distinguish between two main "souls." On the one hand, there are the so-called "secular feminists," who promote women's rights and gender equality relying mainly on international human rights treaties and conventions, specifically the CEDAW. They also call for a separation between temporal power and spiritual power. At the end of the 1990s, they started to discuss several issues that, up until that moment, had represented a real taboo in Islamic societies, such as sex, women's sexual preferences, and domestic violence. These feminists rely on the human rights discourse, look to Western models, and have largely departed from the Islamic religion, tradition, and culture.[253]

On the other hand, a considerable number of feminists in the Arab region can be classified as "Islamist feminists." They argue that women's rights and gender equality can be achieved *within* Islam, through a re-reading of Islamic texts. In their opinion, the patriarchal interpretation of the Quran that has thus far prevailed is a *betrayal* of the true and original meaning of this Holy Book, and therefore women have to regain what has been usurped from them over centuries.[254] Thus, unlike "secular feminists," these "Islamist feminists" very much insist on the fact that it is not necessary to abandon one's tradition and religion to promote equality between men and women.[255]

Over the past few decades, a growing number of Islamist scholars have also focused on discrimination against non-Muslims. For example, in his book *Muwatinun la dhimiyyun* (*Citizens, not Dhimmis*) published in 1985,[256] Fahmy Howeidy argued that, as long as non-Muslims fully participate in all aspects of life in a Muslim community, the *dhimmi* contract should be abolished and replaced by a citizenship contract, in which all people are equal, irrespective of one's religion. Howeidy relied on *ijtihad* (the hermeneutic effort), suggesting a different reading of religious texts. In his opinion, restrictions on non-Muslims' rights should be eliminated so as to guarantee full equality to all citizens.

The approach adopted by the Sudanese Muslim reformer Mahmud Muhammad Taha and by his follower Abdullahi Ahmed An-Na'im is much more radical. According to An-Na'im,

> Modern Muslim traditional reform efforts have attempted to improve the status of women, especially in family law, and sought to rationalize and restrict the inferior

[253] See Ahmed, *Women and Gender*, at p. 196 ff; Renata Pepicelli, "Decolonizzare il femminismo: i movimenti delle donne in Nord Africa" in Corrao and Violante (eds.) 2018, *L'Islam non è terrorismo*, at p. 83ff.

[254] See Juliette Gaté, "Droits des femmes et révolutions arabes" (2014) 6 *La Revue des droits de l'homme*, 10.

[255] See Ahmed, *Women and Gender*, at p. 196ff.; Pepicelli, "Decolonizzare il femminismo," at p. 83ff.; Ziba Mir-Hosseini, "Una via islamica per uscire dal patriarcato" (December 2019) 30 *Oasis. Cristiani e musulmani nel mondo globale*, 14ff.

[256] Fahmy Howeidy, *Muwatinun la dhimiyyun* (Dar al-Shuruq 1985).

> status of non-Muslims. None of these efforts, however, has suggested a way for achieving the necessary degree of reform, namely, achieving *complete legal equality* for women and non-Muslims under *shari'a*. The uncircumventable barrier facing all traditional reform techniques of *shari'a* is the fact that the inequality of women and non-Muslims is entrenched by clear and definite texts of the Qur'an itself (emphasis in original).[257]

The verses of the Quran that, according to An-Na'im, explicitly proclaim the inferior status of women and non-Muslims include, in particular, Sura 4:34 and Sura 9:29 mentioned earlier.[258] Mahmud Muhammad Taha suggested a radical theory that was subsequently embraced by An-Na'im.[259] This theory is based on the idea that both the Quran and the Sunna contain two messages: the primary and permanent message revealed in Mecca, and the subsidiary and traditional message revealed in Medina. Because of the persistent and violent rejection by the people in Mecca of the principle of justice and equality contained in the Mecca message, Islam implemented, as its First Message, the principles of relative justice and equality that were more appropriate to the specific circumstances prevailing at the time the Quran was revealed to Prophet Mohammed, that is, the seventh century. Taha argues that, now that human beings, thanks to God's help, have achieved sufficient advances from a social, economic, and political point of view, it is time to implement the primary and permanent message of Islam, which is, according to a chronological order of implementation, the Second Message of Islam. This means that certain aspects of *sharia* revealed in Medina – including the verses proclaiming the inferior status of women and non-Muslims – should be considered as transitional, and must be replaced by the fundamental principles of the Quran and Sunna of the earlier Mecca period, including those providing for full equality between men and women and between Muslims and non-Muslims. In particular, for non-Muslims, the Quran revealed in Mecca provides for freedom of choice and conscience (e.g., Sura 18:29; Sura 88:21–24). Taha concludes his analysis by stating that if the First Message of Islam, the one revealed in Medina, is no longer implemented, and is replaced by the Second Message of Islam, the one revealed in Mecca, then all discrimination against women and non-Muslims will be eliminated.

In the leaflet issued on December 25, 1984, by Taha and the other members of his organization (the Republicans) against Sudanese President Numeiri's policy of imposed Islamization, it was argued, *inter alia*, that

> These laws [i.e. the September 1983 Laws aimed at imposing sharia in the Sudan] have jeopardized the unity of the country and divided the people in the north and

[257] An-Na'im, "Religious Minorities," at p. 15.

[258] See Section 4.1.

[259] The main book by Mahmud Muhammad Taha is *The Second Message of Islam* (Syracuse University Press 1987) (translation and introduction by Abdullahi Ahmed An-Na'im). For an analysis and assessment of Taha's theory, see also An-Na'im, "Religious Minorities," at p. 15ff., as well as An-Na'im's other works mentioned in footnote 14.

> south [of the country] by provoking religious sensitivity, which is one of the fundamental factors that has aggravated the southern problem [that is, conflict and civil war in the non-Muslim southern part of the country]. It is futile for anyone to claim that a Christian person is not adversely affected by the implementation of Shari'a. A Muslim under Shari'a is the guardian of a non-Muslim in accordance with the "verse of the sword" and the "verse of *jiziah*" [respectively calling the Muslims to use arms to spread Islam, and for the imposition of a humiliating poll tax on the subjugated Christians and Jews – verses 5 and 29 of chapter 9 of the Qur'an]. They do not have equal rights. It is not enough for a citizen today merely to enjoy freedom of worship. He is entitled to the full rights of a citizen in total equality with all other citizens.[260]

Because of these views, which were considered to be "heretical," on January 18, 1985, Taha was convicted of apostasy by the Court of Appeal and sentenced to death. President Numeiri, citing religious and political reasons, confirmed the conviction and the death penalty.[261]

Another scholar who has recently proposed a very innovative interpretation of the Quran with respect to the relationship between Muslims and non-Muslims is the Lebanese theologian, Nayla Tabbara. Relying on a chronological criterion, Tabbara argues that the Quranic relationship with the People of the Book goes through three phases, corresponding to the pedagogical message of the Quran for dealing with diversity.[262] In the first phase, which corresponds to the Meccan period, the Quran (e.g., Sura 21:92–93 and Sura 23:52–53) calls for unity with the Religions of the Book. During this period, Islam is interpreted in a broad sense, that is, an Abrahamic religion that also includes Christianity and Judaism. During the second phase, which corresponds to the Medinan period, the tone of the verses of the Quran changes dramatically. In the first place, Islam is no longer interpreted in a broad sense (namely, as a union with Christianity and Judaism), but rather in a narrow sense (i.e., Islam as a fully separate, autonomous religion). Furthermore, this period is characterized by significant divisions and tensions at the political, religious, and dogmatic level between Muslims and the People of the Book. This explains why the verses of the Quran – including for example the "verse of the sword" and the "verse of the *jizya*" recalled earlier – now openly refer to confrontations and hostility between Muslims and non-Muslims, the latter often being described in negative terms. In addition to the traditional chronological division of the Quran (i.e., into the Meccan and Medinan periods), Tabbara also identifies a third phase, "particularly represented in the last *surah* that was revealed, *al-Ma'ida*, to which we can find prologues in the *surahs* of the three last years of the revelation."[263] Unlike the verses of the second

[260] Cited in Abdullahi Ahmed An-Na'im, "Translator's Introduction" in Taha, *Second Message of Islam*, at p. 11.

[261] On this event, see Abdullahi Ahmed An-Na'im, "The Islamic Law of Apostasy and Its Modern Applicability. A Case From the Sudan" (1986) 16 *Religion*, 197ff.

[262] See Tabbara, "Islam and Other Religions," at p. 71ff.

[263] Ibid., at p. 93.

period, the Quran now promotes openness and conviviality with the People of the Book, and this according to Tabbara is the final message of the Quran regarding religious diversity. While the political and dogmatic differences with respect to other religions are recognized, the Quran's message is to work together for the common good and to accept that other religions also offer paths to salvation, sent by God. According to Tabbara, Muslims and the People of the Book are "invited to live together under the shadow of the divine generosity and hospitality, accepting one another, and adorning themselves with generosity and hospitality in the image of their one God."[264]

4.4.2 *Religious Leaders and Institutions*

The first instances of interreligious dialogue between Muslims and non-Muslims are very old.[265] One can recall, for instance, the visit by Christians of Najran (in southern Arabia, near the border with Hijaz) to Prophet Mohammed in Medina in 631 CE. The delegation of Christians defended their faith in Christ, explaining why they would not convert to Islam. Remarkably, Prophet Mohammed allowed them to pray in the Nabawi mosque (known as the Prophet's Mosque), where Muslims also prayed. This was "the first time that Christians prayed in a mosque. While Prophet Muhammad and the Najrans were not able to reach common ground on all theological issues, he nonetheless gave them a place to stay near his home, and even ordered Muslims to pitch their tent."[266]

Another very important example of interreligious dialogue is the historic meeting between Saint Francis of Assisi and the Sultan of Egypt al-Malik al-Kamil in 1219 near Damietta, a port on the Nile River near where it flows into the Mediterranean Sea. Historian, John V. Tolan, who has written a detailed account of this meeting,[267] underscores that it is impossible to know what the two men said to each other, or what the consequences of this meeting were both for the Crusade and for their personal lives. From a symbolic point of view, however, this meeting was undoubtedly of the utmost importance. Remarkably, 800 years later, in 2019, Pope Francis and the Grand Imam of Al-Azhar, Ahmad al-Tayeb, signed a "Document on Human Fraternity for World Peace and Living Together" (which is analyzed later).[268] During his visit to the United Arab Emirates, where he met with al-Tayeb,

[264] Ibid., at p. 101.

[265] See Mustafa Cenap Aydin, "L'Islam e il dialogo interreligioso" in Corrao and Violante (eds.) 2018, *L'Islam non è terrorismo*, at pp. 111–113.

[266] Craig Considine, "Pluralism and the Najran Christians: How Prophet Muhammad Went Beyond Tolerance," *Huffpost* (February 17, 2016), www.huffpost.com/entry/pluralism-and-the-najran-christians_b_9235554

[267] John V. Tolan, *St. Francis and the Sultan: The Curious History of a Christian-Muslim Encounter* (Oxford University Press 2009).

[268] See Section 4.4.2.6.

Pope Francis stressed that "Providence ordained that the visit be from a Pope named Francis, 800 years after Saint Francis of Assisi's visit to Sultan al-Malik al-Kāmil."[269]

Over the past few decades, initiatives for interfaith dialogue have multiplied. Even prominent religious leaders and institutions (both Muslims and non-Muslims) have been encouraging this form of dialogue, calling for a more egalitarian approach between Muslims and non-Muslims and between men and women. The following sections (Sections 4.4.2.1–4.4.2.8) focus in particular on the 2004 "Amman Message," the 2007 "Common Word Between Us and You" Letter, and the 2016 Discussion Paper on the "Rule of Law and Civil State"; the Documents and Declarations issued by Al-Azhar between 2011 and 2020; the 2015 "Beirut Declaration on Religious Freedom"; the 2016 "Marrakesh Declaration on the Rights of Religious Minorities in Muslim-Majority Lands"; the 2019 "Charter of Mecca"; the 2019 "Document on Human Fraternity for World Peace and Living Together" jointly signed by Pope Francis and the Grand Imam of Al-Azhar, Ahmad al-Tayeb; the meeting between Pope Francis and the Grand Ayatollah Ali al-Husayni al-Sistani in Iraq's holy city of Najaf in March 2021; the 2021 "Inclusive Citizenship in the Arab World" Dialogue Report; and the 2021 document "We Choose Abundant Life. Christians in the Middle East: Towards Renewed Theological, Social, and Political Choices." All of these documents have opened up a twofold path in Muslim thought of the twenty-first century: "on the one hand, the adoption of a modern political lexicon and an interactional reference based on human rights, and on the other hand, the re-reading or reinterpretation of Muslim concepts concerning public life."[270]

4.4.2.1 The "Amman Message," the "Common Word Between Us and You" Letter, and the Discussion Paper on the "Rule of Law and Civil State"

Under the leadership of King Abdullah II, who has promoted interreligious dialogue since the beginning of his reign, Jordan has led a series of initiatives aimed at fostering openness, mutual understanding, and dialogue between Muslims and non-Muslims. The "Amman Message," issued in 2004, stated, *inter alia*, that

> Together, these are principles that provide common ground for the followers of religions and [different] groups of people. That is because the origin of divine religions is one, and Muslims believe in all Messengers of God and do not differentiate between any of them. Denying the message of any one of them is a deviation from Islam. This establishes a wide platform for the believers of [different] religions to meet the other upon common ground, for the service of human society, without

[269] Pope Francis, *General Audience – Apostolic Journey to the United Arab Emirates* (February 6, 2019), www.vatican.va/content/francesco/en/audiences/2019/documents/papa-francesco_20190206_udienza-generale.html

[270] Nayla Tabbara "Dalla fratellanza esclusiva alla fratellanza universale" in Fadi Daou and Nayla Tabbara, *L'ospitalità divina e la fraternità umana* (Edizioni Qiqajon 2022), 235.

> encroaching upon creedal distinctions or upon intellectual freedom [...] Islam honors every human being, regardless of his color, race or religion.[271]

The following year, in 2005, King Abdullah II convened an international Islamic conference of 200 of the world's leading Islamic scholars from fifty countries, with the aim of expanding on some of the key points of the "Amman Message." One of the most important decisions made by these scholars was to prohibit *takfir* (declaration of apostasy) between Muslims. Then, on October 13, 2006, one month to the day after Pope Benedict XVI's Regensburg address of September 12, 2006 ("Faith, Reason and the University – Memories and Reflections"),[272] thirty-eight Islamic authorities and scholars from around the world came together to deliver an answer to the Pontiff in the spirit of open intellectual exchange and mutual understanding. In their Open Letter to the Pope and to all the leaders of the Christian churches and denominations, Muslim scholars spoke with one voice about the true teachings of Islam. The final form of the letter (entitled "A Common Word Between Us and You") was presented at a conference in September 2007 by the Royal Academy of The Royal Aal al-Bayt Institute for Islamic Thought in Jordan, under the patronage of King Abdullah II.[273] The letter called for peace, mutual understanding, and dialogue between Islam and Christianity, arguing that these two religions share the same two supreme commandments, namely "love of the One God, and love of the neighbour."

A few years later, on October 16, 2016, King Abdullah II released his sixth discussion paper on the "Rule of Law and Civil State" in which he developed some of the key concepts of the "Amman Message" and the "Common Word Between Us and You" Letter. The monarch relied in particular on the Charter of Medina, which he regarded as a model in terms of full and equal citizenship for all, irrespective of one's religion:

> The Charter comprised several aspects, including coexistence between all community members in Medina and ensuring social safety for all, equality between the residents of the city as full citizens and active contributors to various domains of public life. It established respect and protection of religious freedom and worship, social solidarity, protecting non-Muslim citizens and non-Muslim minorities as well as exchanging counsel and acts of charity among Muslims, people of monotheistic faiths and others.[274]

[271] The "Amman Message" (2004), https://ammanmessage.com/the-amman-message-full/

[272] Pope Benedict XVI, *Faith, Reason and the University – Memories and Reflections*, University of Regensburg (September 12, 2006), www.vatican.va/content/benedict-xvi/en/speeches/2006/september/documents/hf_ben-xvi_spe_20060912_university-regensburg.html. As is well-known, a number of Islamic political and religious leaders protested against a passage on Islam (taken from a medieval text) quoted by the Pope in the "Regensburg Address," and which they perceived as an insulting mischaracterization of the Islamic religion. The Pontiff then clarified that the quotation did not in any way express his personal thought.

[273] "A Common Word Between Us and You" (2007), www.acommonword.com/the-acw-document/

[274] King Abdullah II, "Rule of Law and Civil State" Discussion Paper (2016), https://kingabdullah.jo/en/discussion-papers/rule-law-and-civil-state

Building on this model, Abdullah II argued that what needs to be established now is a *civil state*, namely a state

> governed by a constitution and laws that apply to all citizens without exception. It is a state of institutions that guarantee separation of powers through a system of checks and balances, preventing any power from encroaching on the other. It is a state built on peace, tolerance and harmony and is distinguished for respecting and safeguarding pluralism, respecting different opinions and protecting all members of the community, regardless of their religious or intellectual affiliation. It is a state that protects rights and guarantees freedoms, where all are equal in their rights and obligations. It is a state to which citizens resort when their rights are violated. It guarantees religious freedom for its citizens and enroots tolerance and respect of others in society. It protects the rights of women and minorities.[275]

4.4.2.2 The Al-Azhar Documents

Between 2011 and 2020, Al-Azhar – which is defined by the 2014 Egyptian Constitution as "the fundamental reference [*al-marja' al-asasi*] for religious sciences and Islamic affairs" (Article 7), and which is considered the most prestigious and influential Sunni institution in the Islamic world – issued some extremely important documents, including "The Future of Egypt" (2011),[276] "Basic Freedoms" (2012),[277] "Countering Extremism and Terrorism" (2014),[278] "Citizenship and Coexistence" (2017),[279] and "Renovation in Islamic Thought" (2020).[280] All of these documents – which were issued under the leadership of the Grand Imam of Al-Azhar Ahmad al-Tayeb with the participation of Muslim and (often) non-Muslim scholars, intellectuals, and thinkers – represent a point of reference for a wide range of key issues, including, *inter alia*, citizenship, fundamental rights and freedoms, the relationship between Muslims and non-Muslims (and in particular between Muslims and Christians), as well as the fight against religious fundamentalism. The content of these documents is to a large extent very innovative. In particular, according to Al-Azhar, one of the most important pillars (if not *the* most important pillar) upon which the Egyptian society should be based is citizenship, interpreted as equal citizenship.

[275] Ibid.

[276] "The Future of Egypt" (2011) in Grote and Röder (eds.) 2016, *Constitutionalism, Human Rights, and Islam*, at pp. 107–109.

[277] "Basic Freedoms" (2012) in Grote and Röder (eds.) 2016, *Constitutionalism, Human Rights, and Islam*, at pp. 109–113.

[278] "Countering Extremism and Terrorism" (2014), https://egyptembassy.net/news/news/al-azhar-conference-calls-for-muslims-to-combat-extremist-ideology/

[279] "Citizenship and Coexistence" (2017), www.azhar.eg/observer-en/details/ArtMID/1153/ArticleID/13505/Al-Azhar-Declaration-on-Citizenship-and-Coexistence-Issued-by-His-Eminence-the-Grand-Imam-of-Al-Azhar

[280] "Renovation in Islamic Thought" (2020), www.azhar.eg/en/Renovation-of-Islamic-Thought/ArtMID/10548/ArticleID/49287/Final-Statement-of-Al-Azhar-International-Conference-on-Renovation

A first reference to citizenship can already be found in the first document on "The Future of Egypt" (2011), which contains proposals and suggestions for building the legal, political, and social basis for the new Egypt. This document refers to the "commitment to fundamental freedoms of thought and opinion with full respect of human, women's and children's rights; to emphasize the principle of pluralism and full respect of divine religions; and to consider citizenship as the basis of responsibility in the society." On the issue of religious freedom, the document sets out a commitment to "ensuring the free exercise of all religious rites without any obstacles, and respect for all aspects of worship in various forms, without slighting the culture of the people or distorting their authentic traditions [...]." The document also seems to suggest a major novelty as far as the right to be elected is concerned. Indeed, it first stresses "support for the establishment of a constitutional national state of modern democracy, which depends on a constitution accepted by the nation. Such constitution shall separate between the state powers and its governing legal institutions; set governance framework; and guarantee the rights and duties of all citizens equally [...]." Furthermore, it "embraces democracy based on free and direct voting which represents the modern formula to achieve the Islamic precepts of *shura* (consultation) [...]." It has been argued that the combination of these two principles would allow (at least theoretically) the candidacy not only of women but also of non-Muslims as head of state.[281] This would represent a significant innovation if one considers that this right (as discussed earlier) is still explicitly denied for non-Muslims within some Arab constitutions (but not in Egypt's).[282]

The second document by Al-Azhar on "Basic Freedoms" (2012) elaborates on some of the points already mentioned in the first document on "The Future of Egypt," including those on citizenship and freedom of belief. It states that "freedom of belief, and the associated right to full citizenship for all based on full equality of rights and duties, is regarded as a cornerstone of modern community-building." Furthermore, "[a]s the Arab world has been the location of divine revelations that embrace (heavenly) religions, it is rigorously committed to the protection of their holiness, the respect of their rituals, and the maintenance of the rights of their believers, with freedom, dignity and brotherhood." From freedom of belief "follows the recognition of the legitimacy of pluralism, the protection of the right to disagree, the obligation of every citizen to respect the feelings of others, as well as equality between citizens. This equality is based on a solid foundation of citizenship, partnership, and equal opportunities in all rights and duties." Moreover, respecting freedom of belief also entails the rejection of *takfir*.

The notion of equal citizenship for all, irrespective of one's religious belief, finds its greatest expression in the document on "Citizenship and Coexistence" (2017).

[281] See Assem Hefny, "Religious Authorities and Constitutional Reform. The Case of Al-Azhar in Egypt" in Grote and Röder (eds.) 2016, *Constitutionalism, Human Rights, and Islam*, at pp. 101–102.

[282] See Sections 4.2 and 4.2.7.

The document begins by declaring that the concept of citizenship is not an imported solution but "has its origin in Islam as it was perfectly applied in the constitutional document of Madinah." It then states that citizenship should not just be an aspiration, but rather a necessity:

> citizenship is not just a desirable solution but rather a necessary recalling of the first Islamic application of the fairest system of governance to the first Muslim community in the state of Madinah. The prophet's application of citizenship was totally free of any discrimination against any category of the society at that time; it featured policies based on religious, racial, and social pluralism. Such pluralism could only prosper in an environment of full citizenship and equality under the constitutional document of Madinah. The document stated clearly that all citizens of Madinah must be treated equally in terms of their rights and responsibilities, that they together constitute one nation, regardless of their different races and religions, and that non-Muslims have the same rights given to Muslims and are required to fulfill the same obligations imposed on Muslims.

Muslims and Christians are regarded as "one nation in which both religions are freely practiced," and any form of discrimination is considered incompatible with "Islam, the divine religions, and the international norms." Citizenship represents a *condicio sine qua non* for the creation of a modern state:

> excluding the concept of citizenship as a sort of contract between citizens and communities will inevitably lead to the failure of the whole state, its religious institutions, and the political and cultural organizations. As a consequence, the comprehensive development and the march of progress will be impeded and the enemies will find their opportunity to destabilize our countries, steal our wealth, and control our future.

It should be noted that the notion of equal citizenship promoted by al-Azhar in these documents has been profoundly influenced by Christian (and most specifically Coptic) thought.[283] For example, the Egyptian Coptic activist Samir Morcos, who participated in the drafting of some of these documents, has long considered citizenship as the cornerstone for future religious relations between Muslims and non-Muslims in the country.[284] In addition to Morcos, other Coptic intellectuals, including George Isaac, Mounir Ayyad, Nabil Ayyad, and Hannah Grace, have produced some important documents, the titles of which are emblematic: "*Citizenship to all Egyptians*" (2007) and "*Renewing Citizenship and Integration*" (2008).[285]

References to the notion of full citizenship can also be found in the declaration issued by Al-Azhar in 2014 on "Countering Extremism and Terrorism" (e.g.,

[283] See Paola Pizzo, "Religione e cittadinanza nella transizione egiziana: tra al-Azhar e Chiesa copta" in Airò and Zaccaria (eds.) 2015, *I confini della cittadinanza nel nuovo Medio Oriente*, at p. 61.

[284] Ibid.

[285] Ibid., at p. 63.

"Muslims and Christians in the East are brothers; they belong to one civilization and one nation; they have lived together for many centuries; and they should continue to live together in national, sovereign and free states, achieve the equality of all citizens and respect freedoms"; "Governance in Islam is based on values of justice and equality and the protection of the rights of citizenship for all citizens without discrimination because of their color, sex or belief"), as well as in the Final Statement of the 2020 "Al-Azhar International Conference on Renovation in Islamic Thought" (e.g., "Full citizenship is an inalienable right of all the citizens of each state with no discrimination among them on the basis of religion, sect, race, or color. It is the basis on which the first Muslim state was established as adopted by the constitution of Madinah. Therefore, all Muslims should revive this basic principle").

Although they are extremely innovative (to the point that the Document on "The Future of Egypt" has been described as a "revolutionary change in Al-Azhar ideology"),[286] these documents by Al-Azhar are not immune from criticism. In the first place, when they declare equal citizenship "for all," they only refer in actual fact to the three "heavenly religions," namely Islam, Christianity, and Judaism. Other religions are thus clearly excluded. Moreover, the concept of "freedom of belief" as recognized in these documents undoubtedly refers to the right to practice one's religion but does not seem to include also freedom of conscience, that is, (as recalled earlier) the right to choose a religion, to change religion, or not to have a religion. It may also be noted that, while special emphasis is placed on non-Muslims, less attention is dedicated to women, who are another extremely vulnerable category of people in the Arab world. More recent initiatives have tried to better address the need to place a greater emphasis on the role of women in Islamic societies. For example, the issue of the magazine published in May 2022 by the Al-Azhar Observatory for Combating Extremism – an institution established in 2015 with a website operating in several different languages[287] – is entirely devoted to Muslim women, with the aim of dispelling misunderstandings and stereotypes.[288]

4.4.2.3 The "Beirut Declaration on Religious Freedom"

The "Beirut Declaration on Religious Freedom,"[289] issued in 2015 by the Philanthropic Islamic Association of Beirut "Makassed," recalls in some respects the abovementioned documents by Al-Azhar. For example, it states that "[r]eligious faith is a free choice and obligation," that Christians and Muslims must enjoy "the same rights and duties," that "no one has the right to judge people for their faith or

[286] Hefny, "Religious Authorities," at p. 102.

[287] See www.azhar.eg/observer-en/

[288] See *Step Forward*, issue no. 2 (May 2022), www.azhar.eg/observer-en/details/ArtMID/1153/ArticleID/62335/Step-Forward-May-2022-Issue-02

[289] "Beirut Declaration on Religious Freedom" (2015), www.lebanonrenaissance.org/assets/Uploads/The-Beirut-Declaration-on-Religious-Freedom.pdf

persecute and discriminate against them on religious or ethnic grounds," and that God himself "upheld the right to be different" as "[n]ever have human societies been one or the same in their attitude and their way of life, or even in their religious beliefs." The Beirut Declaration also rejects the imposition of an Islamic state, thus confirming the previous declaration by Al-Azhar:

> Islam, as the Al-Azhar statement said, does not impose a specific political regime nor does it endorse a religious state. Political systems, in any society, are the creation of the people in that society, be they Muslims and non-Muslims. Based on the shared consent of citizens, a people can choose its own system of government, and can change it according to their free will on the basis of their best interests. Therefore, to consider a specific political system as sacred or infallible, or as a matter for religion, is a misunderstanding of religion and an imposition on people, both Muslims and non-Muslims. All persons are protected by the national state that they have created together, on the basis of respect for the Constitution and the laws that consider them equal in rights and duties.

4.4.2.4 The "Marrakesh Declaration on the Rights of Religious Minorities in Muslim-Majority Lands"

Another very important document focusing on citizenship and non-Muslims' rights in Arab countries is the "Marrakesh Declaration on the Rights of Religious Minorities in Muslim-Majority Lands,"[290] which represented the outcome of a conference held in 2016 in Marrakesh under the auspices of King Mohammed VI. This conference, which was organized by the Ministry of Endowments and Islamic Affairs of Morocco and the Forum for Promoting Peace in Muslim Societies, was attended by hundreds of Muslim and non-Muslim scholars, religious leaders, and heads of state. One of the key assertions of the Marrakesh Declaration is that the Charter of Medina represents the basis and foundation for ensuring the rights of religious minorities in predominantly Muslim states:

> For Muslims, the contemporary societal context makes the "Charter of Medina" the ideal foundation for the institution of citizenship. It provides contractual citizenship and is a just constitution that serves as a model for any society with multiple ethnicities, religions, and languages. It guarantees equal rights for all members of society, whereby all individuals, despite their differences, also bear the same responsibilities, thus forging national unity.

The Declaration invites Muslim scholars and intellectuals around the world "to develop a jurisprudence of the concept of 'citizenship,' which is inclusive of diverse groups," and it also calls on politicians and policymakers "to take the political and legal

[290] "Marrakesh Declaration on the Rights of Religious Minorities in Muslim-Majority Lands" (2016), www.abc-usa.org/wp-content/uploads/2021/05/Marrakesh-Final-04-12-18.pdf

steps necessary to establish a constitutional contractual relationship for its citizenry and to support all institutions and initiatives that aim to strengthen relationships and understanding between the various religious groups in predominantly Muslim lands."

4.4.2.5 The "Charter of Mecca"

The "Charter of Mecca"[291] is a document adopted at the end of a conference held in Mecca in May 2019 organized by the Muslim World League under the patronage of the Saudi King Salman bin Abdulaziz Al Saud. It was approved by 1,200 Muslim religious leaders from 139 countries representing a number of different Muslim communities. This document contains thirty points aimed at offering "Muslims around the world guidance on the principles that speak to the true meaning of Islam." The introductory note to the Charter written by the Secretary General of the Muslim World League states that this document is "the first of its kind in contemporary Islamic history," and second only to the Charter of Medina, a fact that explains why some Muslim scholars regard it as the "Second Constitutional Document of the Islamic *Ummah*." The Charter of Mecca promotes, *inter alia*, dialogue, tolerance, coexistence, and religious and cultural diversity: "All people, regardless of their different ethnicities, races and nationalities, are equal under God" (point 1); "Differences among people in their beliefs, cultures and natures are part of God's will and wisdom" (point 3); "Religious and cultural diversity never justifies conflict [...]" (point 4); "God revealed Himself to all mankind and is the origin of all religious belief, and its various messages and methods, when practiced in their true form. We shall not define any religion by the false political practices of those claiming to be adherents" (point 5); "All world leaders and international organizations should cooperate effectively to achieve safe coexistence among the religious, ethnic and cultural communities of humanity. No individual should be discriminated against based on his or her religion, ethnicity or otherwise when it comes to political, economic or humanitarian assistance" (point 21). Point 25 is specifically dedicated to women: "The empowerment of women should not be undermined by marginalizing their role, disrespecting their dignity, reducing their status, or impeding their opportunities, whether in religious, academic, political or social affairs. Their rights include equality of wages and opportunity."

4.4.2.6 The "Document on Human Fraternity for World Peace and Living Together" and the Meeting Between Pope Francis and the Grand Ayatollah al-Sistani

As far as the relationships between Muslims and Christians are concerned, the past few years have seen some historic initiatives concerning dialogue, mutual understanding, respect, peace, friendship, and fraternity between these two

[291] "Charter of Mecca" (2019), https://themwl.org/sites/default/files/TheCharterofMakkah.pdf

religions.[292] First of all, it must be recalled the "Document on Human Fraternity for World Peace and Living Together" signed by Pope Francis and the Grand Imam of Al-Azhar, Ahmad al-Tayeb, during the apostolic journey of Pope Francis to the United Arab Emirates on February 3–5, 2019.[293] The document is not only addressed to Muslims and Christians but also "invites all persons who have faith in God and faith in *human fraternity* to unite and work together so that it may serve as a guide for future generations to advance a culture of mutual respect in the awareness of the great divine grace that makes all human beings brothers and sisters" (emphasis in original). The content of this document – in terms of both aspirations and lexicon – clearly echoes the Al-Azhar documents recalled earlier.[294] Moreover, the encyclical by Pope Francis "Fratelli tutti. On Fraternity and Social Friendship"[295] (which was published in 2020, the year after the issue of the "Document on Human Fraternity") often draws on this document. Indeed, in that encyclical, the Pontiff states that, when preparing it, he "felt particularly encouraged by the Grand Imam Ahmad Al-Tayyeb," and that the encyclical "takes up and develops some of the great themes raised in the Document [on Human Fraternity] that we both signed."[296]

In the "Document on Human Fraternity," Pope Francis and the Grand Imam al-Tayeb call in particular for a recognition of *full and equal citizenship* to all, irrespective of one's religious belief.

> The concept of *citizenship* is based on the equality of rights and duties, under which all enjoy justice. It is therefore crucial to establish in our societies the concept of *full citizenship* and reject the discriminatory use of the term *minorities* which engenders feelings of isolation and inferiority. Its misuse paves the way for hostility and discord; it undoes any successes and takes away the religious and civil rights of some citizens who are thus discriminated against. (emphasis in original)

It should be noted that the term "minorities" had already been rejected in the Al-Azhar document on "Citizenship and Coexistence," which stressed "the bad consequences of the excessive use of the term 'minorities'. That is because this term has implications of discrimination and separation under the pretext of protecting minorities' rights." On the contrary, in the "Marrakesh Declaration," non-Muslims are usually referred to as "religious minorities." However, the Declaration

[292] See "Dossier: Il tempo propizio" (January-February 2023) 1 *Terra Santa*, 27ff.

[293] "Document on Human Fraternity for World Peace and Living Together" (2019), www.vatican.va/content/francesco/en/travels/2019/outside/documents/papa-francesco_20190204_documento-fratellanza-umana.html

[294] See Section 4.4.2.2.

[295] Pope Francis, *Fratelli tutti: On Fraternity and Social Friendship* (2020), www.vatican.va/content/francesco/en/encyclicals/documents/papa-francesco_20201003_enciclica-fratelli-tutti.html

[296] Ibid., no. 5. On the notion of "fraternity," see Fadi Daou, "La sfida della fratellanza" in Daou and Tabbara 2022, *L'ospitalità divina e la fraternità umana*, at p. 191ff.

itself recognizes that the Charter of Medina "does not use terms such as 'minority' or 'majority'; rather, it refers to different constituents that together form a single nation, i.e., citizens." On the one hand, the rejection of the term "minorities" is a positive step not only because this expression in the Arab world has a negative connotation,[297] but also because it is part of the new approach toward full citizenship. Furthermore, it is for this reason that "[t]he recent Islamic declarations have [...] recognized Christians for who they are by calling them *masīḥiyyūn*, the self-reference which Christians themselves use, instead of *naṣārā*, a term Muslims used throughout the centuries but that Christians of today reject."[298] On the other hand, however, non-Muslims remain *de facto* a minority, subject to prejudice and discrimination on account of their faith. Thus, the practical challenges that this category of people are facing remain those of minorities.

In the "Document on Human Fraternity," Pope Francis and the Grand Imam al-Tayeb also place special emphasis on pluralism and fundamental freedoms, stating that these have divine origin.

> Freedom is a right of every person: each individual enjoys the freedom of belief, thought, expression and action. The pluralism and the diversity of religions, colour, sex, race and language are willed by God in His wisdom, through which He created human beings. This divine wisdom is the source from which the right to freedom of belief and the freedom to be different derives. Therefore, the fact that people are forced to adhere to a certain religion or culture must be rejected, as too the imposition of a cultural way of life that others do not accept.

Although the document only explicitly refers to "freedom of belief," it also declares that people cannot be forced "to adhere to a certain religion or culture," thus possibly suggesting the recognition even of freedom of conscience – a fact that (as discussed earlier) would represent a major novelty in most Arab countries.

The document also calls for the protection of the fundamental rights of other vulnerable categories of people, including children, the elderly, the weak, the disabled, and the oppressed. The document is particularly vocal also when it comes to women's rights:

> It is an essential requirement to recognize the right of women to education and employment, and to recognize their freedom to exercise their own political rights. Moreover, efforts must be made to free women from historical and social conditioning that runs contrary to the principles of their faith and dignity. It is also

[297] Indeed, in the Arab world, the term minority "really has a powerful sense of Otherness, difference, and not belonging" (Elizabeth Monier, "Christians and Other Religious Minorities in the Middle East," *The Century Foundation* (April 18, 2019), https://tcf.org/content/report/christians-religious-minorities-middle-east-questions-elizabeth-monier/?agreed=1). On the origins of the use of this term, see Tadros, "Christianity," at pp. 16–17.

[298] Nayla Tabbara, "Let Us All Choose Abundant Life! A Muslim and Dialogical Perspective" (2022) 43 *Theological Review*, 112.

> necessary to protect women from sexual exploitation and from being treated as merchandise or objects of pleasure or financial gain. Accordingly, an end must be brought to all those inhuman and vulgar practices that denigrate the dignity of women. Efforts must be made to modify those laws that prevent women from fully enjoying their rights.

It is thus explicitly acknowledged that women's dignity is often denigrated, that women do not enjoy full rights, that they are exploited on various grounds, and that current legislation discriminates against them. The Pontiff and al-Tayeb call for addressing these major injustices by guaranteeing women full dignity and rights, thus making them full citizens.

Although the "Document on Human Fraternity" is not yet sufficiently well known, some interesting developments are taking place. It has been reported, for example, that more than two million people in Al-Azhar institutions are studying this document as part of their programs, and that some countries (such as the United Arab Emirates) have also begun to include it within their school or university curricula.[299]

Another extremely important bridge between Muslims and Christians was built thanks to the historic meeting between Pope Francis and the Grand Ayatollah Ali al-Husayni al-Sistani, one of the most influential Shia authorities, in Iraq's holy city of Najaf, on March 6, 2021. This meeting, which took place in Al-Sistani's home, was particularly important not only in further strengthening Christian-Muslim dialogue[300] (specifically between Christians and *Shias*, following the ties established in the past few years with Al-Azhar, the leading *Sunni* institution) but also in shedding light on the extremely difficult conditions of Iraqi Christians (and implicitly of all Christians living in Muslim-majority countries). After the meeting, Grand Ayatollah al-Sistani's office released a statement in which the Shia leader "affirmed his concern that Christian *citizens* should live *like all Iraqis* in peace and security, and with their *full constitutional rights*"[301] (emphasis added). Although it is very concise, this statement is nonetheless full of significance and clearly echoed the words used by Pope Francis and Grand Imam al-Tayeb in the "Document on Human Fraternity." Full rights and citizenship have long been requested by Iraqi Christians. For example, Syriac Catholic Patriarch of Antioch Ignatius Ephrem Joseph III Yonan expressed a hope that Christians "be recognized as real citizens of their own country," and stated that Christians are not looking for "privileges, but rather for the recognition of the same rights granted to Muslim citizens."[302] His words perfectly summarize the

[299] See "A Mediterranean Conversation on Human Fraternity and Inclusive Citizenship" in Fabio Petito, Fadi Daou and Michael D. Driessen (eds.), *Human Fraternity & Inclusive Citizenship: Interreligious Engagement in the Mediterranean* (ISPI – June 2021), 47, www.ispionline.it/en/publication/human-fraternity-and-inclusive-citizenship-interreligious-engagement-mediterranean-30794

[300] It is significant that the official Vatican slogan of the journey was "You are all brothers."

[301] See "Pope Francis Meets Iraq's Shia Leader al-Sistani," *Al Jazeera* (March 6, 2021), www.aljazeera.com/news/2021/3/6/pope-francis-meets-iraqs-shia-leader-al-sistani

[302] See Manuela Borracino, "Basta belle parole" (March–April 2021) 2 *Terra Santa*, 14–15.

requests made by Christians (and more in general by non-Muslims) not only in Iraq but also throughout the Arab world at large.

Over the past few years, Pope Francis has very much insisted on the need to protect Christians who are persecuted and discriminated against in various regions of the world, including North Africa and the Middle East, as well as the need to grant them full citizenship. For example, this was one of the key points in the addresses he gave during the meeting held in Bari, Italy, with the Heads of the Churches and the Christian communities of the Middle East (July 8, 2018),[303] during the apostolic journeys to Morocco (March 30–31, 2019)[304] and to Iraq (March 5–8, 2021),[305] as well as in the Encyclical "Fratelli tutti. On Fraternity and Social Friendship" (2020), in which he stated as follows: "We Christians ask that, in those countries where we are a minority, we be guaranteed freedom, even as we ourselves promote that freedom for non-Christians in places where they are a minority. One fundamental human right must not be forgotten in the journey towards fraternity and peace. It is religious freedom for believers of all religions" (no. 279). In that encyclical, the Pontiff also denounced the discrimination that women are still suffering in various regions of the world: "[…] the organization of societies worldwide is still far from reflecting clearly that women possess the same dignity and identical rights as men. We say one thing with words, but our decisions and reality tell another story" (no. 23).

4.4.2.7 The "Dialogue Report on Inclusive Citizenship"

As shown in the previous sections (Sections 4.4.2.1–4.4.2.6), citizenship has increasingly been at the center of political-religious debate in the Arab world. In 2018, Wilton Park (UK), the Forum for Promoting Peace in Muslim Societies (United Arab Emirates), and the Rashad Centre for Cultural Governance of the Adyan Foundation (Lebanon) launched a series of dialogues among a number of prominent religious institutions and leaders from the region and beyond with a view to developing the idea of inclusive citizenship. In June 2021, this series of meetings resulted in the publication of a "Dialogue Report on Inclusive Citizenship" in the

303 See in particular the address given by the Pope at the conclusion of the meeting in the Esplanade of the Basilica of Saint Nicholas (July 7, 2018), www.vatican.va/content/francesco/en/speeches/2018/july/documents/papa-francesco_20180707_visita-bari-conclusione.html

304 See in particular the address given by the Pope at the Esplanade of the Hassan Tower (Rabat) (March 30, 2019), www.vatican.va/content/francesco/en/speeches/2019/march/documents/papa-francesco_20190330_autorita-marocco.html

305 See in particular the address given by the Pope in Baghdad during the meeting with authorities, civil society, and the diplomatic corps (March 5, 2021), www.vatican.va/content/francesco/en/speeches/2021/march/documents/papa-francesco_20210305_iraq-autorita.html; the address given in the Plain of Ur (March 6, 2021), www.vatican.va/content/francesco/en/speeches/2021/march/documents/papa-francesco_20210306_iraq-incontro-interreligioso.html; and the address given in Qaraqosh (March 7, 2021), www.vatican.va/content/francesco/en/speeches/2021/march/documents/papa-francesco_20210307_iraq-comunita-qaraqosh.html

Arab World.[306] Although it was not possible to agree on the adoption of this document as a final charter, this report still seems to be of the utmost importance as it develops several concepts related to citizenship that have also been expressed in the abovementioned religious documents and declarations over the past few years. The report focuses in particular on the concept of *inclusive citizenship*, which consists in

> an integrated system of policies, legislations and behavior that embodies a comprehensive culture of participation. On the one hand, it aims to ensure the effective participation of citizens in public life, to guarantee that their voices are heard, and that their special needs are met. On the other hand, it also seeks to integrate their cultural specificities into national life.[307]

This idea of inclusive citizenship relies on five principles, namely: (1) human dignity ("This recognition of every human being's dignity requires that it be translated in practice in a way that preserves and protects this dignity from negative discrimination for racial, religious, gender, social or political purposes")[308]; (2) pluralism and inclusive national identity ("This model of citizenship is not based on a monolithic ideology that assimilates citizens into a rigid identity mold, but rather it is based on respect for freedoms and pluralism, and the promotion of a sense of belonging, partnership and integration within the same national community")[309]; (3) comprehensive participation in public life ("This requires transforming citizenship from a mere legal reality into citizenship-based acts, enhancing the ability of all citizens [...] to contribute voluntarily and creatively to achieving the common good")[310]; (4) religious freedom and inviolability of the human conscience ("The conscience constitutes the internal private sphere of every person who has the right to choose the options, attitudes and beliefs they deem appropriate for themselves and achieves their best interest. [...] Religious freedom also includes the right to the expression of faith, the right to interpret it, and the right to practice individual or collective rituals")[311]; (5) a culture of dialogue and respect for difference ("inclusive citizenship should constitute a space for breaking down barriers between citizens, enhancing dialogue among them and building partnerships across their multiple personal affiliations)."[312]

Thus, this notion of inclusive citizenship goes beyond the idea of equal citizenship.[313] According to Silvio Ferrari, for example, equal rights and duties for all is

[306] "Wilton Park Dialogue Report on Inclusive Citizenship" (June 2021), www.wiltonpark.org.uk/app/uploads/2021/06/Inclusive-Citizenship-Dialogue-Report.pdf
[307] Ibid., at p. 14.
[308] Ibid., at p. 16.
[309] Ibid., at p. 17.
[310] Ibid.
[311] Ibid., at p. 19.
[312] Ibid., at p. 20.
[313] On the notion of inclusive citizenship, see also Petito, Daou and Driessen (eds.) 2021, *Human Fraternity*, at p. 1ff.

only the "precondition" for addressing the issue of minorities and their rights.[314] Ferrari argues that equality needs to be complemented by legal pluralism, which refers to the idea that more than one legal system can exist in the same state. State authorities offer all individuals different options for regulating the same legal relationship. This model, Ferrari contends, is available on equal terms to anyone who wishes to use it: Rights are not granted to members of minorities but to all citizens, through a strategy of legal pluralism that regulates "the same legal relationship in the way they consider most appropriate to their convictions."[315]

4.4.2.8 The Document "We Choose Abundant Life. Christians in the Middle East: Towards Renewed Theological, Social, and Political Choices"

It has been rightly emphasized that since the messages of the Catholic Patriarchs of the Orient in the 1990s, there has been "a lack of Arab Christian documents in recent decades on issues related to citizenship, religious freedom, and the meaning of being a Christian in the Middle East."[316] The 2021 document "We Choose Abundant Life. Christians in the Middle East: Towards Renewed Theological, Social, and Political Choices"[317] – drafted by a group of Christians from Lebanon, Palestine, and Jordan, including both women and men, ordained ministers and lay people, belonging to different churches – has the merit of filling this gap. Not surprisingly, the document pays special attention to the issue of full citizenship for all. It first stresses that citizenship "spearheaded the Arab Spring uprisings":

> Popular movements showed that the citizens' rights had been violated and infringed for decades, until this deviant situation turned into the norm, often based on arguments such as religion, confession, race, and region. Hence, the uprisings challenged the concepts of minority and majority in the name of a citizenship based on individual rights, and called for citizenship to be at the centre of political practice and a beacon for political and social reform. (para. 21)

The document continues by stressing that the 2011 uprisings "were the starting point for new ways of looking at the relationship between citizenship and other elements of identity such as religion, confession, race, and colour, based on citizenship as an umbrella that acknowledges, embraces, and respects differences" (para. 23).

In order to build a state based on this idea of citizenship, the document contends that certain legal reforms are required. Thus, the document implicitly suggests a

314 See Silvio Ferrari, "Overcoming the 'Same Rights for All Special Rights for Minorities' Dichotomy: Is Inclusive Citizenship the Right Answer?" in Petito, Daou and Driessen (eds.) 2021, *Human Fraternity*, at p. 139.

315 Ibid., at p. 141.

316 Tabbara, "Let Us All Choose Abundant Life!," at p. 103.

317 "We Choose Abundant Life. Christians in the Middle East: Towards Renewed Theological, Social, and Political Choices" (2021), www.wechooseabundantlife.com

need to reform those constitutions that proclaim Islam (or rather *sharia*) as a source of legislation:

> Islam in most countries of the Middle East is a source of legislation. This poses a structural challenge to the principle of equality among members of the same society, regardless of their cultural, religious, ethnic and linguistic affiliations. Hence, the Christians of the Middle East are required, along with our Muslim brothers and sisters, and our other partners, to delve deep into building a civil state where citizenship can be applied without discrimination or exception. (para. 59)

Thus, the document suggests that a *sharia* clause is incompatible with the existence of *civil* state. Legal reforms are also required in the field of family law: "We call on our Churches to work seriously for the ratification of civil personal status laws based on the equality of all citizens. We invite the Churches to participate actively in drafting these laws, which confirm the neutrality of the state vis-à-vis religions and the commitment of the latter to citizenship and the just legal state for all" (para. 96).

Freedom of conscience – defined as "the crown of all freedoms" – is considered by the authors of the document as a key component of the civil state:

> Freedom of conscience, the crown of all freedoms, is a major challenge in the Middle East and an inalienable, sacred right. It is rooted in the dignity of the person, regardless of origin, religious affiliation, or political choice, as evidenced by the sacred books [...]. Hence the importance of the transition from the idea of tolerance to that of freedom of conscience, which allows us all to live freely according to our options and convictions. (para. 58)

Interestingly, the need to switch "from the idea of tolerance to that of freedom of conscience" mentioned in the document recalls what happened in Europe with the transition from the nineteenth-century "liberal state" to the post–World War II democratic pluralist state. In Italy, for example, the 1848 *Statuto Albertino* (i.e., Italy's first constitutional text) stated that "The Catholic, Apostolic and Roman Religion is the sole Religion of the State. The other religious denominations now existing are *tolerated* in accordance with the laws" (emphasis added) (Article 1). By contrast, the current 1948 constitution stipulates that "All religious denominations are equally free before the law" (Article 8) and that "Anyone is entitled to freely profess their religious belief in any form, individually or with others, and to promote them and celebrate rites in public or in private, provided they are not offensive to public morality" (Article 19). Moreover, the Italian Constitutional Court argued that from these provisions derives *freedom of conscience*.[318]

The document also calls for a radical change in the position of women, guaranteeing full equality between men and women, and denouncing the "patriarchal masculinized system," which is considered to be incompatible with the message and

[318] See, for example, Judgments 117/1979, 234/1989, 149/1995, and 334/1996.

spirit not only of the Universal Declaration of Human Rights but also of the Gospel. This confirms that – in the same manner as Islamic religious texts – Christian religious texts too have often been interpreted in a patriarchal light. It should be noted, however, that unlike the documents and the declarations issued by Islamic leaders and institutions, this document explicitly acknowledges the fact that discriminations against women are the consequence of such a patriarchal interpretation:

> The position of women in our Churches requires a radical change of mentality and practice, taking seriously the dignity of women, their unique value in the eyes of God, and the full equality of women and men (Gen 1:27), in addition to the concept of synodality, with its commitment to togetherness and consultation. A patriarchal masculinized system has imposed viewpoints in our Churches that contradict the position God wants for women. These viewpoints have been justified by social customs and traditions and entrenched through deviant interpretations of some biblical passages. This is the moment for the Churches of the Middle East to free themselves from teachings, structures and practices that reduce women to second-class beings, contrary to the spirit of the Gospel (Galatians 3:28) and the *Universal Declaration of Human Rights*. In this context, note that in the last four years, the Evangelical Churches in Lebanon have taken the remarkable step of ordaining three women to the pastoral ministry.[319] (para 69) (emphasis in original)

4.5 FROM DIFFERENTIATED CITIZENSHIPS TO ONE FULL AND INCLUSIVE CITIZENSHIP?

This chapter has shown that citizenship in the Arab world – with a few, limited exceptions – only exists in plural form. Indeed, there is not one type of citizenship. Rather, at least three types of citizenship can be identified: "full citizenship," "second class citizenship," and "third-class citizenship." "Full citizenship" is only granted to *Muslim men*: They are the only citizens *optimo jure*, as they enjoy full rights. "Second-class citizenship" is granted to *women* (and particularly to *Muslim* women) and to *Christians and Jews* (People of the Book): These people are discriminated against on various grounds, both *de jure* and *de facto*, and do not enjoy full rights. "Third-class citizenship" is the type of citizenship granted to the *followers of religions other than Islam, Christianity, and Judaism* and *non-Muslim women* (they are doubly discriminated against as they are at the same time both women and non-Muslims).[320] In the best-case scenario, these people are tolerated, but usually they are subject to very harsh forms of discrimination, to the point that in some cases they can hardly be classified as citizens of any sort. Although the analysis of

[319] For an in-depth analysis of this document, see Tabbara, "Let Us All Choose Abundant Life!," at p. 103ff.

[320] See Open Doors, *The Persecution of Christian Women and Girls* (2022), media.opendoorsuk.org/document/pdf/Advocacy-Womens-Report-2022.pdf; Marta Petrosillo, "Donne e cristiane. Due volte nel mirino" (July 2018) *Missioni Consolata*, 58ff.

their condition has exceeded the scope of this chapter, other categories of people are also deprived of the status of full citizens, including LGBTQI+ people[321] and Islamic minorities (such as Sufis, 'Alawis, Druze, and Ismaili).[322] These people are also harshly discriminated against, with their status ranging from "second-class" to "third-class citizenship."

The Arab Spring did not produce any major change to the abovementioned tripartition. Indeed, on the one hand, post-2011 constitutions significantly reinforced the provisions on women's rights and gender equality, and in some cases, even the provisions on religious freedom were strengthened (even if Christians and Jews continue to enjoy a privileged position compared to that of the other religious denominations). Despite certain shortcomings, this *formal* improvement represents an important step forward, which should not by any means be underestimated. On the other hand, however, as could easily be predicted, in most cases, words have not been followed by deeds, a fact that has prevented women and non-Muslims (including Christians and Jews) from substantially improving their condition. In some countries, their condition has even worsened. According to the 2019 UNDP Arab Human Development Report (whose emblematic title is "Leaving No One Behind: Towards Inclusive Citizenship in Arab Countries"), "[d]ifferentiated citizenship based on identities determined by religion, gender, race, ethnicity and class extends both vertically and horizontally, where unequal treatment and exclusion are practiced in state–citizen relations and citizen–citizen relations."[323] Referring specifically to the condition of non-Muslims in Arab countries, it has rightly been stressed that

> [...] there is prejudice that is endemic throughout society. This prejudice leads to everyday discrimination. It's in your relationship at work, in school, in bureaucratic settings. So regardless of what the law says, it is not being properly implemented. The people who are implementing the law are acting within a state that has normalized discrimination. Pluralism is acknowledged but it isn't really accepted.[324]

However, there are now reasons to view the future of women and non-Muslims in the Arab region in more optimistic (or at least in less pessimistic) terms compared to the past. Indeed, over the past few years, not only thinkers, scholars, feminists, and reformers but also prominent religious leaders and institutions have been calling for equality between men and women and between Muslims and non-Muslims

[321] See Tommaso Virgili, *Islam, Constitutional Law, and Human Rights: Sexual Minorities and Freethinkers in Egypt and Tunisia* (Routledge 2022); Human Rights Watch, *Audacity in Adversity: LGBT Activism in the Middle East and North Africa* (2018), www.hrw.org/sites/default/files/report_pdf/lgbt_mena0418_web_0.pdf

[322] See Castellino and Cavanaugh, *Minority Rights*, at p. 127ff.

[323] Adel Abdellatif, Paola Pagliani and Ellen Hsu, *Arab Human Development Report Research Paper – Leaving No One Behind. Towards Inclusive Citizenship in Arab Countries* (2019), 5, https://arab-hdr.org/wp-content/uploads/2020/12/UNDP_Citizenship_and_SDGs_report_web.pdf

[324] Monier, "Christians and Other Religious Minorities."

(specifically Christians and Jews), often suggesting a more egalitarian interpretation of religious texts. Interestingly, several Islamic leaders have emphasized that the notion of equal citizenship, far from being alien to Islam, finds in the Charter of Medina the model to be followed. Religious leaders and institutions have issued some extremely important and innovative documents and declarations, which can also be read as forms of *soft-law*. These documents are particularly important, especially if it is considered that religion exerts a profound influence on law and society in Arab-Islamic countries, and that *legal rules are never sufficient in themselves but need to be legitimized by religious discourse*. Therefore, these calls by religious leaders and institutions may help to combat prejudices and stereotypes, favor the enforcement of those provisions that already provide for gender equality and religious freedom, and lead more readily to the adoption of legal reforms aimed at removing (or at least reducing) discrimination against women and non-Muslims, thereby moving toward more inclusive citizenship. Some of these religious documents explicitly declare that these types of legal reform need to be adopted. For example, the "Document on Human Fraternity" by Pope Francis and the Grand Imam al-Tayeb states that "Efforts must be made to modify those laws that prevent women from fully enjoying their rights." Furthermore, some of these documents have already concretely influenced the drafting of new constitutional texts. For instance, the Al-Azhar documents on "The Future of Egypt" and "Basic Freedoms" had quite a considerable impact on the Egyptian Constitutions of 2012 and 2014, as was demonstrated, *inter alia*, by the emphasis placed on the notion of citizenship (interpreted as equal citizenship). However, Al-Azhar's influence is also apparent in a negative light within those constitutional provisions that grant the right to practice religious rituals and establish places of worship only to the followers of the three "heavenly" religions.[325]

Notwithstanding certain limits, calls for a more equality-based approach – especially those contained in the religious documents and declarations issued over the past few years – seem to have significant potential, as they might represent a first step toward replacing the three forms of *differentiated citizenship* mentioned earlier that currently exist within Arab countries with *one single, full, and inclusive citizenship*. The journey toward this goal is likely to be extremely long and complex. However, the direction suggested by this approach seems to be the right one.

[325] It has rightly been pointed out that this approach is "inconsistent with the role of a modern state, which should not meddle in protecting a particular faith, but should protect the freedom of belief itself so that belief will be built on conviction and certainty, not on fear of law" (Hefny, "Religious Authorities," at p. 106).

Conclusions

Constitutional Dissonances

C.1 CONSTITUTIONAL DICHOTOMIES

According to the Oxford English Dictionary, a dissonance is "a combination of musical notes that do not sound pleasant together." One is also left with the impression of a lack of harmony when examining the constitutional systems that emerged after the Arab uprisings. Indeed, as has been shown in the preceding chapters (1, 2, 3, and 4), while some positive innovations were introduced, a number of major democratic shortcomings are still very evident. Thus, the impression one gets when examining the new Arab constitutional systems is akin to that of a spectator attending a concert by an untrained musician: There are some pleasant sounds but also a number of out-of-tune notes, resulting overall in a lack of harmony and a poor result.

In the light of these dissonances, it comes as no surprise that the role and functions of post-2011 constitutions are not very clear, and that several ambiguities, discrepancies, and contradictions can be found. At least three major dichotomies can be identified: (1) The constitution as a "charter of values" or as an "instrument of government"; (2) the integrative function of the constitution vis-à-vis societal fragmentation; and (3) the written and the unwritten constitution.

C.1.1 *Between a "Charter of Values" and an "Instrument of Government"*

Giuseppe de Vergottini has rightly pointed out that a number of countries in the world are attached to the idea of the constitution as an "instrument of government" (*strumento di governo*) but have not yet assimilated the idea of the constitution as a "charter of values" (*tavola dei valori*).[1] According to the former notion (the constitution as an instrument of government), which is typical of illiberal and hybrid regimes, the constitution is used by the ruling regime for instrumental purposes in order to exercise its rule, in a context characterized by a weak separation of powers

[1] Giuseppe de Vergottini, *Le transizioni costituzionali* (il Mulino 1998), 199–200 and 211–212; Giuseppe de Vergottini, *Diritto costituzionale comparato* (XI Edition) (Wolters Kluwer – CEDAM 2022), 209–211.

and little protection for fundamental rights. In this case, the constitution is simply an *instrument of power*: It is a tool aimed to legitimize the political action of the ruler. On the other hand, according to the latter perspective (the constitution as a charter of values), the constitution is the fundamental document in which the supreme and immutable principles and values of the legal system – including those concerning the separation of powers, the system of checks and balances, and the safeguarding of rights and freedoms – are enshrined. In this case (which is typical of those consolidated democracies that have embraced the values of constitutionalism), the constitution is a *limit on power*.

In the context of the Arab world following the 2011 uprisings, the idea of the constitution as a charter of values is more evident than it was in the past. It is sufficient to consider that principles such as human dignity or the separation of powers are now explicitly guaranteed, not to mention the fact that bills of rights have been expanded and mechanisms for the protection of these rights have been reinforced.[2] Thus, these concepts "have become part of the vocabulary of the vast majority of the protagonists of the political scene in [the Arab] world."[3] However, the idea of the constitution as an instrument of government is still largely the dominant one.[4] Indeed, the concentration of powers – both in horizontal and vertical terms – continues to prevail over the separation of powers. Furthermore, as will be analyzed in greater detail later, the implementation of certain parts of constitutions is still very limited, especially those proclaiming and protecting fundamental principles (e.g., equality and dignity) as well as rights and freedoms.

Conclusive evidence that constitutions in the region are still mainly perceived and used as instruments of government is apparent from the fact that Arab rulers have no qualms about adopting new constitutional texts or amending them whenever they feel that the current constitutions limit their powers and prerogatives excessively, or whenever they feel that the content of these documents is not in line with their political vision. Recent practice clearly illustrates this trend. The 2014, 2016, and 2022 constitutional reforms in Jordan significantly expanded the king's prerogatives, especially his powers of appointment. The 2019 constitutional amendments in Egypt consolidated yet further the supremacy of the presidency and the armed forces in the country, to the detriment of the legislative and judicial branches. In Tunisia, Kaïs Saïed's tailor-made 2022 constitution replaced the semi-presidential system provided for under the 2014 constitution with a hyper-presidential regime.

2 On the strengthening of the protection of rights and freedoms in post-2011 constitutions, see Nathalie Bernard-Maugiron, *Droit contemporain des pays arabes* (Sirey 2023), 803ff.

3 Baudouin Dupret, *La charia: Des sources à la pratique, un concept pluriel* (La Découverte 2014), 11.

4 According to Nathalie Bernard-Maugiron, "Religious References in the Constitutions of the Arab World: Islamization of the Constitution or Constitutionalization of Religion?" in Anja Schoeller-Schletter (ed.), *Constitutional Review in the Middle East and North Africa* (Nomos 2021), 289, the constitution in Arab countries "is more an instrument in the hands of the political elite than a tool to organize and limit the power."

All of these examples confirm that "there is [...] no belief in the sanctity of the constitutional text, which can therefore be easily modified whenever it serves the needs of the national leaders of the day."[5]

C.1.2 *Between Integration and Fragmentation*

Constitutions, particularly in divided societies, should aim to unite people, contributing to creating a collective, political, and cultural identity.[6] As stressed by Gertrude Lübbe-Wolff,

> The most fundamental function of a constitution is integration, i.e. the creation and maintenance of political unity and peace among citizens. [...] Constitutions guarantee fundamental liberties and equality rights designed to make coexistence and cooperation of people of different origins, roles, beliefs, convictions, etc. work. [...] The integrative function of constitutions thus goes far beyond what has been contemplated in traditional constitutional theories of integration such as *Rudolf Smend's*, which have tended to concentrate on symbolic expressions of political unity like flags, national anthems, festivities, etc.[7] (emphasis in original)

In other words, constitutions should serve as "the state's charter of identity. By delineating the commonly held core societal norms and aspirations of the people, constitutions [should] provide the citizenry with a sense of ownership and authorship, a sense that 'We the People' includes me."[8] This is the purpose that constitutions served, for example, in Europe in the last century, especially those constitutional charters adopted after the fall of autocratic regimes (such as in Italy, Germany, Greece, Portugal, Spain, and many Central and Eastern European countries). Indeed, these constitutions represented a key instrument of political unification and integration of the masses: They relied on a *Wertordnungen* and were perceived as constituent elements of a foundational and integrative project, as well as of a national identity.[9]

Unfortunately, post-2011 Arab constitutions have reflected the pluralism and fragmentation characterizing Arab societies only to a limited extent. This is a major

5 de Vergottini, *Le transizioni costituzionali*, at p. 200.

6 See Paolo Ridola, *Esperienza costituzioni storia: Pagine di storia costituzionale* (Jovene 2019), 322, 497, and 546.

7 Gertrude Lübbe-Wolff, "Integrating or Polarising? How to Promote Integrative Decision-making in Constitutional Courts" in Anja Schoeller-Schletter (ed.) 2021, *Constitutional Review*, at pp. 189–190. See also Gertrude Lübbe-Wolff, "Verfassung als Integrationsprogramm," *Aus Politik und Zeitgeschichte* (April 12, 2019), www.bpb.de/shop/zeitschriften/apuz/289230/verfassung-als-integrationsprogramm/; Gertrude Lübbe-Wolff, "Integration durch Verfassung" (2009) 12 *Zeitschrift des Deutschen Juristinnenbundes*, 174ff.

8 Hanna Lerner, "Constitution-Writing in Deeply Divided Societies: The Incrementalist Approach" (2010) 16 *Nations and Nationalism*, 69.

9 See Ridola, *Esperienza costituzioni storia*, at p. 497.

flaw, especially if one considers that many of these societies are deeply divided along religious, ethnic, tribal, and cultural lines. These divisions are rooted in history. In the case of Libya, for example, as observed by Karim Mezran, Gaddafi

> emphasized the "Arab" identity of Libyans first to be followed by the "Islamic" one before concluding the end of his rule with the "African" one. Practically everything but a de facto Libyan identity. It was no wonder that the notions of unity and national identity collapsed on the eve of the 2011 revolts, when Libyans went back to the concepts of family and tribe once more. According to this view, today, Libyans are still divided among many tribes and urban centers which are often in rivalry – if not open conflict – with one another. More importantly, the only feeling of unity that is stronger than tribal allegiances is the division between the three ancient regions that divided Libya for centuries: Tripolitania, Cyrenaica, and Fezzan.[10]

Admittedly, there are cases that show the efforts made by constitutional framers to achieve greater integration. For example, the preamble to the 2011 constitution of Morocco declares, *inter alia*, that

> A sovereign Muslim State, attached to its national unity and territorial integrity, the Kingdom of Morocco intends to preserve, in its plenitude and diversity, its one and indivisible national identity. Its unity is forged by the convergence of its Arab-Islamist, Berber and Saharan-Hassanic components, nourished and enriched by its African, Andalusian, Hebraic and Mediterranean influences.

On the one hand, the reference made, in particular, to the "Hebraic" influences must be welcomed, as Morocco has long hosted one of the most important Jewish communities in the Arab world, especially before the birth of the State of Israel in 1948. On the other hand, however, other important components of national religious identity, such as Moroccan Christians and Baha'is, have been omitted. In a similar vein, the 2014 constitution of Egypt grants freedom to practice religious rituals and to establish places of worship only to the followers of "divinely revealed religions" (i.e., Muslims, Christians, and Jews) (Article 64), thus excluding, for example, the Baha'is.

On a positive note, it should also be stressed that the post-2011 constitutional reforms in Morocco and Algeria have strengthened the position of the Berber community. The preamble to the Moroccan Constitution explicitly refers to the Berber component, as does the preamble to the 1996 Algerian Constitution (as amended in 2016 and 2020). Indeed, the preamble to the latter describes Algeria as the "land of Islam, an integral part of the Great Maghreb, and an Arab *and Amazigh*, as well as Mediterranean and African country […]" (emphasis added). Furthermore, *Tamazigh* – the language spoken by the Berber people – has been recognized as an official state language in both Morocco (Article 5) and Algeria (Article 4). This recognition represents, also in

10 Karim Mezran, "Different Nations for One Libya," *ISPI* (December 14, 2021), www.ispionline.it/it/pubblicazione/different-nations-one-libya-32651

symbolic terms, a way of better integrating a segment of the population that has long been discriminated against and that has suffered from long-standing prejudice.

Despite the positive changes introduced in the new constitutional texts, women have also for a long time faced practices of discrimination and exclusion in Arab (patriarchal) societies. In general terms, therefore, it is evident that there are still numerous categories of people that can hardly be considered to form an integral part of society. Obviously, this is not only due to the formal provisions of the respective constitution but also to the integration policies pursued by state institutions, which may be either nonexistent or not sufficiently developed.

C.1.3 *Between the Written Constitution and the Unwritten Constitution*

When analyzing constitutional systems in the Arab world, it must also be considered that official, written constitutions often exist alongside *unwritten* constitutions. These consist in uncodified rules, practices, and conventions followed by the ruling regime with the aim of preserving the *status quo* and achieving the contingent goals of national leaders. Needless to say, these practices are often at odds with official constitutional texts, especially the most democratic aspects of those texts. This binary scheme – written vs unwritten constitution – was particularly evident under pre-2011 constitutional systems, although it seems that it has remained largely in place. Examples abound. In Morocco, for instance, there is a dichotomy between the formal, codified constitution and the constitution of the "*makhzen.*" The *makhzen* (literally "warehouse") represents

> the fulcrum of formal and informal power structures, the family and neo-patrimonial network, and the inner circle of advisers close to the Sovereign […] The Sovereign and the power structure built around him actually occupied the central position in the political system, functioning as an arbiter and a cohesive force among the different political factions.[11]

The constitution of the *makhzen*, which represents a major obstacle to the full implementation of the principles and values proclaimed in the official constitution, aims primarily to ensure that the long-term interests (of various nature) of the monarchy and its inner circle are not affected.

In Algeria, the various written constitutions adopted over the years since the country gained independence in 1962 have had to coexist with the informal rules and practices exercised by the so-called "*Le Pouvoir*," which is a very commonly used term in the country to refer to the "powers behind the throne."[12] This power base,

[11] Silvia Colombo, "Il Marocco tra modernità e tradizione" in Karim Mezran, Silvia Colombo and Saskia Van Genugten (eds.), *L'Africa mediterranea: Storia e futuro* (Donzelli 2011), 80. See also Mohamed Tozy, *Monarchie et Islam politique au Maroc* (Press de Sciences Po 1999), 40ff.

[12] John P. Entelis, "Algeria: The Outlier State?" in Justin O. Frosini and Francesco Biagi (eds.), *Political and Constitutional Transitions in North Africa: Actors and Factors* (Routledge 2015), 132.

which has for a long time determined the fate of the country, consists in the triad of the president of the Republic, the National Liberation Front (which was for a long time the only constitutionally legal party in the country), and the army. *Le Pouvoir*, which operates behind closed doors, has always been firm and resolute in preserving its coercive, economic, and technocratic assets.[13]

In Egypt, the formal constitution has long existed alongside the "security apparatus' constitution," which consists in the rules and practices exercised by the security forces. Having been the chief instrument of Mubarak-era repression, the security forces have remained extremely powerful and influential even under the Al-Sisi administration. Whenever the regime believes there is a serious threat to national security, the formal constitution takes a step back and is immediately replaced by this uncodified constitution, which does not provide for any democratic guarantees: Respect for human dignity and fundamental rights is not contemplated and torture is a standard practice.[14]

In other words, these unwritten constitutions are nothing but the informal norms of the "extra-constitutional state," consisting in the part of the state apparatus that operates outside official constitutional channels – not so much hidden as unaccountable.

C.2 CONSTITUTIONAL ENFORCEMENT

Comparative scholars have long stressed the crucial significance of the distinction between the "law in the books" and the "law in action."[15] This distinction appears to be of the utmost importance, especially when examining the actual enforcement of constitutional provisions, particularly in the context of *constitutional transitions*.[16]

[13] Ibid.

[14] See Human Rights Watch, "Egypt" in *Human Rights Watch World Report 2022* (2022), www.hrw.org/world-report/2022/country-chapters/egypt; Amr Magdi, "Egypt's Response to Torture: Punish the Victims," *Human Rights Watch* (June 10, 2022), www.hrw.org/news/2022/06/10/egypts-response-torture-punish-victims Among the cases that received a great deal of media attention over the past few years, consider that of Giulio Regeni (the Italian Ph.D. researcher who was tortured and then killed in Cairo in 2016 (see Declan Walsh, "Why Was an Italian Graduate Student Tortured and Murdered in Egypt?," *The New York Times Magazine* (August 15, 2017), www.nytimes.com/2017/08/15/magazine/giulio-regeni-italian-graduate-student-tortured-murdered-egypt.html)), and that of Patrick Zaki (the Egyptian Coptic student pursuing a master's degree at the University of Bologna who was arrested in Cairo in 2020 on charge of spreading false news at home and abroad (see "Researcher Patrick Zaki Faces Emergency Trial for Penning 2019 Article on Life as Coptic Christian in Egypt," *Mada Masr* (September 15, 2021), www.madamasr.com/en/2021/09/15/news/u/researcher-patrick-zaki-faces-emergency-trial-for-penning-2019-article-on-life-as-coptic-christian-in-egypt/)).

[15] See, for example, Harold C. Gutteridge, *Comparative Law: An Introduction to the Comparative Method of Legal Study and Research* (Cambridge University Press 1946); Tullio Ascarelli, "Interpretazione del diritto e studio del diritto comparato" in *Saggi di diritto commerciale* (Giuffrè 1955), 508; Karl H. Neumayer, "Law in the Books, Law in Action et les méthodes du droit comparé" in Mario Rotondi (ed.), *Buts et méthodes du droit comparé* (CEDAM 1973).

[16] See de Vergottini, *Le transizioni costituzionali*, at p. 1ff.

Paraphrasing this distinction, one can refer to the difference between the "law *in the constitution*" and the "law in action." Before the 2011 upheavals, in several Arab countries, the gap between the liberal-democratic principles often drawn on as role models in constitutions and their actual transposition and implementation was quite stark.[17] Therefore, it was no surprise that most of these countries were labeled, depending on the circumstances, as "autocratic regimes," "hybrid regimes," or "façade democracies."

In post-2011 constitutional systems, the issue of constitutional enforcement remains extremely problematic, especially with regard to the parts of the constitutions concerning the recognition and protection of fundamental principles and values, as well as rights and freedoms. According to Freedom House, at present not one single Arab state can be classified as a "free" country. Indeed, their respective statuses range from "not free" (e.g., Algeria, Libya, Egypt, Jordan, and Syria) to "partially free" (e.g., Morocco and Tunisia).[18] The only exception was Tunisia, which obtained the status of "free country" in 2015 (thanks to "the adoption of a progressive constitution, governance improvements under a consensus-based caretaker administration, and the holding of free and fair parliamentary and presidential elections, all with a high degree of transparency"),[19] although subsequently lost it in 2022 (when it was classified as "partially free," as "President Kaïs Saïed unilaterally dismissed and replaced the elected government, indefinitely suspended the parliament, and imposed harsh restrictions on civil liberties to suppress opposition to his actions").[20]

The issue of constitutional implementation was a key component of Ferdinand Lassalle's famous lecture held in Berlin in 1862 ("On the Nature of Constitutions"). Indeed, after examining the significance of constitutions, the prominent German socialist came to the following conclusion:

> When is a written constitution good and durable? Manifestly, only when it corresponds […] to the real constitution, that is, to the real relations between the social forces existing in the country. Where the written constitution does not correspond to the real constitution, then a conflict arises, a conflict which cannot be resolved and in which, unconditionally, over time, in the long run, the written constitution, the mere sheet of paper, must subject itself to the real constitution, to the actual relations between the social forces existing in the country.[21]

The tension between the "written" and the "real" constitution – to use Lassalle's words – emerged with full force over the years following the outbreak of the Arab

[17] See Maurizio Oliviero, *Il costituzionalismo dei paesi arabi. Volume I. Le Costituzioni del Maghreb* (Giuffrè 2003), 44.

[18] See Freedom House, *Freedom in the World 2022* (2022), 18–19, https://freedomhouse.org/sites/default/files/2022-02/FIW_2022_PDF_Booklet_Digital_Final_Web.pdf

[19] Freedom House, *Freedom in the World 2015* (2015), 10, https://freedomhouse.org/sites/default/files/01152015_FIW_2015_final.pdf

[20] Freedom House, "Tunisia" in *Freedom in the World 2022* (2022), https://freedomhouse.org/country/tunisia/freedom-world/2022

[21] Ferdinand Lassalle, *Sulla natura delle costituzioni* (Casa Editrice Ambrosiana 1945), 63.

Spring. It must not be forgotten that the slogans chanted during protest demonstrations indicated very clearly what the main goals of the protesters were: "Bread, freedom, and dignity" in Egypt, "Work, freedom, dignity" in Tunisia. These slogans very much recalled Nelson Mandela's famous statement made in 1993:

> A vote without food, shelter and health care would be to create the appearance of equality while actual inequality is entrenched. We do not want freedom without bread, no do we want bread without freedom. While providing the rights associated with democracy, our constitution should also create the basis for an expanding floor of entitlements so as to accord every citizen that measure of dignity intrinsic to being human.[22]

The problem was that the promises made to the population – promises that were incorporated into the texts of the new constitutions (e.g., human dignity, due process, free speech, freedom of assembly and association, and socioeconomic rights) – were in many cases not maintained, as the relevant constitutional provisions in these areas have remained little more than a dead letter. In particular, *social justice is still missing*. This has often generated major resentment, frustration, and anger among Arab people. As a reaction, several countries (including, e.g., Morocco, Jordan, Algeria, and Tunisia) have experienced a new wave of protest demonstrations over the past few years – so much so that some scholars have even used the expression "Arab Spring 2.0."[23]

A variety of reasons explain why several post-2011 constitutions were enforced only to a limited extent, especially with respect to those parts that deal with fundamental principles and rights and freedoms. The first set of reasons has to do with how the constitution is usually interpreted in the region. As analyzed earlier, constitutional texts are often mainly considered as "instruments of government" rather than "charters of values."[24] This means that Arab rulers, who enjoy broad powers and prerogatives, have little interest in promoting the implementation of constitutional norms other than those relating to the system of government and the organization of power. Furthermore, it must be recalled that the "unwritten" constitutions – which embody the interests of the "extra-constitutional state" – *de facto* prevail over the formal, written constitutions (particularly their most democratic aspects), especially in relation to issues that, in the eyes of the regime, are perceived as dangerous to national security.[25]

Another reason accounting for the difficulties in the process of constitutional implementation relates to the fact that, in the Arab world, the principle of the supremacy of the constitution – which is explicitly proclaimed in virtually all constitutional texts – exists more at the formal level than at the substantive level. Indeed,

22 Nelson Mandela, *Acceptance Address by Nelson Mandela at the Clark University Investiture, Atlanta, Georgia – United States* (July 10, 1993), www.mandela.gov.za/mandela_speeches/1993/930710_clark.htm

23 See Marwan Muasher, "Is This the Arab Spring 2.0?," *Carnegie Endowment for International Peace* (October 30, 2019), https://carnegieendowment.org/2019/10/30/is-this-arab-spring-2.0-pub-80220.

24 See Section C.1.1.

25 See Section C.1.3.

statutory legislation *de facto* often prevails over the constitution, particularly when it comes to the implementation of constitutional provisions on rights and freedoms. For this reason, "some authors have spoken of the *legality of the constitution*, that is, of the constitution that follows the evolution of laws, and not, as it should be, of laws that must be under the control of constitutions"[26] (emphasis added). The hierarchy of the sources of law is thus reversed: "Rather than have the constitution limit and define the scope of statutes, statutes define the limits of the constitutional text."[27] Unfortunately, in many cases, laws implementing fundamental rights and freedoms have resulted in the full-scale "hollowing out" of those very rights.

The issue of the normativity of the constitution is another factor that helps to account for the difficulties inherent within the process of constitutional enforcement. In the past, Arab constitutions were more "symbolic or programmatic" documents than "legal" texts.[28] For example, once they became independent, Arab States promulgated constitutions in part as an expression of "national sovereignty," and in part as a way "to organize or augment state authority."[29] This notion of the constitution has changed gradually over time. Nowadays these texts are perceived as being legally binding much more than in the past. An example of this trend toward the "normativization" of the constitutions is evidenced by the fact that the preambles to some constitutional texts (i.e., Morocco, Syria, Tunisia [2014], Egypt, and Algeria) are classified by the constitutions themselves as constituting an "integral part" of the constitution in question, with the result that they may represent a parameter for the constitutional review of legislation. On the other hand, however, full recognition of the normative value of the constitution in most Arab countries has yet to occur. This seems to be particularly evident with respect to the constitutional provisions on socioeconomic rights. These were significantly strengthened following the 2011 uprisings, but their implementation remains problematic. As explained by Zaid Al-Ali, "it is not that negotiators and drafters debated whether socioeconomic rights should be directly enforceable and decided against it. It is that they did not debate the matter at all."[30] The consequence is that the long-standing distinction between civil and political rights (which are considered to be directly enforceable) and socioeconomic rights (which are considered not to be directly enforceable) is still very strong: "The [socioeconomic] rights that are listed in

[26] Yadh Ben Achour, "Conclusions générales" in *Les Constitutions des Pays arabes: Colloque de Beyrouth*, 1998 (Bruylant 1999), 320. The author referred to pre-2011 constitutions, but his observation remains valid even today.

[27] Nathan J. Brown, "Constitutional Reform in the Arab Spring: A New Beginning or an Unhappy Ending?" in Noah Feldman and Nathan J. Brown (eds.), *Two Lectures on the Arab Spring* (Yale Law School – Occasional Papers 2013), 40.

[28] Thierry Le Roy, "Constitutionalism in the Maghreb. Between French Heritage and Islamic Concepts" in Rainer Grote and Tilmann J. Röder (eds.), *Constitutionalism in Islamic Countries: Between Upheaval and Continuity* (Oxford University Press 2012), 110.

[29] Nathan J. Brown, *Constitutions in a Nonconstitutional World: Arab Basic Laws and the Prospects for Accountable Government* (SUNY Press 2002), 91–92.

[30] Zaid Al-Ali, *Arab Constitutionalism: The Coming Revolution* (Cambridge University Press 2021), 216.

the constitutions and that drafters spent so much time rewording are therefore merely intended as a *list of aspirations*" (emphasis added).[31]

The last factor that needs to be considered in order to understand the difficulties associated with the implementation of certain parts of post-2011 constitutions is the following. As is masterfully illustrated by Roberto Gargarella,[32] the "institutional" part of the constitution, that is, the part dealing with the organization of and relations among the various state powers, exerts a very strong influence on the other part of the constitution, that is, the part dedicated to the recognition and protection of rights and freedoms. A "diffuse" power usually has positive effects on the enjoyment of fundamental rights, while a "concentrated" power tends to produce negative effects on the enjoyment of such rights. As Gargarella puts it,

> most new [Latin American] Constitutions have opted to keep the door of the "engine room" of the Constitution closed. The result of this is that the system of concentrated power begins to conflict with the social demands generated in the name of constitutional rights – which ends up implying that a part of the Constitution begins to work against the success of the second.[33]

From a comparative point of view, it appears that quite a clear trend can be observed on a global scale. On the one hand, most new constitutions expressly recognize an extremely large number of rights and freedoms, to a much greater extent than in the past. On the other hand, however, the institutional part of constitutions very often continues to be rather problematic, mainly because of the excessive concentration of power in the hands of the executive and the provision of overly weak mechanisms of checks and balances.[34] Gargarella has described this phenomenon in Latin America, although the excessive concentration of power in the hands of the executive can also be found, for example, in sub-Saharan Africa,[35] and also in the Arab world before the outbreak of the 2011 uprisings.[36]

Post-Arab Spring constitutions seem to confirm this trend. Indeed, on the one hand, important steps have been taken toward achieving greater recognition for rights and freedoms (although there are still many problematic aspects in this area as well); on the other hand, however, aside from the Tunisian Constitution of 2014,

31 Ibid., at 215.

32 See Roberto Gargarella, *Latin American Constitutionalism, 1810–2010: The Engine Room of the Constitution* (Oxford University Press 2013). Spanish version: *La sala de máquinas de la Constitución: Dos siglos de constitucionalismo en América Latina (1810–2010)* (Katz Editores 2014).

33 Gargarella, *Latin American Constitutionalism*, at p. VII.

34 This problem is also emphasized by Antonin Scalia. Referring to the US Constitution, Scalia argues that "it is those other humdrum provisions – the structural, mechanistic portions of the Constitutions that pit, in James Madison's words, 'ambition against ambition,' and make it impossible for any element of government to obtain unchecked power – that convert the Bill of Rights from a paper assurance to a living guarantee" (Antonin Scalia, *The Essential Scalia: On the Constitution, the Courts and the Rule of Law* (Crown Forum 2020), 35).

35 See H. Kwasi Prempeh, "Presidents Untamed" (2008) 19 *Journal of Democracy*, 109ff.

36 See Brown, *Constitutions in a Nonconstitutional World.*

the new constitutional texts have not marked a clear discontinuity with the past with respect to the institutional part (*"la sala de máquinas de la Constitución,"* that is, "the engine room of the Constitution," according to Gargarella's definition), and thus ultimately the system of government. This hyper-concentration of power in the hands of the executive inevitably operates as a factor weakening the implementation of constitutional provisions dealing with fundamental rights and freedoms. This is a major shortcoming that, unfortunately, will not be easy to remedy.

C.3 CONSTITUTIONAL WISHFUL THINKING?

The new constitutions or constitutional reforms adopted between 2011 and 2022 obviously to a certain extent differ from one another. However, they are united by certain underlying characteristics. First of all, they are still squeezed within a context marked by constrained constitutionalism. Therefore, with the partial exception of the 2014 Tunisian Constitution, post-2011 constitutions can only to a limited extent be classified as "garantiste" constitutions, according to Giovanni Sartori's definition. Indeed, in Sartori's view, "garantiste" constitutions are those constitutional texts whose *telos* corresponds to that of constitutionalism, that is, to restrict arbitrary power.[37] Furthermore, these documents are genuinely enforced, that is, the "law in the books" coincides with the "law in action." Unfortunately, despite some improvements compared to the past, post-2011 Arab constitutions continue to be characterized by a weak separation of powers and a weak system of checks and balances. Moreover, the parts of these texts that address the protection of rights and freedoms are often disregarded. For this reason, some features of new Arab constitutions are typical of "façade" or "fake" constitutions (always according to Sartori's definition). Indeed, "façade" constitutions "take the appearance of 'true constitutions.' What makes them untrue is that they are disregarded (at least in their essential garantiste features). Actually they are 'trap-constitutions.' As far as the techniques of liberty and the rights of the power addressees are concerned, they are a dead letter."[38] It should be noted that, despite their democratic shortcomings, post-Arab Spring constitutions can hardly be included in the third category of constitutional texts identified by Sartori, that is, that of "nominal" constitutions. Indeed, these are "merely organizational constitutions, i.e., the collection of rules which organize but do not restrain the exercise of political power in a given polity. They frankly describe a system of limitless, unchecked power. They are not a dead letter. It is only that this letter is irrelevant to the *telos* of constitutionalism."[39] This is not the case for post-Arab Spring constitutions, which do provide for some checks on the executive branch, although these checks are clearly too weak.

37 Giovanni Sartori, "Constitutionalism: A Preliminary Discussion" (1962) 56 *The American Political Science Review*, 855.

38 Ibid., at 861.

39 Ibid. It should be noted that despite the use of a different terminology, Karl Loewenstein, *Political Power and the Governmental Process* (The University of Chicago Press 1957), 147ff., provides for a

The fact that the Arab world had grown "rich in constitutions but poorer in constitutionalism"[40] was noted by Nathan J. Brown as early as 2003. Twenty years later, this observation is still valid. Out of all the countries involved in the Arab Spring, the only one that managed for some time to embark on a serious process of democratization (a process that was later unfortunately abandoned) was Tunisia. All other countries have remained illiberal regimes, or (at best) hybrid regimes.

Another feature (which is closely related to the previous one) uniting post-2011 constitutions – again, with the partial exception of the 2014 Tunisian Constitution – is that these documents cannot be regarded as "transformative" constitutions. While initially having been used to describe South Africa's post-apartheid constitutional order,[41] the idea of a "transformative" constitution refers to "the adoption of a constitutional order which is expected to 'transform' the existing pre-constitutional order. To this extent, these constitutions are aspirational and are meant to empower the newly democratized state to make significant changes to the existing social and economic order."[42] The Kenyan Supreme Court, albeit using different words, expressed a similar idea: "Transformative constitutions are new social contracts that are committed to fundamental transformations in societies. They provide a legal framework for the fundamental transformation required that expects a solid commitment from the society's ruling classes."[43]

Post-Arab Spring constitutions do contain some innovative elements that seek to mark a break with the previous constitutional order. Although, as recalled earlier, they are often not implemented, this has been the case for provisions dealing with fundamental principles (e.g., equality and dignity), as well as rights and freedoms. In other equally important fields, however, continuity with the past is still very strong. Citizenship remains an extremely problematic issue, as certain categories of people (including, e.g., women and non-Muslims) are still not regarded as fully-fledged citizens.[44] It is hoped that the calls made over the past few years by prominent religious leaders and institutions may help to combat prejudices and stereotypes and facilitate the adoption of legal reforms aimed at removing (or at least reducing) discrimination against women and non-Muslims, toward a more inclusive citizenship. Another

classification very similar to that provided for by Sartori. Indeed, Loewenstein calls "normative" the constitutions that Sartori defines as "garantiste"; "nominal" the constitutions that Sartori defines as "façade"; "semantic" the constitutions that Sartori defines as "nominal." See also Dieter Grimm, "Types of Constitution" in Michel Rosenfeld and András Sajó (eds.), *The Oxford Handbook of Comparative Constitutional Law* (Oxford University Press 2012), 105–107.

40 Nathan J. Brown, "Regimes Reinventing Themselves: Constitutional Development in the Arab World" (2003) 18 *International Sociology*, 41.

41 See Karl E. Klare, "Legal Culture and Transformative Constitutionalism" (1998) 14 *South African Journal on Human Rights*, 146ff.

42 Heinz Klug, "Transformative Constitutions and the Role of Integrity Institutions in Tempering Power: The Case of Resistance to State Capture in Post-Apartheid South Africa" (2019) 67 *Buffalo Law Review*, 701.

43 Kenyan Supreme Court, *Communications Commission of Kenya & 5 others* v. *Royal Media Services Limited & 5 others* (2014), para. 377.

44 See Chapter 4.

problematic issue is the overconcentration of powers in the hands of heads of state, which significantly hinders the implementation of those parts of constitutions that deal with rights and freedoms.[45] Thus, rather than following a transformative approach, most countries in the region have, despite the revolutionary context, "opted to pursue an *incremental* approach"[46] (emphasis added) to constitutional reforms.

There are various different reasons for the difficulties in establishing democratic regimes based on the principles of constitutionalism in the Arab region, including a weak constitutional culture, fairly widespread support for one-man rule, the dire economic and social conditions in which most people live, as well as the adherence by some segments of the population to a very conservative (and in some cases even fundamentalist) view of Islam and *sharia*. Many, if not all, of these reasons coincide with the reasons that prevented the establishment of democracy and constitutionalism before 2011. One might thus be tempted to conclude that very little has changed compared to the past. This conclusion may not be too far removed from the truth. Still, one must not overlook the fact that, following the outbreak of the Arab Spring, there was one country – Tunisia – that showed that the possibility of breaking with the tradition of previous autocratic regimes is not simply a mirage. Tunisia adopted a profoundly democratic constitution in 2014 following an equally democratic constitution-making process. Tunisia held free and fair elections and experienced a peaceful alternation of political parties in power. The Tunisian constitutional order was based on the principle of the separation of powers and a system of checks and balances and was characterized by fairly effective protection for civil, political, and religious rights. Even women's rights and the principle of gender equality were strengthened. Obviously, this experience also featured some serious weaknesses and shortcomings, including antagonism and polarization between Islamists and non-Islamists, the failure to implement some crucial parts of the constitution (consider the failure to establish the Constitutional Court or the very weak enforcement of socioeconomic rights),[47] rampant corruption, a high rate of unemployment, and the inability to satisfy people's hopes for improved living standards. Kaïs Saïed relied precisely on these weaknesses in order to re-establish illiberal rule. It seems fair to argue that, during the 2011–2021 decade, Tunisian "garantiste" and "transformative" constitutionalism (as defined earlier) showed its buds, but not its blossoms. With its successes and failures, Tunisia represents a particularly interesting constitutional laboratory in the region. Above all, it shows that the path toward democracy and constitutionalism in the Arab world – despite being extremely tortuous, full of obstacles, and beset by constant risks of democratic backsliding – is nonetheless something more than wishful thinking.

45 See Section C.2.

46 Zaid Al-Ali, "The Arab Spring Constitutions. For Whose Benefit?" in Tom Ginsburg and Aziz Z. Huq (eds.), *Assessing Constitutional Performance* (Cambridge University Press 2016), 388.

47 On the difficulties of the process of constitutional enforcement, see Democracy Reporting International, *La mise en œuvre de la Constitution tunisienne du 27 janvier 2014 au niveau du cadre juridique. Bilan* (September 2022), https://democracyreporting.s3.eu-central-1.amazonaws.com/images/63761f99ace6d.pdf

Bibliography

ACADEMIC LITERATURE AND SCIENTIFIC SOURCES

Abat i Ninet, Antoni, and Tushnet, Mark, *The Arab Spring: An Essay on Revolution and Constitutionalism* (Edward Elgar 2015).

Abbiate, Tania, "The Cross-Cutting Issue of Religion in the Tunisian Participatory Constitution-Making Process" in Tania Abbiate, Markus Böckenförde and Veronica Federico (eds.), *Public Participation in African Constitutionalism* (Routledge 2018).

Abbiate, Tania, *La partecipazione popolare ai processi costituenti: L'esperienza tunisina* (Editoriale Scientifica 2016).

Abdel Fattah, Nabil, "The Political Role of the Egyptian Judiciary" in Nathalie Bernard-Maugiron (ed.), *Judges and Political Reform in Egypt* (The American University in Cairo Press 2008).

Abdelaal, Mohamed, "The Flawed Public Participation in the Egyptian Constitutional Process" in Tania Abbiate, Markus Böckenförde and Veronica Federico (eds.), *Public Participation in African Constitutionalism* (Routledge 2018).

Abdelkafi, Badreddine, "L'Assemblée Nationale Constituante et la société civile: quelle relation?" in *La Constitution de la Tunisie – Processus, principes et perspectives* (UNDP 2016).

Abdellatif, Adel, Pagliani, Paola, and Hsu, Ellen, *Arab Human Development Report Research Paper – Leaving No One Behind: Towards Inclusive Citizenship in Arab Countries* (2019), https://bit.ly/3TkFlbH

Abouchi, El Houssain, "La pratique référendaire dans le régime constitutionnel marocaine, 1962–2011: une analyse du contenu" in *Cinquante ans de vie constitutionnelle au Maroc: quel bilan?* (Publications de l'Association marocaine de Droit constitutionnel 2013).

Abouelenen, Mohamed Maher, "Judges and Acts of Sovereignty" in Nathalie Bernard-Maugiron (ed.), *Judges and Political Reform in Egypt* (The American University in Cairo Press 2008).

Abu-Karaki, Muddather, Faqir, Raed S. A., and Marashdah, Majed Ahmad K., "Democracy & Judicial Controlling in Jordan: A Constitutional Study" (2011) 4 *Journal of Politics and Law*.

Ackerman, Bruce, "The Emergency Constitution" (2004) 113 *The Yale Law Journal*.

Ackerman, Bruce, *We the People: Foundations* (Harvard University Press 1991).

"A Common Word between Us and You" (2007), www.acommonword.com/the-acw-document/

Adnane, Abdelhamid, "Tratamiento jurídico-constitucional de los entes territoriales en Marruecos y los indicadores de la autonomía mermada del poder regional," *Federalismi.it* (June 24, 2020), www.federalismi.it.

Agamben, Giorgio, *State of Exception* (University of Chicago Press 2005).

Ahmed, Leila, *Women and Gender in Islam* (Yale University Press 1992).

Al-Ali, Zaid, "Algeria's Draft Constitution 2020," *IACL-AIDC Blog* (May 14, 2020), https://blog-iacl-aidc.org/2020-posts/2020/5/14/algerias-draft-constitution-2020

Al-Ali, Zaid, *Arab Constitutionalism: The Coming Revolution* (Cambridge University Press 2021).

Al-Ali, Zaid, "The Arab Spring Constitutions: For Whose Benefit?" in Tom Ginsburg and Aziz Z. Huq (eds.), *Assessing Constitutional Performance* (Cambridge University Press 2016).

Al-Ali, Zaid, "Constitutional Legitimacy in Iraq: What Role Local Context?" in Rainer Grote and Tilmann J. Röder (eds.), *Constitutionalism in Islamic Countries: Between Upheaval and Continuity* (Oxford University Press 2012).

Al-Ali, Zaid, "Egypt's Third Constitution in Three Years: A Critical Analysis," *ConstitutionNet* (December 20, 2013), bit.ly/4a3Gnyv

Al-Ali, Zaid, *Libya's Final Draft Constitution: A Contextual Analysis (Version 2)*, International IDEA (December 2020), bit.ly/3IvrQzJ

Al-Ali, Zaid, "The New Egyptian Constitution: An Initial Assessment of Its Merits and Flaws," *Open Democracy* (December 26, 2012), bit.ly/3VeMao8

Al-Ali, Zaid, *The Struggle for Iraq's Future: How Corruption, Incompetence and Sectarianism Have Undermined Democracy* (Yale University Press 2014).

Al-Azhar, "Basic Freedoms" in Rainer Grote and Tilmann J. Röder (eds.), *Constitutionalism, Human Rights, and Islam after the Arab Spring* (Oxford University Press 2016).

Al-Azhar, "Citizenship and Coexistence" (2017), bit.ly/4a7RUgo

Al-Azhar, "Countering Extremism and Terrorism" (2014), bit.ly/3VdvvtI

Al-Azhar, "The Future of Egypt" in Rainer Grote and Tilmann J. Röder (eds.), *Constitutionalism, Human Rights, and Islam after the Arab Spring* (Oxford University Press 2016).

Al-Azhar, "Renovation in Islamic Thought" (2020), bit.ly/3TxKoaF

Al Khatib, Wael, *Decentralization in Jordan* (Konrad Adenauer Stiftung 2020), bit.ly/3wXE7dJ

Al-Mawlawi, Ali, "Salvaging State Legitimacy in Iraq through Decentralization" in Aslı Ü. Bâli and Omar M. Dajani (eds.), *Federalism and Decentralization in the Contemporary Middle East and North Africa* (Cambridge University Press 2023).

Al Momani, Sabah Mousa, "Acts of Sovereignty as a Restriction on Judicial Control" (2020) 13 *Journal of Politics and Law*.

Al Naimat, Tareq, "Constitutional Amendments in Jordan," *Carnegie Endowment for International Peace* (March 1, 2022), https://carnegieendowment.org/sada/86538

Albert, Richard, *Constitutional Amendments: Making, Breaking, and Changing Constitutions* (Oxford University Press 2019).

Albert, Richard, "Does the World Need an International Constitutional Court?" (2023) 3 *Rutgers International Law and Human Rights Journal*.

Aljazy, Ibrahim, and Nasrawi, Laith, "Positive Trends in Jordan: Constitutional Amendments of 2011" (2010–2011) 16 *Yearbook of Islamic and Middle Eastern Law*.

Aljidie, Fawaz, *The Kuwaiti Constitutional System* (Kuwait City 2018).

Alkadiri, Raad, "Federalism and Iraq's Constitutional Stalemate," *Chatham House* (November 2020), bit.ly/3VdqL7A

Allagui, Abdelkrim, *Juifs et musulmans en Tunisie* (Tallandier 2016).

Allegretti, Umberto, Corsi, Cecilia, and Allegretti, Giovanni, "Constituent Process and Constituent Assembly: The Making of Constitutions through the Larger Involvement of Citizens," *Forum costituzionale* (July 27, 2016), www.forumcostituzionale.it

Almutairi, Fawaz, "The Kuwaiti Constitutional Court and Its Role in Protecting the Fundamental Liberties" in Anja Schoeller-Schletter (ed.), *Constitutional Review in the Middle East and North Africa* (Nomos 2021).

Alsarghali, Sanaa, "An (Un)constitutional Hangover? An Analysis of the Current Palestinian Basic Law in Light of Palestine's Constitutional Heritage" (2017) 2017 *University of Illinois Law Review*.

Alsarghali, Sanaa, Mabon, Simon, and Ruished, Adel (eds.), *States of Exception or Exceptional States: Law, Politics and Giorgio Agamben in the Middle East* (Bloomsbury Publishing 2022).

"A Mediterranean Conversation on Human Fraternity and Inclusive Citizenship" in Fabio Petito, Fadi Daou and Michael D. Driessen (eds.), *Human Fraternity & Inclusive Citizenship: Interreligious Engagement in the Mediterranean* (ISPI – June 2021), bit.ly/4abgJrL

Amin, Qasim, "*Al-Mar'a al-gadida*" *in The New Woman: A Document in the Early Debate on Egyptian Feminism* (The American University in Cairo Press 1995).

Amin, Qasim, "*Tahrir al-mar'a*" *in The Liberation of Women: A Document in the History of Egyptian Feminism* (The American University in Cairo Press 1993).

"Amman Message" (2004), https://ammanmessage.com/the-amman-message-full/

An-Na'im, Abdullahi Ahmed, "Beyond *dhimmihood*: Citizenship and Human Rights" in Robert W. Hefner (ed.), *The New Cambridge History of Islam. Volume 6. Muslims and Modernity: Culture and Society since 1800* (Cambridge University Press 2010).

An-Na'im, Abdullahi Ahmed, "Islam, Sharia and Democratic Transformation in the Arab World" (2012) 87 *Die Friedens-Warte*.

An-Na'im, Abdullahi Ahmed, "The Islamic Law of Apostasy and Its Modern Applicability: A Case from the Sudan" (1986) 16 *Religion*.

An-Na'im, Abdullahi Ahmed, "Mahmud Muhammad Taha and the Crisis in Islamic Law Reform: Implications for Interreligious Relations" (1988) 25 *Journal of Ecumenical Studies*.

An-Na'im, Abdullahi Ahmed, "Religious Minorities under Islamic Law and the Limits of Cultural Relativism" (1987) 9 *Human Rights Quarterly*.

An-Na'im, Abdullahi Ahmed, "Translator's Introduction" in Mahmud Muhammad Taha, *The Second Message of Islam* (Syracuse University Press 1987).

Annovi, Claudia, "La fine dell'eccezione tunisina?," *Centro Studi Internazionali* (July 29, 2021), www.cesi-italia.org/it/articoli/la-fine-delleccezione-tunisina

Araabi, Samer, and Hilal, Leila, "Decentralization in State Disintegration: An Examination of Governance Experiments in Syria" in Aslı Ü. Bâli and Omar M. Dajani (eds.), *Federalism and Decentralization in the Contemporary Middle East and North Africa* (Cambridge University Press 2023).

Asad, Talal, and An-Na'im, Abdullahi Ahmed, *Religion, Law, and the Politics of Human Rights: Talal Asad and Abdullahi An-Na'im in Conversation* (September 29, 2009), bit .ly/43sAFEt

Ascarelli, Tullio, "Interpretazione del diritto e studio del diritto comparato" in *Saggi di diritto commerciale* (Giuffrè 1955).

Atassi, Karim, *Syria, the Strength of an Idea: The Constitutional Architectures of Its Political Regimes* (Cambridge University Press 2018).

Auf, Yussef, "Egypt's Constitutional Committees," *Atlantic Council* (September 5, 2013), https://atlanticcouncil.org/blogs/menasource/egypt-s-constitutional-committees/

Auf, Yussef, "Equality in the Jurisprudence of the Supreme Constitutional Court of Egypt" in Anja Schoeller-Schletter and Robert Poll (eds.), *Balancing Individual Rights, Religious Law and Equality: Landmark Decisions from Egypt, Kuwait and Tunisia* (Konrad Adenauer Stiftung – Rule of Law Programme Middle East and North Africa 2021), bit.ly/3TceJsr

Auf, Yussef, "Islam and Sharia Law: Historical, Constitutional, and Political Context in Egypt," *Atlantic Council* (May 2016), www.atlanticcouncil.org/wp-content/uploads/2016/05/Islam_and_Sharia_Law.pdf

Auf, Yussef, "The State of Emergency in Egypt: An Exception or Rule?," *Atlantic Council* (February 2, 2018), bit.ly/4cbRfwg

Auf, Yussef, "What Does the Supreme Constitutional Court's Decision Mean?," *Atlantic Council* (June 5, 2013), www.atlanticcouncil.org/blogs/menasource/what-does-the-supreme-constitutional-court-s-decision-mean/

Aviv, Efrat, "Millet System in the Ottoman Empire" in *Islamic Studies* (Oxford University Press) (November 28, 2016), www.oxfordbibliographies.com/view/document/obo-9780195390155/obo-9780195390155-0231.xml

Avocats Sans Frontières, *The Tunisian Response to the Covid-19 Pandemic – When the State of Exception Overlaps with the State of Emergency* (July 1, 2020), https://asf.be/the-tunisian-response-to-the-covid-19-pandemic-when-the-state-of-exception-overlaps-with-the-state-of-emergency/

Awawda, Osayd, *The Palestinian Constitutional Court: An Assessment of Its Independence Under the Emergency Regime* (Cambridge Scholars Publishing 2022).

Bâli, Asli Ü., and Lerner, Hanna (eds.), *Constitution Writing, Religion and Democracy* (Cambridge University Press 2017).

Bâli, Asli Ü., and Lerner, Hanna, "Designing Constitutions in Religiously Divided Societies" in Asli Ü. Bâli and Hanna Lerner (eds.), *Constitution Writing, Religion and Democracy* (Cambridge University Press 2017).

Bâli, Asli Ü., and Lerner, Hanna, "Introduction" in Asli Ü. Bâli and Hanna Lerner (eds.), *Constitution Writing, Religion and Democracy* (Cambridge University Press 2017).

Ballantyne, William, "Commercial Law: The Conflict in Shar'ia and Secular Law Public Policy" in Sohrab Behdad and Farhad Nomani (eds.), *Islam and the Everyday World: Public Policy Dilemmas* (Routledge 2006).

Bammarny, Bawar, "The Legal Status of the Kurds in Iraq and Syria" in Rainer Grote and Tilmann J. Röder (eds.), *Constitutionalism, Human Rights, and Islam after the Arab Spring* (Oxford University Press 2016).

Baraggia, Antonia, "Constitutional Moment" in Rainer Grote, Frauke Lachenmann and Rüdiger Wolfrum (eds.), *Max Planck Encyclopedia of Comparative Constitutional Law* (Oxford University Press 2020).

Bartu, Peter, and MacEachern, Aidan, "The Devil Is in the Details: Iraqi Kurdistan's Evolving Autonomy" in Aslı Ü. Bâli and Omar M. Dajani (eds.), *Federalism and Decentralization in the Contemporary Middle East and North Africa* (Cambridge University Press 2023).

Basri, Carole, "The Jewish Refugees from Arab Countries: An Examination of Legal Rights – A Case Study of the Human Rights Violations of Iraqi Jews" (2003) 26 *Fordham International Law Journal*.

Bava, Sophie, and Boissevain, Katia, "Migrations africaines et variations religieuses: les églises chrétiennes du Maroc et de Tunisie" (2020) 32 *Migration Société*.

"Beirut Declaration on Religious Freedom" (2015), www.lebanonrenaissance.org/assets/Uploads/The-Beirut-Declaration-on-Religious-Freedom.pdf

Bekhechi, Mohammed Abdelwahab, "Remarques sur l'évolution du droit constitutionnel algérien de l'indépendance à la révision constitutionnelle de 1996" in *Les Constitutions des Pays arabes: Colloque de Beyrouth*, 1998 (Bruylant 1999).

Belaiz, Tayeb, "Allocution de M. Tayeb Belaiz, Président du Conseil Constitutionnel, à l'ouverture de la journée d'étude organisée à Alger, le 22 avril 2013, sur le thème 'L'extension de la saisine du Conseil Constitutionnel'" (2013) 2 *Revue du Conseil Constitutionnel*.

Ben Abda, Hana, "The Provisional Instance of Tunisia: An Insufficient Substitute for a Constitutional Court," *IACL-AIDC Blog* (July 15, 2021), https://blog-iacl-aidc

.org/menaregion/the-provisional-instance-of-tunisia-an-insufficient-substitute-for-a-constitutional-court-ddjlw

Ben Achour, Rafaâ, "La Constitution tunisienne du 27 janvier 2014" (2014) 100 *Revue française de droit constitutionnel.*

Ben Achour, Rafaâ, "La Dyarchie dans la Constitution tunisienne" in *La Constitution de la Tunisie – Processus, principes et perspectives* (UNDP 2016).

Ben Achour, Rafâa, "Le contrôle consultatif de la constitutionnalité des lois par le Conseil constitutionnel tunisien" in *Constitutions et pouvoirs: Mélanges en l'honneur de Jean Gicquel* (Montchrestien – L'extenso éditions 2008).

Ben Achour, Rafaâ, "Vicissitudes du contrôle de constitutionnalité des lois" (1988) 4 *Annuaire international de justice constitutionnelle.*

Ben Achour, Rafaâ, and Ben Achour, Sana, "La transition démocratique en Tunisie: entre légalité constitutionnelle et légitimité révolutionnaire" (2012) 92 *Revue française de droit constitutionnel.*

Ben Achour, Rafâa, and Lachaal, Abdessalem, "Le contrôle de la constitutionalité des lois (état de la question)" (1991) 7 *Annuaire international de justice constitutionnelle.*

Ben Achour, Sana, "Le Code tunisien du statut personnel, 50 ans après: les dimensions de l'ambivalence" (2007) II *L'Année du Maghreb.*

Ben Achour, Yadh, "An International Constitutional Court. Bulwark against the Erosion of Constitutional Democracy" in Rainer Grote and Tilmann J. Röder (eds.), *Constitutionalism, Human Rights, and Islam after the Arab Spring* (Oxford University Press 2016).

Ben Achour, Yadh, "Conclusions générales" in *Les Constitutions des Pays arabes: Colloque de Beyrouth, 1998* (Bruylant 1999).

Ben Achour, Yadh, "La révolution tunisienne dans ses manifestations constitutionnelles. La première phase de transition (14 Janvier 2011–16 Décembre 2011)" in *La Constitution de la Tunisie – Processus, principes et perspectives* (UNDP 2016).

Ben Achour, Yadh, *Tunisie: Une révolution en pays d'Islam* (Cérès éditions 2017).

Benabdallah, Mohammed Amine, "Préface" in Mohammed Benyahya (ed.), *Les grandes décisions de la jurisprudence du Conseil Constitutionnel [1994–2013]* (Publications de REMALD 2013, no. 31).

Benchemsi, Ahmed, "Mohammed VI, despote malgré lui" (2013) 145 *Pouvoirs.*

Benchikh, Madjid, "The Grip of the Army on Algeria's Political System" in Rainer Grote and Tilmann J. Röder (eds.), *Constitutionalism, Human Rights, and Islam after the Arab Spring* (Oxford University Press 2016).

Bendourou, Omar, "La consécration de la monarchie gouvernante" (2012) VIII *L'Année du Maghreb* (on-line issue).

Bendourou, Omar, "La nouvelle Constitution marocaine du 29 juillet 2011" (2012) 91 *Revue française de droit constitutionnel.*

Bendourou, Omar, "Le Conseil constitutionnel et les droit fondamentaux" (2004) 56 *Revue marocaine d'administration locale et de développement.*

Bennadji, Chérif, "De l'ambigüité des rapports entre le président de la République et le pouvoir judiciaire en Algérie: de l'usage de la formule 'le président de la République, Premier magistrat du pays'" (2007) III *L'Année du Maghreb* (on-line issue).

Bensoussan, Georges, *Les Juifs du monde arabe: La question interdite* (Odile Jacob 2017).

Benyettou, Wissam, "Will Algeria Start 2016 with a New Constitution? Long-awaited Constitutional Revision and the Road to Democratic Transition," *ConstitutionNet* (November 24, 2015), https://constitutionnet.org/news/will-algeria-start-2016-new-constitution-long-awaited-constitutional-revision-and-road

Bernard-Maugiron, Nathalie, *Droit contemporain des pays arabes* (Sirey 2023).

Bernard-Maugiron, Nathalie, "La constitution égyptienne de 2014: quelle réforme constitutionnelle pour l'Égypte?" (2015) 103 *Revue française de droit constitutionnel*.

Bernard-Maugiron, Nathalie, "La Haute Cour constitutionnelle égyptienne, gardienne des libertés publiques" (1999) 2 *Égypte/Monde arabe*.

Bernard-Maugiron, Nathalie, "La place du religieux dans le processus constitutionnel en Égypte après 2011" (2018) 181 *Archives de sciences sociales des religions*.

Bernard-Maugiron, Nathalie, *Le politique à l'épreuve du judiciaire: la justice constitutionnelle en Égypte* (Bruylant 2003).

Bernard-Maugiron, Nathalie, "Religious References in the Constitutions of the Arab World: Islamization of the Constitution or Constitutionalization of Religion?" in Anja Schoeller-Schletter (ed.), *Constitutional Review in the Middle East and North Africa* (Nomos 2021).

Bernard-Maugiron, Nathalie, "State Powers and Constitution Drafting Processes in Post-Revolutionary Transitions in North Africa" in Senén Florensa (ed.), *The Arab Transitions in a Changing World: Building Democracies in Light of International Experiences* (IE Med 2016).

Bernard-Maugiron, Nathalie, "Strong Presidentialism. The Model of Mubarak's Egypt" in Rainer Grote and Tilmann J. Röder (eds.), *Constitutionalism in Islamic Countries: Between Upheaval and Continuity* (Oxford University Press 2012).

Bernoussi, Nadia, "La Constitution de 2011 et le juge constitutionnel" in Centre d'Études Internationales (ed.), *La Constitution marocaine de 2011: Analyses et commentaires* (LGDJ 2012).

Bernoussi, Nadia, "Morocco's Constitutional Court after the 2011 Reforms" in Rainer Grote and Tilmann J. Röder (eds.), *Constitutionalism, Human Rights, and Islam after the Arab Spring* (Oxford University Press 2016).

Bernoussi, Nadia, and El Maslouhi, Abderrahim, "Les chantiers de la 'bonne justice'. Contraintes et renouveau de la politique judiciaire au Maroc" (2012) 91 *Revue française de droit constitutionnel*.

Bessalah, Aymen, "Kaïs Saïed's National Monologue on a New Tunisian Constitution," *Project on Middle East Democracy – POMED* (June 2022), https://pomed.org/wp-content/uploads/2022/06/2022_06b_Bessalah_Snapshot.pdf

Biagi, Francesco, "The Algerian Constitutional Reform of 2016: A Critical Analysis" (2017) 17 *Global Jurist*.

Biagi, Francesco, "Constitution Drafting after the Arab Spring: A Comparative Overview" (2022) 29 *Indiana Journal of Global Legal Studies*.

Biagi, Francesco, "Constitutional Review after the Arab Spring: Reforms, Challenges and Perspectives" in Anja Schoeller-Schletter (ed.), *Constitutional Review in the Middle East and North Africa* (Nomos 2021).

Biagi, Francesco, "Constitutional Review in Algeria Following the 2016 Reform: With Particular Reference to the 'Exception of Unconstitutionality'" in Anja Schoeller-Schletter (ed.), *Constitutional Review in the Middle East and North Africa* (Nomos 2021).

Biagi, Francesco, "Estados de emergencia y crisis pandémica: algunas reflexiones sobre el papel de los tribunales constitucionales" (2021) 1 *Asuntos constitucionales*.

Biagi, Francesco, *European Constitutional Courts and Transitions to Democracy* (Cambridge University Press 2020).

Biagi, Francesco, "La Costituzione del Libano" in Luca Mezzetti (ed.), *Codice delle Costituzioni. Paesi islamici. Vol. VI.3* (Wolters Kluwer – CEDAM 2023).

Biagi, Francesco, "The Pilot of *Limited* Change: Mohammed VI and the Transition in Morocco" in Justin O. Frosini and Francesco Biagi (eds.), *Political and Constitutional Transitions in North Africa: Actors and Factors* (Routledge 2015).

Biagi, Francesco, "Religion in Constitution-Making Processes: Comparative Perspectives" in Susanna Mancini (ed.), *Constitutions and Religion* (Edward Elgar 2020).

Biagi, Francesco, "The 2011 Constitution-making Process in Morocco: A Limited and Controlled Public Participation" in Tania Abbiate, Markus Böckenförde and Veronica Federico (eds.), *Public Participation in African Constitutionalism* (Routledge 2018).

Biagi, Francesco, "The Separation and Distribution of Powers under the New Moroccan Constitution" in Rainer Grote and Tilmann J. Röder (eds.), *Constitutionalism, Human Rights, and Islam after the Arab Spring* (Oxford University Press 2016).

Biagi, Francesco, "Tunisi: la primavera araba sfiorisce in stato d'eccezione" (2021) 4 *Quaderni costituzionali*.

Biagi, Francesco, "Tunisia: la Costituzione di Kaïs Saïed," *Diritti Comparati* (July 28, 2022), www.diritticomparati.it/tunisia-la-costituzione-di-kais-saied/

Biagi, Francesco, "Will Surviving Constitutionalism in Morocco and Jordan Work in the Long Run? A Comparison with Three Past Authoritarian Regimes" (2014) 3 *Cambridge Journal of International and Comparative Law*.

Biagi, Francesco, "Women's Rights and Constitutional Implementation in the MENA Region: Challenges and Perspectives" in Claudia Padovani and Francesca Helm (eds.), *Rethinking the Transition Process in Syria: Constitution, Participation and Gender Equality* (Research-Publishing.net 2018).

Bint al-Shati, *The Rhetorical Explanation of the Holy Quran* (Tafsir al-bayani li-l-Quran al-karim, 1962–1968).

Blanc, François-Paul, "La régionalisation et la Constitution de 2011: genèse et prospective" in Centre d'Études Internationales (ed.), *La Constitution marocaine de 2011: Analyses et commentaires* (LGDJ 2012).

Blount, Justin, "Participation in Constitutional Design" in Tom Ginsburg and Rosalind Dixon (eds.), *Comparative Constitutional Law* (Edward Elgar 2011).

Blount, Justin, Elkins, Zachary, and Ginsburg, Tom, "Does the Process of Constitution-making Matter?" in Tom Ginsburg (ed.), *Comparative Constitutional Design* (Cambridge University Press 2012).

Böckenförde, Markus, "Letting the Constituent Power Decide? Merits and Challenges of Referenda in Constitution-making Processes in Africa" in Tania Abbiate, Markus Böckenförde and Veronica Federico (eds.), *Public Participation in African Constitutionalism* (Routledge 2018).

Bognetti, Giovanni, *Dividing Powers: A Theory of the Separation of Powers*, English edition by Antonia Baraggia and Luca Pietro Vanoni (Wolters Kluwer – CEDAM 2017).

Bognetti, Giovanni, *Introduzione al diritto costituzionale comparato* (Giappichelli 1994).

Boissevain, Katia, "Algeria and Tunisia" in Kenneth R. Ross, Mariz Tadros and Todd M. Johnson (eds.), *Christianity in North Africa and West Asia* (Edinburgh University Press 2018).

Boissevain, Katia, "Le baptême adulte de chrétiens tunisiens: rituel public d'un engagement privé" (2014) *Cahiers d'études du religieux. Recherches interdisciplinaires* (on-line), special issue, https://journals.openedition.org/cerri/1408

Borrillo, Sara, "Women's Movements and the Recognition of Gender Equality in the Constitution-Making Process in Morocco and Tunisia (2011–2014)" in Ruth Rubio-Marín and Helen Irving (eds.), *Women as Constitution-Makers: Case Studies from the New Democratic Era* (Cambridge University Press 2019).

Boukhars, Anouar, *Politics in Morocco: Executive Monarchy and Enlightened Authoritarianism* (Routledge 2011).

Boumghar, Mouloud, "Le gant constitutionnel réversible: accessoire de l'uniforme militaire. Regard critique sur la crise constitutionnelle algérienne de 2019" (2019) 21 *L'Année du Maghreb* (online version).

Boutin, Christophe, De Cara, Jean-Yves and Nimer Saint-Prot, Charles, *Les constitutions arabes* (Karthala 2016).

Bras, Jean-Philippe, "Un État 'civil' peut-il être religieux? Débats tunisien" (2016) 156 *Pouvoirs*.

Brown, Nathan J., "Citizenship, Religious Rights, and State Identity in Arab Constitutions: Who is Free and What are They Free to Do?" in Nehal Bhuta (ed.), *Freedom of Religion, Secularism, and Human Rights* (Oxford University Press 2019).

Brown, Nathan J., "Constitutional Reform in the Arab Spring: A New Beginning or an Unhappy Ending?" in Noah Feldman and Nathan J. Brown, *Two Lectures on the Arab Spring* (Yale Law School – Occasional Papers 2013).

Brown, Nathan J., *Constitutions in a Nonconstitutional World: Arab Basic Laws and the Prospects for Accountable Government* (SUNY Press 2002).

Brown, Nathan J., "Egypt: A Constitutional Court in an Unconstitutional Setting" in Justin O. Frosini and Francesco Biagi (eds.), *Political and Constitutional Transitions in North Africa: Actors and Factors* (Routledge 2015).

Brown, Nathan J., "Judicial Review and the Arab World" (1998) 9 *Journal of Democracy*.

Brown, Nathan J., "L'État C'est Qaïs," *Malcolm H. Kerr – Carnegie Middle East Center* (July 13, 2022), https://carnegie-mec.org/diwan/87496

Brown, Nathan J., "Regimes Reinventing Themselves: Constitutional Development in the Arab World" (2003) 18 *International Sociology*.

Brown, Nathan J., *The Rule of Law in the Arab World: Courts in Egypt and the Gulf* (Cambridge University Press 1997).

Brown, Nathan J., "The Unsurprising but Distinctive Nature of Constitution Writing in the Arab World" in David Landau and Hanna Lerner (eds.), *Comparative Constitution Making* (Edward Elgar 2019).

Brown, Nathan J., and Dunne, Michele, "Egypt's Draft Constitutional Amendments Answer Some Questions and Raise Others," *Carnegie Endowment for International Peace* (March 1, 2011), https://carnegieendowment.org/2011/03/01/egypt-s-draft-constitutional-amendments-answer-some-questions-and-raise-others-pub-42817

Brown, Nathan J., and Lombardi, Clark B., "Contesting Islamic Constitutionalism after the Arab Spring: Islam in Egypt's Post-Mubarak Constitutions" in Rainer Grote and Tilmann J. Röder (eds.), *Constitutionalism, Human Rights, and Islam after the Arab Spring* (Oxford University Press 2016).

Brown, Nathan J., and Lombardi, Clark B., "The Supreme Constitutional Court of Egypt on Islamic Law, Veiling and Civil Rights: An Annotated Translation of Supreme Constitutional Court of Egypt Case No. 8 of Judicial Year 17 (May 18, 1996)" (1996) 21 *American University International Law Review*.

Brown, Nathan J., and Waller, Julian G., "Constitutional Courts and Political Uncertainty: Constitutional Ruptures and the Rule of Judges" (2016) 14 *International Journal of Constitutional Law*.

Brown, Nathan J., et al., *Authoritarianism from the Inside: How and When State Institutions Realize Autonomy under Authoritarian Regimes* (forthcoming).

Bulmer, Elliot, *Emergency Powers* (International IDEA 2018), www.idea.int/sites/default/files/publications/emergency-powers-primer.pdf

Burchfield, Emily, "What's Next for Algeria's Popular Movement?," *Atlantic Council* (April 11, 2019), www.atlanticcouncil.org/blogs/menasource/what-s-next-for-algeria-s-popular-movement

Burgis, Michelle L., "Judicial Reform and the Possibility of Democratic Rule in Jordan: A Policy Perspective on Judicial Independence" (2007) 21 *Arab Law Quarterly*.

Camau, Michel, "Un moment populiste tunisien? Temporalité électorale et temporalité révolutionnaire" (2020) 1 *Revue tunisienne de Science politique*.

Campanini, Massimo, "Il concetto ambiguo di 'Stato islamico'" (2014) 3 *Storia del pensiero politico*.
Cappelletti, Mauro, *Dimensioni della giustizia nelle società contemporanee: Studi di diritto giudiziario comparato* (il Mulino 1994)..
Cappelletti, Mauro, "The 'Mighty Problem' of Judicial Review and the Contribution of Comparative Analysis" (1980) 53 *Southern California Law Review*.
Carter Center, *Constitution-making Process in Tunisia: Final Report, 2011–2014* (2015), www.cartercenter.org/resources/pdfs/news/peace_publications/democracy/tunisia-constitution-making-process.pdf
Carter Center, *Syria's Transition Governance & Constitutional Options Under U.N. Security Council Resolution* 2254 (June 2016), www.cartercenter.org/resources/pdfs/peace/conflict_resolution/syria-conflict/principles-and-constitutional-provisions-may-8-2016.pdf
Carter Center, *The 2014 Constitutional Drafting Assembly Elections in Libya: Final Report* (2014), www.cartercenter.org/resources/pdfs/news/peace_publications/election_reports/libya-06112014-final-.pdf
Castellino, Joshua, and Cavanaugh, Kathleen A., *Minority Rights in the Middle East* (Oxford University Press 2013).
Cenap Aydin, Mustafa, "L'Islam e il dialogo interreligioso" in Francesca Maria Corrao and Luciano Violante (eds.), *L'Islam non è terrorismo* (il Mulino 2018).
Center for Constitutional Transitions – International IDEA, *Constitutional Courts after the Arab Spring: Appointment Mechanisms and Relative Judicial Independence* (2014), www.idea.int/sites/default/files/publications/constitutional-courts-after-the-arab-spring.pdf
Chaieri, Hanae, "La armonización del código penal de Marruecos con la constitución de 2011: la tutela del orden público nacional frente a la protección penal de las libertades" in Gerardo José Ruiz-Rico Ruiz et al. (eds.), *Derecho penal y garantías constitucionales: Una perspectiva iberoamericana* (Tirant lo Blanch 2020).
Charrad, Mounira M., *States and Women's Rights: The Making of Postcolonial Tunisia, Algeria, and Morocco* (University of California Press 2001).
Charrad, Mounira M., and Zarrugh, Amina, "Equal or Complementary? Women in the New Tunisian Constitution after the Arab Spring" in Andrea Khalil (ed.), *Gender, Women and the Arab Spring* (Routledge 2015).
"Charter of Mecca," (2019), https://themwl.org/sites/default/files/TheCharterofMakkah.pdf
Cherif, Nedra, *Libya's Constitution: Between Conflict and Compromise* (European University Institute – Middle East Directions (MED) 2021/02) (March 2021), https://cadmus.eui.eu/bitstream/handle/1814/70538/QM-09-21-057-EN-N.pdf?sequence=3&isAllowed=y
Cherif, Nedra, "Libya's Constitutional Quagmire," *Konrad Adenauer Stiftung – Libya Brief no. 10* (June 2021).
Cherif, Nedra, "Participation in the Tunisian Constitution-Making Process" in Tania Abbiate, Markus Böckenförde and Veronica Federico (eds.), *Public Participation in African Constitutionalism* (Routledge 2018).
Chikhaoui, Leïla, "Le renvoi des recours au Président de la République: 'Déni de justice' ou silence dynamique?" in *Mouvances du droit. Études en l'honneur du professeur Rafâa Ben Achour. Tome 1* (Konrad Adenauer Stiftung 2015).
Choudhry, Sujit, and Tushnet, Mark, "Participatory Constitution-Making: Introduction" (2020) 18 *International Journal of Constitutional Law*.
Clarence-Smith, William Gervase, *Islam and the Abolition of Slavery* (Oxford University Press 2006).
Colombo, Silvia, "Il Marocco tra modernità e tradizione" in Karim Mezran, Silvia Colombo and Saskia Van Genugten (eds.), *L'Africa mediterranea: Storia e futuro* (Donzelli 2011).

Conseil Constitutionnel [of Lebanon], *Recueil des décisions du Conseil constitutionnel 1994–2016 – Volume 1: Décisions relatives à la constitutionnalité des lois* (Beirut 2017).

Conseil Constitutionnel [of Lebanon], *Recueil des décisions du Conseil constitutionnel 1994–2016 – Volume 2: Décisions relatives au contentieux électoral* (Beirut 2017).

Conseil Constitutionnel and Fondation Konrad Adenauer (eds.), *Extension des attributions du Conseil constitutionnel au Liban. Actes du séminaire organisé par le Conseil constitutionnel et Fondation Konrad Adenauer le 6/5/2016. Débat autour du Projet élaboré par le Président du Conseil constitutionnel Issam Sleiman* (Beirut 2017).

"Constitutional Jurisprudence on Fundamental Rights: Digest of Selected Cases" in Kevin Boyle and Adel Omar Sherif (eds.), *Human Rights and Democracy: The Role of the Supreme Constitutional Court of Egypt* (Kluwer Law International 1996).

Cristiani, Dario, "Tunisia's Political Landscape a Decade after the Jasmine Revolution," *Atlantic Council* (December 17, 2020), www.atlanticcouncil.org/blogs/menasource/tunisias-political-landscape-a-decade-after-the-jasmine-revolution/

Crouch, Melissa, "Constitution Making and Public Participation in Southeast Asia" in David Landau and Hanna Lerner (eds.), *Comparative Constitution Making* (Edward Elgar 2019).

Cubertafond, Bernard, "La transition marocaine après le printemps arabe et la nouvelle Constitution" (2011) 5 *Les Études et Essais du Centre Jacques Berque*.

"Custodianship over Holy Sites," *King Abdullah II Official Webpage*, https://kingabdullah.jo/en/page/the-hashemites/custodianship-over-holy-sites

Cusumano, Antonino, "Una Madonna di frontiera, tra la Sicilia e la Tunisia" (2020) 44 *Dialoghi mediterranei*, www.istitutoeuroarabo.it/DM/una-madonna-di-frontiera-tra-la-sicilia-e-la-tunisia/

Dahlerup, Drude, and Freidenvall, Lenita, "Gender Quotas in Politics: A Constitutional Challenge" in Susan H. Williams (ed.), *Constituting Equality: Gender Equality and Comparative Constitutional Law* (Cambridge University Press 2009).

Daou, Fadi, "La sfida della fratellanza" in Fadi Daou and Nayla Tabbara, *L'ospitalità divina e la fraternità umana* (Edizioni Qiqajon 2022).

Daraji, Ibrahim, "Syria: The Constitution of the 'Crisis' or the Crisis of the Constitution?", *Journal of Constitutional Law in the Middle East and North Africa*, special issue on "Arab Constitutional Responses to the Revolutions and Transformations in the Region" edited by Rim Turkmani and Tamara El Khoury (December 2023), www.jcl-mena.org

de Esteban, Jorge, "El proceso constituyente español, 1977–1978" in José Félix Tezanos Tortajada, Ramón Cotarelo García and Andrés de Blas Guerrero (eds.), *La transición democrática española* (Editorial Sistema 1989).

de Montalivet, Pierre, "QPC et 'dialogue des juges'" (2018) 116 *Revue française de droit constitutionnel*.

de Vergottini, Giuseppe, *Diritto costituzionale comparato* (Wolters Kluwer – CEDAM 2022).

de Vergottini, Giuseppe, *Le transizioni costituzionali* (il Mulino 1998).

de Visser, Maartje, *Constitutional Review in Europe: A Comparative Analysis* (Hart 2015).

Debbeche, Kaouthar, "The Difficult Path toward Democracy: New Electoral Systems in Egypt, Libya and Tunisia" in Rainer Grote and Tilmann J. Röder (eds.), *Constitutionalism, Human Rights, and Islam after the Arab Spring* (Oxford University Press 2016).

Del Zanna, Giorgio, "Società civile, pluralismo e minoranze in Turchia" in Barbara Airò and Massimo Zaccaria (eds.), *I confini della cittadinanza nel nuovo Medio Oriente* (Viella 2015).

Delledonne, Giacomo, "Appointing and Electing Constitutional Judges: An Evolving Comparative Landscape" in Martin Belov (ed.), *The Role of Courts in Contemporary Legal Orders* (Eleven International Publishing 2019).

Demichelis, Marco, "Citizenship and Equity: An Excursus within the Nahda, Islamic Pluralism and Religious Exclusivism" in Barbara Airò and Massimo Zaccaria (eds.), *I confini della cittadinanza nel nuovo Medio Oriente* (Viella 2015).

Democracy Reporting International, *Assessment of the 1951 Libyan Constitution According to International Standards* (Briefing Paper 28) (July 2012), https://democracy-reporting.org/wp-content/uploads/2016/03/dri-ly-bp28-1951_libya_constitution.pdf

Democracy Reporting International, *Decentralisation in Libya* (August 2013), https://democracy-reporting.org/en/office/libya/publications/report-decentralisation-in-libya

Democracy Reporting International, *La Cour Constitutionnelle tunisienne: Analyse de la physionomie de l'institution après l'adoption de la Loi organique du 3 décembre 2015* (2016).

Democracy Reporting International, *La mise en œuvre de la Constitution tunisienne au niveau du cadre juridique. 30 septembre 2019 – 9eme édition* (2019).

Democracy Reporting International, *La mise en œuvre de la Constitution tunisienne du 27 janvier 2014 au niveau du cadre juridique. Bilan* (September 2022), https://democracyreporting.s3.eu-central-1.amazonaws.com/images/63761f99ace6d.pdf

Democracy Reporting International, *Les effets de l'absence de la Cour constitutionnelle pendant la législature 2014–2019* (December 2019), https://democracyreporting.s3.eu-central-1.amazonaws.com/images/21732020-08-Tunisia-Effets-Abs-CC-Web-Fr.pdf

di Giovanni, Janine, *The Vanishing: The Twilight of Christianity in the Middle East* (Bloomsbury 2021).

Di Gregorio, Angela, *Epurazioni e protezione della democrazia: Esperienze e modelli di "giustizia post-autoritaria"* (Franco Angeli 2012).

Diab Esq, Razi A., "Religion and the Law in Syria," *Arab Center for International Humanitarian Law and Human Rights Education (ACIHL)*, https://acihl.org/articles.htm?article_id=26

Dorsen, Norman et al., *Comparative Constitutionalism: Cases and Materials* (Third Edition) (West Academic Publishing 2016).

Dris, Chérif, "Quatrième mandat de Bouteflika: le parachèvement de la sanctuarisation du pouvoir présidentiel" (2014) 11 *L'Année du Maghreb* (on-line version).

Dupret, Baudouin, *La charia: Des sources à la pratique, un concept pluriel* (La Découverte 2014).

Duverger, Maurice, "A New Political System Model: Semi-presidential Government" (1980) 8 *European Journal of Political Research*.

Ebrahim, Hassen, and Miller, Laurel E., "Creating the Birth Certificate of a New South Africa: Constitution Making after Apartheid" in Laurel E. Miller (ed.), *Framing the State in Times of Transition: Case Studies in Constitution Making* (United States Institute of Peace 2010).

"Egypt: New Church Law Discriminates against Christians," *Human Rights Watch* (September 15, 2016), www.hrw.org/news/2016/09/15/egypt-new-church-law-discriminates-against-christians

Eisenstadt, Todd A., LeVan, A. Carl, and Maboudi, Tofigh, *Constituents before Assembly: Participation, Deliberation, and Representation in the Crafting of New Constitutions* (Cambridge University Press 2017).

el-Hakim, Jacques, and Harding, Taymour, "Syria" (2010–2011) 16 *Yearbook of Islamic and Middle Eastern Law*.

El Khoury, Tamara, "Back to Basics: When Stating the Obvious is Groundbreaking," *IACL-AIDC Blog* (June 22, 2021), https://blog-iacl-aidc.org/menaregion/22-6-21-back-to-basics-when-stating-the-obvious-is-groundbreaking

El Maslouhi, Abderrahim, "Séparation des pouvoirs et régime parlementaire dans la nouvelle Constitution marocaine" in Centre d'Études Internationales (ed.), *La Constitution marocaine de 2011: Analyses et commentaires* (LGDJ 2012).

El Sagezli, Mustafa, "A Return to a Constitutional Monarchy May Solve Libya's Problems," *Atlantic Council* (October 21, 2021), www.atlanticcouncil.org/blogs/menasource/a-return-to-a-constitutional-monarchy-may-solve-libyas-problems/

El-Morr, Awad Mohammad, Nossier, Abd El-Rahman, and Sherif, Adel Omar, "The Supreme Constitutional Court and Its Role in the Egyptian Judicial System" in Kevin Boyle and Adel Omar Sherif (eds.), *Human Rights and Democracy: The Role of the Supreme Constitutional Court of Egypt* (Kluwer Law International 1996).

El-Sadany, Mai, and Omar, Yasmin, "Egypt's Constitutional Court Amendments: The International System on Its Own Terms," *Carnegie Endowment for International Peace* (July 12, 2021), https://carnegieendowment.org/sada/84941

Elassar, Yousri, "Le contrôle de la constitutionnalité des lois au Koweït" in *Les Constitutions des Pays arabes: Colloque de Beyrouth, 1998* (Bruylant 1999).

Elkhatib, Numan A., and Domour, Nesreen M., "The Constitutional Court of Jordan and Its Relation to Ordinary Courts" (2021) 11 *The Lawyer Quarterly*.

Ellena, Katherine, and Brown, Alexandra, "Beyond Constitutional Reform to Elections. Libya Electoral Legal Framework Analysis," *International Foundation for Electoral Systems* (2019), www.ifes.org/sites/default/files/libya_electoral_legal_framework_analysis_november_2019.pdf

Ellis, Mark S., "Purging the Past: The Current State of Lustration Laws in the Former Communist Bloc" (1996) 59 *Law and Contemporary Problems* 4.

Elster, Jon, "Arguing and Bargaining in Two Constituent Assemblies" (2000) 2 *University of Pennsylvania Journal of Constitutional Law*.

Elster, Jon, "Forces and Mechanisms in the Constitution-making Process" (1995) 45 *Duke Law Journal*.

Elster, Jon, "Legislatures as Constituent Assemblies" in Richard W. Bauman and Tsvi Kahana (eds.), *The Least Examined Branch: The Role of Legislatures in the Constitutional State* (Cambridge University Press 2006).

Entelis, John P., "Algeria: The Outlier State?" in Justin O. Frosini and Francesco Biagi (eds.), *Political and Constitutional Transitions in North Africa: Actors and Factors* (Routledge 2015).

Esposito, John L., "Islam and Civil Society" in John P. Esposito and Francois Burgat (eds.), *Modernizing Islam: Religion in the Public Sphere in the Middle East and Europe* (Rutgers University Press 2003).

Esposito, John L., "Takfir" in *The Oxford Dictionary of Islam* (Oxford University Press 2003), www.oxfordreference.com/display/10.1093/acref/9780195125580.001.0001/acref-9780195125580-e-2319

European Parliament, *Annual Report on Human Rights and Democracy in the World and the European Union's Policy on the Matter 2015* (December 14, 2016), www.europarl.europa.eu/doceo/document/TA-8-2016-0502_EN.pdf?redirect

Eyadat, Zaid, and Nasrawin, Laith, *The Constitutional Court of Jordan: Evaluating 10 Years of Service & Future Expectations* (Konrad Adenauer Stiftung – Rule of Law Program Middle East & North Africa 2021).

Ezzat, Amr, "The Fundamental Rights of Baha'is: An Excellent Opportunity to Expand Religious Freedom in Egypt," *Egyptian Initiative for Personal Rights* (January 4, 2022), https://eipr.org/en/blog/amr-ezzat/2022/01/fundamental-rights-baha'-excellent-opportunity-expand-religious-freedom-egypt

Fabbrini, Federico, "Kelsen in Paris: France's Constitutional Reform and the Introduction of a Posteriori Constitutional Review of Legislation" (2008) 9 *German Law Journal*.

Fabius, Laurent, "La question prioritaire de constitutionnalité en France 2010–2017: les principaux enseignements" (2017) 8 *Revue du Conseil Constitutionnel*.

Fadel, Mohammad H., "The Sounds of Silence: The Supreme Constitutional Court of Egypt, Constitutional Crisis, and Constitutional Silence" (2018) 16 *International Journal of Constitutional Law*.

Fares, Qais, "The Syrian Constitution: Assad's Magic Wand," *Malcolm H. Kerr Carnegie Middle East Center* (May 8, 2014), https://carnegie-mec.org/diwan/55541

Farouk, Yasmine, "Writing the Constitution of the Egyptian Revolution: Between Social Contract and Political Contracting (March 2011–July 2013)," *Arab Reform Initiative* (November 2013), https://s3.eu-central-1.amazonaws.com/storage.arab-reform.net/ari/2013/11/02114149/Arab_Reform_Initiative_2013-11_Research_Paper_en_writing_the_constitution_of_the_egyptian_revolution_between_social_contract_and_political_contracting.pdf

Feldman, Noah, *The Fall and Rise of the Islamic State* (Princeton University Press 2012).

Ferrari, Giuseppe Franco, "Comparazione e storia" (2021) 2 *Diritto pubblico comparato ed europeo*.

Ferrari, Silvio, "Overcoming the 'Same Rights for All Special Rights for Minorities' Dichotomy: Is Inclusive Citizenship the Right Answer?" in Fabio Petito, Fadi Daou and Michael D. Driessen (eds.), *Human Fraternity & Inclusive Citizenship: Interreligious Engagement in the Mediterranean* (ISPI – June 2021), www.ispionline.it/en/publication/human-fraternity-and-inclusive-citizenship-interreligious-engagement-mediterranean-30794

Fihri, Youssef Fassi, "Le Conseil constitutionnel marocain et le contrôle du législateur organique" in Omar Bendourou, Rkia El Mossadeq and Mohammed Madani (eds.), *La nouvelle Constitution marocaine à l'épreuve de la pratique* (Friedrich Ebert Stiftung 2014).

Fleyfel, Antoine, *Géopolitique des Chrétiens d'Orient: Défis et avenir des chrétiens arabes* (L'Harmattan 2014).

Fombad, Charles M., "The Evolution of Modern African Constitutions: A Retrospective Perspective" in Charles M. Fombad (ed.), *Separation of Powers in African Constitutionalism* (Oxford University Press 2016).

Frankenberg, Günter, *Political Technology and the Erosion of the Rule of Law: Normalizing the State of Exception* (Edward Elgar 2014).

Freedom House, *Freedom in the World 2015* (2015), https://freedomhouse.org/sites/default/files/01152015_FIW_2015_final.pdf

Freedom House, *Freedom in the World 2022* (2022), https://freedomhouse.org/sites/default/files/2022-02/FIW_2022_PDF_Booklet_Digital_Final_Web.pdf

Freedom House, "Tunisia" in *Freedom in the World 2022* (2022), https://freedomhouse.org/country/tunisia/freedom-world/2022

Frosini, Justin O., *Constitutional Preambles: At a Crossroads between Politics and Law* (Maggioli 2012).

Frosini, Justin O., and Biagi, Francesco (eds.), *Political and Constitutional Transitions in North Africa: Actors and Factors* (Routledge 2015).

Frosini, Justin O., and Biagi, Francesco, "Transitions from Authoritarian Rule following the Arab Uprisings: A Matter of Variables" in Justin O. Frosini and Francesco Biagi (eds.), *Political and Constitutional Transitions in North Africa: Actors and Factors* (Routledge 2015).

Gaddafi, Muammar, *The Green Book* (1975).

Gaddes, Chawki, "Il processo costituente (2011–14): fasi e protagonisti" in Tania Groppi and Irene Spigno (eds.), *Tunisia: La primavera della Costituzione* (Carocci 2015).

Gallala-Arndt, Imen, "Constitutional Jurisdiction and Its Limits in the Maghreb" in Rainer Grote and Tilmann J. Röder (eds.), *Constitutionalism in Islamic Countries: Between Upheaval and Continuity* (Oxford University Press 2012).

Gallala-Arndt, Imen, "Tracing Tunisian Case Law on Freedom of Religion, Equality and Islamic Law" in Anja Schoeller-Schletter and Robert Poll (eds.), *Balancing Individual*

Rights, Religious Law and Equality: Landmark Decisions from Egypt, Kuwait and Tunisia (Konrad Adenauer Stiftung – Rule of Law Programme Middle East and North Africa 2021), www.kas.de/documents/265308/265357/Balancing+Inidividual+Rights%2C+Religious+Law+and+Equality.pdf/5e4cd2b6-372f-f15e-f462-23cdeb1e9a3a?version=1.0&t=1617987215625

Gallala-Arndt, Imen, "Tunisia after the Arab Spring: Women's Rights at Risk?" in Rainer Grote and Tilmann J. Röder (eds.), *Constitutionalism, Human Rights, and Islam after the Arab Spring* (Oxford University Press 2016).

Gamal Ali, Mohamed, "Exclusively for Adherents of 'Divinely Revealed' Religions?! How Did the Preparatory Work for the Egyptian Constitutions Discuss Issues of Freedom of Religion and Belief?," *Religioni, diritti ed economie nello spazio mediterraneo* (REDESM) (September 26, 2022), www.redesm.org/2022/09/26/exclusively-for-adherents-of-divinely-revealed-religions-how-did-the-preparatory-work-for-the-egyptian-constitutions-discuss-issues-of-freedom-of-religion-and-belief/

Gannagé, Pierre, "Le Conseil constitutionnel libanais" in *Les Constitutions des Pays arabes: Colloque de Beyrouth, 1998* (Bruylant 1999).

Gargarella, Roberto, *La sala de máquinas de la Constitución: Dos siglos de constitucionalismo en América Latina (1810–2010)* (Katz Editores 2014).

Gargarella, Roberto, *Latin American Constitutionalism, 1810–2010: The Engine Room of the Constitution* (Oxford University Press 2013).

Garlicki, Lech, "Constitutional Courts versus Supreme Courts" (2007) 5 *International Journal of Constitutional Law*.

Gastineau, Bénédicte, "Légalisation de l'avortement et planification familiale: l'expérience tunisienne," *Séminaire International "Santé de la Reproduction en Afrique"* (Abidjan, November 9–12, 1999), https://horizon.documentation.ird.fr/exl-doc/pleins_textes/2022-03/010029691.pdf

Gaté, Juliette, "Droits des femmes et révolutions arabes" (2014) 6 *La Revue des droits de l'homme*.

"General Presentation of the Project for the Establishment of an International Constitutional Court" in Asma Ghachem and Henri Pallard (eds.), *Une Cour Constitutionnelle Internationale au service du droit démocratique et du droit constitutionnel: Actes du colloque* (Konrad Adenauer Stiftung 2015).

Ghai, Yash, "Civil Society, Participation and the Making of Kenya's Constitution" in David Landau and Hanna Lerner (eds.), *Comparative Constitution Making* (Edward Elgar 2019).

Ghazwi, Mohammed S. M., *The Development of Monitoring the Constitutionality of Laws and Regulations in Light of the Jordanian Constitution of 1952* (Amman 2015).

Ghebouli Labidine, Zine, "Algeria: New Constitution, Old Balances," *Dustour Talk – JCL MENA* (March 23, 2021), http://jcl-mena.org/talk-entry.php?bid=9

Gherairi, Ghazi, "La Constitution de la IIe République: Clartés et ombres," *Leaders* (February 6, 2014), www.leaders.com.tn/article/13304-la-constitution-de-la-iie-republique-clartes-et-ombres

Ginsburg, Tom, *Judicial Review in New Democracies: Constitutional Courts in Asian Cases* (Cambridge University Press 2003).

Ginsburg, Tom, "The Real Winner in the Egyptian Constitution? The Military," *HuffPost* (December 7, 2012), www.huffpost.com/entry/egypt-draft-constitution-military_b_2259798

Ginsburg, Tom, and Bisarya, Sumit, "Introduction: Constitution Makers on Constitution Making" in Tom Ginsburg and Sumit Bisarya (eds.), *Constitution Makers on Constitution Making: New Cases* (Cambridge University Press 2022).

Ginsburg, Tom, and Elkins, Zachary, "Ancillary Powers of Constitutional Courts" (2008) 87 *Texas Law Review*.

Ginsburg, Tom, and Moustafa, Tamir (eds.), *Rule by Law: The Politics of Courts in Authoritarian Regimes* (Cambridge University Press 2008).

Gobe, Eric, "Saïed's Constitution, an Authoritarian Project Behind a Bottom-up Curtain," *ISPI* (July 21, 2022), www.ispionline.it/it/pubblicazione/saieds-constitution-authoritarian-project-behind-bottom-curtain-35847

Goui, Bouhania, "Algerian Angst: Can it Agree on Constitutional Change?," *Arab Reform Initiative – Policy Alternatives* (February 2015), www.arab-reform.net/en/node/494

Graëffly, Romain, "Le Conseil constitutionnel algérien. De la greffe institutionnelle à l'avènement d'un contentieux constitutionnel?" (2005) 5 *Revue de droit publique*.

Grewal, Sharan, Satouri, Salah-Dean, and DeHaven, Ian, "Tunisia's New Constitution Will Only Worsen Its Political Crisis," *The Brookings Institution* (July 6, 2022), www.brookings.edu/blog/order-from-chaos/2022/07/06/tunisias-new-constitution-will-only-worsen-its-political-crisis/

Grimm, Dieter, "Types of Constitution" in Michel Rosenfeld and András Sajó (eds.), *The Oxford Handbook of Comparative Constitutional Law* (Oxford University Press 2012).

Groppi, Tania, "La Constitution tunisienne de 2014: illustration de la globalisation du droit constitutionnel?" (2018) 114 *Revue française de droit constitutionnel*.

Grote, Rainer, "The Arab Republic of Egypt: Introductory Note" in *Oxford Constitutions of the World* (Oxford University Press 2014).

Grote, Rainer, "Constitutional Review in Arab Countries: Down of a New Era?" in Rainer Grote and Tilmann J. Röder (eds.), *Constitutionalism, Human Rights, and Islam after the Arab Spring* (Oxford University Press 2016).

Grote, Rainer, "Models of Institutional Control: The Experience of Islamic Countries" in Rainer Grote and Tilmann J. Röder (eds.), *Constitutionalism in Islamic Countries: Between Upheaval and Continuity* (Oxford University Press 2012).

Grote, Rainer, and Röder, Tilmann J. (eds.), *Constitutionalism in Islamic Countries: Between Upheaval and Continuity* (Oxford University Press 2012).

Grote, Rainer, and Röder, Tilmann J. (eds.), *Constitutionalism, Human Rights, and Islam after the Arab Spring* (Oxford University Press 2016).

Guédira, Ahmed Reda, "Une constituante ni nécessaire ni possible" 27 *Confluent* 67 (January 1963).

Gutteridge, Harold C., *Comparative Law: An Introduction to the Comparative Method of Legal Study and Research* (Cambridge University Press 1946).

Häberle, Peter, *Verfassungslehre als Kulturwissenschaft* (Duncker & Humblot 1998).

Habib, Akram, "Libya" in Kenneth R. Ross, Mariz Tadros and Todd M. Johnson (eds.), *Christianity in North Africa and West Asia* (Edinburgh University Press 2018).

Haddad, Tahar, *Notre femme, la législation islamique et la société* (Editions ANEP 2012).

Haider, Huma, *The Persecution of Christians in the Middle East*, Institute of Development Studies (February 16, 2017), https://opendocs.ids.ac.uk/opendocs/bitstream/handle/20.500.12413/13055/K4D_HDR_Persecution%20of%20Christians%20in%20the%20Middle%20East.pdf;jsessionid=A2BBDB58992018CD5B3E2F28511CB7ED?sequence=142

Hajjar, Sami G., "The Jamahiriya Experiment in Libya: Qadhafi and Rousseau" (1980) 18 *The Journal of Modern African Studies*.

Hallaq, Wael B., *The Impossible State: Islam, Politics, and Modernity's Moral Predicament* (Columbia University Press 2013).

Hammadi, Souhila, "Lois organiques encadrant les élections: Bâclage des procédures et violation de la Constitution," *Algeria-Watch* (September 16, 2019), https://algeria-watch.org/?p=72559

Hammady, Omar, "The Role of Civil Society in the Libyan Constitution-making Process" in Tania Abbiate, Markus Böckenförde and Veronica Federico (eds.), *Public Participation in African Constitutionalism* (Routledge 2018).

Hammouri, Mohammad, "Constitutional Reform and the Rise of Constitutional Adjudication in Jordan. Background, Issues, and Controversies" in Rainer Grote and Tilmann J. Röder (eds.), *Constitutionalism, Human Rights, and Islam after the Arab Spring* (Oxford University Press 2016).

Hanafi, Sari, and Tomeh, Azzam, "Gender Equality in the Inheritance Debate in Tunisia and the Formation of Non-Authoritarian Reasoning" (2019) 3 *Journal of Islamic Ethics*.

Hefny, Assem, "Religious Authorities and Constitutional Reform: The Case of Al-Azhar in Egypt" in Rainer Grote and Tilmann J. Röder (eds.), *Constitutionalism, Human Rights, and Islam after the Arab Spring* (Oxford University Press 2016).

Heller, Peter B., "The Permanent Syrian Constitution of March 13, 1973" (1974) 28 *The Middle East Journal*.

Herb, Michael, "Princes and Parliaments in the Arab World" (2004) 58 *The Middle East Journal*.

Hill, Enid, "Establishing the Doctrine of Judicial Review in Egypt and the United States" in Eugene Cotran and Adel Omar Sherif (eds.), *The Role of the Judiciary in the Protection of Human Rights* (Kluwer Law International 1997).

Hinder, Paul, *Als Bischof in Arabien: Erfahrungen mit dem Islam* (Herder 2016).

Hirschl, Ran, *Comparative Matters: The Renaissance of Comparative Constitutional Law* (Cambridge University Press 2014).

Hirschl, Ran, *Constitutional Theocracy* (Harvard University Press 2010).

Hokayem, Antoine, *La genèse de la Constitution libanaise de 1926: Le contexte du mandat francais, les projets préliminaires, les auteurs, le texte final* (Les éditions universitaires du Liban 1996).

Howeidy, Fahmy, *Muwatinun la dhimiyyun* (Dar al-Shuruq 1985).

Hudson, Alexander, *The Veil of Participation: Citizens and Political Parties in Constitution-Making Processes* (Cambridge University Press 2021).

Human Rights Watch, *Audacity in Adversity: LGBT Activism in the Middle East and North Africa* (2018), www.hrw.org/sites/default/files/report_pdf/lgbt_mena0418_web_0.pdf

Human Rights Watch, "Egypt" in *Human Rights Watch World Report 2022* (2022), www.hrw.org/world-report/2022/country-chapters/egypt

Huntington, Samuel, *The Third Wave: Democratization in the Late 20th Century* (University of Oklahoma Press 1991).

Ibán, Iván C., "God in Constitutions and Godless Constitutions" in W. Cole Durham, Jr. et al. (eds.), *Law, Religion, Constitution: Freedom of Religion, Equal Treatment, and the Law* (Routledge 2013).

International Commission of Jurists, *Flawed and Inadequate: Algeria's Constitutional Amendment Process – A Briefing Paper* (October 2020), www.icj.org/wp-content/uploads/2020/10/Algeria-NewConstitution-Advocacy-Analysis-Brief-2020-ENG.pdf

International Commission of Jurists, *Fundamentally Flawed: Tunisia's 2022 Constitution-making Process* (June 2022), www.icj.org/wp-content/uploads/2022/07/Tunisia-draft-constitution-question-and-answer-briefing-2022-ENG.pdf

International Commission of Jurists, *Tunisia: Judiciary Must Act as a Check on President's Power Grab* (August 3, 2021), www.icj.org/tunisia-judiciary-must-act-as-a-check-on-presidents-power-grab/

International Crisis Group, *Décentralisation en Tunisie: consolider la démocratie sans affaiblir l'État* (Rapport Moyen-Orient et Afrique du Nord, no. 198) (March 26, 2019), www.crisisgroup.org/fr/middle-east-north-africa/north-africa/tunisia/198-decentralisation-en-tunisie-consolider-la-democratie-sans-affaiblir-letat

International Peace Institute, Stimson Center and Security Council Report, *The Situation in Libya: Reflections on Challenges and Ways Forward* (June 2022), www.stimson.org/wp-content/uploads/2022/07/Situation-in-Libya-Meeting-Note-Proofs26.pdf

Jalabi, Mariam, "Rethinking Transition in Syria, Gender Equality, and Constitution" in Claudia Padovani and Francesca Helm (eds.), *Rethinking the Transition Process in Syria: Constitution, Participation and Gender Equality* (Research-Publishing.net 2018).

Jaldi, Abdessalam, "Tunisie: la démocratie à l'épreuve de la crise de la IIème République," *Policy Center for the New South* (February 2022), www.policycenter.ma/sites/default/files/2022-02/PP_03-22_Jaldi%20%281%29.pdf

Jenkins, Philip, *The Lost History of Christianity: The Thousand-Year Golden Age of the Church in the Middle East, Africa and Asia – And How It Died* (HarperOne 2008).

Jenkins, Philip, "Premessa dell'autore all'edizione italiana" in Philip Jenkins (ed.), *La storia perduta del Cristianesimo. Il millennio d'oro della Chiesa in Medio Oriente, Africa e Asia (V-XV secolo). Come è finita una civiltà* (EMI 2016).

Johnson, Darin E. W., "Conflict Constitution-Making in Libya and Yemen" (2017) 39 *University of Pennsylvania Journal of International Law*.

Johnson, Todd M., and Zurlo, Gina A., "Ongoing Exodus: Tracking the Emigration of Christians from the Middle East" (2013–2014) 3 *Harvard Journal of Middle Eastern Politics and Policy*.

Joseph, Edward P., "Libya Needs Its Old Constitution if It Wants to Survive," *The National Interest* (July 4, 2018) https://nationalinterest.org/feature/libya-needs-its-old-constitution-if-it-wants-survive-24952

Journal of Constitutional Law in the Middle East and North Africa, special issue on "Arab Constitutional Responses to the Revolutions and Transformations in the Region" edited by Rim Turkmani and Tamara El Khoury (December 2023), www.jcl-mena.org

Jrad, Eya, "Constitutional or Unconstitutional: Is That the Question?," *Arab Reform Initiative* (August 3, 2021), www.arab-reform.net/pdf/?pid=19421&plang=en

Kaldas, Timothy, "Taking Dictatorship from De Facto to De Jure: Egypt's Constitutional Amendments," *ConstitutionNet* (May 1, 2019), http://constitutionnet.org/news/taking-dictatorship-de-facto-de-jure-egypts-constitutional-amendments

Katz, Andrea Scoseria, "Taming the Prince: Bringing Presidential Emergency Powers under Law in Colombia" (2020) 18 *International Journal of Constitutional Law*.

Kebaish, Karim Adel, "Tiran and Sanafir: A Historical and Constitutional Argument Opposing the Territorial Cession of the Tiran and Sanafir Islands to Saudi Arabia" (2019) 97 *Texas Law Review*.

Kelibi, Salsabil, "Séparation et équilibre des pouvoirs dans la Constitution tunisienne" in *La Constitution de la Tunisie – Processus, principes et perspectives* (UNDP 2016).

Kempe, Frederick, and Massolo, Giampiero, "Preface" in Karim Mezran and Annalisa Perteghella (eds.), *The Politics of Pandemics: Evolving Regime-Opposition Dynamics in the MENA Region* (ISPI-Atlantic Council 2020), www.ispionline.it/en/publication/politics-pandemics-evolving-regime-opposition-dynamics-mena-region-28410

Khalidi, Ismail R., "Constitution of the United Kingdom of Libya: Background and Summary" (1952) 6 *Middle East Journal*.

Khan, Mohsin, and Mezran, Karim, "No Arab Spring in Algeria," *Atlantic Council* (May 2014), www.atlanticcouncil.org/wp-content/uploads/2014/05/No_Arab_Spring_for_Algeria.pdf

Khan, Siraj, "A Comparative Analysis of the Draft Constitutions of Tunisia 2022: Zero-Sum Games," *Konrad Adenauer Stiftung – Rule of Law Programme Middle East and North Africa* (July 2022), www.kas.de/documents/265308/22468903/A+Comparative+Analysis+of+the+Draft+Constitutions+of+Tunisia+2022+Zero-Sum+Games.pdf/4a68ee42-6ca4-31b2-78f2-4aeccca3e3b4?version=1.0&t=1674460240919

Khan, Siraj, "The State of Emergency and COVID-19: The Defence Law of Jordan 1992," unpublished manuscript.

Kherigi, Intissar, "Decentralization Reforms in Post-Revolution Tunisia: The Struggle between Political and Bureaucratic Elites" in Aslı Ü. Bâli and Omar M. Dajani (eds.), *Federalism and Decentralization in the Contemporary Middle East and North Africa* (Cambridge University Press 2023).

King Abdullah II, *Letter to Samir Rifai Entrusting Him with Chairing the Royal Committee to Modernise the Political System* (June 10, 2021), https://kingabdullah.jo/en/letters/letter-samir-rifai-entrusting-him-chairing-royal-committee-modernise-political-system

King Abdullah II, "Rule of Law and Civil State" Discussion Paper (2016), https://kingabdullah.jo/en/discussion-papers/rule-law-and-civil-state

Klare, Karl E., "Legal Culture and Transformative Constitutionalism" (1998) 14 *South African Journal on Human Rights*.

Klein, Claude, and Sajó, András, "Constitution-Making: Process and Substance" in Michel Rosenfeld and András Sajó (eds.), *The Oxford Handbook of Comparative Constitutional Law* (Oxford University Press 2012).

Klug, Heinz, "Transformative Constitutions and the Role of Integrity Institutions in Tempering Power: The Case of Resistance to State Capture in Post-Apartheid South Africa" (2019) 67 *Buffalo Law Review*.

Koch, Cordelia, "The Separation of Powers in a Fragmented State: The Case of Lebanon" in Rainer Grote and Tilmann J. Röder (eds.), *Constitutionalism in Islamic Countries: Between Upheaval and Continuity* (Oxford University Press 2012).

Lambert, Edouard, *Le gouvernement des juges et la lutte contre la législation sociale aux Etats-Unis* (Marcel Giard & Cie 1921).

Lamrabet, Asma, *Women in the Qur'an: An Emancipatory Reading* (Kube Publishing 2016).

Landau, David, "Constituent Power and Constitution Making in Latin America" in David Landau and Hanna Lerner (eds.), *Comparative Constitution Making* (Edward Elgar 2019).

Larbi, Walid, "Le statut du citoyen dans les structures traditionnelles d'appartenance et d'organisation politique islamique" in Rafâa Ben Achour (ed.), *Constitution, citoyenneté et justice constitutionnelle: Entre exigence démocratique et recompositions territoriales* (Centre de publication universitaire 2014).

Laserud, Stina, and Taphorn, Rita, *Designing for Equality: Best-fit, Medium-fit and Non-favourable Combinations of Electoral Systems and Gender Quotas* (International IDEA 2007), www.idea.int/sites/default/files/publications/designing-for-equality.pdf

Lassalle, Ferdinand, *Sulla natura delle costituzioni* (Casa Editrice Ambrosiana 1945).

Le Roy, Thierry, "Constitutionalism in the Maghreb: Between French Heritage and Islamic Concepts" in Rainer Grote and Tilmann J. Röder (eds.), *Constitutionalism in Islamic Countries: Between Upheaval and Continuity* (Oxford University Press 2012).

Legrand, Pierre, *Le droit comparé* (Presses Universitaires de France 1999).

Legrand, Pierre, "The Same and the Different" in Pierre Legrand and Roderick Munday (eds.), *Comparative Legal Studies: Traditions and Transitions* (Cambridge University Press 2003).

Lerner, Hanna, "Constitution-Writing in Deeply Divided Societies: The Incrementalist Approach" (2010) 16 *Nations and Nationalism*.

Les constitutions des pays arabes: Colloque de Beyrouth, 1998 (Bruylant 1999).

Lewis, Bernard, "L'islam et les non-musulmans" (1980) 3–4 *Annales*.

Linz, Juan J., and Stepan, Alfred, *Problems of Democratic Transition and Consolidation: Southern Europe, South America, and Post-Communist Europe* (The Johns Hopkins University Press 1996).

Locchi, Maria Chiara, "La risposta all'emergenza sanitaria Covid-19 nei paesi a maggioranza musulmana: alcune considerazioni comparative" (2020) 2 *DPCE online*.

Loewenstein, Karl, *Political Power and the Governmental Process* (The University of Chicago Press 1957).

Lollini, Andrea, and Palermo, Francesco, "Comparative Law and the 'Proceduralization' of Constitution-Building Processes" in Julia Raue and Patrick Sutter (eds.), *Facets and Practices of State-Building* (Martinus Nijhoff 2009).

Lombardi, Clark B., "The Constitution as Agreement to Agree: The Social and Political Foundations (and Effects) of the 1971 Egyptian Constitution" in Denis J. Galligan and Mila Versteeg (eds.), *Social and Political Foundations of Constitutions* (Cambridge University Press 2013).

Lombardi, Clark B., "Constitutional Provisions Making Sharia 'a' or 'the' Chief Source of Legislation: Where Did They Come from? What Do They Mean? Do They Matter?" (2013) 28 *American University International Law Review*.

Lombardi, Clark B., "Constitutions of Arab Countries in Transition: Constitutional Review and Separation of Powers" in *IEMed Mediterranean Yearbook* (2014), www.iemed.org/wp-content/uploads/2021/02/Constitutions-of-Arab-Countries-in-Transition-Constitutional-Review-and.pdf

Lombardi, Clark B., "Egypt's Supreme Constitutional Court: Managing Constitutional Conflict in an Authoritarian, Aspirationally 'Islamic' State" (2008) 3 *Journal of Comparative Law*.

Longo, Pietro, "L'Islam nella nuova Costituzione: dallo Stato neutrale allo Stato 'protettore'" in Tania Groppi and Irene Spigno (eds.), *Tunisia: La Primavera della Costituzione* (Carocci 2015).

López García, Bernabé, and Fernández Suzor, Cecilia, *Introducción a los regímenes y constituciones árabes* (Centro de Estudios Constitucionales 1985).

Lübbe-Wolff, Gertrude, "Integrating or Polarising? How to Promote Integrative Decision-making in Constitutional Courts" in Anja Schoeller-Schletter (ed.), *Constitutional Review in the Middle East and North Africa* (Nomos 2021).

Lübbe-Wolff, Gertrude, "Integration durch Verfassung" (2009) 12 *Zeitschrift des Deutschen Juristinnenbundes*.

Lübbe-Wolff, Gertrude, "Verfassung als Integrationsprogramm," *Aus Politik und Zeitgeschichte* (April 12, 2019), www.bpb.de/shop/zeitschriften/apuz/289230/verfassung-als-integrationsprogramm/

M'Barek, Mabrouka, "Makers of Our Own History: Upholding the Revolution and Unsettling Coloniality in the Drafting of Tunisia's 2014 Constitution" in Tom Ginsburg and Sumit Bisarya (eds.), *Constitution Makers on Constitution Making: New Cases* (Cambridge University Press 2022).

Maboudi, Tofigh, *The "Fall" of the Arab Spring: Democracy's Challenges and Efforts to Reconstitute the Middle East* (Cambridge University Press 2022).

Maboudi, Tofigh, and Nadi, Ghazal P., "Crowdsourcing the Egyptian Constitution: Social Media, Elites, and the Populace" (2016) 69 *Political Research Quarterly*.

Madani, Mohammed, "Constitutionnalisme sans démocratie: la fabrication et la mise en œuvre de la Constitution marocaine de 2011" in Omar Bendourou, Rkia El Mossadeq and Mohammed Madani (eds.), *La nouvelle Constitution marocaine à l'épreuve de la pratique* (Éditions la Croisée des Chemins 2014).

Madani, Mohammed, "La réforme constitutionnelle sous le règne de Mohammed VI: le processus et l'aboutissement" in Amina El Messaoudi and Manuel José Terol Becerra (eds.), *El poder constituyente en el mundo árabe* (Junta de Andalucía, Instituto Andaluz de Administración Pública 2012).

Magdi, Amr, "Egypt's Response to Torture: Punish the Victims," *Human Rights Watch* (June 10, 2022), www.hrw.org/news/2022/06/10/egypts-response-torture-punish-victims

Maggiolini, Paulo, and Twal, Iyad, "Jordan" in Kenneth R. Ross, Mariz Tadros and Todd M. Johnson (eds.), *Christianity in North Africa and West Asia* (Edinburgh University Press 2018).

Maghraoui, Driss, "Constitutional Reforms in Morocco: Between Consensus and Subaltern Politics" in George Joffé (ed.), *North Africa's Arab Spring* (Routledge 2013).

Mahieddin, Nahas M., "L'évolution du droit de la famille en Algérie: nouveautés et modifications apportées par la loi du 4 mai 2005 au Code algérien de la famille du 9 juin 1984" (2007) II *L'Année du Maghreb*.

Mahmoudi, Said, "International Human Rights Law as Framework for Emerging Constitutions in Arab Countries" in Rainer Grote and Tilmann J. Röder (eds.), *Constitutionalism, Human Rights, and Islam after the Arab Spring* (Oxford University Press 2016).

Mallat, Chibli, *Introduction to Middle Eastern Law* (Oxford University Press 2007).

Mandela, Nelson, *Acceptance Address by Nelson Mandela at the Clark University Investiture, Atlanta, Georgia – United States* (July 10, 1993), www.mandela.gov.za/mandela_speeches/1993/930710_clark.htm

"Map of Military Control across Syria at the End of 2022 and the Beginning of 2023," *Jusoor Center for Studies* (January 2, 2023), https://jusoor.co/en/details/map-of-military-control-across-syria-at-the-end-of-2022-and-the-beginning-of-2023

Marinelli, Stefano, "The 2016 Rojava Social Contract: A Democratic Experiment of Civil and Social Rights in Northern Syria," *International Law Blog* (October 24, 2016), https://internationallaw.blog/2016/10/24/the-2016-rojava-social-contract-a-democratic-experiment-of-civil-and-social-rights-in-northern-syria/

"Marrakesh Declaration on the Rights of Religious Minorities in Muslim-Majority Lands" (2016), www.abc-usa.org/wp-content/uploads/2021/05/Marrakesh-Final-04-12-18.pdf

Maus, Didier, "L'exécutif dans la Constitution marocaine de 2011" in Centre d'Études Internationales (ed.), *La Constitution marocaine de 2011: Analyses et commentaires* (LGDJ 2012).

Max Planck Foundation for International Peace and the Rule of Law, *The Constitutional Court System in the Hashemite Kingdom of Jordan: High-Level Roundtable with the Constitutional Court and the Court of Cassation of Jordan (October 10–13, 2016)* (Heidelberg 2016–2017).

Mekki, Nidhal, "From 'Big Plans' to Improvisation: Where Is the New Tunisian Constituent Process Headed?," *ConstitutionNet* (April 29, 2022), https://constitutionnet.org/news/big-plans-improvisation-where-new-tunisian-constituent-process-headed

Mekki, Nidhal, "The Law on Local and Regional Elections: A Step Towards Local Democracy in Tunisia," *ConstitutionNet* (March 27, 2017), https://constitutionnet.org/news/law-local-and-regional-elections-step-towards-local-democracy-tunisia

Mekki, Nidhal, "The Political Crisis in Tunisia: Is It a Consequence of the Semi-presidential Arrangement?," *ConstitutionNet* (December 7, 2018), https://constitutionnet.org/news/political-crisis-tunisia-it-consequence-semi-presidential-arrangement

Mekki, Nidhal, "The Project of the President's Constitution: Is It Time to Close the Democratic Parenthesis in Tunisia?," *ConstitutionNet* (July 25, 2022), https://constitutionnet.org/news/project-presidents-constitution-it-time-close-democratic-parenthesis-tunisia

Melcangi, Alessia, "Regime Responses in Egypt and Algeria" in Karim Mezran et al. (eds.), *The Impact of COVID-19 on Either Shore of the Mediterranean* (Atlantic Council 2020), www.atlanticcouncil.org/wp-content/uploads/2020/09/Covid-on-Both-Shores-Report_Final.pdf

Melis, Nicola, "Lo statuto giuridico degli ebrei dell'Impero ottomano" in Martino Contu, Nicola Melis and Giovannino Pinna (eds.), *Ebraismo e rapporti con le culture del Mediterraneo nei secoli XVIII–XX* (Giuntina 2003).

Melloni, David, "La Constitution marocaine de 2011: une mutation des ordres politique et juridique marocains" (2013) 145 *Pouvoirs*.

Melloni, David, "Le nouvel ordre constitutionnel marocain: de la 'monarchie gouvernante' à la 'monarchie parlementaire'?" in Centre d'Études Internationales (ed.), *La Constitution marocaine de 2011: Analyses et commentaires* (LGDJ 2012).

Menouni, Abdeltif, "Constitution et séparation des pouvoirs" in Driss Basri, Michel Rousset and Georges Vedel (eds.), *Trente années de vie constitutionnelle au Maroc* (LGDJ 1993).

Merhej, Karim, "Latest Political Reforms in Jordan: Systemic Changes on the Horizon?," *The Tahrir Institute for Middle East Policy* (May 25, 2022), https://timep.org/commentary/analysis/latest-political-reforms-in-jordan-systemic-changes-on-the-horizon/

Merhof, Katrin, "Building a Bridge between Reality and the Constitution: The Establishment and Development of the Colombian Constitutional Court" (2015) 13 *International Journal of Constitutional Law*.

Meyer-Resende, Michael, "Egypt: In-depth Analysis of the Main Elements of the New Constitution," *Directorate-general for the External Policies of the European Union – Policy Department* (2014), www.europarl.europa.eu/RegData/etudes/note/join/2014/433846/EXPO-AFET_NT(2014)433846_EN.pdf

Mezran, Karim, "Constitutional Reforms in Algeria," *Atlantic Council* (January 12, 2016), www.atlanticcouncil.org/blogs/menasource/constitutionalreforms-in-algeria

Mezran, Karim, "Different Nations for One Libya," *ISPI* (December 14, 2021), www.ispionline.it/it/pubblicazione/different-nations-one-libya-32651

Mezran, Karim, and Eljarh, Mohamed, "The Case for a New Federalism in Libya," *Atlantic Council* (December 23, 2014), www.atlanticcouncil.org/publications/issue-briefs/the-case-for-a-new-federalism-in-libya

Mezran, Karim, and Miller, Elissa, "The Promise – And Limits – Of Stabilization through Local Governance in Libya" in Aslı Ü. Bâli and Omar M. Dajani (eds.), *Federalism and Decentralization in the Contemporary Middle East and North Africa* (Cambridge University Press 2023).

Mezran, Karim, and Neale, Erin A., "Algerian Demonstrations: What They Mean for the Future of the Elite and the Country," *Atlantic Council* (February 27, 2019), www.atlanticcouncil.org/blogs/menasource/algerian-demonstrations-what-they-mean-for-the-future-of-the-elite-and-the-country

Mezran, Karim, and Pavia, Alissa, "Tunisia Was the Only Democracy to Blossom from the Arab Spring. Now It's a Mess," *Atlantic Council* (July 28, 2021), www.atlanticcouncil.org/blogs/menasource/tunisia-was-the-only-democracy-to-blossom-from-the-arab-spring-now-its-a-mess/?mkt_tok=NjU5LVdaWCowNzUAAAF-kuKsfoOsxCbduoSHJ1HS2lnFNBdPoSzAK_ns-4w7O7nOfOyhE5ZbjS_4joqyEpj1KaB52eeQPJAvPFbxMV85mkTMApB2BHgaBoyYGpMc

Mezran, Karim, and Pusztai, Wolfgang, "Libya: Exploiting the Achievements of the Libyan Political Agreement," *ISPI* (January 9, 2019), www.ispionline.it/it/pubblicazione/libya-exploiting-achievements-libyan-political-agreement-21962

Mezzetti, Luca, *Diritto islamico: Storia, fonti, istituzioni, società* (Giappichelli 2022).

Mezzetti, Luca, *La libertà decapitata: Dalle Primavere arabe al Califfato* (Editoriale Scientifica 2016).

Micalessin, Gian, *Fratelli traditi. La tragedia dei cristiani in Siria. Cronaca di una persecuzione ignorata* (Cairo Editore 2018).

Mir-Hosseini, Ziba, *Journeys toward Gender Equality in Islam* (Oneworld Academic 2022).

Mir-Hosseini, Ziba, "Una via islamica per uscire dal patriarcato" (December 2019) 30 *Oasis. Cristiani e musulmani nel mondo globale*.

Mohamed-Afify, Ayman, "La Constitution égyptienne de 2014: entre traditions et tendances révolutionnaires" (2015) 101 *Revue française de droit constitutionnel*.

Mohammed, Islam, "The Perpetual State of Emergency and the Reconstruction of National Security Threats in Egypt," unpublished manuscript.

Mohammed, Islam, "Supreme Constitutional Court of Egypt (Al-Mahkamah al-Dustūrīyah al-'Ulyā)" in Rainer Grote, Frauke Lachenmann and Rüdiger Wolfrum (eds.), *Max Planck Encyclopedia of Comparative Constitutional Law* (Oxford University Press 2022).

Molfessis, Nicolas, "La résistance immédiate de la Cour de Cassation à la QPC" (2011) 137 *Pouvoirs*.

Monier, Elizabeth, "Christians and Other Religious Minorities in the Middle East," *The Century Foundation* (April 18, 2019), https://tcf.org/content/report/christians-religious-minorities-middle-east-questions-elizabeth-monier/?agreed=1

Mosebach, Martin, *The 21: A Journey into the Land of Coptic Martyrs* (Plough Publishing House 2019).

Mouaqit, Mohamed, "Disposition culturelle/axiologique du juge et interprétation du nouveau code de la famille" in *Le code de la famille: Perceptions et pratique judiciaire* (Fondation Friedrich-Ebert 2007).

Mousa, Salma, "To Protest or not to Protest? The Christian Predicament in the Syrian Uprising" (2012) 17 *Syrian Studies Association Bulletin*.

Moussebbih, Adil, "L'office du Conseil constitutionnel marocain, juge électoral" (2017) 110 *Revue française de droit constitutionnel*.

Moustafa, Tamir, "The Political Role of the Supreme Constitutional Court: Between Principles and Practice" in Nathalie Bernard-Maugiron (ed.), *Judges and Political Reform in Egypt* (The American University in Cairo Press 2008).

Moustafa, Tamir, *The Struggle for Constitutional Power: Law, Politics, and Economic Development in Egypt* (Cambridge University Press 2007).

Muasher, Marwan, "Is This the Arab Spring 2.0?," *Carnegie Endowment for International Peace* (October 30, 2019), https://carnegieendowment.org/2019/10/30/is-this-arab-spring-2.0-pub-80220

Muasher, Marwan, "Jordan's Proposed Constitutional Amendments – A First Step in the Right Direction," *Carnegie Endowment for International Peace* (August 17, 2011), https://carnegieendowment.org/2011/08/17/jordan-s-proposed-constitutional-amendments-first-step-in-right-direction

Muntasser, Emadeddin, and Fouad, Mohamed, "Libya Should Revive the 1963 Constitution," *MEI@75* (March 28, 2017), www.mei.edu/publications/libya-should-revive-1963-constitution

Nasir, Jamal J. Ahmad, *The Islamic Law of Personal Status: Third Revised and Updated Edition* (Brill 2009).

Nasir, Jamal J. Ahmad, *The Status of Women under Islamic Law and Modern Islamic Legislation: Third Edition of the Revised and Updated Work* (Brill 2009).

Nasrawin, Laith K., "Protecting Human Rights Through Constitutional Adjudication – Jordan as a Case Study" (2016) 25 *Digest of Middle East Studies*.

Nasrawin, Laith K., "Protection against Domestic Violence in Jordanian Law and International Conventions" (2017) 31 *Arab Law Quarterly*.

Nasrawin, Laith K., "Towards the Establishment of an International Constitutional Court" (2017) 10 *Vienna Journal on International Constitutional Law*.

National Human Rights Council, *The Organic Law Relating to the Exception of Unconstitutionality – Memorandum* (Rabat 2013), www.ceja.ch/images/CEJA/DOCS/Bibliotheque/Doctrine/Maroc/CNDH/ENGLISH/Memorandum/The%20exception%20of%20unconstitutionality-%20memorandum.pdf

Neumayer, Karl H., "Law in the Books, Law in Action et les méthodes du droit comparé" in Mario Rotondi (ed.), *Buts et méthodes du droit comparé* (CEDAM 1973).

O'Donnell, Guillermo, and Schmitter, Philippe C., "Tentative Conclusions about Uncertain Democracies" in Guillermo O'Donnell, Philippe C. Schmitter, and Laurence Whitehead (eds.), *Transitions from Authoritarian Rule* (The Johns Hopkins University Press 1986).

Obeidat, Sufian, "The Independence of Constitutional Judges: The Case of Jordan" in Anja Schoeller-Schletter (ed.), *Constitutional Review in the Middle East and North Africa* (Nomos 2021).

Obeidat, Sufian, "Jordan's 2016 Constitutional Amendments: A Return to Absolute Monarchy?," *ConstitutionNet* (May 27, 2016), http://constitutionnet.org/news/jordans-2016-constitutional-amendments-return-absolute-monarchy

Obeidat, Sufian, "Modernizing Jordan's Political System: The Unspoken Motivations," *ConstitutionNet* (July 29, 2021), https://constitutionnet.org/news/modernizing-jordans-political-system-unspoken-motivations

Ochab, Ewelina, "Religious Freedom" in Kenneth R. Ross, Mariz Tadros and Todd M. Johnson (eds.), *Christianity in North Africa and West Asia* (Edinburgh University Press 2018).

Olivetti, Marco, "La forma di governo, tra parlamentarismo razionalizzato e semipresidenzialismo" in Tania Groppi and Irene Spigno (eds.), *Tunisia: La primavera della Costituzione* (Carocci 2015).

Oliviero, Maurizio, *Il costituzionalismo dei paesi arabi. I. Le Costituzioni del Maghreb* (Giuffrè 2003).

Open Doors, *The Persecution of Christian Women and Girls* (2022), https://media.opendoorsuk.org/document/pdf/Advocacy-Womens-Report-2022.pdf

Open Doors, *World Watch List 2022* (2022), https://cms.evangelicalfocus.com/upload/2022-01-19-11:49_MapaWWL2022.pdf

Open Doors International – World Watch Research, *Algeria: Full Country Dossier* (December 2021), https://opendoorsanalytical.org/wp-content/uploads/2022/01/Algeria-Full-Country-Dossier-December-2021.pdf

Open Doors International – World Watch Research, *Egypt: Full Country Dossier* (January 2022), https://opendoorsanalytical.org/wp-content/uploads/2022/01/Egypt-Full-Country-Dossier-Revised-24-January-2022.pdf

Open Doors International – World Watch Research, *Jordan: Full Country Dossier* (December 2021), https://opendoorsanalytical.org/wp-content/uploads/2022/01/Jordan-Full-Country-Dossier-December-2021.pdf

Open Doors International – World Watch Research, *Libya: Full Country Dossier* (January 2022), https://opendoorsanalytical.org/wp-content/uploads/2022/01/Libya-Full-Country-Dossier-Revised-January-2022.pdf

Open Doors International – World Watch Research, *Morocco: Full Country Dossier* (January 2022), https://opendoorsanalytical.org/wp-content/uploads/2022/01/Morocco-Full-Country-Dossier-January-2022.pdf

Open Doors International – World Watch Research, *Syria: Full Country Dossier* (December 2021), https://opendoorsanalytical.org/wp-content/uploads/2022/01/Syria-Full-Country-Dossier-December-2021.pdf

Open Doors International – World Watch Research, *Tunisia: Full Country Dossier* (January 2022), https://opendoorsanalytical.org/wp-content/uploads/2022/01/Tunisia-Full-Country-Dossier-January-2022-revised.pdf

Orozco Henríquez, José de Jesús, *Justicia electoral comparada de América Latina* (Universidad Nacional Autónoma de México 2019).

Ortiz Jiménez, William, "Los Tres Nuevos Procesos Constituyentes en América Latina: Los Cambios Políticos y los Sujetos que los Impulsan" (2013) 38 *Diálogos de Saberes*.

Ottaway, Marina, and Muasher, Marwan, "Arab Monarchies. Chance for Reform, Yet Unmet," *The Carnegie Papers* (December 2011), https://carnegieendowment.org/files/arab_monarchies1.pdf

Papa, Massimo, "L'evoluzione storica del costituzionalismo nei Paesi arabi tra Islam e modernità" in Eberhard Kienle et al. (eds.), *Islam, democrazia e diritti* (Clueb 2007).

Papa, Massimo, "L'Islam e la violenza: un excursus giuridico" in Francesca Maria Corrao and Luciano Violante (eds.), *L'Islam non è terrorismo* (il Mulino 2018).

Papa, Massimo, and Ascanio, Lorenzo, *Shari'a* (il Mulino 2014).

Parolin, Gianluca Paolo, "The Buzz and Fuzz of 'Citizenship' in North African Constitutions" in Barbara Airò and Massimo Zaccaria (eds.), *I confini della cittadinanza nel nuovo Medio Oriente* (Viella 2015).

Parolin, Gianluca Paolo, *Citizenship in the Arab World: Kin, Religion and Nation-State* (Amsterdam University Press 2009).

Parolin, Gianluca Paolo, "Drifting Power Relations in the Egyptian Constitution: The 2019 Amendments" (2020) 3 *DPCE online*.

Parolin, Gianluca Paolo, "Il referendum in Egitto tra rivoluzione e riconfigurazione" (2014) 4 *Diritto pubblico comparato ed europeo*.

Parolin, Gianluca Paolo, "Winter is Coming. Authoritarian Constitutionalism under Strain in the Gulf" in Rainer Grote and Tilmann J. Röder (eds.), *Constitutionalism, Human Rights, and Islam after the Arab Spring* (Oxford University Press 2016).

Partlett, William, "Understanding the Origins of Russia's Constitutional Solution to the Syrian Conflict," *ConstitutionNet* (February 24, 2017), https://constitutionnet.org/news/understanding-origins-russias-constitutional-solution-syrian-conflict

Partlett, William, and Nwokora, Zim, "The Foundations of Democratic Dualism: Why Constitutional Politics and Ordinary Politics Are Different" (2019) 26 *Constellations*.

Pastor y Camarasa, Alicia, "Demystifying How Constitutions Are Made: External Actors' Modes of Actions in the 2014 Tunisian Constitution" (2022) 1 *Michigan Journal of Law & Society*.

Pellegrino, Chiara, "Le autorità religiose islamiche al tempo del Coronavirus," *Fondazione Oasis* (April 30, 2020), www.oasiscenter.eu/it/le-autorita-religiose-islamiche-al-tempo-del-coronavirus

Pepicelli, Renata, "Decolonizzare il femminismo: i movimenti delle donne in Nord Africa" in Francesca Maria Corrao and Luciano Violante (eds.), *L'Islam non è terrorismo* (il Mulino 2018).

Peters, Rudolph, and De Vries, Gert J. J., "Apostasy in Islam" (1976–1977) 17 *Die Welt des Islams*.

Pew Research Center, *Europe's Growing Muslim Population* (November 29, 2017), www.pewresearch.org/religion/2017/11/29/europes-growing-muslim-population/

Philippe, Xavier, "La Constitution Algérienne. Évaluation des Changements Après la Révision de Janvier 2016," *Democracy Reporting International* (June 2016), https://democracyreporting.s3.eu-central-1.amazonaws.com/images/3435DRI-Algerie-EU-BP84-2017-06.pdf

Picchi, Margherita, "A Woman amongst the Sheikhs: The Qur'anic exegesis of Bint al-Shāṭi'," *Fondazione Oasis* (January 13, 2021), www.oasiscenter.eu/en/woman-amongst-sheikhs-quranic-exegesis-bint-al-shati

Pickard, Duncan, "Al-Nahda: Moderation and Compromise in Tunisia's Constitutional Bargain" in Justin O. Frosini and Francesco Biagi (eds.), *Political and Constitutional Transitions in North Africa: Actors and Factors* (Routledge 2015).

Pickard, Duncan, and Meyer-Resende, Michael, "Libya: Comparison of Two Constitutional Texts According to International Standards of Democracy," *Democracy Reporting International* (November 24, 2020), https://democracyreporting.s3.eu-central-1.amazonaws.com/images/2015Constitutional-Comparison_Final_2020-11-17.pdf

Pin, Andrea, "Arab Constitutionalism and Human Dignity" (2017) 50 *The George Washington International Law Review*.

Pin, Andrea, *Religious Freedom without the Rule of Law: Getting the Middle East Right* (Brill, forthcoming).

Pin, Andrea, "Religious Persecution and Constitution Building in the Middle East: The Rule-of-Law Conundrum" (2022) 97 *Notre Dame Law Review Reflection*.

Pizzo, Paola, "Religione e cittadinanza nella transizione egiziana: tra al-Azhar e Chiesa copta" in Barbara Airò and Massimo Zaccaria (eds.), *I confini della cittadinanza nel nuovo Medio Oriente* (Viella 2015).

Pope Benedict XVI, "Faith, Reason and the University – Memories and Reflections," University of Regensburg (September 12, 2006), www.vatican.va/content/benedict-xvi/en/speeches/2006/september/documents/hf_ben-xvi_spe_20060912_university-regensburg.html

Pope Francis, *Address of His Holiness*, Church of "Immaculate Conception" (Qaraqosh, Iraq) (March 7, 2021), www.vatican.va/content/francesco/en/speeches/2021/march/documents/papa-francesco_20210307_iraq-comunita-qaraqosh.html

Pope Francis, *Address of His Holiness*, Esplanade of the Hassan Tower (Rabat, Morocco) (March 30, 2019), www.vatican.va/content/francesco/en/speeches/2019/march/documents/papa-francesco_20190330_autorita-marocco.html

Pope Francis, *Address of His Holiness*, Hall of the Presidential Palace (Baghdad, Iraq) (March 5, 2021), www.vatican.va/content/francesco/en/speeches/2021/march/documents/papa-francesco_20210305_iraq-autorita.html

Pope Francis, *Address of the Pope at the Conclusion of the Meeting*, Esplanade of the Basilica of Saint Nicholas (Bari, Italy) (July 7, 2018), www.vatican.va/content/francesco/en/speeches/2018/july/documents/papa-francesco_20180707_visita-bari-conclusione.html

Pope Francis, *Fratelli tutti: On Fraternity and Social Friendship* (2020), www.vatican.va/content/francesco/en/encyclicals/documents/papa-francesco_20201003_enciclica-fratelli-tutti.html

Pope Francis, *General Audience – Apostolic Journey to the United Arab Emirates* (February 6, 2019), www.vatican.va/content/francesco/en/audiences/2019/documents/papa-francesco_20190206_udienza-generale.html

Pope Francis, *Interreligious Meeting*, Plain of Ur (Iraq) (March 6, 2021), www.vatican.va/content/francesco/en/speeches/2021/march/documents/papa-francesco_20210306_iraq-incontro-interreligioso.html

Pope Francis and Grand Imam Ahmad al-Tayeb, "Document on Human Fraternity for World Peace and Living Together" (2019), www.vatican.va/content/francesco/en/travels/2019/outside/documents/papa-francesco_20190204_documento-fratellanza-umana.html

Prempeh, H. Kwasi, "Presidents Untamed" (2008) 19 *Journal of Democracy*.

Quraishi, Asifa, "The Separation of Powers in the Tradition of Muslim Governments" in Rainer Grote and Tilmann J. Röder (eds.), *Constitutionalism in Islamic Countries: Between Upheaval and Continuity* (Oxford University Press 2012).

Rabbath, Edmond, *La Constitution libanaise: Origines, textes et commentaires* (Publications de l'Université libanaise 1982).

Rashwan, Eman Muhammad, and Lotief, Ahmad Ali, "Egypt" in Richard Albert et al. (eds.), 2019 *Global Review of Constitutional Law* (ICONnect – Clough Center 2020).

Ridola, Paolo, *Esperienza costituzioni storia: Pagine di storia costituzionale* (Jovene 2019).

Risley, David, "What Egypt's Court Ruling on Protest Law Means," *MEI@75* (December 14, 2016), www.mei.edu/publications/what-egypts-court-ruling-protest-law-means

Röder, Tilmann J., "The Separation of Powers in Muslim Countries: Historical and Comparative Perspectives" in Rainer Grote and Tilmann J. Röder (eds.), *Constitutionalism in Islamic Countries: Between Upheaval and Continuity* (Oxford University Press 2012).

Röder, Tilmann J., "State Control over the Military or Military Control over the State? A Comparison of Selected Arab Constitutions" in Rainer Grote and Tilmann J. Röder (eds.), *Constitutionalism, Human Rights, and Islam after the Arab Spring* (Oxford University Press 2016).

Rosenfeld, Michel, *The Identity of the Constitutional Subject: Selfhood, Citizenship, Culture and Community* (Routledge 2009).

Rossi, Ettore, "Il Regno unito della Libia" (October–December 1951) 10/12 *Oriente Moderno*.

Rousset, Michel, "L'interprétation des pouvoirs du roi dans la nouvelle Constitution" in Centre d'Études Internationales (ed.), *La Constitution marocaine de 2011: Analyses et commentaires* (LGDJ 2012).

Royaume du Maroc – Haut-Commissariat au Plan, *Enquête nationale sur la prévalence de la violence à l'égard des femmes au Maroc 2009* (2012), www.abhatoo.net.ma/maalama-textuelle/developpement-economique-et-social/developpement-social/societe/femmes/enquete-nationale-sur-la-prevalence-de-la-violence-a-l-egard-des-femmes-au-maroc-2009

Roznai, Yaniv, *Unconstitutional Constitutional Amendments: The Limits of Amendment Powers* (Oxford University Press 2017).

Ruiz Ruiz, Juan José, "Justicia constitucional transicional y jurisdicción constitucional en la Constitución tunecina de 2014" (2016) 19 *Revista general de derecho público comparado*.

Ruiz Ruiz, Juan José, "La Constitución marroquí de 2011 y el ensayo de parlamentarización de la monarquía" (2014) 164 *Revista de estudios políticos*.

Ruiz Ruiz, Juan José, "Las constituciones de las primaveras árabes y su implementación: el caso de Marruecos" (2018) 179 *Revista de estudios políticos*.

Ryan, Curtis R., *Jordan and the Arab Uprisings: Regime Survival and Politics beyond the State* (Columbia University Press 2018).

Saad, Ragab, "A Constitution That Doesn't Protect Rights and Freedoms: Libya Writes Its Constitution," *Atlantic Council* (August 3, 2017), www.atlanticcouncil.org/blogs/menasource/a-constitution-that-doesn-t-protect-rights-and-freedoms-libya-writes-its-constitution/

Saadi, Donia, "From Mosque to Church: What Challenges Face Tunisian Converts to Christianity," paper presented at the Roundtable on "The Effect of Religious Laws on Rights, Equality and non-Discrimination: Citizenship and Subsidiary Rights Affected by Religious Laws in the MENA Region," organized by the MENA Legal Network and the Konrad Adenauer Stiftung, Lebanon (July 26–27, 2023).

Saati, Abrak, *The Participation Myth: Outcomes of Participatory Constitution Building Processes on Democracy* (Umeå University 2015).

Sadek, George, *Egypt: Supreme Administrative Court Rejects Petition to Obligate Local Administrative Authorities to Allocate Burial Site for Baha'i Religious Minority*, Library of Congress (January 25, 2023), www.loc.gov/item/global-legal-monitor/2023-01-24/egypt-supreme-administrative-court-rejects-petition-to-obligate-local-administrative-authorities-to-allocate-burial-site-for-bahai-religious-minority/

Sadurski, Wojciech (ed.), *Constitutional Justice, East and West: Democratic Legitimacy and Constitutional Courts in Post-Communist Europe in a Comparative Perspective* (Kluwer Law International 2002).

Sadurski, Wojciech, *Rights before Courts: A Study of Constitutional Courts in Postcommunist States of Central and Eastern Europe* (Springer 2014).

Saghieh, Nizar, "Lebanon's Constitutional Council: Access Blocked to Protect the Consensus System?" in Anja Schoeller-Schletter (ed.), *Constitutional Review in the Middle East and North Africa* (Nomos 2021).

Sale, Giovanni, *Isis, Islam e cristiani d'oriente* (Jaca Book 2016).

Sartori, Giovanni, *Comparative Constitutional Engineering: An Inquiry into Structures, Incentives and Outcomes* (Macmillan 1994).

Sartori, Giovanni, "Constitutionalism: A Preliminary Discussion" (1962) 56 *The American Political Science Review*.

SASG *Stephanie Williams' Statement on the High-level Meeting on Libya's Constitutional Track in Geneva* (June 30, 2022), https://unsmil.unmissions.org/sasg-stephanie-williams'-statement-high-level-meeting-libya's-constitutional-track-geneva

Saunders, Cheryl, "International Involvement in Constitution Making" in David Landau and Hanna Lerner (eds.), *Comparative Constitution Making* (Edward Elgar 2019).

Sbailò, Ciro, *Diritto pubblico dell'Islam mediterraneo. Linee evolutive degli ordinamenti nordafricani contemporanei: Marocco, Algeria, Tunisia, Libia, Egitto* (Wolters Kluwer – CEDAM 2022).

Sbailò, Ciro, "Elezioni presidenziali in Egitto: quando le Corti vogliono guidare le transizioni" (2012) 3 *Quaderni costituzionali*.

Sbailò, Ciro, *Principi sciaraitici e organizzazione dello spazio pubblico nel mondo islamico: Il caso egiziano* (CEDAM 2012).

Scalia, Antonin, *The Essential Scalia: On the Constitution, the Courts and the Rule of Law* (Crown Forum 2020).

Scheppele, Kim Lane, "Autocratic Legalism" (2018) 85 *The University of Chicago Law Review*.

Schmitt, Carl, *Political Theology: Four Chapters on the Concept of Sovereignty* (translated by George Schwab) (University of Chicago Press 2005).

Schoeller-Schletter, Anja (ed.), *Constitutional Review in the Middle East and North Africa* (Nomos 2021).

Schwartz, Herman, *The Struggle for Constitutional Justice in Post-Communist Europe* (University of Chicago Press 2000).

Security Council Report, *January 2023 Monthly Forecast*, www.securitycouncilreport.org/monthly-forecast/2023-01/syria-51.php

Serôdio, Diana, "A Comparison of the 2012 and 2014 Constitutions" in Cornelis Hulsman (ed.), *The 2014 Egyptian Constitution: Perspectives from Egypt* (Tectum Verlag 2017).

Serôdio, Diana, "Shaping Egypt's 2014 Constitution: Controversy and Negotiations" in Cornelis Hulsman (ed.), *The 2014 Egyptian Constitution: Perspectives from Egypt* (Tectum Verlag 2017).

Shaar, Karam, and Dasouki, Ayman, "Syria's Constitutional Committee: The Devil in the Detail," *MEI@75* (January 6, 2021), www.mei.edu/publications/syrias-constitutional-committee-devil-detail

Shehabi, Omar Yousef, "'Dans ses Frontières Authentiques'? Morocco's Advanced Regionalization and the Question of Western Sahara" in Aslı Ü. Bâli and Omar M. Dajani (eds.), *Federalism and Decentralization in the Contemporary Middle East and North Africa* (Cambridge University Press 2023).

Silvera, Victor, "Le régime constitutionnel de la Tunisie: la Constitution du 1er juin 1959" (1960) 2 *Revue française de science politique*.

Siriani, Razek, "Syria" in Kenneth R. Ross, Mariz Tadros and Todd M. Johnson (eds.), *Christianity in North Africa and West Asia* (Edinburgh University Press 2018).

Sleiman, Issam, and Poll, Robert, "Towards a Reform in Lebanon? Interview with the President of the Constitutional Council Issam Sleiman," *VerfassungsBlog* (June 20, 2018), https://verfassungsblog.de/towards-a-reform-in-lebanon-interview-with-the-president-of-the-constitutional-council-issam-sleiman/

Spadaro, Antonino, "La transizione costituzionale. Ambiguità e polivalenza di un'importante nozione di teoria generale" in Antonino Spadaro (ed.), *Le "trasformazioni" costituzionali nell'età della transizione* (Giappichelli 2000).

Stefanini, Marthe, *Le filtrage opéré par le Conseil d'État* (Rapport de recherche – Aix-Marseille Université 2013), www.researchgate.net/publication/281356900_Le_filtrage_opere_par_le_Conseil_d'Etat

Stilt, Kristen, "Constitutions in Authoritarian Regimes: The Egyptian Constitution of 1971" in Tom Ginsburg and Alberto Simpser (eds.), *Constitutions in Authoritarian Regimes* (Cambridge University Press 2014).

Sultany, Nimer, *Law and Revolution: Legitimacy and Constitutionalism after the Arab Spring* (Oxford University Press 2017).

"Syrian Arab Republic: 2012 Constitution," *Refworld*, www.refworld.org/docid/5100f02a2.html

Syrians for Truth and Justice, *The Supreme Constitutional Court in Syria: A Formal Independent Tool in the Hands of the President* (August 2022), https://stj-sy.org/wp-content/uploads/2022/08/The-Supreme-Constitutional-Court-in-Syria-.pdf

Tabbara, Nayla, "Dalla fratellanza esclusiva alla fratellanza universale" in Fadi Daou and Nayla Tabbara (eds.), *L'ospitalità divina e la fraternità umana* (Edizioni Qiqajon 2022).

Tabbara, Nayla, "Islam and Other Religions" in Fadi Daou and Nayla Tabbara (eds.), *Divine Hospitality: A Christian-Muslim Conversation* (World Council of Churches Publications 2017).

Tabbara, Nayla, "Let Us All Choose Abundant Life! A Muslim and Dialogical Perspective" (2022) 43 *Theological Review*.

Tabbara, Nayla, *L'Islam pensé par une femme* (Bayard 2018).

Tadros, Mariz, "Christianity in North Africa and West Asia" in Kenneth R. Ross, Mariz Tadros and Todd M. Johnson (eds.), *Christianity in North Africa and West Asia* (Edinburgh University Press 2018).

Tadros, Mariz, "Negotiating Women in Egypt's Post-Mubarak Constitutions (2012–2014)" (2020) 16 *Politics & Gender*.

Tadros, Samuel, "Egypt" in Kenneth R. Ross, Mariz Tadros and Todd M. Johnson (eds.), *Christianity in North Africa and West Asia* (Edinburgh University Press 2018).

Taha, Mahmud Muhammad, *The Second Message of Islam* (Syracuse University Press 1987).

Tarchouna, Lofti, "Il decentramento territoriale: novità e sfide" in Tania Groppi and Irene Spigno (eds.), *Tunisia: La primavera della Costituzione* (Carocci 2015).

Tayebi, Taha, "Religious Minorities in the Sherifian Kingdom of Morocco: Change and Lack of Change" in Hamza Tayebi and Jochen Lobah (eds.), *Dynamics of Inclusion and Exclusion in the MENA Region: Minorities, Subalternity, and Resistance* (Hanns Seidel Foundation 2019).

Terán, Millán, and Antonio, Óscar, "El sistema electoral para la elección de los magistrados del Tribunal Constitucional Plurinacional" (2015) 35 *Ciencia y Cultura*.

"TIMEP Brief: Protest Law," *The Tahrir Institute for Middle East Policy* (November 9, 2018), https://timep.org/reports-briefings/timep-brief-protest-law/

Tolan, John V., *St. Francis and the Sultan: The Curious History of a Christian-Muslim Encounter* (Oxford University Press 2009).

Torki Bani Salameh, Mohammed, and Ali Ananzah, Azzam, "Constitutional Reforms in Jordan: A Critical Analysis" (2015) 24 *Digest of Middle East Studies*.

Torres del Moral, Antonio, *Estado de Derecho y democracia de partidos* (Editorial Universitas 2012).

Tourabi, Abdellah, "Constitutional Reform in Morocco: Reform in Times of Revolution," *Arab Reform Initiative* (November 2011), www.arab-reform.net/en/node/526

Tozy, Mohamed, *Monarchie et Islam politique au Maroc* (Presses de Sciences Po 1999).

Troper, Michel, "Sovereignty" in Michel Rosenfeld and András Sajó (eds.), *The Oxford Handbook of Comparative Constitutional Law* (Oxford University Press 2012).

Tushnet, Mark, "The Inevitable Globalization of Constitutional Law" (2009) 49 *Virginia Journal of International Law*.

U.S. Department of State – Office of International Religious Freedom, *2021 Report on International Religious Freedom: Algeria* (June 2, 2022), www.state.gov/reports/2021-report-on-international-religious-freedom/algeria/

U.S. Department of State – Office of International Religious Freedom, *2021 Report on International Religious Freedom: Egypt* (June 2, 2022), www.state.gov/reports/2021-report-on-international-religious-freedom/egypt/

U.S. Department of State – Office of International Religious Freedom, *2021 Report on International Religious Freedom: Jordan* (June 2, 2022), www.state.gov/reports/2021-report-on-international-religious-freedom/jordan/

U.S. Department of State – Office of International Religious Freedom, *2021 Report on International Religious Freedom: Libya* (June 2, 2022), www.state.gov/reports/2021-report-on-international-religious-freedom/libya/

U.S. Department of State – Office of International Religious Freedom, *2021 Report on International Religious Freedom: Morocco* (June 2, 2022), www.state.gov/reports/2021-report-on-international-religious-freedom/morocco/

U.S. Department of State – Office of International Religious Freedom, *2021 Report on International Religious Freedom: Syria* (June 2, 2022), www.state.gov/reports/2021-report-on-international-religious-freedom/syria/

U.S. Department of State – Office of International Religious Freedom, *2021 Report on International Religious Freedom: Tunisia* (June 2, 2022), www.state.gov/reports/2021-report-on-international-religious-freedom/tunisia/

UNICEF, *Child Marriage in the Middle East and North Africa – Egypt Country Brief* (2017), www.unicef.org/mena/media/1796/file/MENA-CMReport-EgyptBrief.pdf.pdf

United Nations Support Mission in Libya – Report of the Secretary-General (S/2022/632) (August 19, 2022), https://reliefweb.int/report/libya/united-nations-support-mission-libya-report-secretary-general-s2022632-enar

United Nations Women, *Study on Ways and Methods to Eliminate Sexual Harassment in Egypt* (April 2013), https://s3-eu-west-1.amazonaws.com/harassmap/media/uploaded-files/287_Summaryreport_eng_low-1.pdf

UNSMIL Statement on the UN-facilitated Joint HOR/HCS Committee Meeting (March 21, 2022), https://unsmil.unmissions.org/unsmil-statement-un-facilitated-joint-horhcs-committee-meeting

van den Boogert, Maurits H., "Millets: Past and Present" in Anh Nga Longva and Anne Sofie Roald (eds.), *Religious Minorities in the Middle East: Domination, Self-Empowerment, Accommodation* (Brill 2012).

van Lier, Felix-Anselm, "Constitution-Making as a Tool for State-Building? Insights from an Ethnographic Analysis of the Libyan Constitution-Making Process," *Max Planck Institute for Social Anthropology* (Working Paper no. 192) (2018).

Vedaschi, Arianna, *À la guerre comme à la guerre? La disciplina della guerra nel diritto costituzionale comparato* (Giappichelli 2007).

Vedaschi, Arianna, "Da al-Qaida all'IS: il terrorismo internazionale si è fatto Stato?" (2016) 1 *Rivista trimestrale di diritto pubblico*.

Vedaschi, Arianna, "Diritto comparato e interdisciplinarietà: tra innata vocazione e incompiuta realizzazione?" (2021) 2 *Diritto pubblico comparato ed europeo*.

Venice Commission, *Opinion on the Draft Institutional Law on the Constitutional Court of Tunisia* (Opinion no. 817/2015) (October 26, 2015), www.venice.coe.int/webforms/documents/?pdf=CDL-AD(2015)024-e

Venice Commission, *Opinion on the Final Draft Constitution of the Republic of Tunisia* (Opinion no. 733/2013) (October 17, 2013), www.venice.coe.int/webforms/documents/?pdf=CDL-AD(2013)032-e

Venice Commission, *Study on Individual Access to Constitutional Justice* (Study no. 538/2009) (January 27, 2011), www.venice.coe.int/WebForms/documents/default.aspx?pdffile=CDL-AD(2010)039rev-e

Venice Commission, *Tunisia. Urgent Opinion on the Constitutional and Legislative Framework on the Referendum and Elections Announcements by the President of the Republic* (Opinion no. 1085/2022) (May 27, 2022), www.venice.coe.int/webforms/documents/default.aspx?pdffile=CDL-PI(2022)026-e

Venter, Francois, *Constitutionalism and Religion* (Edward Elgar 2015).

Virgili, Tommaso, *Islam, Constitutional Law, and Human Rights: Sexual Minorities and Freethinkers in Egypt and Tunisia* (Routledge 2022).

Voermans, Wim, Stremler, Maarten, and Cliteur, Paul, *Constitutional Preambles: A Comparative Analysis* (Edward Elgar 2017).

Volpi, Frédéric, "Algeria versus the Arab Spring" (2013) 24 *Journal of Democracy*.

Wadud, Amina, *Qur'an and Woman: Rereading the Sacred Text from a Woman's Perspective* (Oxford University Press 1999).

Wahid Hanna, Michael, "Excluded and Unequal. Copts on the Margins of the Egyptian Security State," *The Century Foundation* (May 9, 2019), https://tcf.org/content/report/christian-exclusion-from-egypts-security-state/#easy-footnote-bottom-2

Wahiu, Winluck, *A Practical Guide to Constitution Building: An Introduction* (International IDEA 2011).

Wald, Jack, "Morocco and Western Sahara" in Kenneth R. Ross, Mariz Tadros and Todd M. Johnson (eds.), *Christianity in North Africa and West Asia* (Edinburgh University Press 2018).

Walker, Nigel, "Syria: 2021 Presidential Election and Future Prospects," *House of Commons Library* (June 9, 2021), https://researchbriefings.files.parliament.uk/documents/CBP-9250/CBP-9250.pdf

Waterbury, John, *The Egypt of Nasser and Sadat: The Political Economy of Two Regimes* (Princeton University Press 1983).

"We Choose Abundant Life. Christians in the Middle East: Towards Renewed Theological, Social, and Political Choices" (2021), www.wechooseabundantlife.com

"Wilton Park Dialogue Report on Inclusive Citizenship" (June 2021), www.wiltonpark.org.uk/app/uploads/2021/06/Inclusive-Citizenship-Dialogue-Report.pdf

Wolfrum, Rüdiger, "Legitimacy of Constitution-making Processes. Reflections from the Perspective of International Law" in Rainer Grote and Tilmann J. Röder (eds.), *Constitutionalism, Human Rights, and Islam after the Arab Spring* (Oxford University Press 2016).

Yerkes, Sarah, and Al-Mailam, Mohammad, "Tunisia's New Electoral Law Is Another Blow to Its Democratic Progress," *Carnegie Endowment for International Peace* (October 11, 2022), https://carnegieendowment.org/2022/10/11/tunisia-s-new-electoral-law-is-another-blow-to-its-democratic-progress-pub-88127

Yom, Sean L., "Jordan in the Balance: Evaluating Regime Stability" (January 2013) 6 *CTC Sentinel*, https://ctc.westpoint.edu/jordan-in-the-balance-evaluating-regime-stability/

Yom, Sean L., and Al-Khatib, Wael, "Democratic Reform in Jordan. Breaking the Impasse," *Project on Middle East Democracy – POMED* (February 2022), https://pomed.org/wp-content/uploads/2022/02/Yom_Khatib_Final-1.pdf

Young, Michael, "An Excommunication in Damascus," *Malcolm H. Kerr – Carnegie Middle East Center* (November 19, 2021), https://carnegie-mec.org/diwan/85816

Youssef, Nada, "Le Liban: la transition inachevée vers l'État de droit" (2013) 95 *Revue française de droit constitutionnel*.

Ziadeh, Radwan, "The History of the Syrian Constitution" (2017) 22 *Syrian Studies Association Bulletin*, https://ojcs.siue.edu/ojs/index.php/ssa/article/view/3236/1263.

Zoglin, Katie, "Morocco's Family Code: Improving Equality for Women" (2009) 31 *Human Rights Quarterly*.

Zulueta-Fülscher, Kimana and Bisarya, Sumit, *(S)electing Constitution-Making Bodies in Fragile and Conflict-Affected Settings* (International IDEA 2018).

Zurlo, Gina A., "A Demographic Profile of Christianity in North Africa and West Asia" in Kenneth R. Ross, Mariz Tadros and Todd M. Johnson (eds.), *Christianity in North Africa and West Asia* (Edinburgh University Press 2018).

NEWSPAPERS ARTICLES

Abdi, Mazloum, "If We Have to Choose Between Compromise and Genocide, We Will Choose Our People," *Foreign Policy* (October 13, 2019), https://foreignpolicy.com/2019/10/13/kurds-assad-syria-russia-putin-turkey-genocide/

Ait Akdim, Youssef, "Au Maroc, œil au beurre noir cherche poudre libre pour maquillage de violences," *Le Monde* (December 7, 2016), www.lemonde.fr/afrique/article/2016/12/07/au-maroc-il-au-beurre-noir-cherche-poudre-libre-pour-maquillage-de-violences_5045016_3212.html

Al Sharif, Osama, "Changes to Jordan's Constitution Raise Concerns," *Al-Monitor* (May 4, 2016), www.al-monitor.com/originals/2016/05/jordan-adopts-constitution-amendments-king-powers.html

Al-Ali, Zaid, "Tunisia's Draft Constitution Solidifies One-man Rule," *The Washington Post* (July 8, 2022), www.washingtonpost.com/politics/2022/07/08/tunisia-saied-coup-constitution-backsliding-democracy/

"Algeria's Powerful Military Chief Ahmed Gaid Salah Dies," *BBC News* (December 23, 2019), www.bbc.com/news/world-africa-50891741

"Algérie: l'avant-projet de réforme constitutionnelle laisse un goût d'inachevé," *Jeune Afrique* (May 12, 2020), www.jeuneafrique.com/943997/politique/algerie-lavant-projet-de-reforme-constitutionnelle-laisse-un-gout-dinacheve/

Alkhaldi, Celine, "Jordanian Lawmakers Trade Punches in Parliament Amid Heated Discussion on Women's Rights," *CNN* (December 29, 2021), https://edition.cnn.com/2021/12/29/middleeast/jordan-parliament-fight-intl/index.html

Allouche, Yasmina, "A Breakdown of Algeria's New Constitution," *Middle East Eye* (October 29, 2020), www.middleeasteye.net/news/algeria-new-constitution-breakdown

Aloul, Lena, "Today, History Was Made," *The Jordan Times* (January 2, 2022), www.jordantimes.com/opinion/lena-aloul/today-history-was-made

Anderson, Jon Lee, "The Unravelling. In a Failing State, an Anti-Islamist General Mounts a Divisive Campaign," *The New Yorker* (February 23 and March 2, 2015), www.newyorker.com/magazine/2015/02/23/unravelling

"Appel: Pour une Assemblée Constituante!," *El Watan* (March 3, 2019), www.elwatan.com/edition/actualite/appel-pour-une-assemblee-constituante-03-03-2019

"Au Maroc, des chrétiens se battent pour que leur mariage soit reconnu par les autorités," *Info Chrétienne* (June 12, 2018), www.infochretienne.com/maroc-chretiens-se-battent-mariage-soit-reconnu-autorites/

Badrane, Mohamed, "Moudawana 2023, année de la grande réforme?," *Aujourd'hui le Maroc* (December 28, 2022), https://aujourdhui.ma/actualite/moudawana-2023-annee-de-la-grande-reforme

Belalloufi, Amal, "Le régime en crise de légitimité après l'échec du referendum," *Le Devoir* (November 3, 2020), www.ledevoir.com/monde/afrique/588932/la-reforme-constitutionnelle-est-acceptee-en-algerie-avec-une-abstention-record

Ben Henda, Mokhtar, "Caid Essebsi père et fils: Virage ou mirage dynastique?," *Kapitalis* (September 4, 2018), http://kapitalis.com/tunisie/2018/09/04/caid-essebsi-pere-et-fils-virage-ou-mirage-dynastique/

Bobin, Frédéric, "Guerre des chefs en Tunisie," *Le Monde* (July 25, 2016), www.lemonde.fr/international/article/2016/07/25/guerre-des-chefs-en-tunisie_4974259_3210.html

Borracino, Manuela, "Basta belle parole" (March–April 2021) 2 *Terra Santa*.

Chentouf, Abdelhaif, "Exception d'inconstitutionnalité des lois: le gouvernement contraint de revoir sa copie," *Challenge* (June 24, 2019), www.challenge.ma/exception-dinconstitutionnalite-des-lois-le-gouvernement-contraint-de-revoir-sa-copie-111234/

"Ces candidates qui se voilent la face," *El Watan* (April 14, 2017), www.elwatan.com/actualite/ces-candidates-qui-se-voilent-la-face-14-04-2017-343261_109.php

Considine, Craig, "Pluralism and the Najran Christians: How Prophet Muhammad Went Beyond Tolerance," *Huffpost* (February 17, 2016), www.huffpost.com/entry/pluralism-and-the-najran-christians_b_9235554

"Constitutional Crisis Blocks New Tunisian Ministers from Oath of Office," *The Arab Weekly* (January 30, 2021), https://thearabweekly.com/constitutional-crisis-blocks-new-tunisian-ministers-oath-office

Cremonesi, Lorenzo, "Sconfitta Isis, noi curdi vogliamo ora una Siria federale e democratica," *Il Corriere della Sera* (March 29, 2019), www.corriere.it/esteri/19_marzo_29/sconfitta-isis-noi-curdi-vogliamo-ora-siria-federale-democratica-4b1ef910-5236-11e9-95de-b93fcff37bd3.shtml

Dahmani, Frida, "Tunisie: guerre froide entre Kaïs Saïed et Rached Ghannouchi," *Jeune Afrique* (July 2, 2020), www.jeuneafrique.com/mag/1007068/politique/tunisie-guerre-froide-entre-kais-saied-et-rached-ghannouchi/

Dehnert, Elspeth, "As Lebanon, Jordan, Tunisia End 'Marry-Your-Rapist' Laws, Where Next?," *The New Humanitarian* (August 22, 2017), www.newsdeeply.com/womenandgirls/articles/2017/08/22/as-lebanon-jordan-tunisia-end-marry-your-rapist-laws-where-next

"Dossier Copti" (June 2017) *Missioni Consolata*.

"Dossier Giordania" (November–December 2022) 6 *Terra Santa*.

"Dossier: Il tempo propizio" (January–February 2023) 1 *Terra Santa*.

"Egypt Appoints First Christian President of Supreme Constitutional Court," *Daily News Egypt* (February 9, 2022), https://dailynewsegypt.com/2022/02/09/egypt-appoints-first-christian-president-of-supreme-constitutional-court/

"Egyptian Lawmaker's Call for Virginity Tests Draws Fire," *VOA News* (October 2, 2016), www.voanews.com/a/egyptian-lawmaker-call-for-virginity-tests-draws-fire/3533612.html

Eljarh, Mohamed, "Democracy Fatigue in Libya," *Foreign Policy* (February 26, 2014), https://foreignpolicy.com/2014/02/26/democracy-fatigue-in-libya/

"En Algérie, l'inclusion des femmes en politique reste sélective," *VOA Afrique* (June 9, 2021), www.voaafrique.com/a/en-algérie-l-inclusion-des-femmes-en-politique-reste-sélective-/5922165.html

Farid, Sonia, "Witch-hunt Politics in Egypt," *AlArabiya News* (July 9, 2013), https://english.alarabiya.net/en/views/news/middle-east/2013/07/10/Witch-hunt-politics-in-Egypt

Gardner, Frank, "Iraq's Christians 'close to extinction'," *BBC News* (May 23, 2019), www.bbc.com/news/world-middle-east-48333923

Grewal, Sharan, "Why Algeria's Army Abandoned Bouteflika," *Brookings* (April 10, 2019), www.brookings.edu/blog/order-from-chaos/2019/04/10/why-algerias-army-abandoned-bouteflika/

Hadid, Diaa, "Jordan Tones Down Textbooks' Islamic Content, and Tempers Rise," *The New York Times* (October 14, 2016), www.nytimes.com/2016/10/15/world/middleeast/jordan-tones-down-textbooks-islamic-content-and-tempers-rise.html

Hagedorn, Elizabeth, "US Government Watchdog Calls Out Syria for Religious Freedom Abuses," *Al-Monitor* (April 21, 2021), www.al-monitor.com/originals/2021/04/us-government-watchdog-calls-out-syria-religious-freedom-abuses

Hoffner, Anne-Bénédicte, "Au Maroc, les apostats ne sont plus passibles de la peine de mort," *La Croix* (February 8, 2017), www.la-croix.com/Religion/Islam/Au-Maroc-apostats-sont-plus-passibles-peine-mort-2017-02-08-1200823368

"Iraq's Invalid Supreme Court is Used Against Kurds Again," *Washington Kurdish Institute* (February 26, 2022), https://dckurd.org/2022/02/26/iraqs-invalid-supreme-court/

"Iraqi Court Bars Veteran Zebari from Running for Presidency," *Al Jazeera* (February 13, 2022), www.aljazeera.com/news/2022/2/13/iraqi-court-bars-zebari-from-running-for-presidency-state-media

Ismael, Majida S., "The Federal Supreme Court of Iraq from Interpreting to Amending the Constitution: KRG's Oil Judgement as an Example," *Kurdistan 24* (April 3, 2022), www.kurdistan24.net/en/opinion/27484-The-Federal-Supreme-Court-of-Iraq-from-interpreting-to-amending-the-constitution:--KRG's-oil-judgement-as-an-example

"Jordan Plans to Lift Martial Law," *The New York Times* (December 20, 1989), www.nytimes.com/1989/12/20/world/jordan-plans-to-lift-martial-law.html

Khazbak, Rana, "In Egypt, There Is No Local Government," *Mada Masr* (March 28, 2016), www.madamasr.com/en/2016/03/28/opinion/u/in-egypt-there-is-no-local-government/

"La Constitution de 'l'Algérie nouvelle' ne fait pas consensus," *Le Monde Afrique* (May 12, 2020), www.lemonde.fr/afrique/article/2020/05/12/la-constitution-de-l-algerie-nouvelle-ne-fait-pas-consensus_6039444_3212.html

"Lamp of Peace Awarded in Assisi to King of Jordan," *Ansa.it* (March 29, 2019), www.ansa.it/ansamed/en/news/nations/italy/2019/03/29/lamp-of-peace-awarded-in-assisi-to-king-of-jordan_b132904f-8bd1-4fa2-b585-302ec9754cc8.html

"L'article 522 abrogé, mais ses effets maintenus dans deux situations," *L'Orient Le Jour* (February 16, 2017), www.lorientlejour.com/article/1035419/larticle-522-abroge-mais-ses-effets-maintenus-dans-deux-situations.html

Leduc, Sarah, "Nouvelle Constitution en Algérie: entre 'avancée démocratique' et 'occasion ratée'," *France 24* (February 9, 2016), www.france24.com/fr/20160208-algerie-nouvelle-constitution-interview-hassan-moali-societe-civile-loi-corruption

"Le président Tebboune promulgue la révision de la Constitution," *L'Orient-Le Jour* (January 1, 2021), www.lorientlejour.com/article/1246710/le-president-tebboune-promulgue-la-revision-de-la-constitution.html

"Libya's Eastern Authority Bans Women Travelling Solo," *BBC News* (February 20, 2017), www.bbc.com/news/world-africa-39027619

Lmrabet, Ali, "Maroc: la véritable histoire d'Abderrahman Youssoufi," *Middle East Eye* (August 15, 2020), www.middleeasteye.net/fr/opinion-fr/maroc-abderrahman-youssoufi-nationaliste-socialiste-premier-ministre-histoire

Macleod, Hugh, and Flamand, Annasofie, “Syria Referendum Called ‘a Sham’,” *GlobalPost* (February 27, 2012), www.pri.org/stories/2012-02-27/syria-referendum-called-sham

Makedhi, Madjid, “Le référendum sur la révision de la Constitution en quête de soutiens: Un projet qui peine à convaincre,” *El Watan* (September 28, 2020), www.elwatan.com/edition/actualite/un-projet-qui-peine-a-convaincre-28-09-2020

“Mariage des mineures au Maroc: Un phénomène ‘dur à cuire’,” *La Quotidienne* (August 3, 2022), https://laquotidienne.ma/article/infos-societe/mariage-des-mineures-au-maroc-un-phenomene-dur-a-cuire

Meddeb, Abdelwahab, “Une constitution inacceptable,” *Leaders* (April 27, 2013), www.leaders.com.tn/article/11300-abdelwahab-meddeb-une-constitution-inacceptable

Meddi, Adlène, “Algérie: Tebboune dévoile son projet de réforme constitutionnelle,” *Le Point Afrique* (May 8, 2020), www.lepoint.fr/afrique/algerie-tebboune-devoile-son-projet-de-reforme-constitutionnelle-08-05-2020-2374712_3826.php#

Mihaila, Liliana, “More Withdraw from Constituent Assembly,” *Daily News Egypt* (November 18, 2012), https://dailynewsegypt.com/2012/11/18/more-withdraw-from-constituent-assembly/

“No State Religion Says Tunisia President after Receiving Draft Constitution,” *The Arab Weekly* (June 21, 2022), https://thearabweekly.com/no-state-religion-says-tunisia-president-after-receiving-draft-constitution

Ouanes, Yosra, “Tunisie: le président Saïed refuse de promulguer la loi sur la Cour constitutionnelle,” *Anadolu Ajansı* (April 4, 2021), www.aa.com.tr/fr/afrique/tunisie-le-président-saïed-refuse-de-promulguer-la-loi-sur-la-cour-constitutionnelle-/2197826

Petrosillo, Marta, “Donne e cristiane. Due volte nel mirino” (July 2018) *Missioni Consolata.*

“Pope Francis Meets Iraq’s Shia Leader al-Sistani,” *Al Jazeera* (March 6, 2021), www.aljazeera.com/news/2021/3/6/pope-francis-meets-iraqs-shia-leader-al-sistani

“Proclamation de la liste des professeurs de droit constitutionnel élus,” *Algérie Press Service* (October 18, 2021), www.aps.dz/algerie/129061-cour-constitutionnelle-proclamation-de-la-liste-des-professeurs-de-droit-constitutionnel-elus

“‘Qu’y a-t-il dans la Constitution? Il y a Bonaparte’ Le mot circule dans Paris en 1800,” *L’Histoire en citations*, www.histoire-en-citations.fr/citations/qu-y-a-t-il-dans-la-constitution#cit-1696

“Report: Number of Christians in Syria Dropped from 1.5 Million to 300,000,” *The Syrian Observer* (November 18, 2022), https://syrianobserver.com/news/80226/report-number-of-christians-in-syria-dropped-from-1-5-million-to-300000.html

“Researcher Patrick Zaki Faces Emergency Trial for Penning 2019 Article on Life as Coptic Christian in Egypt,” *Mada Masr* (September 15, 2021) www.madamasr.com/en/2021/09/15/news/u/researcher-patrick-zaki-faces-emergency-trial-for-penning-2019-article-on-life-as-coptic-christian-in-egypt/

“Révision de la Constitution: Tamazight cible des islamistes,” *Algerie Eco* (October 6, 2020), www.algerie-eco.com/2020/10/06/revision-de-la-constitution-tamazight-cible-des-islamistes/

“Révision de la Constitution: Un membre du comité d’experts démissionne,” *Algerie Eco* (April 15, 2020), www.algerie-eco.com/2020/04/15/revision-de-la-constitution-un-membre-du-comite-dexperts-demissionne/

Riccardi, Andrea, “La nuova ‘resurrezione’ cristiana in Medio oriente, *Il Corriere della Sera* (April 21, 2019).

Riccardi, Andrea, “La sconfitta del Califfato sarà il ritorno dei cristiani,” *Il Corriere della Sera* (November 5, 2017).

Rice, Xan, “Egyptians Protest Over ‘Virginity Tests’ on Tahrir Square Women,” *The Guardian* (May 31, 2011), www.theguardian.com/world/2011/may/31/egypt-online-protest-virginity-tests

Robbins, Michael, "Arab Citizens Know Democracy's Not Perfect. They Want It Anyway," *The Washington Post* (July 21, 2022), www.washingtonpost.com/politics/2022/07/21/arab-citizens-know-democracys-not-perfect-they-want-it-anyway/

Sabry, Bassem, "Problems Ahead for Egypt Constitution Debate," *Al Monitor* (September 30, 2013), www.al-monitor.com/pulse/ar/originals/2013/09/egypt-constitution-highlights-new-draft.html

Safdar, Anealla, "Transgender Ruling in Lebanon an 'Empowering' Moment," *Al Jazeera* (February 6, 2016), www.aljazeera.com/features/2016/2/6/transgender-ruling-in-lebanon-an-empowering-moment

Saïd, Arezki, "Algérie: pourquoi les islamistes continuent de s'opposer à l'amazigh," *Jeune Afrique* (October 12, 2020), www.jeuneafrique.com/1057038/politique/algerie-pourquoi-les-islamistes-continuent-de-sopposer-a-lamazigh/

"Saied Slams Venice Commission Over 'Interference' in Tunisia Affairs," *The Arab Weekly* (May 31, 2022), https://thearabweekly.com/saied-slams-venice-commission-over-interference-tunisia-affairs

Sbailò, Ciro, "La svolta inevitabile verso l'autoritarismo della Tunisia," *HuffPost* (July 26, 2022), www.huffingtonpost.it/blog/2022/07/26/news/referendum_in_tunisia_una_svolta_inevitabile-9945102/

Sherwood, Harriet, "Christians in Egypt Face Unprecedented Persecution, Report Says," *The Guardian* (January 18, 2018), www.theguardian.com/world/2018/jan/10/christians-egypt-unprecedented-persecution-report

Souilem, Amira, "Tunisie: après les législatives, un Parlement sans coloration politique bien définie," *RFI* (February 1, 2023), www.rfi.fr/fr/afrique/20230201-tunisie-après-les-législatives-un-parlement-sans-coloration-politique-bien-définie

Suchkov, Maxim A., "Russia Offers Outline for Syrian Constitution," *Al-Monitor* (January 27, 2017), www.al-monitor.com/originals/2017/01/russia-meeting-syria-opposition-moscow-constitution.html

"Témoignage d'un pasteur algérien: 'La foi chrétienne en Algérie est difficile mais Dieu nous donne beaucoup de joie et de courage'," *Info Chrétienne* (February 25, 2022), www.infochretienne.com/temoignage-dun-pasteur-algerien-la-foi-chretienne-en-algerie-est-difficile-mais-dieu-nous-donne-beaucoup-de-joie-et-de-courage/

Toumi, Habib, "Kuwaiti MPs Call for Abolishing Constitutional Court," *Gulf News* (January 7, 2019), https://gulfnews.com/world/gulf/kuwait/kuwaiti-mps-call-for-abolishing-constitutional-court-1.61290332

"Tunisia Expert Drafting New Constitution Says No Reference to Islam," *France 24* (June 6, 2022), www.france24.com/en/live-news/20220606-tunisia-expert-drafting-new-constitution-says-no-reference-to-islam

"Tunisia President Wants Debate on New Political System, Constitutional Amendment," *Reuters* (July 15, 2021), www.reuters.com/world/tunisia-president-wants-debate-new-political-system-constitutional-amendment-2021-06-15/

"Tunisian President Rejects Gender Equality in Inheritance," *The Arab Weekly* (August 14, 2020), https://thearabweekly.com/tunisian-president-rejects-gender-equality-inheritance

"Tunisie: l'auteur de la Constitution désavoue le projet amendé par Kaïs Saïed," *Jeune Afrique* (July 3, 2022), www.jeuneafrique.com/1358718/politique/tunisie-lauteur-de-la-constitution-desavoue-le-projet-amende-par-kais-saied/

"Tunisie/législatives: 154 députés dont 25 femmes au nouveau parlement et 7 sièges encore vacant," *XinhuaNet* (January 31, 2023), https://french.news.cn/20230131/f77f6d59d6414f26a0bb776fb1b8430d/c.html

Vecchi, Gian Guido, "Il viaggio di un francescano tra i cristiani decimati in Iraq," *Il Corriere della Sera* (December 19, 2019).

Walsh, Declan, "Why Was an Italian Graduate Student Tortured and Murdered in Egypt?," *The New York Times Magazine* (August 15, 2017), www.nytimes.com/2017/08/15/magazine/giulio-regeni-italian-graduate-student-tortured-murdered-egypt.html

"War and Economic Crisis in Aleppo Cause Christians to Flee," *Vatican News* (December 13, 2021), www.vaticannews.va/en/church/news/2021-12/syria-war-christian-tobji-joseph.html

"Women Workers Must Receive Annual Pay Increases During Unpaid Maternity Leave: Egypt's Constitutional Court," *Ahram Online* (May 6, 2017), https://english.ahram.org.eg/NewsContent/1/64/268220/Egypt/Politics-/-Women-workers-must-receive-annual-pay-increases-d.aspx

Zecchinelli, Cecilia, "L'ebreo del Marocco che cerca i Giusti fra gli islamici," *Il Corriere della Sera* (November 4, 2007).

Zerrouky, Madjid, "En Algérie, un projet de Constitution loin du rêve du Hirak," *Le Monde* (May 21, 2020), www.lemonde.fr/afrique/article/2020/05/20/en-algerie-un-projet-de-constitution-loin-du-reve-du-hirak_6040259_3212.html

Index

Printed by Integrated Books International,
United States of America